A Biographical Handbook of Hispanics and United States Film

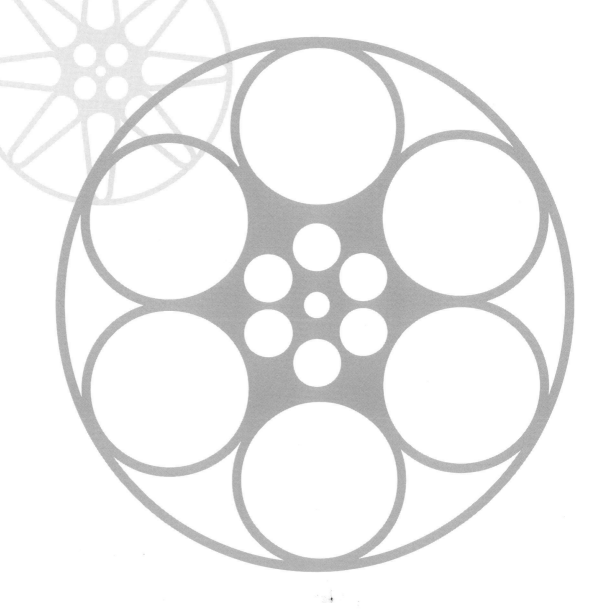

Bilingual Press/Editorial Bilingüe

General Editor
    Gary D. Keller

Managing Editor
    Karen S. Van Hooft

Associate Editors
    Karen M. Akins
    Barbara H. Firoozye

Assistant Editor
    Linda St. George Thurston

Editorial Consultant
    Ingrid Muller

Address:
    Bilingual Review/Press
    Hispanic Research Center
    Arizona State University
    P.O. Box 872702
    Tempe, Arizona 85287-2702
    (602) 965-3867

A Biographical Handbook of Hispanics and United States Film

Gary D. Keller

with the assistance of
Estela Keller

Bilingual Press/Editorial Bilingüe
Tempe, Arizona

ISBN 0-927534-65-7
Printed simultaneously in a softcover edition. ISBN 0-927534-56-8

Library of Congress Cataloging-in-Publication Data

Keller, Gary D.
    A biographical handbook of Hispanics and United States film / Gary
D. Keller.
        p.   cm.
    Includes bibliographical references and index.
    ISBN 0–927534–65–7 (cloth : alk. paper). — ISBN 0–927534–56–8
(pbk. : alk. paper)
    1. Hispanic Americans in the motion picture industry—Biography—
Dictionaries.   2. Hispanic American motion picture actors and
actresses—Credits.   3. Hispanic American motion picture producers
and directors—Credits.   I. Title.
PN1995.9.H47K46   1997
791.43'08968073—dc20   96–41117
                                                          CIP

PRINTED IN THE UNITED STATES OF AMERICA

Cover design, interior by John Wincek, Aerocraft Charter Art Service

CONTENTS

TEXT

PHOTOGRAPHIC THEMES

INTRODUCTION

In 1994, I published the first volume of this two-volume work, *Hispanics and United States Film: An Overview and Handbook,* writing in the introduction (dated March 1994) that the companion book would be published within the year. This is that book, with a slightly different title from what was originally announced (it was going to be called *A Pictorial Handbook*) and almost two years overdue. However, the time has been well spent, permitting the inclusion of a greater number of biographies and other information including dates, film titles, bibliographical entries, photographs, posters, and other images. The considerable expansion of this volume over what had originally been envisioned is due in great part to the diligent research of my mother, Estela Keller, originally trained as an anthropologist and currently converted to researcher of film figures, either celebrated or, more usually, lamentably obscured.

ON PROCEDURES

A general bibliography encompassing both volumes appears at the end of this book. This general bibliography includes all of the titles that were cited in the earlier volume, which was only a fraction of the actual titles that were consulted. In this volume are also two indexes, one of film titles and the other of individuals. Each of the indexes specifies the volume in which the reference appears. *Hispanics and United States Film: An Overview and Handbook* is designated by I, and *A Biographical Handbook of Hispanics and United States Film* by II. The occasional mistakes in the spelling of names and in film titles that appeared in volume I are corrected in the indexes.

There are also some minor corrections of the earlier volume that appear in the text of this volume. For example, here the film *Trial* (starring Glenn Ford) appears correctly, whereas in the earlier volume it was listed as *The Trial.* Similarly listed here is *Stay Away, Joe* (starring Elvis Presley), whereas in the first volume it was incorrectly called *Stay Way, Joe.* Volume I had Héctor Elizondo debuting in film in 1971. In fact, he debuted in 1969. Mrs. George Hernández was referred to in the first volume. She was documentably not Hispanic and does not appear in this book. Other mat-

ters are more subtle. In the first volume I included the actor Juan de la Cruz. He has been eliminated, at least for this edition, on the basis of my documenting that he was born in Copenhagen and that most of his movies were not Hispanic-focused. My working assumption now is that he was not Hispanic, but that could change with more accurate information.

Accents and other orthographic marks are a difficult issue to deal with. It has proved impossible to use one specific policy. To simply follow common United States practice and thus virtually eliminate all diacritical marks with respect to the titles of films and the names of actors and actresses would be to legitimize and perpetuate the crimes against Spanish orthography that have been the hallmark of United States language practice as applied to cinema. This would also violate the editorial standards that the Bilingual Press has maintained in the publication of all its other books. On the other hand, to introduce accents consistently where they should normally be in the Spanish language would generate spellings seen for the first time. For example, even a book published in the Canary Islands (where María Montez grew up) does not spell her surname with an accent, presumably because *she* never did so and also presumably because it would standardize the pronunciation of her last name as MON-tez when in fact she pronounced it, gringo style, Mon-TEZ.

I have opted for a middle course. Juárez is always accented, referring as it does to a historical figure, including in the title of the film *Juárez.* Usually Rio is not accented, given the fact that the majority of the uses refer to the Rio Grande, the Anglicized name of the river (the Mexican name is Río Bravo), or to Rio de Janeiro, Brazil. Raúl Juliá started his career using the accents. Then they were dropped. Was that his decision, or simply the practice of North Americans to which he acquiesced? Upon his death and funeral in Puerto Rico, newspapers on the Island invariably spelled his name correctly, according to Spanish practice. He appears here as Raúl Juliá. On the other hand, the film *Message to Garcia* does not include the accent because while in the movie itself García was pronounced in standard Spanish, this popular film spawned the phrase "message to Garcia" (pronounced gringo style, GAR-cia) that had a life of its own. The widely used, Anglicized pronunciation would be negated by the accent in Spanish. In order not to estrange the reader from the film, the English punctuation of *Viva Zapata!* has been retained, instead of the Spanish-accurate *¡Viva Zapata!*

Thus, in general, numerous accents and orthographic marks (yes, Virginia, there is a difference between *ano* and *año*) have been restored to the Spanish elements of film titles and the names of film professionals, but in certain cases, such as when American-style pronunciation is widespread or where adding previously nonexistent Spanish elements would make a title seem incongruous, the American usage has been maintained.

ON ACCURACY

In general, this second volume represents the most complete information that I have been able to obtain, and therefore it updates and/or corrects information that appeared in the earlier volume in the case of discrepancies between the two volumes. The one exception to this may be in the area of film dates, a seemingly impenetrable thicket. In the first volume, I pointed out that a film's date may vary due to diverse practices such as keying the film on the date of its completion rather than on the date of its original release. In point of fact there are additional dating practices. A third date that complicates matters is neither that of the film's completion nor of its general release but its debut (usually at one cinema house). A fourth practice is the release, as in the case of Italian or Mexican films created for dual markets (e.g., the home market and the United States) in different languages, with different release dates and with either different titles or the same title. Finally, there is one additional complication, this one editorial. The index of film titles was the last element generated for this book; thus, I did not have access in writing my manuscript to cross-references to the films I cited until after the manuscript had been typeset and indexed. The result is that the reader will encounter, from time to time, discrepant dates between the two volumes or even within the same volume that reflect, but unfortunately do not specify, the dating practice used: completion of film, first screening, general release, or release in a new market. However, usually these dates do not vary by more than a year or so. Generally, but not always, dates given by the American Film Institute catalogs (which are usually general release dates) are given precedence. However, it should be noted that no catalogs exist for the years 1941 through 1960 and 1971 through the present. The perceptive reader of the biographies in this book will note that this research work (like all others) is relatively less complete for the period 1941-1960 because the AFI catalogs have not yet been done for those years and will not be done perhaps for decades. For example, if you look at the entry "Joe Yrigoyen," you will find a radical example of missing data. Because only the *AFI Catalog* (as contrasted with other less exhaustive filmographies) would list the credits of a stuntman or bit player, Yrigoyen's credits jump from *Melody Ranch* (1940) to *The Sons of Katie Elder* (1965). Assuredly, Yrigoyen worked in film during the period between 1941 and 1960, but because

no AFI catalog exists to document his credits, it has proved impossible to provide them. The more recent period (1971-present) is not as problematic, however, because of the existence of other filmographies, although, once again, not ones with the completeness of the *AFI Catalog*.

On the other hand, AFI coverage is extraordinarily weak in many ways for the purpose of this research even for the decades for which it is currently available. For example, for the period 1911-1920 only features of four or more reels are catalogued by AFI, with the result that the majority of the films that my research refers to do not appear in the *AFI Catalog* for that decade, including almost all of the "greaser" films. Recently I have done research on the first Alamo film, *The Immortal Alamo* (1911, Star Film Company, dir. Gaston Méliès) and the first Cisco Kid film, *The Caballero's Way* (1914, Eclair). Neither are in the *AFI Catalog* for 1911-1920. Four reels was a very substantial number in the early years of that decade, so much so that as the 1911-1920 *AFI Catalog* points out (p. xv), the first film listed for that decade does not appear until 14 April 1912! An additional shortcoming that affects this research is that, while the AFI project hopes to include short films and newsreels at some later date, at this point they are still merely a glimmer in the camera minder's eye.

With respect to the subject of birthdates, as I pointed out in the first volume, there is a strong professional incentive for actors to represent themselves as younger than they actually are. As a result, not surprisingly, actors' birthdates often vary from source to source, sometimes by as much as a decade or more. In the case of significant variations, I have included the discrepant birthdates given by different sources. Also, in order to provide more accuracy, I have used the terms actor and actress, rather than using actor for females. This procedure makes clear what gender the Guadalupes, Ángels, and others are.

Another element of inaccuracy in film biographies and film research reflects the posture of the writer. Let me cite some relevant examples. In a few recent articles that have focused on the director Gregory Nava and his success with *My Family/Mi familia,* which in turn has opened the door to Nava for new projects, it has been highlighted that a full twelve years transpired between this director's independently produced *El Norte* (1983) and *My Family*. The implication is that despite his great success with the independently produced film, this unfortunate director had to "wait" all this time in order to get a chance to make a "Hollywood" film. This portrait of the deserving but unrecognized Latino director may serve to reinforce Latino notions of discrimination but entirely obscures the truth that Nava did get his chance after *El Norte* and proceeded to produce *A Time of Destiny* (1988, Columbia), which was a stupendous bomb despite its starring such major talents as William Hurt, Timothy Hutton, and Francisco Rabal. I have singled out this one example, but film writing, both popular and academic, is rife with such misrepresentations. The comforting homily of the Latino talent oppressed by racist Hollywood gnomes is perpetuated at the expense of the facts and a deeper understanding of how films are made and how Latinos participate in their making. Unfortunately, there is sufficient discrimination in Hollywood already and no need to fabricate more than exists.

A somewhat different but analogous problem is introduced by Luis Reyes and Peter Rubie's *Hispanics in Hollywood,* which to my mind has a somewhat misleading subtitle, *An Encyclopedia of Film and Television.* Let me state at the outset that this book greatly advances our information base on Hispanics in film and Hispanic-focused film, although the volume, featuring a miniscule bibliography, does not reference all of its sources. However, it is primarily the product of Hollywood publicist Luis Reyes, and as such it often reflects not the work of the academic encyclopedist, dry but aspiring to objectivity and to highlighting that which is documentable, but rather the emotionally heightened art of the publicist. As a result, Reyes and Rubie's book is replete with "firstest with the mostest" sorts of narratives and anecdotes about the great role that was almost in the hands of the actor (Hollywood-style "humongous fish that got away" stories). All the same, the book is really a significant advance.

And then there is inaccuracy through simple carelessness or invention. Here I would like to cite Juan B. Heinink, writing in his "Introducción: Agradecimientos y Reproches" to the book *Cita en Hollywood* by Juan B. Heinink and Robert G. Dickson, another work that is a major advance in our understanding of Hispanic-focused Hollywood. Heinink discusses how he came to do research on Spanish-language films in Hollywood and points out that in doing other, tangential cataloging work, he came across Alfonso Pinto's "Hollywood Spanish-Language Films" in the journal *Films in Review.* Heinink thought at the time that the Pinto article pretty much exhausted the subject, but upon further investigation he found that

Alfonso Pinto también cometió muchas equivocaciones, omisiones, e imperdonables invenciones, que se multiplicaron al pasar de mano en mano. Entonces no me di cuenta de aquellos errores, y no reaccioné a tiempo para evitar que se repitieran en mi obra precedente de catalogación, aunque así aprendí a no utilizar nunca informaciones de segunda mano. En vista de la situación, consideré oportuno hacerme cargo del caso, y comencé de nuevo desde el principio. (10)

Would that we could live in such an Edenic milieu where we would never have to utilize second-hand sources. In my career as a researcher, beginning in 1963, I have never come across such a treacherous and exasperating work as Alfred Charles Richard, Jr.'s three volumes of interpretative filmographies of Hispanic-focused Hollywood films. Carelessness and inventions are compounded by myriad typos, misspellings, inconsistencies, and numbering mistakes that reflect the publisher's willingness to print the author's manuscript without an iota of review or revision. And yet, as I stated in the earlier volume of this work (68), it is a goldmine of information since it goes through thousands of reviews of Hispanic-focused films in a wide variety of magazines and newspapers.

Despite the postmodern convention that emphasizes the pervasive subjectivity of all research, these two volumes do attempt to take the "handbook" component of the title seriously and strive to use only documentable information. Nevertheless, in all probability, just as in Heinink's initial situation, some of what has been garnered from second-hand sources reflects not fact but the primrose path. As I pointed out in the earlier volume, this two-volume work is not a history but rather an overview and handbook that provides for the first time a great deal of new or obscured information in a systematic way. It is my hope that these volumes will go through revised editions, possibly in a form more closely approximating history, and that, in whatever form, the information that is made public here will be corrected, updated, and expanded by additional research by my colleagues and myself. For indeed this field is alive and receiving considerable additional attention.

Additional recent research in the field has produced several titles in book form that have either been published since the 1994 appearance of the earlier tome, or, if published earlier, only became available to me since 1994. My bibliography includes over 2,000 titles, but I do want to make special reference to some particularly important books that I did not have access to for the writing of the earlier volume: Chon Noriega and Ana López, *The Ethnic Eye: Latino Media Arts;* volumes 2 and 3 of Richard's interpretative filmography; volumes 5 and 6 of García Riera's excellent *México visto por el cine extranjero;* and, of course, Juan B. Heinink and Robert G. Dickson's *Cita en Hollywood* and Luis Reyes and Peter Rubie's wonderful *Hispanics in Hollywood.* Recently, Frank Javier García Berumen's *The Chicano/Hispanic Image in American Film* has come across my desk. This is apparently a vanity publication. I have not had the opportunity to read it.

ACKNOWLEDGMENTS

I would like to acknowledge and thank a number of people who have helped bring this book to fruition including Rosemary Hanes and Madeline Matz of the Motion Picture, Broadcasting and Recorded Sound Division of the Library of Congress; the creators of Le Giornate del Cinema Muto (especially Livio Jacob, Piera Patat, and Lorenzo Codelli), which is housed in Gemona and runs the annual silent film festival in Pordenone, Italy, and which has permitted me access to numerous Hispanic-focused silent films that I otherwise would not have been able to view; Peter Lehman of the University of Arizona, who got me involved both in the Society for Cinema Studies and the Pordenone conference; Jack Keller, who has helped me greatly in obtaining film information from Mexico and elsewhere; Michael Olivas, law professor and film devotee par excellence, who has given me numerous film "leads" and elusive articles and other information over the years (decades actually); Karen Van Hooft and Barbara Firoozye of the Bilingual Press, who edited this book and acquired the productive if contagious habit of searching out Hispanic actors, particularly in new releases, and also Karen Akins (marketing manager) and Linda St. George Thurston (assistant editor/typesetter extraordinaire) of the Bilingual Press; Michael Sullivan, my chief operational associate in the minority projects that we have developed together (and this book certainly represents one of them); John Colt in the School of Art and the Hispanic Research Center of Arizona State University; and John Wincek, who did the design and layout of this book.

Orientation to the Listings

While the biographical information provided here is extensive, it is by no means exhaustive. A few of the limitations should be noted. There are certainly figures that deserve inclusion in this biographical listing but that for circumstances beyond the author's control may have been missed. In future editions of this book, it is my hope to add to the listings here with new names and to expand or refine the current listings. All suggestions with respect to additional names or corrections or emendations of the information as published here will be gratefully acknowledged.

In addition to lack of information or oversights, some names do not appear here simply because of limitations on the scope of this handbook. This is particularly true with respect to the actors, filmmakers, and other professionals who participated in the Hollywood Spanish-language film period (approximately between 1929 and 1940). With very few exceptions, this handbook includes only actors or filmmakers who were involved in multiple Hollywood Spanish-language films. For a much more complete list of personages as well as a splendid filmography of (most) of the films themselves, see Juan B. Heinink and Robert G. Dickson, *Cita en Hollywood: antología de las películas habladas en español* and *The American Film Institute Catalog, Feature Films (1931-1940)*.

Another limitation is with respect to either foreigners or non-Hispanic American actors who have undertaken Hispanic roles. This handbook does have very limited coverage of such personages; examples include Carmen Miranda, Pelé, and persons who may (or may not) be entirely non-Hispanic, such as Mimi Aguglia, but who worked extensively in Hollywood Spanish-language film. Of course, there is no complete record of non-Hispanics in Hispanic roles, but additional information on this phenomenon, much beyond what is available in this handbook, is provided in Emilio García Riera's six-volume study, *México visto por el cine extranjero*. Some additional information is also available in Luis Reyes and Peter Rubie, *Hispanics in Hollywood,* who in addition to a few actors provide information on a handful of non-Hispanic directors who cultivated Hispanic themes or settings.

Very recently archival information has become available with respect to primarily silent films that has proven valuable to me for my study of Hispanics in film. This reflects my acquisition of the CD-ROM *International Film Archive* produced by the International Federation of Film Archives, 6 Nottingham Street, London, United Kingdom W1M 3 RB (tel. (0)171 224 0991; fax (0)171 224 1203). In a few cases where the actors or filmmakers are important but have been obscured (e.g., Myrtle González, Soledad Jiménez), I have indicated an archive that holds the film (holding a film usually but does not always carry the implication that the film is available for viewing, due to the condition of early films). In a second edition of this book it is the author's intention to greatly expand this archival information. On the other hand, readers should understand that the majority of all silent films worldwide have been permanently lost and their content has to be interpolated from other sources such as scripts, catalogs, newspaper reviews, and advertisements.

Abbreviations (Publications)

PHH   Piet Hien Honig and Hanns-Georg Rodek, *100001. Die Showbusiness-Enzyklopadie des 20. Jahrhunderts.*

R   Luis Reyes and Peter Rubie, *Hispanics in Hollywood.*

Abbreviations (Archives)

CF   Cineteca del Friuli (Gemona, Italy)
CR   Cinémathèque Royale, Brussels
EH   George Eastman House, Rochester, New York
LC   Library of Congress, Washington, D.C.
MOMA   Museum of Modern Art, New York City
NAC   National Archive of Canada, Ottawa
NFTA   National Film and Television Archive, London

Julio Abadia

Actor; he did a few Hollywood Spanish-language films. He had the role of Armando in *Su última noche* (1931, MGM, dir. Chester M. Franklin, starring Conchita Montenegro and María Alba), a Spanish-language adaptation of *The Gay Deceiver* (1926). He also appeared in *Monerías* (1931, MGM, starring Charley Chase), a Spanish-language adaptation of the short, *Rough Seas* (1931, starring Charley Chase), and *Rosa de Francia* (1935, Fox, starring Rosita Díaz Gimeno, Julio Peña, and Antonio Moreno), a Spanish-language original based on a stage comedy by Eduardo Marquina and Luis Fernández Ardavín.

Natividad Abascal

Actress; she appeared in *Bananas* (1971, dir. Woody Allen).

Victoria Abril

(Victoria Mérida Rojas) Actress, born in Madrid, July 4, 1959. She has appeared in over 60 European films, usually in highly erotic roles. She costarred in *On the Line* (1983, El Iman, S.A., film made in Spain and released in Spanish as *Río abajo*) opposite David Carradine as a Mexican whore fought over by two Mexico-U.S. border guards and in the Pedro Almodóvar films released in English as *Tie Me Up! Tie Me Down!* (1990, Miramax, opposite Antonio Banderas), *High Heels* (1991), and *Kika* (1993). She has also appeared in *Jimmy Hollywood* (1994) opposite Joe Pesci and Christian Slater.

Enrique Acosta

Actor, born in Mexico City, February 26, 1870, died May 22, 1948 [one source has 1949]. Acosta left Mexico during the Revolution of 1910 and found work in Hollywood as a bit player in silent films including *Don Q, Son of Zorro* (1925). During the talking period he worked as a supporting actor in at least 21 Hollywood Spanish-language productions, particularly Laurel and Hardy and Charley Chase vehicles, including, among others: *Sombras de gloria* (1929, Sono-Art Productions, starring José Bohr and Mona

Rico), a Spanish-language version of *Blaze O'Glory* (1929, starring Eddie Dowling and Betty Compson); *Ladrones* (1929, MGM, starring Stan Laurel and Oliver Hardy), a Spanish-language version of *Night Owls* (1929, starring Laurel and Hardy); *El jugador de golf* (1930, MGM, starring Charley Chase), a Spanish-language version of *All Teed Up* (1930, starring Charley Chase); *Tiembla y titubea* (1930, MGM, starring Stan Laurel and Oliver Hardy), a Spanish-language version of *Below Zero* (1930, starring Laurel and Hardy); *Estrellados* (1930, MGM, starring Buster Keaton, Raquel Torres, Don Alvarado, and María Calvo), a Spanish-language version of *Free and Easy* (1930, starring Buster Keaton and Anita Page); *El precio de un beso* (1930, Fox, starring José Mojica, Mona Maris, and Antonio Moreno), a Spanish-language version of *One Mad Kiss* (1930, starring José Mojica, Mona Maris, and Antonio Moreno); *Una cana al aire* (1930, MGM, starring Charley Chase), a Spanish-language version of *Looser Than Loose* (1930, starring Charley Chase); *De bote en bote* (1931, MGM, starring Stan Laurel and Oliver Hardy), a Spanish-language version of *Pardon Us* (1931, starring Laurel and Hardy); *Don Juan diplomático* (1931, Universal, starring Miguel Faust Rocha, Lia Torá, and Celia Montalván), a Spanish-language version of *The Boudoir Diplomat* (1930, starring Betty Compson, Mary Duncan, and Ian Keith); *Politiquerías* (1931, MGM, starring Stan Laurel and Oliver Hardy), a Spanish-language version of *Chickens Come Home* (1931, starring Laurel and Hardy); *Dos noches* (1933, Fanchon Royer Pictures, Inc., presented by J. H. Hoffberg Co., starring José Crespo, Conchita Montenegro, and Romualdo Tirado), a Spanish-language version of *Revenge at Monte Carlo* (1933, starring José Crespo, June Collyer, and Wheeler Oakman); *Una viuda romántica* (1933, Fox, starring Catalina Bárcena, Gilbert Roland, Mona Maris, and Julio Peña), a Spanish-language original based on "El sueño de una noche de agosto" by Gregorio Martínez Sierra (Madrid, 1918); *Tres amores* (1934, Universal, starring José Crespo, Anita Campillo, and Mona Maris), a Spanish-language version of *Bachelor Mother* (1933, starring Evalyn Knapp and James Murray); and *Te quiero con locura* (1935, Fox, starring Rosita Moreno and Raúl Roulien), a Spanish-language original comedy.

Rodolfo "Rudy" Acosta

(Also used Rudolph) Actor, born in Chihuahua, Mexico, July 29, 1920 [R lists 1921], died in Woodland Hills, California, November 7, 1974. As a teenager he lived in both Mexico City and Los Angeles. During World War II, Acosta served in Naval Intelligence with the U.S. Navy. Having worked in Mexican films, he went to Hollywood in the late 1940s and had a secondary role in John Ford's *The*

Above: Rodolfo Acosta struggling with John Wayne in *Hondo* (1954)

Fugitive (1947), which was shot in Mexico. In 1948, he played the role of a gigolo in the Mexican film classic *Salón México,* directed by Emilio Fernández, for which he won an Ariel, Mexico's highest acting award. His career was primarily marked by character roles, specializing in Mexican and Indian villains. His credits include *One Way Street* and *Pancho Villa Returns* (1950); *The Bullfighter and the Lady* (1951); *Horizons West* (1952); *San Antone* and *Destination Gobi* (1953); *Hondo, Passion, Drum Beat,* and *Night People* (1954); *A Life in the Balance* and *The Littlest Outlaw* (1955); *The Proud Ones* and *Bandido* (1956); *The Tijuana Story* (leading role) (1957); *Walk Like a Dragon* (1960); *One-Eyed Jacks, The Last Rebel, Posse from Hell,* and *The Second Time Around* (1961); *How the West Was Won* and *Savage Sam* (1963); *Río Conchos* (1964); *The Greatest Story Ever Told, The Reward,* and *The Sons of Katie Elder* (1965); *Return of the Seven* (1966); *Valley of Mystery* (1967); *Dayton's Devils* (1968); *Impasse* and *Young Bill Young* (1969); *Savage Run, Flap, The Great White Hope,* and *Run, Simon, Run* (1970); and *Pat Garrett and Billy the Kid* (1973).

Teresa Acosta

Actress; she had a supporting role in *Way of a Gaucho* (1952, 20th Century-Fox).

Acquanetta

(Burnu Acquanetta Davenport) Actress, born in Cheyenne, Wyoming, July 17, 1920. She was discovered by Charles Boyer and first appeared in *Arabian Nights* (1942, starring María Montez). She also appeared in *Dead Man's Eyes* (1944, Universal, starring Lon Chaney, Jr.), *Captive Wild Woman* (1943, Universal) and its sequel, *Jungle Woman* (1944, Universal), *Tarzan and the Leopard Woman* (1946, RKO, starring Johnny Weismuller), and *The Lost Continent* (1951). She had a small role in *Grizzly Adams: The Legend Continues* (1990).

Mimi Aguglia

(Mimi Gerolama Aguglia) Internationally recognized actress of Italian descent, born in Palermo, Italy, December 21, 1884, died in Woodland Hills, California, July 31, 1970. She appeared in several Hollywood Spanish-language films in supporting roles including *Mi último amor* (1931, Fox, starring José Mojica and Andrés de Segurola), a Spanish-language version of *Their Mad Moment* (1931, starring Warner Baxter and ZaSu Pitts); *Marido y mujer* (1932, Fox, starring George Lewis, Conchita Montenegro, and José Nieto), a Spanish-language version of *Bad Girl* (1931, dir. Frank Borzage, starring Sally Eilers and James Dunn); *El último varón sobre la tierra* (1932, Fox, starring Raúl Roulien and Rosita Moreno), a Spanish-language version of *The Last Man on Earth* (1924, starring Earle Foxe and Grace Cunard); *Primavera en otoño* (1933, Fox, starring Catalina Bárcena, Raúl Roulien, and Antonio Moreno), a Spanish-language original based on a work by Gregorio Martínez Sierra; *Una viuda romántica* (1933, Fox, starring Catalina Bárcena, Gilbert Roland, and Mona Maris), a Spanish-language original based on "El sueño de una noche de agosto" (Madrid, 1918) by Gregorio Martínez Sierra; *Tres amores* (1934, Universal, starring José Crespo, Anita Campillo, and Mona Maris), a Spanish-language version of *Bachelor Mother* (1933, starring Evalyn Knapp and James Murray); and *Señora casada necesita marido* (1934, Fox, starring Catalina Bárcena, Antonio Moreno, and José Crespo), a Spanish-language original based on the novel *Mi segunda mujer* by Eugenio Heltai. She played a Mexican woman in the English-language Howard Hughes film *The Outlaw* (1940, released 1943).

Antonio Aguilar

Singer, *charro,* and film star, born in Zacatecas, Mexico, June 13, 1922. He appeared in one Hollywood film, playing the Juarista general, Rojas, in *The Undefeated* (1969, 20th Century-Fox, starring John Wayne). He also appeared in one of the most unusual and interesting Mexican films, *Ánimas Trujano,* released in the United States as *The Important Man* (1961, Azteca Films, dir. Ismael Rodríguez, starring Toshiro Mifune); he had the role of Tadeo.

Rico Alanís

(Also Alaniz) Actor. He appeared in minor roles in the 1950s including *Santiago* (1956, Warner, starring Alan Ladd); *Stagecoach to Fury* (1956, 20th Century-Fox); *The Women of Pitcairn Island* (1956, 20th Century-Fox); *Toughest Gun in Tombstone* (1958, United Artists); *War of the Colossal Beast* (1958); *The Magnificent Seven* (1960, Columbia, starring Yul Brynner, Steve McQueen, and Eli Wallach); and *Summer and Smoke* (1961, Paramount, starring Laurence Harvey, Geraldine Page, and Rita Moreno).

Luz Alba

Actress; she had minor roles in *Daughter of the West* (1949, Film Classics) and *Sombrero* (1953, MGM, starring Ricardo Montalbán, with José Greco and Thomas Gómez). The last film, although based on the well-regarded, pre-Chicana novel *Mexican Village* by Josephina Niggli (who shares credit for the screenplay), is grossly stereotypical (bullfighters, gypsies, supplications to an Aztec god, fiesta-loving locals, flamenco, and on and on).

María Alba

(Also used María Casajuana professionally) Actress, born in Barcelona, December 9, 1910. In English-language films, María Alba appeared in *Blindfold* (1928); *Road House* (1928, Fox, starring Lionel Barrymore); *A Girl in Every Port* (1928, Fox, dir. Howard Hawks, costarring opposite Victor McLaglen); *Joy Street* (1929); *Hell's Heroes* (1930); *Mr. Robinson Crusoe* (1932), starring Douglas Fairbanks, Sr., as a man who bets he can survive like Crusoe on a South Sea island; *Chandu on the Magic Island* (1934); and *Return of Chandu (The Magician)* (1934, starring Bela Lugosi as Chandu, the Master of White Magic), a 12-chapter serial. She starred or appeared in at least nine Hollywood Spanish-language films including *Charros, gauchos y manolas* (1930, Hollywood Spanish Pictures Co., dir. Xavier Cugat), as a Spanish *manola; El cuerpo del delito* (1930, Paramount, opposite Antonio Moreno and Ramón Pereda), a Spanish-language version of *The Benson Murder Case* (1930, starring William Powell and Natalie Moorhead); *La fuerza del querer* (1930, James Cruze Productions, presented by Paramount, with Carlos Barbé as costar), a Spanish-language version of *The Big Fight* (1930, starring Lola Lane and Ralph Ince); *Olimpia* (1930, MGM, opposite José Crespo), a Spanish-language version of *His Glorious Night* (1929, dir. Lionel Barrymore, starring John Gilbert and Catherine Dale Owen); *Los que danzan* (1930, Warner, opposite Antonio Moreno), a Spanish-language version of *Those Who Dance*

Above: María Alba as an unfaithful countess and Juan de Landa as her husband in *Su última noche* (1931, MGM)

(1930, starring Monte Blue and Lila Lee); *Su última noche* (1931, MGM, opposite Ernesto Vilches and Conchita Montenegro), a Spanish-language version of *The Gay Deceiver* (1926, starring Lew Cody and Marceline Day); *El código penal* (1931, Columbia, opposite Barry Norton), a Spanish-language version of *The Criminal Code* (1931, dir. Howard Hawks, starring Walter Huston and Constance Cummings); *Del infierno al cielo* (1931, Fox, opposite Juan Torena), a Spanish-language version of *The Man Who Came Back* (1931, dir. Raoul Walsh, starring Janet Gaynor and Charles Farrell); and *La ley del harem* (1931, Fox, opposite José Mojica and Carmen Larrabeiti), a Spanish-language version of *Fazil* (1928, dir. Howard Hawks, starring Charles Farrell and Greta Nissen).

Luis Alberni

Actor, born in Barcelona, October 4, 1886, died in Hollywood, California, December 23, 1962. Upon graduating from the University of Barcelona, he came to the United States as a youth and began a simultaneous career on Broadway and in silent films. After the introduction of sound, he became one of Hollywood's busiest character actors, typically in roles as an excitable Latino. He appeared in both English-language and a few Spanish-language Hollywood films. His English-language credits include *Little Italy* (1921); *The Man From Beyond* (1922); *The Bright Shawl* and *The Valley of Lost Souls* (1923); *The Santa Fe Trail* (1930); *I Like Your Nerve, The Mad Genius, Men in Her Life, One Heavenly Night, Side Show, Svengali, Sweepstakes,* and *The Tip-Off* (all 1931); *The Big Stampede,*

Above: Luis Alberni and Barbara Leonard in
¡Asegure a su mujer! (1934, Fox)

Cock of the Air, The Cohens and Kellys in Hollywood, Guilty or Not Guilty, High Pressure, Hypnotized, Manhattan Parade, A Parisian Romance, The Kid from Spain, Week-end Marriage, and *The Woman in Room 13* (1932); *Above the Clouds, The California Trail, Flying Down to Rio, Goodbye Love, I Love That Man, If I Were Free, Lady Killer, The Last Trail, Man from Monterey, Men Must Fight, The Sphinx, Topaze, Trick for Trick,* and *When Ladies Meet* (1933); *The Black Cat, The Captain Hates the Sea, The Count of Monte Cristo, Glamour, I Believed in You, One Night of Love, Strictly Dynamite,* and *When Strangers Meet* (1934); *Bad Boy, Champagne for Breakfast, The Gay Deception, The Gilded Lily, Goin' to Town, In Caliente, Let's Live Tonight, Love Me Forever, Manhattan Moon, Metropolitan, Music Is Music, Public Opinion, Rendezvous at Midnight, Roberta,* and *The Winning Ticket* (1935); *Anthony Adverse, Colleen, Dancing Pirate, Follow Your Heart, Hats Off,* and *Ticket to Paradise* (1936); *Easy Living, The Great Garrick, Hitting a New High, The King and the Chorus Girl, Love on Toast, Madame X, Manhattan Merry-Go-Round, Sing and Be Happy, Two Wise Maids, Under Suspicion,* and *When You're in Love* (1937); *I'll Give a Million* (1938); *The Amazing Mr. Williams, The Great Man Votes, The Housekeeper's Daughter, Let Freedom Ring, Miracle on Main Street,* and *Naughty but Nice* (1939); *Elsa Maxwell's Public Deb No. 1, Enemy Agent, The Lone Wolf Meets a Lady, Scatterbrain,* and *So You Won't*

Talk (1940); *The Lady Eve* and *That Hamilton Woman* (1941); *Babes on Broadway* (1942); *Harvest Melody* (1943); *A Bell for Adano* (1945); and *What Price Glory* (1952). His Spanish-language credits include *Hombres en mi vida* (1932, Columbia, starring Lupe Vélez and Gilbert Roland), a Spanish-language version of *Men in Her Life* (1931, starring Lois Moran and Charles Bickford); *La ciudad de cartón* (1933, Fox), a Spanish-language original; *La buenaventura* (1934, First National Pictures, starring Enrico Caruso, Jr., and Anita Campillo), a Spanish-language original; and *¡Asegure a su mujer!* (1934, Fox, starring Raúl Roulien, Conchita Montenegro, Antonio Moreno, and Mona Maris), a Spanish-language original.

Edward Albert

(Eddie Albert, Jr.) Actor, son of Margo and Eddie Albert, born in Los Angeles, February 20, 1951. He made his motion picture debut in *The Fool Killer* (1965, Allied Artists) as a 12-year-old runaway and has starred or appeared in *Butterflies Are Free* (1972); *Forty Carats* (1973); *Death Cruise* (1974); *Midway* (1976); *The Purple Taxi* and *The Domino Principle* (1977); *The Greek Tycoon* (1978, starring Anthony Quinn); *Silent Victory: The Kitty O'Neil Story* (1979); *When Time Ran Out!* (1980); *Galaxy of Terror* (1981); *Butterfly* (1982); *A Time to Die* (1983); *Ellie* (1984); *The House Where Evil Dwells* (1985); *Getting Even* and *Terminal Entry* (1986); *Distortions* (1987); *The Rescue, Fist Fighter* (costarring opposite Jorge Rivero), and *The Heist* (1988); *Mindgames, Accidents,* and *Wild Zone* (1989); *Exiled in America* (1990); *Out of Sight, Out of Mind* (1991); *Body Language* (1992); and *Shootfighter: Fight to the Death* (1993). He has also made numerous television appearances.

Rafael Alcaide

(Also Alcayde) Actor. He costarred in one Hollywood Spanish-language film, *Castillos en el aire* (1938, Monogram Pictures, opposite Cristina Téllez), a Spanish-language original based on a screenplay by Jaime Salvador. He also appeared in supporting roles in *Ten Days to Tulara* (1958, United Artists, starring Sterling Hayden and Rodolfo Hoyos) and *Villa!* (1958, 20th Century-Fox, starring Brian Keith and César Romero).

José Alcalá

Child actor; he had the leading role in *. . . and the earth did not swallow him* (1995, dir. Severo Pérez).

José Alcántara

(Pepe Alcántara) Actor; he appeared in supporting roles in a few Hollywood Spanish-language films including *Cuerpo y alma* (Fox, 1931, starring George Lewis, Ana María Custodio, and José Nieto), a Spanish-language version of *Body and Soul* (1931, starring Charles Farrell, Elissa Landi, Humphrey Bogart, and Myrna Loy); *Hay que casar al príncipe* (1931, Fox, starring José Mojica and Conchita Montenegro), a Spanish-language version of *Paid to Love* (1927, dir. Howard Hawks, starring George O'Brien and Virginia Valli); and *Mamá* (1931, Fox, dir. Benito Perojo, starring Catalina Bárcena and Rafael Rivelles), a Spanish-language original based on a work by Gregorio Martínez Sierra.

Luana Alcañiz

(Lucrecia Ana Úbeda) Major Spanish-language actress, born in Madrid, May 8, 1906. She appeared either as the lead or in a major role in at least 14 Hollywood Spanish-language films including *Del mismo barro* (1930, Fox, opposite Mona Maris and Juan Torena), a Spanish-language version of *Common Clay* (1930, starring Constance Bennett and Lew Ayres); *Cupido Chauffeur* (1930, Fox, costarring Richard Keene and Manuel Arbó), a Spanish-language original based on "Border Love" by Paul Pérez and Max Constant; *El último de los Vargas* (1930, Fox, opposite George Lewis and Vicente Padula), a Spanish-language version of *Last of the Duanes* (1930, starring George O'Brien, Lucille Brown, and Myrna Loy); *El presidio* (1930, MGM, starring José Crespo and Juan de Landa), a Spanish-language version of *The Big House* (1930, starring Chester Morris and Wallace Beery); *La llama sagrada* (1931, Warner, starring Elvira Morla and Martín Garralaga), a Spanish-language version of *The Sacred Flame* (1929, starring Pauline Frederick and Conrad Nagel); *La dama atrevida* (1931, First National Pictures, costarring Ramón Pereda and Martín Garralaga), a Spanish-language version of *The Lady Who Dared* (1931, starring Billie Dove and Conway Tearle); *El pasado acusa* (1931, Columbia, costarring Barry Norton and Carlos Villarías), a Spanish-language version of *The Good Bad Girl* (1931, starring Marie Prevost and James Hall); *Primavera en otoño* (1933, Fox, starring Catalina Bárcena and Raúl Roulien), a Spanish-language original based on a work by Gregorio Martínez Sierra; *Julieta compra un hijo* (1935, Fox, opposite Catalina Bárcena and Gilbert Roland), a Spanish-language original based on a work by Gregorio Martínez Sierra; *Contra la corriente* (1935, RKO Radio Pictures, dir. Ramón Novarro, costarring José Caraballo), a Spanish-language original

based on a screenplay by Alfredo Le Pera; *La última cita* (1935, Columbia, opposite José Crespo), a Spanish-language original based on a screenplay by René Borgia; and *Verbena trágica* (1938, Columbia, opposite Fernando Soler), a Spanish-language original based on a screenplay by Jean Bart. She had minor roles in *Frontiers of '49* (1939) and *Doctor Zhivago* (1965, MGM), as Mrs. Sventytski.

Julio Aldama

Actor. He was very active in the Mexican film industry and also seen in the United States in *The Pearl of Tlayucán* (1964, Mexican production) and *Guns for San Sebastian* (1968, MGM, starring Anthony Quinn).

Norma Aleandro

Actress, playwright, and director, born in Argentina in 1941. Known best for her performance in the Academy Award-winning Best Foreign Film *The Official Story* (1985), for which she was named best actress at Cannes. She has also acted in *Gaby—A True Story* (1987), *Cousins* (1989), *Vital Signs* (1990), and *One Man's War* (1991, for cable TV), and she continues to do Spanish-language film.

Gabriel Algaro

(Algara in *AFI Catalog*) Actor, born in 1888, died in Zaragoza, Spain, in 1951. He had supporting roles in a few Hollywood Spanish-language films including *La incorregible* (1931, Paramount, starring Enriqueta Serrano and Tony D'Algy), a Spanish-language version of *Manslaughter* (1930, starring Claudette Colbert and Fredric March); *Entre noche y día* (1931, United Artists, starring Alfonso Granada and Helena D'Algy), a Spanish-language version of *77 Park Lane* (1931, starring Dennis Neilson-Terry and Betty Keen); *Un caballero de frac* (1931, Paramount, starring Roberto Rey and Gloria Guzmán), a Spanish-language version of *Evening Clothes* (1927, starring Adolphe Menjou, Virginia Valli, and Noah Beery); and *El hombre que asesinó* (1931, Paramount British, starring Rosita Moreno and Ricardo Puga), a Spanish-language version of *Stamboul* (1931, starring Rosita Moreno and Warwick Ward).

Ana Alicia

(Ana Alicia Ortiz) Actress, born in Mexico City, December 10, 1956. She attended high school in El Paso and graduated with a degree in drama from the University of Texas. First a contract player for Universal television, in 1980 she was cast as Melissa Cumson in the television series *Falcon Crest*. She was in *Coward of the County* (1981, TV film) and played the wife of an aristocrat in *Romero* (1989).

Fernando Allende

Actor, born in Cuba, November 10, 1954, and raised in Mexico. He was a leading man in a number of Mexican films in the 1970s and 1980s. He played opposite Joanne Woodward as a gang tough in the television film *The Streets of L.A.* (1979), appeared in an independent feature film, *Heartbreaker* (1983), and continues to work in U.S. television and in international productions.

Néstor Almendros

(Also used an alias, John Nestor) Director of photography, born in Barcelona, October 30, 1930, raised in Cuba, died in New York City, March 4, 1992. After working as a cameraman or director on several documentaries of the early Castro era, he then moved to France where he worked for television and on film shorts. In the mid-1960s, he began collaborating regularly with director Eric Rohmer and later with director François Truffaut. Beginning in the late 1970s, he participated in numerous U.S. productions. He won an Academy Award for Best Cinematography for the 1978 film *Days of Heaven* and was director of photography of *Madame Rosa* (1977), which won the Academy Award for Best Foreign Film. Selected films: *The Wild Racers* (U.S., 1968), *Six in Paris* (1968), *Gun Runner* (U.S., 1968), *Ma nuit chez Maud/My Night at Maud's* (Fr., 1969), *More* (1969), *L'enfant sauvage/The Wild Child* (Fr., 1970), *Le genou de Claire/Claire's Knee* (Fr., 1971), *L'amour l'après-midi/Chloe in the Afternoon* (Fr., 1972), *L'histoire d'Adèle/The Story of Adele H.* (Fr., 1975), *Days of Heaven* (U.S., 1978), *Goin' South* (1978), *Kramer vs. Kramer* (1979), *The Blue Lagoon* (1980), *Sophie's Choice* (1982), *Places in the Heart* (1984), *Nadine* (1987), and *Billy Bathgate* (1991). He codirected *Improper Conduct* (1984) and *Nobody Listened*.

Chelo Alonso

Cuban-born actress, born in 1938. She appeared in a number of Italian epics of the 1960s that were released in the United States in English versions. Credits include *Goliath and the Barbarians* and *Sign of the Gladiators* (1960); *Morgan the Pirate* and *The Pirate and the Slave Girl* (1961); *The Huns* and *Son of Samson* (1962); *Atlas Against the Cyclops* (1963); and a small part in *The Good, the Bad, and the Ugly* (1967).

Above: Cinematographer Néstor Almendros

María Conchita Alonso

Actress and singer, born in Cienfuegos, Cuba, May 13, 1957. She moved to Venezuela at the age of five and began her career as a beauty-pageant winner (Miss Teenager of the World 1971 and Miss Venezuela 1975), subsequently becoming one of South America's best-selling recording artists. She established herself in Hollywood with her role in *Moscow on the Hudson* (1984, opposite Robin Williams). Her credits include *Fear City* (1984); *Touch and Go* and *A Fine Mess* (1986); *The Running Man* (1987, opposite Arnold Schwartzenegger); *Extreme Prejudice,* as a Mexican cantina singer, and *Blood Ties* (1987); *Colors* (1988); *Vampire's Kiss* (1989); *Predator 2* (1990), as a Latina cop; *McBain* (1991); *Teamster Boss: The Jackie Presser Story* (1992); and *Roosters* (1995, dir. Robert Young).

John A. Alonzo

Actor and cinematographer, born in Dallas, Texas, January 3, 1934. He worked as a cameraman at a local Dallas television station and moved to Los Angeles in 1957, doing bit parts in movies and television, often as a *bandido*. He began his career as an actor in *The Magnificent Seven* (1960) and was in *The Long Rope* (1961), *Hand of Death* (1962), *Terror at Black Falls* (1962), and *Invitation to a Gunfighter* (1964). The latter was shot by Joe MacDonald, who encouraged him to pursue a career in cinematography. Alonzo assisted in the film *Seconds* (1966), directed by John Frankenheimer, who later hired him as his cameraman on *Black Sunday* (1977). Other credits as a cinematographer include *Bloody Mama* (1970), *Harold and Maude* (1971), *Lady Sings the Blues* (1972), *Sounder* (1972), *Chinatown* (1974, for which he was nominated for an Academy Award in Cinematography), *Norma Rae* (1979), *Blue Thunder* (1983), *Scarface* (1983), *Runaway Train* (1985), and *Steel Magnolias* (1989).

Carlos Alvarado

(Carlos Page) Agent, born June 22, 1901, in New Mexico, died June 22, 1983; the brother of Don Alvarado. He founded a talent agency in 1943 that specialized in promoting Latinos.

Don Alvarado

(José Page) Actor, born November 4, 1904 [1900 according to PHH, 1905 according to R], in Albuquerque, died March 31, 1967, in Hollywood. Also known professionally as Don Page, he got his first role as an extra in *Mademoiselle Midnight* (1924) and soon became an established "Latin Lover" type in many late silents and early talkies, particularly musicals. He was cast in non-Hispanic parts as well. In the 1940s he became an assistant director for Warner Brothers. His English-language film acting credits include *The Pleasure Buyers* (Warner Brothers), *Satan in Sables,* and *The Wife Who Wasn't Wanted* (all 1925); *The Night Cry* (Warner Brothers), *A Hero of the Big Snows,* and *His Jazz Bride* (1926); *The Monkey Talks* (1927, Fox, dir. Raoul Walsh [film held at EH]); *Loves of Carmen* (1927, Fox, dir. Raoul Walsh, opposite Dolores del Río [film held at MOMA]); *Breakfast at Sunrise* (1927); *The Scarlet Lady* and *No Other Woman* (both 1928); *The Battle of the Sexes* (1928, United Artists, presented by Joseph M. Schenck, dir. D. W. Griffith); *Drums of Love* (1928, Feature Productions, Inc., dir. D. W. Griffith, opposite Mary Philben and Lionel Barrymore [film held at LC]); *The Apache* (1928, Columbia); *Rio Rita* (1929, RKO); *The Bridge of San Luis Rey* (1929, MGM); *The Bad One* (1930, United Artists); *Captain Thunder* (1930, Warner Brothers); *Beau Ideal* (1931); *Bachelor's Affairs, The King Murder, Lady With a Past,* and *Westward Passage* (1932); *La Cucaracha* (1932, Pioneer); *Under Secret Orders* and *Black Beauty* (1933); *Morning Glory* (1933, opposite Katharine Hepburn); *A Demon for Trouble, Once to Every Bachelor,* and *Sweet Adeline* (1934); *The Devil Is a Woman* (1935,

Above: Don Alvarado in 1927

Below: Don Alvarado

Paramount, starring Marlene Dietrich and with César Romero); *I Live for Love* (1935); *Rose of the Rancho* (1936, Paramount); *Federal Agent* and *Rio Grande Romance* (1936); *The Lady Escapes, Love Under Fire,* and *Nobody's Baby* (1937); *Rose of the Rio Grande* and *A Trip to Paris* (1938); *Cafe Society* and *Invisible Stripes* (1939); *Knute Rockne—All American* and *One Night in the Tropics* (1940); and *The Big Steal* (1949). As an assistant director his credits, under the name Don Page, include *Rebel Without a Cause* (1955), *The Old Man and the Sea* (1958), and *Auntie Mame* (1958). He also starred or had major roles in the following Hollywood Spanish-language productions: *Un fotógrafo distraído* (1930, Hollywood Spanish Pictures Co., dir. Xavier Cugat, opposite Romualdo Tirado and Carmen Guerrero), a Spanish-language original; *La rosa de fuego* (1930, Tom White Productions, costarring Renée Torres), a Spanish-language original; *Estrellados* (1930, MGM, opposite Buster Keaton and Raquel Torres), a Spanish-language version of *Free and Easy* (1930, starring Buster Keaton and Anita Page); *Amor que vuelve* (1934, Latin American Pictures, Inc., presented by Kinematrade, costarring Renée Torres), a Spanish-language original; and *Rosa de Francia* (1935, Fox, starring Rosita Díaz Gimeno and Julio Peña), a Spanish-language original based on a comedy by Eduardo Marquina and Luis Fernández Ardavín. His former wife, Ann Page, later married Jack L. Warner, studio chief of Warner Brothers.

Fernando Alvarado

Mexican American child actor. He had roles in *A Medal for Benny* (1945), *Without Reservations* (1946), and *Wake of the Red Witch* (1948).

Magalí Alvarado

Actress, born in Puerto Rico and raised in New Jersey. She made her motion picture debut in *Salsa* (1988) and appeared in *Mi Vida Loca* (1994).

Trini Alvarado

Actress and dancer, born in Puerto Rico in 1967. She began performing as a flamenco dancer at age seven with her parents' dance troupe in New York. She made her film debut at age 11 in *Rich Kids* (1979), was in *A Movie Star's Daughter* (1979) and *Private Contentment* (1983), played Diane Keaton's daughter in *Mrs. Soffel* (1984), and had leading roles in *Times Square* (1980), *The Chair* and *Sweet Lorraine* (1987), *Nitti: The Enforcer* and *Satisfaction* (1988), *Stella* (1990), *The Babe* and *American Blue Note* (1991), *American*

Above: Trini Alvarado (right) and Bette Midler in *Stella* (1990)

Friends (1993), the highly regarded *Little Women* (1994), *The Pérez Family* (1995), and *The Frighteners* (1996).

Ángel Álvarez

Actor. He appeared in supporting roles in a few films of the 1960s and 1970s made in Spain or Italy and released in the United States in English-language versions including *Not On Your Life* (1965, Pathé Contemporary Films), *Operation Delilah* (1966), *Navajo Joe* (1967, United Artists, starring Burt Reynolds), *Django* (1968), and *The Mercenary* (1970, United Artists).

Pablo Álvarez

Actor; he had supporting roles in a few Hollywood Spanish-language films including *Sombras habaneras* (1929, Hispania Talking Film Corp., presented by All-Star Exchange, starring René Cardona and Jacqueline Logan), a Spanish-language original based on a screenplay by René Nestor; *Monsieur Le Fox* (1930, MGM, dir. Hal Roach, starring Gilbert Roland and Rosita Ballesteros), a Spanish-language version of *Men of the North* (1930, dir. Hal Roach, starring Gilbert Roland, Barbara Leonard, Robert Elliott, and Nina Quartaro); and *La voluntad del muerto* (1930, Universal, starring Lupita Tovar and Antonio Moreno), a Spanish-language version of *The Cat Creeps* (1930, starring Helen Twelvetrees and Raymond Hackett).

Pablo Álvarez Rubio

Actor and journalist, born in Madrid, June 7, 1900. He had two supporting roles in Hollywood Spanish-language films: *Los que danzan* (1930, Warner), as Juan, and *Drácula* (1931, Universal), as Renfield.

Domingo Ambriz

Actor, born in Texas, February 29, 1948. He had the starring role as an illegal immigrant in the notable independent Chicano production *Alambrista!* (1977, dir. Robert M. Young, costarring Trinidad Silva, Ned Beatty, and Edward James Olmos). He also appeared in *Walk Proud* (1979), *Green Ice* (1981), and *Young Guns II* (1990), and he had a supporting role in *American Me* (1992, dir. and starring Edward James Olmos, costarring William Forsythe, Pepe Serna, and Danny de la Paz).

Sonia Amelio

Actress; she had a supporting role in *The Wild Bunch* (1969, Warner Brothers) and was seen on a limited basis by American audiences in a few Mexican films released in the United States including *Fearmaker* (1989, starring Katy Jurado).

Ramsay Ames

(Rosemary Phillips; also Rosemary Ames) Actress, born March 30, 1924 [PHH has 1919], in New York City of a Spanish mother and an English father. She was first a night-club singer and leader of her own rumba orchestra. She appeared in *I Believed in You, Pursued,* and *Such Women Are Dangerous* (1934); *The Great Hotel Murder, One More Spring,* and *Our Little Girl* (1935); *Two Señoritas from Chicago* (1943); *Ali Baba and the Forty Thieves* (1944); *Beauty and the Bandit* (1946); *Alexander the Great* (1956); *The Running Man* (1963); and three serials: *G-Men Never Forget* (1948) at Republic, *The Vigilante* (1947) at Columbia, and *Black Widow* (1954).

Leo Anchóriz

(Leopoldo Anchóriz Fustel) Actor, born in Almería, Spain, 1932. He had principal parts in numerous action films in the 1960s and 1970s made in Spain or Italy for primary release in the United States in English-language versions, including *The Invincible Gladiator* (1963), *Commando* (1964), *Finger on the Trigger* and *Sandokan the Great* (1965), *Up the MacGregors* (1967), *Seven Guns for the MacGregors* (1968), *A Bullet for Sandoval* (1970, starring Ernest Borgnine), and *Kill Them All and Come Back Alone* (1970).

Marita Ángeles

Actress; she had supporting roles in a few Hollywood Spanish-language films including *La incorregible* (1931,

Paramount, starring Enriqueta Serrano and Tony D'Algy), a Spanish-language version of *Manslaughter* (1930, starring Claudette Colbert and Fredric March); *Un caballero de frac* (1931, Paramount, starring Roberto Rey and Gloria Guzmán), a Spanish-language version of *Evening Clothes* (1927, starring Adolphe Menjou, Virginia Valli, and Noah Beery); and *Las luces de Buenos Aires* (1931, Paramount, starring Carlos Gardel and Sofía Bazán), a Spanish-language original based on a work by Manuel Romero and Luis Bayón Herrera.

Ira Angustain

Actor, born August 6, 1958, in Glendale, California. He was a child actor beginning at age 11, appearing in television shows including *Dan August, Ironside,* and *Lancer.* He is best known for his role as Gómez in the CBS television serial *The White Shadow.* He appeared in *80 Steps to Jonah* (1969, Warner, starring Wayne Newton) and played comedian Freddie Prinze in the television movie *Can You Hear the Laughter? The Story of Freddie Prinze* (1979).

Art Aragón

Actor; he had the role of fighting buddy Sánchez in the autobiographical film *To Hell and Back* (1955), starring Audie Murphy.

Ángel Aranda

(Ángel Pérez Aranda) Actor; born in Jaén, Spain. He had principal parts in numerous action films in the 1960s and 1970s made in Spain or Italy for primary release in the United States in English-language versions, including *The Colossus of Rhodes* (1961), *Goliath Against the Giants* (1963), *Planet of the Vampires* (1965), *El Greco* (1966, 20th Century-Fox, starring Mel Ferrer), and *The Hellbenders* (1967).

Alfonso Arau

Mexican actor and director, born 1932. He has played bandits, drug dealers, Mexican army officers, and similarly stereotypical parts. His acting credits include *The Wild Bunch* (1969), *Scandalous John* and *El Topo* (1971), *Posse* (1975), *Romancing the Stone* (1984), *¡Three Amigos!* (1986), and *Used Cars* (1989). In addition to appearing in dozens of Mexican films he directed *Como agua para chocolate/Like Water for Chocolate,* released in the United States in 1993 to great critical and popular reception, and most recently *A Walk in the Clouds* (1995), starring Aitana Sánchez-Gijón and Anthony Quinn.

Manuel Arbó

(Manuel Arbó del Val) Actor, born in Madrid, July 18, 1898. He starred as Charlie Chan in a Spanish-language Fox film, *Eran trece* (1931), and had major or supporting roles in at least 16 other Hollywood Spanish-language films including *Cupido Chauffeur* (1930, Fox, opposite Luana Alcañiz and Richard Keene), a Spanish-language original based on the screenplay "Border Love" by Paul Perea and Max Constant; *El dios del mar* (1930, Paramount, starring Ramón Pereda and Rosita Moreno), a Spanish-language version of *The Sea God* (1930, starring Richard Arlen and Fay Wray); *Oriente y occidente* (1930, Universal, opposite Lupe Vélez and Barry Norton), a Spanish-language version of *East is West* (1930, starring Lupe Vélez, Lew Ayres, and Edward G. Robinson); *Drácula* (1931, Universal, starring Carlos Villarías and Lupita Tovar), a Spanish-language version of *Dracula* (1931, starring Bela Lugosi and Helen Chandler); *El código penal* (1931, Columbia, starring Barry Norton and María Alba), a Spanish-language version of *The Criminal Code* (1931, dir. Howard Hawks, starring Walter Huston and Constance Cummings); *La mujer X* (1931, MGM, dir. Carlos F. Borcosque, starring María Ladrón de Guevara and Rafael Rivelles), a Spanish-language version of *Madame X* (1929, dir. Lionel Barrymore, starring Ruth Chatterton and Lewis Stone); *El tenorio del harem* (1931, Universal, starring Slim Summerville and Lupita Tovar), a Spanish-language version of *Arabian Knights* (1931, starring Slim Summerville and Tom Kennedy); *Cheri-Bibi* (1931, MGM, dir. Carlos F. Borcosque, starring Ernesto Vilches and María Ladrón de Guevara), a Spanish-language version of *The Phantom of Paris* (starring John Gilbert and Leila Hyams); *Hay que casar al príncipe* (1931, Fox, starring José Mojica and Conchita Montenegro), a Spanish-language version of *Paid to Love* (1927, dir. Howard Hawks, starring George O'Brien and Virginia Valli); and *Eran trece* (1931, Fox, costarring Juan Torena and Ana María Custodio), a Spanish-language version of *Charlie Chan Carries On* (1931, starring Warner Oland and John Garrick). He also appeared in the European-made epic for primary release in the United States: *Goliath Against the Giants* (1963).

Pilar Arcos

Actress; she had supporting roles as mothers or aunts in several Hollywood Spanish-language productions including *Castillos en el aire* (1938, Eduardo Le Baron Productions, presented by Monogram, starring Cristina Téllez and Rafael Alcaide), a Spanish-language original based on a screenplay by Jaime Salvador; *Verbena trágica* (1938, Columbia, starring Fernando Soler and Luana Alcañiz), a Spanish-language original based on a screenplay by Jean Bart; *El otro soy yo* (1939, Paramount, starring Tito Guízar and Amanda Varela), a Spanish-language original based on a screenplay by Mortimer Braus; *Cuando canta la ley* (1939, Paramount, starring Tito Guízar and María Luisa Pineda), a Spanish-language original based on a screenplay by Jack Natteford, Enrique Uhthoff, and Richard Harlan; and *El milagro de la Calle Mayor* (1939, Fox, starring Margo, Arturo de Córdova, and José Crespo), a Spanish-language version of *A Miracle on Main Street* (1939, starring Margo and Walter Abel). She was in the English-language film *The Firefly* (1937).

Antonia Arévalo

Actress; she had supporting roles in two Hollywood Spanish-language films: *Sombras del circo* (1931, Paramount, as Señora Elsie) and *Su noche de bodas* (1931, Paramount).

Imperio Argentina

(Magdalena Nile del Río) Actress and singer, born in Buenos Aires, December 26, 1906. She starred or had major roles in at least seven Hollywood Spanish-language productions including *Su noche de bodas* (1931, Paramount, costarring Pepe Romeu), a Spanish-language version of *Her Wedding Night* (1930, starring Clara Bow and Ralph Forbes); *Lo mejor es reír* (1931, Paramount, costarring Tony D'Algy and Rosita Díaz Gimeno), a Spanish-language version of *Laughter* (1930, starring Nancy Carroll and Fredric March); *¿Cuándo te suicidas?* (1931, Paramount, costarring opposite Fernando Soler), a Spanish-language version of the French film *Quand tues-tu?* (1931, starring Robert Burnier and Simone Vaudry); *El cliente seductor* (1931, Paramount, costarring opposite Maurice Chevalier), a Spanish-language original; *Melodía de arrabal* (1933, Paramount, costarring Carlos Gardel), a Spanish-language original based on a screenplay by Alfredo Le Pera; *La casa es seria* (1933, Paramount, costarring Carlos Gardel), a Spanish-language original based on a screenplay by Alfredo Le Pera; and *Buenos días* (1933, Paramount, costarring Rafael Jáimez), a Spanish-language original based on a screenplay by Jesús Rey.

José Argüelles

Actor; he had a few supporting roles in Hollywood Spanish-language productions including *El hombre que asesinó* (1931, Paramount British, starring Rosita Moreno and Ricardo Puga), a Spanish-language version of *Stamboul* (1931, starring Rosita Moreno and Warwick Ward); *Espérame* (1933, Paramount, starring Carlos Gardel and Goyita Herrero), a Spanish-language original based on a screenplay by Louis

Gasnier; and *Melodía de arrabal* (1933, Paramount, starring Imperio Argentina and Carlos Gardel), a Spanish-language original based on a screenplay by Alfredo Le Pera.

Juan Aristi Eulate

Actor; he had a few starring or supporting roles in Hollywood Spanish-language productions including *Olimpia* (1935, MGM, starring José Crespo and María Alba), a Spanish-language version of *His Glorious Night* (1929, dir. Lionel Barrymore, starring John Gilbert and Catherine Dale Owen); *El barbero de Napoleón* (1930, Fox, costarring Manuel París), a Spanish-language version of *Napoleon's Barber* (1928, dir. John Ford, starring Otto Matiesen and Frank Reicher); *Don Juan diplomático* (1931, Universal, opposite Miguel Faust Rocha, Lia Torá, and Celia Montalván), a Spanish-language version of *The Boudoir Diplomat* (1930, starring Betty Compson and Mary Duncan); *Del infierno al cielo* (1931, Fox, starring Juan Torena and María Alba), a Spanish-language version of *The Man Who Came Back* (1931, dir. Raoul Walsh, starring Janet Gaynor and Charles Farrell); and *El impostor* (1931, Fox, starring Juan Torena and Blanca de Castejón), a Spanish-language version of *Scotland Yard* (1930, starring Edmund Lowe, Joan Bennett, and Donald Crisp).

Yareli Arizmendi

Actress, born in Mexico. She costarred in the notable Mexican film *Como agua para chocolate/Like Water for Chocolate* (1993 U.S. release) in the role of Rosaura, the older sister. She appeared in *The Cisco Kid* (1994) as Pancho's wife and as a Latina mother in *Beverly Hills Cop III* (1994). She was also in Walt Disney's *The Big Green* (1995).

Pedro Armendáriz

Actor, born May 9, 1912, in Mexico City to a Mexican father, Pedro Armendáriz, Sr., and an American mother, Della Hastings. He was educated in San Antonio, Texas, and at California Polytechnic. He died June 18, 1963, in Los Angeles of a self-inflicted gunshot after learning he had cancer. One of Mexico's most successful film stars, he appeared in over 40 local films, many directed by Emilio "El Indio" Fernández and featuring the cinematography of Gabriel Figueroa, and he frequently costarred with Dolores del Río. He was internationally recognized for *María Candelaria* (1943) and for his work with major directors including Luis Buñuel and John Ford. His son Pedro Armendáriz, Jr., is also an actor. In the United States he only appeared as a supporting actor. Selected films (primarily

Above: Pedro Armendáriz with María Elena Marqués in *La perla/The Pearl* (1946)

Below: John Wayne, Pedro Armendáriz (center), and Harry Carey, Jr., in *Three Godfathers* (1948, MGM)

Above: Pedro Armendáriz in *Border River* (1954)

U.S.): *María Candelaria* (Mex., 1943); *La perla/The Pearl* (U.S. and Mex., 1945); *The Fugitive* (1947); *Fort Apache* (1948); *Three Godfathers* (1949); *We Were Strangers* (1949), as a Cuban police officer; *Tulsa* (1949), as an American Indian; *The Torch* (1950); *Lucrece Borgia* (1953); *Border River* (1954), as a Mongol warrior; *Diane* and *The Conqueror* (1955); *The Littlest Outlaw* (U.S. and Mex., 1955); *The Little Savage* and *The Wonderful Country* (1959); *Beyond All Limits* and *Francis of Assisi* (1961); *My Son, the Hero* and *Captain Sinbad* (1963); and his final film, *From Russia with Love* (1963), as the agent Kerim Bey opposite Sean Connery.

Pedro Armendáriz, Jr.

(Pedro Armendáriz Bohr) Actor, born April 6, 1940, son of Pedro Armendáriz and Carmen Pardo. He has appeared in over 100 Mexican and U.S. films including *Bandits* (1967), *Guns for San Sebastian* (1968), *The Undefeated* (1969), *Chisum* (1970), *Macho Callahan* (1970), *Don't Be Afraid of the Dark* (1973, TV movie), *Earthquake* (1974), *Walker*

(1987), *License to Kill* (1989), and *Old Gringo* (1989). He has also appeared on many television programs including *The High Chaparral, Columbo,* and *Murder, She Wrote.*

Armida

(Armida Vendrell) Actress whose father was Spanish and mother Mexican, born in 1913 [May 21, 1911, according to PHH], in Sonora, Mexico [others state Mexico City, in 1912]. Noted as a stereotypical Latin lady in Hollywood B pictures of the 1930s and 1940s, her selected films include *Mexicana* (1929, a short); *General Crack* (1929); *On the Border, The Texan,* and *Border Romance* (1930); *Under a Texas Moon* (1930, the first Western totally in Technicolor); *The Marines Are Coming* (1934); *Under the Pampas Moon* (1935); *Border Café* and *Rootin' Tootin' Rhythm* (1937); *La Conga Nights* (1940); *South of Tahiti* and *Fiesta* (1941); *Always in My Heart* (1942); *The Girl from Monterey* and *Gaiety* (1943); *Machine Gun Mama* (1944); *South of the Rio Grande* (1945); *Bad Men of the Border* (1946); *Fiesta* (1947); *Jungle Goddess* (1948); and *Rhythm Inn* (1951).

Desi Arnaz

(Desiderio Alberto Arnaz y de Acha III) Actor and musician, born March 2, 1917 [R lists March 17, 1912], in Santiago, Cuba, died December 2, 1986, in Del Mar, California. Living in the United States from age 16, he became a popular singer and bongo player and in 1940 married Lucille Ball, who was his costar in *Too Many Girls,* his screen debut. The 1950s television series *I Love Lucy,* in which he and Lucille Ball starred, was enormously popular. With the success of *I Love Lucy,* he and Lucille Ball purchased the bankrupt facilities of RKO Studios and created the successful Desilu Production Company, which produced numerous television series including *The Untouchables, Make Room for Daddy, Star Trek,* and *The Mothers-in-Law.* He and Ms. Ball were divorced in 1960; their son Desi Arnaz, Jr. is also an actor. Selected films: *Too Many Girls* (1940), *Father Takes a Wife* (1941), *Four Jacks and a Jill* (1941), *The Navy Comes Through* (1942), *Bataan* (1943), *Cuban Pete* (1946), *Holiday in Havana* (1949), *The Long*

Long Trailer (1954), *Forever Darling* (1956), and *The Scarface Mob* (1962). He also had an appearance in *The Escape Artist* (1982, starring Raúl Juliá and Teri Garr).

Desi Arnaz, Jr.

(Desiderio Alberto Arnaz IV) Actor, born in Los Angeles, January 19, 1953, son of Desi Arnaz and Lucille Ball. He first appeared on the *Here's Lucy* show. He was part of a performance group, "Dino, Desi & Billy," which appeared in *Murderers' Row* (1966, Columbia, starring Dean Martin in his Matt Helm role) and *Follow Me* (1969). He appeared in *Red Sky at Morning* (1971), *The Voyage of the Yes* (1972), *Marco* (1973), *Billy Two Hats* (1973, starring Gregory Peck), *Joyride* (1977), *A Wedding* and *How to Pick up Girls* (1978); *Great American Traffic Jam* and *Fake Out* (1982), and *The Mambo Kings* (1992, cameo appearance in the role of his father). On television he starred in his own series, *Automan* (1983-1984), but his career was hampered in the 1980s by difficulties related to substance abuse.

Lucie Arnaz

(Lucille Desiree Arnaz) Actress, born in Hollywood, July 17, 1951, daughter of Desi Arnaz and Lucille Ball. She began in show business on the *Here's Lucy* show. Her film credits include *Death Scream* and *Who Is the Black Dahlia?* (1975), *Billy Jack Goes to Washington* (1977), *The Jazz Singer* (1980, starring Neil Diamond), *Washington Mistress* (1981), and *Second Thoughts* (1983). She was featured in a short-lived television series in 1985, *The Lucie Arnaz Show,* and in *Sons and Daughters* (1991).

Eduardo Arozamena

Actor, died in 1951. He had supporting roles in at least seven Hollywood Spanish-language films including *Drácula,* in which he played Prof. Van Helsing (1931, Universal, starring Carlos Villarías, Lupita Tovar, and Barry Norton), a Spanish-language version of *Dracula* (1931, starring Bela Lugosi); *Don Juan diplomático* (1931, Universal, starring Miguel Faust Rocha and Lia Torá), a Spanish-language version of *The Boudoir Diplomat* (starring Betty Compson and Mary Duncan); *Resurrección* (1931, Universal, dir. Edwin Carewe, starring Lupe Vélez and Gilbert Roland), a Spanish-language version of *Resurrection* (1931, dir. Edwin Carewe, starring Lupe Vélez and John Boles), based on the novel by Tolstoy; *El tenorio del harem* (1931, Universal, starring Slim Summerville and Lupita Tovar), a Spanish-language version of *Arabian Knights* (1931, starring Slim Summerville and Tom Kennedy); *Cheri-Bibi* (1931, MGM, dir. Carlos F.

Above: Desi Arnaz and Lucille Ball

Borcosque, starring Ernesto Vilches and María Ladrón de Guevara), a Spanish-language version of *The Phantom of Paris* (starring John Gilbert and Leila Hyams); *Carne de cabaret* (1931, Columbia, dir. Christy Cabanne, starring Lupita Tovar and Ramón Pereda), a Spanish-language version of *Ten Cents a Dance* (1931, dir. Lionel Barrymore, starring Barbara Stanwyck and Ricardo Cortez); and *Hombres en mi vida* (1932, Columbia, starring Lupe Vélez and Gilbert Roland), a Spanish-language version of *Men in Her Life* (1931, starring Lois Moran and Charles Bickford).

Isaac Artenstein

Film director, born December 5, 1954, in San Diego. He grew up in Tijuana, studied in the Fine Arts Department at UCLA, and graduated in 1977 with a film/video major from the California Institute of the Arts. He is known for his Chicano productions, some in cooperation with Paul Espinosa. His *Break of Dawn* (1988) is a feature about a Mexican singer and radio announcer of the 1930s, Pedro J. González, who was framed on false charges, deported from the United States, and who continued to work from Tijuana. He has also directed *Ballad of an Unsung Hero* (1983) on the same topic and *Border Brujo* (1990), about performance artist Guillermo Gómez-Peña.

Marco Antonio Arzate

Actor; he had supporting roles, usually as an American Indian, in a few films including *The War Wagon* (1967, Universal, starring John Wayne and Kirk Douglas), in the role of Wild Horse; *The Scalp Hunters* (1968); and *Soldier Blue* (1970, starring Candice Bergen), as a Kiowa brave.

Joe Aubel

Art director and production designer, born November 10, 1939, in East Los Angeles. He began his film career in 1964 as a junior set designer for *The Adventures of Ozzie and Harriet.* Subsequently, he was assistant set designer on various television programs including *The Danny Thomas Hour, The Fugitive,* and *The Mod Squad,* and for films including *The Chase* (1966), *Camelot* (1967), *Cool Hand Luke* (1967), and *The Wild Bunch* (1969). He was art director for *Dead and Buried* (1981) and *The Milagro Beanfield War* (1988) and production designer for *American Me* (1992). Additional film credits: *Viva Max!* (1969), *Close Encounters of the Third Kind* (1977), and *Star Trek IV: The Voyage Home* (1986).

Tina Aumont

(Also uses Tina Marquand professionally; born Marie Christine Salomons) Actress, daughter of María Montez and Jean-Pierre Aumont. Born in Beverly Hills, California, February 1, 1946, she has worked in both American and European films (some of the latter primarily for American release). Her credits include *Modesty Blaise* and *Texas Across the River* (both 1966); *The Game Is Over* (1967, dir. Roger Vadim, starring Jane Fonda), in the role of Anne Sernet; *Partner* (1968, dir. Bernardo Bertolucci, released with English subtitles; she costarred); *Torso* (1973); *Lifespan* (1974, starring Klaus Kinski); and *Malicious* (1974).

Luis Ávalos

Cuban-born actor, born September 21, 1946. He debuted as a junkie in *Badge 373* (1973) and appeared in *Hot Stuff* (1979), *The Hunter* (1980), *Love Child* (1982), *Ghost Fever* (1985), *The Butcher's Wife* (1991), and *Fires Within* (1991). On television he has appeared in numerous series episodes and starred in the series *Condo.* He appeared regularly on *Hangin' With Mr. Cooper* and was featured in *Ned Blessing.*

Elizabeth Avellán

Coproducer of *El Mariachi* (1992) and *Desperado* (1995) with her husband, Robert Rodríguez.

Carlos Ávila

Writer/director, born June 26, 1961, in Lima, Peru. He moved to Los Angeles at an early age and graduated with a master's of fine arts from UCLA's School of Film and Television. He wrote and directed the 1993 PBS "American Playhouse" television film *La Carpa.* His earlier short film, *Distant Water,* won the Grand Prize at the First Film Festival of International Cinema Students, Tokyo, Japan.

Ángel Avilés

Actress; her credits include *Chain of Desire* (1992, dir. by the Venezuelan Temístocles López), *Equinox* (1993), and *Mi Vida Loca* (1994), in the role of "Sad Girl."

Rick Avilés

Actor and comedian. He debuted in *The Cannonball Run* (1981) and was in *Mondo New York* (1987, dir. Harvey Keitel), *Ghost* (1990), as Patrick Swayze's murderer, and *The Saint of Fort Washington* (1993).

Héctor Babenco

(Héctor Eduardo Babenco) Director, born February 7, 1946, in Buenos Aires, Argentina. At age 18, he refused army service in Argentina and spent five years in Spain, eventually working in low-budget "spaghetti Westerns" and subsequently resettling in Brazil in the early 1970s. His first feature film was *The King of the Night* (1975), followed by *Lucio Flavio* (1977), which was well received in Brazil and the first film to expose the Brazilian death squads and the relationship between the paramilitary and the official police. His next film, *Pixote* (1981), about dispossessed children who become delinquents, is of major significance. His first English-language film, *Kiss of the Spider Woman* (1985), starring Raúl Juliá and William Hurt, received four Academy Award nominations (Hurt received the award for Best Actor). Additional film credits: *Ironweed* (1987) and *At Play in the Fields of the Lord* (1991), about a group of missionaries in the Amazon jungle.

Catherine Bach

(Catherine Ann Bachman) Actress of German-Mexican heritage, born March 1, 1954, in Warren, Ohio. She is best known for her sexy role on the television series *Dukes of Hazzard* (1979-85). She has had a number of film roles as well, including *Nicole* (1972), *The Midnight Man* and *Thunderbolt and Lightfoot* (1974), *Hustle* and *Strange New World* (1975), *Cannonball Run II* (1984), *Street Justice* (1987), *Criminal Act* and *Driving Force* (1988), *Masters of Menace* (1990), and *Rage and Honor* (1992).

Salvador Báguez

(Name appears professionally with variations including Salvadore Baquez) Actor; he had supporting roles in *The Hired Gun* (1957, starring Rory Calhoun) and *From Hell to Texas* (1958, 20th Century-Fox).

Rosita Ballesteros

Actress; she starred or had major roles in a few Hollywood Spanish-language productions including *Monsieur Le Fox*

(1930, MGM, dir. Hal Roach, opposite Gilbert Roland), a Spanish-language version of *Men of the North* (1930, dir. Hal Roach, starring Gilbert Roland, Barbara Leonard, Robert Elliott, and Nina Quartaro); *El hombre malo* (1930, First National Pictures, opposite Antonio Moreno, Andrés de Segurola, and Juan Torena), a Spanish-language version of *The Bad Man* (1930, starring Walter Huston and Dorothy Revier); and *Sevilla de mis amores* (1930, MGM, dir. Ramón Novarro, starring Ramón Novarro and Conchita Montenegro), a Spanish-language version of *Call of the Flesh* (1930, dir. Charles Brabin, starring Ramón Novarro and Dorothy Jordan).

Antonio Banderas

Actor, born in Málaga, Spain, 1960. He became internationally known in a series of films by Spanish writer/director Pedro Almodóvar, including *Labyrinth of Passion* (1983), *Law of Desire* (1986), *Matador* and *Women on the Verge of a Nervous Breakdown* (1988), and *Tie Me Up! Tie Me Down* (1990). He debuted in U.S. film in the documentary *Truth or Dare* (1991, starring Madonna) and had leading roles in *The Mambo Kings* (1992); *Philadelphia* (1993); *Interview with the Vampire* and *The House of the Spirits* (1994); and *Desperado* (dir. Robert Rodríguez), *Assassins, Miami Rhapsody, Two Much* (dir. Fernando Trueba), and *Never Talk to Strangers* (all 1995).

Catalina Bárcena

Actress, born in Cienfuegos, Cuba, December 10, 1896, died in Madrid, August 10, 1977. She was a major presence in the Spanish cinema. Her Hollywood Spanish-language film credits, invariably in the leading role, include *Mamá* (1931, Fox, dir. Benito Perojo, costarring Rafael Rivelles), a Spanish-language original based on a work by Gregorio Martínez Sierra; *Primavera en otoño* (1933, Fox, costarring Raúl Roulien and Antonio Moreno), a Spanish-language original based on a work by Gregorio Martínez Sierra; *Una viuda romántica* (1933, Fox, costarring Gilbert Roland and Mona Maris), a Spanish-language original based on "El sueño de una noche de agosto" (Madrid, 1918) by Gregorio Martínez Sierra; *Yo, tú y ella* (1933, Fox, costarring Gilbert Roland and Valentín Parera), a Spanish-language original based on "Mujer" (Madrid, 1926) by Gregorio Martínez Sierra; *La ciudad de cartón* (1933, Fox, costarring Antonio Moreno and José Crespo), a Spanish-language original based on a screenplay by Gregorio Martínez Sierra; *Señora casada necesita marido* (1934, Fox, costarring Antonio Moreno and José Crespo), a Spanish-language original based on the novel *Mi segunda mujer* by Eugenio Heltai; and *Julieta compra un*

Above: Catalina Bárcena and José Crespo in *La ciudad de cartón* (1933, Fox)

Below: Catalina Bárcena and Gilbert Roland in *Julieta compra un hijo* (1936)

hijo (1935, Fox, costarring Gilbert Roland and Luana Alcañiz), a Spanish-language original based on a work by Gregorio Martínez Sierra and Honorio Maura.

Lita Baron

(Isabel Castro) Actress, born in Almería, Spain, August 11, 1929. She came to the United States at the age of four. She began in show business as a singer with Xavier Cugat and subsequently appeared in *That's My Baby* (1944); *Pan-*

Americana (1945, RKO); *A Medal for Benny* (also 1945); *Club Havana*, *The Gay Señorita*, and *Slightly Scandalous* (1946); *Border Incident* (1949); *Savage Drums* (1951); and *Red Sundown* (1956). She appeared in a number of Paramount musical shorts, including *Champagne for Two* (1947), which was nominated for an Academy Award.

Max Barón

(Also Max Wagner) Actor, born November 28, 1901, died in West Los Angeles, California, November 16, 1975 [listed by PHH as Mexican]. He used Max Barón for his roles in Hollywood Spanish-language films and Max Wagner for his English-language films. According to the *American Film Institute Catalog (1931-1940)*, he may have also used Max Waggner and M. Wagner. He appeared in over 100 English-language films including several Charlie Chan vehicles (e.g., *Charlie Chan in Shanghai*, 1935, and *Charlie Chan at the Race Track*, 1936). Some additional English-language credits include *Renegades of the West* and *The World and the Flesh* (1932); *Arizona to Broadway* and *The Last Trail* (1933); *The Lost Jungle* and *Wharf Angel* (1934); *Storm Over the Andes* and *Under the Pampas Moon* (1935); *Dancing Pirate* and *Trapped by Television* (1936); *Black Legion, Border Cafe, San Quentin*, and *You Only Live Once* (1937); *Mr. Moto's Gamble, Painted Desert*, and *Up the River* (1938); *Cafe Society, The Return of the Cisco Kid*, and *The Roaring Twenties* (1939); *The Grapes of Wrath, Men Against the Sky*, and *Pier 13* (1940); and *San Francisco Docks* (1941). He also had a few supporting roles in Hollywood Spanish-language films including *El último de los Vargas* (1930, Fox, starring George Lewis and Luana Alcañiz), a Spanish-language version of *Last of the Duanes* (1930, starring George O'Brien, Lucille Brown, and Myrna Loy); *El valiente* (1930, Fox, starring Juan Torena and Angelita Benítez), a Spanish-language version of *The Valiant* (1929, starring Paul Muni and Marguerite Churchill); *El código penal* (1931, Columbia, starring Barry Norton and María Alba), a Spanish-language version of *The Criminal Code* (1931, dir. Howard Hawks, starring Walter Huston and Constance Cummings); *Cuerpo y alma* (1931, Fox, starring George Lewis and Ana María Custodio), a Spanish-language version of *Body and Soul* (1931, starring Charles Farrell, Elissa Landi, Humphrey Bogart, and Myrna Loy); and *El pasado acusa* (1931, Columbia, starring Luana Alcañiz and Barry Norton), a Spanish-language version of *The Good Bad Girl* (1931, starring Marie Prevost and James Hall).

Steven Bauer

(Steven Rocky Echevarría) Actor, born in Havana, Cuba, December 2, 1956. He arrived in Miami at the age of three. He debuted under the name Rocky Echevarría in the Miami-based PBS series, *Qué Pasa, U.S.A.?* and on several television series including *The Rockford Files, Hill Street Blues, From Here to Eternity,* and *Wiseguy.* He gained film attention as Al Pacino's Cuban gangster comrade in *Scarface* (1983); had the lead role in *Thief of Hearts* (1984); and appeared in *Sword of Gideon* and *Running Scared* (1986); *Two Moon Junction, Wildfire,* and *The Beast* (1988); *Gleaming the Cube* (1989); the television film *Drug Wars: The Camarena Story* (1989); *A Climate for Killing* and *Sweet Poison* (1991); *Drive Like Lightning* (1991, for cable TV); and *False Arrest* and *Raising Cain* (1992). He was married to actress Melanie Griffith.

Above: Alfonso Bedoya (right) with Pedro Armendáriz in *Border River* (1954, Universal)

Below: Alfonso Bedoya in *The Treasure of the Sierra Madre* (1947, dir. John Huston)

José Baviera

(José Baviera Navarro) Actor, born in Valencia, Spain, August 17, 1906, died in Mexico City, August 13, 1981. He was seen in this country in *Viva Maria!* (1965, United Artists, dir. Louis Malle, starring Jean Moreau and Brigitte Bardot) and *The Exterminating Angel* (1967, dir. Luis Buñuel).

Alfonso Bedoya

Actor, born April 16, 1904, in Vicam, Sonora, Mexico, died in Mexico City, December 15, 1957. After a considerable career as a character actor in Mexican films, he made a notable American film debut in 1948 in John Huston's *The Treasure of the Sierra Madre* as the treacherous and mocking stereotypical Mexican bandit, Goldhat. His performance is both recognized and parodied in Luis Valdez's play *I Don't Have to Show You No Stinking Badges.* Selected films (primarily U.S.) include *La perla/The Pearl* (Mex. and U.S., 1945), *The Treasure of the Sierra Madre* (1948), *Streets of Laredo* and *Border Incident* (both 1949), *The Black Rose* (1950), *Man in the Saddle* (1951), *California Conquest* (1952), *Sombrero* and *The Stranger Wore a Gun* (both 1953), *Border River* (1954), *Ten Wanted Men* (1955), and *The Big Country* (1958).

Yerye Beirute

Actress; active in the Mexican film industry, she appeared in a few American releases as well including *Woman's Devotion* (1956), *Face of the Screaming Werewolf* (1965, Diana Films,

starring Lon Chaney, Jr., made in Mexico and originally released as *La casa del terror*), and *Vampire's Coffin* (1965, made in Mexico and originally released as *El ataúd del vampiro*).

Julia Bejarano

Actress; she had a few supporting roles in both Hollywood English-language and Spanish-language productions. Her English-language credits include *The Lone Defender* (1934), *The Prescott Kid* (1934, Columbia), as Juanita, *Cowboy*

Holiday (1935), *Let 'Em Have It* (1935), and *Ramona* (1936), in a very minor role. Her Spanish-language credits include *Hollywood, ciudad de ensueño* (1931, Universal, starring José Bohr and Lia Torá), a Spanish-language original based on a screenplay by Miguel de Zárraga and José Bohr; *Una viuda romántica* (1933, Fox, starring Catalina Bárcena and Gilbert Roland), a Spanish-language original based on "El sueño de una noche de agosto" (Madrid, 1918) by Gregorio Martínez Sierra; and *El diablo del mar* (1935, Theater Classic Pictures, starring Ramón Pereda and Movita Castañeda), a Spanish-language version of *Devil Monster* (1935, starring Jack del Rio, Blanche Mehaffey, and Barry Norton).

Alma Beltrán

Character actress, born in 1927 in Mexico, raised in California and Arizona. She has appeared in *Blue* (1968), *Red Sky at Morning* (1971), *Oh God! Book II* (1980), *Zoot Suit* (1981), and *Herbie Goes Bananas* (1988). Her television work includes *Sánchez of Bel Air, Chico and the Man* (as Freddie Prinze's aunt), and *Sanford and Son* (as Julio Fuentes's mother). She has worked extensively in Los Angeles theater and on Spanish-language radio.

Robert Beltrán

Actor, born November 19, 1953. He debuted with a small role in *Zoot Suit* (1981) and then became well-known for his role as Raoul in the cult film *Eating Raoul* (1982). Subsequently he starred or had major roles in *Lone Wolf McQuade* (1983), *Night of the Comet* (1984), *Latino* (1985), *Streethawk* (1986), the excellent and highly regarded *Gaby—a True Story* (1987), *Scenes from the Class Struggle in Beverly Hills* (1989), *To Die Standing* (1990), and *Kiss Me a Killer* (1991). He is the first Hispanic with a regularly featured role on the *Star Trek* TV series, appearing as Commander Chakatoy in the latest cycle, *Voyager*.

Lolita Benavente

Actress; she had supporting roles in two Hollywood Spanish-language films: *Espérame* (1933, Paramount), as Juanita, and *La casa es seria* (1933, Paramount).

Angelita Benítez

Actress; she costarred in four Hollywood Spanish-language films including *El valiente* (1930, Fox, opposite Juan Torena), a Spanish-language version of *The Valiant* (1929, starring Paul Muni and Marguerite Churchill); *Wu Li Chang* (1930,

Above: Robert Beltrán

MGM, opposite Ernesto Vilches), a Spanish-language version of *Mr. Wu* (1927, starring Lon Chaney and Louise Dresser); *Monerías* (1931, MGM, opposite Charley Chase), a Spanish-language version of *Rough Seas* (1931, starring Charley Chase and Thelma Todd); and *El comediante* (1931, Paramount, opposite Ernesto Vilches), a Spanish-language original based on "Sullivan" by E. V. Domínguez.

Gabriel Beristain

Cinematographer, son of the well-known Mexican actor Luis Beristain (1916-1962), whose last film was Buñuel's *The Exterminating Angel*. Gabriel Beristain's American films include *Waiting for the Light* (1990), *The Distinguished Gentleman* (1992), and *Bound by Honor* (1993, dir. Taylor Hackford). He has numerous other films credits in Latin America and Europe, and at the 1987 Berlin Film Festival he won the Silver Bear for Cinematography for *Caravaggio*, directed by Derek Jarman.

Manuel Bernardos

Actor; he had two supporting roles in Hollywood Spanish-language films: *Entre noche y día* (1931, United Artists), as Carrington, and *Espérame* (1933, Paramount), as Sebastián.

Above: Rubén Blades (left) and Aidan Quinn in *The Lemon Sisters* (1990)

Below: Rubén Blades in *The Milagro Beanfield War* (1988)

Roxann Biggs-Dawson

Actress of Puerto Rican descent, born in Los Angeles. She has a regular role on the *Star Trek* TV series as B'Elanna Torres, the half-human, half-Klingon chief engineer of the starship U.S.S. *Voyager*.

Rubén Blades

Actor, musician, composer, and lawyer, born in Panama City, July 16, 1948 [R lists July 6]. Living for a period alternately between Panama (where he earned a law degree) and New York City (where he performed with various salsa bands), Blades debuted as cowriter and star of *Crossover Dreams* (1985, dir. León Ichaso) and went on to do a number of film performances, including the role of the sheriff in *The Milagro Beanfield War* (1988). Additional film credits include *The Last Fight* (1983); *Critical Condition* and *Fatal Beauty* (1987); *Homeboy* (1988); *Disorganized Crime* and *The Lemon Sisters* (1989); *The Heart of the Deal, Mo' Better Blues, Predator 2*, and *The Two Jakes* (all 1990); and *The Super* (1991, starring Joe Pesci). He also wrote and performed the musical score for *Q & A* (1990). He has done several TV films including HBO's *Dead Man Out* (1989) and *The Josephine Baker Story* (1990), Turner Network Television's *Crazy from the Heart* (1991), and *One Man's War* (1991, cable TV).

Eumenio Blanco

(Also used Eumenco Blanco professionally) Actor, died March 9, 1984. He appeared in three Hollywood Spanish-language productions in supporting roles: *El cuerpo del delito*

(1930, Paramount, starring Antonio Moreno and Ramón Pereda), a Spanish-language version of *The Benson Murder Case* (1930, starring William Powell and Natalie Moorhead); *El precio de un beso* (1930, Fox, starring José Mojica, Mona Maris, and Antonio Moreno), a Spanish-language version of *One Mad Kiss* (1930, with the same three stars); and *Soñadores de la gloria* (1931, United Artists, starring Miguel Contreras Torres and Lia Torá), a Spanish-language original based on a screenplay by Miguel Contreras Torres. He also had minor parts in *Sunset of Power* (1935) and *Green Hell* (1940, Universal, starring Douglas Fairbanks, Jr.), two English-language originals.

Above: José Bohr and Mona Rico in *Sombras de gloria* (1929)

Below: Fortunio Bonanova (as officer) with Anthony Quinn (left) and John Howard in *Bulldog Drummond in Africa* (1938, Paramount)

José Bohr

Actor and director, born in Buenos Aires, 1900. He starred in a few Hollywood Spanish-language films including *Sombras de gloria* (1929, Sono-Art Productions, Ltd., costarring Mona Rico), a Spanish-language version of *Blaze O'Glory* (1929, starring Eddie Dowling and Betty Compson); *Así es la vida* (1930, Sono-Art Productions, Ltd., costarring Lolita Vendrell), a Spanish-language version of *What a Man* (1930, starring Reginald Denny and Miriam Seegar); and *Hollywood, ciudad de ensueño* (1931, Universal, costarring Lia Torá and Donald Reed), a Spanish-language original based on a screenplay by Miguel de Zárraga and José Bohr.

Fortunio Bonanova

(Luis Moll) Actor, born January 13, 1895, in Palma de Mallorca, Spain, died in Woodland Hills, California, April 2, 1969. He debuted in opera at age 17 and became internationally known as an opera star. Having starred in the Spanish film *Don Juan Tenorio* (1921), and first appearing in the United States in Broadway theater, in 1927 he made his American film debut in *The Loves of Sunya* with Gloria Swanson. He was the star, writer, producer, and director of 12 Spanish-language shorts made at the Fort Lee Studios in New Jersey. In addition to starring in several Spanish-language films made in Spain, Mexico, or South America, in 1932 he began appearing in English-language productions, followed by Hollywood Spanish-language films. His English-language film credits, mostly as a character actor, include *Careless Lady* and *A Successful Calamity* (both

1932); *Bulldog Drummond in Africa, Romance in the Dark,* and *Tropic Holiday* (1938); *Down Argentine Way, I Was an Adventuress,* and *The Mark of Zorro* (1940); *That Night in Rio, Citizen Kane,* as the opera singing teacher, and *Blood and Sand* (1941); *For Whom the Bell Tolls* (1943), as a Spanish guerrilla; *Double Indemnity* and *Going My Way* (1944); *Kiss Me Deadly* (1955); and *The Running Man* (1963). His Hollywood Spanish-language film credits include *El capitán tormenta* (1936, MGM, costarring opposite Lupita Tovar), a Spanish-language version of *Captain Calamity* (1936, starring George Houston and Marion

Nixon); *El carnaval del diablo* (1936, MGM, costarring Blanca de Castejón), a Spanish-language version of *The Devil on Horseback* (1936, starring Del Campo and Lili Damita); and *La Inmaculada* (1939, United Artists, costarring Andrea Palma), a Spanish-language original based on Catalina D'Erzell's novel *La Inmaculada.*

Carlos F. Borcosque

(Carlos Francisco Borsosque Sánchez) Actor and director, born in Valparaíso, Chile, September 9, 1894, died in Buenos Aires, September 5, 1965. He was active as an assistant director or director in numerous Hollywood Spanish-language films including *Olimpia* (1930, MGM, as an assistant director), *Sevilla de mis amores* (1930, MGM, as an assistant director), *En cada puerto un amor* (1931, MGM, as dialogue director), *La mujer X* (1931, MGM, as director), *Cheri-Bibi* (1931, MGM, as director), *Dos noches* (1933, Fanchon Royer Pictures, Inc., presented by J. H. Hoffberg Co., as director), *Alas sobre el Chaco* (1935, Universal, dir. Christy Cabanne, as assistant director), and *El carnaval del diablo* (1936, MGM, as dialogue director). Borcosque also directed one English-language original: *The Fighting Lady* (1935, Fanchon Royer Pictures, Inc., starring Peggy Shannon and Jack Mulhall), based on an original play by Robert Ober.

María Borello

Actress; she had a few supporting roles in Hollywood Spanish-language productions including *Tres amores* (1934, Universal, starring José Crespo and Anita Campillo), a Spanish-language version of *Bachelor Mother* (1933, starring Evalyn Knapp and James Murray); *El trovador de la radio* (1938, Paramount, starring Tito Guízar and Robina Duarte), a Spanish-language original based on a screenplay by Bernard Luber and Nenette Noriega; and *La Inmaculada* (1939, United Artists, starring Fortunio Bonanova and Andrea Palma), a Spanish-language original based on Catalina D'Erzell's novel, *La Inmaculada.*

Agostino Borgato

(Also used Al Borgato professionally) Actor of (possibly completely) Italian descent, born in Venice, Italy, June 30, 1871, died in Hollywood, California, March 14, 1939. He had numerous supporting roles in Hollywood Spanish-language films including *La voluntad del muerto* (1930, Universal, starring Lupita Tovar and Antonio Moreno), a Spanish-language version of *The Cat Creeps* (1930, starring Helen Twelvetrees and Raymond Hackett); *Primavera en otoño* (1933, Fox); *La melodía prohibida* (1933, Fox,

starring José Mojica and Conchita Montenegro), a Spanish-language original based on a screenplay by Eve Unsell; *Julieta compra un hijo* (1935, Fox); and *El capitán tormenta* (1936, MGM). He also appeared in a large number of English-language films including *The Maltese Falcon* (1931), *Murders in the Rue Morgue* (1932), *Christopher Strong* (1933), *Now and Forever* (1934), *The Gay Deception* (1935), *In Caliente* (1935), *Love on the Run* (1936), *The Bride Wore Red* (1937), *Lloyd's of London* (1937), *Daughter of Shanghai* (1938), *Hotel Imperial* (1939), and *The Three Musketeers* (1939).

Graciela Borges

Actress, born in Buenos Aires, 1936. In addition to being active in the Argentine film industry, she appeared in a U.S/Argentine-made film distributed by MGM: *Monday's Child* (1967, starring Arthur Kennedy and Geraldine Page).

Jesse Borrego

Actor, born August 1, 1962, in San Antonio, Texas. He appeared in the Martin Scorsese segment of *New York Stories* (1989) and had major roles in *Bound by Honor* (1993), the well-received *I Like It Like That* (1994, starring Lauren Vélez), and *Mi Vida Loca* (1994). He played the Mexican American dancer Jesse on the television series *Fame,* and he had the lead in the TV movie *Tecumseh* (1995).

Sonia Braga

Actress, born in Maringa, Brazil, 1949. Her childhood shaken by her father's death when she was 8, she quit school at 14 and by age 18 was working in the theater, where she created a sensation by taking her clothes off on stage in a production of *Hair.* In 1968 she starred in a television soap opera, *The Girl of the Blue Sailboat,* followed by a series of soap operas for the leading Brazilian television network, TV Globo (including *Gabriela* and *Dancin' Days*), which made her a star. She first became known in the United States for her roles in *Doña Flor and Her Two Husbands* (1977), *I Love You* (1981), and *Gabriela* (1983), opposite Marcello Mastroianni. *Kiss of the Spider Woman* (1985) was her first English-language film, and she costarred in *The Milagro Beanfield War* (1988, dir. Robert Redford) and *Moon Over Parador* (1988). Other film credits include *Lady on the Bus* (1978), the notable *The Man Who Broke 1000 Chains* (1987, costarring opposite Val Kilmer), *The Rookie* (1990), the excellent *The Last Prostitute* (1991, for cable TV), and *Roosters* (1995, dir. Robert Young).

Benjamin Bratt

(Benjamin Bratt Banda) Actor, born December 16, 1963. He studied acting as an undergraduate at the University of California at Santa Barbara and in the master's program at San Francisco's American Conservatory Theater. He has had major roles as an inexperienced detective in *One Good Cop* (1991), in *Demolition Man* (1993), and as Paco in *Bound by Honor* (1993). Other credits include the films *Bright Angel, Rope of Sand,* and *Chains of Gold* (all 1991) and main or costarring roles in the television series pilot *Juárez,* the ABC-TV series *Knightwatch,* NBC's *Nasty Boys,* and the NBC series *Law and Order.*

Peter Bratt

Producer/director, brother of Benjamin Bratt. His independent feature *Follow Me Home* debuted at the 1996 Sundance Film Festival.

J. Robert Bren

Film producer and writer, born 1903 in Guanajuato, Mexico. He made his film-writing debut in 1934 with *Looking for Trouble* and wrote the screenplays for *In Old California* (1942), *The Great Sioux Uprising* (1953), and *The Siege at Red River* (1954).

Romney Brent

(Rómulo Larralde) Actor, born January 26, 1902, in Saltillo, Mexico, died September 24, 1976. He was a stage actor in New York and London. He made his film debut in a British production released in the United States, *East Meets West* (1936, Gaumont-British Picture Corp. of America). Other film credits include *Dreaming Lips, Dinner at the Ritz, Head Over Heels in Love, The Dominant Sex,* and *Under the Red Robe* (all 1937); and *The Adventures of Don Juan* (1949).

Ruth Britt

Actress of Puerto Rican descent; she appeared in *The Nude Bomb* (1980) and *Night School* (1981). She also made numerous guest appearances in television series and TV movies and was a regular on the television series *Operation Petticoat* as a native island girl.

Claudio Brook

Actor, born in Mexico City, August 27, 1927. Highly active in the Mexican film industry, he appeared in several Luis Buñuel films released in the United States including *The Young One* (1961), *Simon of the Desert* (1965), *The Exterminating Angel* (1967), and *The Milky Way* (1969), as well as the following productions made abroad but released in English-language versions: *The Last Rebel* (1961, Mexico), *The Upper Hand* (1967, multinational European, starring Jean Gabin and George Raft), *Don't Look Now* (1969, French/British), and *Peking Blonde* (1969, multinational European).

George Stanford Brown

Actor/director, born June 24, 1943, in Havana, Cuba, raised in Harlem, New York. As an actor he was a tough cop on the television series *The Rookies* and appeared in both *Roots* and *Roots: The Next Generation.* His film credits include *The Comedians* (1967), *Bullitt* (1968), *Dayton's Devils* (1968), *The Forbin Project* (1970), *The Man* (1972), *Stir Crazy* (1980), *The Kid with the Broken Halo* (1982, TV film), *The Jesse Owens Story* (1984, TV film), and *House Party 2* (1991). He has directed numerous television productions; his credits include *Family, Starsky and Hutch, Charlie's Angels, Hill Street Blues,* and *Cagney & Lacey.*

Argentina Brunetti

Actress, born August 31, 1907 [PHH has 1917], in Argentina (her mother was the internationally known stage and film actress Mimi Aguglia), known for her roles as mothers or *dueñas.* Her film credits include *California* (1946); *Miracle on 34th Street* (1947); *Broken Arrow* (1950), as Cochise's Indian squaw; *The Lawless* (1950), as the mother of the Mexican youth in trouble; *The Caddy* (1953), as an Italian mother; *King of the Khyber Rifles* (1953); *Three Violent People* (1956); *The Brothers Rico* (1957); *The George Raft Story* (1961); *The Horizontal Lieutenant* and *The Pigeon That Took Rome* (both 1962); *7 Faces of Dr. Lao* and *Stage to Thunder Rock* (1964); *The Money Trap* (1966); and *The Appaloosa* (1966, with Marlon Brando). She also appeared for three years on the daytime television soap opera *General Hospital.*

Quintín Bulnes

Actor. Active in the Mexican film industry, he also appeared in a few Mexican productions or American/Mexican coproductions released in English in the United States. Film credits include *The Queen's Swordsmen* (1963), *Little Red Riding Hood and the Monsters* (1965), *The Living Coffin* (1965), *Rage* (1966, U.S./Mexico coproduction, released by

Columbia, starring Glenn Ford, Stella Stevens, and David Reynoso), and *The Curse of the Doll People* (1968).

Luis Buñuel

Internationally known Spanish filmmaker, born in Calanda, Spain, February 2, 1900, died in Mexico City, July 29, 1983. In 1940, Buñuel worked as a technical advisor for an uncompleted pro-Spanish Loyalist film at MGM Studios in Hollywood and from 1941 to 1944 he worked in the film department at the Museum of Modern Art in New York City. Many of Buñuel's Spanish-language films (either produced in Mexico or in Spain) have been well received in the United States (often in English-language as well as Spanish-language versions) including *Los Olvidados* (1950), *The Young One* (1961), *Viridiana* (1961), *The Criminal Life of Archibaldo de la Cruz* (1962), *Nazarín* (1962), *Diary of a Chambermaid* (1965), *Simon of the Desert* (1965), *The Exterminating Angel* (1967), *Belle de*

Above: Luis Buñuel

jour (1967), *The Milky Way* (1969), *Tristana* (1970), and his final film, *That Obscure Object of Desire* (1977).

Robert Cabal

Actor of Filipino descent. His film credits include *Crisis* (1950), *Mara Maru* (1952), and *The Man Behind the Gun* (1952). He also appeared in the role of Hey Soos on the television series *Rawhide.*

David Cadiente

Actor/stuntman. He has appeared in *Donovan's Reef* (1963), *Rampage* (1963), *Ride the Wild Surf* (1964), *The Sting II* (1983), and *Stick* (1985). On television, his credits include *Adventures in Paradise, The Gallant Men,* and *The A-Team.*

Joseph Calleia

(Joseph Spurin Calleja; also used Joseph Spurin Calleia professionally) Actor of English and Spanish parents, born in Malta, August 4, 1897, died in Malta, October 31, 1975. A character actor, he had considerable range including numerous Latin roles. His credits include *His Woman* and *My Sin* (both 1931); *The Divorce Racket* (1932); *Public Hero Number 1* (1935); *After the Thin Man, Robin Hood of El Dorado, Sinner Take All,* and *Tough Guy* (all 1936); *The Bad Man of Brimstone* and *Man of the People* (1937); *Algiers* and *Marie Antoinette* (1938); *Golden Boy* and *Juárez* (1939); *My Little Chickadee* and *Wyoming* (1940); *For Whom the Bell Tolls* (1943); *Gilda* (1946); *Branded* (1950); *The Treasure of Pancho Villa* and *The Littlest Outlaw* (1955); *Serenade* (1956); *Touch of Evil* (1958); *Cry Tough* (1959); *The Alamo* (1960); and *Johnny Cool* (1963). He wrote the script for MGM for *The Robin Hood of El Dorado* (1936), starring Warner Baxter.

María Luz Callejo

Actress, born in Madrid, July 31, 1909. She had several starring or major roles in Hollywood Spanish-language films including *Un hombre de suerte* (1930, Cinéstudio Continental Paramount, dir. Benito Perojo, opposite Roberto Rey), a Spanish-language version of a French original, *Un trou dans le mur* (1930, starring Jean Murat and Dolly Davis), based on a comedy by Yves Mirandé and

Above: María Luz Callejo and Jack Castello in *La fruta amarga* (1931, MGM)

Gustave Quinson; *La fruta amarga* (1931, MGM, opposite Virginia Fábregas and Juan de Landa), a Spanish-language version of *Min and Bill* (starring Marie Dressler and Wallace Beery); *Cheri-Bibi* (1931, MGM), in a supporting role; and *Mamá* (1931, Fox, dir. Benito Perojo, opposite Catalina Bárcena and Rafael Rivelles), a Spanish-language original based on an original work by Gregorio Martínez Sierra.

María Calvo

Actress, born in Zaragoza, Spain, 1892. She was one of the most productive Hollywood Spanish-language actresses, with supporting roles as *señoras,* or even an occasional mother or mother superior, in at least 23 films including *El cuerpo del delito* (1930, Paramount, starring Antonio Moreno); *Estrellados* (1930, MGM, starring Buster Keaton); *Amor audaz* (1930, Paramount, starring Adolphe Menjou and Rosita Moreno); *Del mismo barro* (1930, Fox, starring Mona Maris); *La voluntad del muerto* (1930, Universal, starring Lupita Tovar and Antonio Moreno); *Sevilla de mis amores* (1930, MGM, dir. and starring Ramón Novarro); *El alma de la fiesta* (1931, MGM, starring Charley Chase); *El código penal* (1931, Columbia, starring Barry Norton); *Politiquerías* (1931, MGM, starring Stan Laurel and Oliver Hardy); *Carne de cabaret* (1931, Columbia, dir. Christy Cabanne, starring

Above: Buster Keaton, María Calvo, and Raquel Torres in *Estrellados* (1930, MGM)

Lupita Tovar); *El pasado acusa* (1931, Columbia, starring Luana Alcañiz); *Granaderos del amor* (1934, Fox, starring Raúl Roulien); *Angelina o el honor de un brigadier* (1935, Fox, starring Rosita Díaz Gimeno); and *Rosa de Francia* (1935, Fox, starring Rosita Díaz Gimeno). She had a small role in the English-language film *A Devil with Women* (1930).

Rafael Calvo

Actor who had supporting roles in several Hollywood Spanish-language films including *Sombras del circo* (1931, Paramount, starring Amelia Muñoz and Tony D'Algy); *Cuerpo y alma* (1931, Fox, starring George Lewis and Ana María Custodio); *Esclavas de la moda* (1931, Fox, starring Carmen Larrabeiti and Félix de Pomés); *Hay que casar al príncipe* (1931, Fox, starring José Mojica and Conchita Montenegro); *¿Conoces a tu mujer?* (1931, Fox, starring Rafael Rivelles and Carmen Larrabeiti); *La ley del harem* (1931, Fox, starring José Mojica and Carmen Larrabeiti); *Eran trece* (1931, Fox, starring Manuel Arbó and Juan Torena); and *Mamá* (1931, Fox, dir. Benito Perojo, starring Catalina Bárcena and Rafael Rivelles).

Anita Campillo

Actress. She starred or had major roles in various Hollywood Spanish-language films including *La cruz y la espada* (1933, Fox, opposite José Mojica), a Spanish-language original based on a screenplay by Miguel de Zárraga; *La buenaventura* (1934, First National Pictures, opposite Enrico Caruso, Jr.), a Spanish-language original based on Victor Herbert's operetta

The Fortune Teller; Cuesta abajo (1934, Paramount, starring Carlos Gardel and Mona Maris), a Spanish-language original based on a screenplay by Alfredo Le Pera; *Tres amores* (1934, Universal, opposite José Crespo), a Spanish-language version of *Bachelor Mother* (1933, starring Evalyn Knapp and James Murray); *Julieta compra un hijo* (1935, Fox, starring Catalina Bárcena and Gilbert Roland), a Spanish-language original based on a work by Gregorio Martínez Sierra and Honorio Maura; *Un hombre peligroso* (1935, Producciones Latinas Ltd., presented by Criterion Films, costarring Paul Ellis), a Spanish-language original; and *La vida bohemia* (1937, Columbia, starring Rosita Díaz Gimeno and Gilbert Roland), a Spanish-language original based on Henri Murger's novel *Scènes de la vie de bohème* (1851). She also appeared in two English-language films: *The Man from Utah* (1934) and *The Desert Trail* (1935; her participation in this film is unconfirmed according to the *AFI Catalog, 1931-1940*).

Rafael Campos

Actor, native of the Dominican Republic, born May 13, 1936, died of cancer in Woodland Hills, California, July 9, 1985. He came to the United States with his family in 1949 and attend-

Above: Rafael Campos in the mid-1950s

ed the High School for the Performing Arts in New York City, where he was cast with other little-known actors (Sidney Poitier, Paul Mazursky, Vic Morrow, and Jamie Farr) in *Blackboard Jungle* (1955, MGM). His credits include *Trial* (1955), as the Mexican American boy accused of murder; *The Sharkfighters* (1956); *This Could Be the Night* (1957); *The Light in the Forest* (1958); *Savage Sam* (1963); *Lady in a Cage* (1964); *Agent for H.A.R.M., Mister Buddwing, Tonka*, and *The Appaloosa* (all 1966); *The Astro-Zombies* and *Girl in Gold Boots* (1968); *Oklahoma Crude* (1973); *The Hanged Man* (1974); *Slumber Party '57* (1976); and *The Return of Josey Wales* (1986). On television he appeared in *Studio One, Playhouse 90, Alcoa Theatre, Rhoda* (as Ramón Díaz), and the epic miniseries *Centennial* (1978), as Nacho Gómez, the trail cook.

Víctor Campos

Actor, born in New York City, January 15, year unknown. He appeared in *Newman's Law* (1974), *The Master Gunfighter* (1975), and *Five Days from Home* (1978). On television he has appeared in *Doctors' Hospital* and *Cade's County.*

Larry Cano

Executive producer of *Silkwood* (1983).

Cansino family

(Eduardo, father; Volga, mother; Rita [Rita Hayworth]; Eduardo, Jr.; Sonny; José; and others) Family of performers, especially dancers. They appeared as the Royal Cansinos or under other names in films that included *Dancing Pirate* (1936), *Four Men and a Prayer* (1938), *Masked Rider* (1941, using the name José Cansino Dancers), and *Too Many Blondes* (1941). José and Vernon Cansino had minor roles in *The Loves of Carmen* (1948, Columbia, starring Rita Hayworth and Glenn Ford).

"Cantinflas"

(Mario Moreno Reyes) Actor, born August 12, 1911, in Mexico City, died April 20, 1993. He began as a circus clown, bullring buffoon, and tent show song-and-dance man. Debuting in Mexican film in 1936, he became one of the most recognized comic actors of the Hispanic world. He appeared in numerous Mexican films but only two American films: *Around the World in 80 Days* (1956) and *Pepe* (1960).

Above: Elsa Cárdenas (right), Elvis Presley, and Ursula Andress in *Fun in Acapulco* (1963)

Irene Cara

Actress, singer, and dancer born to Cuban and Puerto Rican parents on March 18, 1958, in the Bronx, New York. She appeared in *Aaron Loves Angela* (1975), *Sparkle* (1976), *Fame* (1980), *For Us, the Living: The Medgar Evers Story* (1983, orig. for television), *D.C. Cab* and *City Heat* (1984), *Certain Fury* and *Killing 'Em Softly* (1985), *Busted Up* (1986), *Caged in Paradiso* (1989), and *Happily Ever After* (1993). In 1984, she won an Academy Award for cowriting the Best Original Song, "Flashdance . . . What a Feeling," the title song (which she also recorded) to *Flashdance* (1983). She also has had a considerable television career, including a role in *Roots: The Next Generation* (1979).

Tony Carbajal

Actor, active in the Mexican film industry. He also appeared in *Of Love and Desire* (1963, 20th Century-Fox, starring Merle Oberon; filmed in Mexico) and *The Last Rebel* (1961, Mexican production, dir. Miguel Contreras Torres).

Elsa Cárdenas

Actress, born in Tijuana, Mexico, August 31, 1935, and raised in Mexico City. She made her film debut in 1954 in the Mexican film *Magdalena*. Her American films include *The Brave One* (1956), *Giant* (1956), as Juana Benedict, wife of the son of the oil rancher played by Rock Hudson, *Fun in Acapulco* (1963), *Of Love and Desire* (1963), *Taggart* (1964, Universal), and *The Wild Bunch* (1969).

Annette Cardona

Actress who played the role of Cha Cha in *Grease* (1978) and costarred in *Latino* (1985).

René Cardona (André Dux)

Actor and producer, born in Havana, September 8, 1905, died in Mexico City, 1988. He is the father of Mexican director René Cardona, Jr. (who also simply uses René Cardona professionally, especially for the U.S. release of his Mexican films), assistant director of *Two Mules for Sister Sara* (1970). The senior Cardona starred in and produced the first Hollywood Spanish-language production, *Sombras habaneras* (1929, Hispania Talking Film Corporation, presented by All-Star Exchange, costarring Jacqueline Logan, Paul Ellis, and Juan Torena). This melodrama debuted in Los Angeles on December 4, 1929, in Mexico City on December 6, 1929, and in San Juan, Puerto Rico, on February 18, 1930. He also costarred or had major roles in *Del mismo barro* (1930, Fox, starring Mona Maris and Luana Alcañiz), a Spanish-language version of *Common Clay* (1930, starring Constance Bennett and Lew Ayres); *Cuando el amor ríe* (1930, Fox, opposite José Mojica and Mona Maris), a Spanish-language version of *The Love Gambler* (1922, starring John Gilbert and Carmel Myers); and *Carne de cabaret* (1931, Columbia, dir. Christy Cabanne, opposite Lupita Tovar and Ramón Pereda), a Spanish-language version of *Ten Cents a Dance* (1931, dir. Lionel Barrymore, starring Barbara Stanwyck and Ricardo Cortez). Ríos-Bustamante (1992, 27) claims that Cardona also had supporting roles in English-language films such as *Gentlemen Prefer Blondes.* This is not confirmed by the *AFI Catalog,* which contrary to Ríos-Bustamante lists *Gentlemen Prefer Blondes* as 1928, not 1935.

Ismael ("East") Carlo

Actor, born January 19, 1942, in Puerto Rico and raised in New York. He played drug kingpins, concerned fathers, or corrupt officials on television and in film. His film credits include *A Piece of the Action* (1977), *Defiance* (1980), and *One Man Out* (1989). On television he has appeared in *The A-Team, Murder, She Wrote,* and *Crime Story.*

Julie Carmen

Actress, born April 4, 1954 [R has 1960], in Milburn, New Jersey [some sources give Mt. Vernon, New York]. She has done some television (*Falcon Crest, Condo)* and a considerable number of films, including the role of the wife in *The Milagro Beanfield War.* Film credits include *Can You Hear the Laughter? The Story of Freddie Prinze* (1979); *Night of the Juggler* (1980); *Gloria* (1980, dir. John Cassavetes), for which she won the Best Supporting Actress prize at the Venice Film Festival; *She's in the Army Now* and *Fire on the Mountain* (1981); *Last Plane Out* (1983); *Blue City* (1986); *The Milagro Beanfield War* and *The Penitent* (1988); *The Neon Empire, Paint It Black,* Gore Vidal's *Billy the Kid,* and *Fright Night II* (all 1989); *Kiss Me a Killer* and *The Hunt for the Night Stalker* (1991); and *Curaçao* (1993).

Ada Carrasco

Actress. Active in the Mexican film industry (e.g., she appeared in *Nazarín,* released in the United States in 1962), she also appeared in *Two Mules for Sister Sara* (1970) and *Like Water for Chocolate* (1993).

Carlos Carrasco

Actor, born in Panama. He has appeared in *"Crocodile" Dundee II* (1988), *The Fisher King* (1991), and *Bound by Honor* (1993).

Joaquín Carrasco

Actor, born in Barcelona, 1881. He had supporting roles playing the gardener, the doctor, or the like in several Hollywood Spanish-language films including *Un hombre de suerte* (1930, Cinéstudio Continental Paramount, dir. Benito Perojo, starring Roberto Rey and María Luz Callejo); *Toda una vida* (1930, Paramount, starring Carmen Larrabeiti and Tony D'Algy); *Entre noche y día* (1931, United Artists, starring Alfonso Granada and Hélèna D'Algy); and *La pura verdad* (1931, Paramount, starring José Isbert and Enriqueta Serrano).

Barbara Carrera

Actress, born December 31, 1945 [PHH lists December 31, 1939], in Managua, Nicaragua, to an American employee of the U.S. embassy and a Nicaraguan mother. She first became a high-fashion model, debuted on the screen in 1970 in *Puzzle of a Downfall Child* (Universal, starring Faye Dunaway and Viveca Lindfors), and later appeared as a Spanish *señorita* in *The Master Gunfighter* (1975). Additional film credits: *Embryo* (1976); *The Island of Dr. Moreau* (1977); *When Time Ran Out!* (1980); *Condorman* (1981); *I, the Jury* (1982); *Never Say Never Again* and *Lone Wolf McQuade* (1983); *Wild Geese II* (1985); *Love at Stake* and *The Underachievers* (1988); and *The Wicked Stepmother* and *Loverboy* (1989). On television she played the Indian woman, Clay Basket, in the miniseries *Centennial* (1978) and had a notable role as a Jewish woman in the miniseries *Masada* (1981), starring Peter O'Toole.

Above: Barbara Carrera

Edward Carrere

Art director and production designer, born in 1905 in Mexico City of a Spanish mother and a French father, died in 1979. He is the brother of Fernando Carrere and father of Leon Carrere. He won an Academy Award for Art Direction for *Camelot* (1967). During his career at Warner Brothers he worked on *The Adventures of Don Juan, The Fountainhead,* and *White Heat* (all 1949); *Sunrise at Campobello* (1960); and *The Wild Bunch* (1969). He worked with Hecht-Hill-Lancaster on *Separate Tables* and *Run Silent, Run Deep* (both 1958). Additional credits include *Francis of Assisi* (1961); *Taras Bulba* (1962); *Act One, Critic's Choice,* and *Island of Love* (1963); *The Pleasure Seekers* (1964); *Never Too Late* and *The Third Day* (1965); *Not With My Wife, You Don't!* (1966); and *There Was a Crooked Man* (1970).

Fernando Carrere

Art director and production designer, as was his older brother, Edward Carrere; born December 31, 1910, in Mexico City of a Spanish mother and a French father. He designed sets for *The Pride and the Passion* (1957), *Birdman of Alcatraz* (1962), *The Great Escape* (1963), and several Pink Panther films. In 1961, he was nominated for an Academy Award for *The Children's Hour* (dir. William Wyler). Additional credits: *Jack the Giant Killer* (1962), *The Pink Panther* and *The Young Lovers* (both 1964), *The Great Race* (1965), *What Did You Do in the War, Daddy?* (1966), *Gunn* and *Waterhole # 3* (1967), *The Party* (1968), and *Darling Lili* (1970).

Leon Carrere

Television film editor and director, born February 26, 1935, son of Edward Carrere. His television credits include *Charlie's Angels* (both as editor and director), *The Rookies,* and *In the Heat of the Night.*

Robert Carricart

Character actor, born January 18, 1917, in Bordeaux, France, of a Spanish mother and a French father. He initially worked on the Broadway stage, moving to Hollywood in 1957 and appearing in *Black Orchid* (1959); *Blueprint for Robbery* and *Run Across the River* (1961); *Follow That Dream* (1962); *Fun in Acapulco* and *Dime with a Halo* (1963); *Robin and the 7 Hoods* and *Blood on the Arrow* (1964); *Black Spurs* (1965); *Apache Uprising* and *What Did You Do in the War, Daddy?* (1966); *The Pink Jungle, The Wicked Dreams of Paula Schultz,* and *Villa Rides* (1968); *Land Raiders* (1970); and *The Milagro Beanfield War* (1988). On television he costarred in the series *T.H.E. Cat.*

Elpidia Carrillo

Actress, born August 16, 1961, in Michoacán, Mexico. She debuted in *The Border* (1982), opposite Jack Nicholson, as a Guatemalan immigrant whose baby is stolen. She has appeared in *Beyond the Limit* and *Under Fire* (1983), *Salvador*

character actors of the 1930s and 1940s. In the early 1950s, he played Pancho, Duncan Renaldo's sidekick, in *The Cisco Kid* television series. Some of the over 100 films he appeared in include *Mister Antonio* (1929); *Hell Bound, The Homicide Squad, The Guilty Generation,* and *Lasca of the Rio Grande* (all 1931); *Deception, Girl of the Rio, The Broken Wing,* and *Men Are Such Fools* (1932); *Before Morning, Moonlight and Pretzels, Obey the Law, Parachute Jumper,* and *Racetrack* (1933); *Villa Villa!, Manhattan Melodrama, The Band Plays On, Four Frightened People,* and *The Gay Bride* (1934); *In Caliente, Love Me Forever, If You Could Only Cook,* and *The Winning Ticket* (1935); *The Gay Desperado, Moonlight Murder,* and *It Had to Happen* (1936); *Manhattan Merry-Go-Round, The Barrier, 52nd Street, Hotel Haywire, I Promise to Pay,* and *History Is Made at Night* (1937); *The Girl of the Golden West, Blockade, City Streets, Flirting with Fate, Little Miss Roughneck,* and *Too Hot to Handle* (1938); *The Arizona Wildcat, Chicken Wagon Family, Fisherman's Wharf, Society Lawyer, The Girl and the Gambler,* and *Rio* (1939); *Lillian Russell, One Night in the Tropics, Captain Caution, Wyoming,* and *20 Mule Team* (1940); *Horror Island* and *Barnacle Bill* (1941); *Sin Town, American Empire* (1942); *Crazy House, Follow the Band, Frontier Badmen,* and *Phantom of the Opera* (1943); *Ghost Catchers, Bowery to Broadway, Gypsy Wildcat,* and *Moonlight and Cactus* (1944); *Crime Incorporated* and *Mexicana* (1945); *The Fugitive* (1947); and *The Girl from San Lorenzo* and *Pancho Villa Returns* (1950).

Lynda Carter

Actress, born July 24, 1951, in Phoenix, Arizona, of German-Hispanic heritage. She is known for her 1970s television series *Wonder Woman*. She has appeared in *Bobbie Jo and the Outlaw* (1976), *Last Song* (1980), *Hotline* (1982), *Rita Hayworth: The Love Goddess* (1983, TV film), and *I Posed for Playboy* (1991).

Blanca Castejón

(Also used Blanca de Castejón professionally) Mexican actress, born in New York City, May 13, 1914, died in Mexico City, December 26, 1969. She had one leading and several costarring or supporting roles in Hollywood Spanish-language productions including *Resurrección* (1931, Universal, dir. Edwin Carewe, starring Lupe Vélez and Gilbert Roland); *El impostor* (1931, Fox, costarring opposite Juan Torena), a Spanish-language version of *Scotland Yard* (1930, starring Edmund Lowe and Joan Bennett); *Esclavas de la moda* (1931, Fox, starring Carmen Larrabeiti and Félix de Pomés); *Eran trece* (1931, Fox, starring Manuel Arbó and Juan Torena); *El carnaval del diablo* (1936, MGM, costarring opposite Fortunio Bonanova), a Spanish-language version of *The Devil*

Above: Elpidia Carrillo and Jimmy Smits in *My Family/Mi familia* (1995)

(1986), *Let's Get Harry* and *Predator* (1987), *Assassin* (1989), *The Lightning Incident* (1991, cable TV), and *My Family/Mi familia* (1995), once again as an undocumented immigrant.

Leo Carrillo

(Also used Leo Carillo professionally) Actor, born August 6, 1880 [R has 1881], in Los Angeles, died September 10, 1961, in Santa Monica, California. A member of one of the most prominent original Californio families, he went to Santa Monica High School (his father, Juan José, was once mayor of Santa Monica) and St. Vincent's (now Loyola Marymount) University. He began as a cartoonist before becoming a dialect comedian in vaudeville and later a successful Broadway actor. Debuting in Hollywood in 1929 with *Mr. Antonio* (Tiffany-Stahl Productions, Inc., costarring Virginia Valli), he became one of Hollywood's busiest

LEO CARRILLO, CHARACTER ACTOR

Leo Carrillo, a descendent of a long-standing *californio* family, did not mind playing stereotypical Hispanic roles for decades, including Cisco Kid's sidekick.

Left: Leo Carrillo (left), Ida Lupino, and Nino Martini in *The Gay Desperado* (1936, United Artists)

Below: Leo Carrillo (right) and Nino Martini (middle) in *The Gay Desperado* (1936, United Artists)

Left: Leo Carrillo (right) as the sidekick and Duncan Renaldo (center) as the Cisco Kid

Below: Leo Carrillo (right) in *Timber*

on Horseback (1936, starring Del Campo and Lili Camita); *Mis dos amores* (1938, Paramount, costarring opposite Tito Guízar), a Spanish-language original based on a screenplay by José Antonio Miranda; and *Los hijos mandan* (1939, 20th Century-Fox, in a starring role, with Fernando Soler and Arturo de Córdova costarring), a Spanish-language original based on "El caudal de los hijos" (Madrid, 1921) by José López Pinillos.

Antonio Castillo

Theatrical costume designer, Spanish-born. He won an Academy Award for his work on *Nicholas and Alexandra* (1972).

Enrique Castillo

(Also E. J. Castillo) Mexican American actor, born January 10, 1949. He has appeared in *Borderline* (1980), *Losin' It* (1983), and *Bound by Honor* (1993). His television credits include *The Waltons* and the television film *Fighting Back: The Rocky Bleier Story* (1980).

Eduardo Castro

Film and stage costume designer. He designed costumes for *Shout* (1991) and was codesigner on *Bird on a Wire* (1990). He designed the 1987 season of the television series *Miami Vice*.

Larry Ceballos

Choreographer, born November 21, 1887, in Iquique, Chile, where he was raised, died September 12, 1978. He was one of Hollywood's most recognized dance directors in the late 1920s and early 1930s, working for Warner Brothers and RKO on feature films and Vitaphone shorts. The dance sequences that he choreographed appeared, among many other films, in *Gold Diggers of Broadway, On With the Show,* and *Show of Shows* (all 1929); *Hold Everything, No, No Nanette,* and *Sally* (1930); *Kiss Me Again* (1931); *Sitting Pretty* (1933); *The Cat's-Paw* and *Transatlantic Merry-Go-Round* (1934); *Redheads on Parade* and *Sweet Surrender* (1935); *Follow Your Heart* (1936); *Make a Wish* (1937); *Outside of Paradise* (1938); *Laugh It Off* and *Rio* (1939); *One Night in the Tropics* and *Sing, Dance, Plenty Hot* (1940); and *Spring Parade* (1941).

Gary Cervantes

Mexican American character actor, known for his roles as criminals. He has appeared in *Boulevard Nights* and *Walk*

Above: Choreographer Larry Ceballos at work with chorus girls

Below: From left to right: (standing) Gary Cervantes, Pepe Serna, Robby Benson, Luis Reyes, and Tony Alvaranga; (front) Trinidad Silva and Ángel Salazar in *Walk Proud* (1970, Universal)

Proud (both 1979), *Scarface* (1983), *Commando* and *Stick* (1985), *Extreme Prejudice* and *Fatal Beauty* (1987), *Colors* (1988), *Grand Canyon* (1991), and *A Low Down Dirty Shame* (1994). He has also appeared on numerous television episodes.

Jorge Cervera, Jr.

Actor. He has appeared in *Papillon* (1973), *The Big Fix* (1978), *Black Marble* (1979), *True Confessions* (1981), *Waltz Across Texas* (1982), *¡Three Amigos!* (1986), and *Stones for Ibarra* (1988, TV film). He has done considerable television work including costarring on the television series *Viva Valdez.*

Damian Chapa

Actor of Mexican American and German heritage. He appeared in *Under Siege* (1992) and had the leading role of Miklo in *Bound by Honor* (1993).

Charlita

(María Diego) Actress and dancer, born in Cuba, noted for her torrid, sexy roles. She appeared in *Brimstone* (1949, Republic); *Come Fill the Cup* (1951, Warner, starring James Cagney); *Let's Go Navy* (1951); *South of Caliente* (1951, Republic, starring Roy Rogers and Dale Evans), in the role of the evil horse trainer; *Rancho Notorious* (1952, RKO, dir. Fritz Lang, starring Marlene Dietrich and Mel Ferrer), as a "dark lady"; *Toughest Man in Arizona* (1952, Republic); *Massacre Canyon* (1954, Columbia), as Nita the Naughty; *Green Fire* (1955, starring Grace Kelly and Stewart Granger); *Billy the Kid vs Dracula* (1966); and *El Dorado* (1966, dir. Howard Hawks, starring John Wayne, Robert Mitchum, and James Caan).

Charo

(María Rosario Pilar Martínez) Actress and musician (classical guitar), born January 15, 1951 [1944 according to PHH], in Murcia, Spain. She had the role of Aunt Charo (1977-78) on the television series *Chico and the Man* and became well known primarily on television talk and variety shows in the 1970s as an updated version of the discombobulated, malaprop-spouting, hot-blooded Latina. She received her start in the United States with Xavier Cugat, to whom she was married. Her film credits include *Tiger by the Tail* (1970), *Airport '79* (1979), and *Moon Over Parador* (1988).

Richard Chaves

Actor, born in Jacksonville, Florida, October 9, 1951. He cowrote the successful stage play *Tracers,* based on his Vietnam War experience. He appeared in *Cease Fire* (1985), costarred in *Predator* (1987) as Poncho, and was in *Night Eyes 2* (1991). He also costarred in the television film *Fire on the Mountain* (1981) with Buddy Ebsen and has appeared in numerous television series episodes.

José Chávez

Actor, active in the Mexican film industry. He has been seen in the United States in both Mexican films in English-language versions and U.S. movies that were filmed in Mexico or on the border. Credits include *The Important Man* (1961, Mexican production, starring Toshiro Mifune), *The Mighty Jungle* (1964), *The Professionals* (1966, Columbia, starring Burt Lancaster, Lee Marvin, and Robert Ryan), *Guns for San Sebastian* (1968), *Tarzan's Deadly Silence* (1970), and *Two Mules for Sister Sara* (1970).

Linda Christian

(Blanca Rosa Welter) Actress, born November 13, 1924, in Tampico, Mexico, of Dutch parents. She debuted in *Holiday in Mexico* (1946). She became well known when she married actor Tyrone Power in 1949, whom she divorced in 1955. She was also married to Edmund Purdom. Film credits include *Green Dolphin Street* (1947), *Tarzan and the Mermaids* (1948), *Battle Zone* and *The Happy Time* (both 1952), *Slaves of Babylon* (1953), *Athena* and *Casino Royale* (both 1954), *Thunderstorm* (1956), *The House of Seven Hawks* (1959), *The Devil's Hand* (1961), *Full Hearts and Empty Pockets* and *The V.I.P.s* (1963), *The Moment of Truth* (1965), *Contest Girl* (1966), and *How to Seduce a Playboy* (1968).

Cynthia Cidre

Cuban-born screenwriter, born in 1957. Her credits include *Country* (1989, coscripted), *Fires Within* (1991), and *The Mambo Kings* (1992).

Aurora Clavel

Actress, active in the Mexican film industry (e.g., she appeared in the notable *Tarahumara*, 1965, starring Ignacio López Tarso). She appeared in several U.S. films including *Major Dundee* (1965), *Guns for San Sebastian* (1968), *The Wild Bunch* (1969), and *Soldier Blue* (1970).

Alex Colón

Actor, born January 26, 1941, in Puerto Rico, and raised in New York. Colón has worked in theater, film, and television. He appeared in *The Cross and the Switchblade* (1970); *The Hospital* (1971); *Harry and Tonto, The Super Cops,* and *The Taking of Pelham One Two Three* (all 1974); *The Ultimate Warrior* (1975); *Special Delivery* (1976); *When You Comin' Back, Red Ryder?* (1979); *Back Roads* (1981); *Deal of the Century* (1983); *Invasion U.S.A.* and *Death of an Angel* (1985); *Deep Cover* (1988); and *The Mighty Quinn* and *Red Scorpion* (1989). His television credits include *The Law* (1974), *Hustling* (1975), *Raid on Entebbe* (1977), *Women of San Quentin* (1983), and the epic miniseries *Centennial* (1978).

Miriam Colón

Actress, born in Ponce, Puerto Rico, 1925 [PHH lists August 20, 1936]. She studied drama at the University of Puerto Rico and subsequently was admitted to New York's prestigious Actor's Studio, studying under Lee Strasberg and Elia Kazan. She is the founder and artistic director of New York's Puerto Rican Traveling Theatre. As a character actor, she has appeared in a number of U.S. films including *Battle at Bloody Beach, The Outsider,* and *One-Eyed Jacks* (all 1961); *Harbor Lights* and *Thunder Island* (1963); *The Appaloosa* (1966); *The Possession of Joel Delaney* (1972); *Back Roads* (1981); *Scarface* (1983), as the gangster leader's mother; *A Life of Sin* (1992); *The House of the Spirits* (1994); *Sabrina* (1995); and *Lone Star* (1996, dir. John Sayles).

Anjanette Comer

Actress, born in Dawson, Texas, August 7, 1942. She has appeared in *Quick, Before It Melts* and *The Loved One* (both 1965); *The Appaloosa* (1966); *Banning* (1967); *Guns for San Sebastian* and *In Enemy Country* (1968); *Rabbit, Run* and *The Firechasers* (1970); *The Baby* and *The Manchu Eagle Murder Caper Mystery* (1973); *Lepke* (1975); *Fire Sale* (1978); *The Long Summer of George Adams* (1982); and *The Underneath* (1995).

Above: Miriam Colón in *Scarface* (1983)

James Contreras

Film sound man, born in 1923, died 1990. His credits include *The Night of the Iguana* (1964), *Psych-Out* (1968), and *Easy Rider* (1969). On television he worked on the series *Kung Fu* and *The Streets of San Francisco.* He was the brother of actor Roberto Contreras.

Luis Contreras

Mexican American actor, born September 18, 1950. He often played stereotypical sleazy Latino characters in both films and television. His film credits include *Coming Home*

(1978); *Borderline* and *The Long Riders* (both 1980); *Barbarosa* (1982); *Pee-Wee's Big Adventure, Red Heat,* and *Stand Alone* (1985); *Blue City* (1986); *Extreme Prejudice* and *Walker* (1987); and *Bound by Honor* (1993). His television credits include *Gunsmoke,* the original *Mission: Impossible, Hill Street Blues, Dallas,* the new *Adam 12,* and *MacGyver.* He is the son of actor Roberto Contreras.

Roberto Contreras

Actor, born in St. Louis and raised in Mexico City. He began his acting career at age eight, appearing in Mexican film and television. His U.S. film credits include *The Sun Also Rises* (1957), *The Magnificent Seven* (1960), *Gold of the Seven Saints* (1961), *California* (1963), *Mara of the Wilderness* and *Ship of Fools* (both 1965), *The Appaloosa* and *The Professionals* (1966), *Topaz* (1969), *Barbarosa* (1982), *Scarface* (1983), and *Streets of Fire* (1984). He had a regular role as a ranch hand on *The High Chaparral* television series. He is the brother of sound man James Contreras and the father of actor Luis Contreras.

Miguel Contreras Torres

(Also Miguel C. Torres) Director and actor, born in Cotija, Michoacán, 1890, died in Mexico City, June 7, 1981. He directed and starred in *Soñadores de la gloria* (1931, Imperial Art Films, presented by United Artists, costarring Lia Torá and Manuel Granado), a Spanish-language original for which he also wrote the screenplay. He also directed, produced, and wrote the screenplay for *No matarás* (1935, Hispano International Film Corporation, starring Ramón Pereda and Adriana Lamar), a Spanish-language original. He directed *The Mad Empress* (1939, Warner Brothers, starring Medea Novara, Lionel Atwill, and Conrad Nagel), which began as an independent film production in Mexico but was completed with funds provided by Warner so that Warner could protect its major film *Juárez* (1939) from competition with another studio. He also directed the Mexican film released in English in the United States as *The Last Rebel* (1961).

Tito Coral

Actor. He had major parts in two Hollywood Spanish-language films: *Un capitán de cosacos* (1934, Fox), as Nick Baglieff, and *Señora casada necesita marido* (1934, Fox), as *el cantante.* He was also in *365 Nights in Hollywood* (1934) and *Goin' to Town* (1935).

Caesar Córdova

Character actor, born May 16, 1936, in Puerto Rico. His film credits include *Shark's Treasure* (1975), *Where the* *Buffalo Roam* (1980), *Nighthawks* (1981), and *Scarface* (1983). On television he appeared on *East Side/West Side* and *Kojak.*

Linda Córdova

Actress; she appeared as an easy waitress in *The Long Rope* (1961) and in the role of Mrs. Delgado in *Hombre* (1967, 20th Century-Fox, starring Paul Newman and Fredric March).

Mapy Cortés

(Also Mapy Cortez; born María del Pilar Cordero) Actress, born in San Juan, Puerto Rico, March 1, 1919 [PHH has March 1, 1913]. She performed in Spanish-language theater in Latin America and Spain as well as appearing in films in both Spain and Mexico, where she was highly popular. Coming to Hollywood in 1942, she appeared in *Seven Days' Leave* (1942, RKO), a musical revue with Victor Mature and Lucille Ball.

David Cota

Actor; he appeared in Hispanic roles in *Perilous Holiday* (1946, Columbia) and *Crisis* (1950, MGM, starring Cary Grant, Gilbert Roland, and José Ferrer).

Jim Cota

Agent of Mexican heritage, partner in The Artists' Agency. In the industry since 1971, his clients include Edward James Olmos, Pepe Serna, and Jon Mercedes III and Josefina López (a writer/producer team).

Manny Coto

(Also Cota, Cotto) Writer and director, born in Havana, Cuba, and raised in Orlando, Florida. He directed *Playroom* (1989), *Cover-Up* (1990), and *Dr. Giggles* (1992), and, on television, episodes of HBO's *Tales from the Crypt* and the syndicated series *Monsters.*

José Crespo

(José Crespo Ferraz) Actor, born in Murcia, Spain, November 7, 1902. He had starring or major roles in at least 16 Hollywood Spanish-language films including *Olimpia* (1930, MGM, costarring María Alba), a Spanish-language version of *His Glorious Night* (1929, dir. Lionel Barrymore, starring John Gilbert and Catherine Dale Owen); *Wu Li*

Chang (1930, MGM, starring Ernesto Vilches and Angelita Benítez); *El presidio* (1930, MGM, costarring Juan de Landa and Luana Alcañiz), a Spanish-language version of *The Big House* (1930, starring Chester Morris and Wallace Beery); *En cada puerto un amor* (1931, MGM, costarring Conchita Montenegro), a Spanish-language version of *Way for a Sailor* (1930, starring John Gilbert and Wallace Beery); *El proceso de Mary Dugan* (1931, MGM, costarring opposite María Ladrón de Guevara), a Spanish-language version of *The Trial of Mary Dugan* (1929, starring Norma Shearer and Lewis Stone); *Dos noches* (1933, Fanchon Royer Pictures, Inc., presented by J. H. Hoffberg Co., Inc., dir. Carlos F. Borcosque, costarring Conchita Montenegro), a Spanish-language version of *Revenge at Monte Carlo* (1933, starring José Crespo and June Collyer); *La ciudad de cartón* (1933, Fox, starring Catalina Bárcena and Antonio Moreno); *Tres amores* (1934, Universal, costarring Anita Campillo and Mona Maris), a Spanish-language version of *Bachelor Mother* (1933, starring Evalyn Knapp and James Murray); *Señora casada necesita marido* (1934, Fox, starring Catalina Bárcena and Antonio Moreno); *Angelina o el honor de un brigadier* (1935, Fox, costarring opposite Rosita Díaz Gimeno), a Spanish-language original based on a work by Enrique Jardiel Poncela; *La última cita* (1935, Columbia, costarring Luana Alcañiz), a Spanish-language original based on a screenplay by René Borgia; *Alas sobre el Chaco* (1935, Universal, dir. Christy Cabanne, costarring Lupita Tovar and Antonio Moreno), a Spanish-language version of *Storm Over the Andes* (1935,

dir. Christy Cabanne, starring Jack Holt and Antonio Moreno); *Tengo fe en ti* (1940, RKO-Radio Pictures, costarring opposite Rosita Moreno), a Spanish-language original based on a screenplay by John Reinhardt and Carmen Brown and a plot by Rosita Moreno; *La vida bohemia* (1937, Columbia, starring Rosita Díaz Gimeno and Gilbert Roland); and *El milagro de la Calle Mayor* (1939, 20th Century-Fox, starring Margo and Arturo de Córdova). He also appeared in the following English-language films: *Revenge at Monte Carlo* (1933), *Hollywood Hoodlum* (1934), and *Rascals* (1938).

Linda Cristal

(Marta Victoria Moya Burges) Actress, born February 24, 1935, in Buenos Aires [1934 according to PHH] and orphaned at 13. She played leads in Mexican film from the age of 16 and debuted in Hollywood in the mid-1950s in both films and TV (*The High Chaparral*) as a leading lady. Her film credits (U.S.) include *Comanche* (1956); *The Perfect Furlough*, *The Fiend Who Walked the West,* and *The Last of the Fast Guns* (all 1958); *Cry Tough* (1959); *The Alamo* (1960); *The Pharaoh's Woman* (1961); *Two Rode Together* (1961, dir. John Ford), as a Mexican woman captured by Indians; *Panic in the City* (1968); *Mr. Majestyk* (1974); *The Dead Don't Die* (1975, TV film); *Hughes and Harlow: Angels in Hell* (1977); and *Love and the Midnight Auto Supply* (1978).

Vladimir Cruz

Cuban actor. He costarred in the notable Cuban film released in the United States as *Strawberry and Chocolate* about the politics of gay love in contemporary Cuba.

Alfonso Cuarón

Mexican director. His American cinematic debut, *A Little Princess* (1995), won the Los Angeles Film Critics award for that year. His earlier Mexican film *Love in the Time of Hysteria* was released in the United States.

Xavier Cugat

(Francisco de Asís Javier Cugat Mingall) Bandleader and film director, born January 1, 1900, in Barcelona, died October 27, 1990, in Barcelona. He came to the United States from Havana, where he was raised from the age of three. He was married to and divorced Rita Montaner, Carmen Castillo, Lorraine Allen, Abbe Lane, and Charo Baeza. In the 1930s and 1940s, he was known as America's

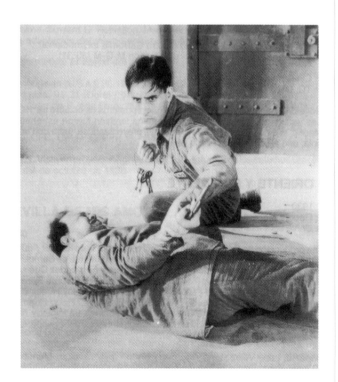

Above: José Crespo in *El presidio* (1930, MGM)

"Rumba King" and was instrumental in popularizing Latin music in the United States. He also helped, by featuring beautiful singers with his band, to launch the careers of Lina Romay, Margo, Abbe Lane, and Charo. Early in his career he made a short-subject film with his band and Rita Cansino (later Rita Hayworth). He appeared in occasional films, usually playing himself and leading his orchestra, "The Gigolos," in MGM musicals of the 1940s. His films include *Go West Young Man* (1936); *You Were Never Lovelier* (1942), which reunited him in film with Rita Hayworth; *The Heat's On* and *Stage Door Canteen* (both 1943); *Bathing Beauty* and *Two Girls and a Sailor* (1944); *Weekend at the Waldorf* (1945); *Holiday in Mexico* and *No Leave, No Love* (1946); *This Time for Keeps* (1947); *A Date with Judy*, *Luxury Liner*, and *On An Island With You* (1948); *Neptune's Daughter* (1949, starring Esther Williams); *Chicago Syndicate* (1955); *The Monitors* (1969); and *The Phynx* and *Tiger by the Tail* (both 1970). He directed and appeared in two Hollywood Spanish-language films: *Charros, gauchos y manolas* (1930, Hollywood Spanish Pictures Company, featuring numerous Hispanic entertainers including Carmen Castillo, Delia Magaña, Paul Ellis, Carmen Granada, María Alba, and Martín Garralaga) and *Un fotógrafo distraído* (1930, Hollywood Spanish Pictures Company, starring Romualdo Tirado, Carmen Guerrero, Don Alvarado, and Delia Magaña).

Antonio Cumellas

Actor; he had a few supporting roles in Hollywood Spanish-language productions including *En nombre de la amistad* (1930, Fox, starring George Lewis and Andrés de Segurola); *Soñadores de la gloria* (1931, Imperial Art Films, presented by United Artists, dir. and starring Miguel Contreras Torres); *Marido y mujer* (1932, Fox, starring George Lewis and Conchita Montenegro); and *Dos noches* (1933, Fanchon Royer Pictures, Inc., presented by J. H. Hoffberg, Inc., dir. Carlos F. Borcosque, starring José Crespo and Conchita Montenegro). He was also in the English-language film *Bad Girl* (1931).

Above: Xavier Cugat and Lina Romay in *Two Girls and a Sailor* (1944)

Ana María Custodio

(Ana María Muñoz Custodio) Actress, born in Ecija, Sevilla, Spain, March 19, 1907, died in Madrid, April 10, 1976. She starred or had major roles in a few Hollywood Spanish-language productions including *Cuerpo y alma* (1931, Fox, costarring opposite George Lewis), a Spanish-language version of *Body and Soul* (1931, starring Charles Farrell, Elissa Landi, Humphrey Bogart, and Myrna Loy); *¿Conoces a tu mujer?* (1931, Fox, starring Rafael Rivelles and Carmen Larrabeiti); *Eran trece* (1931, Fox, costarring opposite Manuel Arbó and Juan Torena), a Spanish-language version of *Charlie Chan Carries On* (1931, starring Warner Oland and John Garrick); and *Mi último amor* (1931, Fox, costarring opposite José Mojica), a Spanish-language version of *Their Mad Moment* (1931, starring Warner Baxter, Dorothy Mackaill, and ZaSu Pitts).

D

Hélèna D'Algy

(Also Helen) Actress, born in Spain, sister of Tony D'Algy. She appeared in both English-language and Spanish-language productions. English-language films she appeared in include *Lend Me Your Husband, A Sainted Devil, Let No Man Put Asunder* (all 1924); *Confessions of a Queen, Daddy's Gone a-Hunting, The Fool,* and *Pretty Ladies* (1925); *Don Juan, The Exquisite Sinner, The Silver Treasure, The Cowboy and the Countess* [film held at MOMA], and *Siberia* (1926). She also had supporting roles in several Hollywood Spanish-language productions including *Un hombre de suerte* (1930, Cinéstudio Continental Paramount, dir. Benito Perojo, starring Roberto Rey and María Luz Callejo); *Dos mentiras* (1930, Cinéstudio Continental Paramount, starring Carmen Larrabeiti and Félix de Pomés); *Entre noche y día* (1931, United Artists, costarring opposite Alfonso Granada), a Spanish-language version of *77 Park Lane* (1931, with Dennis Neilson-Terry and Betty Stockfield); *El hombre que asesinó* (1931, Paramount British, starring Rosita Moreno and Ricardo Puga); and *Melodía de arrabal* (1933, Paramount, starring Imperio Argentina and Carlos Gardel).

Tony D'Algy

(Also used Antonio; born Antonio Guedes Infante) Spanish actor, born in Angola, 1904, died April 29, 1977, brother of Hélèna D'Algy. He appeared in both English-language and Spanish-language productions. His English-language films include *Meddling Women, The Rejected Woman,* and *A Sainted Devil* (all 1924); *Soul Mates* (1925); and *The Boob, The Gay Deceiver,* and *Monte Carlo* (1926). He had leading roles in several Hollywood Spanish-language films including *El secreto del doctor* (1930, Paramount, starring Eugenia Zuffoli and Félix de Pomés); *Toda una vida* (1930, Paramount, costarring opposite Carmen Larrabeiti), a Spanish-language version of *Sarah and Son* (1930, starring Ruth Chatterton and Fredric March); *La fiesta del diablo* (1930, Paramount, costarring opposite Carmen Larrabeiti), a Spanish-language version of *The Devil's Holiday* (1930, starring Nancy Carroll and Phillips Holmes); *Sombras del circo* (1931, Paramount, costarring opposite Amelia Muñoz), a Spanish-language version of *Half-way to Heaven* (1929, starring Jean Arthur and Charles

Above: Hélèna D'Algy (left) and Rosita Moreno on the set of *El hombre que asesinó* (1930, Warner Brothers)

"Buddy" Rogers); *La incorregible* (1931, Paramount, costarring opposite Enriqueta Serrano), a Spanish-language version of *Manslaughter* (1930, starring Claudette Colbert and Fredric March); and *Lo mejor es reír* (1931, Paramount, costarring opposite Imperio Argentina), a Spanish-language version of *Laughter* (1930, starring Nancy Carroll and Fredric March).

Bertila Damas

Cuban-Puerto Rican actress; she appeared opposite Jimmy Smits in *Fires Within* (1991) and also appeared in *Nothing But Trouble* (1991) and *Stop! or My Mom Will Shoot* (1992).

Mona Darkfeather

Actress, Hispanic in whole or part (see García Riera, vol. I, 59; however, Buscombe [1988] claims she was Seminole), married first to Frank Montgomery, who directed her in *A Spanish Madonna* and *The Western Border* (1915), and subsequently to the Mexican actor and stuntman Art Ortega. She was very active in silent film, usually as the leading star, playing an American Indian or Hispanic. Additional credits, all in leading roles, include *A Savage Girl's Devotion* (1911, Bison, dir. Fred J. Balshofer [film held at MOMA]); *Massacre of the Fourth Cavalry* (1912, Bison, dir. Frank E. Montgomery [film held at MOMA]); *A Crucial Test* (1912, Selig Polyscope [film held at LC]); *Juanita* (1913, Nestor); *The Oath of Conchita* (1913, Nestor); *The Vengeance of the Skystone* (1913, 101 Bison, dir. Frank E. Montgomery [film held at EH]); *The Apache Father's Vengeance* (1913, Bison [film held at NFTA]); *At the End of the Rope* (1914, Kalem, dir. Frank E. Montgomery [film held at LC]); and *Defying the Chief* (1914, Kalem, dir. Frank E. Montgomery [film held at EH]).

Henry Darrow

(Enrico Thomas Delgado) Actor, born September 15, 1933 [R has 1931], in New York City, he starred in *The High Chaparral* television series (1967-71); had the role of Alex Monténez (1973-74) on *The New Dick Van Dyke Show;* was Detective Lt. Manny Quinlan (1974-1975) on *Harry-O*, a dramatic TV series; played Don Diego de la Vega (Zorro Sr.) on *Zorro and Son,* a TV comedy (1983); and was Lt. Rojas (1985) on *Me and Mom,* a TV dramatic series. His film credits include *Holiday for Lovers* (1959), where he debuted on film with a small role, *Badge 373* (1973), *The Invisible Man* (1975), *Computer Wizard* and *Where's Willy* (both 1977), *Walk Proud* (1979), *Attica* (1980), *Seguín* (1982), *Losin' It* (1983), *Death Blow* (1987), *In Dangerous Company* (1988), *L.A. Bounty* (1989), *The Last of the Finest* (1990), and *Percy and Thunder* (1992).

Tito Davison

(Also Tito H. Davison) Actor, writer, and director, born in Chillén, Chile, November 14, 1912, died in Mexico City, March 21, 1985. He helped adapt some scripts into Spanish for Hollywood and had numerous supporting roles in Hollywood Spanish-language films including *Sombras de gloria* (1929, Sono-Art Productions, Ltd., starring José Bohr and Mona Rico); *Así es la vida* (1930, Sono-Art Productions, Ltd., starring José Bohr and Lolita Vendrell); *La fuerza del querer* (1930, Paramount, starring María Alba and Carlos Barbé); *Los que danzan* (1930, Warner, starring Antonio Moreno and María Alba); *El presidio* (1930, MGM, starring José Crespo and Juan de Landa); *La gran jornada* (1931, Fox, starring George Lewis and Carmen Guerrero); *Cheri-Bibi* (1931, MGM, dir. Carlos F. Borcosque, starring Ernesto Vilches and María Ladrón de Guevara); *Granaderos del amor* (1934, Fox, starring Raúl Roulien and Conchita Montenegro); and *Rosa de Francia* (1935, Fox, starring Rosita Díaz Gimeno, Julio Peña, and Antonio Moreno). He also had directorial roles in a few English-language productions including *Neighbors' Wives* (1933, as assistant director), *The Fighting Lady* (1935, as assistant director), and *Ramona* and *Sutter's Gold* (1936, both as technical advisor). He had bit parts, in each case as a bellhop, in *Stamboul Quest* and *Laughing Boy* (both 1935).

Chico Day

(Also used Francisco Day; born Francisco Alonso) Assistant director and production manager, the younger brother of Gilbert Roland, born in Juárez, Mexico, 1907, and raised in El Paso and Los Angeles. Day was apparently the first Mexican American in the Directors Guild of America. He was an important role model for other Latino production people, working for over 30 years at Paramount Studios (see Reyes, *DGA Magazine,* 1995). His film credits include *The Plainsman* (1936), *The Big Broadcast of 1938* (1938), *Lady in the Dark* (1944), *Whispering Smith* (1948), *Streets of Laredo* (1949), *Samson and Delilah* (1949), *The Ten Commandments* (1956), *Teacher's Pet* (1958), and *One-Eyed Jacks* (1961). Subsequently, he became a unit production manager with credits on such films as *The Magnificent Seven* (1960); *Battle at Bloody Beach* and *The Last Time I Saw Archie* (both 1961); *Escape from Zahrain* (1962); *The Fool Killer* and *Major Dundee* (1965); *The Last of the Secret Agents?* and *Seconds* (1966); *Valley of the Dolls* (1967); *The Sweet Ride* (1968); *Hello, Dolly!* (1969); and *Patton* (1970).

Pedro de Córdoba

Actor, born September 28, 1881, in New York, to Cuban-French parents, died September 16, 1950, in Sunland, California. A former stage actor, he played character parts in numerous silent and sound films, usually as either a benevolent or malevolent Latin aristocrat. Selected films: *Carmen* (1915, Jesse L. Lasky Feature Play Co. [film held at EH and MOMA]), as Escamillo opposite Geraldine Farrar and Wallace Reid; *Temptation* (1915); *Maria Rosa* (1916); *The New Moon* (1919); *The World and His Wife* (1920 [film held

Above: Pedro de Córdoba (second from left) with (left to right) Ernest Joy, Geraldine Farrar, and Wallace Reid in *María Rosa* (1916, Lasky)

Above: Pedro de Córdoba in 1918

Above: Arturo de Córdova (right) and J. Carrol Naish in *A Medal for Benny* (1945, Paramount)

at LC]); *The Dark Mirror* (1920, Famous Players-Lasky Corp., costarring opposite Dorothy Dalton); *The Inner Chamber* (1921); *Just a Song at Twilight, The Young Diana, When Knighthood Was in Flower* (all 1922); *The Enemies of Women* and *The Purple Highway* (1923); *The Bandolero* (1924); *The Desert Sheik* and *The New Commandment* (1925); *Through the Centuries* (1933); *The First World War* (1934); *Condemned to Live, The Crusades,* and *Captain Blood* (1935); *Rose of the Rancho, Anthony Adverse, The Devil-Doll, His Brother's Wife, Moonlight Murder, Professional Soldier, Trouble for Two, Ramona,* and *The Garden of Allah* (1936); *The Firefly, Girl Loves Boy, Maid of Salem,* and *Marriage Forbidden* (1937); *Dramatic School, Gold Diggers in Paris, Heart of the North, Storm over Bengal, International Settlement,* and *Keep Smiling* (1938); *Chasing Danger, City in Darkness, Devil's Island, Escape to Paradise, Law of the Pampas, Man of Conquest, Range War, Winner Take All,* and *Juárez* (1939); *Before I Hang, Earthbound, The Ghostbreakers, The Light That Failed, My Favorite Wife, Phantom Submarine, South of Pago Pago, The Mark of Zorro,* and *The Sea Hawk* (1940); *Romance of the Rio Grande, Blood and Sand,* and *Aloma of the South Seas* (1941); *The Corsican Brothers, Son of Fury,* and *Saboteur* (1942); *The Song of Bernadette* and *For Whom the Bell Tolls* (1943); *Uncertain Glory* (1944); *The Keys of the Kingdom* (1945); *Swamp Fire* (1946); *Mexican Hayride* (1948); *Samson and Delilah* (1949); and *Comanche Territory* and *Crisis* (1950).

Arturo de Córdova

(Arturo García Rodríguez) Actor, born May 8, 1908, in Mérida, Yucatán, Mexico, died November 3, 1973, in Mexico City. He debuted in Mexican films in the early 1930s and played "Latin Lovers" in Hollywood during the 1940s, then returned to Spanish-language film. Selected films (primarily U.S.): *Cielito lindo* (Mex., 1936); *La zandunga* (Mex., 1937); *Son's Command* (1938); *For Whom the Bell Tolls* (1943); *Frenchman's Creek* (1944); *Masquerade in Mexico, A Medal for Benny, Duffy's Tavern,* and *Incendiary Blonde* (all 1945); *New Orleans* (1947); *Adventures of Casanova* (1948); *Stronghold* (1951); *Él* (released in the United States as *This Strange Passion,* 1952, dir. Luis Buñuel); and *The Violent and the Damned* (1962). His Hollywood Spanish-language film credits include *Los hijos mandan* (1939, 20th Century-Fox, opposite Blanca de Castejón and Fernando Soler), a Spanish-language original based on "El caudal de los hijos" (Madrid, 1921) by José López Pinillos, and *El milagro de la Calle Mayor* (1939, 20th Century Fox, costarring opposite Margo), a Spanish-language version of *A Miracle on Main Street* (1940, starring Margo and Walter Abel).

Frederick De Córdova

Director, born October 27, 1910, in New York City. He entered films from the stage in 1944, working for Warner Brothers first as a dialogue director. He directed many unexceptional medium-budget features through the mid-1960s, including the now notable *Bedtime for Bonzo* (1951, starring Ronald Reagan), *Bonzo Goes to College* (1952), *Yankee Buccaneer* (1952), and *Frankie and Johnny* (1966, starring Elvis Presley), but he was primarily active in television after

Above Arturo de Córdova in *Adventures of Casanova* (1948)

the mid-1950s. From 1971 until his retirement in May 1992, he was the producer of NBC's *The Tonight Show Starring Johnny Carson.*

Josie de Guzmán

Puerto Rican stage actress working on Broadway. She was featured in the film *F/X* (1986).

Juan de Homs

Actor. He appeared in supporting roles in several Hollywood Spanish-language films including *Estrellados* (1930, MGM, starring Buster Keaton, Raquel Torres, and Don Alvarado); *Olimpia* (1930, MGM, starring José Crespo and María Alba); *El presidio* (1930, MGM, starring José Crespo and Juan de Landa); *La llama sagrada* (1931, Warner, starring Elvira Morla and Martín Garralaga); *La fruta amarga* (1931, MGM, starring Virginia Fábregas and Juan de Landa); and *El príncipe gondolero* (1931, Paramount, starring Roberto Rey and Rosita Moreno).

Joe de la Cruz

(Also used José; also Joe Dellacruz) Actor, born in Mexico, March 19, 1892, died December 14, 1961. He had supporting roles, often in Westerns, where he usually played a bandit or a vaquero. Film credits include *The Bearcat* (1922, starring Hoot Gibson); *Western Yesterdays* (1924); *Call of the West, Hell's Heroes,* and *A Devil with Women* (all 1930); *The Hidden Valley, Law and Lawless,* and *Trailing the Killer* (1932); *The Battling Buckaroo* and *Four Frightened People* (1934); *Lawless Border, Sunset of Power, Unconquered Bandit,* and *The Cactus Kid* (1935); *Ramona* (1936); *Frontiers of '49, Gunga Din, Oklahoma Frontier,* and *Zorro's Fighting Legion,* a 12-episode serial (1939); *The Westerner* (1940); and *The Black Scorpion* (1957).

Juan de Landa

(Juan Pisón Pagoaga) Actor and singer, born in Motrico, Spain, January 27, 1894, died in Motrico, February 17, 1968. He began as an opera singer and later migrated to Hollywood, where he started his acting career in Hollywood Spanish-language films. He appeared as a costar or in major roles in the following: *¡De frente, marchen!* (1930, MGM, starring Buster Keaton and Conchita Montenegro, as Sargento Gruñón), a Spanish-language version of *Doughboys* (1930, starring Buster Keaton and Sally Eilers); *El último de los Vargas* and *El valiente* (both 1930, Fox); *El presidio* (1930, MGM, costarring opposite José Crespo), a Spanish-language version of *The Big House* (1930, starring Chester Morris and Wallace Beery); *Su última noche* (1931, MGM), in the role of Aquiles Desano; *En cada puerto un amor* (1931, MGM, costarring opposite José Crespo and Conchita Montenegro), a Spanish-language version of *Way for a Sailor* (1930, starring John Gilbert and Wallace Beery); *La fruta amarga* (1931, costarring opposite Virginia Fábregas), a Spanish-language version of *Min and Bill* (1930, starring Marie Dressler and Wallace Beery); and *El proceso de Mary Dugan* (1931, MGM), in the role of Inspector Hunt. He was also in *The Man Who Wagged His Tail* (1961, Spanish-Italian production, starring Peter Ustinov).

Jack Delano

Director of several Puerto Rican films including *Los peloteros* (1951) and *Las manos del hombre* (1952), about the dignity and value of different kinds of manual labor.

Danny de la Paz

Actor, born April 13, 1957. He played the role of a Chicano gang member in *Boulevard Nights* (1979) and appeared in *Cuba* (1979), *Blood Barrier* (1979, British production starring Telly Savalas, originally titled *The Border*), *Seguín* and *Barbarosa* (both 1982), *City Limits* (1985), *3:15* (1986), *The Wild Pair* (1987), *Miracle Mile* (1989), and *American Me* (1992), as Puppet, a prison gang member who kills his own brother in deference to the gang code.

George de la Peña

Dancer, born 1958 [PHH has 1956], in New York, of Russian-Argentine parentage. He performs with the American Ballet Theatre. He portrayed the renowned Russian dancer in *Nijinsky* (1980). He was in *Cowboy and the Ballerina* (1984), *Kuffs* (1992), had a major role in *Brain Donors* (1992, starring John Turturro), and appeared in *Mighty Aphrodite* (1995).

Above: Danny de la Paz (left) with Gilbert Roland in *Barbarosa* (1982, Universal)

Alfredo Del Diestro

Actor, died 1951. He appeared in supporting roles in at least ten Hollywood Spanish-language films including *Los que danzan* (1930, Warner, starring Antonio Moreno and María Alba); *A media noche* (1930, Fox, starring Lia Torá and Juan Torena); *La dama atrevida* (1931, First National Pictures, starring Luana Alcañiz and Ramón Pereda); *El código penal* (1931, Columbia, starring Barry Norton and María Alba); *La mujer X* (1931, MGM, dir. Carlos F. Borcosque, starring María Ladrón de Guevara and Rafael Rivelles); *Soñadores de la gloria* (1931, United Artists, dir. Miguel Contreras Torres, starring Miguel Contreras Torres and Lia Torá); *El pasado acusa* (1931, Columbia, starring Luana Alcañiz and Barry Norton); and *Nada más que una mujer* (1934, Fox, starring Berta Singerman and Juan Torena).

Marcus de León

Director/writer of Mexican American and German heritage. A native of Los Angeles, he directed a short student film, *Xavier,* that won UCLA's prestigious Best Film Award. De León and several of his UCLA classmates made the film *Border Radio* (1988), and de León wrote and directed the independent feature *Kiss Me a Killer* (1991).

Marcel Delgado

Model maker and sculptor, born 1900 in La Parrita, Mexico, died 1976. Delgado moved with his family to California in 1909. Self-educated, he worked on many films including *King Kong* (1933, RKO), for which he was chief model maker and sculptor. Other film credits include *The Lost World* (1925), *Son of Kong* (1934), *Mighty Joe Young* (1949), *Jack the Giant Killer* (1962), *It's a Mad Mad Mad Mad World* (1963), and *Fantastic Voyage* (1966).

Roger Delgado

(Roger Caesar Delgado) Actor, born in London, March 1918, died June 17, 1973. He appeared often in Hispanic or other exotic roles in films (often British productions) such as *Sea Fury* (1958, Rank), as a Hispanic tugboat captain; *The Terror of the Tongs* (1961); *In Search of the Castaways, The Singer Not the Song,* and *The Road to Hong Kong* (all 1962); *The Running Man* (starring Laurence Harvey), in the role of a Spanish doctor, *Khartoum* (starring Charlton Heston), and *The Mind Benders* (all 1963); *Agent 8-3/4* and *Masquerade* (1965); *The Mummy's Shroud* and *The Assassination Bureau* (1967); *Underground* (1970); and *Antony and Cleopatra* (1973, dir. and starring Charlton Heston).

Marcia del Mar

Actress; her film credits include *Under Fire* (1983) and *Body Double* (1984), and she costarred in the USA cable network television series *Sánchez of Bel Air.*

Pilar del Rey

Actress. Her film credits include *Mark of the Renegade* (1951, with Ricardo Montalbán), *The Miracle of Our Lady of Fatima* (1952, starring Gilbert Roland), *The Naked Jungle* (1953), *Black Horse Canyon* (1954), *Giant* (1956), as the mother of Sal Mineo, *Lonely Are the Brave* (1962), and *. . . And Now Miguel* (1966).

Dolores del Río

(Lolita Dolores Martínez Asunsolo López Negrete) Actress, born August 3, 1905 [PHH has 1904], in Durango, Mexico, died April 11, 1983, in Newport Beach, California. She was educated in a convent; by age 16 she was married to writer Jaime del Río. Director Edwin Carewe was struck by her beauty and invited her to Hollywood, where she appeared in *Joanna* in 1925. She became a star, appearing in many silent films, but her career suffered from frequent typecasting in ethnic and exotic roles, particularly after the advent of sound. Dissatisfied with Hollywood, she returned to Mexico in 1943, doing many important films of the 1940s including *María*

Above: Dolores del Río

Candelaria and John Ford's *The Fugitive* (filmed on location in Mexico). She finally returned to Hollywood in character parts in the 1960s. Selected films: *Joanna* (1925); *Pals First* (1926, her first lead); *What Price Glory* (1926, Fox, dir. Raoul Walsh, costarring opposite Victor McLaglen and Edmund Lowe [film held at EH and MOMA]); *Resurrection* (1927); *The Loves of Carmen* (1927, Fox, dir. Raoul Walsh, costarring Victor McLaglen and Don Alvarado [film held at CR and MOMA]); *The Gateway of the Moon, No Other Woman,* and *Ramona* (all 1928); *Revenge* (1928, Edwin Carewe Productions, dir. Edwin Carewe, costarring James Marcus [film held at EH]); *The Red Dance* (1928, Fox, dir. Raoul Walsh, costarring opposite Charles Farrell [film held at CR and MOMA]); *Evangeline* (1929, Edwin Carewe-Feature Productions, Inc., dir. Edwin Carewe, costarring Roland Drew [film held at LC]); *The Trail of '98* (1929); *The Bad One* (1930); *Bird of Paradise* and *Girl of the Rio* (1932); *Flying Down to Rio* (1933); *Madame Du Barry* and *Wonder Bar* (1934); *I Live for Love* and *In Caliente* (1935); *Widow from Monte Carlo* (1936); *Ali Baba Goes to Town, Lancer Spy,* and *The Devil's Playground* (1937); *International Settlement* (1938); *The Man from Dakota* (1940); *María Candelaria* (Mex., 1943); *The Fugitive* (1947); *Doña Perfecta* (Mex., 1950); *La cucaracha* (Mex., 1958); *Flaming Star* (1960); *Cheyenne Autumn* (1964); *More Than a Miracle* (1967); and *The Children of Sánchez* (1978).

Benicio del Toro

Puerto Rican actor, born 1967. He appeared in *License to Kill* and *Big Top Pee-Wee* (both 1989); *Christopher Columbus: The Discovery* (1992), as an Indian slave master; *Fearless* (1993); *Money for Nothing* (1993, dir. Ramón Menéndez); *China Moon* (1994); *Swimming with Sharks* and *The Usual Suspects* (1995); and *Basquiat* (1996). On television his credits include *Miami Vice* and the miniseries *Drug Wars: The Camarena Story.*

Guillermo del Toro

Director and writer. His *Cronos* (1992, Mexican production, starring Ron Perlman, Claudio Brook, and Margarita

Above: Dolores del Río in *In Caliente* (1935)

Isabel), a Christian vampire fable about a romance between a deformed man who inhabits the sewers under a meat market and the daughter of the market's owner, was very well received.

Félix de Pomés

(Félix de Pomés Soler) Actor and film director, born in Barcelona, February 5, 1889, died in Barcelona, July 17, 1969, father of actress Isabel de Pomés. He had several roles as a starring or principal actor in Hollywood Spanish-language films including *Doña Mentiras* (1930, Cinéstudio Continental Paramount, costarring opposite Carmen Larrabeiti), a Spanish-language version of *The Lady Lies* (1929, starring Walter Huston and Claudette Colbert); *El secreto del doctor* (1930, Paramount, costarring opposite

Eugenia Zuffoli), a Spanish-language version of *The Doctor's Secret* (1929, starring Ruth Chatterton and H. B. Warner); *Toda una vida* (1930, Paramount), as John Ashmore; *La fiesta del diablo* (1930, Paramount, costarring opposite Carmen Larrabeiti and Tony D'Algy), a Spanish-language version of *The Devil's Holiday* (1930, starring Nancy Carroll and Phillips Holmes); *Sombras del circo* (1931, Paramount, costarring opposite Amelia Muñoz and Tony D'Algy), a Spanish-language version of *Half-way to Heaven* (1929, dir. George Abbott, starring Jean Arthur and Charles "Buddy" Rogers); *Cuerpo y alma* (1931, Fox), as Comandante Knowles; *Esclavas de la moda* (1931, Fox, costarring opposite Carmen Larrabeiti), a Spanish-language version of *On Your Back* (1930, starring Irene Rich and Raymond Hackett); and *Mamá* (1931, Fox, dir. Benito Perojo), in the role of Mauricio.

Enrique de Rosas

(Also DeRosas) Actor, born in Buenos Aires, July 14, 1888, died in Ituzango/Buenos Aires, January 20, 1948. He had several costarring or principal roles in Hollywood Spanish-language films including *¿Cuándo te suicidas?* (1931, Paramount); *Angelina o el honor de un brigadier* (1935, Fox), as Brigadier Marcial Ortiz; *Tango Bar* (1935, Paramount, costarring opposite Carlos Gardel and Rosita Moreno), a Spanish-language original based on a screenplay by Alfredo Le Pera; *Te quiero con locura* (1935, Fox, costarring opposite Rosita Moreno and Raúl Roulien), a Spanish-language original based on "La cura de reposo" (Madrid, 1927) by Pedro Muñoz Seca and Enrique García Velloso; *Piernas de seda* (1935, Fox), as Mr. Baxter; *Rosa de Francia* (1935, Fox), as Mariscal de Tesse; and *El carnaval del diablo* (1938, MGM, costarring opposite Fortunio Bonanova and Blanca de Castejón), a Spanish-language version of *The Devil on Horseback* (1936, starring Del Campo and Lili Damita). He appeared in a few English-language releases as well including *Hi, Gaucho!* (1935); *The Devil on Horseback* (1936); and *Sandflow, Timberesque, When You're in Love,* and *Swing High, Swing Low* (all 1937).

Nick de Ruiz

(Also Nicholas) Actor. He appeared in dozens of feature films in the 1920s and 1930s in a variety of roles ranging from Mexican bandits to sultans including *The Shark Master* and *Morals* (both 1921); *The Altar Stairs, Another Man's Shoes, East Is West, The Half Breed, Wolf Law,* and *A Wonderful Wife* (all 1922); *Bavu, The Hunchback of Notre Dame* (starring Lon Chaney), *Fools and Riches,* and *Slave of Desire* (1923); *Forbidden Paradise, Mademoiselle Midnight,*

and *The Night Hawk* (1924); *His Supreme Moment* and *Lord Jim* (1925); *The Girl from Montmartre* and *Old Ironsides* (1926); *The Unknown* (starring Lon Chaney) and *The Man Who Laughs* (1927); *Rio Rita* (1929); *Call of the West, Golden Dawn, Isle of Escape,* and *Wings of Adventure* (1930); *Viva Villa!* (1934); *I Live My Life* (1935); *Banjo on My Knee, Love Before Breakfast, Robin Hood of El Dorado,* and *White Fang* (1936); and *Madame X* (1937).

José de San Antonio

Puerto Rican actor. He appeared in two films shot in Puerto Rico: *Thunder Island* (1963, with Miriam Colón) and *Harbor Lights* (1963, also with Miriam Colón).

Joe de Santis

(Joseph V. de Santis) Actor, born in New York City, June 15, 1909, died August 30, 1989. His credits include *Deadline U.S.A.* (1952); *Marty* (1955); *Dino* (1957); *Buchanan Rides Alone* (1958, starring Randolph Scott); *The Flying Fontaines* and *Al Capone* (1959); *Cry Tough* (also 1959, starring John Saxon and Linda Cristal, an early film on the problems of second-generation Puerto Ricans); *The George Raft Story* and *A Cold Wind in August* (1961); *An American Dream, Beau Geste, Madame X, The Professionals,* and *And Now Miguel* (1966); *The Venetian Affair* (1967); *Blue* (starring Ricardo Montalbán), *Chubasco* (troubled motorcycle gang member redeems himself working on honest tuna boat), and *The Brotherhood* (all 1968); *Night Chase* (1970); *Honor Thy Father* (1971, TV film); and *Little Cigars* (1973).

Andrés de Segurola

(Also André and Andreas; born Andrés Perello de Segurola) Actor, born in Valencia, Spain, March 27, 1874, died in Barcelona, January 23, 1953. He began as an operatic basso and made his first appearance in the United States at the Metropolitan Opera (1901-02 season). He appeared in numerous films starring Gloria Swanson, John Barrymore, Grace Moore, and others, including *The Loves of Sunya* (1927); *Glorious Betsy, My Man, Bringing Up Father,* and *The Cardboard Lover* (1928); *Behind Closed Doors, The Red Dance, General Crack, Careers,* and *Mamba* (1929); *Song o' My Heart* (1930); *One Night of Love* and *We're Rich Again* (1934); *Goin' to Town* and *Public Opinion* (1935); *One Hundred Men and a Girl* and *First Love* (1937); *Three Smart Girls Grow Up* (1939); and *Spring Parade* (1940). During his acting career, which ran from the late 1920s through the 1930s, he wore a monocle, which became his trademark. He appeared in principal roles (costarring in two) in at least 18 Hollywood Spanish-language films including *El cuerpo del delito* (1930, Paramount), as Antonio Benson; *La fuerza del querer* (1930, Paramount), as Chuck; *El hombre malo* (1930, First National Pictures, costarring opposite Antonio Moreno), a Spanish-language version of *The Bad Man* (1930, starring Walter Huston and Dorothy Revier); *Cascarrabias* (1930, Paramount); *En nombre de la amistad* (1930, Fox, costarring opposite George Lewis), a Spanish-language original based on Eugene Walter's screenplay "Friendship"; *La voluntad del muerto* (1930, Universal); *El príncipe gondolero* (1931, Paramount), as Príncipe Dantarini; *Mamá* (1931, Fox), as Fernando; *Mi último amor* (1931, Fox), as Lord Harry; *El caballero de la noche* (1932, Fox); *No dejes la puerta abierta* (1933, Fox); *La ciudad de cartón* (1933, Fox), as Morrison; *Granaderos del amor* (1934, Fox), as Barón Von Keller; *Un capitán de cosacos* (1934, Fox), as Fedor Petrovich; *Dos más uno, dos* (1934, Fox), as Sir Edward Bentley; *Tres amores* (1934, Universal); *Angelina o el honor de un brigadier* (1935, Fox); and *Castillos en el aire* (1938, Monogram, dir. Jaime Salvador).

Aura de Silva

Actress; she had a few supporting roles in Hollywood Spanish-language films including *Angelina o el honor de un brigadier* (1935, Fox); *Rosa de Francia* (1935, Fox); and *El crimen de media noche* (1935, Reliable), as Kate. She was also in the English-language film *Sutter's Gold* (1936).

Rosana de Soto

Actress, born September 2, 1947, in San Jose, California. She studied drama at San Jose State University. Originally with the Northern California Light Opera company, she moved to repertory theater, television, and feature films. She appeared in *The In-Laws* (1979) and *Cannery Row* (1982), had the role of the translator in *The Ballad of Gregorio Cortez* (1982), and was recognized by reviewers for her role as Ritchie Valens's mother in *La Bamba* (1987). She appeared as Fabiola Escalante in *Stand and Deliver* (1987), as Dustin Hoffman's wife in *Family Business* (1989), and as a Klingon in *Star Trek VI: The Undiscovered Country* (1991). On television she was a regular on *The Redd Fox Show* and *A.E.S. Hudson Street,* and she has appeared in many TV movies and as a guest star in various series.

Steven E. de Souza

Writer of Spanish and Portuguese background. His screenplays include *48HRS.* (1982), *Die Hard* (1988), *Die Hard 2* (1990), and both *Terminator* films (1984, 1991). He has done many television series as a contract writer for Universal Studios.

Carlos J. de Valdez

(Also Carlos de Valdez) Peruvian-born stage and screen actor, born in Arica, Peru, March 19, 1894 [PHH lists August 7, 1888], died November 30, 1939. He appeared in numerous films including *All Men Are Enemies, Little Man, What Now?, Music in the Air, Paris Interlude, The Prescott Kid,* and *Viva Villa!* (1934); *Anna Karénina, Bonnie Scotland, The Florentine Dagger,* and *The Night Is Young* (1935); *Anthony Adverse, The Bold Caballero,* and *The Robin Hood of El Dorado* (1936); *Drums of Destiny, Espionage, The Last Train from Madrid, Men in Exile, Old Louisiana, Sudden Bill Dorn, Thin Ice, Conquest,* and *Lancer Spy* (1937); *Gold Diggers in Paris, Romance in the Dark,* and *Suez* (1938); *Bridal Suite, Midnight, The Llano Kid, The Girl from Mexico,* and *Juárez* (1939); *British Intelligence* (1940); and *Fiesta* (1941).

José de Vega, Jr.

Actor, born in San Diego, California, in 1933 to a Filipino father and a Colombian mother, died in Westwood, California, April 8, 1990. He appeared in *Blue Hawaii* (1962), in a minor role; *The Spiral Road* (1962); *Island of the Lost* and *A Covenant with Death* (1967); and *Ash Wednesday* (1973). He is best known for having played Chino in the Broadway and film versions of *West Side Story* (1961).

Jaime Devesa

Actor. He had several supporting roles in Hollywood Spanish-language films including *Espérame* (1933, Paramount, starring Carlos Gardel and Goyita Herrero); *Melodía de arrabal* (1933, Paramount, starring Imperio Argentina and Carlos Gardel); *Cuesta abajo* (1934, Paramount, starring Carlos Gardel and Mona Maris); *El tango en Broadway* (1934, Paramount, starring Carlos Gardel and Trini Ramos); *Milagroso Hollywood* (1935, Royal Films, starring Tito Guízar and Nenette Noriega); *Un hombre peligroso* (1935, Producciones Latinas Ltd., presented by Criterion Films, starring Anita Campillo and Paul Ellis); and *El crimen de media noche* (1935, Reliable Pictures, starring Ramón Pereda and Adriana Lamar).

Miguel de Zárraga

Writer and publicist, born 1885, died December 26, 1941. He worked on at least 13 Hollywood Spanish-language films in the 1930s, mostly as a translator from English into Spanish, occasionally writing screenplays. He then worked in the foreign publicity department at Columbia.

Miguel de Zárraga, Jr.

Sound technician, writer, and assistant director, died January 1, 1971, in Montebello, California. He worked on at least six Hollywood Spanish-language films in one or more of the above-mentioned capacities. He also was one of the founders of the Hollywood Foreign Press Association.

Don Diamond

Actor, born 1917, in Brooklyn, New York. He played El Toro, the Mexican sidekick, on the television series *The Adventures of Kit Carson* (1951-1955), Corporal Reyes on Walt Disney's *Zorro* (1958-1959), and Crazy Cat on the series *F Troop* (1965-1967). His film credits include *Swingin' Along* (1962), *Irma La Douce* (1963), *How Sweet It Is!* (1968), *Viva Max!* (1969), and *Hit Man* (1972).

Cameron Díaz

Cuban-American actress and model. She auditioned for a bit-part in *The Mask* (1994, starring Jim Carrey) and won the female lead. An overnight success, she is in *The Last Supper* (1996), which debuted at the Sundance Film Festival, and *She's the One* (also 1996).

Edith Díaz

Puerto Rican-born actress. She appeared in *Scenes from the Class Struggle in Beverly Hills* and *Born on the Fourth of July* (1989), and she was one of the singing nuns in *Sister Act* (1992). On television she starred in the series *Popi* in the 1970s and was Desi Arnaz's mother in the telefilm *Lucy and Desi: Before the Laughter* (1991).

Ken Díaz

Makeup artist; he was nominated for an Academy Award for his work on *Dad* (1989, starring Jack Lemmon).

Vic Díaz

Filipino actor. He appeared in numerous films produced or coproduced by Philippine film companies beginning in the 1960s in supporting roles, usually as a Filipino or Vietnamese, including *Moro Witch Doctor* (1964), *Operation CIA* and *The Ravagers* (both 1965), *Flight to Fury* (1966, starring Jack Nicholson), *Mission Batangas* and *The* *Passionate Strangers* (1968), *Impasse* (1969), *Beast of the Yellow Night* and *The Losers* (1970), *Superbeast* (United Artists) and *Daughters of Satan* (both 1972), *Deathhead Virgin* (1974), *Too Hot to Handle* (1976), *The Boys in Company C* (1978, Columbia), *The Children of An Lac* (1980), *Raw Force* (1982, also released as *Shogun Island*), *Eye of the Eagle* (1987), as Anglo-hating, Vietnamese Col. Trang, and *Bloodfist* (1989).

Carlos Díaz de Mendoza

Actor, born in Madrid, 1898, died 1959. He had one costarring and a few supporting roles in Hollywood Spanish-language films including *Toda una vida* (1930, Paramount, starring Carmen Larrabeiti and Tony D'Algy); *La carta* (1930, Paramount, costarring opposite Carmen Larrabeiti), a Spanish-language version of *The Letter* (1929, starring Jeanne Eagels and Herbert Marshall); *La fiesta del diablo* (1930, Paramount, starring Carmen Larrabeiti and Tony D'Algy); and *Eran trece* (1931, Fox, starring Manuel Arbó and Juan Torena).

Luis Díaz Flores

Actor. He had a few supporting roles in Hollywood Spanish-language films including *Hollywood, ciudad de ensueño* (1931, Universal, starring José Bohr and Lia Torá); *Contra la corriente* (1935, RKO-Radio Pictures, dir. Ramón Novarro, starring Luana Alcañiz and José Caraballo); *Alas sobre el Chaco* (1935, Universal, dir. Christy Cabanne, starring José Crespo, Lupita Tovar, and Antonio Moreno; he also had a minor role in the English-language original, *Storm Over the Andes*); and *La inmaculada* (1939, United Artists, starring Fortunio Bonanova and Andrea Palma).

Rosita Díaz Gimeno

Actress, born in Madrid, 1911, died in New York City, August 1986. She starred or had major roles in several Hollywood Spanish-language productions including *Su noche de bodas* (1931, Paramount, starring Imperio Argentina and Pepe Romeu); *Lo mejor es reír* (1931, Paramount, costarring opposite Imperio Argentina and Tony D'Algy), a Spanish-language version of *Laughter* (1930, starring Nancy Carroll and Fredric March); *Un caballero de frac* (1931, Paramount, starring Roberto Rey and Gloria Guzmán); *El cliente seductor* (1931, Paramount, starring Maurice Chevalier and Imperio Argentina); *Angelina o el honor de un brigadier* (1935, Fox, costarring José Crespo), a Spanish-language original based on a work by Enrique Jardiel Poncela; *Rosa de Francia* (1935, Fox, costarring Julio Peña and Antonio Moreno), a Spanish-language original based on a comedy by Eduardo Marquina

Above: Imperio Argentina, Carlos San Martín, Rosita Díaz Gimeno, and José Luis Salado at the Paramount studio in Joinville, France, early 1930s

Above: Beatrice Domínguez in *Under Crimson Skies* (1919, Universal, dir. Rex Ingram)

and Luis Fernández Ardavín; and *La vida bohemia* (1937, Columbia, costarring Gilbert Roland), a Spanish-language original based on the novel by Henri Murger, *Scènes de la vie de bohème* (1851).

Larry Domasin

Child actor. He appeared, usually as a Mexican moppet, in *Dime with a Halo* (1963), *Fun in Acapulco* (1963, Paramount), *Island of the Blue Dolphins* (1964), *The Rare Breed* (1966, Universal), *Ride Beyond Vengeance* (1966, Columbia), and *Valley of Mystery* (1967).

Plácido Domingo

Internationally recognized opera star, born in Spain, January 21, 1941, and raised in Mexico. He appeared in Franco Zeffirelli's *La Traviata* (1982) as Alfredo, in *Bizet's Carmen* (1984) as Don José, and in *Otello* (1986) in the title role.

Beatrice Domínguez

Actress and dancer (she was Rudolph Valentino's tango partner in *The Four Horsemen of the Apocalypse*), born in California, September 6, 1897, died in Los Angeles, February 27, 1921, of appendicitis. She appeared opposite Myrtle González in *The Masked Dancer* (1914, Vitagraph), and she was also in *The Light of Victory* and *The Sundown Trail* (1919) and *Under Crimson Skies* (1920).

Columba Domínguez

Actress, born in Guaymas, Mexico, March 4, 1929, married to director and actor Emilio "El Indio" Fernández. She was seen in the United States in a few Mexican productions, notably *Ánimas Trujano* (released in the United States as *The Important Man*, costarring opposite Japanese star Toshiro Mifune) and *The Weaver of Miracles* (1962, costarring opposite Pedro Armendáriz).

José Domínguez

(Also Joe Domínguez; José J. Domínguez) Actor, born in Chihuahua, Mexico, March 19, 1894, died in Woodland Hills, California, April 11, 1970. Domínguez had numerous supporting roles in Hollywood films including *Mason of the Mounted* and *Riders of the Desert* (both 1932); *Flying Down to Rio* (1933); *The Captain Hates the Sea* and *Marie Galante* (1934); *Red Salute* and *Under the Pampas Moon* (1935); *The Gay Desperado, The Texas Rangers, Under Two Flags,* and *Woman Trap* (all 1936); *When You're in Love* (1937); *Adventure in Sahara, The Girl of the Golden West, Out West with the Hardys,* and *Yellow Jack* (1938); *Blackmail, Mexicali Rose,* and *Down Argentine Way* (1939); *Gaucho Serenade* and *Geronimo* (1940); *Outlaws of the Rio Grande* (1941); *Perilous Holiday* and *Thrill of Brazil* (both 1946, Columbia); *Bandit Queen* (1950); *The Hitch-Hiker* (1953, RKO); *Green Fire* (1955, MGM); *One-Eyed Jacks* (1961); and *I Love You, Alice B. Toklas!* (1968). He also had a supporting role in one Hollywood Spanish-language film, playing Luciano in *El hombre malo* (1930, First National Pictures), and he was *ayudante de dirección* on *La fruta amarga* (1932, MGM, dir. Arthur Gregor).

Luis Miguel Dominguín

Internationally recognized Spanish matador. He had a cameo role in *Around the World in 80 Days* (1956, United Artists) and a major role together with other bullfighters in the notable docudrama *Bullfight* (1956, Janus).

"Don Catarino"

(Chevo Pirrín) Comic actor. He costarred in one and had a few supporting roles in other Hollywood Spanish-language productions including *Entre platos y notas* (1930, Fox, opposite Delia Magaña), a Spanish-language original based on the screenplay "Waiting for Love" by Paul Pérez and Max Constant; *Desconcierto matrimonial* (1930, Fox, starring Delia Magaña); *Gente alegre* (1931, Paramount, starring Roberto Rey and Rosita Moreno); *El príncipe gondolero* (1931, Paramount, starring Roberto Rey and Rosita Moreno); and *El cantante de Nápoles* (1934, Warner, starring Enrico Caruso, Jr., and Mona Maris).

Benji Donniger

Director of several Puerto Rican films including *El cacique* (1957, written by Emilio Díaz Valcárcel), about a rural community dealing with an authoritarian and greedy leader, and *Modesta* (1956, winner at the Venice Film Festival that same year), about the physical abuse of women in the Puerto Rican countryside.

Susan DosAmantes

Actress. She appeared in a supporting role with future major film executive Sherry Lansing as, respectively, María Carmen and Amelita, victims of rape and disfiguration in *Río Lobo* (1970, dir. Howard Hawks, starring John Wayne and Jorge Rivero). DosAmantes also had supporting roles in *Target Eagle* (1984), *Counterforce* (1987), and *Day of the Assassin* (1988, starring Glenn Ford).

Robina Duarte

Actress. She costarred in one and had supporting roles in two other Hollywood Spanish-language films: *El trovador de la radio* (1938, Paramount, opposite Tito Guízar), a Spanish-language original based on a screenplay by Bernard Luber and Nenette Noriega; *El otro soy yo* (1939, Paramount, starring Tito Guízar and Amanda Varela), a Spanish-language original based on a screenplay by Dana Wilma; and *El milagro de la Calle Mayor* (1939, 20th Century-Fox, starring Margo and Arturo de Córdova), a Spanish-language version of *A Miracle on Main Street* (1940, starring Margo and Walter Abel).

Marta Du Bois

Actress of French-Panamanian heritage; she grew up in the United States. She had the role of Shady in *Boulevard Nights* (1979), was in *Johnnie Mae Gibson: FBI* (1986, TV film), *The Trial of the Incredible Hulk* (1989), and *Fear* (1990), and, on television, has guest starred on numerous episodic series including *Magnum P.I.*

Suzanne Duller

Actress; she had supporting roles in several Hollywood Spanish-language films including *Cuesta abajo* (1934, Paramount, starring Carlos Gardel and Mona Maris); *El tango en Broadway* (1934, Paramount, starring Carlos Gardel and Trini Ramos); *El día que me quieras* (1935, Paramount, starring Carlos Gardel and Rosita Moreno); *Tango Bar* (1935, Paramount, starring Carlos Gardel and Rosita Moreno); and *Milagroso Hollywood* (1935, Royal Films, starring Tito Guízar and Nenette Noriega). She was also in the English-language productions *Gold Diggers in Paris* and *Jezebel* (both 1938).

Larry Durán

Actor/stuntman, born July 26, 1925, in Los Angeles. He was recognized when he was a boxer by Marlon Brando, who befriended and encouraged him. He had roles in *Viva Zapata!* (1952), *Guys and Dolls* (1955), *The Young Lions* (1958), *The Magnificent Seven* (1960), *One-Eyed Jacks* (1961), *The Hallelujah Trail* (1965), *The Last of the Secret Agents?* (1966), and *Good Times* (1967).

Juan Duval

Spanish actor and director, born April 28, 1899, died April 1, 1954. He has at least 11 Hollywood Spanish-language film credits, one as director, one as costar, and the others in supporting roles. His credits include *Sombras de gloria* (1929, Sono-Art Productions, Ltd., starring José Bohr and Mona Rico); *Cascarrabias* (1930, Paramount, starring Ernesto Vilches and Carmen Guerrero); *Los que danzan* (1930, Warner Brothers, starring Antonio Moreno and María Alba); *Amor que vuelve* (1934, Latin American Pictures, Inc., presented by Kinematrade, Inc., costarring opposite Don Alvarado and Renée Torres), a Spanish-language original based on a screenplay by Eustace Hale Ball; *Un capitán de cosacos* (1934, Fox, starring José Mojica and Rosita Moreno); *El diablo del mar*, as director (1935, Theater Classic Pictures, starring Ramón Pereda and Movita Castañeda), a Spanish-language version of *Devil Monster* (1935, starring Jack del Rio, Blanche Mehaffey, and Barry Norton); and *No matarás* (1935, Hispano International Film Corpora-tion, starring Ramón Pereda and Adriana Lamar). He also had numerous bit parts in English-language films including *Flying Down to Rio* and *The California Trail* (both 1933); *In Caliente* and *Storm Over the Andes* (1935); *Anthony Adverse, Under Two Flags,* and *A Message to Garcia* (1936); *Renfrew on the Great White Trail* (1938); *Mr. Moto in Danger Island* (1939); and *Down Argentine Way, Rhythm of the Rio Grande,* and *Arise, My Love,* (1940).

VERSIONS OF *RAMONA*

Above right: Mary Pickford and Kate Bruce
(as the mother) in *Ramona* (1910, dir. D. W.
Griffith)

Below right: Mary Pickford and Francis Grandin
(*Ramona,* 1910 version)

Bottom right: Mary Pickford and Henry B.
Walthall (*Ramona,* 1910 version)

Below left: Dolores del Río and Roland Drew
(1928 version)

Above left: Monroe Salisbury and Adda Gleason
(*Ramona*, 1916, W. H. Clune)

Below left: Dolores del Río (1928 version)

Below right: Cover of sheet music for *Ramona*
(1928) associated with Dolores del Río

Left: Warner Baxter and Dolores del Río
(1928, United Artists)

Below left: Film poster, Dolores del Río in
Ramona (1928)

Chuy Elizondo

Cinematographer, born December 25, 1942, in Torreón, Mexico. He was brought to the United States at age 12. Starting as a camera assistant at Universal Studios, he began to work for John Alonzo as a camera operator on such films as *Chinatown* (1974), *Conrack* (1974), *Farewell, My Lovely* (1975), and *The Bad News Bears* (1976). He became director of photography on the feature *Shadow of Kilimanjaro* (1987). On television his credits include *La Pastorela* (1991), *Bodies of Evidence* (1992), and *Terror in the Towers* (1993).

Héctor Elizondo

Actor, born December 22, 1936, in Puerto Rico, raised in New York City. He made his film debut in *The Vixens* (1969). His other film credits include *The Landlord* (1970); *Valdez Is Coming* (1971, starring Burt Lancaster), as a Mexican bandit; *Born to Win* (1971); *Deadhead Miles, Pocket Money,* and *Stand Up and Be Counted* (all 1972); *The Taking of Pelham One Two Three* (1974), as a psychopathic killer; *Report to the Commissioner* (1975); *Thieves* (1977); *Cuba* (1979); *American Gigolo* (1980); *The Fan* (1981); the comedy *Young Doctors in Love* (1982), as a mafioso forced to dress as a woman; *The Flamingo Kid* (1984); *Nothing in Common* (1986); *Leviathan* (1989); *Pretty Woman,* as a warmhearted hotel manager, and *Taking Care of Business* (both 1990); *Frankie and Johnny, Necessary Roughness,* and *Final Approach* (all 1991); *There Goes the Neighborhood* and *Samantha* (1992); and *Exit to Eden, Beverly Hills Cop III, Being Human,* and *Getting Even with Dad* (1994). On television he has starred in six television series: *Freebie and the Bean, Popi, Casablanca, A.K.A. Pablo* (on which he made his directorial

THE VERSATILE HÉCTOR ELIZONDO

A major talent, Héctor Elizondo's career, in both film and television, has accelerated over the decades.

Left: Héctor Elizondo with (from left to right) Anthony Pérez, Edith Díaz, and Dennis Vázquez in the TV comedy series *Popi*

Above: Héctor Elizondo (left) and Tom Mason in the TV series *Freebie and the Bean*

Above: Héctor Elizondo (with weapon) in *The Taking of Pelham One Two Three* (1974)

Below: Héctor Elizondo (right) and Sean Connery in *Cuba* (1979)

debut), *Foley Square,* and *Chicago Hope.* He has appeared on many other television shows and in the TV films *The Impatient Heart* (1971), *Wanted: The Sundance Woman* (1976), *The Dain Curse* (1978), *Honeyboy* (1982), *Casablanca* and *Women of San Quentin* (both 1983), *Out of the Darkness* (1985, opposite Martin Sheen), *Private Resort* and *Murder: By Reason of Insanity* (also 1985), *Courage* (1986), *Power, Passion, and Murder* (1987), *Forgotten Prisoners: The Amnesty Files* (1990), *Chains of Gold* and *Finding the Way Home* (1991), and *The Burden of Proof* (1992).

Paul Ellis

(Manuel Granado) Actor and screenplay writer, born in Buenos Aires, November 6, 1896. He had a significant career in silent and English-language Hollywood films and in Spanish-language sound films as well. Among his silent or English-language credits are *The Pace That Thrills* and *Pretty Ladies* (1925); *The Dancer of Paris* (1926); *Bitter Apples* and *Three Hours* (1927); *The Charge of the Gauchos* (1928); *The Bridge of San Luis Rey* and *In Old California* (1929); *The Common Law* (1931); *No Man of Her Own* (1932); *Secret Sinners* and *Under Secret Orders* (1933); *The Merry Widow, One Night of Love,* and *The Woman Condemned* (1934); *Captured in Chinatown, Fighting, Public Opinion, Never Too Late, Rip Roaring Riley, Rumba, $20 a Week,* and *Women Must Dress* (1935); *Fatal Lady, The House of a Thousand Candles, Marihuana, Wife vs. Secretary,* and *Murder at Glen Athol* (1936); *Heroes of the Alamo, Love Under Fire,* and *Timberesque* (1937); *California Frontier* (1938); *Nick Carter, Master Detective* (1939); and *Arizona Gang Busters* and *Down Argentine Way* (1940). He had a few costarring and numerous supporting roles in Hollywood Spanish-language films, including the first Hollywood Spanish-language film, *Sombras habaneras* (1929, Hispania Talking Film Corp., presented by All-Star exchange, costarring opposite René Cardona and Jacqueline Logan), a Spanish-language original based on a screenplay by René Nestor; *Charros, gauchos y manolas* (1930, Hollywood Spanish Pictures Co., dir. Xavier Cugat, starring in the *cuadro argentino* part of the film); as screenplay writer and star (using his Spanish name) of *Alma de gaucho* (1930, Chris Pillis Productions, presented by Edward L. Klein Corporation, also starring Mona Rico), a Spanish-language original based on a screenplay by Paul Ellis; *La voluntad del muerto* (1930, Universal, costarring opposite Lupita Tovar and Antonio Moreno); *El pasado acusa* (1931, Columbia, starring Luana Alcañiz and Barry Norton); *Hombres en mi vida* (1932, Columbia, starring Lupe Vélez and Gilbert Roland); *Dos noches* (1933, Fanchon Royer Pictures, presented by J. H. Hoffberg Co., Inc., dir. Carlos F. Borcosque, starring José Crespo and Conchita Montenegro); *Un hombre peligroso* (1935, Producciones Latinas Ltd., presented by Criterion Films, costarring opposite Anita Campillo); *Di que me quieres* (1938, RKO-Radio Pictures, costarring opposite George Lewis and Eva Ortega), a Spanish-language original based on dialogs by Francisco J. Ariza; *Papá soltero* (1939, Paramount, costarring opposite Tito Guízar, Armanda Varela, and Tana), a Spanish-language original based on a screenplay by Dana Wilma; and *Cuando canta la ley* (1939, Paramount, costarring opposite Tito Guízar, Tana, and Martín Garralaga), a Spanish-language original based on a screenplay by Jack Nattleford adapted into Spanish by Enrique Uhthoff.

René Enríquez

Actor, born November 25, 1933 [PHH has 1931], died March 23, 1990, in Tarzana, California. Born in San Francisco and raised in Nicaragua, he appeared in *Bananas* (1971), *Ants* (1977), *Gridlock* (1980, TV film), *Under Fire* (1983), *Choices of the Heart* (1983, TV film), *The Evil That Men Do* (1984), and *Bulletproof* (1988). He is best known for his role as Lt. Ray Calletano in the television series *Hill Street Blues*.

Félix Enríquez Alcalá

Director of photography. He has worked extensively in television, directing episodes of television series including *I'll Fly Away, Homefront,* and *South Beach.*

Moctesuma Esparza

Producer and director, born March 12, 1949, in Los Angeles, one of the best-known Chicanos in the film industry. He

Above: René Enríquez in the TV series *Hill Street Blues*

attended UCLA, where he received a B.A. and M.F.A. in film. During his college years he was involved in civil rights and antiwar activities (he was one of the "L.A. Thirteen" indicted in 1968), and he also helped to found the Chicano Research Center at UCLA. As a graduate student he worked on the production of bilingual films for *Sesame Street,* and his master's thesis, a 1973 documentary for NBC entitled *Cinco Vidas/Five Lives,* won an Emmy. In 1974, he formed Moctesuma Esparza Productions, which did documentaries and children's films. In 1977, Esparza was nominated for an Academy Award in the Best Documentary Short category for *Águeda Martínez,* a portrait of an elderly New Mexican woman. Beginning in the late 1970s he concentrated on feature films, the most notable of which have been *The Ballad of Gregorio Cortez* (1983) and *The Milagro Beanfield War* (1988). More recently, he formed a production company, Esparza/Katz, which has raised considerable funds to produce a number of feature-length motion pictures, some of them with Latino themes. Thus far Esparza/Katz has produced *Gettysburg* (1993) for Turner Entertainment and *The Cisco Kid* (1994) for Turner Network Television. Selected credits as producer or coproducer: *Only Once in a Lifetime* (1978), *The Ballad of Gregorio Cortez* (1983), *Radioactive Dreams* (1986), *The Milagro Beanfield War* (1988), *The Ambulance* (1990), and *The Cisco Kid* (1994).

José Ángel Espinosa, "Ferrusquilla"

Actor, born in Choix, Sinaloa, Mexico. Active in the Mexican film industry, he appeared in supporting roles in *Bandido*

(1956, United Artists, starring Robert Mitchum and Gilbert Roland); the Louis Malle film *Viva Maria!* (1965, United Artists); *Rage* (1966); *Guns for San Sebastian* (1968); *Río Lobo* (1970); and *Two Mules for Sister Sara* (1970).

Paul Espinosa

Producer and director, long affiliated with KPBS Television, San Diego. He has produced and directed exceptional documentaries and docudramas including *Los mineros* (1990, Héctor Galán, coproducer), a stirring view of the history of labor struggle by Arizona Mexican American miners from the turn of the century to the present. He produced for the American Playhouse series a dramatic adaptation of Tomás Rivera's masterpiece . . . *and the earth did not swallow him* (1995, Severo Pérez, director/writer). Other credits include *The Trail North* (1983); *Ballad of an Unsung Hero* (1983), about a scandalous case of discrimination and deportation of a well-known Chicano radio figure; *The Lemon Grove Incident* (1985), about separate and unequal education of Chicanos in California; *Vecinos desconfiados/Uneasy Neighbors* (1989), about tensions between migrant workers and affluent homeowners in San Diego, and *The Hunt for Pancho Villa* (1993, as writer and coproducer), a documentary about Pancho Villa's raid on Columbus, New Mexico, and its aftermath.

Above: Emilio Estévez and Demi Moore in *Wisdom* (1986)

Richard Espinoza

Assistant director, born April 4, 1948, in Texas. He has worked on *North Dallas Forty* (1979), *The Border* (1982), *Remo Williams* (1985), *American Me* (1992), and *Dr. Giggles* (1992). His television work includes *Jake and the Fatman, Baywatch,* and *Beauty and the Beast.*

Emilio Estefan

Composer, born March 4, 1950, husband of Cuban American singer Gloria Estefan. He has produced the scores of numerous successful films including *Top Gun* (1986) and *Three Men and a Baby* (1987).

Emilio Estévez

Actor, director, and screenwriter, born May 12, 1962, in New York City, son of Martin Sheen and brother of Charlie Sheen and Ramón and Renée Estévez; formerly married to Paula Abdul. The fair-haired and blue-eyed Estévez, who decided to use the original family surname, has been able to secure roles in mainstream pictures. His accomplishments as an actor are many and varied; much of his work

Above: Emilio Estévez in *Freejack* (1992)

Above: Renée Estévez

has been recognized for its excellence. Appearing first in television dramas such as *In the Custody of Strangers* (1982), he debuted in film in *Tex* (1982), followed by *The Outsiders* (1983, dir. Francis Ford Coppola) and *Nightmares* (1983), achieving wide recognition in *Repo Man* (1984). He has appeared, usually as star or costar, in *St. Elmo's Fire, The Breakfast Club,* and *That Was Then . . . This Is Now* (all 1985); *Wisdom* and *Maximum Overdrive* (1986); *Stakeout* (1987); *Never on Tuesday* (1988, cameo role); *Young Guns* (1988); *Nightbreaker* (1989); *Men at Work* and *Young Guns II* (1990); *Freejack* and *The Mighty Ducks* (1992); *Another Stakeout, Judgment Night,* and *National Lampoon's Loaded Weapon I* (1993); and *D2: The Mighty Ducks* (1994). Estévez has written several screenplays and directed two of them, including *Wisdom* (1986) and *Men at Work* (1990).

Ramón Estévez

Actor, youngest son of Martin Sheen and brother of Charlie Sheen and Emilio and Renée Estévez. He has appeared in *Blood on the Badge* (date unknown, an action

thriller about Libyan terrorists), *Cadence* (1989, dir. Martin Sheen, starring Charlie Sheen and Martin Sheen), and *Beverly Hills Brats* (1991, starring Martin Sheen).

Renée Estévez

Actress, daughter of Martin Sheen, sister of Charlie Sheen and Emilio and Ramón Estévez. She has had major roles in a number of films, primarily of the murder thriller or revenge variety, including *Bulldance* (starring Lauren Hutton), *Intruder, For Keeps,* and *Sleepaway Camp 2: Unhappy Campers* (all 1988); *Forbidden Sun* (starring Lauren Hutton) and *Marked for Murder* (1989); *Touch and Die* (1991, in the lead role, costarring Martin Sheen); and *Cheatin' Hearts* and *Deadfall* (1993).

Angelina Estrada

Character actress, born February 28, 1931. She appeared first as an extra and had a minor part in *Only Angels Have Wings* (1939). A recognized Hawaiian dancer, she danced with Elvis Presley in *Blue Hawaii* (1961); she also appeared in *Aloma of the South Seas* (1941), *The Jungle Book* (1942), *A Medal for Benny* (1945), *One-Eyed Jacks* (1961), *Paint Your Wagon* (1969), and *Ghost* (1990).

Erik Estrada

(Henry Enrique Estrada) Actor, born March 16, 1949 [PHH lists 1944], in New York City, to Puerto Rican parents. Estrada first began performing in New York City parks with a group called The Kids from San Juan as part of a cultural program sponsored by Mayor John Lindsay's administration. In his first film role, he carried a switchblade in the Pat Boone film *The Cross and the Switchblade* (1972). He became widely recognized in the role of Frank "Ponch" Poncherello in the TV series *CHiPs* (1977-83). He had some interesting roles in the films he did in the 1970s, but his 1990s films especially have been primarily trashy violence and sexploitation vehicles. Additional selected films: *Jailbreakin'* and *The New Centurions* (1972); *Airport 1975* (1974); *Midway* (1976), as the stereotypical aviator, Chili Bean Ramos; and *The Longest Drive* and *Trackdown* (also 1976); *Fire!* (1977); *The Line* (1980); *Honeyboy* (1982); *Lightblast* (1985); *Hour of the Assassin* (1986); *The Dirty Dozen: The Fatal Mission* (1988, TV film); *Caged Fury, Alien Seed,* and *Andy and the Airwave Rangers* (1989); *Guns, Night of the Wilding, Spirits, The Last Riders, Twisted Justice,* and *A Show of Force* (1990); *Do or Die* and *The Divine Enforcer* (1991); and *National Lampoon's Loaded Weapon I* (1993).

Éster Estrella

Actress. She had typical pretty *señorita* roles in several B movies including *Light of Western Stars* (1940, Paramount), *Three Men from Texas* (1940, Paramount, starring Hopalong Cassidy), and *Prairie Pioneers* (1941, Republic, a "Three Mesquiteers" film).

Above: Erik Estrada with Morgan Fairchild in *Honeyboy* (1982, TV film)

Manolo Fábregas

Actor, born in Vigo, Spain, 1921. Very active in Mexican film and theater, he had supporting roles in *Candy Man* (1968), as a Mexican policeman, and *Two Mules for Sister Sara* (1969), in the role of Col. Beltrán.

Virginia Fábregas

(María Barragán) Actress, born in Yautepec, Morelos, Mexico, 1870, died in Mexico City, November 17, 1950. The grandmother of Manolo Fábregas, she began her career on the stage in 1902. She had one Hollywood Spanish-language film appearance, starring in *La fruta amarga* (1931, MGM, costarring Juan de Landa and María Luz Callejo), a Spanish-language version of *Min and Bill* (1930, starring Marie Dressler and Wallace Beery).

Antonio Fargas

Actor, born August 14, 1946, in New York City. He initially worked with various New York theater groups, landing a role in the Broadway production of *The Great White Hope,* starring James Earl Jones. He had a solid role in the notable film *Putney Swope* (1969) and has had a good career since with major roles, usually as a character actor, in films that include *Shaft* (1971); *Across 110th Street* (1972); *Cleopatra Jones* (1973); *Conrack* and *Busting* (1974); *Huckleberry Finn* (1975, TV film); *Car Wash* and *Next Stop, Greenwich Village* (1976); *Pretty Baby* (1978); *Nurse* (1980, TV film); *The Ambush Murders* (1982); *Streetwalkin'* (1985); *Florida Straits* (1986, HBO); *Shakedown* (1988); *I'm Gonna Get You Sucka* and *Night of the Sharks* (1989); *Howling VI: The Freaks* (1990); *Whore* and *The Borrower* (1991); and *Percy and Thunder* (1992).

Miguel Faust Rocha

Actor. He appeared in two Hollywood Spanish-language films, one as star: *Don Juan diplomático* (1931, Universal, dir. George Melford, costarring Lia Torá), a Spanish-language version of *The Boudoir Diplomat* (1930, starring Betty Compson and Mary Duncan); and *Resurrección* (1931, Universal, dir. Edwin Carewe, starring Lupe Vélez and Gilbert Roland), in the role of Capitán Shenbok.

María Félix

(María de los Ángeles Félix Gutiérrez) Internationally recognized Mexican actress, born in Los Alamos, Sonora, April 8, 1915, married first to singer Jorge Negrete and then to composer Agustín Lara. She was seen in the United States in several original Spanish-language Mexican films (e.g., *La cucaracha,* which was also released in English) and in a few English-language releases of Mexican films including *Tumult of Sentiments* (1959, costarring opposite Jack Palance and Pedro Armendáriz), *Beyond All Limits* (1961, costarring opposite Jack Palance and Pedro Armendáriz), and *The Empty Star* (1962).

Ábel Fernández

Actor, born July 14, 1930, in East Los Angeles. He appeared in many television series of the 1950s including *Lassie* and *Rin-Tin-Tin,* usually as an Indian or a Mexican. He is best known for his portrayal of the Native American treasury agent, Youngfellow, on *The Untouchables* TV series (1959-1963). His film credits include *The Scarface Mob* (1962) and *Apache Uprising* (1966).

Emilio "El Indio" Fernández

Director and actor, born March 26, 1904, in El Seco, Coahuila, Mexico, died August 6, 1986, in Mexico City. One of the most important figures of Mexican cinema, he was born to a Spanish-Mexican father and an Indian mother (hence the nickname "El Indio"). At 19 he took part in the Mexican Revolution; in 1923 he was sentenced to 20 years of imprisonment but escaped to California, where he played bit parts and supporting roles. His first role apparently was in *The Land of Missing Men* (1930, Tiffany), which occasioned a review praising him for his "realistic appearance" and for his Spanish, since when he spoke he did so "with a Spanish accent that sounds real and no doubt so" (Richard, vol. I, 410-11). He returned to Mexico first as an actor, debuting in the role of an Indian in *Janitzio* (1934), and then as Mexico's most prominent director. His film *María Candelaria* won Grand Prize at Cannes, and *La perla/The Pearl* won the International Prize at San Sebastian. As a Hollywood actor, he had a few notable parts in Sam Peckinpah films. Selected films as director: *Soy puro mexicano* (1942), *Flor silvestre* and *María Candelaria* (1943), *Bugambilia* (1944), *La perla/The Pearl* (Mex. and U.S., 1946), *El gesticulador* (1957), and *A Loyal Soldier of Pancho Villa* (U.S., 1966). Selected films as an actor: *The Land of Missing Men* and *Oklahoma Cyclone* (both

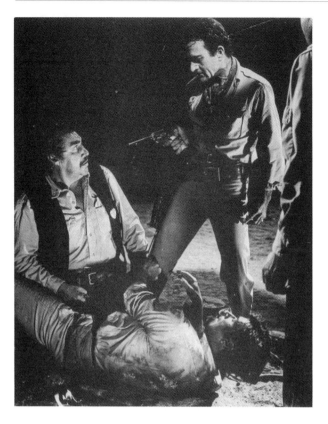

Above: Emilio Fernández (crouching) and
Gilbert Roland (with gun) in *The Reward* (1965)

1930); *Western Code* (Columbia, starring Tim McCoy) and
Flying Down to Rio (1933); *Janitzio* (Mex., 1934); *The
Reward* (1965); *The Appaloosa* and *Return of the Seven*
(1966); *A Covenant with Death* and *The War Wagon* (1967);
The Wild Bunch (1969), as the sadistic General Mapache; *Pat
Garrett and Billy the Kid* (1973); *Bring Me the Head of Alfredo
García* (1974); *Lucky Lady* (1975); *Under the Volcano* (1984);
and *Pirates* (1986). He had the supporting role of Boris in
the Hollywood Spanish-language film *La buenaventura*
(1934, First National Pictures).

Escamillo Fernández

(First name spelled with variations including E. L.,
Escamilo, Escarmillo) Actor. He appeared in numerous
films including *The Two Orphans* (1915), *Audrey* (1916),
Heart of the Wilds and *Woman* (1918), *Hit or Miss* (1919),
The Fortune Teller (1920), *Love's Redemption* (1921), and *The
Man from Glengarry* (1923).

Esther Fernández

(Also *Éster*) Actress, born April 23, 1920, in Mexico City
[PHH has Mascota, Jalisco, Mexico], where she was highly
successful in films, including her starring role in *Santa*
(1943, opposite Ricardo Montalbán). She did one film in
the United States, *Two Years Before the Mast* (1946, opposite
Alan Ladd), and appeared in the Mexican production *Pancho
Villa Returns* (1950, dir. Miguel Contreras Torres, starring
Leo Carrillo).

Evelina Fernández

Actress, born April 28, 1954. She appeared in *Downtown*
(1989), *Flatliners* (1990), and *Postcards from the Edge* (1990)
and costarred opposite Edward James Olmos as Julie in
American Me (1992). On television she appeared frequently
as Juanita Herrera, a factory coworker, on the first season of
the series *Roseanne*.

Jaime Fernández

Actor, born in Monterrey, Mexico. Active in the Mexican
film industry, he costarred in Luis Buñel's *Adventures of
Robinson Crusoe* (1952, Mex.) and appeared in supporting
roles in *Massacre* (1956), *A Bullet for the General* (1968), and
Guns for San Sebastian (1968).

Juan Fernández

Character actor; he appeared in *The Amazing Transplant*
(1970), *Uncommon Valor* (1983), *Fear City* (1984), *Salvador*
(1986), *"Crocodile" Dundee II* and *Bulletproof* (1988),
Kinjite: Forbidden Subjects (1989), *Cat Chaser* (1990), and
Liquid Dreams (1991).

Nelly Fernández

Actress. She had one starring and several supporting roles in
Hollywood Spanish-language productions including *Del
mismo barro* (1930, Fox, starring Mona Maris and Juan
Torena); *El último de los Vargas* (1930, Fox, starring George
Lewis and Luana Alcañiz); *El barbero de Napoleón* (1930,
Fox, starring Juan Aristi Eulate and Manuel París); *La ser-
pentina* (1930, Iberia Productions, Inc., in a starring role,
with Alfonso de Larios and Julián Rivero costarring), a
Spanish-language original based on a screenplay by Arturo S.
Mom; *Politiquerías* (1931, James W. Horne, starring Stan
Laurel and Oliver Hardy); and *Esclavas de la moda* (1931,
Fox, starring Carmen Larrabeiti and Félix de Pomés).

José Ferrer

(José Vicente Ferrer de Otero y Cintrón) Actor and director, born January 8, 1912 [PHH lists 1909], in Santurce,

Above: José Ferrer

Forbid Them Not and *Lawrence of Arabia* (1962), *Nine Hours to Rama* (1963), *Stop Train 349* (1964), *The Greatest Story Ever Told* and *Ship of Fools* (1965), *Enter Laughing* (1966), *Cervantes* (1967, also known as *Young Rebel*), *Behind the Iron Mask* and *The Sentinel* (1977), *Fedora* (1978), *The 5th Musketeer* (1979), *The Big Brawl* (1980), *A Midsummer Night's Sex Comedy* (1982), *To Be or Not to Be* (1983), *The Evil That Men Do* (1984), *Dune* (1985), *Strange Interlude* (1988), and *A Life of Sin* and *Old Explorers* (both 1990). As director: *Cockleshell Heroes* (1955), *Green Mansions* (1959), *Return to Peyton Place* (1961), and *State Fair* (1962). He both directed and starred in *The Shrike* (1955), *The Great Man* (1957), *I Accuse!* (1957), and *The High Cost of Living* (1958). His television credits include the original *Kojak* pilot, *The Marcus Nelson Murders,* in addition to *Kismet, A Case of Libel, Gideon, The Return of Captain Nemo, The Dream Merchant, Evita Perón, Fame,* and the miniseries *Blood & Orchids.*

Mel Ferrer

(Melchior Gastón Ferrer) Actor, director, and producer, born August 25, 1917, in Elberon, New Jersey, son of a Cuban-born surgeon and a Manhattan socialite. He attended Princeton University but dropped out to become an actor, debuting on Broadway in 1938 as a chorus dancer. He made his screen acting debut in 1949 and appeared in many films as a leading man. His third (1954-68) of four wives was actress Audrey Hepburn, whom he directed in *Green Mansions* (1959). Selected films as actor: *Lost Boundaries* (1949), *Born to Be Bad* (1950), *The Brave Bulls* (1951), *Rancho Notorious* and *Scaramouche* (both 1952), *Lili* and

Puerto Rico, died January 26, 1992, in Coral Gables, Florida. He discovered dramatics at Princeton and made his Broadway debut in 1935, receiving considerable attention for his Broadway role as Iago opposite Paul Robeson's *Othello* in 1942. He debuted on the screen in *Joan of Arc* (1948), as the Dauphin opposite Ingrid Bergman, for which he received an Oscar nomination, and he received a Best Actor nomination for his role as Toulouse-Lautrec in *Moulin Rouge* (1952, dir. John Huston). The first Hispanic American actor to win an Academy Award (for the title role of *Cyrano de Bergerac*), he also received two Oscar nominations for Best Actor and one for Best Supporting Actor, and he received five Tony Awards. His third wife was singer Rosemary Clooney. Selected films: *Joan of Arc* (1948), *Whirlpool* (1949), *Crisis* and *Cyrano de Bergerac* (1950), *Anything Can Happen* and *Moulin Rouge* (1952), *Miss Sadie Thompson* (1953), *The Caine Mutiny* and *Deep in My Heart* (1954),

Above: Mel Ferrer (right) and Anthony Quinn
in *The Brave Bulls* (1951, Columbia)

Above: Mel Ferrer in the title role of *El Greco* (1964)

Knights of the Round Table (1953), *Elena and Her Men* (1956, Fr., dir. Jean Renoir), and *War and Peace* (1956), *The Sun Also Rises* (1957), *The World, the Flesh and the Devil* (1959), *Fall of the Roman Empire* and *Sex and the Single Girl* (1964), *El Greco* (1966), *Brannigan* (1975), *Eaten Alive* (1977), *The Norseman* (1978), *The Visitor* and *Guyana: Cult of the Damned* (1979), *City of the Walking Dead* and *Emerald Jungle* (1980), *Lili Marleen* (1981, Ger., dir. Rainer Werner Fassbinder), *One Shoe Makes It Murder* (1982), *Seduced* (1985, TV film), and *Revenge* (1990). As director: *The Girl of the Limberlost* (1945), *The Secret Fury* and *Vendetta* (1950), and *Green Mansions* (1959). He also produced *Wait Until Dark* (1967). Mel Ferrer did one non-Hollywood movie, *El Greco* (1964), and gained wide exposure in the role of a lawyer on television's *Falcon Crest.*

Miguel Ferrer

Actor, son of José Ferrer and Rosemary Clooney. He has appeared in *Heartbreaker* (1983); *Flashpoint, Lovelines,* and *Star Trek 3: The Search for Spock* (all 1984); *RoboCop* and *Valentino Returns* (1987); *C.A.T. Squad: Python Wolf* (1988); *Shannon's Deal* (1989, TV film); *Deepstar Six* (1989); *Revenge* and *The Guardian* (1990); *Twin Peaks: Fire Walk with Me* (1992); *Another Stakeout, The Harvest, Point of No Return, Scam,* and *Hot Shots! Part Deux* (1993); and *Blank Check* (1994). His television credits include starring in two brief series, *Broken Bridges* and *Unsub,* and occasional appearances on *Twin Peaks* (in role of Albert Rosenfeld, FBI agent).

Pablo Ferro

Special effects director for films and television commercials, born January 15, 1935, in Havana, raised in New York City. He pioneered split-screen images in *The Thomas Crown Affair* (1968) and was recognized for split-second intercutting in *A Clockwork Orange* (1971). Other credits include *Midnight Cowboy* (1969), *Darkman* (1990), and *Mobsters* (1991). He directed *Me, Myself and I* (1991, starring George Segal).

Paul Fierro

Actor. Active in the Mexican film industry, he had the role of the murderer, Lou García, in *Waco* (1952), and also appeared in *Fighter Attack* (1953).

Efraín Figueroa

Actor; he appeared in *Tequila Sunrise* (1988) and *Pretty Woman* (1990).

Gabriel Figueroa

Director of photography, born April 24, 1907, in Mexico. An orphan, he was forced to seek work as a boy, yet was able to pursue painting and photography on his own. In 1935, he went to Hollywood to study motion picture photography and returned to Mexico the following year to begin a prolific career as the cameraman on over 100 films. He worked for Buñuel, John Ford, and Emilio Fernández and ranks among the leading directors of photography in world cinema. Selected films (primarily Mexican): *Allá en el rancho grande* (1936), *Flor silvestre* and *María Candelaria* (1943), *Bugambilia* (1944), *La perla/The Pearl* (Mex. and U.S., 1946), *The Fugitive* (U.S., 1947), *Los olvidados* (1952), *La cucaracha* (1958), *Nazarín* (1959), *Macario* (1960), *Ánimas Trujano* (1961), *El ángel exterminador* (1962), *The Night of the Iguana* (U.S., 1964), *Simón del desierto* (1965), *Two Mules for Sister Sara* (U.S., 1970), *The Children of Sánchez* (U.S., 1978), and *Under the Volcano* (U.S., 1984).

Above: Gabriel Figueroa (left) and Emilio Fernández in 1943 on the set of *Flor silvestre*

William A. Fraker

Cinematographer and director, born in 1923 in Los Angeles to a Mexican mother and an American father, graduated from University of Southern California Film School. He worked as director of photography on *Rosemary's Baby* and *Bullitt* (1968), *Paint Your Wagon* (1969), *Looking for Mr. Goodbar* (1977), and *Heaven Can Wait* (1978). He debuted as a director with *Monte Walsh* (1970) and also directed *A Reflection of Fear* (1973) and *The Legend of the Lone Ranger* (1981).

Ábel Franco

Actor, born in 1922. He has appeared in *The Searchers* (1956), *Zoot Suit* (1981), *El Norte* (1984), *The Falcon and the Snowman* (1985), and *¡Three Amigos!* (1986). His script *Canción de la Raza* (PBS daytime drama) won an Emmy Award.

Ramón Franco

Actor, born in 1963 in Caguas, Puerto Rico. His credits include *Boardwalk* (1979), *Heartbreak Ridge* (1986), *Tour of Duty* (1987), *Bulletproof* (1988), and *Kiss Me a Killer* (1991). On television he had the role of Private Ruiz on the Vietnam War television series *Tour of Duty*.

Jesús Franco Manera

(Uses numerous aliases) Director and screenwriter, born in Madrid, May 12, 1930. His numerous aliases include Roland Marciegnac, A. L. Mariaux, A. L. Marioux, John O'Hara, Dan Simon, David Tough, Robert Zimmerman, Clifford Brown, Toni Falt, Jess Franck, J. Franck Mandra, Jess Franco, Jesús Franco, A. M. Franck, Jess Frank, James Gardner, Jack Griffin, Frank Hollmann, Frank Holman, B. F. Johnson, James P. Johnson, David Khunne, David Kuhnne, David Kunne, John A. Lazar, and A. Malriaux. He has directed (and often has cast himself in) numerous exploitation films such as *Castle of Fu Manchu* and *Against All Odds* (1968); *Deadly Sanctuary, Count Dracula* (starring Christopher Lee and Klaus Kinski), and *Venus in Furs* (1970); *Virgin Among the Living Dead* (1971); *Women in Cellblock 9* (1977); *Demoniac* and *Jack the Ripper* (1979); *Ilsa, The Wicked Warden* (1980); and *Erotikill* and *Bloody Moon* (1981; a clip from this last film was used in Pedro Almodóvar's *Matador*). Many of these exploitation films have been re-released multiple times with different titles.

Hugo Fregonese

Argentine-born director and screenwriter, born April 8, 1909, died January 25, 1987, in Buenos Aires. He first worked in the film industry in Argentina; two of his films, *Where Words Fail* (1948) and *Hardly a Criminal* (1949), were dubbed into English and released in the United States. Beginning in the 1950s, he directed films in Hollywood including *One Way Street* and *Saddle Tramp* (both 1950, MGM), *Apache Drums* (1951, MGM), *Mark of the Renegade* (1951, MGM, with Ricardo Montalbán and Gilbert Roland), *Untamed Frontier* (1952, MGM), *My Six Convicts* (1952, Columbia, starring Gilbert Roland), and *Man in the Attic* (1953, Fox). Although he mainly directed B films, he made a major feature, *Blowing Wild* (1953, Columbia, with Barbara Stanwyck, Gary Cooper, and Anthony Quinn). He also did a number of primarily Italian-based films including *Decameron Nights* (1953, RKO), *Black Tuesday* and *The Raid* (1954), *The Beast of Marseilles* (1957, RKO), *Marco Polo* (1962, RKO) *Shatterhand* and *Savage Pampas* (1967, RKO), and *Dracula vs. Frankenstein* (1989).

Antonio Fuentes

Matador, he starred in one of the earliest films, *The Great Bullfight* (1902, Edison Mfg. Co.).

VERSIONS OF CARMEN

Above right: Geraldine Farrar, *Carmen* (1915, Lasky-Paramount, dir. Cecil B. DeMille)

Below right: Geraldine Farrar and Wallace Reid (1915, Lasky-Paramount)

Below left: Victoria Lepanto, *Carmen* (1910, Pathé)

Left: Geraldine Farrar and Jeanie MacPherson (1915, Lasky-Paramount)

Below left: Theda Bara, *Carmen* (1915, Fox, dir. Raoul Walsh)

Bottom left: Edna Purviance and Charles Chaplin, *Charlie Chaplin's Burlesque on "Carmen"* (1916, Essenay)

Below right: Theda Bara with Einar Linden, *Carmen* (1915, Fox, dir. Raoul Walsh)

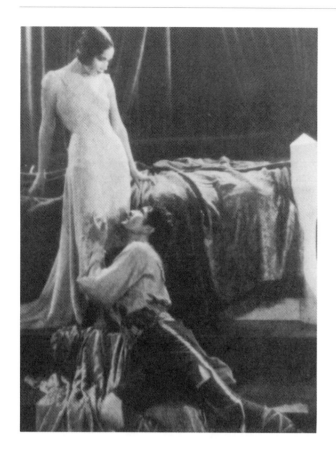

Above left, above right: Dolores del Río and
Don Alvarado, *Loves of Carmen* (1927, Fox)

Below left: Rita Hayworth and a wooden Glenn
Ford as Don José in *The Loves of Carmen* (1948)

Below right: Dorothy Dandridge and Harry
Belafonte in *Carmen Jones* (1954)

Jenny Gago

Actress. Her credits include *Under Fire* (1983); *Irreconcilable Differences* (1984); *No Man's Land, Innerspace,* and *Best Seller* (1987); *Old Gringo* (1989); *Sweet 15* (1990); and *My Family/Mi familia* (1995). On television she had the role of María for three years on *Knots Landing;* she also guest starred on *Cagney & Lacey* and *Falcon Crest* and had a recurring role on *Dallas.*

Héctor Galán

Director and producer, born in San Angelo, Texas. He did *Vaquero: The Forgotten Cowboy* (1987), tracing the American

Below: Jenny Gago and Eduardo López Rojas in *My Family/Mi familia* (1995)

cowboy to the Mexican American vaquero; *Los mineros* (1990), about Mexican American miners in Arizona; *The Hunt for Pancho Villa* (1993, coproduced with Paul Espinosa), about Pancho Villa's raid on Columbus, New Mexico, in 1916 and the failed efforts of the U.S. government to capture him; and *Songs of the Homeland* (1995), about Tejano music. He was a series producer for the documentary *Chicano!* (1996), on the history of the Mexican American civil rights movement. Galán has produced numerous pieces for PBS's *Frontline.*

Nelly Galán

Producer. After gaining experience at HBO and cofounding its Latino division, she made a major deal with Fox TV in late 1994 to finance her company, GaLAn Entertainment, in order to develop programs. She is one of the few Hispanic women with significant influence in entertainment, particularly television. She produced the National Council of La Raza's *BRAVO Awards,* which appeared on Fox in 1995.

Nacho Galindo

Character actor, born in Guadalajara, Mexico, November 7, 1908, died June 22, 1973. He appeared in films from

the 1940s through the 1960s including *Tycoon* (1946), *South of St. Louis* (1949), *Borderline* (1950), *Border River* and *Broken Lance* (1954), *Wetbacks* (1956, starring Lloyd Bridges), in the role of a nice bar owner, *Born Reckless* (1959), *One-Eyed Jacks* (1961), *El Dorado* (1967), and *The Pink Jungle* (1968).

Silvana Gallardo

Actress, born January 13, 1953, in New York City, to Venezuelan-Cuban parents. Her credits include *Windwalker* (1980), *Death Wish II* (1982), *Out of the Dark* (1988), and *Solar Crisis* (1993). On television she was in the TV movies *Silence of the Heart* and *The Calendar Girl Murders* (1984), *Copacabana* (1986), and *Prison Stories: Women on the Inside* (1991). She also made guest appearances on various episodic series.

Gina Gallego

Mexican American actress, born November 30, 1959, in Los Angeles. Her credits include *Lust in the Dust* (1984, with César Romero), a parody of Hispanic-focused Westerns, *The Men's Club* (1986), and *My Demon Lover* (1987). On television she had the role of Santana on the daytime soap opera *Santa Barbara,* appeared in the soap opera *Rituals,* and was a regular on the TV series *Flamingo Road.* She was in *Personals* (1990) and costarred in a Showtime TV film, *Keeper of the City* (1991).

Pedro Galván

Actor, active in the Mexican film industry. He had supporting roles in *The Black Scorpion* (1957), as a priest, *The Big Cube* and *The Candy Man* (1969), and *Two Mules for Sister Sara* (1970).

Joaquín Garay II

Vaudeville song and dance performer, born in 1911, died in 1990. He appeared with Jack Benny and later Dean Martin and Jerry Lewis. He was one of the featured singers in *It Happened One Night* (1934) and provided the voice of Panchito (the parrot) in Walt Disney's *The Three Caballeros* (1944).

Allan García

Actor, born March 18, 1887, died September 4, 1938. He began as a casting director at Chaplin Studios and then became an actor; his first major role was as a circus proprietor in Chaplin's *The Circus* (1923). He was the butler in Chaplin's *City Lights* (1931) and the factory boss in *Modern Times* (1936). Additional credits include *Reputation* and *The Idle Class* (both 1921); *The Three Buckaroos* and *Pay Day* (1922); *Morgan's Last Raid* (1929); *The Cisco Kid* and *The Deceiver* (1931); *The Gay Caballero* (1932); *Under the Tonto Rim* and *The California Trail* (1933); *Under the Pampas Moon* (1935); *Robin Hood of El Dorado* and *The Gay Desperado* (1936); *Blossoms on Broadway, I'll Take Romance,* and *The Last Train from Madrid* (1937); and *Blockade* and *In Old Mexico* (1938). He had two principal parts in Hollywood Spanish-language films: *La gran jornada* (1931, Fox), as Flack "El Rojo", and *Marido y mujer* (1932, Fox), as Dr. Burgess.

Andy García

(Andrés Arturo Garci-Menéndez) Actor, born April 12, 1956, in Havana. He and his family moved to Miami in 1961. He worked in Florida regional theater, moved to Los Angeles, and turned in a superb performance as a cocaine boss in *8 Million Ways to Die* (1986). In 1987, he received

Above: Andy García in *Dead Again* (1991)

widespread recognition as an earnest FBI agent in Brian De Palma's *The Untouchables*. In 1990, he achieved star status as the good cop in *Internal Affairs* and was nominated for an Academy Award for Best Supporting Actor for his role as the illegitimate son of Sonny Corleone in *The Godfather, Part III*. Additional credits include *Blue Skies Again* and *A Night in Heaven* (1983), *The Mean Season* (1985), *Blood Money: The Story of Clinton and Nadine* (1987, TV film), *Stand and Deliver* (1987), *American Roulette* (1988), *Black Rain* (1989), *A Show of Force* (1990), *Dead Again* (1991), *Hero* (1992), *Jennifer 8* (1993), *When a Man Loves a Woman* (1994), and *Things to Do in Denver When You're Dead* (1996).

Above: John George, Rosita García, Hughie Mack, and Shorty Ben Mairech in *Mare Nostrum* (1926, MGM, dir. Rex Ingram)

Juan García

Actor, active in the Mexican film industry. He had a few supporting roles in U.S. films including *Blowing Wild* (1953, starring Gary Cooper, Barbara Stanwyck, and Anthony Quinn), in the role of El Gavilán, a "Gold Hat" type à la Alfonso Bedoya in *Treasure of the Sierra Madre* (see García Riera, vol. 3, 107-108); *The Tall Men* (1955, dir. Raoul Walsh, starring Clark Gable and Jane Russell), as Gable's loyal sidekick; and *The Undefeated* (1969).

Rick García

American-born actor. He appeared in the parody *Blazing Saddles* (1974), where he played a Mexican who repeated the lines from *The Treasure of the Sierra Madre*, "Badges? We don't need no stinkin' badges," and in *Tough Guys* (1986).

Ron García

Cinematographer. His credits include *Disorganized Crime* (1989), *Side Out* (1990), and *Twin Peaks: Fire Walk with Me* (1992). In television his credits include the series *Crime Story* and *Hunter*. He was nominated for an Emmy Award in 1993 for his cinematography on the television miniseries *Murder in the Heartland*.

Rosita García

(Rosita Ramírez) Actress, reputed to be a granddaughter of a former president of Cuba. She was discovered as a juvenile by director Rex Ingram, who cast her in *Where the Pavement Ends* (1923, Metro, filmed in Florida and Cuba, starring Ramón Novarro and Alice Terry). Subsequently, she had the leading role in Ingram's *Baroud/Love in Morocco* (1931). She appeared in some later films including *The Private Life of Don Juan* (1934, dir. Alexander Korda, starring Douglas Fairbanks) and *The Beachcomber* (1939) before fading from the screen.

Stella García

Actress; she costarred in the films *The Last Movie* (1971) and *Joe Kidd* (1972).

Tito García

Actor. He had several supporting roles in Italian or Spanish productions released in English-language versions including *Finger on the Trigger* (1965), *Lightning Bolt* and *Up the MacGregors* (both 1967), *The Ugly Ones* (1968), *God Forgives—I Don't* (1969), *The Mercenary* (1970), and *With Friends, Nothing Is Easy* (1971).

Pascual García Peña

Actor, active in the Mexican film industry. He was one of the supportive compatriots of Chu Chu Ramírez, played by Ricardo Montalbán, in *My Man and I* (1952, costarring Shelly Winters), and appeared as a doctor in *The Black Scorpion* (1957).

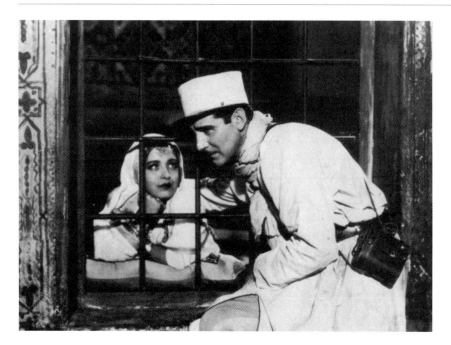

Above: Rosita García and Rex Ingram in *Baroud* (1931, Rex Ingram Productions, dir. Rex Ingram)

José García Torres

Puerto Rican filmmaker. He made several films from an *independentista* perspective including *The Oxcart* (1970), *Los nacionalistas/The Nationalists* (1973), and *The Life and Poetry of Julia de Burgos* (1979).

Carlos Gardel

(Charles Romuald Gardes) Internationally recognized singer, composer, and movie star, born in Toulouse, December 11, 1887, died in Medellín, Colombia, June 24, 1935, as the result of a plane crash. One of Argentina's most beloved singers and movie stars and popularizer of the tango, he made several Spanish-language films in Joinville, France, for Paramount, and later, in New York, for that same company. His numerous starring roles in Hollywood Spanish-language films include *Las luces de Buenos Aires* (1931, Paramount Pictures, costarring Sofía Bazán and Gloria Guzmán), a Spanish-language original based on an original work by Manuel Romero and Luis Bayón Herrera; *Espérame* (1933, Paramount, costarring Goyita Herrero and Lolita Benavente), a Spanish-language original based on a screenplay by Louis Gasnier (who directed); *Melodía de arrabal* (1933, Paramount, costarring opposite Imperio Argentina), a Spanish-language original based on a screenplay by Alfredo Le Pera; *La casa es seria* (1933, Paramount, costarring opposite Imperio Argentina), a Spanish-language original based on a screenplay by Alfredo Le Pera; *Cuesta abajo* (1934, Paramount, costarring

Mona Maris and Vicente Padula), a Spanish-language original based on a screenplay by Alfredo Le Pera; *El tango en Broadway* (1934, Paramount, costarring Trini Ramos and Blanca Vischer), a Spanish-language original based on a screenplay by Alfredo Le Pera; *El día que me quieras* (1935, Paramount, costarring Rosita Moreno), a Spanish-language original based on a screenplay by Alfredo Le Pera; and *Tango Bar* (1935, Paramount, costarring Rosita Moreno), a Spanish-language original based on a screenplay by Alfredo Le Pera.

Juanita Garfias

Actress. She had a supporting role as Pepita in both the English-language film *Storm Over the Andes* (1935, Universal) and its Hollywood Spanish-language version, *Alas sobre el Chaco* (1935, Universal).

Martín Garralaga

Actor and singer, born November 10, 1898 [1894 according to PHH], in Spain, died in Woodland Hills, California, June 12, 1981. Beginning his career in Barcelona as a singer, he did concerts and opera in South and North America and eventually both Spanish- and English-language films in Hollywood, where he appeared in a very large number of films in supporting roles. His first important English-speaking role was in *A Message to Garcia* (1936). He played both comic parts, including Pancho, the Cisco Kid's sidekick in several films with Duncan Renaldo, as well as villains. Other English-language film credits include *The Gay Caballero* (1932); *Sweet Adeline* (1934); *George White's 1935 Scandals, In Caliente, The Law of 45's, Lawless Border,* and *Under the Pampas Moon* (all 1935); *Anthony Adverse, The Charge of the Light Brigade,* and *Song of the Gringo* (1936); *Another Dawn, Boots of Destiny, Love Under Fire, Riders of the Rockies,* and *The Sheik Steps Out* (1937); *Four Men and a Prayer, Outlaw Express, Starlight Over Texas,* and *Rose of the Rio Grande* (1938); *Another Thin Man, Code of the Secret Service, Mutiny on the Blackhawk, The Fighting Gringo,* and *Juárez* (1939); *Legion of the Lawless, Meet the Wildcat, Rangers of Fortune, Stage to Chino, Wagon Train,* and *Rhythm of the Rio Grande* (1940); *In Old California* and *The Lady Has Plans* (1942); *For Whom the Bell Tolls* (1943); *In Old New Mexico* and *South of the Rio Grande* (1945); *South of Monterey* (1947); *The Feathered Serpent* (1948); *Susanna Pass* and *The Big*

Sombrero (1949); *African Treasure* and *The Fighter* (1952); *Man in the Shadow* (1957); *The Left-Handed Gun* (1958); *The Last Angry Man* (1959); *Lonely Are the Brave* (1962); *Island of the Blue Dolphins* (1964); and *Whatever Happened to Aunt Alice?* (1969).

He was one of the most prolific actors in Hollywood Spanish-language films, appearing in numerous productions, costarring in a few, and obtaining major supporting roles in many others. His Hollywood Spanish-language film credits include *Charros, gauchos y manolas* (1930, Hollywood Spanish Pictures Co., dir. Xavier Cugat, costarring opposite María Alba in the *cuadro español*), a Spanish-language original based on a screenplay by Xavier Cugat; *El precio de un beso* (1930, Fox, starring José Mojica, Mona Maris, and Antonio Moreno); *El hombre malo* (1930, First National Pictures, starring Antonio Moreno and Andrés de Segurola); *El rey del jazz* (1930, Universal, a musical review in which he and Lupita Tovar functioned as *maestros de ceremonias*), a Spanish-language version of *The King of Jazz* (1930); *¡De frente, marchen!* (1930, MGM, starring Buster Keaton and Conchita Montenegro); *El último de los Vargas* (1930, Fox, starring George Lewis and Luana Alcañiz); *Wu Li Chang* (1930, MGM, starring Ernesto Vilches and Angelita Benítez); *Los que danzan* (1930, Warner Brothers, starring Antonio Moreno and María Alba); *Sevilla de mis amores* (1930, MGM, dir. Ramón Novarro, starring Ramón Novarro and Conchita Montenegro); *La llama sagrada* (1931, Warner, costarring opposite Elvira Morla), a Spanish-language version of *The Sacred Flame* (1929, dir. Archie L. Mayo, starring Pauline Frederick and Conrad Nagel); *La dama atrevida* (1931, First National Pictures, starring Luana Alcañiz and Ramón Pereda); *La gran jornada* (1931, Fox, starring George Lewis and Carmen Guerrero); *Cuerpo y alma* (1931, Fox, starring George Lewis and Ana María Custodio); *Eran trece* (1931, Fox, starring Manuel Arbó and Juan Torena); *Marido y mujer* (1932, Fox, starring George Lewis and Conchita Montenegro); *El rey de los gitanos* (1933, Fox, starring José Mojica and Rosita Moreno); *Dos noches* (1933, Fanchon Royer Pictures, Inc., presented by J. H. Hoffberg, dir. Carlos F. Borcosque, starring José Crespo and Conchita Montenegro); *No dejes la puerta abierta* (1933, Fox, starring Raúl Roulien and Rosita Moreno); *Yo, tú y ella* (1933, Fox, starring Catalina Bárcena and Gilbert Roland); *La cruz y la espada* (1933, Fox, starring José Mojica and Anita Campillo); *El cantante de Nápoles* (1934, Warner, starring Enrico Caruso, Jr., and Mona Maris); *Angelina o el honor de un brigadier* (1935, Fox, starring Rosita Díaz Gimeno and José Crespo); *Piernas de seda* (1935, Fox, starring Rosita Moreno and Raúl Roulien); *Rosa de Francia* (1935, Fox, starring Rosita Díaz Gimeno, Julio Peña, and Antonio Moreno); *De la sartén al fuego* (1935, 20th Century-Fox, starring Rosita Moreno and Juan Torena); *Mis dos amores* (1938, Paramount, starring Tito Guízar and Blanca de Castejón); *Di que me quieres* (1938, RKO-Radio Pictures, starring George Lewis and Eva Ortega); *El trovador de la radio* (1938, Paramount, starring Tito Guízar and Robina Duarte); *Papá soltero* (1939, Paramount, starring Tito Guízar and Amanda Varela); *El otro soy yo* (1939, Paramount, starring Tito Guízar and Amanda Varela); and *Cuando canta la ley* (1939, Paramount, costarring opposite Tito Guízar and Tana), a Spanish-language original based on a screenplay by Jack Natteford, Enrique Uhthoff, and Richard Harlan.

John Gavin

(Jack Golenor) Actor, born April 8, 1931 [1928 according to PPH], in Los Angeles, the son of a Mexican mother and American father. He went to Stanford and then joined the Navy. He was often cast as a tall, dark, and handsome leading man. He debuted in film in *Behind the High Wall* (1956), was in *Four Girls in Town* (1956), *Quantez* (1957), and *Psycho* (1960, dir. Alfred Hitchcock), and had the role of Julius Caesar in *Spartacus* (1960). Additional film credits include *A Time to Love & a Time to Die* (1958); *Imitation of Life* (1959); *A Breath of Scandal* and *Midnight Lace* (both 1960); *Romanoff and Juliet, Back Street*, and *Tammy, Tell Me True* (all 1961); *Thoroughly Modern Millie* (1967); *The Madwoman of Chaillot* (1969); *Murder for Sale* and *Pussycat, Pussycat, I Love You* (1970); *Jennifer* (1978); *Sophia Loren: Her Own Story* (1980, TV film); *History of the World: Part 1* (1981); and *House of Shadows* (1983). In the 1970s, he left film and was appointed the United States ambassador to Mexico.

Tony Genaro

Supporting actor whose credits include *The Milagro Beanfield War* (1988), *Tremors* (1989), and *Bound by Honor* (1993).

Mike Gómez

Character actor, born April 18, 1951, in Dallas, Texas. He appeared in *Zoot Suit* (1981) as Joey, one of the pachucos, *The Border* (1982), and *Heartbreak Ridge* (1986).

Panchito Gómez

Actor, born November 2, 1963, in Spanish Harlem, New York. He has been acting since age four. He is known for his roles as a tough Latino youth, appearing in *Paco* (1975, starring José Ferrer), *Uncle Joe Shannon* and *Run for the Roses* (both 1978), *Walk Proud* (1979), *Borderline* (1980), *Sweet 15* (1990), and as the teenage Santana in Edward James Olmos's *American Me* (1992). On television he has appeared in *Barney Miller*, *CHiPs*, *Simon and Simon*, and *Baretta*.

Thomas Gómez

(Sabino Thomas Gómez) Actor, born in New York City, July 10, 1905, died in Santa Monica, California, June 18, 1971. His paternal grandparents were Spaniards and his maternal grandfather, Frank Thomas, was a sea captain who fought under Admiral David Farragut in the capture of New Orleans in the Civil War. Following considerable stage experience including seven years with Alfred Lunt and Lynn Fontanne, he began his film career in the 1940s, debuting in *Sherlock Holmes and the Voice of Terror* (1942). This heavyset character actor appeared typically as a crafty villain. He was nominated for a Best Supporting Actor Academy Award for his role in *Ride a Pink Horse* (1947). His film credits include *Arabian Nights, Pittsburgh,* and *Who Done It?* (1942); *White Savage, Corvette K-225,* and *Crazy House* (1943); *Phantom Lady, In Society, Can't Help Singing, Dead Man's Eyes,* and *The Climax* (1944); *I'll Tell the World* and *Frisco Sal* (1945); *A Night in Paradise* (1946); *Johnny O'Clock, Singapore,* and *Captain from Castile* (1947); *Angel in Exile, Casbah, Key Largo,* and *Force of Evil* (1948); *Sorrowful Jones* and *That Midnight Kiss* (1949); *The Woman on Pier 13* (originally released as *I Married a Communist*), *The Eagle and the Hawk, The Furies,* and *Kim* (1950); *The Harlem Globetrotters* and *Anne of the Indies* (1951); *Macao, The Sellout, The Merry Widow,* and *Pony Soldier* (1952); *Sombrero* (1953); *The Gambler from Natchez* and *The Adventures of Haji Baba* (1954); *The Magnificent Matador, Night Freight, The Looters,* and *Las Vegas Shakedown* (1955); *The Conqueror* and *Trapeze* (1956); *John Paul Jones* and *But Not for Me* (1959); *Summer and Smoke* (1961); *Stay Away, Joe* (1968); and *Beneath the Planet of the Apes* (1970).

Vicente Gómez

Composer of Spanish gypsy music, born in 1915 in Madrid. In 1941 he was brought to Hollywood by director Rouben Mamoulian to compose gypsy music and play guitar for motion pictures.

Peter Gonzales

(Peter Gonzales Falcón) Texas-born actor; he played the young Fellini in *Fellini's Roma* (1972) and appeared in *The End* (1973).

Above: Thomas Gómez in *Casbah* (1948) as the chief of the French police

Cordelia González

Actress. She had a principal role in the notable Puerto Rican film production *La gran fiesta* (1987, starring Miguelangelo Suárez, with Raúl Juliá in a cameo as a poet). She was a prostitute in *Born on the Fourth of July* (1989, dir. Oliver Stone, starring Tom Cruise), appeared in *Homeboy* (1989), and had a minor role in *The Mambo Kings* (1992).

Félix González

Actor, active in the Mexican film industry. He also appeared in *Of Love and Desire* (1963) and *The Candy Man* (1969).

Myrtle González

(Also Myrtle Gonzales) Early film star, born September 23, 1891, died of influenza October 22, 1918, at the age of 27. She grew up in Los Angeles and was a player at Vitagraph Studios in 1913. She costarred with William Duncan in many Westerns. Her film credits include *Deception* (1913, Vitagraph, dir. William J. Baumann, costarring Jane Novak [film held at NFTA]); *The Masked Dancer* (1914, Vitagraph); *Captain Alvarez* (also 1914); *The Chalice of Courage* (1915); *A Natural Man* (1915, Vitagraph Co. of America, dir. Ulysses Davis, starring Alfred Vosburgh, costarring Otto Lederer [film held at LC]); *The Girl of the*

Lost Lake, It Happened in Honolulu, A Romance of Billy Goat Hill, and *The Secret of the Swamp* (all 1916); *The End of the Rainbow* (1916, Bluebird Photoplays, Inc., dir. Lynn F. Reynolds, costarring George Hernández and Val Paul [film held at MOMA and NAC]); *The Heart of Bonita* (1916,

Above: Myrtle González in 1916

Below: Myrtle González and William Desmond Taylor in *Captain Álvarez* (1917)

Laemmle); *God's Crucible, The Greater Law, Mutiny,* and *Southern Justice* (all 1917); and *The Show Down* (1917, Bluebird Photoplays, Inc., dir. Lynn F. Reynolds, costarring George Hernández and Arthur Hoyt [film held at LC]).

José González-González

(Also written without the hyphen) Actor, born December 21, 1926, identical twin brother of Pedro. He followed his brother to Hollywood and did similar roles as a short, comical Mexican. His credits include *Cha-Cha-Cha Boom* (1956), *Panama Sal* (1957), *The Mermaids of Tiburón* (1962), *For Love or Money* (1963), and *The Aqua Sex* (1965).

Pedro González-González

(Also written without the hyphen) Actor, born in Aguilares, Texas, December 21, 1926 [PHH lists May 24, 1925], a San Antonio comic. His career was aided by his appearance on the 1950s television game show, *You Bet Your Life* with Groucho Marx, where he was celebrated for his "Sí, señor," dumb Mexican routine. He made his screen debut as a comic revolutionary in *Wings of the Hawk* (1953), followed by *The High and the Mighty* (1954), *I Died a Thousand Times* and *Strange Lady in Town* (both 1955), *The Sheepman* (1958), *Río Bravo* (1959), *The Adventures of Bullwhip Griffin* and *Hostile Guns* (1967), and *Hook, Line and Sinker* and *The Love Bug* (1969). He also made numerous television and nightclub appearances.

Carmen Granada

Actress. She appeared in a few Spanish-language films including *Charros, gauchos y manolas* (1930, Hollywood Spanish Pictures Co., dir. Xavier Cugat, costarring opposite Paul Ellis in the *cuadro argentino),* a Spanish-language original based on a screenplay by Xavier Cugat; *Una cana al aire* (1930, MGM, costarring opposite Charley Chase and Carmen Guerrero), a Spanish-language version of *Looser Than Loose* (1930, starring Charley Chase and Thelma Todd); *La cautivadora* (1930, Iberia Productions, Inc., starring Nelly Fernández and Alfonso de Larios); and *Politiquerías* (1931, MGM, starring Stan Laurel and Oliver Hardy).

Rosita Granada

Actress. She had numerous supporting roles in Hollywood Spanish-language films including *¡De frente marchen!* (1930, MGM, starring Buster Keaton and Conchita Montenegro); *Entre platos y notas* (1930, Fox, starring Delia Magaña and "Don Catarino"); *Cuando el amor ríe* (1930, Fox, starring

José Mojica and Mona Maris); *En cada puerto un amor* (1931, MGM, starring José Crespo and Conchita Montenegro); *El pasado acusa* (1931, Columbia, starring Luana Alcañiz and Barry Norton); *Marido y mujer* (1932, Fox, starring George Lewis and Conchita Montenegro); *No dejes la puerta abierta* (1933, Fox, starring Raúl Roulien and Rosita Moreno); *Yo, tú y ella* (1933, Fox, starring Catalina Bárcena and Gilbert Roland); *Piernas de seda* (1935, Fox, starring Rosita Moreno and Raúl Roulien); and *El trovador de la radio* (1938, Paramount, starring Tito Guízar and Robina Duarte). She also appeared in the English-language production *The Buccaneer* (1938).

José Greco

Dancer, choreographer, and actor, born in 1919 in Italy, raised in Brooklyn, New York. He performed in New York City nightclubs and subsequently became the touring partner of "La Argentinita," a highly recognized Spanish dancer, until her untimely death in 1945. He later went to Spain where he became a sensation (the Spaniards dismissed the notion that he was an Italian from Brooklyn and he was accepted as a Spanish flamenco dancer). In 1946, he choreographed and led a notable flamenco dance sequence in the Spanish film *Manolete*. He also appeared in Hollywood films including *Sombrero* (1953), *Around the World in 80 Days* (1956), *Holiday for Lovers* (1959), *Ship of Fools* (1965), as a Gypsy pimp, and *The Proud and the Damned* (1973). He was in a few Italian productions released in the United States in English including *Duel of the Titans, Goliath and the Sins of Babylon,* and *The Rebel Gladiators* (all 1963).

José Guardiola

(José García Guardiola) Actor, born in Murcia, Spain, December 7, 1921. He had supporting roles in *Spanish Affair* (1958, Paramount), *Desert Warrior* (1961), *The Ceremony* (1963, United Artists), and *A Bullet for Sandoval* (1970).

Castulo Guerra

Argentine actor, born August 24, 1945. He appeared in *Two of a Kind* (1983), *Stick* (1985), *Where the River Runs Black* (1986), and *Terminator 2: Judgment Day* (1991). On television he was a regular for a season on *Falcon Crest* and he has guest-starred on a number of weekly series.

Carmen Guerrero

Actress, born in 1911 in Mexico. She had starring or principal roles in numerous Hollywood Spanish-language films. She also did the original English-language version of one Charley Chase film (see below). Her credits include *Un fotógrafo distraído* (1930, Hollywood Spanish Pictures Company, dir. Xavier Cugat, costarring opposite Romualdo Tirado and Don Alvarado), a Spanish-language original produced by Xavier Cugat and Rodolfo Montes; *Amor audaz* (1930, Paramount, starring Adolphe Menjou and Rosita Moreno); *Locuras de amor* (1930, MGM, costarring opposite Charley Chase), a Spanish-language version of *Fast Work* (1930, starring Charley Chase and June Marlowe); *¡Huye, faldas!* (1930, MGM, costarring opposite Charley Chase), a Spanish-language version of *Girl Shock* (1930, starring Charley Chase, Carmen Guerrero, and Edgar Kennedy); *Cascarrabias* (1930, Paramount, costarring opposite Ernesto Vilches and Barry Norton), a Spanish-language version of *Grumpy* (1930, dir. George Cukor and Cyril Gardner, starring Cyril Maude and Phillips Holmes); *Una cana al aire* (1930, MGM, costarring opposite Charley Chase), a Spanish-language version of *Looser Than Loose* (1930, starring Charley Chase and Thelma Todd); *El alma de la fiesta* (1931, MGM, costarring opposite Charley Chase), a Spanish-language version of *Thundering Tenors* (1932, starring Charley Chase and Lillian Elliott); *Drácula* (1931, Universal, starring Carlos Villarías and Lupita Tovar); *La gran jornada* (1931, Fox, costarring opposite George Lewis), a Spanish-language version of *The Big Trail* (1930, dir. Raoul Walsh, starring John Wayne and Marguerite Churchill); and *Carne de cabaret* (1931, Columbia, dir. Christy Cabanne, starring Lupita Tovar and Ramón Pereda).

Dan Guerrero

Producer. He began as a New York theatrical agent and now heads his own Guerrero and Company. He coproduced *El Show de Paul Rodríguez* for Univisión and produced the first annual *VIDA Awards* (NBC TV in collaboration with *Hispanic Magazine*).

Evelyn Guerrero

Actress, born in East Los Angeles, February 24, 1949. She appeared in *Lenny* (1974), *The Toolbox Murders* (1978), *On the Nickel* (1980), and *Bound by Honor* (1993). She had the recurring role of the sexy dream girl, Donna, in *Cheech and Chong's Next Movie* (1980), *Cheech and Chong's Nice Dreams* (1981), and *Cheech and Chong: Things Are Tough All Over* (1982). On television she played Dora's sister Marisol on the TV series *I Married Dora,* and she starred as Lupe Cordero in the Luis Valdez-directed TV series pilot *Fort Figueroa* (1988).

Lalo Guerrero

Singer, composer, and musician, born in Tucson, December 24, 1916. He has written and composed songs in a myriad of styles (mariachi, norteño, pachuco, and social protest songs, etc.) but is probably best known for his parodies of English-language songs (e.g., "Pancho López," to the tune of "The Ballad of Davy Crockett"). He has appeared in a few films including *Boots and Saddles* (1935, starring Gene Autry), *Arizona* (1945, starring William Holden), *His Kind of Woman* (1948), and *The Sun Also Rises* (1950), and he has appeared on television programs ranging from *The Steve Allen Show* and *The Art Linkletter Show* (both in 1955) to Luis Valdez's *La Pastorela* (1991), *El Show de Paul Rodríguez* (cohost, 1993 season), and *Culture Clash* (1994, Fox).

Tito Guízar

(Federico Tito Guízar) Singer, songwriter, and film star, born April 8, 1908, in Mexico City. He starred in the highly successful Mexican musical *Allá en el rancho grande* (1936). Beginning in 1938, he appeared in several Hollywood English-language musicals, usually making guest appearances as himself. His English-language Hollywood credits include *Flame of Mexico* (1932), *Under the Pampas Moon* (1935), *The Big Broadcast of 1938* and *Tropic Holiday* (both 1938), *The Llano Kid* and *Saint Louis Blues* (1939), *Blondie Goes Latin* (1941), *Brazil* (1944), *The Thrill of Brazil* (1946), *On the Old Spanish Trail* (1947), and *The Gay Ranchero* (1948). He also had numerous Spanish-language Hollywood film credits in starring roles, including *Milagroso Hollywood* (1935, Royal Films, costarring Nenette Noriega), a Spanish-language original based on a screenplay by Raúl Gurruchaga; *Mis dos amores* (1938, Paramount, costarring Blanca de Castejón), a Spanish-language original based on a screenplay by José Antonio Miranda; *El trovador de la radio* (1938, Paramount, costarring Robina Duarte and Tana), a Spanish-language original based on a screenplay by Bernard Luber and Nenette Noriega; *Papá soltero* (1939, Paramount, costarring Amanda Varela and Tana), a Spanish-language original based on a screenplay by Dana Wilma; *El otro soy yo* (1939, Paramount, costarring Amanda Varela and Tana), a Spanish-language original based on a screenplay by Mortimer Braus and Dana Wilma; and *Cuando canta la ley* (1939, Paramount, costarring Tana and Martín Garralaga), a Spanish-language original based on a screenplay by Jack Natteford, Enrique Uhthoff, and Richard Harlan.

Efraín Gutiérrez

One of the earliest Chicano filmmakers, noted for his dramas and documentaries (see Barrios, 1985), several of which,

including *Please Don't Bury Me Alive!/Por favor, ¡No me entierren vivo!* (1977), *Amor chicano es para siempre/Chicano Love Is Forever* (1978), and *Run Junkie/Tecato Run* (1979), were filmed in 16mm and released in 35mm color in the 1970s in regional distribution in the Chicano community. His documentaries include *El Juanio* (screened at the 1979 San Antonio film festival), about the drug problems, mostly paint sniffing, of youngsters in the barrios of San Antonio, and *La onda chicana* (screened at the 1981 San Antonio film festival), a review of a 1976 Chicano concert.

Vincent R. Gutiérrez

Television scriptwriter. He did a number of episodes of *Little House on the Prairie* and *Highway to Heaven.*

Tomás Gutiérrez Alea

Cuban filmmaker, born December 11, 1928, died April 2, 1996. He was best known for his film *Memories of Underdevelopment* (1968), in which an antirevolutionary, Europeanized intellectual takes a stand against Fidel Castro's regime. His *Strawberry and Chocolate* (1993, released in the United States in 1995) depicts an older man who is gay who falls for a younger man who is not, set against the background of Cuban politics and attitudes toward homosexuality.

Claudio Guzmán

Television art director, producer, and film and television director, born in 1931, in Santiago, Chile, the brother of Pato Guzmán. He came to the United States in 1952 and studied at the University of Southern California. He was the art director at Desilu Studios for *The Life of Riley, The Danny Thomas Show, Official Detective, Wyatt Earp, December Bride, I Love Lucy,* and *Our Miss Brooks.* Also at Desilu he created, produced, and directed *The Victor Borge Comedy Hour,* and he directed episodes of *I Love Lucy, The Dick Van Dyke Show, The Fugitive, The Patty Duke Show,* and *The Untouchables.* He also produced and directed four years of the series *I Dream of Jeannie* and episodes of *The Wackiest Ship in the Army, Love on a Rooftop, The Flying Nun,* and *The Iron Horse.* He directed the following films: *Antonio* (1973, starring Trini López and Larry Hagman), *Willa* (1979), and *The Hostage Tower* (1980, starring Peter Fonda).

Gloria Guzmán

Actress. She costarred opposite Roberto Rey in *Un caballero de frac* (1931, Paramount), a Spanish-language version of *Evening Clothes* (1927, starring Adolphe Menjou and

Virginia Valli), and she also costarred opposite Carlos Gardel and Sofía Bazán in *Las luces de Buenos Aires* (1931, Paramount), a Spanish-language original based on an original work by Manuel Romero and Luis Bayón Herrera.

Luis Guzmán

Actor, often appearing as a streetwise Latino. His credits include *Short Eyes* (1977); *Family Business, True Believer, Rooftops,* and *Black Rain* (all 1989); *Q & A* and *Cadillac Man* (1990); *The Hard Way* (1991); *Jumpin' at the Boneyard* and *Innocent Blood* (1992); *Guilty as Sin* and *Carlito's Way* (1993); *The Burning Season* (1994, TV film); and *The Cowboy Way* (1994).

Pato Guzmán

Producer and production designer, born in Santiago, Chile, 1934, died January 2, 1991. Guzmán came to the United States in the late 1950s and worked in the design department at Desilu Studios, doing all its pilots as well as *The Danny Thomas Show, The Dick Van Dyke Show,* and *Star Trek.* After working on *The President's Analyst* (1967), he began a 20-year relationship with Paul Mazursky as a producer and production designer, with credits including *I Love You, Alice B. Toklas* (1967), *Bob & Carol & Ted & Alice* (1969), *Blume in Love* (1973), *An Unmarried Woman* (1978), *Tempest* (1982), *Moscow on the Hudson* (1984), and *Enemies, a Love Story* (1989). Guzmán also designed *The In-Laws* (1979) and *Hide in Plain Sight* (1990).

HISTORY AS A FUNCTION OF INTERRACIAL SEX

History according to Hollywood: the battle of the Alamo was the result of attempted interracial sexual abuse (see *Martyrs of the Alamo,* 1915); the Aztecs were defeated because an Aztec princess betrayed them out of love for a Spaniard (see the surrounding stills from *The Woman God Forgot* [1917, dir. Cecil B. DeMille]).

Above left: Wallace Reid and an "Aztec" in *The Woman God Forgot*

Above right: Theodore Kosloff (far left), Geraldine Farrar, and Wallace Reid

Right: Raymond Hatton, Theodore Kosloff, Geraldine Farrar, and Wallace Reid

Richard Harlan

Director, born in Lima, Peru, April 19, 1900. He worked as an assistant director in several English-language films and was the director of a number of Hollywood Spanish-language films. His English-language directorial credits include *The Devil Is a Woman* (1935); *My American Wife, Poppy,* and *The Preview Murder Mystery* (1936); *Double or Nothing, The Plainsman,* and *Waikiki Wedding* (1937); *Artists and Models Abroad, The Buccaneer, You and Me,* and *Bulldog Drummond's Peril* (1938); and *Ambush* and *Mercy Plane* (1939). His credits as director of Hollywood Spanish-language films include *En nombre de la amistad* (1930, Fox, starring George Lewis and Andrés de Segurola), a Spanish-language version of *Friendship* (1929, dir. Eugene Walter, starring Donald Gallaher and Robert Edeson); *El valiente* (1930, Fox, starring Juan Torena and Angelita Benítez), a Spanish-language version of *The Valiant* (1929, dir. William K. Howard, starring Paul Muni and Marguerite Churchill); *Del infierno al cielo* (1931, Fox, starring Juan Torena and María Alba), a Spanish-language version of *The Man Who Came Back* (1931, dir. Raoul Walsh, starring Janet Gaynor and Charles Farrell); *El trovador de la radio* (1938, Paramount, starring Tito Guízar and Robina Duarte), a Spanish-language original based on a screenplay by Bernard Luber and Nenette Noriega; *Papá soltero* (1939, Paramount, starring Tito Guízar and Amanda Varela), a Spanish-language original based on a screenplay by Dana Wilma; *El otro soy yo* (1939, Paramount, starring Tito Guízar and Amanda Varela), a Spanish-language original based on a screenplay by Mortimer Braus and Dana Wilma; and *Cuando canta la ley* (1939, Paramount, starring Tito Guízar and Tana), a Spanish-language original based on a screenplay by Jack Natteford, Enrique Uhthoff, and Richard Harlan.

Daniel A. Haro

Actor, born in Los Angeles, May 27, 1955. He appeared in *Stand and Deliver* (1988), *American Me* (1992), and *Talent for the Game* (1993).

Salma Hayek

Actress of Arab/Hispanic descent. She made a name for herself in Mexican *telenovelas* and then gained fame as the female lead in Robert Rodríguez's *Roadracers* (1994, TV film), as the girlfriend who gives "wild one" David Arquette problems, *Desperado* (1995), *From Dusk to Dawn* (1995), and *Fled* (1996).

Rita Hayworth

(Margarita Carmen Cansino) Actress, born October 17, 1918, in Brooklyn, New York, died May 14, 1987, in New York City. The daughter of Spanish-born dancer Eduardo Cansino and his "Ziegfeld Follies" partner Volga Haworth, she danced professionally by the age of 13 at Mexican night spots in Tijuana and Agua Caliente, where she was eventually noticed by Hollywood. She made her screen debut in 1935, playing bit parts under her real name. In 1937, she married Edward Judson, under whose guidance she changed her name and was transformed into an auburn-haired sophisticate. For the remainder of the 1930s she was limited to leads in B pictures, but through much of the 1940s, beginning with the widespread recognition she achieved in her role as Doña Sol, a heartless temptress opposite Tyrone Power in *Blood and Sand* (1941), she became the undisputed sex goddess of Hollywood films and the hottest star at Columbia Studios. Her fame reached its pinnacle with *Gilda* (1946), in which she performed a sensuous striptease number. Her tempestuous personal life included marriages to Edward C. Judson, Orson Welles, Prince Aly Khan, singer and actor Dick Haymes, and producer James Hill. Her career was attenuated by erratic behavior and memory lapses, which was ultimately diagnosed as Alzheimer's disease. Selected films (as Rita Cansino): *Under the Pampas Moon, Charlie Chan in Egypt, Dante's Inferno,* and *Paddy O'Day* (all 1935); *Rebellion, Human Cargo,* and *Meet Nero Wolfe* (1936); *Trouble in Texas, Old Louisiana,* and *Hit the Saddle* (1937).

As Rita Hayworth: *The Shadow* (1937); *Only Angels Have Wings* (1939); *Music in My Heart, Susan and God, The Lady in Question,* and *Angels Over Broadway* (1940); *Strawberry Blonde, Blood and Sand,* and *You'll Never Get Rich* (1941); *You Were Never Lovelier* and *My Gal Sal* (1942); *Cover Girl* (1944); *Tonight and Every Night* (1945); *Gilda* (1946); *Down to Earth* (1947); *The Lady from Shanghai* and *The Loves of Carmen* (1948); *Affair in Trinidad* (1952); *Salome* and *Miss Sadie Thompson* (1953); *Fire Down Below* and *Pal Joey* (1957); *Separate Tables* (1958); *They Came to Cordura* (1959); *The Happy Thieves* (1962); *Circus World* (1964); *The Poppy Is*

Also a Flower and *The Money Trap* (1966); *The Love Goddesses* (1967); *Head* (1968); *The Naked Zoo* and *Road to Salina* (1970); *The Wrath of God* (1972); and *Circle* (1976).

Pepe Hern

(Pepe Hernández) Actor, born in Spain; he came to the United States as a youth. He appeared in a number of films in the 1950s including *Borderline* (1950), *The Ring* (1952), *Summer and Smoke* (1961), and *13 West Street* (1962).

George F. Hernández

Actor, born in Placerville, California, June 6, 1863, died in Los Angeles, January 2, 1923; married to actress Anna Hernández, born in River Falls, Wisconsin, October 19, 1867, died in Los Angeles, California, May 4, 1945. Hernández was in numerous films during the silent period, and he had major roles in *When Helen Was Elected* (1912); *Mutiny, God's Crucible, Southern Justice,* and *The Greater Law* (all 1917); and *Arabia* and *Flaming Hearts* (1922). Additional film credits include *The Little Widow* (1911, Selig Polyscope Co., dir. Frank "Francis" Boggs, also starring Sydney Ayres and Herbert Rawlinson [film held at LC]); *The Making of Bobby Burnit* (1914); *The Circular Staircase, The Rosary,* and *Rosemary* (1915); *The End of the Rainbow* (Bluebird Photoplays, Inc., dir. Lynn F. Reynolds, also starring Myrtle González and Val Paul [film held at MOMA]), *The Girl of the Lost Lake, It Happened in Honolulu, A Romance of Billy Goat Hill, The Secret of the Swamp, A Son of the Immortals,* and *Unto Those Who Sin* (all 1916); *Broadway Arizona* (Triangle Film Corp., dir. Lynn F. Reynolds, also starring Olive Thomas and George Chesebro [film held at EH]), *The Show Down* (Bluebird Photoplays, Inc., dir. Lynn F. Reynolds, also starring Myrtle González and Arthur Hoyt [film held at LC]), *Mr. Opp,* and *Up or Down* (all 1917); *Betty Takes a Hand, The Hopper, Mlle. Paulette, The Man Who Woke Up, The Vortex,* and *You Can't Believe Everything* (1918); *The Silver Girl* (Anderson Brunton Co., dir. Frank Keenan, also starring Frank Keenan and Catherine Adams [film held at NAC]), *Be a Little Sport, The Courageous Coward, The Lost Princess, Mary Regan, Miss Adventure, The Rebellious Bride, A Taste of Life,* and *Tin Pan Alley* (1919); *The Daredevil, The Honey Bee, The House of Toys, Just Out of College, The Money-Changers, Seeds of Vengeance, The Third Woman,* and *The Village Sleuth* (1920); *After Your Own Heart, First Love, The Innocent Cheat, The Lure of Egypt,* and *The Road Demon* (1921); *Billy Jim* (1922, Fred Stone Productions, dir. Frank Borzage, also starring Fred Stone and Millicent Fisher [film held at CR]); *Bluebeard, Jr.* (1922, James Livingston, dir. Scott R. Dunlap, also starring Mary Anderson and Jack Connolly [film held at NFTA]); and *Man Under Cover* (1922, Universal, dir. Tod Browning, also starring Herbert Rawlinson and William Courtright [film held at MOMA]).

Juano Hernández

(Juan G. Hernández) Actor, born in 1898 in Puerto Rico, died July 19, 1970. He usually played African American or African film characters. Lacking formal education, he taught himself to read and write in several languages. Originally in minstrel shows, vaudeville, Broadway musicals, and serious theater, he debuted in film as the black sharecropper in *Intruder in the Dust* (1949). Other credits include *Young Man with a Horn,* as an aging jazz musician, *The Breaking Point,* and *Stars in My Crown* (all 1950); *Trial,* as an African American judge, and *Kiss Me Deadly* (1955); *Ransom* (1956); *Something of Value,* as an African Mau Mau leader, and *The Mark of the Hawk* (1957); *St. Louis Blues* (1958); *The Sins of Rachel Cade* and *Sergeant Rutledge* (1960); *Two Loves* (1961); *Hemingway's Adventures of a Young Man* (1962); *The Pawnbroker* (1965); *Uptight* (1968); *The Extraordinary Seaman* and *The Reivers* (1969); and *They Call Me MISTER Tibbs!* (1970).

Tom Hernández

Actor, died June 2, 1984. He had supporting roles in *The Third Voice* (1960, 20th Century-Fox) and *Fun in Acapulco* (1963).

Goyita Herrero

Actor. He had two roles in Hollywood Spanish-language films: *La pura verdad* (1931, Paramount), as Sabel, and *Espérame* (1933, Paramount, costarring opposite Carlos Gardel), a Spanish-language original based on a screenplay by Louis Gasnier (who also directed).

Laura Herring

(Laura Martínez Herring) Actress, born in Los Mochis, Sinaloa, Mexico, March 3, year unknown. An ex-Miss USA, she has appeared in *Silent Night, Deadly Night III—Better Watch Out!* (1989) and *The Forbidden Dance* (1990).

Lance Hool

Producer, writer, and director, born in Mexico City, educated in Mexico and the United States. His credits include *10 to Midnight* (1983), *The Evil That Men Do* and *Missing in Action* (1984), *Missing in Action II: The Beginning* (1985), *Steel Dawn* (1987), and *Pure Luck* (1991).

Rudolfo Hoyos, Jr.

(Also Rodolpho Hoyas, Jr.) Actor, born in Mexico City in 1914, died in Los Angeles, April 15, 1983. He was brought by his father, the opera star, to the United States in the late 1920s, where he debuted as a 14-year-old in Howard Hughes's *Hell's Angels* (1930, starring Jean Harlow). He was a character actor, usually playing a villain or a stern father. Credits include *The Fighter* (1952); *Second Chance* (1953); *The Americano* (1955); *Secret of Treasure Mountain, The Brave One, Timetable, The First Texan,* and *The Three Outlaws* (1956); *Ghost Diver* (1957); *Villa!* and *Ten Days to Tulara* (1958); *The Little Savage* (1959); *Operation Eichmann* (1961); *California* and *The Gun Hawk* (1963); *Seven Days in May* (1964); *Return of the Gunfighter* (1967); and *Change of Habit* (1969). His television credits include appearances in over 300 television episodes; he also worked for the last 10 years of his life as the Spanish-language broadcaster of the Los Angeles Dodgers.

Rudolfo Hoyos, Sr.

(Also Rodolfo Hoyos, Rudolfo Hoyos) Singer, born in 1895 in Mexico City, died in Los Angeles, California, May 24, 1980. He first came to the United States in the late 1920s to perform at New York's Metropolitan Opera. Hoyos appeared and sang in *Grand Canary* and *One Night of Love* (1934); *A Night at the Opera* (1935, starring the Marx Brothers); and *The Girl of the Golden West* (1938). He portrayed Ricky Ricardo's uncle in an episode of *I Love Lucy.* A Rodolfo Hoyos is credited as a supporting actor in three Hollywood Spanish-language musicals: *Carne de cabaret* (1931, Columbia, dir. Christy Cabanne, starring Lupita Tovar and Ramón Pereda); *Un capitán de cosacos* (1934, Fox, starring José Mojica and Rosita Moreno); and *Piernas de seda* (1935, Fox, starring Rosita Moreno and Raúl Roulien). It is presumed that these roles were played by Rodolfo Hoyos, Sr. His son, Rudolfo Hoyos, Jr., was also a Hollywood actor.

MARGARITA CANSINO BECOMES SEXY RITA HAYWORTH

Margarita Cansino "repositioned" herself from Latina to Anglo and became immensely successful.

Above: Phil Silvers, Rita Hayworth, and Gene Kelly in *Cover Girl* (1944)

Right: Rita Hayworth and Fred Astaire in *You'll Never Get Rich* (1941)

Left: Margarita Cansino before she became Rita Hayworth

Below: Rita Hayworth doing her famous striptease number in *Gilda* (1946)

León Ichaso

Director, son of well-known television and film director Justo Rodríguez Santos. Born in 1949 in Cuba, he left the island at age 14 and finished his education in the United States. He began with commercials, documentaries, and industrial films, then directed independent films including *El Super* (1979), *Power, Passion, and Murder* (1983), *Crossover Dreams* (1985), *The Take* (1990), *The Fear Inside* (1992), and *Sugar Hill* (1994).

Eugene Iglesias

Character actor, born December 3, 1926, in San Juan, Puerto Rico. He attended Columbia University, and he began his career in the theater. His film credits include *The Brave Bulls,* as lighthearted Pepe Bello, and *The Mask of the Avenger* (both 1951); *War Cry* (1952, also released as *Indian Uprising*); *East of Sumatra* (1953); *The Naked Dawn* (1955), as a bandit; *Frontier Uprising* (1961); *Safe at Home!* (1962); *Apache Rifles* (1964); and *Harper* and *The Money Trap* (1966).

Eddie Infante

Filipino actor. He had supporting roles in films set in the Philippines or elsewhere in the Pacific including *No Place to Hide* (1956), *No Man Is an Island* (1962), *Cavalry Command* (1963), *Warkill* (1967), and *Ethan* (1971).

Gloria Irrizary

Puerto Rican character actress. She was in *Cargo of Love* (1968), played María, Buddy Holly's Puerto Rican mother-in-law, in *The Buddy Holly Story* (1978), and played another Puerto Rican mother in *Q & A* (1990). She has numerous television credits.

Isabelita

Singer and actress. She had a few stereotypical roles, often singing a song or two, in films during the 1940s including *Club Havana* (1945), *Don Ricardo Returns* (1946), *Slightly Scandalous* (1946, Universal), and *Samba Mania* (1948, Paramount), in the role of a jealous Latin dancer.

José Isbert

(José Isbert Alvarruiz) Actor and veteran film star, born in Madrid, March 3, 1886, died in Madrid, November 28, 1966, married to actress María Isbert Soriano and grandfather of actor Tony Isbert. He appeared in 120 Spanish-language films. He also appeared in a few European or coproductions released in various languages including English: *The Man Who Wagged His Tail* (1961), *Not on Your Life* (1965), and *Operation Delilah* (1966). He starred in two Hollywood Spanish-language films: *La pura verdad* (1931, Paramount, dir. Manuel Romero, costarring Enriqueta Serrano), a Spanish-language version of *Nothing But the Truth* (1929, starring Richard Dix and Helen Kane); and *¿Cuándo te suicidas?* (1931, Paramount), as Petavey.

Al Israel

Actor and musician, born in New York City. His film credits include *Scarface* (1983), *Body Double* (1984), *Marked for Death* (1990), and *Carlito's Way* (1993).

José Iturbi

(José de Iturbi) Pianist and conductor, born in Valencia, Spain, November 28, 1895, died in Hollywood, California, June 28, 1980. A child prodigy, he soon became a world-renowned pianist. He appeared as himself in a number of MGM musical films including *Thousands Cheer* (1943), *Two Girls and a Sailor* and *Music for Millions* (1944), *Anchors Aweigh* (1945), *Holiday in Mexico* (1946), *Three Daring Daughters* (1948), and *That Midnight Kiss* (1949). He played the piano for actor Cornel Wilde in the role of Chopin in *A Song to Remember* (1945). His recording of Chopin's "A-flat Polonaise" from this film became the first classical record to sell over a million copies.

Rebeca Iturbide

(Rebeca Iturbide de Sendel) Actress, born in El Paso, Texas. She had supporting roles in *The Last Rebel* (1961) and *Of Love and Desire* (1963).

ONE, TWO, MANY EXOTICS: THE VARIED ROLES OF DOLORES DEL RÍO AND ANTHONY QUINN

Dolores del Río and Anthony Quinn were able to break out of strictly Hispanic roles. However, they primarily did exotic characters.

Left: Dolores del Río as a gypsy bear trainer in *Revenge* (1928)

Below left: In her gypsy costume with José Crespo in *Revenge* (1928)

Below right: Dolores del Río as a South Sea island girl and Joel McCrea in *Bird of Paradise* (1932)

Opposite page, top: Dolores del Río and Joel McCrea in *Bird of Paradise* (1932)

Below left: Dolores del Río dressed up anachronistically *a la española* (with Norman Foster) in the border movie, *Girl of the Rio* (1931)

Below right: As an American Indian, with Gilbert Roland playing her son, in *Cheyenne Autumn* (1964, Warner Brothers, dir. John Ford)

Above left: Dolores del Río as a Russian in *The Red Dance* (1928)

Above right: Dolores del Río as a French courtesan in *Madame Dubarry* (1934,Warner Brothers, dir. William Dieterle)

Below left: Anthony Quinn as a Spanish bullfighter with J. Carrol Naish and Tyrone Power in *Blood and Sand* (1941, 20th Century-Fox)

Below right: Anthony Quinn as Alexis Zorba in *Zorba the Greek* (1964, 20th Century-Fox)

Above left: Anthony Quinn as Yellow Hand with Joel McCrea in *Buffalo Bill* (1944, 20th Century-Fox)

Above right: As an Irish-looking Al Jackson in *Irish Eyes Are Smiling* (1944, 20th Century-Fox)

Below left: Anthony Quinn as Attila in *Attila* (1954)

Below right: As a Chinese soldier in *China Sky* (1945)

Above left: Anthony Quinn as Barabbas in
Barabbas (1962)

Above right: As Kiang, chief of a South Sea
island, in *East of Sumatra* (1953, Universal)

Below left: As Gauguin in *Lust for Life* (1956)

Below right: As Quasimodo in *The Hunchback
of Notre Dame* (1957, Allied Artists)

Above left: Anthony Quinn as an opportunistic sheik, Auda Abu Tayi, in *Lawrence of Arabia* (1962)

Above right: Anthony Quinn as Pope Kiril I (of Russian extraction) in *The Shoes of the Fisherman* (1968, MGM)

Below left: As an Eskimo with Yoko Tanai in *The Savage Innocents* (1960, Paramount)

Marabina Jaimes

Television moderator; she won an Emmy Award for Best Host or Moderator of a TV Series for her work on KCET's *Storyline.*

Enrique Jardiel Poncela

Prolific playwright and actor. He had a few supporting roles in Hollywood Spanish-language films including *Primavera en otoño* (1933, Fox, starring Catalina Bárcena, Raúl Roulien, and Antonio Moreno) and *Una viuda romántica* (1933, Fox, starring Catalina Bárcena and Gilbert Roland). He also composed music for Hollywood Spanish-language films including *La melodía prohibida* (1933, Fox, starring José Mojica and Conchita Montenegro), and he wrote the screenplay for *Angelina o el honor de un brigadier* (1935, Fox, starring Rosita Díaz Gimeno and José Crespo).

Carmen Jiménez

Actress; she had a few supporting roles in Hollywood Spanish-language films including *¡Salga de la cocina!* (1930, Paramount, starring Roberto Rey and Amparo Miguel Ángel); *Sombras del circo* (1931, Paramount, starring Amelia Muñoz and Tony D'Algy); and *Mamá* (1931, Fox, dir. Benito Perojo, starring Catalina Bárcena and Rafael Rivelles).

Neal Jiménez

Scriptwriter and director, born May 22, 1960. He wrote the screenplays for *Where the River Runs Black* and *River's Edge* (both 1986), cowrote *For the Boys* (1991), and wrote and directed his autobiographical film *The Waterdance* (1992), which deals with his permanent paralysis. He also wrote the script for the box-office and critical failure *Dark Wind* (1994) and cowrote *Hideaway* (1995, starring Jeff Goldblum).

Soledad Jiménez

(Also numerous variants on spelling) Spanish character actress, born in Santander, Spain, February 28, 1874, died in Woodland Hills, California, October 17, 1966. In her long and varied film-acting career, she appeared in the Jesse L. Lasky Feature Play Co. American production of *Carmen* (1915, starring Geraldine Farrar), and she was in the first talking Western, *In Old Arizona* (1929, with Warner Baxter), and *The Robin Hood of El Dorado* (1936, also with Warner Baxter). John Ford used her in many of his productions, in which she played both comedy and dramatic roles. Additional silent or Hollywood English-language film credits include *The Cock-Eyed World* and *Romance of the Rio Grande* (1929); *The Arizona Kid, A Devil With Women,* and *The Texan* (1930); *The Broken Wing* (1932); *Bordertown, The Cyclone Ranger, In Caliente, Rumba,* and *Under the Pampas Moon* (1935); *The Bold Caballero, Phantom of the Range,* and *The Traitor* (1936); *Kid Galahad, Law and Lead, Man of the People, When You're in Love,* and *Live, Love and Learn* (1937); *California Frontier* and *Forbidden Valley* (1938); *Girl from Rio, The Real Glory, The Return of the Cisco Kid,* and *Rough Riders Round-Up* (1939); and *Seven Sinners* (1940). She also had several supporting roles in Hollywood Spanish-language films including *La voluntad del muerto* (1930, Universal, starring Lupita Tovar and Antonio Moreno); *Resurrección* (1931, Universal, dir. Edwin Carewe, starring Lupe Vélez and Gilbert Roland); *Carne de cabaret* (1931, Columbia, dir. Christy Cabanne, starring Lupita Tovar and Ramón Pereda); *La cruz y la espada* (1933, Fox, starring José Mojica and Anita Campillo); *Tres amores* (1934, Universal, starring José Crespo and Anita Campillo); *Julieta compra un hijo* (1935, Fox, starring Catalina Bárcena and Gilbert Roland); and *La última cita* (1935, Columbia, starring José Crespo and Luana Alcañiz).

Raúl Juliá

(Raúl Rafael Carlos Juliá y Arcelay) Actor, born in San Juan, Puerto Rico, March 9, 1940, died October 24, 1994. He became one of the best-known Hispanic actors for his roles in Shakespearean and other classical stage dramas and musicals as well as film. He moved from Puerto Rico to New York in 1964 and became closely associated with Joseph Papp's New York Shakespeare Festival (he received Tony nominations for *Two Gentlemen of Verona* and *The Threepenny Opera*) and then with Broadway theater. In 1971, spelling his name Raul Julia, he debuted in small parts in *The Organization, Been Down So Long It Looks Like Up to Me,* and *Panic in Needle Park.* Juliá appeared in *The Gumball Rally* (1976), *Eyes of Laura Mars* (1978), and achieved national attention as the costar in the notable *Kiss of the Spider Woman* (1985), from the novel by Argentine Manuel Puig. Additional credits: *One from the Heart* (dir. Francis Ford Coppola), *Tempest,* and *The Escape Artist* (all 1982); *Compromising Positions* (1985), as a Hispanic detective; *The Morning After* (1986); *Trading Hearts* (1987); *La*

Above left: Raúl Juliá in *Tequila Sunrise* (1988)

Below left: Raúl Juliá in *Kiss of the Spider Woman* (1985)

Below: Raúl Juliá

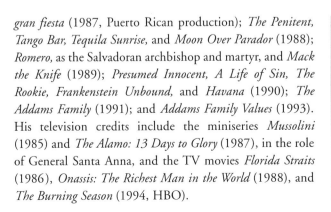

gran fiesta (1987, Puerto Rican production); *The Penitent, Tango Bar, Tequila Sunrise,* and *Moon Over Parador* (1988); *Romero,* as the Salvadoran archbishop and martyr, and *Mack the Knife* (1989); *Presumed Innocent, A Life of Sin, The Rookie, Frankenstein Unbound,* and *Havana* (1990); *The Addams Family* (1991); and *Addams Family Values* (1993). His television credits include the miniseries *Mussolini* (1985) and *The Alamo: 13 Days to Glory* (1987), in the role of General Santa Anna, and the TV movies *Florida Straits* (1986), *Onassis: The Richest Man in the World* (1988), and *The Burning Season* (1994, HBO).

Tito Junco

Actor, born in Veracruz, Mexico, 1915, died in Mexico City, December 9, 1983; brother of Víctor Junco. Active in the Mexican film industry, he was seen in the United States in a few Mexican films released in English-language versions. Credits include *Gina* (1956, also released as *Diamond Hunters,* dir. Luis Buñuel), *The Empty Star* (1962), *The Invasion of the Vampires* (1965), and *The Exterminating Angel* (1967, dir. Luis Buñuel).

Víctor Junco

(Gutiérrez Zamora) Actor, born in Veracruz, Mexico; brother of Tito Junco. Active in the Mexican film industry, he was seen in the United States in *The Big Cube* and *The Undefeated* (both 1969).

Katy Jurado

(María Cristina Jurado García) Actress, born January 16, 1924, in Guadalajara, Mexico. Having become a well-known Mexican film star in the 1940s (her most successful Mexican film was *La vida inútil de Pito Pérez,* 1943), she began her Hollywood career as a columnist for Mexican publications and played "dark lady" roles, either as a Mexican, American Indian, or "half breed," in a variety of films, most memorably *High Noon* and *One-Eyed Jacks.* She was nominated for an Oscar for her supporting role in *Broken Lance.* Between 1959 and 1964 she was married to actor Ernest Borgnine. Credits include *The Bullfighter and the Lady* (1951), as the wife of an aging bullfighter played by Gilbert Roland; *High Noon,* in the role of Helen Ramírez, and *The Brute* (both 1952); *Arrowhead,* as an Apache-Mexican, and *San Antone* (both 1953); *Broken Lance* (1954), as Spencer Tracy's Indian wife; *The Racers* and *Trial* (both 1955); *Trapeze* and *The Man from Del Rio* (1956); *Dragoon Wells Massacre* (1957); *The Badlanders* (1958); *One-Eyed Jacks* (1961); *Barabbas* (1962); *Smoky* and *A Covenant with Death* (1966); *Stay Away, Joe* (1968); *Once Upon a Scoundrel* and *Pat Garrett and Billy the Kid* (1973); *El recurso del método* (Mex.) and *The Children of Sánchez* (1978); *Evita Perón* (1981, TV film, starring Faye Dunaway); *Under the Volcano* (1984); and *Fearmaker* (1989). On television she was the mother in the Paul Rodríguez sitcom *A.K.A. Pablo.*

Above: Katy Jurado

Opposite page, above: Katy Jurado and Grace Kelly in *High Noon* (1952)

Opposite page, below: Katy Jurado in *Pat Garrett and Billy the Kid* (1952)

DANCING SEÑORITAS

The Cantina Dancer was one of only three Hispanic female roles in the early cinema; the type has been retained over time through Dolores del Río (even though she couldn't dance), Margarita Cansino/Rita Hayworth, Carmen Miranda, and contemporary salsa films.

Below: Pola Negri in *The Spanish Dancer* (1923, Paramount)

Above: The role might have reached its acme with Carmen Miranda, here in a number from *The Gang's All Here* (1943)

Below left: Dolores del Río in *In Caliente* (1935)

Below right: Lupe Vélez in *Lady of the Pavements* (1929)

Pancho Kohner

Producer, born January 7, 1939, son of agent Paul Kohner and Mexican actress Lupita Tovar and brother of actress Susan Kohner. He has produced *St. Ives* (1976), *The White Buffalo* (1977), *The Evil That Men Do* (1984), *Death Wish 4: The Crackdown* (1987), and *Kinjite: Forbidden Subjects* (1989).

Susan Kohner

Actress, born in Los Angeles, November 11, 1936, daughter of agent Paul Kohner and Mexican actress Lupita Tovar.

She was educated at UCLA and debuted as María in *To Hell and Back* (1955, starring Audie Murphy). She was in *The Last Wagon* (1956), *Trooper Hook* and *Dino* (1957), *The Gene Krupa Story* and *The Big Fisherman* (1959), *All the Fine Young Cannibals* (1960), *By Love Possessed* (1961), and *Freud* (1962). She was nominated for an Academy Award for Best Supporting Actress for her role as a young black woman who tries to pass for white in *Imitation of Life* (1959).

Apollonia Kotero

(Patricia Apollonio Kotero) Mexican American actress, singer, and dancer, born in Santa Monica, California, August 2, 1961. She costarred with Prince in *Purple Rain* (1984), and on television she had the role of a character called Apollonia on *Falcon Crest* for a season. Additional credits include *Heartbreaker* (1983), *Tricks of the Trade* (1988), *Ministry of Vengeance* (1989), *Back to Back* (1990), and *Black Magic Woman* (1991).

THE MEXICAN CONNECTION

Mexican actors and filmmakers have made a significant contribution to international filmmaking, participating in the development of the Hollywood film industry and its depiction style.

Above: *Like Water for Chocolate* (1992), the best-selling Mexican film in the U. S. market to date

Right: Mario Moreno "Cantinflas" with Margarito in the enormously popular *Ahí está el detalle* (1949, dir. Juan Bustillo Oro)

Above: Donald Reed (left), Lupita Tovar, and Juan José Martínez Casado in Mexico's first sound film, *Santa* (1931, dir. Antonio Moreno)

Left: Alma Delia Fuentes and Miguel Inclán in *Los olvidados/The Young and the Damned* (1950)

Top left: Jorge Negrete (left, with Carmelita González) and Pedro Infante (right, with Yolanda Varela) in *Dos tipos de cuidado* (1952, dir. Ismael Rodríguez)

Above left: María Luisa Zea and Lupe Vélez in *La zandunga* (1937, dir. Fernando de Fuentes)

Above right: Germán Valdés, "Tin-Tan," the first film pachuco, in *Hotel de verano* (1943, dir. René Cardona)

Below right: Pedro Armendáriz and Dolores del Río in *María Candelaria* (1943, dir. Fernando de Fuentes)

Left: Tito Guízar and Esther Fernández in the supremely popular *Allá en el Rancho Grande* (1936, dir. Fernando de Fuentes)

Below left: María Félix and Agustín Isunza in *Doña Bárbara* (1943, dir. Fernando de Fuentes)

Bottom left: María Félix as a heroic rural teacher in *Río Escondido* (1946, dir. Emilio Fernández)

Bottom right: Víctor Parra and David Silva in *Espaldas mojadas* (1953, dir. Alejandro Galindo)

Carlos LaCámara

Actor, born in 1957 in Havana, Cuba. He moved to the United States at age two. He earned a B.A. from UCLA and works in television, where he is best known for his role as Paco, an orderly on the series *Nurses.*

María Ladrón de Guevara

(María Ladrón de Guevara y Trápanga) Actress, born in Madrid, 1896, died in Madrid, April 25, 1974, married to Spanish actor Rafael Rivelles. She starred in a few Hollywood Spanish-language films including *La mujer X* (1931, MGM, dir. Carlos F. Borcosque, costarring her husband, Rafael Rivelles), a Spanish-language version of *Madame X* (1929, dir. Lionel Barrymore, starring Ruth Chatterton and Lewis Stone); *Cheri-Bibi* (1931, MGM, dir. Carlos F. Borcosque, costarring opposite Ernesto Vilches), a Spanish-language version of *The Phantom of Paris* (1931, starring John Gilbert and Leila Hyams); and *El proceso de Mary Dugan* (1931, MGM, costarring José Crespo), a Spanish-language version of *The Trial of Mary Dugan* (1929, starring Norma Shearer and Lewis Stone).

Adriana Lamar

(Also Monina Lamar) Actress. She costarred or had supporting roles in a few Hollywood Spanish-language films including *Cheri-Bibi* (1931, MGM, dir. Carlos F. Borcosque, starring Ernesto Vilches and María Ladrón de Guevara); *No matarás* (1935, Hispano International Film Corporation, dir. Miguel Contreras Torres, costarring opposite Ramón Pereda), a Spanish-language original based on a screenplay by Miguel Contreras Torres; and *El crimen de media noche* (1935, Reliable Pictures, costarring opposite Ramón Pereda), a Spanish-language version of *The Midnight Phantom* (1935, starring Reginald Denny and Claudia Dell). She was also in *The Phantom of Paris* (1931).

Fernando Lamas

Actor, born January 9, 1915, in Buenos Aires, died October 8, 1982, in Los Angeles. A star in Argentina, he was import-

Above: Fernando Lamas

ed to Hollywood by MGM and typecast as a sporty Latin Lover in a number of light films, some of which featured his singing. He married Pearla Mux, Lydia Babachi, Arlene Dahl (1954-60), and Esther Williams (in 1967). Film credits include *The Avengers* (1950); *The Law and the Lady* and *Rich, Young and Pretty* (1951); *The Merry Widow* (1952); *Dangerous When Wet, Sangaree, The Girl Who Had Everything,* and *The Diamond Queen* (all 1953); *Jívaro* and *Rose Marie* (1954); *The Girl Rush* (1955); *The Lost World* (1960); *A Place Called Glory* (1966, German); *The Violent Ones, Valley of Mystery,* and *Kill a Dragon* (1967); *100 Rifles* and *Backtrack* (1969); *Powder Keg* (1970, TV film); *Murder on Flight 502* (1975, TV film); and *The Cheap Detective* (1978). He directed scores of television episodes including several of the series *Falcon Crest* featuring his son, Lorenzo Lamas. Comedian Billy Crystal parodied his character on the television show *Saturday Night Live,* making use of a stock phrase, "You look maahvelous!"

Lorenzo Lamas

Actor, son of Fernando Lamas and Arlene Dahl, born in Santa Monica, California, January 20, 1958. He has appeared in *Grease* and *Take Down* (both 1978); *Body Rock* (1984);

Above: Fernando Lamas (with Lana Turner) in *The Merry Widow* (1952)

Below: Dorothy Lamour in *Man About Town* (1939)

1996. Debuting in *College Holiday* (1936, bit part) and then *The Jungle Princess* (1936), she became an overnight star at Paramount, partly because of her sexy costume, the sarong, which became her trademark. She received considerable recognition for her role in *The Hurricane* (1937, dir. John Ford), and she was noted for her singing and comic talents in the series of *Road to . . .* films with Bob Hope and Bing Crosby. Among her many other films, she played a Latina in *A Medal for Benny* (1945) and was in *Masquerade in Mexico* (1945) and *The Road to Rio* (1947). She played a Spaniard in *The Last Train from Madrid* (1937). Additional credits: *High, Wide and Handsome* and *Swing High, Swing Low* (both 1937); *The Big Broadcast of 1938, Her Jungle Love, Spawn of the North, Thrill of a Lifetime,* and *Tropic Holiday* (all 1938); *Disputed Passage, Man About Town,* and *Saint Louis Blues* (1939); *Chad Hanna, Johnny Apollo, Moon Over Burma, Road to Singapore,* and *Typhoon* (1940); *Caught in the Draft, Road to Zanzibar,* and *Aloma of the South Seas* (1941); *Road to Morocco, The Fleet's In,* and *Beyond the Blue Horizon* (1942); *They Got Me Covered, Dixie,* and *Riding High* (1943); *And the Angels Sing* and *Rainbow Island* (1944); *Duffy's Tavern* and *Road to Utopia* (1945); *My Favorite Brunette, Wild Harvest,* and *Variety Girl* (1947); *On Our Merry Way, Lulu Belle,* and *The Girl From Manhattan* (1948); *Lucky Stiff* (1949); *Here Comes the Groom* (1951); *The Greatest Show on Earth* and *Road to Bali* (1952); *Hollywood Goes to War* (1954); *The Road to Hong Kong* (1962); *Donovan's Reef* (1963); *Pajama Party* (1964); *The Love Goddesses* (1965); *The Phynx* (1970); *Won Ton Ton, the Dog Who Saved Hollywood* (1976); and *Creepshow* (1987).

Elena Landeros

Actress. She had a few supporting roles in Hollywood Spanish-language films including *En cada puerto un amor* (1931, MGM, starring José Crespo and Conchita Montenegro); *El príncipe gondolero* (1931, Paramount, starring Roberto Rey and Rosita Moreno); and *Hollywood, ciudad de ensueño* (1931, Universal, starring José Bohr and Lia Torá).

William Douglas Lansford

Writer, born July 13, 1922, in East Los Angeles, to a Mexican mother and an Anglo father. His credits, all in television, include episodes of *Bonanza, The Virginian, The High*

SnakeEater and *SnakeEater 2: The Drug Buster* (1989); *Night of the Warrior* (1990, with his mother Arlene Dahl); *Killing Streets* and *Final Impact* (1991); and *SnakeEater 3: His Law, C.I.A.: Code Name Alexa,* and *The Swordsman* (all 1992). On television he is best known for his role as Lance Cumson on *Falcon Crest*; he also starred in the TV series *Renegade* (1992).

Dorothy Lamour

(Mary Leta Dorothy Slaton Kaumeyer) Actress of French, Scotch-Irish, and Spanish descent, born in New Orleans, December 10, 1914, died in N. Hollywood, September 22,

Chaparral, Fantasy Island, The Rookies, Matt Houston, and *CHiPs.* He also wrote the television films *The Deadly Tower* (1975) and *Don't Look Back: The Story of Leroy "Satchel" Paige* (1981).

Carmen Larrabeiti

Actress, born in Bilbao, Spain, May 2, 1906. Her sister was Mariana Larrabeiti, also an actress, born in Bilbao in 1904. Carmen starred or costarred in seven Hollywood Spanish-language films including *Doña Mentiras* (1930, Cinéstudio Continental Paramount, costarring Félix de Pomés), a Spanish-language version of *The Lady Lies* (1929, starring Walter Huston and Claudette Colbert); *Toda una vida* (1930, Paramount, costarring Tony D'Algy), a Spanish-language version of *Sarah and Son* (1930, starring Ruth Chatterton and Fredric March); *La carta* (1930, Paramount, costarring Carlos Díaz de Mendoza), a Spanish-language version of *The Letter* (1929, starring Jeanne Engels and Herbert Marshall); *La fiesta del diablo* (1930, Paramount, costarring Tony D'Algy), a Spanish-language version of *The Devil's Holiday* (1930, starring Nancy Carroll and Phillips Holmes); *Esclavas de la moda* (1931, Fox, with Félix de Pomés), a Spanish-language version of *On Your Back* (1930, starring Irene Rich and Raymond Hackett); *¿Conoces a tu mujer?* (1931, Fox, costarring opposite Rafael Rivelles), a Spanish-language version of *Don't Bet on Women* (1931, starring Edmund Lowe and Jeanette MacDonald); and *La ley del harem* (1931, Fox, costarring opposite José Mojica), a Spanish-language version of *Fazil* (1928, dir. Howard Hawks, starring Charles Farrell and Greta Nissen).

Mario Larrinaga

Scenic artist, born in California. He worked at RKO and is best known for his contribution to the 1933 production of *King Kong.*

Raúl Lechuga

(Also Raoul) Actor. He had numerous supporting roles in Hollywood Spanish-language films including *La rosa de fuego* (1930, Tom White Productions, starring Don Alvarado and Renée Torres); *Monsieur le Fox* (1930, MGM, starring Gilbert Roland and Rosita Ballesteros); *El valiente* (1930, Fox, starring Juan Torena and Angelita Benítez); *Desconcierto matrimonial* (1930, Fox, starring Delia Magaña and Raoul de León); *¿Conoces a tu mujer?* (1931, Fox, starring Rafael Rivelles and Carmen Larrabeiti); *El crimen de media noche* (1935, Reliable Pictures, starring Ramón Pereda and Adriana Lamar); *Papá soltero* (1939, Paramount, starring

Above: John Leguizamo in *Whispers in the Dark* (1992)

Tito Guízar and Amanda Varela); and *Cuando canta la ley* (1939, Paramount, starring Tito Guízar and Tana). He was also in several English-language films including *Under the Pampas Moon* (1935), *Love Under Fire* and *When You're in Love* (both 1937), and *Only Angels Have Wings* (1939).

John Leguizamo

Actor and comic, born in Bogotá, Colombia, raised in Jackson Heights, Queens, New York. He first became well known for his 1990 one-man comic show, *Mambo Mouth,* a satire of Latino stereotypes which he produced and wrote and in which he starred. It appeared on HBO cable network in 1991. He followed this with *Spic-O-Rama* (1992), also on HBO, a similarly acerbic satire. He has appeared in several films including *Casualties of War* (1989); *Street Hunter, Revenge,* as a Mexican mountain boy, and *Die Hard 2* (all 1990); *Regarding Henry* (1991), as a street hood; *Whispers in the Dark* (1992), as a Soho artist; *Super Mario Brothers* (1993), in which he costarred; *Carlito's Way* (1993), also as a hood; and *To Wong Foo, Thanks for Everything, Julie Newmar* and *A Pyromaniac's Love Story* (1995). He had a major role in the memorable independent feature *Hangin' with the*

Homeboys (1991, dir. Joseph B. Vásquez). He had a recurring role in the TV series *Miami Vice* and starred in the short-lived series *House of Buggin'* (1995, Fox).

Barbara Leonard

Actress, born in San Francisco, January 9, year unknown. She had supporting roles in three Hollywood Spanish-language films: *Señora casada necesita marido* (1934, Fox, starring Catalina Bárcena and Antonio Moreno); *¡Asegure a su mujer!* (1934, Fox, starring Raúl Roulien and Conchita Montenegro); and *Julieta compra un hijo* (1935, Fox, starring Catalina Bárcena and Gilbert Roland). She was also in numerous English-language films including *Bought* and *City Streets* (both 1931); *Beauty and the Boss, The Crash, Love Affair, The Man from Yesterday, One Hour with You,* and *A Successful Calamity* (all 1932); *Desirable, Flirtation Walk,* and *The Merry Widow* (1934); *Folies Bergère de Paris* (1935); *The White Angel* (1936); *Espionage* (1937); *City in Darkness* (1939); and *Women Without Names* (1940).

Emilia Leovalli

Actress. She had several supporting roles in Hollywood Spanish-language films including *La buenaventura* (1934, First National Pictures, starring Enrico Caruso, Jr., and Anita Campillo); *Tres amores* (1934, Universal, starring José Crespo and Anita Campillo); *El cantante de Nápoles* (1934, Warner, starring Enrico Caruso, Jr., and Mona Maris); *Te quiero con locura* (1935, Fox, starring Rosita Moreno and Raúl Roulien); *Castillos en el aire* (1938, Monogram Pictures, dir. Jaime Salvador, starring Cristina Téllez and Rafael Alcaide); *Mis dos amores* (1938, Paramount, starring Tito Guízar and Blanca de Castejón); and *Los hijos mandan* (1939, 20th Century-Fox, dir. Gabriel Soria, starring Blanca de Castejón and Fernando Soler).

Alfredo Le Pera

(Also Alfred) Screenwriter; his credits include numerous screenplays (*guiones* or *argumentos*) or other writing (*diálogos*) for Hollywood Spanish-language films including *Espérame, Melodía de arrabal,* and *La casa es seria* (all 1933, Paramount); *Cuesta abajo* and *El tango en Broadway* (both 1934, Paramount); and *El día que me quieras* and *Tango Bar* (both 1935, Paramount).

George Lewis

(Also Jorge) Character actor. He presents particular difficulties in establishing his film credits, since this Mexican actor is often confused with George J. Lewis [as in R (1994)], a different actor who appeared in Zorro films and Zorro productions on television in addition to other Hispanic-focused films. Lewis's films are listed from the 1931-1940 and 1961-1970 (only one film) periods since these have definitely been established by the *American Film Institute Catalog* for those years. His films between 1941 and 1960 are not listed because he is difficult to distinguish from George J. Lewis. He was born December 10, 1903, in Guadalajara, Mexico, and died December 29, 1977. Among his film credits are *Heart Punch, A Parisian Romance,* and *South of the Rio Grande* (1932); *Her Resale Value* (1933); *Lazy River, The Merry Widow, Red Morning,* and *Two Heads on a Pillow* (1934); *The Headline Woman, Storm Over the Andes,* and *Under the Pampas Moon* (1935); *Captain Calamity, The Pecos Dandy,* and *Ride, Ranger, Ride* (1937); and *Happy Birthday, Davy* (1970). Lewis also had a significant career in Hollywood Spanish-language films, starring or appearing in numerous productions including *En nombre de la amistad* (1930, Fox, costarring Andrés de Segurola and Luana Alcañiz), a Spanish-language version of *Friendship* (1929, starring Donald Gallaher and Robert Edeson); *El último de los Vargas* (1930, Fox, costarring Luana Alcañiz), a Spanish-language version of *Last of the Duanes* (1930, starring George O'Brien, Lucille Brown, and Myrna Loy); *La gran jornada* (1931, Fox, costarring Carmen Guerrero), a Spanish-language version of *The Big Trail* (1930, dir. Raoul Walsh, starring John Wayne and Marguerite Churchill); *Cuerpo y alma* (1931, Fox, costarring Ana María Custodio), a Spanish-language version of *Body and Soul* (1931, starring Charles Farrell, Elissa Landi, Humphrey Bogart, and Myrna Loy); *Marido y mujer* (1932, Fox, costarring Conchita Montenegro), a Spanish-language version of *Bad Girl* (1931, dir. Frank Borzage, starring Sally Eilers and James Dunn); *No dejes la puerta abierta* (1933, Fox, starring Raúl Roulien and Rosita Moreno); *Alas sobre el Chaco* (1935, Universal, dir. Christy Cabanne, starring José Crespo and Lupita Tovar); *El capitán tormenta* (1936, MGM, starring Lupita Tovar and Fortunio Bonanova); *El carnaval del diablo* (1936, MGM, starring Fortunio Bonanova and Blanca de Castejón); and *Di que me quieres* (1938, RKO-Radio Pictures, costarring Eva Ortega), a Spanish-language original based on a screenplay by Francisco J. Ariza.

Miguel Ligero

(Miguel Ligero Rodríguez) Actor, born in Madrid, October 21, 1897, died in Madrid, February 26, 1968. He had numerous major supporting roles, primarily as a character actor, in Hollywood Spanish-language films including

Above: Miguel Ligero and Ana María Custodio in *¿Conoces a tu mujer?* (1931, Fox)

Doña Mentiras (1930, Cinéstudio Continental Paramount, starring Carmen Larrabeiti and Félix de Pomés); *La fiesta del diablo* (1930, Paramount, starring Carmen Larrabeiti and Tony D'Algy); *¡Salga de la cocina!* (1930, Paramount, dir. Jorge Infante, starring Roberto Rey and Amparo Miguel Ángel); *Sombras del circo* (1931, Paramount, starring Amelia Muñoz and Tony D'Algy); *Su noche de bodas* (1931, Paramount, starring Imperio Argentina and Pepe Romeu); *Hay que casar al príncipe* (1931, Fox, starring José Mojica and Conchita Montenegro); *¿Conoces a tu mujer?* (1931, Fox, starring Rafael Rivelles and Carmen Larrabeiti); *La ley del harem* (1931, Fox, starring José Mojica and Carmen Larrabeiti); *Eran trece* (1931, Fox, starring Manuel Arbó and Juan Torena); and *La vida bohemia* (1937, Columbia, starring Rosita Díaz Gimeno and Gilbert Roland).

Luis Llaneza

Actor. He had numerous supporting roles in Hollywood Spanish-language films including *Olimpia* (1930, MGM, starring José Crespo and María Alba); *El presidio* (1930, MGM, starring José Crespo and Juan de Landa); *El alma de la fiesta* (1931, MGM, starring Charley Chase and Carmen Guerrero); *Los calaveras* (1932, MGM, starring Stan Laurel and Oliver Hardy); *La señorita de Chicago* (1931, MGM, starring Charley Chase and Mona Rico); *La mujer X* (1931, MGM, dir. Carlos F. Borcosque, starring María Ladrón de Guevara and Rafael Rivelles); *Monerías* (1931, MGM, starring Charley Chase and Angelita Benítez); and *El hombre que asesinó* (1931, Paramount British, starring Rosita Moreno and Ricardo Puga).

Luis Lloréns Torres

Writer; he organized the Tropical Film Company in Puerto Rico in 1917, which produced the early film *Paloma del monte* before it ceased business with the entry of the United States into World War I.

Luis Llosa

Peruvian filmmaker. He debuted as a director in the United States with *Hour of the Assassin* (1986, starring Erik Estrada) and has also directed *Crime Zone* (1988), *Eight Hundred Leagues Down the Amazon* (1993, starring Daphne Zúñiga), *Sniper* (1993), and *The Specialist* (1994, starring Sylvester Stallone and Sharon Stone).

Gerry López

Surfer and actor, born in 1948 in Honolulu; his father is of Cuban-German descent and his mother is of Japanese descent. He was featured in *Big Wednesday* (1978) as himself, costarred in *Conan the Barbarian* (1982) as Subotai the Mongol, and appeared in *North Shore* (1987) and *Farewell to the King* (1989).

Jennifer López

Actress. She started as one of the energetic dancers, "The Fly Girls," on the TV comedy series *In Living Color* (1990-1994, Fox) and subsequently appeared in *South Central, Hotel Malibu,* and *Second Chances.* She then began a movie career, appearing in the role of the young mother in *My Family/Mi familia* (1995), followed by a supporting role in *The Money Train* (also 1995). She recently costarred opposite Robin Williams in the Francis Ford Coppola film *Jack* (1996).

Kamala López

(Also Kamala López Dawson) Actress, born in 1965 in New York City to an Indian mother and a Venezuelan father. She debuted professionally on television's *Sesame Street,* where she spent two seasons before entering Yale University. She had the female lead, Dolores, in *Born in East L.A.* (1987), appeared in *Exiled in America* (1990), about Central American refugees, and was in the TV film *Crazy from the Heart* (starring Rubén Blades) and *Dollman* (both 1991). On television, her credits include guest-star appearances on *Spenser: For Hire, Miami Vice,* and *The Cosby Show.*

Manuel López

Actor. He had roles in *Scream in the Night* (1935), *Anthony Adverse* and *Ramona* (both 1936), *For Whom the Bell Tolls* (1943), and *Maracaibo* (1958). Presumably (if this is the same actor), he was also in two musicals: a short subject,

101

Above: Jennifer López in *My Family/Mi familia* (1995)

Priscilla López

Dancer, singer, and actress, born in the Bronx, New York, February 26, 1948, and raised in New York City. She won an Obie Award and was nominated for a Tony for her performance on Broadway in *A Chorus Line,* and she won the Tony for Featured Actress in a Musical in 1980 for *A Day in Hollywood, A Night in the Ukraine.* She was in the sexist and racist film *Cheaper to Keep Her* (1980), in *Revenge of the Nerds II: Nerds in Paradise* (1987), as the beat-up proprietor of a Hispanic motel, and in *Jesse* (1988, TV film). On television, she was a regular on the series *In the Beginning* as Sister Agnes and in *Kay O'Brien* as nurse Rosa Villanueva. She has guest starred on *All in the Family, Trapper John, M.D.,* and *Family.*

Cuban Madness (1945, Universal), and, with the name Manny López, *Cha-Cha-Cha-Boom* (1956, Columbia), appearing in different musical numbers.

Perry López

Actor, born July 31, 1931, in New York City, the son of Puerto Rican parents. He went to high school in New York and attended New York University. He began his career in the theater and had his first film role under the direction of Raoul Walsh in *Battle Cry* (1954), in the role of Spanish Joe Gómez, a good marine willing to die for the colors. This was followed by *Drum Beat* (1954), *The McConnell Story* (1955), and *Mister Roberts* (1955, dir. John Ford). He was a gang tough who menaces James Dean in *Rebel Without a Cause* (1955), starred as a young ex-con in *The Steel Jungle* (1956), and costarred in *Taras Bulba* (1962). His most memorable role was as Detective Luis Escobar in *Chinatown* (1974, dir. Roman Polanski). Additional credits include *I Died a Thousand Times, Hell on Frisco Bay,* and *The Lone Ranger* (1955); *The Young Guns* (1956); *Omar Khayyam* (1957); *The Deep Six* (also 1957), as a Chicano, Al Mendoza, helping Alan Ladd fight the Japanese; *Violent Road* (1958); *Cry Tough* (1959); *Flaming Star* (1960); *Man Trap* (1961); *McLintock!* (1963); *The Rare Breed* (1966); *Daring Game, Sol Madrid,* and *Bandolero!* (all 1968); *Che!* and *Deadlock* (1969); *Kelly's Heroes* (1970); *Death Wish 4: The Crackdown* (1987); *Kinjite: Forbidden Subjects* (1989); and *The Two Jakes* (1990).

Rafael López

(Also Raphael) Actor, born in 1948. He was a juvenile actor in the 1960s, appearing in *The Young Savages* (1961), *Dime with a Halo* (1963), *The Reward* (1965), and *Trackdown* (1976).

Sal López

Mexican American actor, born November 8, 1954. He debuted in *Zoot Suit* (1981, dir. Luis Valdez), was both the Butler and Juan in Luis Valdez's *Corridos* (1987, TV film), played a young recruit in *Full Metal Jacket* (1987, dir. Stanley Kubrick), was in *Pucker Up and Bark Like a Dog* (1990), played Santana's father in *American Me* (1992), was in *The Fire Next Time* and *Return of the Living Dead III* (1993), and was El Mojado in *. . . and the earth did not swallow him* (1995).

Sylvia López

Spanish-born actress; she worked in Italian epics of the 1960s that were dubbed into English and released in the United States including *Hercules Unchained* (1960), *Herod the Great* (1961), *Son of the Red Corsair* (1963), and *The Moralist* (1964).

Trini López

(Trinidad López) Mexican American singer and actor, born in Dallas, May 15, 1937. He did not finish high school, but he was discovered by Frank Sinatra, for whose Reprise records he recorded several million-copy sellers including "If I Had a Hammer" and "La Bamba." He played himself in *Marriage on the Rocks* (1965) and *The Poppy Is Also a Flower* (1966), and he had the role of Private Pedro Ramírez in *The Dirty Dozen* (1967). Additional film credits: *Made in Paris* (1966), *The Phynx* (1970), *There Was a Crooked Man . . .* (1970), and *Antonio* (1973, dir. Claudio Guzmán).

Carlos López Moctezuma

Actor, born in Mexico City, November 19, 1909, died in Aguascalientes, Mexico, July 14, 1980. Active in the Mexican film industry, he appeared in a few European or Mexican films released in English in the United States including *The Proud and the Beautiful* (1956), *The Empty Star* (1962), *Viva María* (1965), and *The Curse of the Crying Woman* (1969).

José López Rodero

Assistant director, born November 20, 1937, in Madrid, Spain. He has worked on over 100 films, primarily in Europe. His credits as first or second assistant director include *Solomon and Sheba* (1959); *Spartacus* (1960); *King of Kings* and *El Cid* (1961); *55 Days at Peking* and *Cleopatra* (1963); *Circus World* and *The Fall of the Roman Empire* (1964); *Battle of the Bulge* (1965); *A Funny Thing Happened on the Way to the Forum* and *Return of the Seven* (1966); *How I Won the War* (1967); *Deadfall* (1968); *The Great White Hope, Land Raiders,* and *Patton* (1970); *Papillon* (1973); *The Boys from Brazil* (1978); and *Conan the Barbarian* (1982). He was associate producer of *Dune* (1984).

José López Rubio

Director and screenwriter, born in Motril, Granada, Spain, December 13, 1903. He was involved in at least 24 Hollywood Spanish-language films as the translator or adapter of English-language screenplays into Spanish, as *director de diálogos,* or in allied writing roles including *El proceso de Mary Dugan* (1931, MGM); *Mamá* (1931, Fox); *Eran trece, El caballero de la noche,* and *El último varón sobre la tierra* (all 1932, Fox); and *La vida bohemia* (1937, Columbia).

Linda Loredo

(Herlinda Loredo) Mexican American actress, born in 1908 in Los Angeles, died August 11, 1931. She did bit parts in silent films and appeared prominently in several Spanish-language Laurel and Hardy and Charley Chase comedy short subjects. In English-language productions she appeared in *Great Gobs* (1929) and *Come Clean* (1931), as Stan Laurel's wife. She had that role in most of the Laurel and Hardy Spanish-language productions, but other actresses, especially Thelma Todd, had the wife's role in the English-language originals. Her Hollywood Spanish-language film credits include *La vida nocturna* (1930, MGM, starring Stan Laurel and Oliver Hardy), a Spanish-language version of *Blotto* (1930); *¡Pobre infeliz!* (1930, MGM, starring Harry Langdon and Thelma Todd); *El jugador de golf* (1930, MGM, costarring opposite Charley Chase), a Spanish-language version of *All Teed Up* (1930, starring Charley Chase and Thelma Todd); *Radiomanía* (1930, MGM, starring Stan Laurel and Oliver Hardy), a Spanish-language version of *Hog Wild* (1930); *El alma de la fiesta* (1931, MGM, starring Charley Chase and Carmen Guerrero); *Los calaveras* (1931, MGM, starring Stan Laurel and Oliver Hardy), a Spanish-language version of *Be Big* (1930); *La señorita de Chicago* (1931, MGM, starring Charley Chase and Mona Rico); and *Politiquerías* (1931, MGM, starring Stan Laurel and Oliver Hardy).

Enrique Lucero

Actor, born in Ciudad Juárez, Mexico, 1919, died in Mexico City, May 9, 1989. He appeared in the famous Mexican film *Macario* (1961) and in several American or Mexican films released in the United States, including *Beyond All Limits* (1961); *The Bloody Vampire, Love Has Many Faces,* and *Major Dundee* (all 1965); *Guns for San Sebastian* (1968); *The Curse of the Crying Woman* and *Shark!* (1969); *Two Mules for Sister Sara* (1970); *The Woman Hunter* (1972); *The Return of a Man Called Horse* (1976); *Mr. Horn* (1979); and *The Evil That Men Do* (1984).

Laurette Luez

Actress, born in Honolulu, Hawaii, August 19, 1927. She had native Island girl, harem girl, and other exotic roles and appeared in the "Bomba" jungle boy series. Credits include *Killer Shark* and *Prehistoric Women* (both 1950), *African Treasure* (1952), *Siren of Bagdad* (1953, starring Patricia Medina), *Jungle Gents* (1954), *Fu Manchu* (1956), *Flower Drum Song* (1961), and *Ballad of a Gunfighter* (1963).

Barbara Luna

Actress, born in New York City, March 2, 1939, of mixed heritage including Spanish, Filipino, Hungarian, Italian, and Jewish. She often played ethnic roles including Latinas, Japanese Geishas, Chinese, and Island girls. She was first recognized as a child actress in the original Broadway production of *South Pacific* (1949). Her film credits include *Cry Tough* (1959), *The Devil at 4 O'Clock* (1961), *Five Weeks in a Balloon* (1962), *Dime with a Halo* (1963*), Mail Order Bride* (1964), *Synanon* and *Ship of Fools* (both 1965), *Firecreek* (1968), *Che!* (1969), *The Gatling Gun* (1972), *Gentle Savage* (1973), *The Hanged Man* (1974), and *The Concrete Jungle* (1982). On television she has appeared in over 400 series episodes and in Movies of the Week. She married actor Doug McClure.

Margarito Luna

Mexican actor; he appeared in a few American-made films and Mexican films released in English-language versions, including *One Way Street* (1950), *The Last Sunset* (1961), *The Vampire* (1968), and *Two Mules for Sister Sara* (1970).

Tito Lusiardo

Comic actor, born in San Telmo, Buenos Aires, Argentina, 1896, died in Buenos Aires, July 1982. He appeared in two Hollywood Spanish-language films: *El día que me quieras* (1935, Paramount), as Rocamora, and *Tango Bar* (1935, Paramount), as Puccini.

Julio Macat

Argentine-born cinematographer. He immigrated with his family to the United States at age 14. He shot *Home Alone* (1990) and *Only the Lonely* (1991).

Paco Madrid

(Francisco Madrid) Actor. He had a few supporting roles in Hollywood Spanish-language films including *Monseiur le Fox* (1930, MGM, starring Gilbert Roland and Rosita Ballesteros); *¡De frente, marchen!* (1930, MGM, starring Buster Keaton and Conchita Montenegro); and *Di que me quieres* (1938, RKO-Radio Pictures, starring George Lewis and Eva Ortega).

Delia Magaña

Actress, born in Mexico City, February 12, 1913, married to actor Roberto Soto. She had numerous major and a few starring parts in Hollywood Spanish-language films including *Charros, gauchos y manolas* (1930, Hollywood Spanish Pictures Co., dir. Xavier Cugat, costarring in the *cuadro mexicano* part), a Spanish-language original based on a screenplay by Xavier Cugat; *Un fotógrafo distraído* (1930, Hollywood Spanish Pictures Co., dir. Xavier Cugat, starring Romualdo Tirado and Carmen Guerrero); *Así es la vida* (1930, Sono-Art Productions, starring José Bohr and Lolita Vendrell); *El hombre malo* (1930, First National Pictures, starring Antonio Moreno and Andrés de Segurola); *Cascarrabias* (1930, Paramount, starring Ernesto Vilches and Carmen Guerrero); *Entre platos y notas* (1930, Fox, costarring "Don Catarino" and Marujita Pirrín), a Spanish-language original based on the screenplay "Waiting for Love" by Paul Pérez and Max Constant; *Desconcierto matrimonial* (1930, Fox, costarring Raoul de León), a Spanish-language original based on the short story "The Boy Friend" by Paul Pérez; *La dama atrevida* (1931, First National Pictures, starring Luana Alcañiz and Ramón Pereda); *Gente alegre* (1931, Paramount, starring Roberto Rey and Rosita Moreno); and *El proceso de Mary Dugan* (1931, MGM, starring María Ladrón de Guevara and José Crespo).

Fred Malatesta

Actor; he appeared in both English-language and Spanish-language Hollywood films in supporting roles. His English-language film credits include *All Dolled Up, Little Lord Fauntleroy,* and *The Mask* (all 1921); *White Shoulders* and *The Woman He Loved* (1922); *The Girl Who Came Back, The Man Between,* and *Refuge* (1923); *Broadway or Bust, Forbidden Paradise, Honor Among Men, The Lullaby, The Night Hawk,* and *The Reckless Age* (1924); *Without Mercy* (1925); *Bardelys the Magnificent* (1926); *The Gate Crasher* and *The Wagon Show* (1928); *The Peacock Fan* (1929); *Wings of Adventure* (1930); *Caught Cheating* (1931); *A Farewell to Arms, Get That Girl,* and *The Man from Yesterday* (1932); *Picture Brides* and *What's Your Racket* (1933); *Call It Luck, Enter Madame!, The Gay Bride, Riptide, Student Tour,* and *The Thin Man* (1934); *The Crusades, Dressed to Thrill, Fighting Shadows, Let's Live Tonight, The Lone Wolf Returns, Love Me Forever, A Night at the Opera, $1,000 a Minute,* and *Under the Pampas Moon* (1935); *Anthony Adverse, Lady of Secrets, Love on the Run, Mary of Scotland, Modern Times, Señor Jim,* and *Under Two Flags* (1936); *Beg Borrow or Steal, The Bride Wore Red, Conquest, Espionage, The Gold Racket* (as Ricardo, a Mexican flunky set up by smugglers), and *Mama Steps Out* (1937); *Artists and Models Abroad, The Black Doll, Four Men and a Prayer, I'll Give a Million, International Settlement, Port of Seven Seas, Sharpshooters, Submarine Patrol,* and *Suez* (1938); *The Arizona Wildcat, Blackwell's Island,* and *Juárez* (1939); *Argentine Nights, Down Argentine Way, The Mark of Zorro, Rangers of Fortune,* and *Road to Singapore* (1940). His Spanish-language credits include *El precio de un beso* (1930, Fox, starring José Mojica and Mona Maris); *La mujer X* (1931, MGM, dir. Carlos F. Borcosque, starring María Ladrón de Guevara and Rafael Rivelles); and *Granaderos del amor* (1934, Fox, starring Raúl Roulien and Conchita Montenegro).

Bill Maldonado

Propmaker and construction coordinator, born May 25, 1921. He supervised a number of films including *Man of the West* (1958), *Some Like It Hot* (1959), *The Great Escape* and *Kings of the Sun* (both 1963), *Hawaii* (1966), *Hour of the Gun* (1967), *Gaily, Gaily* (1969), *Fiddler on the Roof* (1971), and *The Milagro Beanfield War* (1988). He is retired.

Luis Mandoki

Director, born in Mexico, August 17, 1954. He has directed Mexican films and the following U.S. productions: *Gaby—A True Story* (1987), *White Palace* (1990), *Born*

Yesterday (1993), and *When a Man Loves a Woman* (1994, starring Andy García).

Adele Mara

(Adelaida Delgado) Actress, born April 28, 1923, in Highland Park, Michigan. She began as a singer-dancer with Xavier Cugat's orchestra and played "dark lady/other woman" parts in scores of low-budget films in the 1940s and 1950s. Credits include *Navy Blues* (1941); *Shut My Big Mouth, You Were Never Lovelier,* as Rita Hayworth's younger sister, *Alias Boston Blackie,* and *Blondie Goes to College* (1942); *Atlantic City* (1944); *The Tiger Woman, Bells of Rosarita, Girls of the Big House, Vampire's Ghost,* and *Song of Mexico* (1945); *The Catman of Paris, I've Always Loved You,* and *The Inner Circle* (1946); *Twilight on the Rio Grande, Robin Hood of Texas, Blackmail,* and *Exposed* (1947); *Campus Honeymoon, Night Time in Nevada, Wake of the Red Witch,* and *Angel in Exile* (1948); *Sands of Iwo Jima, The Avengers,* and *California Passage* (1950); *The Sea Hornet* (1951); *Count the Hours* (1953); *Back from Eternity* (1956); *Curse of the Faceless Man* (1958); and *The Big Circus* (1959).

Francisco Marán

(Also Francesco; also Francisco Morán) Actor. He appeared in supporting roles in numerous English-language films and several Hollywood Spanish-language films including the second such produced, *Sombras de gloria* (1929, Sono-Art Productions, starring José Bohr and Mona Rico). His English-language film credits include *Flying Down to Rio* (1933); *Hell in the Heavens* and *Riptide* (both 1934); *His Night Out, The Man Who Broke the Bank at Monte Carlo, The Melody Lingers On,* and *Storm Over the Andes* (1935); *Down to the Sea, The Golden Arrow, The Invisible Ray, The Rest Cure,* and *Woman Trap* (1936); *The Bride Wore Red, Conquest, Espionage, I Met Him in Paris, Madame X, Mama Steps Out,* and *Maytime* (1937); *Artists and Models Abroad, Four Men and a Prayer, The Shopworn Angel, Yellow Jack,* and *Rich Man, Poor Girl* (1938); *Beasts of Berlin, Mutiny on the Blackhawk,* and *Only Angels Have Wings* (1939); *Down Argentine Way, The Ghost Breakers,* and *The Mark of Zorro* (1940). Additional Spanish-language film credits include *Granaderos del amor* (1934, Fox, starring Raúl Roulien and Conchita Montenegro); *La buenaventura* (1934, First National Pictures, starring Enrico Caruso, Jr., and Anita Campillo); *El cantante de Nápoles* (1934, Warner, starring Enrico Caruso, Jr., and Mona Maris); *Alas sobre el Chaco* (1935, Universal, dir. Christy Cabanne, starring José Crespo and Lupita Tovar); and *No*

Above: Adele Mara and Gene Barry

matarás (1935, Hispano International Film Corporation, dir. Miguel Contreras Torres, starring Ramón Pereda and Adriana Lamar).

Margo

(Marie Marguerita Guadalupe Teresa Estela Bolado Castilla y O'Donnell) Actress, born May 10, 1918, in Mexico City, died in Pacific Palisades, California, July 17, 1985. Coached as a child by Eduardo Cansino, Rita Hayworth's father, she danced professionally with her uncle Xavier Cugat's band in Mexican nightclubs and at New York's Waldorf-Astoria, where they triumphed in introducing the rumba. After 1934 she became known as a dramatic actress, often typecast as a tragic, suffering woman. She married Eddie Albert in 1945 and is the mother of actor Eddie Albert, Jr. In 1974, she was appointed Commissioner of Social Services for the city of Los Angeles; she was deeply involved with Mexican American community issues and helped found La Plaza de la Raza, a

Above: Margo with Lou Gilbert, Anthony Quinn, and Marlon Brando in *Viva Zapata!* (1952, 20th Century-Fox, dir. Elia Kazan)

Below: Margo with Dennis O'Keefe in *The Leopard Man* (1943)

theater and cultural center in East Los Angeles. Credits include *Crime Without Passion* (1934), where she debuted as a discarded mistress; *Rumba* (1935); *The Robin Hood of Eldorado* and *Winterset* (1936); *Lost Horizon* (1937, dir. Frank Capra), in her most memorable role as a girl who ages and dies as she flees the valley of Shangri-La; *Miracle on Main Street* (1939, costarring Walter Abel); *Cat People* (1942); *Gangway for Tomorrow, The Leopard Man,* in which she plays an ill-fated "Spanish" dancer in a New Mexican town, and *Behind the Rising Sun* (all 1943); *The Falcon in Mexico* (1944); *A Bell for Adano* (1945); *Viva Zapata!* (1952); *I'll Cry Tomorrow* (1955); *From Hell to Texas* (1958); and *Who's Got the Action?* (1962). She also starred in one Hollywood Spanish-language film, the Spanish-language version of her starring role in *Miracle on Main Street,* which was entitled *El milagro de la Calle Mayor* (1939, 20th Century-Fox, costarring Arturo de Córdova).

Chinta Marín

Singer and dancer. She appeared in two American films during the wartime "Good Neighbor" period: *Mexicana* (1945, Republic) and *Rhythm of the Rhumba* (1945, Warner).

Richard "Cheech" Marín

Actor and writer, born July 13, 1946, in Watts, Los Angeles. He earned a bachelor's degree in English from California State University at Northridge. Cheech (short for *chicharrón,* deep-fried pork rinds) began in show business in 1970 as part of the comedy team "Cheech and Chong," later bringing their stoned and hippy routines (from three very successful comedy albums) to the screen with *Cheech and Chong's Up in Smoke* (1978), which was the highest grossing film of the year. Following the split-up of the duo in 1985, Marín continued to appear in films and wrote, directed, and starred in *Born in East L.A.* (1987). Film credits include *Cheech and Chong's Up in Smoke* (1978); *Cheech and Chong's Next Movie* (1980); *Cheech and Chong's Nice Dreams* (1981); *It Came from Hollywood* and *Cheech and Chong: Things Are Tough All Over* (both 1982); *Cheech and Chong: Still Smoking* and *Yellowbeard* (1983); *Cheech and Chong's the Corsican Brothers* (1984); *After Hours* (1985, dir. Martin Scorsese); *Echo Park* (1986); *Born in East L.A.* (1987); *Fatal Beauty* (starring Whoopi Goldberg, also with Rubén Blades), *Ghostbusters II, Rude Awakening, Far Out Man* (dir. and starring Thomas Chong), and *Troop Beverly Hills* (all 1989); *The Shrimp on the Barbie* (1990); *La Pastorela* (1991, PBS production, dir. Luis Valdez, starring Linda Ronstadt, also with

Above: Cheech Marín (right) and Tommy Chong in *Up In Smoke* (1978)

Paul Rodríguez, Robert Beltrán, Freddy Fender, and singer Flaco Jiménez); *Ring of the Musketeer* (1993); *A Million to Juan* (1994, starring Paul Rodríguez, also with Edward James Olmos and Rubén Blades); *Charlie's Ghost* (1994, as the ghost, also with Daphne Zúñiga); *Desperado* (1995); and *Tin Cup* (1996). He also did the voice of Tito, the streetwise chihuahua, for the Disney animated film *Oliver and Company* (1988) and provided voice in *FernGully . . . The Last Rainforest* (1992) and *The Lion King* (1994). On television he played Pancho in *The Cisco Kid* (1994, cable TV film, dir. Luis Valdez, starring Jimmy Smits), was one of the stars of the TV sitcom *The Golden Palace*, and costars opposite Don Johnson in *Nash Bridges*.

Ada Maris

Actress, born June 13, 1963, in East Los Angeles, where she was raised. She starred as Gina Cuevas, an immigrant nurse, for three seasons on the TV series *Nurses*. She costarred with Tony Orlando in a series pilot that aired as an episode of *The Cosby Show*.

Above: Cheech Marín selling illegal green cards in *Born in East L.A.* (1987)

Below: Mona Maris and Carlos Gardel, early 1930s

Mona Maris

(María Capdevielle) Actress, born November 7, 1903 [some sources have 1908], in Buenos Aires and convent-educated in France. She appeared in several British (e.g., *The Little People*, 1926) and German films before embarking upon a

Hollywood career in the late 1920s and 1930s in the usual sultry, exotic type of role. She did both English- and Spanish-language films including both versions of *One Mad Kiss* (1930, the screen debut of José Mojica, tenor for the Chicago Opera Company). Additional credits include *Romance of the Rio Grande* (1929); *Under a Texas Moon, The Arizona Kid,* and *A Devil with Women* (1930); *Seas Beneath* (1931); *The Man Called Back, South of the Rio Grande, The Passionate Plumber,* and *Once in a Lifetime* (1932); *The Death Kiss* and *Secrets* (1933); *Kiss and Make-Up* and *White Heat* (1934); *Love on the Run* (1936); *Underground, A Date with the Falcon, Flight from Destiny,* and *Law of the Tropics* (1941); *My Gal Sal, Pacific Rendezvous, I Married an Angel,* and *Berlin Correspondent* (1942); *Tampico* and *The Falcon in Mexico* (1944); *Heartbeat* and *Monsieur Beaucaire* (1946); and *The Avengers* (1950). Her numerous starring or principal Hollywood Spanish-language roles include *El precio de un beso* (1930, Fox, costarring opposite José Mojica), a Spanish-language version of *One Mad Kiss* (1930, also starring José Mojica and Antonio Moreno); *Del mismo barro* (1930, Fox, costarring Juan Torena), a Spanish-language version of *Common Clay* (1930, starring Constance Bennett and Lew Ayres); *Cuando el amor ríe* (1930, Fox, costarring opposite José Mojica), a Spanish-language version of *The Love Gambler* (1922, starring John Gilbert and Carmel Myers); *El caballero de la noche* (1932, Fox, costarring opposite José Mojica), a Spanish-language version of *Dick Turpin* (1925, starring Tom Mix and Kathleen Myers); *Una viuda romántica* (1933, Fox, costarring opposite Catalina Bárcena and Gilbert Roland), a Spanish-language original based on "El sueño de una noche de agosto" (Madrid, 1918) by Gregorio Martínez Sierra; *La melodía prohibida* (1933, Fox, costarring opposite José Mojica and Conchita Montenegro), a Spanish-language original based on a screenplay by Eve Unsell; *No dejes la puerta abierta* (1933, Fox, starring Raúl Roulien and Rosita Moreno); *Yo, tú y ella* (1933, Fox, starring Catalina Bárcena and Gilbert Roland); *Un capitán de cosacos* (1934, Fox, starring José Mojica and Rosita Moreno); *Cuesta abajo* (1934, Paramount, costarring opposite Carlos Gardel), a Spanish-language original based on a screenplay by Alfredo Le Pera; *Tres amores* (1934, Universal, starring José Crespo and Anita Campillo); *El cantante de Nápoles* (1934, Warner, costarring opposite Enrico Caruso, Jr.), a Spanish-language original based on a novel by Armon Chelieu; and *¡Asegure a su mujer!* (1934, Fox, starring Raúl Roulien and Conchita

Montenegro). She had a supporting role in the Argentine Spanish-language production *Camila* (1984, dir. María Luisa Bemberg).

María Elena Marqués

Mexican film star [see García Riera, 1988, vol. 3], born in Mexico City, 1926. She played an American Indian in two Hollywood features: *Wide Missouri* (1951) and *Ambush at Tomahawk Gap* (1952), the first opposite Clark Gable and the second opposite Ricardo Montalbán, who also played an American Indian. She costarred opposite Pedro Armendáriz in *La perla/The Pearl* (1948, dir. Emilio "El Indio" Fernández).

William Márquez

Cuban actor, born March 14, 1943. He appeared in *Deal of the Century* (1983) and has numerous television credits including *Hart to Hart, Land's End, Quincy, M.E.,* and *CHiPs.*

Christopher "Chris-Pin" Martin

(Ysabel Ponciana Chris-Pin Martín Píaz) Actor. The numerous variations on his name include Christopher Martin, Chris Martin, Chris King Martin, Chris Pin Martin, Chris-pin, and Chrispin. He was born November 19, 1893, in Tucson, Arizona, to Toro "Bull" Martin, a Yaqui Indian, and his wife Florence Morales Martin, a Mexican. He died in Montebello, California, June 27, 1953. His father returned to the Yaqui tribe at the turn of the century and is thought to have died in battle during the Mexican-Yaqui conflicts of that period. Chris-Pin had very little formal education and began in motion pictures as a runner, recruiting Mexican and Indian extras. He is best known for providing comic relief in the Cisco Kid series (as the sidekick, Pancho, opposite César Romero) and in many other Westerns. Film credits include *The Rescue* (1929); *Billy the Kid* (1930); *The Squaw Man, Lasca of the Rio Grande,* and *The Cisco Kid* (1931); *Girl Crazy, Outlaw Justice, The Painted Woman, The Stoker,* and *South of Santa Fe* (1932); *The California Trail* (1933); *Chained, Four Frightened People, Grand Canary, Lazy River, Marie Galante, The Marines Are Coming, Rawhide Mail,* and *Viva Villa* (1934); *Coronado, Escape from Devil's Island, Red Salute, Under the Pampas Moon,* and *Bordertown* (1935); *The Bold Caballero, A Tenderfoot Goes West, The Border Patrolman,* and *The Gay Desperado* (1936); *Boots and Saddles, A Star Is Born, Under Strange Flags, Wallaby Jim of the Islands,* and *Swing High, Swing Low* (1937); *Billy the Kid Returns, Flirting with Fate, Four Men and a Prayer, The Renegade*

Above: Chris-Pin Martin as Cisco Kid's sidekick (Gilbert Roland as Cisco) in *Robin Hood of Monterey* (1947, dir. Christy Cabanne)

Ranger, Too Hot to Handle, Tropic Holiday, and *The Texans* (1938); *Stagecoach, The Cisco Kid and the Lady, The Arizona Wildcat, Code of the Secret Service, Espionage Agent, The Fighting Gringo, The Girl and the Gambler, The Llano Kid, Rio, Stagecoach, Frontier Marshal,* and *The Return of the Cisco Kid* (1939); *Charter Pilot, The Gay Caballero, Viva Cisco Kid, Lucky Cisco Kid, Down Argentine Way, Charlie Chan in Panama,* and *The Mark of Zorro* (1940); *Weekend in Havana* and *Romance of the Rio Grande* (1941); *Tombstone* (1942); *The Ox-Bow Incident* (1943); *Ali Baba and the 40 Thieves* (1944); *San Antonio* (1945); *The Fugitive* and *Robin Hood of Monterey* (1947); *Mexican Hayride* (1948); *The Beautiful Blonde from Bashful Bend* (1949); and *Ride the Man Down* (1952).

Richard "Chito" Martin

(Herbert Pinney) Actor, born December 12, 1918 [PHH has 1917], in Spokane, Washington. He is generally thought to be partially of Hispanic descent, but according to R he is not Latino but grew up in a predominantly Mexican American neighborhood of Los Angeles. He is best known for the role of Chito José Bustamante Rafferty, the Mexican-Irish sidekick to Western hero Tim Holt, who did 29 films in the late 1940s and 1950s. Selected credits: *The Falcon in Danger, Tender Comrade,* and *Bombardier* (1943); *Marine Riders* (1944); *The Tonto Rim* (1947); *Guns of Hate* and *Arizona Ranger* (1948); *Mysterious Desperado, Mysterious Desperado/Rider from Tucson* (double feature), *Brothers in the Saddle, The Rustlers,* and *Riders of the Range* (1949); *Riders of the Range/Storm Over Wyoming* (double feature), *Storm Over*

Above: A Martínez in the TV series *L.A. Law*

Wyoming, Rider from Tucson, and *Dynamite Pass* (1950); *Gun Play, Gun Smugglers/Hot Lead* (double feature, 1951); *Road Agent* and *The Raiders* (1952).

A Martínez

(Adolfo Martínez III) Actor, born in California, September 27, 1948, attended UCLA. He debuted in *Born Wild* (1971), followed by a role as a Mexican American cowhand, Cimarron, in *The Cowboys* (1972, starring John Wayne). His film credits include *Once Upon a Scoundrel* and *Starbird and Sweet William* (both 1973), *Joe Panther* (1976), *Shoot the Sun Down* (1981), *Beyond the Limit* and *Walking Edge* (1983), *Born in East L.A.* (1987), *Pow Wow Highway* (1989), as a Native American activist, and *She-Devil* (1989). On television he is well known for having starred for eight years as Cruz Castillo on the TV soap opera *Santa Barbara,* for which he won a Daytime Emmy Award for Best Actor in a Daytime Drama in 1990. In the fall of 1992 he joined the television series *L.A. Law* in the role of attorney David Morales. Also on television he was in *Death Among Friends* (1975); appeared in the Chicano independent feature *Seguín* (1982, dir. Jesús Salvador Treviño, released by PBS American Playhouse); was a police detective in the TV film *Manhunt: Search for the Night Stalker* (1989); worked in *Not of this World* (1991), *Criminal Behavior* (1992), and *Deconstructing Sarah* (1994, starring Rachel Ticotin); costarred opposite

Connie Sellecca in *She Led Two Lives* (1996, TV film); and starred in *Grand Avenue* (1996, HBO, executive prod. Robert Redford, also starring Irene Bedard and Alexis Cruz). He has had many TV guest starring appearances including *Barney Miller, Quincy, M.E., Police Story,* and *The Streets of San Francisco,* and he had an important role in the miniseries *Centennial* (1978).

Alma Martínez

Actress, born March 18, 1953. She appeared in *Zoot Suit* (1981, dir. Luis Valdez), as Della, the younger sister; *Barbarosa* (1982), as Willy Nelson's daughter; *Under Fire* (1983), as a rebel disguised as a secretary; Luis Valdez's *Corridos* (1987, TV film), as Elizabeta and the Mother; and *Born in East L.A.* (1987). On television she was featured in over 50 episodes as a police sergeant in the series *Adam 12.*

Carmen Martínez

Actress, born in 1933; she appeared in *Heartbreaker* (1983) and *Fires Within* (1992) and in many television episodes.

Joaquín Martínez

Mexican actor, born November 5, 1932. He came to the United States and appeared in Moonfire (1970), and *Joe Kidd* (1972); played the title role of an Indian renegade in *Ulzana's Raid* (1972, dir. Robert Aldrich, starring Burt Lancaster); and costarred as a friendly Mexican peasant, Mauro, in *Revenge* (1990, starring Kevin Costner). He has also made numerous guest appearances on television.

Patrice Martínez

(Patrice Camhi) Actress, born June 12, 1963, in Albuquerque, New Mexico. She first appeared in film in *Convoy* (1978, dir. Sam Peckinpah), followed by *¡Three Amigos!* (1986), in the role of Carmen, and an appearance in *Beetlejuice* (1988). On television she had a major role for four seasons on the new *Zorro* series starring Duncan Regehr, and she guest starred twice on *Magnum, P.I.*

Ron Martínez

First assistant director, subsequently executive production manager, born November 17, 1943, in Santa Ana, California. He began and advanced at Universal Studios, working on *Red Sky at Morning* (1971), *Dillinger* (1973), *The Yakuza* (1975), *Walk Proud* (1979), and *Little Miss Marker* (1980). His television credits include *Quincy, M.E.* and *Little House on the*

Prairie. He is currently executive production manager for Universal Television and has been responsible for *Murder, She Wrote, Major Dad, Coach,* and *Quantum Leap.*

Tony Martínez

Puerto Rican character actor, born January 27, 1920. In addition to considerable stage experience, he had the role of Pepino the Mexican farm worker for six seasons on the 1950s television series *The Real McCoys.*

Velia Martínez

Actress. She appeared in *The Big Boodle* (1957, starring Errol Flynn and Pedro Armendáriz), a mystery set in Havana, and the exploitation film about white slavery in Tijuana, *The Devil's Sisters* (1966).

Carlos Martínez Baena

Actor, born in Madrid May 7, 1889. He had a few supporting roles in Hollywood Spanish-language films including *Un caballero de frac* (1931, Paramount, starring Roberto Rey and Gloria Guzmán); *Las luces de Buenos Aires* (1931, Paramount, starring Carlos Gardel and Sofía Bazán); *¿Cuándo te suicidas?* (1931, Paramount, dir. Manuel Romero, starring Fernando Soler and Imperio Argentina); and *El cliente seductor* (1931, Paramount, starring Maurice Chevalier and Imperio Argentina).

Jorge Martínez de Hoyos

Actor, born in Mexico City, September 25, 1920. Active in the Mexican film industry, he had supporting roles in several American or Mexican productions released in the United States including *The Magnificent Seven* (1960, Columbia); *Beyond All Limits, Gina,* and *Little Angel* (all 1961); *The Pearl of Tlayucán* (1964); *The Professionals* and *Smoky* (1966); *Guns for San Sebastian* (1968); and *The Adventurers* (1970).

Juan Martínez Pla

(Giovanni Martino) Actor. He had a number of supporting roles in Hollywood Spanish-language films including *La fruta amarga* (1931, MGM, starring Virginia Fábregas and Juan de Landa); *La mujer X* (1931, MGM, dir. Carlos F. Borcosque, starring María Ladrón de Guevara and Rafael Rivelles); *Cheri-Bibi* (1931, MGM, dir. Carlos F. Borcosque, starring Ernesto Vilches and María Ladrón de Guevara); *Primavera en otoño* (1933, Fox, starring Catalina Bárcena and Raúl Roulien); *Dos noches* (1933, Fanchon Royer

Pictures, Inc., presented by J. H. Hoffberg Co., starring José Crespo and Conchita Montenegro); *Una viuda romántica* (1933, Fox, starring Catalina Bárcena and Gilbert Roland); *La melodía prohibida* (1933, Fox, starring José Mojica and Conchita Montenegro); and *Las fronteras del amor* (1934, Fox, starring José Mojica and Rosita Moreno). He was also in the English-language production *Music in the Air* (1934).

Gregorio Martínez Sierra

Spanish film and theater director and author, born 1881, died 1947. A number of his works were adapted into Hollywood Spanish-language films, including *Mamá* (1931, Fox, dir. Benito Perojo); *Primavera en otoño* (1933, Fox); *Una viuda romántica* (1933, Fox), based on his "El sueño de una noche de agosto" (Madrid, 1918); *Yo, tú y ella* (1933, Fox), based on his "Mujer" (Madrid, 1926); *La ciudad de cartón* (1933, Fox); and *Julieta compra un hijo* (1935, Fox). In addition, he had the following credits on films not based on his own original authorial work: *El proceso de Mary Dugan* (1931, MGM), for which he did *dirección de diálogos*, and *Señora casada necesita marido* (1934, Fox), on which he was credited with *supervisión escénica.* His play *Canción de cuna* (Madrid, May 26, 1911) was adapted into an English-language film, *Cradle Song* (1933, Paramount, starring Dorothea Wieck).

Julián Mateos

(Julián Mateos Pérez) Actor, born in Robledillo de Trujillo, Spain. He had supporting roles, mostly as an evil Mexican, in American- or European-produced films including *The Unsatisfied* (1964); *Return of the Seven* (1966, starring Yul Brynner, with a large cast of Hispanics including Emilio "El Indio" Fernández, Rodolfo Acosta, and Elisa Montes); *10:30 P.M. Summer* (1966, U.S.-Spain coproduction, based on a Marguerite Duras novel); *Hellbenders* (1967); *Shalako* (1968, Brit., starring Sean Connery and Brigitte Bardot); *Three Silver Dollars* (1968, Ital.), as the menacing bandit, Hondo; *Four Rode Out* (1969, Ital.), as the Mexican outlaw who rapes the character played by Sue Lyon; *Kashmiri Run* and *Krakatoa, East of Java* (both 1969); *Ann and Eve* (1970); and *Catlow* (1971, starring Yul Brynner), in the role of Recalde.

Alfredo Mayo

(Alfredo Fernández Martínez) Actor, born in Barcelona, May 17, 1911, died in Palma de Mallorca, May 19, 1985, married to actress Amparo Rivelles. He was active in the Spanish film industry, appearing in the Carlos Saura film *La caza* (1966, released in 1967 in the United States as *The Hunt*). He had supporting roles in *The Teacher and the*

Miracle (1961), *55 Days at Peking* (1963), *Commando* and *Revolt of the Mercenaries* (both 1964), *The Hunt* and *Mission Bloody Mary* (1967), *Madigan's Millions* (1969), and *Bell from Hell* (1974).

Rachel McLish

(Rachel Elizondo) Bodybuilder and actress, born in Harlingen, Texas, to Mexican parents. She debuted in the documentary *Pumping Iron 2: The Women* (1985) and co-starred opposite Louis Gossett, Jr., in *Aces: Iron Eagles III* (1992).

Ofelia Medina

Actress. She portrayed a Chicana in *The Big Fix* (1978, starring Richard Dreyfuss) and appeared in *Diplomatic Immunity* as a Salvadoran community worker (1991, Canadian production). She also starred in the well-recognized film on Frida Kahlo, *Frida* (1984, dir. Paul Leduc).

Patricia Medina

Actress, born July 19, 1920. The daughter of a Spanish-born barrister, Laureano Medina, and an Englishwoman, Gouda Strode, she attended school in England and France. She was married to actors Joseph Cotten and Richard Greene. She appeared in *Hotel Reserve* (1944, starring James Mason) and *The Secret Heart* (1946) and has over 40 film credits including *Foxes of Harrow* (1947); *Francis* and *The Flying O'Flynn* (both 1949); *Abbott and Costello in the Foreign Legion, Francis, the Talking Mule, The Jackpot,* and *Fortunes of Captain Blood* (1950); *The Lady and the Bandit, The Magic Carpet,* and *Valentino* (1951); *Aladdin and His Lamp, Captain Pirate, Lady in the Iron Mask,* and *Desperate Search* (1952); *Plunder of the Sun, Sangaree, Siren of Bagdad,* and *Botany Bay* (1953); *Drums of Tahiti, Phantom of the Rue Morgue,* and *The Black Knight* (1954); *Pirates of Tripoli* and *Mr. Arkadin* (1955); *Miami Expose, Stranger at My Door, Uranium Boom,* and *The Beast of Hollow Mountain* (1956); *Count Your Blessings* (1959); *Snow White and the Three Stooges* (1961); *The Killing of Sister George* (1968); *Latitude Zero* (1969, Japanese production, starring Joseph Cotten and César Romero); and *The Big Push* (1975). She was on the television series *Thriller* (starring Boris Karloff) in the early 1960s.

Bill Meléndez

(José Cuauhtémoc Meléndez) Animator, born in 1917 in Mexico. He came to Hollywood in 1938 and worked on the Walt Disney production of *Fantasia* (1940). Considered a top independent animator, he has produced the *Peanuts* television specials and numerous other specials.

Tina Menard

Character actress and bit player for 50 years; she coordinated Mexican extras and bit players for *Giant* (1956). Her English-language film appearances include *The Cactus Kid* (1934), *Cheyenne Tornado* (1935), *The Traitor* (1936), *The Devil's Playground* (1937), *Daughter of Shanghai* (1938), *Another Thin Man* (1939), *The Long Voyage* (1940), *Man of the West* (1958, starring Gary Cooper), and *Dime With a Halo* (1963). She had a few supporting roles in the following Hollywood Spanish-language films: *Tres amores* (1934, Universal); *Julieta compra un hijo* (1935, Fox, starring Catalina Bárcena and Gilbert Roland); and *La vida bohemia* (1937, Columbia, starring Rosita Díaz Gimeno and Gilbert Roland).

John Mendoza

Comedian and actor, born in 1953 in New York City. A half-Puerto Rican, half-Irish stand-up comedian, he starred in the NBC situation comedy that premiered in 1993, *The Second Half.*

Víctor Manuel Mendoza

Actor, born in Tala, Jalisco, Mexico, October 19, 1913. Active in the Mexican film industry (he was in the 1951 Luis Buñuel film *Susana*), he also played a treacherous Mexican in *Garden of Evil* (1953), was a pirate in *The Black Pirates* (1954, Lippert Films, Mexican production, also featuring Alfonso Bedoya), appeared in the European production *The Proud and the Beautiful* (1956), was the loyal Mexican in *Cowboy* (1957), and was General Marcos in *The Wonderful Country* (1959, starring Robert Mitchum).

Ramón Menéndez

Cuban-born director. He studied at the American Film Institute and directed the highly recognized film *Stand and Deliver* (1988, starring Edward James Olmos and Lou Diamond Phillips). He also directed *Money for Nothing* (1993), a critical and box-office failure.

Héctor Mercado

Puerto Rican actor, born in 1953. He appeared in *Nomads* (1986) in addition to *Slow Dancing in the Big City* and *Delta Force 2: Operation Stranglehold* (both 1990).

Ricardo Mestres

Film industry executive, born in New York City, January 23, 1958, graduated from Harvard University. He started as a production assistant and became a creative executive at Paramount Pictures in 1981. He was promoted at that studio in 1982 to executive director of production, in 1984 to vice president of production, Motion Picture Group, and in 1986 became senior vice president of motion picture production, Walt Disney Pictures. In 1988, he became president of Walt Disney's Hollywood Pictures, a position he held until 1994.

Beatriz Michelena

Actress, born in New York City, February 22, 1890, died in San Francisco, October 10, 1942. She was the sister of Vera Michelena. Her picture appeared on the cover of the December 9, 1914, *New York Dramatic Mirror* and on the January 1915 issue of *Motion Picture World* with the caption, "Beatriz Michelena, Greatest and Most Beautiful Artist Now Appearing in Motion Pictures." She was in *Mrs. Wiggs of the Cabbage Patch* and *Salomy Jane* (both 1914); *The Lily of Poverty Flat, Mignon, A Phyllis of the Sierras,* and *Salvation Nell* (all 1915); *The Unwritten Law* and *The Woman Who Dared* (1916); *The Heart of Juanita, Just Squaw,* and *The Price Woman Pays* (1919); and *The Flame of Hellgate* (1920).

Vera Michelena

Actress, born June 16, 1884, died August 26, 1961, in Bayside, New York, sister of Beatriz Michelena. She was in *Driftwood* (1916) and *The Devil's Playground* (1917-18).

Lita Milán

Actress, born in New York City, 1935. She appeared in stereotypical Latina roles in such films as *The Violent Men* (1954), as the jealous Elena, *The Toughest Man Alive* (1955), *The Ride Back* (1957, costarring as a sensual Mexican opposite Anthony Quinn), *Naked in the Sun* and *Poor White Trash* (both 1957), *Never Love a Stranger* and *Girls on the Loose* (1958), *I, Mobster* (1958, dir. Roger Corman), and *The Left-Handed Gun* (1958, dir. Arthur Penn, starring Paul Newman as Billy the Kid), in the role of the seduced wife of the Kid's Mexican friend played by Martín Garralaga.

Tomás Milián

(Tomás Rodríguez) Actor, born March 3, 1937, in Havana. He immigrated to the United States in the mid-1950s. He

Above: Beatriz Michelena, William Nigh, and House Peters in *Salomy Jane* (1914, Alco)

Below: Beatriz Michelena in 1914

appeared in over 100 Italian films and worked primarily in Europe for almost 20 years, receiving the Nastro d'Argento, Italy's equivalent to an Oscar, for his role as the schoolteacher in Bernardo Bertolucci's *Luna* (1979). He costarred with Rod Steiger and Shelly Winters in Francesco Maseli's *Time of Indifference* (1965), starred in Michelangelo Antonioni's *Identification of a Woman* (1983), and starred or appeared in a number of American films including *Cat Chaser* (1989), *Revenge* and *Havana* (both 1990), and *The Burning Season* (1994, cable TV, starring Raúl Juliá, Sonia Braga, and

Edward James Olmos). Additional film credits: *Boccaccio '70* (1962, Italian production); *A Fine Pair* (1969); *Counter Punch* (1971); *Compañeros!* (1971, Ital., dir. Sergio Corbucci, starring Jack Palance); *Ripped Off* (1971); *Sonny and Jed* (1973, Ital., dir. Sergio Corbucci, costarring Telly Savalas); *Cop in Blue Jeans* (1976); *Winter Kills, Almost Human,* and *Blood and Guns* (1979); *Monsignor* (1982); *Salome* (1985); *JFK* (1991); *Nails* (1992, starring Dennis Hopper); and *The Cowboy Way* (1994, starring Woody Harrelson).

Víctor Millán

Mexican American actor, born August 1, 1920, in East Los Angeles. He served in World War II and used the GI Bill to study at UCLA. In film, he appeared in *Battle Cry* (dir. Raoul Walsh) and *Drum Beat* (both 1954), *Giant* (dir. George Stevens) and *Walk the Proud Land* (1956), *The Ride Back* (1957), *Touch of Evil* (dir. Orson Welles) and *Terror in a Texas Town* (1958), *The FBI Story* (1959), *The Pink Jungle* (1968), and *Boulevard Nights* (1979). On television, he has guest starred for over 40 years on numerous series and was a regular on *Ramar of the Jungle* and on *Broken Arrow* in the role of Taza, son of Cochise. He served for 30 years as a drama professor and was department head at Santa Monica College.

Yvette Mimieux

Actress, born January 8, 1939, of French parentage on her father's side and Mexican on her mother's. She debuted in film in 1960 in *The Time Machine* and has appeared in numerous films including *Platinum High School* and *Where the Boys Are* (both 1960); *The Four Horsemen of the Apocalypse, Light in the Piazza,* and *The Wonderful World of the Brothers Grimm* (1962); *Diamond Head* and *Toys in the Attic* (1963); *Looking for Love* (1964); *Joy in the Morning* and *The Reward* (1965); *The Caper of the Golden Bulls* and *Monkeys, Go Home!* (1967); *Dark of the Sun* and *3 in the Attic* (1968); *The Delta Factor* (1970); *The Neptune Factor* (1973); *Journey into Fear* and *Hit Lady* (1974); *Legend of Valentino* (1975); *Jackson County Jail* (1976); *Snowbeast*

(1977); *Outside Chance* and *Devil Dog: The Hound of Hell* (1978); *The Black Hole* (1979); *Forbidden Love* and *Brainwash* (1982); *Night Partners* and *Obsessive Love* (1983); *Circle of Power* (1983, also released as *Mystique*); and *The Fantasy Film Worlds of George Pal* (1985, documentary).

Aurora Miranda

Actress, born in 1918, the younger sister of Carmen Miranda. She appeared in *Phantom Lady, Brazil,* and *The Three Caballeros* (all 1944).

Carmen Miranda

(Maria Do Carmo Miranda Da Cunha) Brazilian actress, born in Marco de Canavezes, Portugal, February 9, 1904, raised and educated in Brazil, died in Beverly Hills, California, August 5, 1955. Having achieved widespread

Above: Carmen Miranda, with Groucho Marx

success in Latin America as a singer on the radio, in night-clubs, on concert tours, and in four film musicals, she came to the United States in 1939 where she debuted in the Broadway musical *The Streets of Paris*. Her first film appearance was *Down Argentine Way* (1940); it was followed by *That Night in Rio* and *Week-end in Havana* (1941); *Springtime in the Rockies* (1942); *The Gang's All Here* (1943); *Four Jills in a Jeep, Greenwich Village,* and *Something for the Boys* (all 1944); *Doll Face* (1945); *If I'm Lucky* (1946); *Copacabana* (1947); *A Date with Judy* (1948); *Nancy Goes to Rio* (1950); *Scared Stiff* (1953); and *Hollywood Goes to War* (1954, five collected shorts for the entertainment of GIs overseas). The video *Gotta Dance, Gotta Sing* (1984, a compilation of memorable dance routines from great Hollywood films) includes portions of her films. Many of the Technicolor musicals in which she appeared were part of an effort to encourage the Good Neighbor Policy between the United States and Latin America during World War II. She had many guest appearances on early television in the United States. She died of a heart attack after taping a mambo dance sequence for television's *The Jimmy Durante Show* in 1955.

Robert Miranda

Actor. His film credits include *The Untouchables* (1987), *Midnight Run* (1988), *My Blue Heaven* (1990), *Chips, the War Dog* (1990, TV film), *The Rocketeer* and *Stop! Or My Mom Will Shoot* (1991), *Sister Act* (1992), *Lost in Yonkers* (1993), and *Motorcycle Gang* (TV film) and *Monkey Trouble* (1994). He has appeared often on television and has had a recurring role on the series *Roseanne*.

Susana Miranda

Actress, born in 1949 in East Los Angeles. She made her film debut in *Flap* (1970), costarring opposite Anthony Quinn. She was a dancer on the television series *Rowan and Martin's Laugh-In* and with the José Greco Dance Company.

CARMEN MIRANDA AND HER IMITATORS

Carmen Miranda was so memorable that she was imitated and parodied by entertainers from Jerry Lewis to Mickey Rooney to Willard Scott.

Above left: Film poster for *Weekend in Havana* (1941)

Above right: Carmen Miranda

Above left: Jerry Lewis parodying Carmen Miranda in *Scared Stiff* (1953)

Above right: An actor plays a GI aping Carmen Miranda in the war film *Winged Victory* (1941).

Miroslava

(Miroslava Stern) Actress, born February 26, 1928 [PHH lists 1926], in Prague, Czechoslovakia, died in Mexico City, March 10, 1955. She and her family moved to Mexico before World War II; she entered the Mexican film industry in 1946, where she became one of the leading stars. She costarred in two Hollywood films, *The Brave Bulls* (1951), starring Mel Ferrer and Anthony Quinn, and *Stranger on Horseback* (1955). She committed suicide, allegedly as a result of an unhappy affair with the noted Spanish bullfighter Luis Miguel Dominguín.

Jorge Mistral

(Also George, Georges; Modesto Llosas Rosell) Actor and film director, born in Aldama, Valencia, Spain, November 24, 1920, died in Mexico City, April 20, 1972. He appeared in a number of Mexican films (including Luis Buñuel's Spanish-language *Wuthering Heights,* which was released in the United States with English subtitles) and a few European or U.S. coproductions released in the United States including *The Devil Made a Woman* (1962), *Love on the Riviera* (1964), and *Gunfighters of Casa Grande* and *Scheherazade* (both 1965).

José Mojica

(Francisco Mojica) Actor and tenor, born in San Miguel de Allende, Mexico, September 14, 1896, died in Lima, Peru,

Above: Carmen Miranda showing Mickey Rooney how to imitate her for *Babes on Broadway* (1941)

September 20, 1974. An opera singer, he debuted in the English-language, Hollywood-produced film musical *One Mad Kiss* (1930, Fox, costarring Mona Maris and Antonio Moreno) and its Spanish-language version *El precio de un beso* (1930, Fox, costarring Mona Maris and Antonio Moreno). He starred in numerous other Hollywood Spanish-language films including *Cuando el amor ríe* (1930, Fox, costarring Mona Maris), a Spanish-language version of *The Love Gambler* (1922, starring John Gilbert and Carmel Myers); *Hay que casar al príncipe* (1931, Fox, costarring Conchita Montenegro), a Spanish-language version of *Paid to Love* (1927, dir. Howard Hawks, starring George O'Brien and Virginia Valli); *La ley del harem* (1931, Fox, costarring Carmen Larrabeiti), a Spanish-language version of *Fazil* (1928, dir. Howard Hawks, starring Charles Farrell and Greta Nissen); *Mi último amor* (1931, Fox, costarring Ana María

Above: Miroslava with Anthony Quinn in *The Brave Bulls* (1951, Columbia)

Custodio), a Spanish-language version of *Their Mad Moment* (1931, starring Warner Baxter, Dorothy Mackaill, and ZaSu Pitts); *El caballero de la noche* (1932, Fox, costarring Mona Maris), a Spanish-language version of *Dick Turpin* (1925, starring Tom Mix and Kathleen Myers); *El rey de los gitanos* (1933, Fox, costarring Rosita Moreno), a Spanish-language original based on a screenplay by Llewellyn Hughes; *La melodía prohibida* (1933, Fox, costarring Conchita Montenegro and Mona Maris), a Spanish-language original based on a screenplay by Eve Unsell; *La cruz y la espada* (1933, Fox, costarring Anita Campillo), a Spanish-language original based on a screenplay by Miguel de Zárraga; *Un capitán de cosacos* (1934, Fox, costarring Rosita Moreno), a Spanish-language original based on a screenplay by Joaquín Artegas; and *Las fronteras del amor* (1934, Fox, costarring Rosita Moreno), a Spanish-language original based on a screenplay by Bernice Mason. He also had a minor role in the English-language film *The World Moves On* (1934).

Víctor Mojica

Puerto Rican actor, born in New York, July 15, 1940. He appeared in *Harbor Lights* (1963), *The Final Countdown* (1980), *Ghost Dance* (1983), and *Bound by Honor* (1993). His television credits include guest star roles on *Murder, She Wrote, Hill Street Blues, The Streets of San Francisco,* and *The Six Million Dollar Man.*

Above: José Mojica in *La cruz y la espada* (1933, Fox)

Alfred Molina

Actor, born in London, May 24, 1953. He appeared first in a number of British productions and subsequently in American films including *Raiders of the Lost Ark* (1981), *Ladyhawke* (starring Michelle Pfeiffer) and *Letter to Brezhnev* (both 1985), *Prick Up Your Ears* (1987), *Manifesto* (1988), *Not Without My Daughter* (1990, starring Sally Field), *Enchanted April* (1992), *The Trial* (1992, written by Harold Pinter and based on Franz Kafka's novel), *American Friends* (1993), *Maverick* and *White Fang 2: Myth of the White Wolf* (both 1994), and *The Pérez Family* and *Hideaway* (both 1995).

Ángela Molina

(Ángeles Molina) Actress, born in Madrid in 1953; her brother is singer Antonio Molina. She has appeared primarily in European productions released in the United States. Her films include *That Obscure Object of Desire* (1977, dir. Luis Buñuel); *Demons in the Garden* (1982, Spanish with English subtitles); *The Eyes, the Mouth* (1983, Italian with English subtitles); *Streets of Gold* (1986); *Camorra* (1986, dir. Lina Wertmuller), starring in the role of an ex-prostitute

on trial; *Half of Heaven* (1986, Spanish with English subtitles); and *1492: Conquest of Paradise* (1992).

Carmen Molina

Singer and dancer. She appeared in two "Good Neighbor" period films: *The Three Caballeros* and *Song of Mexico* (both 1945).

Carlos Montalbán

Actor, born March 28, 1904, died April 4, 1991, older brother of Ricardo Montalbán. He appeared in *Flying Down to Rio* (1933), *A Message to Garcia* (1936), *Love Under Fire* and *When You're in Love* (both 1937), *The Harder They Fall* (1956, starring Humphrey Bogart), *Beyond All Limits* (1961), *Love Has Many Faces* (1965), and *The Out-of-Towners* (1970, starring Jack Lemmon). He is best known in the role of the general in Woody Allen's *Bananas* (1971). He also had numerous supporting roles in Hollywood Spanish-language films including *La cruz y la espada* (1933, Fox, starring José Mojica and Anita Campillo); *Un capitán de cosacos* (1934, Fox, starring José Mojica and Rosita Moreno); *Dos más uno, dos* (1934, Fox, starring Rosita Moreno and Valentín Parera); *Tres amores* (1934, Universal, starring José Crespo and Anita Campillo); *Milagroso Hollywood* (1935, Royal Films, starring Tito Guízar and Nenette Noriega); *Rosa de Francia* (1935, Fox, starring Rosita Díaz Gimeno and Julio Peña); *El crimen de media noche* (1935, Reliable Pictures, starring Ramón Pereda and Adriana Lamar); *El carnaval del diablo* (1936, MGM, starring Fortunio Bonanova and Blanca de Castejón); *Papá soltero* (1939, Paramount, starring Tito Guízar and Amanda Varela); and *Cuando canta la ley* (1939, Paramount, starring Tito Guízar and Tana).

Ricardo Montalbán

Actor, born November 25, 1919, in Mexico City. He was brought to the United States by his older brother, Carlos, and finished high school in Hollywood. He began his career in the theater and played bit roles in several Broadway productions before debuting on the screen in Mexico in the early 1940s. He made 13 Spanish-language films in Mexico in four years and was nominated for the Ariel, the Mexican equivalent of the Oscar, for the film *Santa* (1943), in which he played a bullfighter. Subsequently, he was recruited as a "Latin Lover" type (in fact, he starred in a film titled *Latin Lovers*) by MGM in 1947, debuting opposite Esther Williams in *Fiesta* (1947). Films during this period include *On an Island with You* (1948), *Neptune's Daughter* (1949),

119

Above: Ricardo Montalbán (left) and Gilbert
Roland in *Mark of the Renegade* (1951)

Below: Ricardo Montalbán and June Allyson in
Right Cross (1950)

Above: Ricardo Montalbán in the TV series
Fantasy Island

Two Weeks with Love (1950), and *Latin Lovers* (1953).
However, he was also given an opportunity to demonstrate a
wider acting range as evidenced by several action films,
including *Battleground* (1949) and *Across the Wide Missouri*
(1951), and social problem films in which he played a troubled Latino, such as *Border Incident* (1949) and *Right Cross*
(1950). Beginning in the late 1950s and 1960s, his roles
became even more varied as in *Sayonara* (1957), where he
appeared as a Japanese Kabuki dancer, *Sweet Charity* (1969),
which he described as a "satire on a Latin Lover" [R, 449],
and *Cheyenne Autumn* (1964), where he played an American
Indian, Little Wolf. Additional film credits include *The
Kissing Bandit* (1948); *Mystery Street* (1950), as a Hispanic
police officer on Cape Cod; *Mark of the Renegade* (1951); *My
Man and I* (1952); *Sombrero* (1953); *The Saracen Blade*
(1954); *A Life in the Balance* (1955); *Three for Jamie Dawn*
and *The Queen of Babylon* (both 1956); *Let No Man Write
My Epitaph* (1960); *Desert Warrior* (1961); *Hemingway's
Adventures of a Young Man* and *The Reluctant Saint* (1962);
Rage of the Buccaneers and *Love Is a Ball* (1963); *Pirate*

Warrior (1964); *The Singing Nun* (1965); *Alice through the Looking Glass, The Money Trap,* and *Madame X* (1966); *The Longest Hundred Miles* (1967); *Iron Cowboy, Blue,* and *Sol Madrid* (1968); *Black Water Gold* and *Sweet Charity* (1969); *Escape from the Planet of the Apes, Ride to Glory,* and *The Deserter* (1971); *Fireball Forward* and *Conquest of the Planet of the Apes* (1972); *Train Robbers* (1973); *The Mark of Zorro* (1974); *Fantasy Island* (TV film that launched the series) and *Joe Panther* (1976); *Return to Fantasy Island* (1977, TV film); *Mission to Glory* (1979); *Star Trek II: The Wrath of Khan* (1982), in the role of Khan; *Cannonball Run II* (1984); and *The Naked Gun: From the Files of Police Squad!* (1988).

On television his credits include numerous made-for-television films, segments of *The Loretta Young Show, Playhouse 90, Climax, Wagon Train, Ben Casey, Riverboat, Combat, The Name of the Game,* and most importantly, his seven-year success as the mysterious Mr. Roarke on the television series *Fantasy Island.* After *Fantasy Island,* he costarred as a Greek tycoon on *The Colbys.* He won an Emmy Award for his role as Chief Satangkai in the miniseries *How the West Was Won* (1977). Montalbán has also been a strong force in Hollywood for the establishment of better opportunities for Hispanics; in 1969 he helped found a group of Hispanic actors, NOSOTROS, devoted to improving the conditions for Hispanic actors and to bettering the image of Hispanics in Hollywood films.

Johnny Monteiro

Actor. He has appeared in several films, often Filipino American productions. Credits include *Lost Battalion* (1961, U.S.-Philippine coproduction), *Back Door to Hell* and *The Kidnappers* (both 1964), and *Curse of the Vampires* (1970, U.S.-Philippine coproduction).

Conchita Montenegro

(Concepción Andrés) Actress, born September 11, 1912, in San Sebastián, Spain. A former dancer, she played "dark lady" leads in several English-language Hollywood films of the early 1930s before resuming her European film and stage career. Film credits include *The Caballero* (1930); *Strangers May Kiss, Never the Twain Shall Meet* (costarring opposite Leslie Howard as the uninhibited Latina), and *The Cisco Kid* (all 1931); *The Gay Caballero* (1932); *Laughing at Life* (1933); *Handy Andy, Caravan,* and *Hell in the Heavens* (1934); and *Insure Your Wife* (1935). She also starred in several Hollywood Spanish-language films including *¡De frente, marchen!* (1930, MGM, costarring opposite Buster Keaton), a Spanish-language version of *Doughboys* (1930, starring Buster Keaton and Sally Eilers); *Sevilla de mis amores* (1930,

Above: Conchita Montenegro and José Alcántara in *Hay que casar al príncipe* (1931, Fox)

MGM, dir. Ramón Novarro, costarring opposite Ramón Novarro), a Spanish-language version of *Call of the Flesh* (1930, starring Ramón Novarro and Dorothy Jordan); *Su última noche* (1931, MGM, costarring opposite Ernesto Vilches), a Spanish-language version of *The Gay Deceiver* (1926, starring Lew Cody and Marceline Day); *En cada puerto un amor* (1931, MGM, costarring opposite José Crespo), a Spanish-language version of *Way for a Sailor* (1930, starring John Gilbert, Wallace Beery, and Leila Hyams); *Hay que casar al príncipe* (1931, Fox, costarring opposite José Mojica), a Spanish-language version of *Paid to Love* (1927, dir. Howard Hawks, starring George O'Brien and Virginia Valli); *Marido y mujer* (1932, Fox, costarring opposite George Lewis), a Spanish-language version of *Bad Girl* (1931, dir. Frank Borzage, starring Sally Eilers and James Dunn); *Dos noches* (1933, Fanchon Royer Pictures, Inc., presented by J. H. Hoffberg Co., Inc., dir. Carlos F. Borcosque, costarring opposite José Crespo), a Spanish-language version of *Revenge at Monte Carlo* (1933, starring José Crespo and June Collyer); *La melodía prohibida* (1933, Fox, costarring opposite José Mojica), a Spanish-language original based on a screenplay by Eve Unsell; *Granaderos del amor* (1934, Fox, costarring opposite Raúl Roulien), a Spanish-language original based on a screenplay by John Reinhardt and William Kernell; and *¡Asegure a su mujer!* (1934, Fox, costarring opposite Raúl Roulien), a Spanish-language original based on a work by Julio J. Escobar.

Rosenda Monteros

Actress, born in Veracruz, Mexico, August 31, 1935. Active in the Mexican film industry (she appeared in Luis Buñuel's *Nazarín*), she also appeared in several productions, mostly multinational, released in the United States, including *The*

White Orchid (1954), as María, the murdered blackmailer; *Battle Shock* and *A Woman's Devotion* (both 1956); *Villa!* (1958); *Tiara Tahiti* (1962, British production); *The Mighty Jungle* (1964); *She* (1965, British production); *Savage Pampas* and *Cauldron of Blood* (1967); *Eve* (1968); and *Popi* (1969, starring Alan Arkin).

Cora Montes

(Corazón Montes) Actress. She starred in one and appeared in supporting roles in a few Hollywood Spanish-language films including *Monsieur le Fox* (1930, MGM); *Las campanas de Capistrano* (1930, Producciones Latinas Ltd., presented by J. H. Hoffberg Co., Inc., costarring Luis de Ibargüen), a Spanish-language original based on a screenplay by León De La Mothe; *Contra la corriente* (1935, RKO-Radio Pictures); and *De la sartén al fuego* (1935, 20th Century-Fox). She was also in *Three Blind Mice* (1938).

Elisa Montés

(Eliza Ruiz Penella) Actress, born in Granada, Spain, sister of actresses Emma and Terele Penella, married to actor Antonio Puchol. She appeared in a few European productions released in the United States including *As If It Were Raining* (1963); *Return of the Seven* (1966); *Island of the Doomed, The Cobra,* and *Man-Eater of Hydra* (all 1967); and *99 Women* (1969).

Rodolfo Montes

Producer. He coproduced with René Cardona the first Hollywood Spanish-language film, *Sombras habaneras* (1929, Hispania Talking Film Corp., presented by All-Star Exchange, starring René Cardona and Jacqueline Montes), a Spanish-language original based on a screenplay by René Nestor. He also produced two other early Hollywood Spanish-language features: *Charros, gauchos y manolas,* coproduced with Xavier Cugat (1930, Hollywood Spanish Pictures Co., dir. Xavier Cugat), a Spanish-language original based on a screenplay by Xavier Cugat, and *Un fotógrafo distraído,* coproduced with Xavier Cugat (1930, Hollywood Spanish Pictures Co., starring Romualdo Tirado and Carmen Guerrero), a Spanish-language original.

María Montez

(María África Gracia Vidal de Santos Silas) Actress, born June 6, 1912, in Barahona, Dominican Republic, died in "Les Copeaux," outside Paris, September 7, 1951. Her father was a Spanish consul and had various posts in Europe, the Canary Islands (where she went to school for several years), and Europe. One of the most notable, exotic "dark ladies," she was affectionately called "The Queen of Technicolor." She was discovered in New York and started her screen career doing bit parts in Universal films including *The Invisible Woman* and *Boss of Bullion City*

Above: María Montez in *Cobra Woman* (1944)

Above: María Montez in *Siren of Atlantis* (1947)

(both 1941). Her first major success was in the role of a jungle beauty in *South of Tahiti* (1941). Although inordinately unskilled at acting, she nevertheless became immensely popular in a string of color adventure tales, often costarring fellow exotics Jon Hall, Sabu, or Turhan Bey. During World War II, she was a favorite pin-up girl of servicemen, and she ranked with Dorothy Lamour as a glamorous, sexy star. She married French actor Jean-Pierre Aumont (her daughter is actress Tina Aumont) and moved to Europe, where she did a few French-Italian films, cutting short her American film career. She remains the object of an extensive fan cult thirsting for nostalgia and high camp. Additional film credits include *Lucky Devils, That Night in Rio, Moonlight in Hawaii,* and *Raiders of the Desert* (1941); *Arabian Nights,* in the role of Scheherazade, *Bombay Clipper,* and *The Mystery of Marie Roget* (1942); *White Savage* (1943); *Ali Baba and the Forty Thieves, Follow the Boys, Cobra Woman,* in the role of twin sisters, one good and one evil, *Gypsy Wildcat,* and *Bowery to Broadway* (all 1944); *Sudan* (1945); *Tangier* (1946); *The Exile* and *Pirates of Monterey* (1947); *Siren of Atlantis* (1948); *The Wicked City* (1950); and *Revenge of the Pirates* (1951, Italian production).

Sarita Montiel

(María Antonita Abad Fernández) Singer and actress, born March 10, 1925, in Campo de Criptana, Spain. Extremely popular in the Hispanic world (she did a considerable number of Mexican films in the early 1950s), she also appeared in several Hollywood films. She was once married to director Anthony Mann. Film credits include *That Man from Tangier* (1953), *Vera Cruz* (1954, starring Gary Cooper and Burt Lancaster), *Serenade* (1956), *Run of the Arrow* (1957), in the role of an Indian maiden, and *The Devil Made a Woman* (1962, Spanish production).

Alex P. Montoya

Character actor, born October 19, 1907, in El Paso, Texas, died September 25, 1970. He usually played badman or bandit roles. His film credits include *West to Glory* (1947), *Conquest of Cochise* and *Escape from Fort Bravo* (both 1953), *Apache Ambush,* as the Mexican Joaquín Jiroza who wants to return Texas to Mexico, and *Escape to Burma* (1955), *The Magnificent Seven* (1960), *Dangerous Charter* (1962), *Island of the Blue Dolphins* (1964), *The Flight of the Phoenix* (1965), *The Appaloosa* (1966, starring Marlon Brando), in the role of the villainous Mexican, Bizco, *The King's Pirate* (1967), and *Daring Game* (1968).

Above: Sarita Montiel in the Mexican film *Piel canela*

123

Danny Mora

Stand-up comedian and comedy writer. He began his writing career on the *Laverne and Shirley* TV series.

Hipólito Mora

Actor. He appeared in supporting roles in a few Hollywood Spanish-language films including *El último de los Vargas* (1930, Fox), *El código penal* (1931, Columbia), *¿Conoces a tu mujer?* (1931, Fox), *Esclavas de la moda* (1931, Fox), and *Soñadores de la gloria* (1932, United Artists).

Carmen Morales

Actress; she appeared as a tropical temptress in *The Long Voyage Home* (1940, dir. John Ford, starring John Wayne) and in *Primrose Path* (1940).

Esai Morales

Puerto Rican actor, born in Brooklyn, New York, October 1, 1962. He attended New York's High School of Performing Arts and began his acting career on the stage, notably in *Short Eyes*. His first film was an appearance in *Forty Deuce* (1982). He gained considerable attention as the costar in *Bad Boys* (1983, starring Sean Penn), followed by *La Bamba* (1987), in the role of Bob Morales, Ritchie Valens's half-brother. Additional film credits include *L.A. Bad* and *Rainy Day Friends* (both 1985); *The Principal* (1987), as the leading thug; *Bloodhounds of Broadway* (1989, PBS production); *Naked Tango* (1991); *Freejack* (starring Emilio Estévez) and *Ultraviolet* (1992); *In the Army Now, Rapa Nui,* as an evil Easter Islander, *The Burning Season* (TV film starring Raúl Juliá and Edward James Olmos), and *Don't Do It* (all 1994); and *My Family/Mi familia* (1995), as the brother who is shot down by the police. On television he played an Iranian opposite Burt Lancaster in the television miniseries *On Wings of Eagles* (1986) and appeared in *The Equalizer, Fame, Miami Vice,* and an Emmy Award-winning After School Special, *Great Love Experiment* (1984).

Above: Esai Morales in *La Bamba* (1987)

Jacobo Morales

Puerto Rican writer, director, and actor. He appeared in several television soap operas and theater productions in Puerto Rico and had brief roles in *Bananas* (1971, dir. Woody Allen) and *Up the Sandbox* (1972). In 1980 he directed his first film, *Dios los cría,* a satirical depiction of contemporary Puerto Rico, followed by *Nicolás y los demás* (1985). His first 35mm feature film was *Whatever Happened to Santiago* (1989), about a widower who starts a new life after retirement. It was nominated for the Best Foreign Language Film Academy Award in 1990.

Santos Morales

Puerto Rican character actor, born June 1, 1935. He appeared as a Marine drill instructor in *The Boys in Company C* (1978), in *Cannery Row* (1982), and in *Hot to Trot* (1988). He also has had numerous television appearances.

Sylvia Morales

One of the best-recognized Chicana directors. She has directed the short film *Chicana* (1979), about the changing roles of women in Hispanic/Chicano society from pre-Columbian times to the present; *Los Lobos: And A Time to Dance* (1984), a short musical special produced for PBS that profiles the musical group Los Lobos; *Esperanza* (1985), a one-hour narrative drama, directed under the Women Filmmakers Program at the American Film Institute, about a young immigrant girl whose mother is arrested and who has to cope on her own; *SIDA Is AIDS*, a one-hour video documentary for PBS broadcast in both Spanish and English; *Values: Sexuality and the Family*, a half-hour documentary on health issues affecting the Latino community broadcast in Spanish and English; and *Faith Even to the Fire*, a one-hour video documentary for PBS profiling three nuns whose conscience motivated them to speak out on issues of social justice, sexism, racism, and classism within the Catholic church. She was one of the directors of the highly regarded three-part television documentary series *A Century of Women* (1994, Turner Broadcasting System, starring Jane Fonda, Sally Field, Meryl Streep, Jessica Lange, and Glenn Close).

Francisco Morán

(Also Frank) Actor; he appeared in a few multinational films released in the United States including *King of Kings* (1961), *The Castilian* (1963, starring César Romero), *Pyro* (1964), and *The Drums of Tabu* (1967).

Antonio Moreno

(Antonio Garrido Monteagudo Moreno) Actor, born September 26, 1887, in Madrid, died in Beverly Hills, California, February 15, 1967. A dapper Latin Lover of Hollywood silent films, he began his career in 1912 under D. W. Griffith and was extremely popular during the 1920s, appearing in hundreds of films and ranking only behind Rudolph Valentino as a screen lover. He played leads opposite such actresses as Gloria Swanson, Greta Garbo, Pola Negri, and Bebe Daniels. His foreign accent limited his career in English-language talkies, where he was seen mainly in character roles. He starred in Mexico's first sound film, *Santa* (1932). Selected English-language films include *Voice of the Million, Daughters of Eve,* and *The Musketeers of Pig Alley* (all 1912); *By Man's Law, The Wedding Gown* [film held at LC, MOMA], and *The House of Discord,* (1913); *The Song of the Ghetto, His Father's House, Strongheart, Memories in Men's Souls, Politics and the Press, The Loan Shark King, In the Latin Quarter, The Peacemaker* (starring Norma Talmadge [film held at MOMA]), and *Sunshine and Shadows* (1914); *The Quality of Mercy, Love's Way, The Dust of Egypt, The Island of Regeneration, On Her Wedding Night, A Price for Folly, Youth,* and *The Gypsy Trail* (1915); *Kennedy Square, The Devil's Prize, The Shop Girl, The Supreme Temptation, The Tarantula,* and *Rose of the South* (1916); *The Magnificent Meddler, The Angel Factory, By Right of Possession, The Captain of the Gray Horse Troop, Her Right to Live, The Mark of Cain, Money Magic, A Son of the Hills,* and *Aladdin from Broadway* (1917); *The House of Hate* (serial), *The First Law, The Naulahka,* and *The House of a Thousand Candles* (1918); *The Invisible Hand* (serial) and *The Veiled Mystery* (1920); *A Guilty Conscience, The Secret of the Hills,* and *Three Sevens* (1921); *My American Wife* (1922); *The Trail of the Lonesome Pine, The Exciters, Look Your Best, The Spanish Dancer* (starring Pola Negri, also with Adolphe Menjou [film held at EH]), and *Lost and Found on a South Sea* (all 1923); *The Border Legion, Flaming Barriers, The Story Without a Name, Tiger Love,* and *Bluff* (1924); *Her Husband's Secret, Learning to Love* (starring Constance Talmadge [film held at LC]), and *One Year to Live* (1925); *Mare Nostrum, Beverly of Graustark* (starring Marion Davies [film held at LC]), *The Flaming Forest, The Temptress* (starring Greta Garbo [film held at EH]), and *Love's Blindness* (1926); and *Come to My House, It* (starring Clara Bow [film held at EH, LC]), *Madame Pompadour* (starring Dorothy Gish [film held at NFTA]), and *Venus of Venice* (1927); *Adoration, The Midnight Taxi, Nameless Men,* and *The Whip Woman* (1928); *The Air Legion, Careers, Synthetic Sin,* and *Romance of the Rio Grande* (1929); *Rough Romance* and *One Mad Kiss* (1930); *Storm Over the Andes* (1935); *The Bohemian Girl* (1936, starring Stan Laurel and Oliver Hardy); *Rose of the Rio Grande* (1938); *Ambush* (1939); *Seven Sinners* (1940); *They Met in Argentina* (1941); *Valley of the Sun* (1942); *Gaiety* (1943); *Tampico* (1944); *Notorious* (1946); *Fiesta* and *Captain from Castille* (1947); *Crisis, Saddle Tramp,* and *Dallas* (1950); *Untamed Frontier* (1952); *Thunder Bay* and *Wings of the Hawk* (1953); *Creature from the Black Lagoon* (1954); and *The Searchers* (1956).

He starred or had principal parts in at least 11 Hollywood Spanish-language films including *El cuerpo del delito* (1930, Paramount, costarring Ramón Pereda and

María Alba), a Spanish-language version of *The Benson Murder Case* (1930, starring William Powell and Natalie Moorhead); *El precio de un beso* (1930, Fox, costarring opposite José Mojica and Mona Maris), a Spanish-language version of *One Mad Kiss* (1930, starring José Mojica, Mona Maris, and Antonio Moreno); *El hombre malo* (1930, First National Pictures, costarring Andrés de Segurola), a Spanish-language version of *The Bad Man* (1930, starring Walter Huston and Dorothy Revier); *La voluntad del muerto* (1930, Universal, costarring opposite Lupita Tovar), a Spanish-language version of *The Cat Creeps* (1930, starring Helen Twelvetrees and Raymond Hackett); *Los que danzan*

SPANISH FILM SUPERSTAR ANTONIO MORENO

Antonio Moreno emigrated to Hollywood from Spain and became second only to Rudolph Valentino as a star.

Right: Antonio Moreno, Rex Ingram, Vicente Blasco Ibáñez, and Alice Terry with script of *Mare Nostrum* (1926, MGM, dir. Rex Ingram)

Below left: Antonio Moreno in 1920

Below right: Antonio Moreno and Clara Bow in *It* (1927)

Above left: Antonio Moreno (left), Gilbert Roland, and Ramón Novarro in *Crisis* (1950)

Above right: Antonio Moreno in the clutches of Greta Garbo, *The Temptress* (1926)

(1930, Warner Brothers, costarring María Alba), a Spanish-language version of *Those Who Dance* (1930, starring Monte Blue and Lila Lee); *Primavera en otoño* (1933, Fox, costarring opposite Catalina Bárcena and Raúl Roulien), a Spanish-language original based on a work by Gregorio Martínez Sierra; *La ciudad de cartón* (1933, Fox, costarring opposite Catalina Bárcena), a Spanish-language original based on a screenplay by Gregorio Martínez Sierra; *Señora casada necesita marido* (1934, Fox, costarring opposite Catalina Bárcena), a Spanish-language original based on the novel *Mi segunda mujer* by Eugenio Heltai; *¡Asegure a su mujer!* (1934, Fox, costarring opposite Raúl Roulien and Conchita Montenegro), a Spanish-language original based on a work by Julio J. Escobar; *Rosa de Francia* (1935, 20th Century-Fox, costarring opposite Rosita Díaz Gimeno and Julio Peña), a Spanish-language original based on a comedy by Eduardo Marquina and Luis Fernández Ardavín; and *Alas sobre el Chaco* (1935, Universal, dir. Christy Cabanne, costarring opposite José Crespo and Lupita Tovar), a Spanish-language version of *Storm Over the Andes* (1935, dir. Christy Cabanne, starring Jack Holt, Antonio Moreno, and Mona Barrie).

Hilda Moreno

Actress, born in Cuba. She had supporting roles in both English-language and Spanish-language films. Her English-language credits include *Law and Lawless* (1932), *Mr. Broadway* (1933), and *Old Spanish Custom* (1936, British-U.S. coproduction, starring Buster Keaton). She was in two Hollywood Spanish-language films: *El último varón sobre la tierra* (1932, Fox) and *Primavera en otoño* (1933, Fox).

José Elías Moreno

Actor, born in La Unión de San Antonio, Mexico, November 12, 1910, died in Mexico City, July 15, 1969. Active in the Mexican film industry, he appeared in a few Mexican or American films released in the United States including *Kings of the Sun* (1963, United Artists, starring Yul Brynner), *Little Red Riding Hood and the Monsters* (1965, Mexican production), *Rage* (1966, Columbia, starring Glenn Ford), and *Tom Thumb* (1967, Mexican production).

Liza Moreno

Filipina actress. She appeared in two films in 1963, both related to the Philippines: *Cry of Battle* (starring Van Heflin and Rita Moreno) and *The Raiders of Leyte Gulf.*

Paco Moreno

Actor, born in 1885, died in Beverly Hills, California, October 15, 1941. Father of Rosita Moreno (who was married to Antonio Moreno), he had an extensive career in Hollywood Spanish-language films, playing older male parts such as the doctor, the inspector, the valet, or the father. He appeared in at least 24 such films (several of them with his daughter Rosita Moreno) including *Amor audaz* (1930, Paramount, starring Adolphe Menjou and Rosita Moreno); *Cascarrabias* (1930, Paramount); *El dios del mar* (1930, Paramount, starring Ramón Pereda and Rosita Moreno); *La ley del harem* (1931, Fox), in the role of the *primer eunuco*; *El rey de los gitanos* (1933, Fox, starring José Mojica and Rosita Moreno); *La cruz y la espada* (1933, Fox), in the role of Hermano Pedro; *Piernas de seda* (1935, Fox, starring Rosita Moreno and Raúl Roulien); *El trovador de la radio* (1938, Paramount, starring Tito Guízar and Robina Duarte); *Papá soltero* (1939, Paramount, starring Tito Guízar and Amanda Varela); and *La inmaculada* (1939, United Artists, starring Fortunio Bonanova and Andrea Palma). He was in a few English-language productions including *The Devil Is a Woman* and *Storm Over the Andes* (1935); *I Met Him in Paris* (1937); *Artists and Models Abroad* (1938); *The Magnificent Fraud* (1939); and *Charter Pilot, I Want a Divorce,* and *The Mark of Zorro* (1940).

Rita Moreno

(Rosa Dolores Alverio) Actress, dancer, and singer, born December 11, 1931, in Humacao, Puerto Rico. A dancer from childhood, she reached Broadway at 13, making her theater debut in *Skydrift* (1945). She won a 1961 Academy Award as Best Supporting Actress for *West Side Story,* the first Hispanic actress to win an Oscar. Contrary to her expectations, she was only offered conventional Hispanic female roles after winning the award, roles which she refused as demeaning. Her film career in the early and mid-1960s suffered as a result, but she was active in the Broadway and London theater in those years, and her film career picked up after her highly successful role as Googie Gómez in

The Ritz on Broadway, for which she won a Tony. She has been in several films important for understanding the Hollywood depiction of Hispanics, including *The Ring* and *Popi.* She is one of a select few artists to win an Oscar, an Emmy, a Grammy, and a Tony. Film credits include *Pagan Love Song, The Toast of New Orleans,* and *So Young, So Bad,* (1950); *Singin' in the Rain* (bit part), *Ma and Pa Kettle on Vacation* (bit part), *Cattle Town,* and *The Ring* (1952); *Latin Lovers, El Alamein,* and *Fort Vengeance* (1953); *Jívaro, The Yellow Tomahawk,* and *Garden of Evil* (1954); *Seven Cities of Gold* and *Untamed* (1955); *The King and I* (in the role of Tuptim), *The Vagabond King,* and *The Lieutenant Wore Skirts* (1956); *The Deerslayer* (1957); *This Rebel Breed* (1960); *West Side Story* and *Summer and Smoke* (1961); *Samar* (1962); *Cry of Battle* (1963); *Popi, The Night of the Following Day,* and *Marlowe* (1969); *Carnal Knowledge* (1971); *The Ritz* (1976); *The Boss's Son* (1978); *Anatomy of*

Above: Rita Moreno

a Seduction (1979); *Happy Birthday, Gemini* (1980); *Evita Perón* (TV film) and *The Four Seasons* (1981); *Portrait of a Showgirl* (1982, TV film); *Age Isn't Everything* and *Life in the Food Chain* (1991); and *I Like It Like That* (1994). On television she won an Emmy for her performance in an episode of *The Rockford Files* and a second Emmy as Best Supporting Actress on a Variety Show for *The Muppet Show* (1977). She starred for two seasons (1982-83) on *9 to 5* (as Violet), played Burt Reynolds's ex-wife on *B. L. Stryker* for two seasons (1989-90), was Alixandra Stone in *Top of the Heap*, a situation comedy (1991, Fox), and played Angie Corea on *The Cosby Mysteries* (1994-95, NBC). She won a Grammy Award for her work on the record album of *The Electric Company,* a children's educational television series on which she appeared regularly.

Rosita Moreno

(Gabriela Carmen Victoria Viñolas) Actress, born in Madrid, March 18, 1905, married to Antonio Moreno, and daughter of Paco Moreno. She had one of the most extensive careers in Hollywood Spanish-language films, starring or appearing in principal roles in at least 19 films including *Amor audaz* (1930, Paramount, costarring opposite Adolphe Menjou), a Spanish-language version of *Slightly Scarlet* (1930, starring Evelyn Brent and Clive Brook); *Galas de la Paramount* (1930, Paramount, multiple directors and performers), a Spanish-language version of *Paramount on Parade* (1930); *El dios del mar* (1930, Paramount, costarring opposite Ramón Pereda), a Spanish-language version of *The Sea God* (dir. George Abbott, starring Richard Arlen and Fay Wray); *Gente alegre* (1931, Paramount, costarring opposite Roberto Rey), a Spanish-language original based on a screenplay by Henry Myers; *El príncipe gondolero* (1931, Paramount, costarring opposite Roberto Rey), a Spanish-language version of *Honeymoon Hate* (1927, starring Florence Vidor and Tullio Carminati); *El hombre que asesinó* (1931, Paramount British, costarring Ricardo Puga), a Spanish-language version of *Stamboul* (1931, starring Rosita Moreno and Warwick Ward); *El último varón sobre la tierra* (1932, Fox, costarring opposite Raúl Roulien), a Spanish-language version of *The Last Man on Earth* (starring Earle Foxe and Grace Cunard); *El rey de los gitanos* (1933, Fox, costarring opposite José Mojica), a Spanish-language original based on a screenplay by Llewellyn Hughes; *No dejes la puerta abierta* (1933, Fox, costarring opposite Raúl Roulien), a Spanish-language version of *Pleasure Cruise* (1933, starring Genevieve Tobin and Roland Young); *Yo, tú y ella* (1933, Fox, starring Catalina Bárcena and Gilbert Roland); *Un capitán de cosacos* (1934, Fox, costarring opposite José Mojica), a Spanish-language original based on a screenplay

Above: Adolph Menjou and Rosita Moreno in *Amor audaz* (1930, Paramount)

by Joaquín Artegas; *Dos más uno, dos* (1934, Fox, costarring Valentín Parera), a Spanish-language version of *Don't Marry* (1928, starring Lois Moran and Neil Hamilton); *Las fronteras del amor* (1934, Fox, costarring opposite José Mojica), a Spanish-language original based on a screenplay by Bernice Mason; *El día que me quieras* (1935, Paramount, costarring opposite Carlos Gardel), a Spanish-language original based on a screenplay by Alfredo Le Pera; *Tango Bar* (1935, Paramount, costarring opposite Carlos Gardel), a Spanish-language original based on a screenplay by Alfredo Le Pera; *Te quiero con locura* (1935, Fox, costarring Raúl Roulien), a Spanish-language original based on Pedro Muñoz Seca and Enrique García Velloso's play *La cura de reposo* (Madrid, 1927); *Piernas de seda* (1935, Fox, costarring Raúl Roulien), a Spanish-language version of *Silk Legs* (1927, starring Madge Bellamy and James Hall); *De la sartén al fuego* (1935, 20th Century-Fox, costarring Juan Torena), a Spanish-language version of *We're in the Legion Now* (1935, also released as *The Rest Cure,* starring Reginald Denny and Esther Ralston); and *Tengo fe en ti* (1940, RKO-Radio Pictures, costarring José Crespo), a Spanish-language original based on a plot by Rosita Moreno and a screenplay by John Reinhardt and Carmen Brown. She was also in a number of English-language productions including *Stamboul* (1931), *Ladies Should Listen* (1934), *The Scoundrel* (1935), and *The House of a Thousand Candles* (1936).

Rosita Moreno

Actress, born in Pachuca, Mexico [see García Riera, 1987, vol. I, 168]. She appeared in *The Santa Fe Trail* and *Her Wedding Night* (both 1930) and *Walls of Gold* (1933). In

1945, after several years working in Mexican films, she returned to the United States and did a small part in *A Medal for Benny*.

Rubén Moreno

Character actor. He usually played Indians or Mexican bandits as in the film *El Dorado* (1967) and the television series *Bonanza* and *The Big Valley*. Other film credits include *Sullivan's Empire* (1967), *Backtrack* (1969), and *Little Big Man* (1970).

Alberto Morín

(Also Albert) Character actor, born November 26, 1902, in Puerto Rico, died April 7, 1989, in Burbank, California. He moved to Europe at an early age and in the 1920s studied acting in Mexico. He moved to Hollywood in the 1930s. His credits include *Storm Over the Andes* (1935); *Nobody's Fool* (1936); *Café Metropole, Espionage, I Met Him in Paris, Mama Steps Out, One in a Million,* and *Thin Ice* (1937); *Alexander's Ragtime Band, Always Goodbye, The Girl of the Golden West, Suez, Too Hot to Handle, The Toy Wife,* and *A Trip to Paris* (1938); *Another Thin Man, Bridal Suite, Everybody's Hobby, Honolulu, It's a Wonderful World, News Is Made at Night, Outpost of the Mounties, Secret Service of the Air, Wings of the Navy,* and *Gone With the Wind* (1939); *Charlie Chan in Panama, Drums of the Desert, Earthbound, Flight Command,* and *The Lone Wolf Keeps a Date* (1940); *Casablanca* (1942); *Rio Grande* (1949, dir. John Ford, starring John Wayne), as a friendly Mexican lieutenant; *It's Only Your Money* (1962); *Fun in Acapulco* (1963); *For Those Who Think Young* (1964); *Hellfighters* (1968); *Backtrack* (1969); *The Cheyenne Social Club, Chisum,* and *Two Mules for Sister Sara* (1970); and *The Milagro Beanfield War* (1988, dir. Robert Redford). On television he appeared in numerous series including *Hopalong Cassidy, I Love Lucy,* and *The Jack Benny Show*.

Elvira Morla

Actress. She had one starring and a few supporting roles in Hollywood Spanish-language films including *Olimpia* (1930, MGM, starring José Crespo and María Alba); *La llama sagrada* (1931, Warner, in a starring role, with Martín Garralaga costarring), a Spanish-language version of *The Sacred Flame* (1929, dir. Archie L. Mayo, starring Pauline Frederick and Conrad Nagel); *La fruta amarga* (1931, MGM, starring Virginia Fábregas and Juan de Landa); *El proceso de Mary Dugan* (1931, MGM, starring María Ladrón de Guevara and José Crespo); and *Mi último amor* (1931, Fox, starring José Mojica and Ana María Custodio).

Above: Elvira Morla, José Crespo, and Carmen Rodríguez in *Olimpia* (1930, MGM)

Michael Moroff

(Also Mike) Mexican American character actor. He appeared in *La Bamba* (1987), *Angel Town* and *The Cage* (both 1989), and had the role of Pancho Villa in a TV episode of *The Young Indiana Jones Chronicles*.

Bob Morones

Production professional, born January 6, 1943. He was casting director and associate producer for *Salvador* (1986) and casting director for Academy Award-winning *Platoon* (1986, dir. Oliver Stone) and *American Me* (1992, dir. Edward James Olmos).

Movita

(Also other variations; María Luisa Castañeda) Mexican American actress, born April 12, 1916, in Nogales, Arizona, married at one time to Marlon Brando. She has used a number of variations on her name including María Luisa Castañeda, Mawita Castaneda, and Movita Castañeda. She made her film debut in *Flying Down to Rio* (1933), followed by the role of a native girl in the MGM production of *Mutiny on the Bounty* (1935, starring Clark Gable and Charles Laughton). Other English-language film credits include *The Tia Juana Kid* and *Captain Calamity* (both 1936); *The*

Hurricane (dir. John Ford), again as a native island girl, and *Paradise Isle* (1937); *Rose of the Rio Grande* (1938); *Girl From Rio* and *Wolf Call* (1939); *The Tower of Terror* (1942); *Fort Apache* (1948); *Red Light* (1949); *Kim* and *Wagon Master* (1950); *Saddle Legion* (1951); *Last of the Comanches* (1952); *Dream Wife* (1953, starring Cary Grant); and *Panic in Echo Park* (1977). She also starred in one and appeared in supporting roles in several Hollywood Spanish-language films including *La buenaventura* (1934, First National Pictures, starring Enrico Caruso, Jr., and Anita Campillo); *Tres amores* (1934,

Above: Movita with Clark Gable in *Mutiny on the Bounty* (1935)

Below: Movita and Ramón Pereda in *El diablo del mar* (1935)

Universal, starring José Crespo and Anita Campillo); *Señora casada necesita marido* (1934, Fox, starring Catalina Bárcena and Antonio Moreno); *El diablo del mar* (1935, Theater Classic Pictures, dir. Juan Duval, costarring opposite Ramón Pereda), a Spanish-language version of *Devil Monster* (1935, starring Jack del Rio, Blanche Mehaffey, and Barry Norton); and *El capitán tormenta* (1936, MGM, starring Lupita Tovar and Fortunio Bonanova).

Amelia Muñoz

Spanish actress, born in 1909, died in 1930 in Paris while working on Spanish director Benito Perojo's *Lo mejor es reír,* which was completed by Imperio Argentina. She was the daughter of actor Alfonso Muñoz and sister of actress Pilar Muñoz. She had two supporting roles in Hollywood Spanish-language films and then starred in *Sombras del circo* (which was completed in November 1930 and premiered posthumously). Her Hollywood credits are *Un hombre de suerte* (1930, Cinéstudio Continental Paramount, dir. Benito Perojo, starring Roberto Rey and María Luz Callejo); *La fiesta del diablo* (1930, Paramount, starring Carmen Larrabeiti and Tony D'Algy); and *Sombras del circo* (1931, Paramount, costarring Tony D'Algy and Félix de Pomés), a Spanish-language version of *Half-way to Heaven* (1929, dir. George Abbott, starring Jean Arthur and Charles "Buddy" Rogers).

Ramón Muñoz

Actor. He appeared in supporting roles in several Hollywood Spanish-language films including *La jaula de los leones* (1930, Producciones Ci-Ti-Go, presented by J. H. Hoffberg Co., Inc., starring Romualdo Tirado and Matilde Liñán); *Tres amores* (1934, Universal); *El diablo del*

mar (1935, Theater Classic Pictures, dir. Juan Duval, starring Ramón Pereda and Movita); *Te quiero con locura* (1935, 20th Century-Fox); and *El crimen de media noche* (1935, Reliable Pictures, starring Ramón Pereda and Adriana Lamar).

Corrina Mura

(Corrina Wall) Actress and singer, born in San Antonio, Texas, in 1910, died in Mexico City, August 1, 1965. She had the role of Andrea, the French singer at Rick's Café, in *Casablanca* (1942, starring Humphrey Bogart and Ingrid Bergman), and she was also in *Call Out the Marines* (1942).

Karmin Murcelo

Cuban-born actress. She appeared in *Walk Proud* (1979), *Borderline* (costarring opposite Charles Bronson) and *Stir Crazy* (both 1980), *The Big Score* (1983), *Seduced* (1985), *Revenge* (1990), and *Bound by Honor* (1993). She has appeared in numerous television series episodes, in the miniseries *Centennial,* and in the made-for-television movie *The Blue Knight* (1973).

Carlos Múzquiz

Actor, born in 1905, died in Mexico City, February 1960. Active in the Mexican film industry, he also appeared in *The Black Scorpion* (1956), as a Mexican scientist helping to beat the giant beast, and in *Ten Days to Tulara* (1958, starring Sterling Hayden).

Rick Nájera

Writer and comic, one of the founders of the comedy troupe Latins Anonymous; he has worked as a writer on Fox's *In Living Color.*

Gregory Nava

Director and writer, born in San Diego, April 10, 1949, a graduate of UCLA film school. He is known for his outstanding film *El Norte* (1983, independent production associated with American Playhouse), which he directed and also coauthored with his wife, Anna Thomas, about Guatemalan Indians who flee oppression, seeking but not finding comfort in the United States. Subsequently he directed *A Time of Destiny* (1988, starring William Hurt and Timothy Hutton), a revenge film that was not well received, and *My Family/Mi familia* (1994, starring Jimmy Smits), a successful evocation of three generations of Mexican Americans in Los Angeles. He directed and again coauthored the script of *My Family* with Anna Thomas.

Carlos Navarro

(Also Carlos de Navarro) Actor and director, died in Mexico City, February 12, 1969. Active in the Mexican film industry, he appeared in *The Brave One* (1956, for which an Academy Award for Best Original Story went to "Robert Rich," a pseudonym for blacklisted Dalton Trumbo, who did not claim it until 1975), and *The Empty Star* (1962). He directed the notable Mexican film *Janitzio* (1934).

Mario Navarro

Actor; he appeared as the child, Juanito, in *The Black Scorpion* (1957) and was also in *Geronimo* (1962).

Ralph Navarro

(Rafael Navarro) Actor. He appeared in at least 16 Hollywood Spanish-language films including *El cuerpo del delito* (1930, Paramount); *Monsieur le Fox* (1930, MGM), as the sergeant; *Don Juan diplomático* (1931, Universal, dir.

George Melford), as Emilio, secretary to the marquis; *Del infierno al cielo* (1931, Fox, costarring opposite Juan Torena and María Alba), a Spanish-language version of *The Man Who Came Back* (1931, dir. Raoul Walsh, starring Janet Gaynor, Charles Farrell, and William Holden); *Esclavas de la moda* (1931, Fox); *La ley del harem* (1931, Fox, starring José Mojica and Carmen Larrabeiti); *Mamá* (1931, Fox, dir. Benito Perojo, starring Catalina Bárcena and Rafael Rivelles); and *Tres Amores* (1934, Universal), as the lawyer.

Taylor Negrón

Actor and comedian of Puerto Rican and Italian heritage, born in Glendale, California, August 1, year unknown. He has often appeared as an oversexed Latino youth. He debuted in *Young Doctors in Love* (1982), playing a love-struck intern, and appeared in *Fast Times at Ridgemont High* (1982); *Easy Money* (1983), as Rodney Dangerfield's Puerto Rican son-in-law; *Bad Medicine* and *Better Off Dead* (both 1985); *Punchline* (1988); *The Last Boy Scout,* as a psychotic hitman, and *Nothing But Trouble* (both 1991); *Mr. Jones* (1993); and *Angels in the Outfield* and *Inevitable Grace* (1994). On television he was in the situation comedies *Detective School* (1979, ABC) and *Frannie's Turn* (1992, CBS).

José Nieto

(José García Nieto) Actor, born in Murcia, Spain, May 3, 1902, died in Matalascañas, Huelva, Spain, August 8, 1982. He began in Hollywood Spanish-language films but went on to appear in numerous English-language productions. He had one costarring and a few other principal or supporting roles in Hollywood Spanish-language films including *Cuerpo y alma* (1931, Fox, starring George Lewis and Ana María Custodio); *Eran trece* and *Mamá* (both 1931, Fox); *Marido y mujer* (1932, Fox, costarring opposite George Lewis and Conchita Montenegro), a Spanish-language version of *Bad Girl* (1931, dir. Frank Borzage, starring Sally Eilers and James Dunn); and *Tango Bar* (1935, Paramount). His English-language credits, many of them supporting roles in films that were produced multinationally and released in the United States, include the following: *Three Blind Mice* (1938); *King of Kings* and *The Revolt of the Slaves* (both 1961); *The Savage Guns* (1962); *As If It Were Raining* (1963, also with Elisa Montes); *The Ceremony* and *55 Days at Peking* (1964); *The Son of Captain Blood* and *Doctor Zhivago* (1965); *Kid Rodelo* (1966); *Falstaff, Flame Over Vietnam, The Hellbenders,* and *Savage Pampas* (1967); and *The Young Rebel* (1969).

Above: José Nieto with Catalina Bárcena in
Mamá (1931, Fox, dir. Benito Perojo)

Marcela Nivón

Actress. She had a few supporting roles in Hollywood
Spanish-language films including *Así es la vida* (1930, Sono-
Art Productions, Ltd.); *Wu Li Chang* (1930, MGM, starring
Ernesto Vilches and Angelita Benítez); *Oriente y occidente*
(1930, Universal, dir. George Melford, starring Lupe Vélez
and Barry Norton); and *La buenaventura* (1934, First
National Pictures).

Eduardo Noriega

Actor, born in Mexico City, 1918. Active in the Mexican
film industry, he also appeared in a number of productions,
many multinational, that were released in the United
States, including *Honeymoon* (1947, starring Shirley
Temple), *El Paso* (1949), *Captain Scarlett* (1953), *Seven
Cities of Gold* and *Hell's Island* (both 1955), *The Beast of
Hollow Mountain* (1956, U.S.-Mexican production, star-
ring Patricia Medina), *The Last Rebel* (1961), *Geronimo*
(1962), *Of Love and Desire* (1963), and *Tarzan and the
Valley of Gold* (1966).

Manuel Noriega

Actor and film director, born in 1880, died in Mexico City,
August 12, 1961. He appeared in supporting roles in three
Hollywood Spanish-language films: *Dos noches* (1933,
Fanchon Royer Pictures, presented by J. H. Hoffberg Co.,
Inc.); *No dejes la puerta abierta* (1933, Fox), as the barber;
and *Yo, tú y ella* (1933, Fox).

Nenette Noriega

Actress and songwriter. She had one costarring and one supporting role in the following Hollywood Spanish-language
films: *Te quiero con locura* (1935, Fox) and *Milagroso
Hollywood* (1935, Royal Films, costarring opposite Tito
Guízar), a Spanish-language original based on a screenplay by
Raúl Gurruchaga. She composed lyrics for several Hollywood
Tito Guízar vehicles during the Spanish-language production
period. She also composed songs for *Saint Louis Blues* (1939),
in which Tito Guízar appeared.

Barry Norton

(Alfredo Birabén) Actor, born June 16, 1905, in Buenos
Aires, died in Hollywood, California, August 24, 1956. A
romantic lead of late silent and early Hollywood films, he
later appeared in Hollywood-made Spanish-language or
Mexican productions, sometimes directing his own films.
Film credits include *The Lily, What Price Glory* (starring
Victor McLaglen and Dolores del Río), and *The Canyon of
Light* (all 1926); *Ankles Preferred, The Wizard, The Heart of
Salome,* and *Sunrise—A Song of Two Humans* (1927); *Mother
Knows Best, Fleetwing, Sins of the Fathers,* and *Legion of the
Condemned* (1928); *Four Devils* and *The Exalted Flapper*
(1929); *Dishonored* (1931); *Cocktail Hour, Luxury Liner,
Only Yesterday,* and *Lady for a Day* (1933); *Grand Canary,
Imitation of Life, Let's Be Ritzy, Unknown Blonde, The World
Moves On,* and *Nana* (1934); *Anna Karénina, Devil Monster,*
and *Storm Over the Andes* (1935); *The Criminal Within,
Captain Calamity,* and *Murder at Glen Athol* (1936); *History
Is Made at Night, I'll Take Romance, Rich Relations, She's
Dangerous,* and *Timberesque* (1937); *The Buccaneer* (1938);
Should Husbands Work? (1939); and *Around the World in 80
Days* (1956, cameo). He starred or had principal roles in at
least 14 Hollywood Spanish-language films including *El
cuerpo del delito* (1930, Paramount, starring Antonio Moreno
and Ramón Pereda); *Amor audaz* (1930, Paramount);
Cascarrabias (1930, Paramount, costarring opposite Ernesto
Vilches and Carmen Guerrero), a Spanish-language version
of *Grumpy* (1930, dir. George Cukor and Cyril Gardner,

Above: Barry Norton in 1927

his earliest movies he used the name Ramón Samaniegos. A romantic idol of Hollywood silents of the 1920s, he began as a singing waiter and vaudeville performer before breaking into films as an extra in 1917. By 1922 he had become a star "Latin Lover" but was overshadowed by Valentino in that role; he soon sought a broader range and less exotic image, and later he did character parts. His most famous part was the title role of the 1925 *Ben-Hur.* He was found beaten to death by intruders on October 31, 1968. Selected English-language films: *A Small Town Idol* (1921); *Eyes of Turpin Are Upon You!* (a currently marketed videotape consisting of two Ben Turpin comedies, *Idle Eyes* and *A Small Town Idol*), *Mr. Barnes of New York* (billed as Ramón Samaniegos), *The Prisoner of Zenda* (dir. Rex Ingram, billed as Ramón Samaniegos), and *Trifling Women* (all 1922); *Scaramouche* [film held at EH] and *Where the Pavement Ends* (1923); *The Arab* [film held at CR], *Thy Name Is Woman* [film held at EH], and *The Red Lily* (1924); *The Midshipman* [film held at EH], *Ben-Hur* (dir. Fred Niblo [film held at CF, EH]); and *A Lover's Oath* (1925); *The Student Prince in Old Heidelberg* [film held at CF, EH, MOMA], *The Road to Romance,* and *Lovers?* (1927); *A Certain Young Man, Across to Singapore,* and *Forbidden Hours* (1928); *Devil-May-Care, The Flying Fleet,* and *The Pagan* (1929); *In Gay Madrid* and *Call of the Flesh* (1930); *Son of India, Mata Hari* (costarring opposite Greta Garbo), and *Daybreak* (1931); *Huddle* and *The Son-Daughter* (1932); *The Barbarian* (1933); *The Cat and the Fiddle* and *Laughing Boy* (1934); *The Night Is Young* (1935); *The Sheik Steps Out* (1937); *A Desperate Adventure* (1938); *We Were Strangers* (dir. John Huston) and *The Big Steal* (1949); *The Outriders* and *Crisis* (1950); and *Heller in Pink Tights* (1960). During the Hollywood Spanish-language period he directed and starred in *Sevilla de mis amores* (1930, MGM, costarring Conchita Montenegro), a Spanish-language version of *Call of the Flesh* (1930, starring Ramón Novarro and Dorothy Jordan); and he directed, produced, and wrote the screenplay for *Contra la corriente* (1935, RKO-Radio Pictures, starring Luana Alcañiz and José Caraballo), a Spanish-language original.

starring Cyril Maude and Phillips Holmes); *Oriente y occidente* (1930, Universal, dir. George Melford, costarring opposite Lupe Vélez), a Spanish-language version of *East Is West* (1930, dir. Monta Bell, starring Lupe Vélez, Lew Ayres, and Edward G. Robinson); *Drácula* (1931, Universal, dir. George Melford, costarring in the role of Juan Harker opposite Carlos Villarías and Lupita Tovar), a Spanish-language version of *Dracula* (1931, starring Bela Lugosi, David Manners, and Helen Chandler); *El código penal* (1931, Columbia, in a starring role, with María Alba costarring), a Spanish-language version of *The Criminal Code* (1931, dir. Howard Hawks, starring Walter Huston and Constance Cummings); *El comediante* (1931, Paramount); *El pasado acusa* (1931, Columbia, costarring opposite Luana Alcañiz), a Spanish-language version of *The Good Bad Girl* (1931, starring Marie Prevost and James Hall); *El diablo del mar* (1935, Theater Classic Pictures), in the role of Roberto; *Alas sobre el Chaco* (1935, Universal), in the role of Pablo Díaz; *El capitán tormenta* (1936, MGM), in the role of Karl; *El trovador de la radio* (1938, Paramount), in the role of *el reportero;* and *Papá soltero* (1939, Paramount), in the role of Ricardo.

Ramón Novarro

(José Ramón Gil Samaniegos) Actor and film director, born February 6, 1899, in Durango, Mexico, died in Hollywood Hills, California, October 31, 1968. In a few of

Jay Novello

Actor, born August 22, 1904, died in North Hollywood, California, September 2, 1982. He had numerous supporting roles, usually cast as a Hispanic or other exotic. Credits include *Boys Town, Flirting with Fate,* and *Tenth Avenue Kid* (1938); *Calling All Marines* and *Sergeant Madden* (1939); *The Border Legion,* as the bad bandit opposed to Roy Rogers, the good-bad bandit, *Colorado, Girl from Havana,* as Manuel, the loyal, doomed Hispanic, and *The Devil's*

Pipeline (1940); *The Great Train Robbery, Robin Hood of the Pecos, Two Gun Sheriff,* as Albo, the truly evil bandit, and *Sheriff of Tombstone* (1941); *King of the Mounties* (1942, Republic, 12-episode serial featuring Duncan Renaldo and Jay Novello); *Mystery of the River Boat* (1944, Universal, 13-episode serial); *Perilous Holiday* (1946); *Smuggler's Island* (1951), as the loyal sidekick, Espinosa; *Captain Pirate* (1952), as a Spanish villain; *The Miracle of Our Lady of Fatima* (also 1952, starring Gilbert Roland); *Sabaka* (1953); *The Prodigal* (1955); *Lisbon* (1956); *This Rebel Breed* (1960); *Atlantis, the Lost Continent* and *Pocketful of Miracles* (1961); *Escape from Zahrain* (1962); *The Man from the Diners' Club* (1963); *The Art of Love, A Very Special Favor, Sylvia,* and *Harum Scarum* (1965); *What Did You Do in the War, Daddy?* (1966); *The Caper of the Golden Bulls* (1967); and *The Comic* (1969).

Danny Núñez

Character actor and bit player. He appeared in *Viva Zapata!* (1952), *The Professionals* (1966), *Close Encounters of the Third Kind* (1977), and *The Legend of the Lone Ranger* (1981). He has numerous television credits dating from the 1950s.

THE ALL-TIME MOST POPULAR MEXICAN ACTOR IN HOLLYWOOD: RAMÓN NOVARRO

Ramón Novarro stands as Hollywood's most popular actor from Mexico. He vied with Rudolph Valentino and Antonio Moreno as a Latin Lover.

Above: Cover of sheet music for *Devil May Care* (1929), starring Ramón Novarro

Left: Ramón Novarro in 1930

Above left: Ramón Novarro in *Ben Hur* (1926)

Above right: Ramón Novarro in 1923

Below left: Ramón Novarro and Barbara La Marr in *The Prisoner of Zenda* (1922, Metro)

Below right: Ramón Novarro and Greta Garbo in *Mata Hari* (1932)

Above left: Ramón Novarro and Alice Terry in *Where the Pavement Ends* (1923, Metro, dir. Rex Ingram)

Above right: Ramón Novarro and Myrna Loy in *The Barbarian* (1933)

Below left: Ramón Novarro and Joan Crawford in *Across to Singapore* (1928)

Below right: Ramón Novarro and Barbara La Marr in *Trifling Women* (1922, Metro, dir. Rex Ingram)

Maria O'Brien

Daughter of actor Edmond O'Brien and actress Olga San Juan, born in 1950. She appeared in *Smile* (1975) as an aggressive beauty pageant contestant attempting to capitalize on her Mexican American heritage and was also in *Escort Girls* (1974), *Promised a Miracle* (1988, TV film), and *In a Stranger's Hand* (1992, TV film).

Manuel Ojeda

(Also Michael R.) Mexican actor. He worked in the Mexican film industry and also appeared in the following American productions: *The Law of the North* (1918); *The Man Who Turned White* and *Rustling a Bride* (both 1919); and *A Double Dyed Deceiver, Pinto,* and *The Scuttlers* (1920). A Manuel R. Ojeda, presumably the same actor, appeared in *The Last Rebel* (1961) and *The Queen's Swordsman* (1963).

Juan Olaguibel

Actor. He appeared in a few European productions released in the United States including *The Ceremony* (1963, starring Lawrence Harvey), *Kid Rodelo* (1966, costarring Janet Leigh), *House of a Thousand Dolls* (1967, starring Vincent Price in a white slavers vehicle set in Tangiers), and *God Forgives—I Don't* (1969, a Western).

Edward James Olmos

Mexican American actor, composer, producer, and director, born February 21, 1946 [PHH has February 24, 1947], in East Los Angeles, graduated from Montebello High School, and attended East Los Angeles Community College and California State University. Olmos began his career as a rock singer and subsequently became an actor in small theater productions and as a bit player on television. He debuted on film in *aloha, bobby and rose* (1975) in a bit part. He auditioned for and won the role of El Pachuco in Luis Valdez's musical play *Zoot Suit*, which opened in 1978 and was a great success. He earned a Los Angeles Drama Critics Circle Award for his performance in *Zoot Suit,* which he reprised on Broadway and in the 1981 film version. He became nationally known as Lt. Castillo on TV's *Miami Vice* (1984-89), for which he won an Emmy Award as Best Supporting Actor in a Continuing Drama Series. He was nominated for a Best Actor Oscar for his lead role as a committed Latino teacher of calculus to East Los Angeles high school students in *Stand and Deliver* (1988). The film also helped propel him to the cover of *Time* magazine, perhaps the only Chicano to have attained that sort of recognition. Having directed an episode of *Miami Vice* years earlier, he debuted as a film director in *American Me* (1992), which he also starred in and produced, a film that evokes gang life in Los Angeles. Additional film credits include *Alambrista!* (1977, dir. Robert M. Young), *Virus* (1980), *Wolfen* (1981), as an American Indian high-beam steelworker, *Blade Runner* (1982), as a police detective, *The Ballad of Gregorio Cortez* (1982, dir. Robert M. Young), *Saving Grace* (1986), *Triumph of the Spirit* (1989), *Maria's Story* (1990), *A Talent for the Game* (1991), *A Million to Juan* (1993), *Roosters* (1995, dir. Robert M. Young), as an ex-con and breeder of fighting cocks, and *My Family/Mi familia* (1995). On television, in addition to *Miami Vice,* he has made guest appearances on *Police Story* and *Hawaii Five-O,* appeared in *Evening in Byzantium* (1978), costarred with Tony Orlando and Pepe Serna in the made-for-television film *Three Hundred Miles for Stephanie* (1981), played General Santa Anna in *Seguín* (1982, dir. Jesús Salvador Treviño, released through PBS's American Playhouse), had a role in *The Nightingale* (1983, a Faerie Tale Theater production, starring Mick Jagger and Barbara Hershey), costarred in the miniseries based on Mario Puzo's *The Fortunate Pilgrim* (1988), costarred in *Menéndez: A Killing in Beverly Hills* (1994, CBS), appeared in *The Burning Season* (1994), and starred in *The Limbic Region* (1996, TV film).

Lupe Ontiveros

Mexican American character actress. She has appeared in *Zoot Suit* (1981), *The Border* and *El Norte* (both 1982), *The Goonies* (1985), *Born in East L.A.* (1987), *My Family/Mi familia* (1995), and *. . . and the earth did not swallow him* (1995), as the baker's deceitful wife. She has numerous television and stage credits.

Tony Orlando

(Michael Anthony Orlando Cassevitis) Singer, songwriter, and actor of Puerto Rican and Greek heritage, born April 12,

Above: Lupe Ontiveros (top row, second from right) with (top row, left to right) Constance Marie, Elpidia Carrillo, Jimmy Smits, Enrique Castillo, (bottom row, left to right) Edward James Olmos, Jenny Gago, and Eduardo López Rojas in *My Family/Mi familia* (1995)

1944, in New York City. He hosted his own musical variety show on television, *Tony Orlando and Dawn,* starred in the television film *Three Hundred Miles for Stephanie* (1981) as a Mexican American police officer, costarred opposite Sondra Locke in *Rosie: The Rosemary Clooney Story* (1982, TV film), and appeared on several episodes of *The Cosby Show* as a social worker.

Francisco Ortega

Actor. He appeared in two films set on the Mexican coast: *The Third Voice* (1960, 20th Century-Fox, starring Edmond O'Brien, with Olga San Juan playing a blonde prostitute) and *Fun in Acapulco* (1963, starring Elvis Presley).

Kenny Ortega

Choreographer and director, born in Palo Alto, California, to Spanish parents. He has become one of the foremost choreographers for modern popular music. On film his first work was on *The Rose* (1979, starring Bette Midler), followed by contributing to the choreography of *Xanadu* (1980, starring Olivia Newton-John and Gene Kelly). He was the choreographer for *One From the Heart* (1982), *St. Elmo's Fire* (1985), *Ferris Bueller's Day Off* and *Pretty in Pink* (1986), *Dirty Dancing* (1987), and *Salsa* (1989). On television he directed the short-lived series *Dirty Dancing* (1988) and *Hull High* (1990), and he has directed two feature films, a television musical, *Newsies* (1992), and *Hocus Pocus* (1993, starring Bette Midler).

Sophie Ortega

(Also Sophia Ortiga, Sophia Artega) Actress. She appeared in *Revenge* (1928, starring Dolores del Río), *Sadie Thompson* (1928), and played an old native woman in *Bird of Paradise* (1932, starring Dolores del Río).

Art Ortego

(Also Ortega and many other variations) Actor and stunt-man, born in California, February 9, 1890, died July 24, 1960. Other variations on his name include Artie, Arthur, and Art Artego. In his long career he played mostly stereotypical desperados and bandits. He appeared in numerous films without being officially listed. Ortego was married to Mona Darkfeather, with whom he appeared in several films early in his career. Credits include *The Vengeance of the Skystone* (1913, 101 Bison, dir. Frank E. Montgomery, starring Mona Darkfeather and Art Ortega [film held at EH]); *Defying the Chief* (1914, Kalem, dir. Frank E. Montgomery, starring Mona Darkfeather, Art Ortega, and Rex Downs [film held at EH]); *The Girl of the Golden West* (1915), in the role of Antonio; *American Aristocracy* (1916); *The Avenging Trail* (1917); *Broadway Bill* (1918); *Skyfire* (1920); *Riding With Death* (1921); *Two-Fisted Jones* (1925); *Under Western Skies, The Valley of Bravery, The Fighting Boob*, in the role of a desperado, and *Stacked Cards* (1926); *Spurs* (1930); *Galloping Thru, Near the Trail's End, Nevada Buckaroo, Oklahoma Jim, Partners of the Trail,* and *The Riding Fool* (1931); *Boiling Point, Cornered,* and *The Riding Tornado* (1932); *Blue Steel, The Fighting Trooper, The Lawless Frontier, The Lucky Texan, The Man from Utah, Man Trailer, 'Neath the Arizona Skies, The Prescott Kid, Randy Rides Alone, The Star Packer, The Trail Beyond, West of the Divide,* and *Wheels of Destiny* (1934); *Between Men, Circle of Death, The Code of the Mounted, The Desert Trail, Fighting Caballero, The Laramie Kid, Lightning Triggers, North of Arizona, Northern Frontier, Pals of the Range, Rough Riding Ranger, The Test,* and *Tombstone Terror* (1935); *Aces and Eights, The Bold Caballero, Border Caballero, Code of the Range, The Crooked Trail, Custer's Last Stand, Ghost Patrol, King of the Royal Mounted, Lightnin' Bill Carson, Roarin' Guns,* and *Song*

CHICANO FILMS

Left: Poster for Eastern Michigan University's Chicano Film Exhibition and Festival

Eastern Michigan University
Second Annual
Chicano Film Exhibition and Festival

April 14, 15, & 16, 1983
Theme: Major Dramas and Docu-Dramas on the Chicano Experience

The Exhibition/Festival will feature both a retrospective screening of many major dramas and docu-dramas on the Chicano experience (including **Zoot Suit, The Ballad of Gregorio Cortez, Alambrista, Chulas fronteras, Seguin, Chicana, Salt of the Earth, Angel and Big Joe, El grito de las madres dolorosas,** and many others) as well as a juried selection of new productions. A scholarly colloquium on Chicano film will be held concurrently with the Exhibition/Festival and the **Bilingual Review** will have published a special issue dedicated to Chicano cinema.

The Exhibition/Festival will be one of the components of the Eleventh Annual Conference of the National Association for Chicano Studies, a historic event since it is meeting for the first time in the Midwest. Both the Exhibition/Festival and the NACS Conference as well as a Chicano fine and popular arts exhibition, theatrical performance of **La víctima, Hijos,** and **Música** by the nationally recognized Teatro de la Esperanza, publishers' exhibits of Chicano materials, literary readings broadcast live from the Conference, and numerous social activities including dances and mariachis will be held at Eastern Michigan University's campus in Ypsilanti.

For information on how to enter a film in the Festival, participate in any of the NACS events, or simply to attend, write or telephone: Gary D. Keller, Dean, Graduate School, Eastern Michigan University, Ypsilanti, MI 48197 (313) 487-0042

of the Trail (1936); *Blazing Sixes, The Cherokee Strip, Empty Holsters, Hopalong Rides Again,* and *Land Beyond the Law* (1937); *Heart of the North* and *Sergeant Murphy* (1938); *The Kansas Terrors, The Kid from Texas,* and *Stagecoach* (1939); and *Pioneers of the West* (1940).

Dyana Ortelli

Actress, born May 1, 1961, in Nuevo Laredo, Mexico, and raised in California. She has done a number of Latina characters, including a Mexican village girl in *¡Three Amigos!* (1986), a hooker in *La Bamba* (1987), and a Tijuana beggar girl in *Born East L.A.* (1987). She also appeared in *Alienator* (1989) and as a zoot suiter in *American Me* (1992). She costarred as a comic maid, Lupe López, in the short-lived television series *Marblehead Manor.*

Humberto Ortiz

Child actor, born October 12, 1979, in Laredo, Texas, and raised in California. He has appeared in *¡Three Amigos!* (1986), *Salsa* (1989), *Dollman* (1991), and *Kickboxer II* (1991). He also costarred with his mother, Dyana Ortelli, on the TV series *Marblehead Manor.*

Marina Ortiz

Actress. She had a few supporting roles in Hollywood Spanish-language films including *Sombras de gloria* (1929, Sono-Art Productions, Ltd.), *Charros, gauchos y manolas* (1930, Hollywood Spanish Pictures Co.), and *Contra la corriente* (1935, RKO-Radio Pictures).

CHICANO FILMS

Continued.

Below: Lydia Mendoza performing in *Chulas fronteras* (1976)

Above: The group Los Alegres de Terán playing in *Chulas fronteras* (1976)

Below: David Villalpando and Zaide Silvia Gutiérrez in *El Norte* (1984, dir. Gregory Nava)

Above left: Edward James Olmos as Gregorio Cortez with his screen family, in *The Ballad of Gregorio Cortez* (1982)

Above right: Edward James Olmos in *The Ballad of Gregorio Cortez* (1982)

Below right: Edward James Olmos as Santa Anna in *Seguín* (1982)

Above: Marilyn Mulford and Mario Barrera's *Chicano Park* (1989)

Left: Scene from *Raíces de sangre* (1977, dir. Jesús Salvador Treviño)

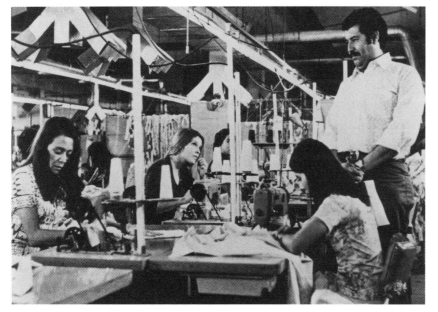

Above: Edward James Olmos (center) in *American Me* (1992)

Right: Scene from *Raíces de sangre* (1977)

Crossing the border **(above)** and *piscando* **(below)**: two scenes from *Alambrista* (1977)

Above left: Poster for *Zoot Suit* (1981)

Above right: Cheech Marín and Paul Rodríguez in *La Pastorela* (1991)

Below left: Poster for *Raíces de sangre* (1977, dir. Jesús Salvador Treviño)

Manuel Padilla, Jr.

(Also Manuel Padilla) Juvenile actor of the 1960s and 1970s, born in 1956. He appeared in *Dime with a Halo* and *The Young and the Brave* (1963); *Robin and the Seven Hoods* (1964); *Black Spurs, Sylvia,* and *Taffy and the Jungle Hunter* (1965); *Tarzan and the Valley of Gold* (1966); *Tarzan and the Great River* (1967); *A Man Called Horse, The Great White Hope, Tarzan's Jungle Rebellion,* and *Tarzan's Deadly Silence* (1970); and *American Graffiti* (1973), as a low-riding Mexican American teenager. He costarred in the television series *Tarzan.* He has been inactive in recent years except for a small role in *Scarface* (1983).

Vincent Padula

(Also Padule; Vicente Padula) Argentine actor, born in 1893, died in Glendale, California, January 16, 1967. He had an extensive career in Hollywood Spanish-language films, occasionally costarring, mostly appearing in principal parts in at least 13 productions, including *Charros, gauchos y manolas* (1930, Hollywood Spanish Pictures Co.); *El cuerpo del delito* (1930, Paramount), as Sargento Heath; *La fuerza del querer* (1930, Paramount), as Steve; *Monsieur le Fox* (1930, MGM); *Amor audaz* (1930, Paramount), as Silvestre Corbett; *Del mismo barro* (1930, Fox), as Señor Fullerton; *El último de los Vargas* (1930, Fox, costarring opposite George Lewis and Luana Alcañiz), a Spanish-language version of *Last of the Duanes* (1930, starring George O'Brien, Lucille Brown, and Myrna Loy); *El presidio* (1930, MGM), as Dunn; *Gente alegre* (1931, Paramount), as Max; *Las luces de Buenos Aires* (1931, Paramount), as Ciriaco; *Melodía de arrabal* (1933, Paramount, costarring opposite Imperio Argentina and Carlos Gardel), a Spanish-language original based on a screenplay by Alfredo Le Pera; *Cuesta abajo* (1934, Paramount, costarring opposite Carlos Gardel and Mona Maris), a Spanish-language original based on a screenplay by Alfredo Le Pera; and *El tango en Broadway* (1934, Paramount), as Juan Carlos. In English-language films he appeared in *Winds of the Pampas* (1927) and *The Flame Barrier* (1958).

Anita Page

(Also Ann Page and Anita Rivera; born Anita Pomares) Actress of Spanish descent, born in Murray Hill, Long Island, New York, August 4, 1910. She was a leading lady of Hollywood films in the 1920s and early 1930s. She began as an extra in 1924 and gained considerable notoriety in *The Broadway Melody* (1929), an early musical about two stage-struck sisters. The film was the first musical to win an Academy Award for Best Picture. Additional film credits: *Our Dancing Daughters, Telling the World* (MGM [film held at NFTA]); and *While the City Sleeps* (all 1928); *The Flying Fleet, The Hollywood Revue of 1929, Navy Blues, Our Modern Maidens,* and *Speedway* (1929); *Caught Short, Free and Easy, The Little Accident, Our Blushing Brides,* and *War Nurse* (1930); *The Easiest Way, Gentleman's Fate, Reducing,* and *Sidewalks of New York* (1931); *Are You Listening?, Night Court, Prosperity, Skyscraper Souls,* and *Under 18* (1932); *The Big Cage, I Have Lived, Jungle Bride,* and *Soldiers of the Storm* (1933); and *Hitch Hike to Heaven* and *The Rest Cure* (1936).

Joy Page

(Also Joy Ann Page) Actress, born in 1921, the daughter of Don Alvarado and Ann Boyer (who later married Jack Warner). Her best-known role is as the young Hungarian girl who offers herself to Colonel Renault in Warner Brothers' *Casablanca* (1942, starring Humphrey Bogart and Ingrid Bergman). Additional film credits include *Kismet* (1944), *The Bullfighter and the Lady* (1951), *Fighter Attack* and *Conquest of Cochise* (1953), *The Shrike* (1955), and *Tonka* (1958).

Andrea Palma

(Guadalupe Bracho Gavilán) Actress, born in Durango, Mexico, April 16, 1903, died in Mexico City, November 10, 1987. She was married to film director Julio Bracho. She appeared in a few Hollywood Spanish-language films including *La última cita* (1935, Columbia, costarring opposite José Crespo and Luana Alcañiz), a Spanish-language original based on a screenplay by René Borgia, and *La Inmaculada* (1939, United Artists, costarring opposite Fortunio Bonanova), a Spanish-language original based on the novel *La Inmaculada* by Catalina D'Erzell. She also was in two important Mexican films: *Sor Juana Inés de la Cruz* (1936), playing the title role of the renowned feminist nun, and *The Criminal Life of Archibaldo de la Cruz* (1955, dir. Luis Buñuel).

Valentín Parera

Actor, born in Granada, Spain, August 14, 1895, married to singer Grace Moore. He costarred or had principal roles in a few Hollywood Spanish-language films including *Un hombre de suerte* (1930, Cinéstudio Continental Paramount); *Yo, tú y ella* (1933, Fox, costarring opposite Catalina Bárcena and Gilbert Roland), a Spanish-language original based on "Mujer" (Madrid, 1926) by Gregorio Martínez Sierra; *Granaderos del amor* (1934, Fox, costarring opposite Raúl Roulien and Conchita Montenegro), a Spanish-language original based on a screenplay by John Reinhardt and William Kernell; *Dos más uno, dos* (1934, Fox, costarring opposite Rosita Moreno), a Spanish-language version of *Don't Marry* (1928, starring Lois Moran and Neil Hamilton); and *Señora casada necesita marido* (1934, Fox), in the role of Antoñito Orbok.

Manuel París

(Manuel Conesa) Spanish actor, born July 27, 1894, died in Woodland Hills, California, November 19, 1959. He had an extensive career in both Hollywood English-language and Spanish-language films. His English-language credits include *Trapped in Tia Juana* (1932, starring Duncan Renaldo); *Flying Down to Rio* (1933), in a bit part as a man at the aviator club; *The Man Who Broke the Bank at Monte Carlo* (1935); *Fatal Lady* and *A Message to Garcia* (both 1936); *I'll Take Romance, When You're In Love,* and *Wise Girl* (1937); and *Artists and Models Abroad, Charlie Chan at Monte Carlo, Four Men and a Prayer, I'll Give a Million, Sharpshooters, Submarine Patrol,* and *Miracles for Sale* (1939). In Hollywood Spanish-language films he used both the names Manuel París and Manuel Conesa in no discernible pattern either as an actor, dialog writer, or translator. He has credits on at least 21 Hollywood Spanish-language productions including the first such film, *Sombras habaneras* (1929, Hispania Talking Film Corp., presented by All-Star Exchange, starring René Cardona and Jacqueline Logan). Additional credits as an actor (one as a costar but often in unnamed roles) include *Charros, gauchos y manolas* (1930, Hollywood Spanish Pictures Co.); *El cuerpo del delito* (1930, Paramount); *El barbero de Napoleón* (1930, Fox, costarring as the *barbero* opposite Juan Aristi Eulate), a Spanish-language version of *Napoleon's Barber* (1928, dir. John Ford, starring Otto Matiesen and Frank Reicher); *Cheri-Bibi* (1931, MGM); *El caballero de la noche* (1932, Fox), as Tom King; *Espérame* (1933, Paramount); *Melodía de arrabal* (1933, Paramount), as Maldonado; *Piernas de seda* (1935, Fox); and *Rosa de Francia* (1935, Fox).

Virginia Paris

Actress. She appeared in the role of Chairwoman Ortega, who opposes Jaime Escalante, played by Edward James Olmos, in *Stand and Deliver* (1987). She has made numerous appearances on television series including *Have Gun Will Travel, Ironside, Medical Center, Police Story,* and *Quincy, M.E.*

Gil Parrondo

Production designer, born in 1921 in Luarca, Spain. He began as an assistant director in the Spanish film industry and subsequently pursued his interests as an art director. His international film career includes *El Cid* (1961), *Mr. Arkadin* (1962), *Doctor Zhivago* (1965), *Patton* (1970), *Nicholas and Alexandra* (1971), *Travels with My Aunt* (1972), *The Wind and the Lion* (1975), *The Boys from Brazil* (1978), *Cuba* (1979), *Lionheart* (1987), and *Farewell to the King* (1989). He twice won Academy Awards for Production Design and Art Direction (for *Patton* and *Nicholas and Alexandra*) and was nominated a third time for an Oscar in the same category for *Travels with My Aunt.*

Alfonso Pedroza

(Also Alphonso) Actor. He appeared in several Hollywood Spanish-language films (often in comic roles) including *Tiembla y titubea* (1930, MGM, starring Stan Laurel and Oliver Hardy), as Señor Verdugo; *La jaula de los leones* (1930, Producciones Ci-Ti-Go, presented by J. H. Hoffberg Co., Inc.); *Locuras de amor* (1930, MGM, starring Charley Chase and Carmen Guerrero); *¡Huye faldas!* (1930, MGM, starring Charley Chase and Carmen Guerrero); *Noche de duendes* (1930, starring Stan Laurel and Oliver Hardy), in the role of *el detective jefe*; *Una cana al aire* (1930, MGM, starring Charley Chase), as *el cliente*; *La buenaventura* (1934, First National Pictures), as Sandor; *El cantante de Nápoles* (1934, Warner), as Fortuni; and *Di que me quieres* (1938, RKO-Radio Pictures). He also appeared in a few Hollywood English-language films including *In Caliente, Metropolitan,* and *Storm Over the Andes* (all 1935); *Desire, The Gay Desperado,* and *Moonlight Murder* (1936); and *Lover Under Fire, Submarine D-1,* and *Waikiki Wedding* (1937).

Pelé

(Edison Arantes de Nascimento) Soccer star, born in 1940 in an impoverished village in Brazil. He appeared in *Victory*

(1981, dir. John Huston) as a British soldier from Trinidad. He has made other film appearances in European and Brazilian productions.

Pilar Pellicer

Mexican actress, sister of Pina Pellicer. Active in the Mexican film industry, she appeared in the notable *Nazarín* (1962, dir. Luis Buñuel) and in the American film *Day of the Evil Gun* (1968, MGM, starring Glenn Ford).

Pina Pellicer

(Josefina Yolanda Pellicer López Liergo) Actress, born April 3, 1940, in Mexico City, died December 7, 1964, in Mexico City. She is known for her role in the first Mexican film to win an Oscar nomination, *Macario* (1960). She played the lead role of Luisa in *One-Eyed Jacks* (1961) opposite Marlon Brando, with whom she had a stormy affair, and won the Best Actress award at the San Sebastián Film Festival for her work in that film. In 1963, she returned to

Above: Pina Pellicer

the United States for a brief period, starring in "The Life Work of Juan Díaz" episode of *The Alfred Hitchcock Hour*. Suffering from depression, she committed suicide in 1964.

Manuel Peluffo

Actor. He had a few supporting roles in Hollywood Spanish-language films including *Cuesta abajo* (1934, Paramount); *El tango en Broadway* (1935, Paramount); *El día que me quieras* (1935, Paramount), as Saturnino; *Tango Bar* (1935, Paramount), as Manuel González; *Te quiero con locura* (1935, Fox), as Willy McRay; and *Piernas de seda* (1935, Fox). He also appeared in a few English-language films including *The Eternal Jew* (1933); *The Gay Desperado, A Message to Garcia,* and *The Rest Cure* (all 1936); and *Love Under Fire* (1937).

Elizabeth Peña

Actress, born in Cuba, September 23, 1959. She came to the United States at eight years of age and was brought up in New York, where her parents, Mario and Margarita Peña, founded and still run the Latin American Theater Ensemble. Her first major role was in the independent feature *El Super* (1979, dir. León Ichaso), followed by a costarring role in *Crossover Dreams* (1985, starring Rubén Blades). She has also appeared in *They All Laughed* (1981), as a murderously jealous ex-girlfriend; *Down and Out in Beverly Hills* (1986), as a sensuous maid; as the jilted Rosie in *La Bamba* (1987); as Marissa in **batteries not included* (1987, dir. Steven Spielberg); as a tempestuous *ecuatoriana* in *Vibes* (1988); and as Jezzie in *Jacob's Ladder* (1990). Additional credits include *Times Square* (1980), *Thief* (1981), *Shannon's Deal* (1989, pilot for TV series), *Blue Steel* (1990), *The Waterdance* (1992), *Dead Funny* and *Free Willy II* (1995), and *Lone Star* (1996, dir. John Sayles). On television she starred in the series *I Married Dora,* was in the series *Tough Cookies,* and appeared in the John Sayles-directed series *Shannon's Deal.*

José Peña, "Pepet"

Actor, he had a very extensive career in Hollywood Spanish-language films in supporting parts, appearing in at least 34 films including *Charros, gauchos y manolas* (1930, Hollywood Spanish Pictures Co.); *La jaula de los leones* (1930, Producciones Ci-Ti-Go, presented by J. H. Hoffberg Co., Inc.) as *el secretario*; *El dios del mar* (1930, Paramount), as Nick, *el perlero*; *El tenorio del harem* (1931, Universal), as *un soldado*; *El príncipe gondolero* (1931, Paramount), as Salustiano Green; *Yo, tú y ella* (1933, Fox),

Above: Elizabeth Peña

as *el fotógrafo*; *Señora casada necesita marido* (1934, Fox), as Julio; *Rosa de Francia* (1935, Fox), as Valouse; *El crimen de media noche* (1935, Reliable Pictures), as doctor McNeill; *La vida bohemia* (1937, Columbia), as Durand; *Mis dos amores* (1938, Paramount), as Manuel Paniagua; and *La Inmaculada* (1939, United Artists). He also was in the English-language films *The Criminal Code* (1931) and *A Message to Garcia* (1936).

Julio Peña

(Julio Peña Muñoz) Actor, born in Santander, Spain, June 20, 1918, died in Madrid, March 29, 1977. He costarred in one and appeared in principal or supporting roles in numerous other Hollywood Spanish-language films including *Doña Mentiras* (1930, Cinéstudio Continental Paramount), as Roberto Duvall; *La fruta amarga* (1931, MGM), as Dick; *Esclavas de la moda* (1931, Fox), as Mario; *Mamá* (1931, Fox), as José María; *Primavera en otoño* (1933, Fox), as Manolo Fresnada; *Un capitán de cosacos* (1934, Fox), as Ivan Trainoff; *Julieta compra un hijo* (1935, Fox), as Guillermo Solsona; *Rosa de Francia* (1935, Fox, costarring opposite Rosita Díaz

Gimeno), a Spanish-language original based on a comedy by Eduardo Marquina and Luis Fernández Ardavín; and *Alas sobre el Chaco* (1935, Universal), as Mitchell. It is presumed but unconfirmed that this is the same actor who appeared in a number of 1960s films, often produced in Spain, including *The Happy Thieves* and *The Revolt of the Slaves* (both 1961); *The Castilian* (1963); *Kid Rodelo, Minnesota Clay, Sunscorched,* and *Web of Violence* (1966); *Falstaff, The Hellbenders,* and *Savage Pampas* (1967); *Satanic* (Spanish-Italian production) and *One Step to Hell* (1969); and *El Cóndor* (1970).

Ramón Pereda

(Ramón Pereda Saro) Actor, director, and producer, born in Esles de Cavón, Santander, Spain, died in 1986. He had starring or principal roles in a number of Hollywood Spanish-language films including *El cuerpo del delito* (1930, Paramount, costarring opposite Antonio Moreno), a Spanish-language version of *The Benson Murder Case* (1930, starring William Powell and Natalie Moorhead); *Amor audaz* (1930, Paramount, costarring opposite Adolphe Menjou and Rosita Moreno), a Spanish-language version of *Slightly Scarlet* (1930, starring Evelyn Brent and Clive Brook); *El dios del mar* (1930, Paramount, costarring Rosita Moreno), a Spanish-language version of *The Sea God* (1930, dir. George Abbott, starring Richard Arlen and Fay Wray); *La dama atrevida* (1931, First National Pictures, costarring opposite Luana Alcañiz), a Spanish-language version of *The Lady Who Dared* (1931, starring Billie Dove and Conway Tearle); *Carne de cabaret* (1931, Columbia, dir. Christy Cabanne, costarring opposite Lupita Tovar), a Spanish-language version of *Ten Cents a Dance* (1931, dir. Lionel Barrymore, starring Barbara Stanwyck and Ricardo Cortez); *El proceso de Mary Dugan* (1931, MGM, costarring opposite María Ladrón de Guevara and José Crespo), a Spanish-language version of *The Trial of Mary Dugan* (1929, starring Norma Shearer and Lewis Stone); *Hombres en mi vida* (1932, Columbia, costarring opposite Lupe Vélez and Gilbert Roland), a Spanish-language version of *Men in Her Life* (1931, starring Lois Moran and Charles Bickford); *El diablo del mar* (1935, Theater Classic Pictures, dir. Juan Duval, costarring Movita), a Spanish-language version of *Devil Monster* (1935, starring Jack del Rio, Blanche

Above: Ramón Pereda and Rosita Moreno
in *El dios del mar* (1930, Paramount)

Mehaffey, and Barry Norton); *No matarás* (1935, Hispano International Film Corp., dir. Miguel Contreras Torres, costarring Adriana Lamar), a Spanish-language original based on a screenplay by Miguel Contreras Torres; and *El crimen de media noche* (1935, Reliable Pictures, costarring Adriana Lamar), a Spanish-language version of *The Midnight Phantom* (1935, starring Reginald Denny and Claudia Dell).

José Pérez

Diminutive Puerto Rican actor, born in 1940 in New York City. He began as a child actor on Broadway and has worked in film and television for over 40 years. His film credits include *A Life in the Balance* (1955), in which he plays a young boy, *Short Eyes* (1977, dir. Robert M. Young), *One Shoe Makes It Murder* (1982), *The Sting II* (1983), *Stick* (1985), *Courage* (1986), and *Miami Blues* (1990), in which he is cast as an adult.

Manuel Pérez

Animator for Warner Brothers Cartoon Studios, active during the 1940s and 1950s.

Paul Pérez

Scriptwriter. He wrote the screenplays, dialogs, translations into Spanish, or did allied work on at least 15 Hollywood Spanish-language films including *El valiente* (1930, Fox), *El rey de los gitanos* (1933, Fox), and *La Inmaculada* (1939, United Artists).

Pepito Pérez

Clown, born in Barcelona, Spain. After becoming famous in Spain and elsewhere in Europe, he appeared in the United States in vaudeville and at the New York Hippodrome. In Hollywood he performed in the circus sequence of *Lady in the Dark* (1944) and appeared in *A Medal for Benny* (1945). He was in the pilot episode of the *I Love Lucy* TV series.

Rosie Pérez

Actress and choreographer, born in 1966 in New York City to Puerto Rican parents, raised in Brooklyn. She made her film debut in Spike Lee's notable film *Do the Right Thing* (1989) as Tina, the lover of Mookie, played by Lee. She followed this performance by appearing in the off-beat *Night on Earth* (1991) as a *puertorriqueña*, and she costarred as Gloria in *White Men Can't Jump* (1992) in a notable performance as a streetwise but vulnerable Latina who aspires to become a game show contestant. In *Untamed Heart* (1993) she played a waitress, in *Fearless* (1993) she played a young mother who loses her baby, and in *It Could Happen to You* (1994) she played a greedy but naive wife of a police officer who wins the lottery. On television she played a Hispanic crack addict in the made-for-television film *Criminal Justice* (1990), and she has appeared on the television series *21 Jump Street* and *WIOU*. She was nominated for an Academy Award as Best Supporting Actress in *Fearless* and for an Emmy for her choreography on the television series *In Living Color*.

Severo Pérez

Writer, producer, and director. He produced *Seguín* (1982, dir. Jesús Salvador Treviño), directed *Tierra* (1994), and wrote and directed the dramatic adaptation of Tomás Rivera's masterpiece *. . . and the earth did not swallow him* (1995, prod. Paul Espinosa). All three films were part of the American Playhouse drama series on PBS. He is also known for his documentaries: *Los Piñateros* (1987), on the traditions of that craft in San Antonio; *There Goes the Neighborhood* (1987), on the conflicts between long-time residents of neighborhoods with recent immigrants; and *Between Friends* (1990), which examines the transmission of AIDS through unprotected sex and drug abuse.

Above: Rosie Pérez in *White Men Can't Jump* (1992)

Below: Jorge Perugorría (right), as Diego, and Vladimir Cruz in *Strawberry and Chocolate* (1994)

Benito Perojo

(Benito Perojo González) Director, producer, and cine-matographer, one of Spain's most noted filmmakers, born in Madrid, June 14, 1894, died in Madrid, November 11, 1974. He directed two Hollywood Spanish-language films: *Un hombre de suerte* (1930, Cinéstudio Continental Paramount, starring Roberto Rey and María Luz Callejo), a Spanish-language version of *Un trou dans le mur* (1930, Cinéstudio Continental Paramount, dir. René Barberis, starring Jean Murat, Dolly Davis, and Marguerite Moreno); and *Mamá* (1931, Fox, starring Catalina Bárcena and Rafael Rivelles), a Spanish-language original based on a work by Gregorio Martínez Sierra. In the 1960s, through

his production company, Producciones Benito Perojo, he produced a number of films made in Spain and released in the United States including *Desert Warrior* (1961), *The Devil Made a Woman* (1962), *The Adventures of Scaramouche* and *The Son of Captain Blood* (both 1964), *Backfire* (1965), and *That Man George* (1967).

Jorge Perugorría

Actor. He costarred in the Cuban film released in the United States as *Strawberry and Chocolate* about gay love in contemporary Cuba.

Alex Phillips, Jr.

Cinematographer, born in Mexico, the son of Hollywood cinematographer Alex Phillips, Sr. He has contributed to over 50 films as cinematographer including *Buck and the Preacher* (1972), *Bring Me the Head of Alfredo García* and *The Savage Is Loose* (both 1974), *Caboblanco* and *Fade to Black* (1980), *Little Treasure* (1985), and the television miniseries *Evita Perón* (1981).

Lou Diamond Phillips

(Lou Upchurch) Actor of mixed European (including Spanish), American Indian, and Filipino heritage, born in Kuby Point, Philippines, February 17, 1962. Appearing first in *Harley* (1985) as an L.A. motorcycle hood who is sent to a Texas ranch for rehabilitation rather than a juvenile detention center, he became a star as the result of his role as Ritchie Valens in *La Bamba* (1987, dir. Luis Valdez). He then starred or had major roles in *Trespasses* (1987); *Stand and Deliver, Dakota,* and *Young Guns* (all 1988); *Disorganized Crime, Renegades,* and *The First Power* (1989); *A Show of Force* and *Young Guns II* (1990); *Ambition* (1991); *Extreme Justice, Dangerous Touch, Teresa's Tattoo,* and *Shadow of the Wolf* (1993); *Sioux City* and *The Dark Wind* (1994); and the critically acclaimed *Courage Under Fire* (1996).

Ernesto Piedra

Actor and songwriter. He had a few supporting roles in Hollywood Spanish-language films including *Sombras de gloria* (1929, Sono-Art Productions, Ltd.) and *Así es la vida* (1930, Sono-Art Productions), as "Sapo." He was also in *Flying Down to Rio* (1933) and *Under Your Spell* (1936).

Above: Lou Diamond Phillips (left) and Esai Morales in *La Bamba* (1987)

Silvia Pinal

Internationally recognized actress, born in Guaymas, Mexico, February 12, year unknown, married to producer Gustavo Alatriste. Very active in the Mexican film industry, she starred in several Luis Buñuel films including *Viridiana* (1961), *The Exterminating Angel* (1962), and *Simon of the Desert* (1965) and also was seen in the United States in *Guns for San Sebastian* and *Shark!* (both 1968).

Federico Pinero

(Also Fred) Actor. He starred in a few low-budget films including *The Devil's Sisters,* about white slavers in Tijuana, and *Death Curse of Tartu* (both 1967), and *The Horse in the Gray Flannel Suit* (1968).

Miguel Piñero

(Miguel Antonio Gómez Piñero, Jr.) Playwright and actor, born December 19, 1946, in Guarabo, Puerto Rico, died in

New York City, June 17, 1988. His play *Short Eyes,* written while he was serving prison time in 1973 at Sing Sing, won an Obie Award and a New York Drama Critics Circle Award as best American play in 1974. A violent portrait of prison life, it was made into a film in 1977 (retitled *Slammer*), directed by Robert M. Young. Piñero wrote the screenplay and appeared in the film. Additional film credits include *Times Square* (1980), *Fort Apache, The Bronx* (1981), *Breathless* (1983, a remake of the Godard film, starring Richard Gere), *Deal of the Century* (1983), *Almost You* and *Alphabet City* (both 1984), and *The Pick-Up Artist* (1987). On television, Piñero wrote scripts and/or appeared in *The Streets of L.A.* (1979, TV film) and the series *Baretta, Kojak,* and *Miami Vice.*

Tony Plana

Actor, born in Cuba, April 19, 1954. He has appeared in a variety of roles including *The Streets of L.A.* (1979, TV film, starring Joanne Woodward, also with Pepe Serna, Isela Vega, and Miguel Piñero); *An Officer and a Gentleman* (1982), as the cadet Dellaserra; *El Norte* (1984), as the jealous Chicano waiter; *Latino* (1985), as a gung-ho Green Beret; *Salvador*

(1986), as Major Max; *¡Three Amigos!* (1986), as the parodic Mexican bandit; *Disorderlies* (1987); *Born in East L.A.* (1987), in the role of Feo; *Break of Dawn* (1988, dir. Isaac Artenstein); *Romero* (1989), as the guerrilla priest; *Buy & Cell* (1989); *The Case of the Hillside Strangler* (1989, TV film); *The Rookie, Havana,* as the journalist, and *Why Me?* (1990); *One Good Cop* and *JFK* (1991); *Live Wire* (1992); and *A Million to Juan* (1993). On television he has appeared in *Listen to Your Heart* (1983), the miniseries *Drug Wars: The Camarena Story* (1989), the PBS drama *Sweet 15,* and an episode of *L.A. Law.*

Begonia Plaza

Actress, born in 1962 in Colombia. She lived in Spain and moved with her family to Los Angeles at the age of nine. She has appeared in *48 Hours* (1982), *Heartbreak Ridge* (1986), *Maid to Order* (1987), *Born on the Fourth of July* (1989), *Delta Force 2: Operation Stranglehold* (1990), and *Dark Justice* (1991, TV film).

Fernando Poe, Jr.

Filipino actor and producer. He appeared in two films depicting the Filipino resistance against the Japanese in World War II: *The Walls of Hell* (1964) and *The Ravagers* (1965).

Lourdes Portillo

Filmmaker. She directed *Después del terremoto* (1979), a film in *telenovela* format on issues related to immigration and gender politics within the barrio; *Las madres de la Plaza de Mayo* (codir. Susana Muñoz); *La ofrenda: The Days of the Dead* (codir. Susana Muñoz), an exploration of the roots and history of the present-day celebrations of the Day of the Dead; *Vida* (1990), about a single Latina who confronts AIDS and finds a new sense of her self and awareness of her sexuality; and *El diablo nunca duerme/The Devil Never Sleeps* (1994), a complex, autobiographical reaction to and analysis of the violent death of the filmmaker's uncle.

Rose Portillo

Actress, born in Los Angeles, November 7, 1953. She appeared in *Exorcist II: The Heretic* (1977), *Walk Proud* (1979), *Where the Buffalo Roam* (1980), *Zoot Suit* (1981), *The Mean Season* (1985), and *. . . and the earth did not swallow him* (1995), as the boy's mother. On television her credits include the series *Eisenhower and Lutz* and the PBS American Playhouse presentation *Seguín* (1982, dir. Jesús Salvador Treviño); she also guest starred on *Police Story.*

Jaime Prades

Born in Uruguay: he was vice president of Samuel Bronston Productions and was associate producer on Bronston films including *El Cid* (1961) and *King of Kings* (1961).

Victoria Principal

(Concettina Principale) Actress, partially of Hispanic heritage, born January 3, 1945 [some sources give 1950], in Fukuoka, Japan, the daughter of an American career army officer. She is best known as Pamela Barnes Ewing, a central character she played for nine years on the TV series *Dallas.* She has also had various roles in films and TV series episodes and was an agent for other actors, including comedian Dick Martin, in the 1970s. Film credits include *The Life and Times of Judge Roy Bean* (1972), as Paul Newman's Mexican mistress; *The Naked Ape* (1973); *Earthquake* (1974); *Fantasy Island* (starring Ricardo Montalbán, the basis for the TV series), *I Will, I Will . . . For Now,* and *Vigilante Force* (all 1976); and *Pleasure Palace* (1980). On television she has starred in television films including *Mistress* (1987), *Naked Lie* (1989), *Blind Rage* (1990), *Nightmare* and *Don't Touch My Daughter* (1991), and *The Burden of Proof* (1992, starring Héctor Elizondo).

Freddie Prinze

Comedian of Puerto Rican and Hungarian heritage, born June 22, 1954, in New York City, died in Los Angeles, January 29, 1977. He starred in the popular television series *Chico and the Man* and appeared in the made-for-television film *The Million Dollar Rip-Off* (1976). He also made guest appearances on the television variety show *Tony Orlando and Dawn.*

Tito Puente

(Ernesto Antonio Tito Puente) Musician, born in New York City to Puerto Rican parents, April 23, 1920. After serving in the Navy in World War II, he emerged as one of the most popular bandleaders of Latin music. In film he appeared in *Armed and Dangerous* (1986) and *Radio Days* (1987, dir. Woody Allen), as a bandleader; in both *Salsa* (1989) and *The Mambo Kings* (1992) he played himself. He also provided the opening theme music for several seasons of the television series *The Cosby Show.*

Luis Puenzo

Director, born in Argentina in 1946. He directed commercials from an early age in Argentina, followed by films. He

Above: Freddie Prinze (right) and Tony Orlando

THE HOLLYWOOD SPANISH-LANGUAGE FILMS

Right: Film poster of *El tenorio del harem* (1931, Universal)

Below: Publicity shot of Imperio Argentina during the filming of *¿Cuándo te suicidas?* (1931, Paramount)

produced, directed, and cowrote *The Official Story* (1985), which won an Academy Award for Best Foreign-Language Film. Subsequently he directed and cowrote *Old Gringo* (1989, starring Gregory Peck, Jimmy Smits, and Jane Fonda) and *The Plague* (1991, starring William Hurt, Robert Duvall, and Raúl Juliá).

Eva Puig

Actress, born February 3, 1894, died in Panorama City, California, October 6, 1968. She appeared in *The Crime of Dr. Forbes* (1936); *Bowery Boy, Forty Little Mothers, I Want a Divorce, Texas Rangers Ride Again* (starring Akim Tamiroff, with Anthony Quinn as evil Joe Yuma), and *North West Mounted Police* (all 1940); *Hold Back the Dawn* and *Romance of the Rio Grande* (1941); and *Snafu* (1945).

Above left: Film poster for *Contra la corriente* (1935, RKO-Radio Pictures, prod. and dir. Ramón Novarro)

Above right: The actors in the lead roles of the multilingual versions of *Men of the North* (1930, MGM). Bilingualism was worth an extra role for Gilbert Roland, who did the English and Spanish versions.

Below right: Film poster of *Eran trece* (1931, Fox), with Manuel Arbó in the role of Charlie Chan

157

Above left: Antonio Moreno and José Crespo in *Alas sobre el Chaco* (1935, Universal, dir. Christy Cabanne)

Above right: Film poster of *El presidio* (1930, MGM)

Below left: Rosita Díaz Gimeno and Gilbert Roland in *La vida bohemia* (1937, Colombia)

Below right: Film poster of *El día que me quieras* (1936, Paramount)

Nina Quartaro

(Also Nena Quartero; Nina Quartero; Gladys Quartaro) Actress. She appeared, usually in starring or principal roles, in *Drifting Sands* (1928); *The Red Mark* (1928, James Cruze, Inc., dir. James Cruze, starring Nina Quartaro, Gaston Glass, and Gustav Von Seyffertitz [film held at LC]); *The Eternal Woman, Frozen River, The Redeeming Sin*, and *One Stolen Night* (all 1929); *Golden Dawn, Men of the North* (starring Gilbert Roland), and *Isle of Escape* (1930); *Arizona, Arizona Terror, The Bachelor Father, The Fighting Sheriff, God's Gift to Women, New Moon*, and *Trapped* (1931); *The Devil's Brother, Man from Monterey, The Monkey's Paw, Sons of the Desert*, and *Under Secret Orders* (1933); *The Cyclone Ranger* and *Vagabond Lady* (1935); *The Phantom of Santa Fe, The Three Mesquiteers, Two in a Crowd*, and *Wife vs. Secretary* (1936); *Left-Handed Law* and *Submarine D-1* (1937); *Torchy Blane in Panama* (1938); and *Green Hell* (1940).

Milo Quesada

(Raúl García) Actor, born in Buenos Aires, 1930. Active in the Argentine film industry, he appeared in a few films released in the United States including *The Young Racers* (1963), *Evil Eye* (1964), *The 10th Victim* (1965), *House of a Thousand Dolls* (1967), *Savage Pampas* (1967, Argentine production, starring Robert Taylor, also with Rosenda Monteros), and *The Mercenary* (1970, Italian production).

Anthony Quinn

(Anthony Rudolph Oaxaca Quinn) Actor, born during the Mexican Revolution on April 21, 1915, in Chihuahua, Mexico, of Irish-Mexican parentage. In the United States from childhood, he entered films in 1936, debuting in *Parole!* (1936) as a convict. The following year he married Cecil B. De Mille's adopted daughter, Katherine (they are now divorced), but his father-in-law did little to advance his career, which did not attain star status until his Academy Award-winning role as Zapata's brother in the 1952 film *Viva Zapata!* Quinn went on to win a second Academy Award for his portrayal of painter Paul Gaugin in *Lust for Life* (1956). He received Academy Award nominations for

his depictions of an Italian American rancher in *Wild Is the Wind* (1957) and Zorba in *Zorba the Greek* (1964). His career was also boosted by his role as circus strongman Zampano in *La Strada* (1954), which won the Academy Award for Best Foreign-Language Film in 1956. He has often been cast in roles emphasizing his earthy and exotic qualities. In addition to playing a Mexican or Mexican American, he has had roles as a Greek, Arab, American Indian, Levantine, and, occasionally, as in *East of Sumatra* (1953), an Asian. He has appeared in over 100 films and has written an autobiography titled *The Original Sin* (1972).

Film credits include *Sworn Enemy, Night Waitress,* and *Parole!* (1936); *The Last Train from Madrid, The Plainsman, Partners in Crime, Swing High, Swing Low, Daughter of Shanghai,* and *Waikiki Wedding* (1937); *The Buccaneer, Hunted Men, Tip-Off Girls, Dangerous to Know, Bulldog Drummond in Africa,* and *King of Alcatraz* (1938); *King of Chinatown, Television Spy, Union Pacific,* and *Island of Lost Men* (1939); *City for Conquest, The Road to Singapore, Emergency Squad, Parole Fixer, The Ghost Breakers,* and *Texas Rangers Ride Again* (1940); *Knockout, Bullets for O'Hara, The Perfect Snob, Thieves Fall Out,* and *Blood and Sand* (1941); *The Black Swan, The Road to Morocco, Larceny, Inc.,* and *They Died with Their Boots On* (1942); *The Ox-Bow Incident,* and *Guadalcanal Diary* (1943); *Irish Eyes Are Smiling, Ladies of Washington, Roger Touhy—Gangster,* and *Buffalo Bill* (1944); *China Sky, Where Do We Go from Here?,* and *Back to Bataan* (1945); *California, Sinbad the Sailor, Tycoon, The Imperfect Lady,* and *Black Gold* (1947); *Mask of the Avenger* and *The Brave Bulls* (1951); *Viva Zapata!, The World in His Arms, The Brigand,* and *Against All Flags* (1952); *Ride Vaquero!, City Beneath the Sea, Fatal Desire, Seminole, Blowing Wild,* and *East of Sumatra* (1953); *The Long Wait* and *La Strada* (1954, Italian production, dir. Federico Fellini); *The Naked Street, Seven Cities of Gold, Ulysses,* and *The Magnificent Matador* (1955); *Lust for Life, Angels of Darkness, The Wild Party, Hunchback of Notre Dame,* and *Man from Del Rio* (1956); *The River's Edge, Wild Is the Wind,* and *The Ride Back* (1957); *Hot Spell* and *The Black Orchid* (1958); *Warlock* and *Last Train from Gun Hill* (1959); *The Savage Innocents, Portrait in Black,* and *Heller in Pink Tights* (1960); *The Guns of Navarone* and *Barabbas* (1961); *Requiem for a Heavyweight* and *Lawrence of Arabia* (1962); *Behold a Pale Horse, The Visit,* and *Zorba the Greek* (1964); *Marco the Magnificent* and *A High Wind in Jamaica* (1965); *Lost Command* (1966); *The 25th Hour* and *The Happening* (1967); *The Shoes of the Fisherman, Guns for San Sebastian,* and *The Magus* (1968); *A Dream of Kings* and *The Secret of Santa Vittoria* (1969); *Flap, A Walk in the Spring Rain,* and *R.P.M. (Revolutions Per Minute)* (1970); *Arruza* (documentary, narrator) and *Across 110th Street* (1972); *Deaf Smith and Johnny Ears* (Italian production) and *The Don Is Dead* (1973); *The Destructors* (1974); *High Risk, Target of an Assassin,* and *The Inheritance* (1976); *Mohammed, Messenger of God* (Arab production, also with Irene Papas), *Jesus of Nazareth,* and *The Con Artists* (1977); *The Greek Tycoon, African Rage, Caravans,* and *The Children of Sánchez* (1978); *The Passage* (1979); *High Risk, Tigers Don't Cry, Lion of the Desert,* and *The Salamander* (1981); *Regina* (1983); *The Switch* (1989); *Ghosts Can't Do It* and *Revenge* (1990); *Mobsters, Jungle Fever,* and *Only the Lonely* (1991); *Last Action Hero* (1993); and *A Walk in the Clouds* (1995, dir. Alfonso Arau). On television he starred in the 1971 television series *The Man and the City* as the Mexican American mayor of a southwestern city. He was nominated for an Emmy as Best Supporting Actor in a Miniseries for his role as Aristotle Onassis's father in *Onassis: The Richest Man in the World* (1988). In two notable made-for-television movies, he played the lead role in *The Old Man and the Sea* (1990) and appeared in *This Can't Be Love* (1994) opposite Katharine Hepburn. His children Kathleen, Duncan, Francesco, Lorenzo, and Daniel Quinn are actors.

Daniel Quinn

Actor, born April 16, 1964, son of Anthony Quinn and Jolanda Addolari. He has appeared in *Conagher* (1991, TV film), *The Last Outlaw* (1993, TV film), *Scanner Cop* (1994), *Scanners: The Showdown* (1994), and *The Avenging Angel* (1995, TV film).

Duncan Quinn

Actor, born in 1945, son of Anthony Quinn and Katherine De Mille. He appeared in *The Children of Sánchez* (1978, starring Anthony Quinn).

Francesco Quinn

Actor, born March 22, 1962, son of Anthony Quinn and Jolanda Addolari. He has appeared in: *Quo Vadis?* (1985, Italian production, TV film), *Platoon* (1986), *Priceless Beauty* (1988), *Indio* (1990), *Dead Certain* and *Deadly Rivals* (both 1992), and *Top Dog* (1995).

Lorenzo Quinn

Actor, born May 1966, son of Anthony Quinn and Jolanda Addolari. He appeared in *Onassis: The Richest Man in the World* (1988, TV film, starring Anthony Quinn).

Adolfo "Shabba Doo" Quiñones

Breakdancer; he has appeared in *Breakin'* and *Breakin' 2: Electric Boogaloo* (both 1984).

CHICANO/LATINO ROLES OF ANTHONY QUINN

Among his many roles, Anthony Quinn had several as a Chicano or other U.S. Latino.

Left: Anthony Quinn as José Esqueda, a ruthless bandido, in *Ride, Vaquero!* (1953, MGM)

Opposite page, above: Anthony Quinn as Mountain Rivera in *Requiem for a Heavyweight* (1962, Columbia)

Opposite page, below: Anthony Quinn as sociology professor "Paco" Pérez in *R.P.M. (Revolutions Per Minute)* (1970, Columbia, dir. Stanley Kramer)

Ana María Quintana

Scriptwriter, born in Chile; her credits include *The Formula* (1980), *The Falcon and the Snowman* (1985), *Remo Williams: The Adventure Begins* (1985), and *Jurassic Park* (1993).

José Quintero

Director, born in Panama, October 15, 1924. He is recognized for his interpretations of Eugene O'Neill and Tennessee Williams. He directed only one film, *The Roman Spring of Mrs. Stone* (1961, starring Vivien Leigh and Warren Beatty).

Héctor Quiroga

Spanish actor, born in La Coruña, Spain, 1933, died in New York City, 1984. He appeared in a few films released in the United States including *Murieta* (1965); *Lost Command, Return of the Seven,* and *Son of a Gunfighter* (all 1966); *Savage Pampas* (1967); and *The Narco Men* (1969).

Francisco Rabal

(Francisco Rabal Valera) Internationally recognized actor, born in Aquilas, Murcia, Spain, March 8, 1925, married to actress María Asunción Balaguer. He has been seen in the United States in a number of films, primarily ones produced elsewhere and released in the United States, including *The Wide Blue Road* (1956, Italian production, starring Yves Montand); *The Mighty Crusaders* (1957, Ital.); *Nazarín* (1958, Mex., dir. Luis Buñuel); *Viridiana* (1961, Span., dir. Luis Buñuel); *Eclipse* (1962); *The Hand in the Trap* (1963); *The Nun* (1966); *Young Rebel* (1967, multinational, starring Horst Buchholz, Gina Lollobrigida, and José Ferrer); *Belle de jour* (1967, Fr.-Ital., dir. Luis Buñuel); *The Female: Seventy Times Seven* and *The Witches* (both 1968); *El Che Guevara* and *Ann and Eve* (1970); *Eagles Over London* (1970, Ital., also with Van Johnson); *Saddle Tramps* (1971); *Exorcism's Daughter* (1974); *The Devil Is a Woman* (1975, Ital., starring Glenda Jackson); *Sorcerer* (1977); *Reborn* (1978); *Stay as You Are* (1978, Fr., starring Marcello Mastroianni and Nastassia Kinski); *Treasure of the Four Crowns* (1983, Span.); *City of the Walking Dead* (1983, Span.-Ital., starring Mel Ferrer); *The Stilts, The Holy Innocents,* and *Diary of a Rebel* (1984); *Camorra* (1986, Ital., dir. Lina Wertmuller, also with Harvey Keitel); *A Time of Destiny* (1988, dir. Gregory Nava); and *Tie Me Up! Tie Me Down!* (1990, Span., dir. Pedro Almodóvar, starring Victoria Abril and Antonio Banderas).

Enrique Rambal

Actor, born in Madrid, May 8, 1924, died in Mexico City, December 15, 1971. He appeared in a few movies released in the United States including *The Exterminating Angel* (1962, Mex., dir. Luis Buñuel), *The Empty Star* (1962), and *The Man and the Monster* (1965).

Carlos Ramírez

Opera singer, born in 1915 in Colombia, died in Miami, December 11, 1986. He did specialty musical numbers in several MGM musicals of the 1940s and 1950s including *Two Girls and a Sailor* and *Bathing Beauty* (both 1944); *Anchors Aweigh* and *Where Do We Go From Here?* (1945); *Easy to Wed* and *Night and Day* (1946); and *Latin Lovers* (1953).

Loyda Ramos

Actress, born in New York, November 5, 1958, to Puerto Rican parents. She has appeared in *¡Three Amigos!* (1986), *Deal of the Century* (1983), and *Best Seller* (1987).

Rudy Ramos

Actor, born in Lawton, Oklahoma, September 19, 1950. He appeared in *Defiance* (1980), *Quicksilver* (1986), *Open House* (1987), *Colors* (1988), and *Blindsided* (1992). On television he was a regular cast member in the last season of *The High Chaparral.*

Vic Ramos

Casting director. He has been responsible for the casting of a number of major television shows and feature films in New York since the 1960s including *The Godfather: Part II* (1974).

Rafael Ramos Cobián

Owner of the largest chain of movie theaters in Puerto Rico in the 1930s. He backed a few productions, mostly in Mexico, including *Mis dos amores* (1938, featuring Puerto Rican actress Blanca de Castejón and Mexican Tito Guízar) and *Los hijos mandan* (1939, with Blanca de Castejón and Arturo de Córdova).

Daniel F. Rea

Actor. He had a few supporting roles in Hollywood Spanish-language films including *El hombre malo* (1930, First National Pictures); *Oriente y occidente* (1930, Universal Pictures), as Lo Sang Ki; *El diablo del mar* (1935, Theater Classic Pictures); *Un hombre peligroso* (1935, Criterion Films); *Papá soltero* (1939, Paramount); and *La Inmaculada* (1939, United Artists), as Homobono.

Alma Real

Actress. She had a few supporting roles in Hollywood Spanish-language films including *El presidio* (1930, MGM), as Señora Marlowe; *La fruta amarga* (1931, MGM); *Mamá* (1931, Fox); *Tres amores* (1934, Universal); *Contra la corriente* (1935, RKO-Radio Pictures), as Señora Martin; and *Alas sobre el Chaco* (1935, Universal), as *la enfermera.* She was also in a few Hollywood English-language films: *Yankee Don* (1931), *Storm Over the Andes* (1935), and *Dancing Pirate* (1936).

Donald Reed

(Also Ernest Gillen; born Ernesto Ávila Guillén) Actor, born in Mexico City, July 23, 1901, died February 27, 1973. He was a leading man during the silent era but turned to supporting roles, usually as a Latin Lover or gigolo, during the sound period. Film credits include *Convoy* and *Naughty But Nice* (both 1927); *Mad Hour, The Night Watch,* and *Show Girl* (all 1928); *Evangeline, Hardboiled, Little Johnny Jones,* and *A Most Immoral Lady* (1929); *The Texan* (1930); *Aloha* and *Playthings of Hollywood* (1931); *Flame of Mexico, The Racing Strain,* and *Westward Passage* (1932); *The Man from Monterey* (1933, starring John Wayne); *Happy Landing* and *Uncertain Lady* (1934); *The Cyclone Ranger, The Devil Is a Woman, Vanishing Riders,* and *Six Gun Justice* (1935); *Ramona* (1936); *Crusades Against Rackets, The Firefly, The Last Train from Madrid, Law and Lead, Renfrew of the Royal Mounted, Slaves in Bondage, Special Agent K-7,* and *Under Strange Flags* (1937); and *Juvenile Court* (1938). He also costarred opposite José Bohr and Lia Torá in the Hollywood Spanish-language original, *Hollywood, ciudad de ensueño* (Universal), based on a screenplay by José Bohr.

George Regas

(Also Rigas; also Jorge Rigas) Actor, born in Sparta, Greece, November 9, 1890 [R has 1900], died December 13, 1940. He came to the United States as a young adult with his brother, Pedro Regas, and worked first on the stage. He debuted on film in 1921 and appeared in numerous films including *The Dangerous Moment* and *The Love Light* (both 1921); *Omar the Tentmaker* (1922); *Fashionable Fakers* and *The Rip-Tide* (1923); *"That Royle Girl"* (1925); *Beau Geste, Desert Gold,* and *The Wanderer* (1926); *Acquitted, Redskin, The Rescue, Sea Fury,* and *Wolf Song* (1929); *The Lonesome Trail* (1930); *Beau Ideal, Caught Cheating, Forbidden Adventure, Hell Bent for Frisco, Mounted Fury, Riders of the North,* and *Trapped* (1931); *The Golden West* (1932); *Blood Money, Central Airport, Destination Unknown,* and *The Way to Love* (1933); *Bulldog Drummond Strikes Back, The Fighting Trooper, Grand Canary, Kid Millions, The Marines Are Coming, Viva Villa!, Sixteen Fathoms Deep,* and *Riptide* (1934); *Bordertown, Eight Bells, Here's to Romance, In Caliente, The Lives of a Bengal Lancer, Night Cargo, Pursuit, Red Blood of Courage,* and *Under Pressure* (1935); *The Charge of the Light Brigade, Daniel Boone, The Girl from Mandalay, Hell-Ship Morgan, Isle of Fury, Robin Hood of El Dorado,*

Rose-Marie, Sworn Enemy, and *Under Two Flags* (1936); *Ali Baba Goes to Town, Another Dawn, The Bad Man of Brimstone, The Californian, Charlie Chan on Broadway, Left-Handed Law, The Legion of Missing Men, Love Under Fire,* and *Waikiki Wedding* (1937); *Arrest Bulldog Drummond, Clipped Wings, Four Men and a Prayer, Hawaiian Buckaroo, Mr. Moto Takes a Chance, Penrod's Double Trouble, Torchy Blane in Panama,* and *The Toy Wife* (1938); *The Adventures of Sherlock Holmes, The Oklahoma Kid, Beau Geste, The Cat and the Canary, Code of the Secret Service, Gunga Din, The Rains Came,* and *Union Pacific* (1939); and *The Light That Failed, The Mark of Zorro, North West Mounted Police, Torrid Zone,* and *Virginia City* (1940). He was also in the Hollywood Spanish-language films *La rosa de fuego* (1930, Tom White Productions, starring Don Alvarado) and *Alma de gaucho* (1930, Chris Phillis Productions, presented by Edward L. Klein Corporation, starring Manuel Granado and Mona Rico). He died of throat cancer.

Pedro Regas

(Also Pedro Riga; also Peter; born Panagiotis Regas) Actor, born in Sparta, Greece, April 12, 1882 [R has 1899], died August 10, 1974. Older brother of George Regas, he did many character roles in films that included *The Riding Renegade* (1928); *Two-Fisted Justice* (1931); *Scarface* and *Tiger Shark* (both 1932); *Flying Down to Rio* (1933); *Grand Canary* and *Viva Villa!* (1934); *Black Fury, Under the Pampas Moon,* and *West of the Pecos* (1935); *Sutter's Gold* and *The Traitor* (1936); *Midnight Taxi* and *Waikiki Wedding* (1937); *The Girl of the Golden West* and *Tropic Holiday* (1938); *Code of the Secret Service, The Rains Came,* and *Only Angels Have Wings* (1939); *Road to Singapore* and *They Drive by Night* (1940); *To Have and Have Not* (1944); *Viva Zapata!* (1952); *Lonely Are the Brave* (1962); *Madmen of Mandoras* (1963); *The Hell With Heroes* (1968); *Angel Unchained* and *Flap* (1970); and *High Plains Drifter* (1973). He was in one Hollywood Spanish-language film, *Politiquerías* (1931, MGM, starring Stan Laurel and Oliver Hardy). On television he appeared in over 100 series episodes over the decades.

Duncan Renaldo

(Vasile Dumitree Coghleanas) Actor, a foundling thought to have been born in Spain on April 23, 1904 [acc. to PHH, born in Romania], died in Santa Barbara, California, September 3, 1980. He arrived in the United States in the early 1920s and was a Hollywood leading man and supporting player. He debuted with MGM in 1928 and by the early 1940s had found a niche in Westerns as the Latin

Above: Duncan Renaldo

Mountain Rangers (1940); Don Amigo/Stage to Chino (double feature, date uncertain but early 1940s, featuring Duncan Renaldo as Cisco Kid and Leo Carrillo as Pancho); Outlaws of the Desert, King of the Texas Rangers (serial), Panama Menace, and Down Mexico Way (1941); King of the Mounties (1942, serial); Secret Service in Darkest Africa (also released as a serial with the title Manhunt in the African Jungle), Border Patrol, Tiger Fangs, and For Whom the Bell Tolls (1943); Perils of the Darkest Jungle (also released as Tiger Woman, serial), Western Double Feature 12 (a Three Mesquiteers film, starring Bob Livingston, Wild Bill Elliot, and Duncan Renaldo as U.S. envoys sent to the Caribbean [available on videotape]), San Antonio Kid, and The Fighting Seabees (all 1944); Guns of Fury, South of the Rio Grande, In Old New Mexico, and The Cisco Kid Returns (1945); Jungle Flight (1947); Sword of the Avenger (1948); Satan's Cradle, We Were Strangers, The Gay Amigo, and The Daring Caballero (1949); The Capture (1950); Manhunt in the African Jungle (1954); and Zorro Rides Again (1959). On television he started the Cisco Kid series in 1950, which was a great success and the first Western to be specially produced for color television. A total of 156 episodes were produced through 1955.

Beginning in 1931 Renaldo was prosecuted by the federal government for being an illegal alien, and he spent several years in litigation and court trials, and one year in a detention center, before being granted a presidential pardon in 1936 by Franklin D. Roosevelt. He became a U.S. citizen in 1941.

Tito Renaldo

Actor; he appeared in Ramona (1936), Old Los Angeles (1948), and The Bribe (1949).

María Teresa Renner

Actress. She had a few supporting roles in Hollywood Spanish-language films including El cuerpo del delito (1930, Paramount); El último de los Vargas (1930, Fox); and Los que danzan (1930, Warner), as Nelly.

Rosaura Revueltas

Mexican actress, born in Durango, Mexico, in 1920, died in Cuernavaca, Mexico, April 30, 1996. Active in Mexican films in the 1950s, she was in Islas Marías and Muchachas de uniforme (both 1950). She starred in the remarkable and controversial union and feminist film Salt of the Earth (1954). Branded a communist and deported by U.S. authorities, she returned to Mexico, spending her later years as a dance teacher and yoga instructor in Cuernavaca.

member (Rico) of the Three Mesquiteers. The series was popular both in the United States and Latin America. Subsequently, he became the screen's fourth Cisco Kid, first with Martín Garralaga as his sidekick and then with Leo Carrillo in that role. Film credits include The Naughty Duchess and Clothes Make the Woman (1928); Pals of the Prairie and The Bridge of San Luis Rey (1929), in the leading role of Esteban; Trader Horn (1931), the first Hollywood film shot on location in Africa; Trapped in Tia Juana (1932); Public Stenographer (1933); Rough Riders' Roundup and The Moth (1934); Lady Luck, Rebellion, Two Minutes to Play, and Moonlight Murder (1936); Crack-Up, The Painted Stallion, Roaring Speedboats, Mile-a-Minute-Love, Special Agent K-7, Jungle Menace (serial), and Zorro Rides Again (serial) (1937); Ten Laps to Go, Tropic Holiday, Spawn of the North, and Rose of the Rio Grande (1938); The Lone Ranger Rides Again (serial), Zaza, Cowboys from Texas, The Mad Empress, Rough Riders Round-Up, South of the Border, and The Kansas Terrors (1939); Covered Wagon Days, Gaucho Serenade, Heroes of the Saddle, Oklahoma Renegades, Pioneers of the West, and Rocky

Alejandro Rey

Actor, born in Buenos Aires, February 8, 1930, died May 21, 1987. He appeared in a number of films including *Solomon and Sheba* (1959); *The Pacific Connection* (1960); *Battle at Bloody Beach* (1961); *Fun in Acapulco* (1963); *Synanon* (1965); *Blindfold* (1966); *The Stepmother* (1971); *Mr. Majestyk* (1974); *Satan's Triangle* (TV film, starring Kim Novak) and *Breakout* (both 1975); *High Velocity* (1977); *Sunburn* (starring Farrah Fawcett-Majors and Charles Grodin), *The Ninth Configuration,* and *Cuba* (all 1979); *Moscow on the Hudson* (1984); *Terror Vision* (1986); and *Stickfighter* (1989). On television he played the role of Carlos Ramírez on *The Flying Nun* opposite Sally Field from 1967 until 1970, and he had guest-star appearances on *Naked City, Gunsmoke, Bob Hope Presents the Chrysler Theatre, The High Chaparral, Fantasy Island,* and *The Love Boat.* He played Rita Hayworth's father, Eduardo Cansino, in the television film *Rita Hayworth: The Love Goddess* (1983).

Fernando Rey

(Fernando Casado Arambillet Veiga) Actor, born in La Coruña, Galicia, Spain, September 20, 1915 [R has 1918], died March 9, 1994. Rey worked continuously over a 50-year period in Spanish films or international productions filmed in Spain. His association with director Luis Buñuel brought him international recognition beginning with his role as Don Lope, the elderly guardian, opposite Catherine Deneuve in *Tristana* (1970). He also appeared in *Viridiana* (1961), *The Discreet Charm of the Bourgeoisie* (1972), and *That Obscure Object of Desire* (1977) directed by Buñuel. In American film he is noted for his roles as the French drug dealer in the Academy Award-winning *The French Connection* (1971) and *The French Connection II* (1975). Additional film credits include *Pantaloons* (1957, French production); *Last Days of Pompeii* (1960); *Goliath Against the Giants* (Ital.) and *The Revolt of the Slaves* (1961); *The Savage Guns* (1962); *The Castilian, The Ceremony,* and *The Running Man* (1963); *Face of Terror* (1964); *Backfire* and *Scheherazade* (1965); *El Greco, Son of a Gunfighter* (Span., starring Russ Tamblyn), and *Return of the Seven* (1966); *The Viscount* (multinational), *Attack of the Robots, Chimes at Midnight, Navajo Joe* (Ital.-Span., starring Burt Reynolds), *Run Like a Thief* (Span.), and *Falstaff* (1967); *The Desperate One, The Immortal Story* (Fr., starring Orson Welles and Jeanne Moreau), and *Villa Rides* (1968); *The Young Rebel* and *Guns of the Magnificent Seven* (1969); *The Adventurers* and *Land Raiders* (1970); *The Light at the Edge of the World* (1971, Span., starring Kirk Douglas and Yul Brynner); *A Town Called Hell* (1971, Brit.-Span., starring Robert Shaw

Above: Fernando Rey in *The French Connection II* (1975)

and Telly Savalas); *Compañeros* (1971, multinational, also with Tomás Milián); *White Fang* (1972, multinational); *White Sister* (starring Sophia Loren) and *High Crime* (both 1973, Ital.); *Antony and Cleopatra* (1973, starring Charlton Heston); *La Grande Bourgeoise* (1974, Fr., starring Catherine Deneuve, also with Tina Aumont); *Seven Beauties* (1976, Ital.); *The Assignment* (1977, Swed.); *Quintet* (1979, starring Paul Newman); *Caboblanco* (1980, starring Charles Bronson, also with Gilbert Roland); *Honey* (1981, Ital.-Span.); *Monsignor* (starring Christopher Reeve) and *Insanity* (1982); *The Hit* (Brit.) and *Black Arrow* (1984); *Rustler's Rhapsody* (1985); *Star Knight* (Span., starring Klaus Kinski and Harvey Keitel), *Saving Grace* (also with Edward James Olmos), and *Angel of Death* (1986); *Moon Over Parador* (1988); *The Tunnel* (1989); *Naked Tango* (1991, also with Esai Morales); *Breath of Life* (1992, Ital., starring Vanessa Redgrave and Franco Nero); and *1492: Conquest of Paradise* (1992, multinational prod., starring Gerard Depardieu and Sigourney Weaver).

Florián Rey

(Antonio Martínez del Castillo) Actor and screenwriter, born in La Coruña, Spain, September 20, 1915, died in

Alicante, Spain, April 11, 1962, married to actress and singer Imperio Argentina. He worked on a number of screenplays of Hollywood Spanish-language films.

Nita Rey

Actress; she appeared as a sexy señorita in *Oklahoma Cyclone* (1930, Tiffany) and as the Don's pretty daughter in *Rancho of the Don* (1930).

Roberto Rey

(Roberto Colás Iglesias) Actor, director, and singer, born in Valparaíso, Chile, February 15, 1905, died in Madrid, May 30, 1972. He starred in five Hollywood Spanish-language films: *Un hombre de suerte* (1930, Cinéstudio Continental Paramount, dir. Benito Perojo, costarring María Luz Callejo), a Spanish-language version of *Un trou dans le mur* (1930, starring Jean Murat, Dolly Davis, and Marguerite Moreno); *¡Salga de la cocina!* (1930, Paramount, dir. Jorge Infante, costarring Amparo Miguel Ángel), an English-language version of *Honey* (1930, starring Nancy Carroll and Stanley Smith); *Gente alegre* (1931, Paramount, costarring Rosita Moreno), a Spanish-language original based on a screenplay by Henry Myers; *El príncipe gondolero* (1931, Paramount, costarring Rosita Moreno), a Spanish-language version of *Honeymoon Hate* (1927, starring Florence Vidor and Tullio Carminati); and *Un caballero de frac* (1931, Paramount, costarring Gloria Guzmán), a Spanish-language version of *Evening Clothes* (1927, starring Adolphe Menjou, Virginia Valli, and Noah Beery).

Rosa Rey

Spanish actress, born September 4, 1892, died April 7, 1969. She had several supporting roles in Hollywood Spanish-language films including *La buenaventura* (1934, First National Pictures); *Tres amores* (1934, Universal); *El cantante de Nápoles* (1934, Warner), as Doña Rosa; *Julieta compra un hijo* (1935, Fox); *El crimen de media noche* (1935, Reliable Pictures), as Señora Ryan; and *El capitán tormenta* (1936, MGM). She was also in the English-language films *Grand Canary* (1934) and *Song of the Gringo* (1936).

Ernie Reyes, Jr.

Actor, born in San Jose, California, January 15, 1972, primarily of Filipino heritage. He is a recognized martial arts

Above: Roberto Rey with Carmen Jiménez in *¡Salga de la cocina!* (1930, Paramount)

expert who has appeared in *The Last Dragon* and *Red Sonja* (both 1985), *Teenage Mutant Ninja Turtles II: The Secret of the Ooze* (1991), and *Surf Ninjas* (1993). On television he starred in his own TV series, *Sidekicks.*

Julián Reyes

New York-born actor of Puerto Rican parents. He appeared in *Die Hard 2* (1990), *Point Break,* as an FBI agent, and *Alligator II: The Mutation* (both 1991), and *Mi Vida Loca/My Crazy Life* (1994, dir. Allison Anders, starring Ángel Avilés and Seidy López). On television he appeared on *Miami Vice* as a guest star and was a regular in the series *What a Country.*

David Reynoso

Well-known Mexican actor; he has appeared in over 100 Mexican films and in the United States appeared in *Invasion of the Vampires* (1965), *Rage* (1966), and *Stick* (1985).

Alfonso Ribeiro

Actor, born in 1968 of Dominican parentage. He debuted at age eight on the PBS series *Oye Willie,* appeared on television as a teenager in the *Silver Spoons* series, and plays Carlton Banks on the series *Fresh Prince of Bel Air.* He was in the film *Infested* (1993) and the PBS TV film *The Mighty Pawns* (1987, Wonderworks family movie series).

Branscome Richmond

Stuntman and actor of mixed heritage including European (French and Spanish), Hawaiian, and Aleutian Indian, born August 8, 1955, in Los Angeles. He has appeared in over 100 films and over 300 television episodes including *Star Trek III: The Search for Spock* and *Thief of Hearts* (both 1984), *Commando* (1985), *License to Kill* (1989), *Hard to Kill* (1990), *Grand Canyon* and *The Taking of Beverly Hills* (1991), *DaVinci's War* and *Batman Returns* (1992), *Jericho Fever* (1993, TV film), and *Renegade* (1993, pilot film for TV series starring Lorenzo Lamas).

María Richwine

Actress, born in Cali, Colombia, June 22, year unknown, and raised in California. She costarred as Buddy Holly's Puerto Rican wife in the Academy Award-nominated film *The Buddy Holly Story* (1978) and was a judge brutally raped in *Sex Crimes* (1992). She also costarred on the TV series *A.K.A. Pablo*.

Mona Rico

(María Enriqueta Valenzuela) Actress, born in Mexico City, July 15, 1909. She costarred in three Hollywood Spanish-language films: *Sombras de gloria* (1929, Sono-Art Productions, Ltd., opposite José Bohr), a Spanish-language version of *Blaze O' Glory* (1929, starring Eddie Dowling and Betty Compson); *Alma de gaucho* (1930, Chris Phillis Productions, presented by Edward L. Klein Corporation, opposite Manuel Granado), a Spanish-language original based on a screenplay by Paul Ellis; and *La señorita de Chicago* (1931, MGM, opposite Charley Chase), a Spanish-language version of *The Pip from Pittsburgh* (1931, starring Charley Chase and Thelma Todd). She was also in the Hollywood English-language films *A Devil with Women* and *Just Imagine* (both 1930), *Thunder Below* (1932), and *Goin' to Town* (1935).

Elvira Ríos

(Elvira Gallegos) Actress and singer, born in Mexico City, November 16, 1914. She appeared in *Tropic Holiday* (1938) and *The Real Glory* and *Stagecoach* (both 1939).

Lalo Ríos

(Edward C. Ríos) Actor, born in Sonora, Mexico, February 7, 1927, died March 14, 1973. He moved to Los Angeles at an early age and while working in construction was discovered by director Joseph Losey, who gave him a major role in the notable Chicano-focused film *The Lawless* (1950) as a Mexican youth falsely accused of a crime. He then starred in the role of a young Mexican American boxer from East Los Angeles in *The Ring* (1952). Aside from these two independently produced films, he was never able to obtain a leading role again. He had small roles in *Mark of the Renegade* (1951), *One Minute to Zero* (1952), as soldier Chico Mendoza fighting in Korea, *Lonely Are the Brave* (1962), as a bracero looking for work (Martín Garralaga appeared in an identical role), and *City Beneath the Sea* (1970), and important parts in *Giant* (1956) and *Touch of Evil* (1958, dir. Orson Welles).

Carlos Riquelme

Actor, born in Mexico City, May 13, 1914. Active in the Mexican film industry, his best-known film was *The Criminal Life of Archibaldo de la Cruz* (1962, dir. Luis Buñuel). He also appeared in *The Milagro Beanfield War* (1988).

Carlos Rivas

Actor, born in Mexico, February 16, 1925. He was both a leading man in Mexican films and a supporting actor in the United States, popular in the mid-1950s and early 1960s. His film credits include *The King and I,* as Tuptim's lover, and *The Beast of the Hollow Mountain* (both 1956); *The Black Scorpion, The Deerslayer,* as an American Indian, *Panama Sal,* and *The Big Boodle* (all 1957); *Machete* (1958); *The Miracle* (1959); *The Unforgiven* (dir. John Huston), as an Indian chief, and *Pepe* (1960); *The Madman of Mandoras* and *They Saved Hitler's Brain* (1963); *Tarzan and the Valley of Gold* (1966); *Hang Your Hat on the Wind, True Grit, Topaz* (dir. Alfred Hitchcock), as a Cuban, and *The Undefeated* (1969); and *The Gatling Gun* (1971, also *King Gun*, Broadway Enterprises). On television he guest-starred on many major television series of the past 35 years, and he has starred in over 20 Mexican films.

Carlos Rivas

Sound technician. He won three Academy Awards for technical advancements in sound. He worked for MGM from 1943 until his retirement in 1965.

Gabry Rivas

(Gabriel Rivas) Actor. He had a few supporting roles in Hollywood Spanish-language films including *Olimpia* (1930, MGM); *¡De frente, marchen!* (1930, MGM), as *el comandante*; and *El presidio* (1930, MGM). He was also in *Thunder Below* (1932).

Geoffrey Rivas

Actor. His film credits include *La Bamba* and *Born in East L.A.* (both 1987) and *Bound by Honor* (1993).

Rafael Rivelles

(Rafael Rivelles Guillén) Actor, son of actor Jaime Rivelles, married to María Ladrón de Guevara and father of actress Amparo Rivelles, born in El Cabañal, Valencia, Spain, December 23, 1898, died in Madrid, December 3, 1971. He starred or had principal parts in a few Hollywood Spanish-language films including *La mujer X* (1931, MGM, dir. Carlos F. Borcosque, costarring opposite his wife, María Ladrón de Guevara), a Spanish-language version of *Madame X* (1929, dir. Lionel Barrymore, starring Ruth Chatterton and Lewis Stone); *El proceso de Mary Dugan* (1931, MGM, starring María Ladrón de Guevara and José Crespo), in the role of *el fiscal*; *¿Conoces a tu mujer?* (1931, Fox, costarring Carmen Larrabeiti), a Spanish-language version of *Don't Bet on Women* (1931, starring Edmund Lowe and Jeanette MacDonald); and *Mamá* (1931, Fox, dir. Benito Perojo, costarring opposite Catalina Bárcena), a Spanish-language original based on a work by Gregorio Martínez Sierra.

Chita Rivera

(Dolores Conchita del Rivero) Actress and dancer of Puerto Rican descent, born in Washington, D.C., January 23, 1933. She appeared in *Sweet Charity* (1969), *Once Upon a Brothers Grimm* (1977), *Pippin* (1981, video version of the stage musical), *That's Singing: The Best of Broadway* (1984, performances of memorable songs), and *Mayflower Madam* (1987, TV film, starring Candice Bergen), in the role of the madam's lawyer.

Geraldo Rivera

Television broadcast journalist, of Puerto Rican and Jewish descent, born July 4, 1943, in New York City. He has been a journalist, television producer, and talk show host for over 20 years.

José Rivera

Screenwriter and playwright, born in Puerto Rico, March 24, 1955. His play *The House of Ramón Iglesias* was produced for the PBS American Playhouse series in 1986. He was a writer on the TV series *A.K.A. Pablo*, has written episodes for the sitcom *Family Matters,* and was cocreator and producer of the 1991-92 series *Eerie, Indiana.*

Above: Chita Rivera, Shirley MacLaine, and Paula Kelly in *Sweet Charity* (1969)

Luis Rivera

Actor. He appeared in a number of 1960s Westerns including *Sunscorched* (1966), *House of a Thousand Dolls* and *Run Like a Thief* (both 1967), *Custer of the West* and *A Few Bullets More* (1968), and *Guns of the Magnificent Seven* (1969).

Edmundo Rivera Álvarez

(Also E. R. Álvarez) Actor; he appeared in low-budget thrillers including *Counterplot* (1959, United Artists), *Creature from the Haunted Sea* (1961, dir. Roger Corman), and *Fiend of Dope Island* (1961, Essenjay Films).

Charles Rivero

Actor. He was in *Mexican Hay Ride* (1948, starring Abbott and Costello) and was one of over 40 Hispanic players in *Crisis* (1950, starring Cary Grant and José Ferrer), about an American doctor held in a South American country to treat an ailing dictator.

Jorge Rivero

(Also George Rivero) Actor, born in 1940. A well-known leading man in Mexico, he has also appeared in a few American films including *Soldier Blue* (1970), as an American Indian; *Río Lobo* (1970, dir. Howard Hawks, starring John

Above: Chita Rivera

Lawless, Lucky Larrigan, The Man from Hell's Edges, The Night Rider, Son of Oklahoma, and Winner Take All (1932); Flying Down to Rio, Man of Action, and Via Pony Express (1933); Burn-'Em-Up Barnes, Viva Villa!, and The Westerner (1934); Born to Battle, Cowboy Holiday, Diamond Jim, Goin' to Town, Gun Play, The Melody Lingers On, Red Salute, Riddle Ranch, The Sagebrush Troubadour, Western Justice, and Hi, Gaucho! (1935); Dancing Pirate, Lawless Land, Phantom Patrol, Song of the Saddle, The Traitor, and Woman Trap (1936); Heroes of the Alamo, in the role of Santa Anna, Land Beyond the Law, Love Under Fire, The Mighty Treve, Ridin' the Lone Trail, and Wells Fargo (1937); Flight to Nowhere and Outlaw Express (1938); The Arizona Wildcat, Code of the Secret Service, Drifting Westward, The Girl and the Gambler, The Mad Empress, and South of the Border (1939); Arizona Gang Busters, Billy the Kid's Gun Justice, Death Rides the Range, Down Argentine Way, Gaucho Serenade, Green Hell, Meet the Wildcat, Riders of Black Mountain, The Westerner, and Young Buffalo Bill (1940); Billy the Kid's Fighting Pals and Billy the Kid's Range War (1941); Valley of Vanishing Men (1942, serial); Hands Across the Border and The Outlaw (1943); The Falcon in Mexico (1944); Trail to Mexico (1946); Robin Hood of Monterey and Captain from Castile (1947); Mexican Hay Ride, The Treasure of the Sierra Madre, as the man who gives Bogart a haircut,

Wayne), as Pierre Cardona, a confederate captain; *The Sin of Adam and Eve* (1972, Mexican production); *The Last Hard Men* (1976), as the bandido César Menéndez; *Bordello* (TV film, also with Isela Vega), *Priest of Love* (Brit., about writer D. H. Lawrence), and *Day of the Assassin* (all 1981); *Conquest* (1983); *Target Eagle* (1984, Span.-Mex., costarring George Peppard and Max von Sydow); *Killing Machine* (1986, Span., costarring Margaux Hemingway); *Counterforce* (1987); and *Fist Fighter* (1988, dir. Frank Zúñiga), in which he starred as a professional bare-knuckle fighter.

Julián Rivero

Actor and director, born in San Francisco, July 25, 1890, died in Hollywood, California, February 24, 1976. First working on the Broadway stage before entering the Hollywood film industry, he directed a few comedies and Westerns for World Film Co. and Canadian film companies. He debuted as an actor in *The Bright Shawl* (1923, First National), which was filmed in Cuba. He appeared in numerous films, often as a Mexican bandit, a sidekick, or a Hispanic don. His film credits include *Fast and Fearless* (1924); *The Night Ship* (1925); *The Border Whirlwind* (1926); *Dugan of the Badlands, God's Country and the Man,* and *Yankee Don* (all 1931); *Beyond the Rockies, The Broken Wing, The Kid from Spain, Law and*

Above: Gabby Hayes, Julián Rivero, and Harry Carey in *The Night Rider* (1932)

and *Old Los Angeles* (1948); *Border Treasure* and *Killer Shark* (1950); *The Texas Rangers* (1951); *Wild Horse Ambush* (1952); *Shadows of Tombstone* (1953); *Broken Lance* (1954); *Thunder Over Arizona* (1956); *Don't Go Near the Water* (1957); *The Reward* (1965), in the role of "El Viejo"; and *The Red Pony* (1973, starring Henry Fonda and Maureen O'Hara). He appeared in varied roles in several Hollywood Spanish-language films including *Los fantasmas* (1930, MGM, starring "Our Gang"), in the role of *el padre de Jackie*, a Spanish-language version of *When the Wind Blows* (1930, starring "Our Gang" and Edgar Kennedy); *Así es la vida* (1930, Sono-Art Productions, Ltd.); *El presidio* (1930, MGM), as Oliver; *La cautivadora* (1930, Iberia Productions, Inc.); *La cruz y la espada* (1933, Fox), as "El Mestizo"; and *Nada más que una mujer* (1934, Fox), as Hansen. On television he appeared in episodes of *The Cisco Kid, The Lone Ranger, Wyatt Earp, Marcus Welby, M.D.,* and *The Bold Ones.*

Victor Rivers

(Víctor Rivas) Actor, born in Cuba in 1956. He debuted in *8 Million Ways to Die* (1986) as a gang member, was in *Black Magic Woman* (1991, also with Apollonia), costarred as Amando in *The Distinguished Gentleman* (1992, starring Eddie Murphy), and appeared in *Bound by Honor* (1993).

Carmen Rodríguez

(Also spelled with other variations) Actress, born in Madrid, February 1899. She had supporting roles as *tías, señoras, doctoras, doñas,* and so on in at least 16 Hollywood Spanish-language films including *Olimpia* (1930, MGM); *El último de los Vargas* (1930, Fox); *La mujer X* (1931, MGM), as Rosa; and *Tango Bar* (1935, Paramount).

Estelita Rodríguez

(Also simply Estelita) Singer and actress, born in 1913 in Guanajay, Cuba, died in Van Nuys, California, March 12, 1966. She starred or appeared in major roles in numerous Westerns for Republic Studios, often as costar to singing cowboy Roy Rogers. Her film credits include *Mexicana* and *Along the Navajo Trail* (both 1945); *Gay Ranchero* (costarring opposite Roy Rogers and Tito Guízar) and *On the Old Spanish Trail* (1947); *Susanna Pass* (also with Martín Garralaga) and *The Golden Stallion* (1949); *Federal Agent at Large, Twilight in the Sierras, California Passage,* and *Belle of Old Mexico* (1950); *Hit Parade of 1951, Cuban Fireball* (with Estelita attempting to replicate the Lupe Vélez Latina screwball comic persona; unfortunately, a box-office failure), *Havana Rose* (starring as a Lupe Vélez type from the fiction-

al island of Lower Salamia with Fortunio Bonanova as the father), and *In Old Amarillo* (1951); and *The Fabulous Señorita* (with Rita Moreno appearing as the younger sister) and *Pals of the Golden West* (1952).

Freddy Rodríguez

Actor of Puerto Rican descent. He grew up in Chicago and began acting at age 12 when he was chosen to join the Whirlwind Performance Company, a theater group for inner-city youth. He was in Robin Givens's syndicated TV program *Angel Street* and then was the host for a children's sports show, *Energy Express,* which won an Emmy in 1993. He appeared in the films *A Walk in the Clouds* (1995, dir. Alfonso Arau) and *Dead Presidents* (1995).

Ismael Rodríguez

Film director, born in Mexico City in 1917. He directed two U.S. productions, *The Beast of Hollow Mountain* (1956, codirected with Edward Nassour) and *Daniel Boone: Trail Blazer* (1956, starring Lon Chaney, Jr.), as well as a few Mexican films released in the United States: *The Important Man* (originally titled *Ánimas Trujano,* a notable film starring Toshiro Mifune as a Mexican peasant) and *La cucaracha* (both 1961) and *The Mighty Jungle* (1964).

Marco Rodríguez

Actor, born July 10, 1953. He appeared in *The Baltimore Bullet* (1980); *Zoot Suit* (1981), in the role of Smiley; *Disorderlies* (1987); *Internal Affairs* and *The Rookie* (both 1990); and *. . . and the earth did not swallow him* (1995), as the father. He has appeared in numerous television series episodes including *Hill Street Blues,* and he had a regular role in the short-lived *The Bay City Blues* (1983, NBC).

Paul Rodríguez

Comedian, actor, director, and producer, born in Mazatlán, Mexico, January 19, 1955, the son of immigrant farm workers. He starred in the TV series *A.K.A. Pablo* (1984), followed by *Trial and Error* (1988), *Grand Slam* (1990), and the PBS production *La Pastorela* (1991, dir. Luis Valdez, also starring Linda Ronstadt and Cheech Marín, with Robert Beltrán and Freddy Fender). His HBO and Fox comedy specials have been very popular. His film credits include *D.C. Cab* (1984); *Miracles, Ponce de León and the Fountain of Youth, Quicksilver,* and *The Whoopee Boys* (all 1986), *Born in East L.A.* (1987), *Made in America* (1993), and *A Million to Juan* (1994), which he directed and in which he starred.

Above: Paul Rodríguez (left) and Eddie Vélez in the TV series *Trial and Error* (1988)

Percy Rodríguez

Actor, born in Montreal, Canada. He often played digni-fied African American parts in U.S. films and television episodes. His film credits include *The Plainsman* (1966), *The Sweet Ride* (1968), and *The Heart Is a Lonely Hunter* (1968). On televi-sion he has guest starred on *Naked City, Peyton Place, Route 66, The Man From U.N.C.L.E., Benson,* and *Dynasty,* and he was in the 1979 TV film *The Night Rider* (ABC, a pilot that was not picked up).

Robert Rodríguez

Director, born in 1968 in Texas. He directed the independent film feature *El Mariachi* (1992, starring Carlos Gallardo and Consuelo Gómez), which was made for a mere $7,000. It was distributed by Columbia Pictures, which has had him under contract. Subse-quently he directed *Roadracers* (1994, Showtime TV film starring

David Arquette, John Hawkes, and Salma Hayek), about a wild small-town guy having problems with a sheriff; *Desperado* (1995, starring Antonio Banderas and Salma Hayek, also with Cheech Marín and Carlos Gallardo), a $7 million sequel to *El Mariachi,* coproduced with his wife, Elizabeth Avellán, and Carlos Gallardo; *Four Rooms* (1995), a four-part film depicting characters staying in different rooms of the same hotel (Allison Anders, director of *Mi Vida Loca,* directs one of the four blocks); and *From Dusk 'til Dawn* (1996, with the appearance of Quentin Tarantino, who also wrote the script), about two con-men brothers who kidnap a family and wind up in a Mexican biker bar infested with vampires.

Jaime Rogers

Choreographer and director of Puerto Rican descent, born in 1935. He appeared as a dancer in *West Side Story* (1961). He has directed and choreographed numerous television shows featuring top performing artists as well as directing the TV series *Fame* and the musical numbers for the film *Breakin'* (1984).

Manuel Rojas

(Also Emmanuel) Actor, active in the Mexican film indus-try. He also appeared in a number of U.S. films released in the 1950s and 1960s including *Buchanan Rides Alone* (1958, starring Randolph Scott), as the Mexican buddy; *Buccaneer* (1958, dir. Anthony Quinn, starring Yul Brynner), as a men-acing but loyal Hispanic pirate; *The Steel Claw* (1961); *Out*

Above: Paul Rodríguez in *The Whoopee Boys* (1986)

Above: Paul Rodríguez flanked by Kirk Ward and Kinan Valdez in *La Pastorela* (1991)

of the Tiger's Mouth and *Samar* (1962); *A Yank in Viet-Nam* (1964); *Ambush Bay* (1966); *Kill a Dragon* (1967); and *Madigan's Millions* (1969).

Gilbert Roland

(Luis Antonio Dámaso de Alonso) Actor, born in Juárez on December 11, 1903, died May 15, 1994. The son of bullfighter Francisco Alonso, he trained for the *corrida* but chose a career in film after his family moved to the United States. Gilbert Roland (who took his stage name from two of his favorite actors, John Gilbert and serial star Ruth Roland) was one of the most durable Latino actors, spanning both the silent and sound periods in roles as a leading man as well as various supporting and character parts. As a

teenager, he debuted in film as an extra and subsequently played a Latin Lover on both the silent and sound screen. His big opportunity came as the second lead in *The Plastic Age* (1925, starring Clara Bow). He became a star in the role of the young Frenchman Armand in *Camille* (1927, starring Norma Talmadge). He survived the transition from silent to sound film, but his career as a leading man began to wane in the 1930s. After World War II, during which he served in the U.S. Army, he starred in a series of Cisco Kid films at Monogram Studios, and subsequently he had numerous supporting roles through the 1970s. His film credits through the 1930s, usually as a Latin Lover leading man, include *Blood and Sand* (1922), as an extra; *The Phantom of the Opera,* as an extra, *The Midshipman,* as Ramón Novarro's double, and *The Plastic Age* (all 1925); *The Blonde Saint* and *The Campus Flirt* (1926); *The Dove* (Norma Talmadge Film Co., dir. Roland West, starring Norma Talmadge, Noah Beery, and Gilbert Roland [film held at LC]), *Camille, The Love Mart,* and *Rose of the Golden West* (1927); *The Woman Disputed* (1928); *New York Nights* (1929); *Men of the North* (1930); *Resurrection* (1931, opposite Lupe Vélez); *Call Her Savage* (starring as a "half breed" opposite Clara Bow); *Life Begins, No Living Witness, A Parisian Romance, The Passionate Plumber,* and *The Woman in Room 13* (1932); *After Tonight, Gigolettes of Paris, She Done Him Wrong* (starring Mae West), as a South American gigolo, and *Our Betters* (1933); *Elinor Norton* (1934); *Ladies Love Danger* and *Mystery Woman* (1935); and *Thunder Trail* and *Midnight Taxi* (1937).

Beginning in the late 1930s he alternated leading parts and supporting roles, with film credits that include *The Last Train from Madrid* (1937, opposite Lew Ayres, Dorothy Lamour, and Anthony Quinn); *Gateway* (1938), in a supporting role; *Juárez* (1939), in a supporting role; *The Sea Hawk* (1940), in a supporting role; *Gambling on the High Seas, Isle of Destiny,* and *Rangers of Fortune* (1940); *Angels with Broken Wings* and *My Life with Caroline* (1941); and *Enemy Agents Meet Ellery Queen* and *Isle of Missing Men* (1942). After World War II, Roland appeared in a number of

Cisco Kid films between 1946 and 1948 and, beginning with his appearance as a cynical revolutionary in *We Were Strangers* (1949, dir. John Huston), in strong supporting roles. His film credits during this period include *Captain Kidd* (1945); *The Gay Cavalier, South of Monterey,* and *Beauty and the Bandit* (1946, all as Cisco Kid); *High Conquest, The Other Love, Pirates of Monterey, Riding the California Trail,* and *Robin Hood of Monterey* (1947); *The Dude Goes West* (1948); *We Were Strangers* and *King of the Bandits* (1949); *The Desert Hawk, The Furies, Malaya, The Torch,* and *Crisis* (1950); *Ten Tall Men, The Bullfighter and the Lady,* as an aging bullfighter, and *Mark of the Renegade* (1951); *The Bad and the Beautiful, Apache War Smoke, Glory Alley, My Six Convicts,* in a comic role as prison boss Punch Piñero, and *The Miracle of Our Lady of Fatima* (1952); *Thunder Bay, The Diamond Queen,* and *Beneath the 12-Mile Reef* (1953); *The French Line* (1954); *The Racers, That Lady, The Treasure of Pancho Villa,* and *Underwater!* (1955); *Three Violent People, Around the World in 80 Days,* and *Bandido* (1956); *The Midnight Story* (1957); *The Last of the Fast Guns* (1958); *The Big Circus, Catch Me If You Can,* and *The Wild and the Innocent* (1959); *The Pacific Connection* and *Guns of the Timberland* (1960); *Samar* (1962); *Cheyenne Autumn* (1964), in the role of Chief Dull Knife; *The Reward* (1965); *The Poppy Is Also a Flower* (1966); *Any Gun Can Play* (1967); *Go Kill and Come Back* (1968); *The Ruthless Four* (1969, Italian-German production, starring Van Heflin); *The Christian Licorice Store* (1971); *Between God, the Devil & a Winchester* and *Johnny Hamlet* (1972); *Running Wild* (1973); *Treasure of Tayopa* and *The Mark of Zorro* (1974); *Islands in the Stream* and *The Black Pearl* (1977); *The Sacketts* (1979, TV film); *Caboblanco* (1981, cameo role); and *Barbarosa* (1982).

Roland also starred or costarred in several Hollywood Spanish-language films including *Monsieur le Fox* (1930, MGM, dir. Hal Roach, costarring Rosita Ballesteros), a Spanish-language version of *Men of the North* (1930, dir. Hal Roach, starring Gilbert Roland, Barbara Leonard, Robert Elliott, and Nina Quartaro); *Resurrección* (1931, Universal, dir. Edwin Carewe, costarring opposite Lupe Vélez), a Spanish-language version of *Resurrection* (1931, dir. Edwin Carewe, starring Lupe Vélez and John Boles); *Hombres en mi vida* (1932, Columbia, costarring opposite Lupe Vélez), a Spanish-language version of *Men in Her Life* (1931, starring Lois Moran and Charles Bickford); *Una viuda romántica*

Above: Gilbert Roland (opposite Norma Talmadge) in *Camille* (1927)

Below: Gilbert Roland in 1925

(1933, Fox, costarring opposite Catalina Bárcena), a Spanish-language original based on "El sueño de una noche de agosto" (Madrid, 1918) by Gregorio Martínez Sierra; *Yo,*

tú y ella (1933, Fox, costarring opposite Catalina Bárcena), a Spanish-language original based on "Mujer" (Madrid, 1926) by Gregorio Martínez Sierra; *Julieta compra un hijo* (1935, Fox, costarring opposite Catalina Bárcena), a Spanish-language original based on a work by Gregorio Martínez Sierra and Honorio Maura; and *La vida bohemia* (1937, Columbia, costarring opposite Rosita Díaz Gimeno), a Spanish-language original based on the novel *Scènes de la vie de bohème* (1851) by Henri Murger. On television he appeared on *Zorro, Wagon Train, Medical Center, The High Chaparral, Kung Fu, Hart to Hart,* and *The Sacketts.*

Emma Roldán

Actress. She had a few supporting roles in Hollywood Spanish-language films including *El impostor* (1931, Fox), *Soñadores de la gloria* (1931, United Artists), and *¿Conoces a tu mujer?* (1931, Fox).

Phil Román

Well-known animator and president of Film Roman, born in 1930 and raised in Fresno. He began at Disney and then went to Warner Brothers. The principal animator and director of Charlie Brown cartoons, some of his credits include *Be My Valentine, Charlie Brown* (1975); *It's Your First Kiss, Charlie Brown* and *Someday You'll Find Her, Charlie Brown* (1977); *Life Is a Circus, Charlie Brown, You're the Greatest, Charlie Brown,* and *She's a Good Skate, Charlie Brown* (1980); *It's Magic, Charlie Brown, Charlie Brown's All-Stars,* and *A Charlie Brown Thanksgiving* (1981); *Good Grief, Charlie Brown* (1983); *It's Three Strikes, Charlie Brown* (1986); *It's a Mystery, Charlie Brown* (1987); and *Tom and Jerry: The Movie* (1992). His company also does the animation for *The Simpsons* and did the animation for *The Mask* (1994).

Lina Romay

(Elena Romay) Singer and actress. The Brooklyn-born daughter of a Mexican diplomat, she was affiliated with Xavier Cugat's band and billed as Cugie's Latin Doll. She appeared in *You Were Never Lovelier* (1942, starring Rita Hayworth); *The Heat's On* (1943, starring Mae West); *Two Girls and a Sailor* and *Bathing Beauty* (both 1944);

Yolanda and the Thief, Adventure (starring Clark Gable), in the stereotypical role of the "hot tamale," loved and left behind in favor of the character played by Greer Garson, and *Weekend at the Waldorf* (1945); *Love Laughs at Andy Hardy* (1946, starring Mickey Rooney); *Honeymoon* (1947); *Señor Droopy* (1949, cartoon, with Lina Romay in a real-life cameo role); *Big Wheel* (1949, starring Mickey Rooney); *Caballero Droopy* (1952, cartoon, same format as *Señor Droopy*); and *The Man Behind the Gun* (1952, starring Randolph Scott), as the singing Chona Degnon who ran the local cantina.

Lina Romay

Actress. She appeared in exploitation and soft porn films, primarily directed by Jess Franco (Jesús Franco). Her credits include *Ilsa, the Wicked Warden* (1978, dir. Jess Franco, also released as *Greta the Mad Butcher*), *Demoniac* (1979, dir. Jess Franco, also released as *Ripper of Notre Dame* and in a hardcore version, *Exorcism & Black Masses*), *The Loves of Irina* (date unknown but 1980s, dir. Jess Franco, original Spanish release titled *Erotikill*), and *Oasis of the Zombies* (1982, dir. Jess Franco).

Carlos Romero

Character actor, born in Los Angeles in 1927. He appeared in *They Came to Cordura* (1959), *Deadly Duo* (1962), *Island of the Blue Dolphins* (1964), and *The Professionals* (1966).

Above: Lina Romay and Mickey Rooney in *Love Laughs at Andy Hardy* (1946)

On television he had recurring roles in two series, *Falcon Crest* and *Wichita Town,* and he guest-starred in *Wagon Train, The F.B.I.,* and *Maverick.*

César Romero

Actor, born February 15, 1907, in New York City, of Cuban parentage (his grandfather was allegedly José Martí), died January 1, 1994. He began in show business in 1927 as a ballroom dancer in New York theaters and nightclubs, followed by work in the legitimate theater as an actor. He debuted on film with a bit part in *The Shadow Laughs* (1933), followed by a small role in *The Thin Man* (1934) and a leading role in *British Agent* (1934). He often played a Latin Lover in Hollywood films of the 1930s through the 1950s as well as playing parts as a gangster, rogue, Indian prince, or sophisticated Frenchman; later he did suave supporting character roles. He played the Cisco Kid in the late 1930s and early 1940s and was the first Hispanic actor to do so (the earlier Ciscos were Anglos such as Warner Baxter). In the 1940s he did a number of musicals opposite Betty Grable, Alice Faye, and Carmen Miranda. Beginning in 1950 he moved primarily into television and was notable as the comic villain "The Joker" in the *Batman* series of the mid-1960s. Additional film credits include *Cheating Cheaters* and *Strange Wives* (1934); *Clive of India, The Devil Is a Woman, Diamond Jim, Hold 'Em Yale, Metropolitan, Rendezvous, Show Them No Mercy!, The Good Fairy,* and

Above: César Romero

Cardinal Richelieu (1935); *15 Maiden Lane, Nobody's Fool, Public Enemy's Wife,* and *Love Before Breakfast* (1936); *Ali Baba Goes to Town, Armored Car, Dangerously Yours, She's Dangerous,* and *Wee Willie Winkie* (1937); *Five of a Kind, My Lucky Star, Always Goodbye* (starring Barbara Stanwyck), and *Happy Landing* (1938); *Charlie Chan at Treasure Island, The Little Princess, Frontier Marshal, The Return of the Cisco Kid, The Cisco Kid and the Lady,* and *Wife, Husband, and Friend,* (1939); *Lucky Cisco Kid, Viva Cisco Kid, The Gay Caballero,* and *He Married His Wife* (1940); *Romance of the Rio Grande, Ride on Vaquero, The Great American Broadcast, Dance Hall, Weekend in Havana,* and *Tall, Dark, and Handsome* (1941); *Springtime in the Rockies, Orchestra Wives, A Gentleman at Heart,* and *Tales of Manhattan* (1942); *Wintertime* and *Coney Island* (1943); *Carnival in Costa Rica* (1947); *Deep Waters, That Lady in Ermine, Captain from Castile,* in the role of Hernán Cortez opposite Tyrone Power and Jean Peters, and *Julia Misbehaves* (1948); *The Beautiful Blonde from Bashful Bend* (1949, starring Betty Grable, also with Olga San Juan); *Once a Thief* and *Love That Brute* (1950); *FBI Girl, The Lost Continent,* and *Happy Go Lovely* (1951); *Scotland Yard Inspector* and *The Jungle* (1952); *The Shadow Man* and *Prisoners of the Casbah* (1953); *Vera Cruz* (1954); *The Americano* and *The Racers* (1955); *The Leather Saint* and

Above: César Romero and Marlene Dietrich in *The Devil Is a Woman* (1935)

Above: César Romero (right), Carmen Miranda, and John Payne in *Springtime in the Rockies* (1942)

Around the World in 80 Days (1956); *Villa!* (1958); *Pepe* (cameo) and *Ocean's Eleven* (1960); *Seven Women from Hell* (1961); *If a Man Answers* (1962); *Donovan's Reef, We Shall Return,* and *The Castilian* (1963, Spanish production); *A House Is Not a Home* (1964); *Two on a Guillotine, Sergeant Deadhead,* and *Marriage on the Rocks* (1965); *Batman* (1966); *Skidoo* and *Hot Millions* (1968); *Gun Crazy, A Talent for Loving, How to Make It, Madigan's Millions,* and *Midas Run* (1969); *The Red, White and Black, Sophie's Place, Target: Harry, Latitude Zero, Crooks and Coronets,* and *The Computer Wore Tennis Shoes* (1970); *Now You See Him, Now You Don't* and *Soul Soldier* (1972); *The Spectre of Edgar Allen Poe* and *The Proud and the Damned* (1973); *The Big Push* and *The Strongest Man in the World* (1975); *Won Ton Ton, the Dog Who Saved Hollywood* (1976); *Mission to Glory* (1980); *Lust in the Dust* (1985); *Judgment Day* (1988); *Simple Justice* (1989); and *Mortuary Academy* (1991). On television, in addition to *Batman,* Romero starred in his own TV series, *Passport to Danger,* had the role of a Greek billionaire on *Falcon Crest,* and appeared on many popular shows over the years including *Bonanza* and *Zorro.* In 1992, on his 85th birthday, he appeared as a guest star along with Mickey Rooney on an episode of the TV series *Jack's Place* (starring Hal Linden).

Eddie Romero

(Also Edgar; also E. F. Romero) Producer and director, known as the Roger Corman of Philippine exploitation films. His credits include *Lost Battalion* (1961); *Cavalry Command, Cry of Battle,* and *The Raiders of Leyte Gulf* (1963); *The Kidnappers, Moro Witch Doctor,* and *The Walls of Hell* (1964); *The Ravagers* (1965); *Flight to Fury* (1966); *Brides of Blood, Brides of the Beast,* and *The Passionate Strangers* (1968); *Mad Doctor of Blood Island* (1969); *Beast of Blood, Beast of the Yellow Night,* and *Beast of the Dead* (1970); *Twilight People, Woman Hunt* (U.S.-Philippine prod.), and *Black Mama, White Mama* (1972); *Beyond Atlantis* (1973); *Sleeping Dragon* (1976); *Desire* (1983, starring John Saxon); and *White Force* (1988).

George A. Romero

Screenwriter, director, and producer, born in New York City in 1940. He studied in the drama department of Carnegie-Mellon University in Pittsburgh. After graduation he founded a film production company and became a leading producer of commercials. His feature film debut was the low-budget horror classic *Night of the Living Dead* (1969). Working in Pittsburgh, he has become one of the most original regional filmmakers, specializing in horror films that are often set in the suburbs. Additional films include *The Crazies, Season of the Witch,* and *Code Name: Trixie* (all 1973); *Martin* (1977); *Dawn of the Dead* (1979); *Knightriders* (1981); *Creepshow* (1982); *Day of the Dead* (1985); *Monkey Shines: An Experiment in Fear* (1988); *Two Evil Eyes* (1991); and *The Dark Half* (1993). He wrote the script for the remake of *Night of the Living Dead* (1990), which, with its misplaced ironies, was less successful than the original.

Manuel Romero

Film director, born in Buenos Aires, September 21, 1891, died in Buenos Aires, October 3, 1954. He was an important director in the Argentine film industry beginning in the mid-1930s and in the 1940s. Earlier, however, he received training doing Hollywood Spanish-language films. He was *ayudante de dirección* on *Las luces de Buenos Aires* (1931, Paramount, dir. Adelqui Millar); directed *La pura verdad* (1931, Paramount, starring José Isbert and Enriqueta Serrano), a Spanish-language version of *Nothing but the Truth* (1929, dir. Victor Schertzinger, starring Richard Dix and Helen Kane); and directed *¿Cuándo te suicidas?* (1931, Paramount, starring Fernando Soler and Imperio Argentina), a Spanish-language version of *Quand te tues-tu?* (1931, dir. Roger Capellani, starring Robert Burnier and Simone Vaudry).

Ned Romero

Actor, born in Louisiana. He has primarily played American Indians in films and on television. He played the Hispanic detective partner opposite Burt Reynolds in the TV series *Dan August* (1970). Credits include *I Will Fight No More Forever* (1975, TV film), *The Medicine Hat Stallion* and *Last of the Mohicans* (both 1977, TV films), *The Deerslayer* (1978), *Stranger on my Land* (1988, TV film, starring Tommy Lee Jones), *House 4: Home Deadly Home* (1991), and *Children of the Corn II—The Final Sacrifice* (1993).

Oscar Roncal

Actor; he appeared in two films set in the Philippines: *Cry of Battle* (1963, starring Van Heflin and Rita Moreno) and *The Walls of Hell* (1964).

Linda Ronstadt

Mexican American singer, born in Tucson, Arizona, July 15, 1946. She has been in a few films including *The Pirates of Penzance* (1983), *FM* (1987), *Chuck Berry Hail! Hail! Rock 'n' Roll* (1987, docudrama, starring Chuck Berry), *Corridos* (1987, TV film, dir. Luis Valdez), in the roles of La Chata and Adelita, and *La Pastorela* (1991, PBS production, dir. Luis Valdez).

Thomas Rosales, Jr.

(Also Tom Rosale) Stuntman and actor. He has worked in numerous films and television shows since 1977 including *Walk Proud* (1979), *Hunter* (1980), *Commando* (1985), *The Bedroom Window* and *Extreme Prejudice* (both 1987), *Bail Out* and *Kindergarten Cop* (1990), and *American Me* (1992).

Bert Rosario

Character actor, born November 17, 1945, in Juncos, Puerto Rico. His film credits include *S.O.B.* (1981, dir. Blake Edwards), *Stick* (1985), *Who's That Girl?* (1987), *Cold Justice* (1989), and *A Million to Juan* (1993). On television he costarred in the series *A.K.A. Pablo, Sword of Justice,* and *Black Jack Savage,* and he guest-starred on *Baretta, Hill Street Blues, Paradise, Knight Rider,* and *Murder, She Wrote.*

Raúl Roulien

(Raúl Pepe Acolti Gil) Actor and singer, also director and producer, born in Rio de Janeiro, October 8, 1905. He

Above: Linda Ronstadt

starred or had major roles in various Spanish-language productions for Fox in the 1930s and also appeared in English-language productions. He was married to actress Tosca Roulien (born 1910, died in Hollywood, California, September 27, 1933). His Hollywood Spanish-language film credits include *Eran trece* (1931, Fox), as Max Minchin; *El último varón sobre la tierra* (1932, Fox, costarring Rosita Moreno), a Spanish-language version of *The Last Man on Earth* (1924, starring Earle Foxe and Grace Cunard); *Primavera en otoño* (1933, Fox, costarring opposite Catalina Bárcena), a Spanish-language original based on a work by Gregorio Martínez Sierra; *No dejes la puerta abierta* (1933, Fox, costarring Rosita Moreno), a Spanish-language version of *Pleasure Cruise* (1933, starring Genevieve Tobin and Roland Young); *Granaderos del amor* (1934, Fox, costarring Conchita Moreno), a Spanish-language original based on a screenplay by John Reinhardt and William Kernell; *¡Asegure a su mujer!* (1934, Fox, costarring Conchita Montenegro), a Spanish-language original based on a work by Julio J. Escobar; *Te quiero con locura* (1935, Fox, costarring opposite Rosita Moreno), a Spanish-language original based on "La cura de reposo" (Madrid, 1927) by Pedro Muñoz Seca and Enrique García

Above: Raúl Roulien had a principal role in *Flying Down to Rio,* starring Dolores del Río; the film established the careers of Ginger Rogers and Fred Astaire.

Velloso; and *Piernas de seda* (1935, Fox, costarring opposite Rosita Moreno), a Spanish-language version of *Silk Legs* (1927, starring Madge Bellamy and James Hall). He was also in a few English-language films including *Delicious* (1931); *Careless Lady, The Painted Woman,* and *State's Attorney* (all 1932); *Flying Down to Rio* (starring Dolores del Río) and *It's Great to Be Alive* (1933); *The World Moves On* (1934, dir. John Ford); and *Music Is Magic* (1935).

Mercedes Ruehl

Actress of Spanish-Irish descent. She won an Academy Award as Best Supporting Actress for her role in *The Fisher King* (1991). She gained attention as the Mafia wife in the film *Married to the Mob* (1988). She won a Tony award on Broadway for her role as Aunt Bella in *Lost in Yonkers,* which she reprised in the 1993 film version. Additional credits: *The Warriors* (1979); *Four Friends* (1981); *Heartburn* (1986); *Leader of the Band, Radio Days, The Secret of My Success,* and *84 Charing Cross Road* (all 1987); *Big* (1988); *Slaves of New York* (1989); *Crazy People* (1990); *Another You* (1991); and *Last Action Hero* (1993).

José Luis Ruiz

Producer and director in film and television since 1970. He has been highly recognized for his documentaries, including *Cinco vidas* (1972), *The Unwanted* (1974, depicting the problems of undocumented workers and their families), *Guadalupe* (1975, a screen adaptation of the play of the same title by El Teatro de la Esperanza), and *Yo soy/I Am* (1985, with Jesús Salvador Treviño, a review of Chicano progress in politics, education, and other areas). He was executive producer of the documentary miniseries *Chicano! History of the Mexican American Civil Rights Movement* (1996). He is currently director of the National Latino Communications Center in Los Angeles, a media arts and production center and provider of Latino programming to public television. His television programs have earned him 11 Emmy nominations and 4 Emmy awards.

Virginia Ruiz

(Virginia Zurí) Actress; she had a few supporting roles in Hollywood Spanish-language films including *Wu Li Chang* (1930, MGM); *Del infierno al cielo* (1931, Fox); and *Hombres en mi vida* (1931, Columbia). She was also in *Men in Her Life* (1931).

Juan Ruiz Anchia

Cinematographer, born in Spain in 1949. He graduated from the Escuela Oficial de Cinematografía in 1972 and from the American Film Institute in 1981. His credits as cinematographer on U.S. films include *Reborn* (1978), *The Stone Boy* and *María's Lovers* (both 1984), *That Was Then . . . This Is Now* (1985), *At Close Range* (1986), *House of Games* (1987), and *Things Change* (1988).

Jorge Russek

Actor, active in the Mexican film industry. He has had several appearances in American films, especially as a result of his work for director Sam Peckinpah. His American film credits include *Hour of the Gun* (1966), in the role of Látigo; *The Wild Bunch* (1969, dir. Sam Peckinpah), in the role of Zamorra, one of Mapache's evil men; *Convoy* (1978, dir. Sam Peckinpah), in the role of Texas sheriff Tiny Álvarez; *Miracles* (1986, starring Teri Garr, also with Paul Rodríguez); and *Pure Luck* (1991, starring Martin Short pratfalling in Mexico).

Andy Russell

(Andrés Robago) Singer, born in East Los Angeles, September 16, 1919, died in Phoenix, Arizona, April 16, 1992. He was known for his renditions of popular songs such as "Bésame mucho" and "What a Difference a Day Makes." He appeared as himself in several musical films including *The Stork Club* (1945), *Make Mine Music* and *Breakfast in Hollywood* (both 1946), and *Copacabana* (1947).

Manuel Russell

Actor. He had supporting roles in a few Hollywood Spanish-language films including *La fiesta del diablo* (1930, Paramount), in the role of Dr. Reynolds; *Su noche de bodas* (1931, Paramount), as Francis Calvet; *Lo mejor es reír* (1931, Paramount), as Charles Lagrange; *La pura verdad* (1931, Paramount), in the role of Roberto; and *¿Cuándo te suicidas?* (1931, Paramount), as León Mirol.

ZORRO, CISCO, AND OTHER HEROIC SOCIAL BANDITS

Right: Douglas Fairbanks, Sr., (left) in *The Mark of Zorro* (1920)

Below right: Warner Baxter in *Return of the Cisco Kid* (1939)

Below left: Warner Baxter as Joaquín Murrieta in *Robin Hood of El Dorado* (1936)

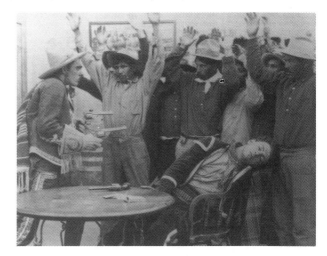

Above: Film poster, *Zorro Rides Again*

Below left: Douglas Fairbanks, Sr., in *Don Q, Son of Zorro* (1925)

Below right: Herbert Stanley Dunn, the original Cisco Kid, in *The Caballero's Way* (1914, Eclair)

Above left: Tyrone Power and Linda Darnell in *The Mark of Zorro* (1940)

Above right: César Romero in *The Cisco Kid and the Lady* (1939)

Left: Gilbert Roland as the Cisco Kid

S

Roberto Saa Silva

Actor. He appeared in supporting roles in several Hollywood Spanish-language films including *Sombras de gloria* (1929, Sono-Art Productions, Inc.), *Monsieur le Fox* (1930, MGM), *Las campanas de Capistrano* (1930, Producciones Latinas, Ltd., presented by J. H. Hoffberg Co.), and *El presidio* (1930, MGM).

Orlando Sacha

Actor. He appeared in a few films, often produced or shot in Peru. His credits include *No Exit* (1962, U.S.-Argentine production based on Jean-Paul Sartre's *Huis clos,* starring Viveca Lindfors), *Interpol Calling Lima* (1969, Peruvian production), *Hour of the Assassin* (1987, dir. Luis Llosa, starring Erik Estrada), *Crime Zone* (1988, dir. Luis Llosa), *Full Fathom Five* (1990), and *To Die Standing* (1991).

Armando Sáenz

Actor, active in Mexican films; he was in *Sierra Baron* (1958).

Eddie Sáenz

(Edwin Matthew Sáenz) Stuntman, born September 21, 1922, in Santa Monica, California, died April 28, 1971. He was the youngest of five brothers who, like their father, Cy, a local boxing promoter and owner of the Culver City Boxing Arena, were all known for their athletic prowess. An outstanding football player at Loyola University (1940-42) and subsequently, as a Navy reservist, the leading rusher for the University of Southern California, he was the first Mexicano to play in the Rose Bowl (1944; his team beat Washington). In 1946, he joined the Washington Redskins, where he played for six years and won recognition as the National Football League's most dangerous kickoff and punt return specialist. Although he never publicly complained about it, he was the object of considerable anti-Mexicano discrimination during his career, which was cut short by injuries at the end of the 1951 season. He then returned to California and became a leading stuntman in the film industry. Sáenz became a specialist in fights and falls, working as a double for Tyrone Power, Steve Cochran, Anthony Quinn, Charles Bronson, and many more in numerous Westerns and other films.

Ábel Salazar

Actor, born in Mexico City. He appeared in a number of Mexican films released in the United States. His credits include *The Man and the Monster* and *Vampire's Coffin* (both 1965); *The Living Dead, The Vampire,* and *The Witch's Mirror* (1968); and *The Brainiac* and *The Curse of the Crying Woman* (1969).

Leopoldo Salcedo

Filipino actor. He appeared in a few films primarily set in the Philippines. Credits include *Lost Battalion* (1961, dir. Eddie Romero), *Cry of Battle* (1963, starring Van Heflin and Rita Moreno), *The Raiders of Leyte Gulf* (1963), *W.I.A. (Wounded in Action)* (1966), and *Mission Batangas* (1968).

Theresa Saldaña

Actress, partly of Hispanic extraction, adopted as an infant and raised by an Italian American couple in New York. She appeared in *Nunzio* and *I Wanna Hold Your Hand* (both 1978), *Defiance* and *Raging Bull* (1980), *The Evil That Men Do* (1984), *The Night Before* (1988), and *Double Revenge* and *Angel Town* (1989). On television she was in *Sophia Loren: Her Own Story* (1980), played herself in the TV movie *Victims for Victims: The Theresa Saldaña Story* (1984), costarred in the series *The Commish* (ABC), and has made numerous appearances in episodic series.

Aldo Sambrell

(Also Aldo Sambrel; Harold Sambrel) Actor, born in Madrid in 1935. He appeared in a number of Westerns, mostly Italian or Spanish productions, including films directed by Sergio Leone and Sergio Corbucci. He was often cast as an amoral or psychopathic killer bandit, enamored of violence for its own sake. His credits include *Gunfight at Red Sands* (1963); *Gunfighters of Casa Grande* (1965); *Lost Command, A Place Called Glory, Dynamite Jim, Son of a Gunfighter,* and *The Texican* (1966); *For a Few Dollars More, The Hellbenders, The Long Duel, Navajo Joe, The Sea Pirate,* and *The Good, the Bad, and the Ugly* (1967); *Awkward Hands, A Bullet for the General,* and *A Minute to Pray, A Second to Die* (1968); *100 Rifles* (1969); *A Town Called Hell* (1971); *Bad Man's River* (1972); *Yellow Hair and the Fortress of Gold* (1984); *Tex and the Lord of the Deep* (1985); and *Hot Blood* and *Voodoo Black Exorcist* (1989).

Above: Jaime Sánchez (second from left; Ernest Borgnine and William Holden are to his right) in *The Wild Bunch* (1969)

Elvira Sánchez

Actress; she appeared in *Law and Lawless* (1932, also with Julián Rivero) and *Torrid Zone* (1940).

Jaime Sánchez

Actor, born December 19, 1938, in Puerto Rico. He gained recognition in the role of Chino in the Broadway production of *West Side Story*. He made his film debut in *David and Lisa* (1963) and appeared in *The Pawnbroker* (dir. Sidney Lumet), in the role of Jesús Ortiz, and *Heroina* (both 1965); *Beach Red* (1967); *The Wild Bunch* (1969), as Ángel, the idealistic Mexican member of the gang; *Bobby Deerfield* (1977); and *Florida Straits* (1986, starring Raúl Juliá).

Marco Sánchez

Actor. He played the role of Sensor Chief Miguel Ortiz on the NBC TV series *seaQuest DSV.*

Mark Sánchez

Makeup artist, born in 1955 in Los Angeles. He has worked in numerous television series and specials including *Sanford and Son, Chico and the Man* (1976-78), *The Tonight Show Starring Johnny Carson* (between 1976 and 1986), and *The Joan Rivers Show,* for which he won an Emmy in 1992 for his makeup work.

Pedro Sánchez

Actor, not to be confused with the Italian actor Ignazio Spalla, a 1960s "Spaghetti Western" player who used this alias. He appeared in *White Fang and the Hunter* (1985) and *Night and the City* (1992, starring Robert De Niro).

Aitana Sánchez-Gijón

(Victoria Aragón) Actress, born in Rome, Italy, and raised in Madrid. She has appeared in numerous Spanish films, plays, and television programs. She debuted in the United States in *A Walk in the Clouds* (1995), opposite Keanu Reeves.

183

Above: Aitana Sánchez-Gijón (right), Keanu Reeves (center), and Anthony Quinn in *A Walk in the Clouds* (1995, dir. Alfonso Arau)

Fernando Sancho

(Fernando Sancho Les) Actor, born in Zaragoza, Spain, January 7, 1916, died in Madrid, July 31, 1990. He had numerous appearances beginning in the 1960s, primarily in European productions released in the United States. His credits include *King of Kings* (1961); *Lawrence of Arabia* (1962); *55 Days at Peking* and *Goliath Against the Giants* (both 1963); *The Son of Captain Blood* (1964); *Backfire* and *Gunmen of the Rio Grande* (1965); *Minnesota Clay, A Pistol for Ringo,* and *Django Shoots First* (1966); *The Sea Pirate* (1967); *The Big Gundown, The Man from Nowhere,* and *Seven Guns for the MacGregors* (1968); *The Boldest Job in the West* (1969); *Blood at Sundown* (date not known, probably 1960s); *Duel in the Eclipse* (date not known, probably 1960s); and *Voodoo Black Exorcist* (1989).

Miguel Sandoval

Actor, born in New Mexico, January 16, 1951. He has appeared in *Repo Man* (1984); *Walker* (1987); *El Diablo* (1990, TV film starring Louis Gossett, Jr.); *Ricochet* (1991);

White Sands (1992); *Jurassic Park* (1993); *Dancing with Danger* (TV film), *Girls in Prison* (TV film), and *Clear and Present Danger* (all 1994); and *Up Close and Personal* (1996). He also appeared in the 1995-96 season of the TV series *Murder One* (ABC) and played Lester on *The Marshal* (ABC).

Bel Sandre

(Also Bel Hernández) Mexican American actress, born December 20, 1956. She had important roles in *Losin' It* (1983) and *Colors* (1988), and she appeared in *My Family/Mi familia* (1995). On television she was featured in the miniseries *The Alamo: 13 Days to Glory* (1987) and in the PBS American Playhouse presentation *La Carpa* (1993). She is one of the founders and the current editor-in-chief of *Latin Heat*, which provides information on Latinos in the film, television, and entertainment industries and promotes advocacy work to expand opportunities for Latinos.

Olga San Juan

Nightclub performer and actress, born March 18, 1927, in New York City to Puerto Rican parents (who moved to Puerto Rico when she was three years old and later returned to New York). As a teenager she established herself as a

Above: Olga San Juan and Fred Astaire in *Blue Skies* (1946)

nightclub performer at the Copacabana, El Morocco, and other important clubs and was billed as a competitor to Carmen Miranda as "The Puerto Rican Pepperpot." She made her film debut in *Rainbow Island* (1944), appeared in *Duffy's Tavern* (1945), and costarred in *Blue Skies* (1946, opposite Bing Crosby and Fred Astaire). Additional credits: *Variety Girl* (1947); *One Touch of Venus, Are You With It,* and *The Countess of Monte Cristo* (all 1948); *The Beautiful Blonde from Bashful Bend* (1949); and *The Third Voice* (1959, 20th-Century Fox, starring Edmond O'Brien), playing a blonde prostitute. After marrying actor Edmond O'Brien, she retired from active involvement in the industry. Her daughter is actress Maria O'Brien.

Carlos San Martín

Actor and director. He appeared in supporting roles in a few Hollywood Spanish-language films including *Un hombre de suerte* (1930, Cinéstudio Continental Paramount); *Lo mejor es reír* (1931, Paramount), as Henri Gilbert; and *El hombre que asesinó* (1931, Paramount British), as Coronel De Sevigné. He codirected with Roger Capellani *Un caballero de frac* (1931, Paramount, starring Roberto Rey and Gloria Guzmán), a Spanish-language version of *Evening Clothes* (1927, dir. Luther Reed, starring Adolphe Menjou, Virginia Valli, and Noah Beery). He was also in a few English-language films: *The Charge of the Light Brigade* and *Fatal Lady* (both 1936) and *Marked Woman* (1937).

Conrado San Martín

(Also Sanmartín) Actor and boxer, born in Higuera de las Dueñas, Spain, in 1921. He appeared in *Contraband Spain* (1955, Associated British Pathé production), *The Colossus of Rhodes* and *King of Kings* (both 1961), and *The Awful Dr. Orlof* (1964).

Reni Santoni

Actor of Italian and Hispanic heritage, born in New York City, April 21, 1940. His film credits include *Enter Laughing* (1967), *Anzio* (1968, multinational production), *Guns of the Magnificent Seven* (1969), *The Student Nurses* (1970), *Dirty Harry* (1971), *Indict and Convict* (1973), *I Never Promised You a Rose Garden* (1977), *They Went That-A-Way and That-A-Way* (1978), *Dead Men Don't Wear Plaid* (1982), *Bad Boys* (1983), *Cobra* (1986), *Second Serve* (1986, TV film), *The Package* (1989), and *The Brady Bunch Movie* (1995). On television he starred in the series *Sánchez of Bel Air* and appeared as a guest star in numerous shows including *Life Goes On, The Senator,* and *Owen Marshall, Counselor at Law.*

Joe Santos

Actor of Puerto Rican and Italian heritage, born in New York City, June 9, 1931 [R has 1933]. His film credits include *Moonlighting Waves* (1966); *My Body Hungers* (1967); *The Gang That Couldn't Shoot Straight* (1971); *Shaft's Big Score!* (1972); *The Blue Knight, Blade,* and *Shamus* (all 1973); *Zandy's Bride* (1974); *Blue Thunder* (1983); *Fear City* (1984); *The Detective* (1985); *Revenge* (1990); *Deadly Desire* (1991); *Sinatra* (TV film) and *Mo' Money* (1992); and *Trial by Jury* (1994). On television he is best known for his role as Detective Dennis Becker on *The Rockford Files,* and he had numerous guest appearances on such series as *Police Story* and *Magnum, P.I.*

Lita Santos

(Angelita Santos) Actress. She appeared in supporting roles in a few Hollywood Spanish-language films including *El caballero de la noche* (1932, Fox); *Dos noches* (1933, Fanchon Royer Pictures, Inc., presented by J. H. Hoffberg Co.); *Granaderos del amor* (1934, Fox); *La buenaventura* (1934, First National Pictures), as *la gitana*; and *Di que me quieres* (1938, RKO-Radio Pictures).

Isabel Sarli

Argentine actress. She appeared in a number of sexploitation films produced in Argentina and released in the United States. Credits include *Woman and Temptation* (1967); *The Female: Seventy Times Seven* and *Put Up or Shut Up* (both 1968); *Fuego* (1969); and *Heat, Muhair* (apparently a phonetic rendition of *mujer*, original Spanish release was titled *La mujer de mi padre*), and *Tropical Ecstasy* (1970).

Lalo Schifrin

Composer and jazz musician, born in Buenos Aires, Argentina, June 21, 1932. He has been nominated six times for an Academy Award for the scores of *Cool Hand Luke* (1967), *The Fox* (1968), *Voyage of the Damned* (1976), *The Amityville Horror* (1979), *The Competition* (1980), and *The Sting II* (1983). He also scored *The Cincinnati Kid* (1965), *Bullitt* (1968), *Dirty Harry* (1971), *Magnum Force* (1973), and *The Mean Season* (1985). He has done many television scores including the theme for *Mission: Impossible*.

Luz Segovia

Actress. She had a few supporting roles in Hollywood Spanish-language films including *Su última noche* (1931, MGM), as Clara; *El último varón sobre la tierra* (1932, Fox); and *El trovador de la radio* (1938, Paramount), as *la enfermera jefe*.

Amelia Senisterra

Actress; she had two supporting roles in Hollywood Spanish-language films: *Drácula* (1931, Universal), as Marta, and *Resurrección* (1931, Universal), as Sofía.

Assumpta Serna

(Assunta Rodes Serna) Actress, born in Barcelona, in 1957. She has appeared in *Matador* (1986, Spanish production, dir. Pedro Almodóvar, costarring Antonio Banderas), *Wild Orchid* (1990, starring Mickey Rourke and Jacqueline Bisset), *Revolver* and *Chain of Desire* (both 1992), and *Nostradamus* (1994, British-German production).

Above: Pepe Serna

Pepe Serna

Actor, born July 23, 1944, in Corpus Christi, Texas. He has played a wide variety of supporting roles, often as a Chicano. His film credits include *The Student Nurses* (1970); *Red Sky at Morning, Shootout*, and *Johnny Got His Gun* (all 1971); *Sniper, The Killer Inside Me, The Deadly Tower*, and *The Day of the Locust* (1975); *Car Wash, The Streets of L.A.* (TV film, also with Miguel Piñero and Isela Vega), *A Force of One*, and *Walk Proud* (1979); *Honeysuckle Rose* and *Inside Moves* (1980); *Vice Squad* (1982); *Scarface*, as Al Pacino's buddy who is killed with a chainsaw, and *Deal of the Century* (1983); *Red Dawn*, as the father of one of the rebellious boys, and *The Adventures of Buckaroo Banzai Across the Eighth Dimension* (1984); *Fandango* (1985, about five Vietnam-era college kids who go on a wild fling before graduation as they face military service); *Silverado* (also 1985), in the role of Scruffy, a hired gun; *Out of Bounds* (1986); *The Forgotten* (1989); *The Rookie*, as Clint Eastwood's police superior, *Postcards from the Edge*, in a bit part as a revolutionary, and *Bad Jim* (1990); *American Me* (1992); and *A Million to Juan* (1993). On television he has appeared in four PBS American Playhouse presentations: *Hot Summer Wind* (1976), *Seguín* (1982), *The Ballad of Gregorio Cortez* (1983), and *Break of Dawn* (1989). He also appeared in the miniseries *Sadat* (1983, starring Lou Gossett, Jr.) in the role of Atif, the Egyptian president's brother, and was in the TV film *Conagher* (1993).

Pastor Serrador

(Heriberto Pastor Serrador) Actor, born in Cuba. In addition to being active in the Mexican and Spanish film industries, he was in two films released in the United States: *Charleston* (1960, Mexican production) and *The Treasure of Makuba* (1967).

Enriqueta Serrano

Actress. In Hollywood Spanish-language films she starred in *La incorregible* (1931, Paramount, costarring Tony D'Algy), a Spanish-language version of *Manslaughter* (1930, dir. George Abbott, starring Claudette Colbert and Fredric March), and she costarred in *La pura verdad* (1931, Paramount, dir. Manuel Romero, starring José Isbert), a Spanish-language version of *Nothing But the Truth* (1929, starring Richard Dix and Helen Kane).

María Serrano

Actress; she appeared in *Serenade* (1956, starring Mario Lanza, costarring Sarita Montiel).

Néstor Serrano

Actor; he appeared in *Hangin' with the Homeboys* (1991, dir. Joseph B. Vásquez) and *Brenda Starr* (1992, starring Brooke Shields).

Virginia Serret

Actress, born in Veracruz, Mexico, died May 2, 1958. She appeared in *Boom in the Moon* (1946, Mexican production, starring Buster Keaton).

Mercedes Servet

Actress. She had supporting roles in a few Hollywood Spanish-language films including *Doña Mentiras* (1930, Cinéstudio Continental Paramount), in the role of Amelia Renaud; *El secreto del doctor* (1930, Paramount), in the role of Señora Redding; *La carta* (1930, Paramount); and *La fiesta del diablo* (1930, Paramount), as Tía Betty.

Carmen Sevilla

(María del Carmen García Gallisteo) Actress, born in Sevilla, Spain, October 16, 1930. One of the leading actresses in Spain during the 1960s, she appeared in films released in the United States including *Pantaloons* (1957, French production, starring Fernandel); *Spanish Affair* (1958, Spanish

Above: Carmen Sevilla, Spanish film star, 1940s

production); *King of Kings,* in the role of Mary Magdalene, and *Desert Warrior* (1961); *European Nights* (1963); and *The Boldest Job in the West* (1971).

Charlie Sheen

(Carlos Irwin Estévez) Actor, born in New York City, September 3, 1965, son of Martin Sheen, brother of Emilio, Ramón, and Renée Estévez. He made his acting debut at the age of nine in the TV film *The Execution of Private Slovik* (1974), which starred his father, and was an extra in *Apocalypse Now* (1979). He attained major star status beginning with his leading role in the Academy Award-winning *Platoon* (1986, dir. Oliver Stone). Additional film credits include *Silence of the Heart* (TV film) and *Red Dawn* (1984); *The Boys Next Door* (1985); *Lucas, Wisdom* (cameo appearance), *Ferris Bueller's Day Off* (cameo appearance), and *The Wraith* (1986); *Amazing Stories, Book 3* (he appears in one of

Above: Charlie Sheen (left) and Michael Douglas
in *Wall Street* (1987)

the three TV programs), *Wall Street* (dir. Oliver Stone, costarring Michael Douglas), *No Man's Land,* and *Three for the Road* (1987); *Young Guns, Never on Tuesday* (together with Emilio Estévez, both in cameo roles), and *Eight Men Out* (1988); *Courage Mountain, Tale of Two Sisters,* and *Backtrack* (1989); *Major League, Navy SEALS, The Rookie,* and *Men at Work* (1990); *Cadence* and *Hot Shots!* (1991); *Deadfall, Beyond the Law, The Three Musketeers, National Lampoon's Loaded Weapon 1* (starring Emilio Estévez), and *Hot Shots! Part Deux* (1993); *Major League II, The Chase,* and *Terminal Velocity* (1994); and *The Arrival* (1996).

Martin Sheen

(Ramón Estévez) Actor, born August 3, 1940, in Dayton, Ohio, to a Spanish immigrant father and Irish mother. He began at the New York Living Theater and debuted on the screen in 1967 as a punk terrorizing subway passengers in *The Incident.* He has achieved major star status for such films as *Badlands* (1973), *Apocalypse Now* (1979), *That Champi-*

onship Season (1982), and *Gandhi* (1982), in which he played an American journalist. He was named Best Actor at the San Sebastián Film Festival for his role in *Badlands.* He is the father of film actors Emilio Estévez, Renée Estévez, Ramón Estévez, and Charlie Sheen. Additional film credits include *The Subject Was Roses* (1968); *Catch-22* (1970); *When the Line Goes Through* and *No Drums, No Bugles* (1971); *Rage, Where the Eagle Flies, Pursuit,* and *Pickup on 101* (1972); *Legend of Earl Durand* (1974); *Sweet Hostage* (1975); *The Little Girl Who Lives Down the Lane* (1976, Canadian production); *The Cassandra Crossing* (1977); *Eagle's Wing* (1979); *Loophole* (British production) and *The Final Countdown* (1980); *Enigma* (British-French production) and *In the King of Prussia* (1982); *The Dead Zone* and *Man, Woman, and Child* (1983); *Firestarter* and *The Guardian* (1984); *Broken Rainbow* (documentary; he was narrator for this Oscar-winning film on the relocation and resistance of the Navajos in Arizona), and *Fourth Wise Man* (1985); *A State of Emergency* (1986); *Conspiracy: The Trial of the Chicago Eight, The Believers, Wall Street* (starring Charlie Sheen), and *Siesta* (1987); *Judgment in Berlin* and *Da* (1988); *Beyond the Stars, Cold Front,* and *Beverly Hills Brats* (1989); *Touch and Die* (costarring opposite Renée Estévez), *Shattered Spirits, Original Intent* (brief role as a homeless man), and

Above: Charlie Sheen

Below: Martin Sheen in *Apocalypse Now* (1979)

The Maid (1991); *Trigger Fast, Hear No Evil, Gettysburg,* in the leading role as Robert E. Lee, and *When the Bough Breaks* (1993); *Boca* and *Ghost Brigade* (1994); and *The American President* (1995). On television he has appeared in *The Andersonville Trial* (1970); *That Certain Summer* and *Pursuit* (both 1972); *Catholics* (1973); *The California Kid, Missiles of October,* as Robert Kennedy, and *The Execution of Private Slovik* (1974); *Blind Ambition* (1979), as John Dean; *In the Custody of Strangers* (1982, also with Emilio Estévez); *Kennedy* (1983), in the role of JFK; *Choices of the Heart* (also 1983, about the murder of nuns in 1980 in El Salvador); *The Atlanta Child Murders, Out of the Darkness* (costarring Héctor Elizondo), and *Consenting Adults* (1985); *Samaritan: The Mitch Snyder Story, Shattered Spirits,* and *News at Eleven* (1986); *Nightbreaker* (1989, with Emilio Estévez costarring as the same character as a young man); and *Roswell* (1994). He debuted as a director in the film *Cadence* (1989), in which he and his son Charlie Sheen both appeared.

Gregory Sierra

Actor, born in New York City, January 25, 1937. He worked for a considerable period in New York theater, often doing Shakespeare. He moved to California in 1969. His film credits include *Beneath the Planet of the Apes* and *Getting Straight* (1970); *Pocket Money* (1972, starring Paul Newman, also with Héctor Elizondo); *The Wrath of God* (also 1972, starring Rita Hayworth); *The Clones, Papillon* (starring Steve McQueen and Dustin Hoffman), and *The Thief Who Came to Dinner* (1973); *The Castaway Cowboy* and *The Towering Inferno* (1974); *Mean Dog Blues* (1978); *The Prisoner of Zenda* (1979, starring Peter Sellers); *The Gambler, Part II—The Adventure Continues* (1983, TV film); *Miami Vice* (1984, pilot for TV series); *Let's Get Harry* (1986); *Code Name: Dancer* (TV film) and *The Trouble with Spies* (1987); *Dynamite and Gold* (1988, TV film, also with Alfonso Arau); *Honey, I Blew Up the Kid* and *Deep Cover* (1992); *Hot Shots! Part Deux* (1993); and *A Low Down Dirty Shame* (1994). On television he appeared in *Evening in Byzantium* (1978, starring Glen Ford) and *Unspeakable Acts* (1990, about child abuse), and he had roles on *The Flying Nun, Sanford and Son, Barney Miller,* and *Soap* (as Carlos "El Puerco" Valdez). He starred in the short-lived series *A.E.S. Hudson Street* and has had numerous appearances in episodic television series.

Above: Martin Sheen in the role of John F. Kennedy in *Kennedy* (1983, TV film)

José Sierra de Luna

Actor. He had a few supporting roles in Hollywood Spanish-language films including *La fiesta del diablo* (1930, Paramount), as Hammond; *Entre noche y día* (1931, United Artists); and *La pura verdad* (1931, Paramount).

David Silva

Actor, born in Mexico City, October 9, 1917, died in Mexico City, September 21, 1976. Active in the Mexican film industry, he appeared in the United States in *The First Texan* (1956), in the role of Santa Anna, *Rage* (1966, starring Glenn Ford and an all-Mexican cast), *The Brainiac* (1969), and *Sisters of Satan* (1975).

Geno Silva

Character actor, born in New Mexico. His film credits include *The Cheyenne Social Club* (1970), *1941* (1979, dir. Steven Spielberg), *Scarface* (1983, dir. Brian De Palma), *Sunset* (dir. Blake Edwards) and *Tequila Sunrise* (both 1988), *Night Eyes 2* (1991), and *Drug Wars 2: The Cocaine Cartel* (1992, also with Julie Carmen). He has appeared in many television series episodes including *Miami Vice, Hunter, Simon and Simon,* and *Murder, She Wrote.*

Henry Silva

Actor, born in 1927 in Brooklyn, New York, to Puerto Rican and Italian parents. He began his career on Broadway and was nominated for a Tony award for his role as a drug dealer in *A Hatful of Rain* (1956). He made his film debut in *Viva Zapata!* (1952). Boasting an extraordinary number of film credits, he usually plays a heavy or a villain. Additional

Above: Trinidad Silva (right) with Robert Duvall in *Colors* (1988)

credits include *The Tall T* (1957, starring Randolph Scott); *A Hatful of Rain* (also 1957, dir. Fred Zinnemann); *Ride a Crooked Trail, The Bravados,* and *The Law and Jake Wade* (1958); *Green Mansions* (dir. Mel Ferrer) and *The Jayhawkers* (1959); *Cinderfella* (starring Jerry Lewis) and *Ocean's Eleven* (1960); *Sergeants 3* and *The Manchurian Candidate* (1962); *A Gathering of Eagles* and *Johnny Cool* (1963); *The Secret Invasion* (1964, dir. Roger Corman); *The Return of Mr. Moto* (British production, in the title role), *The Reward* (also with Gilbert Roland, Emilio Fernández, and Rodolfo Acosta), and *Hail, Mafia* (1965); *The Plainsman* (1966); *Matchless* (Italian production) and *The Hills Run Red* (1967); *Never a Dull Moment* (1968); *Assassination* (1969); *The Animals* (1970); *Killers* (date unconfirmed, but 1970s); *Cry of a Prostitute: Love Kills, Wipeout!,* and *Man and Boy* (1972); *Hired to Kill, Hit Men,* (Ital.), and *The Italian Connection* (1973, Ital.); *Almost Human* (1974, Ital., starring Tomás Milián); *Shoot* (1976, Canadian); *Contract on Cherry Street* (1977, TV film, starring Frank Sinatra); *Love and Bullets* (Brit.), *Crimebusters, Thirst* (Australian), and *Buck Rogers in the 25th Century* (1979); *Virus* (Japanese) and *Alligator* (1980); *The Desperados* (date not confirmed but 1980s, starring Keenan Wynn); *Day of the Assassin* (1981); *Deadly Sting, Wrong Is Right, Sharkey's Machine,* and *Megaforce* (1982); *Violent Breed* and *Chained Heat* (1983); *Cannonball Run II* (1984); *Lust in the Dust, Escape from the Bronx* (Ital.), *Shoot,* and *Code of Silence* (1985); *The Manhunt* (1986, Ital.); *Allan Quatermain and The Lost City of Gold* (1987); *Bulletproof* (1988); *Above the Law* (1989); *Dick Tracy* (1990); *Three Days to a Kill* and *The Colombian Connection* (1991); and *The Harvest* (starring Miguel Ferrer) and *Possessed by the Night* (1993).

Trinidad Silva

Actor, born in 1950 in Mission, Texas, died July 31, 1988, killed by a drunk driver, in Whittier, California. He began as an extra in *The Master Gunfighter* (1975) and obtained his first major role in *Alambrista!* (1977, dir. Robert M. Young). Additional credits include *Walk Proud* (1979, also with Domingo Ambriz and Pepe Serna), in the role of Dagger; *El Norte* (1983), as a friendly illegal; *Crackers* (1984); *Jocks* (1987); *The Night Before* (starring Keanu Reeves, also with Theresa Saldaña), *Stones for Ibarra* (TV film, also with Alfonso Arau), *Colors* (starring Robert Duvall and Sean Penn), in the role of the streetwise gang member, Frog, and *The Milagro Beanfield War,* (1988); and *UHF* (1989, starring "Weird Al" Yankovic). On television he had the role of gang member Jesús Martínez in the Emmy Award-winning series *Hill Street Blues*.

Frank Silvera

(Frank Alvin Silvera) Actor, born in Kingston, Jamaica, July 24, 1914 [R has 1917], died June 11, 1970, the result of an electrical accident. The son of a Spanish Jewish father and a Jamaican mother, he was raised in Boston and studied at Northeastern University and Boston University. His film credits include *Viva Zapata!,* in the role of a Mexican general, *The Fighter, The Miracle of Our Lady of Fatima,* as a Portuguese policeman, and *White Mane* (all 1952); *Fear and Desire* (1953); *Killer's Kiss* (1955); *Death Tide* (1958); *Crime and Punishment, USA* (1959); *Heller in Pink Tights, The Mountain Road,* as a Chinese general, and *Key Witness* (1960); *Mutiny on the Bounty* (1962), as a Tahitian chieftain; *Lonnie* and *Toys in the Attic* (1963); *The Appaloosa* (1966); *Hombre,* as a Mexican bandit, and *The St. Valentine's Day Massacre* (1967); *The Stalking Moon* (starring Gregory Peck) and *Uptight* (1968); *Che!* and *Guns of the Magnificent Seven* (1969); and *Valdez Is Coming* (1971, also with Héctor Elizondo). On television he had the role of Don Sebastián Montoya in the series *The High Chaparral*.

Armando Silvestre

Actor. Active in the Mexican film industry, he was also seen in the following films released in the United States: *The White Orchid* (1954), *For the Love of Mike* (1960), *Geronimo* (1962), *Kings of the Sun* (1963), *Doctor of Doom* (1965), *Smoky* and *Rage* (both 1966), *The Scalphunters* (1968), *Two Mules for Sister Sara* (1970), and *The Last Raiders* and *The Killing Zone* (1990).

Jimmy Smits

Actor, a Brooklyn native of Puerto Rican extraction, born July 9, 1955. He earned a degree at Brooklyn College and a Master of Fine Arts degree from Cornell University. He began as an actor in the New York Shakespeare Festival Public Theater, under the direction of Joseph Papp. He made his film debut in *Running Scared* (1986) and has appeared in *The Believers* (1987, starring Martin Sheen), as a police detective terrified of voodoo; *Old Gringo* (1989), in the leading role as the revolutionary general; *Vital Signs* (1990), as a surgeon instructor; *Fires Within* (1991), as a Cuban political prisoner; *Switch* (1991, dir. Blake Edwards), as a young advertising executive; and *My Family/Mi familia* (1995), in a leading role. On television he had the role of idealistic attorney Víctor Sifuentes in *L. A. Law,* (1986-91), went after a serial murderer in *Stamp of a Killer* (1987), was a detective in the forgettable *Glitz* (1988, TV film), had the leading role in the Stephen King thriller *The Tommyknockers* (1993), played the title role in the TV film *The Cisco Kid* (1994, also with Cheech Marín and Pedro Armendáriz, Jr.), was Solomon in *Solomon and Sheba* (1995, dir. Robert M. Young; while it was a mediocre film, it was notable that Sheba was played by a black woman, Halle Berry), and received an Emmy award for his starring role in the series *NYPD Blue*. He also has guest-starred on *Spenser: For Hire* and *Miami Vice*.

Above: Jimmy Smits in *My Family/Mi familia* (1995)

son of actor Domingo García Soler and Irene Pavia, brother of actors Andrés, Fernando, and Julián Soler. Active in the Mexican film industry, he was also seen in two films released in the United States: *Beyond All Limits* (1961) and *The Pearl of Tlayucan* (1964). He was in the Hollywood Spanish-language film *Perfidia* (1940).

Andrés Soler

Actor, born in Saltillo, Coahuila, Mexico, November 18, 1898, died in Mexico City, July 26, 1969. He was the brother of actors Fernando, Julián, and Domingo Soler, son of actor Domingo García Soler and Irene Pavia, and married to actress Irene Soler. He was active in the Mexican film industry and was seen in a few films released in the United States including *The Brute* (1952), *The Mighty Jungle* (1964), and *The Pearl of Tlayucan* (1964).

Enriqueta Soler

Actress. She had several supporting roles in Hollywood Spanish-language films including *¡Salga de la cocina!* (1930, Paramount), as Rosario; *Cuerpo y alma* (1931, Fox), as Alice Lester; *Esclavas de la moda* (1931, Fox), as Gaby; *¿Conoces a tu mujer?* (1931, Fox), as Lita; and *Mamá* (1931, Fox), as Juana.

Domingo Soler

(Domingo Díaz Pavia) Actor, born in Guerrero, Mexico, April 17, 1902, died in Acapulco, Mexico, June 13, 1961,

Fernando Soler

(Fernando Díaz Pavia) Actor and director, born in Saltillo, Coahuila, Mexico, May 24, 1896, died in Mexico City,

Above: Jimmy Smits (right) with Jane Fonda and Gregory Peck in *Old Gringo* (1989)

October 25, 1979, son of actor Domingo García Soler and Irene Pavia, brother of actors Andrés, Domingo, and Julián Soler. During the Hollywood Spanish-language period he starred in three films: *¿Cuándo te suicidas?* (1931, Paramount, dir. Manuel Romero, costarring Imperio Argentina), a Spanish-language version of *Quand te tues-tu?* (1931, starring Robert Burnier and Simone Vaudry); *Verbena trágica* (1938, Columbia, costarring Luana Alcañiz), a Spanish-language original based on a screenplay by Jean Bart; and *Los hijos mandan* (1939, 20th Century-Fox, dir. Gabriel Soria, costarring opposite Blanca de Castejón), a Spanish-language original based on José López Pinillos's "El caudal de los hijos" (Madrid, 1921). He was also in two Mexican films released in the United States: *The Great Madcap* (1949, dir. Luis Buñuel) and *Susana* (1951, dir. Luis Buñuel).

Julián Soler

(Julián Díaz Pavia) Actor and director, born in Ciudad Jiménez, Mexico, February 17, 1905, died in Mexico City, May 5, 1977, son of Domingo García Soler and Irene Pavia, brother of actors Andrés, Domingo, and Fernando Soler. He appeared in a supporting role in one Hollywood Spanish-language film: *Los hijos mandan* (1939, 20th Century-Fox, dir. Gabriel Soria).

Christina Solís

Actress, raised in Oxnard, California (her parents were agricultural workers). She has appeared in *Out for Justice* (1991, starring Steven Seagal) and *Mi Vida Loca* (1994, also with Ángel Avilés, Seidy López, Jacob Vargas, Jessie Borrego, and Magalí Alvarado).

José Soriano Viosca

Actor. He had supporting roles in at least 10 Hollywood Spanish-language films including *Entre platos y notas* (1930, Fox); *Wu Li Chang* (1930, MGM), as Señor Gregory; *Los que danzan* (1930, Warner); *El presidio* (1930, MGM), as Detective Donlin; *Oriente y occidente* (1930, Universal); *Sevilla de mis amores* (1930, MGM), as Tío Esteban; *Drácula* (1931, Universal), as Doctor Seward; *Cheri-Bibi* (1931, MGM), as Papá Duval; *El proceso de Mary Dugan* (1931, MGM), as *el juez*; and *El comediante* (1931, Paramount), as Mr. Jenkins.

Fernando Soto

Mexican actor; he appeared in the Mexican production *Boom in the Moon* (1946, starring Buster Keaton), a film almost unseen until its video release in the 1980s.

Luis Soto

Television director, born in New York of Puerto Rican heritage. He has worked on the series *The Equalizer* and *Miami Vice*.

Richard Soto

(Ricardo Soto) Producer. He began his career as a documentary filmmaker. He produced two episodes for the PBS Wonderworks series, *Maricela* (1986, dir. Christine Burrill), the story of a young Salvadoran girl who emigrates to Los Angeles, and *Sweet 15,* which won an Emmy award. He was associate producer and supervising editor for the film *The Ballad of Gregorio Cortez* (1983). Soto is well known for his documentaries including *A la brava* (1973), describing the conditions of Chicano *pintos* in Soledad prison, *A Political Renaissance* (1974), which examines the contemporary emergence of Chicano political power, and his four documentaries on the conditions of undocumented workers and migrant labor: *Cosecha* (1976), *Migra* (1976), *Al otro paso* (1976), and *Borderlands* (1983).

Above: Talisa Soto

Talisa Soto

Model and actress, born in New York City, ca. 1966, of Puerto Rican extraction. She debuted in *Spike of Bensonhurst* (1988) as India, a Puerto Rican girl who falls in love with an aspiring Italian boxer; appeared as Lupe Lamora in the James Bond film *License to Kill* (1989); and was featured in *The Mambo Kings* (1992). Additional credits: *Silhouette* (1990, TV film, starring Faye Dunaway), *Prison Stories: Women on the Inside* (1991, TV film, also with Rachel Ticotin and Silvana Gallardo), *Hostage* (1992, British prod., dir. Robert M. Young), and *Don Juan DeMarco* (starring Marlon Brando and Johnny Depp, also with Rachel Ticotin) and *Mortal Kombat* (both 1995).

Charles Stevens

(Also Charlie, Charley; possibly also C. Stevens) Actor, born May 26, 1893, in Solomonsville, Arizona, to a Welsh father and a Mexican Indian mother who was allegedly a daughter of Geronimo, died in Hollywood, August 22, 1964. He specialized in villains, either American Indian or Hispanic, and appeared in many of Douglas Fairbanks, Sr.'s films including *The Mark of Zorro* (1920). He was in Harold Lloyd's first great success, *Grandma's Boy* (1922), and also in *Hot Water* (1924, starring Harold Lloyd). He played Spanish Ed in *The Virginian* (1929) and Diabolito in *Ambush* (1949). His last film was *Sergeants 3* (1962). Additional English-language credits: *Fatherhood* (1915, credit is C. Stevens); *The Americano, The Man from Painted Post,* and *Wild and Woolly* (all 1917); *Six Shooter Andy* (1918); *The Mollycoddle* (1920); *The Three Musketeers* (1921); *Captain Fly-by-Night* (1922); *Where the North Begins* (1923); *Empty Hands* and *The Thief of Bagdad* (1924); *Recompense, A Son of His Father, The Vanishing American,* and *Don Q, Son of Zorro* (1925); *Across the Pacific, The Black Pirate,* and *Mantrap* (1926); *The King of Kings* and *Woman's Law* (1927); *Diamond Handcuffs, The Gaucho,* and *Stand and Deliver* (1928); *The Iron Mask* and *The Mysterious Dr. Fu Manchu* (1929); *The Big Trail* and *Tom Sawyer* (1930); *The Cisco Kid* and *The Conquering Horde* (1931); *Chandu the Magician, Mystery Ranch, South of the Rio Grande,* and *The Stoker* (1932); *The California Trail, Drum Taps, Fury of the Jungle, Police Call,* and *When Strangers Marry* (1933); *Behold My Wife!, Call of the Coyote, Grand Canary, The Trumpet Blows,* and *Viva Villa!* (1934); *The Call of the Wild, The Lives of a Bengal Lancer, Rumba, Under the Pampas Moon,* and *West of the Pecos* (1935); *Aces and Eights, The Bold Caballero, The Country Beyond, Give Us This Night, Here Comes Trouble, Robin Hood of El Dorado, Rose of the Rancho,* and *Three Godfathers* (1936); *Ebb Tide, Fair Warning, The Last Train from Madrid, The Plainsman,* and *Swing High, Swing Low* (1937); *The Crime of Doctor Hallet, Forbidden Valley, The Renegade Ranger,* and *Tropic Holiday* (1938); *The Arizona Wildcat, Desperate Trails, Frontier Marshal, The Girl and the Gambler, The Real Glory,* and *Union Pacific* (1939); *Behind the News, Charlie Chan in Panama, Geronimo, Kit Carson, The Man Who Wouldn't Talk, The Mark of Zorro, South to Karanga, Untamed,* and *Wagons Westward* (1940); *Border Bandits* (1946); *Buffalo Bill Rides Again* (1947); and *The Outsider* (1961). He appeared in one Hollywood Spanish-language film, *La gran jornada* (1931, Fox), as López.

Rafael Storm

(Rafael Alvir) Actor. He had roles in both Hollywood English-language and Spanish-language films. His English-language credits include *Behold My Wife!, Kiss and Make-Up,* and *One Night of Love* (1934); *Broadway*

Gondolier, Fighting Pilot, Goin' to Town, Here Comes Cookie, It Happened in New York, Lady Tubbs, Metropolitan, Music Is Magic, Ruggles of Red Gap, Rumba, and *Under the Pampas Moon* (1935); *The Golden Arrow, The House of a Thousand Candles, Pepper,* and *They Met in a Taxi* (1936); *The Bride Wore Red, Nobody's Baby, Thanks for Listening,* and *Wise Girl* (1937); *Always Goodbye, Annabel Takes a Tour,* and *Straight Place and Show* (1938); *Another Thin Man* and *Island of Lost Men* (1939); and *I Take This Woman, Mexican Spitfire Out West,* and *New Moon* (1940). He also had a few supporting roles in Hollywood Spanish-language films including *Gente alegre* (1931, Paramount); *El impostor* (1931, Fox); *Dos más uno, dos* (1934, Fox), as Henry; *La última cita* (1935, Columbia), as Enrique Soria; and *Rosa de Francia* (1935, Fox), as Marqués de Santa Cruz.

Madeleine Stowe

Actress, born in 1964 in Los Angeles, the daughter of a Costa Rican mother and American father. She had the role of Hetty Hutter in *The Deerslayer* (1978, TV film), played a Latina in *Stakeout* (1987, starring Richard Dreyfuss and Emilio Estévez), and played a Latin American woman in *Revenge* (1990, opposite Kevin Costner). She also starred or had major roles in *Tropical Snow* (1988); *Worth Winning* (1989); *The Two Jakes* (1990, dir. and starring Jack Nicholson, also with Rubén Blades); *Closet Land* (1991); *The Last of the Mohicans,* in the role of Cora Munro, and *Unlawful Entry* (both 1992); *Another Stakeout* and *Short Cuts* (1993); and *Blink, China Moon,* and *Bad Girls* (1994). On television or video she appeared in *The Nativity* (1978), *Gangster Wars* (1981, a video version of the television miniseries *The Gangster Chronicles*), *The Amazons* (1984), and the miniseries *Blood and Orchids* (1986).

Miguelángel Suárez

(Also Miguel) Actor, born in Puerto Rico. He appeared in *Che!* (1969), *Bananas* (1971, dir. Woody Allen), and was a prison convict in *Stir Crazy* (1980, dir. Sidney Poitier, starring Gene Wilder and Richard Pryor). On television he starred in the PBS series *Mundo Real.* He costarred in the independent Puerto Rican film *La gran fiesta* (1987, dir. Marcos Zurinaga, also with Daniel Lugo, and Raúl Juliá).

SOME NOTABLE STEREOTYPES

Right: Wallace Beery plays a childish, ignorant, savage, patriotic, and exuberant Pancho Villa in *Viva Villa!* (1934)

Below: William S. Hart (pointing), leading his band of "greaser" *bandidos* in *The Aryan* (1916)

Above: Poster for *Bordertown,* in which Paul Muni plays a Mexican American lawyer who can't transcend the circumstances of his ethnicity and second-class status in American society

Left: Stan Laurel and Oliver Hardy as mustachioed, serape-wearing, earthy Mexicans in *Pick a Star* (1937)

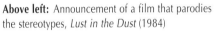

Above left: Announcement of a film that parodies
the stereotypes, *Lust in the Dust* (1984)

Above right: The cartoon character Speedy Gonzales

Tana

(Tana Devodier) Actress. She costarred or had principal roles in several Hollywood Spanish-language films including *El trovador de la radio* (1938, Paramount, costarring opposite Tito Guízar and Robina Duarte), a Spanish-language original based on a screenplay by Bernard Luber and Nenette Noriega; *Papá soltero* (1939, Paramount, costarring opposite Tito Guízar and Amanda Varela), a Spanish-language original based on a screenplay by Dana Wilma; *El otro soy yo* (1939, Paramount); *Cuando canta la ley* (1939, Paramount, costarring opposite Tito Guízar), a Spanish-language original based on a screenplay by Jack Natteford, Enrique Uhthoff, and Richard Harlan; *El milagro de la Calle Mayor* (1939, 20th Century-Fox), as Sade; and *La Inmaculada* (1939, United Artists), as María Luisa.

Arthur Tavares

(Also Arturo) Actor and, subsequently, film editor, born in California, January 10, 1884, died May 27, 1954. His film credits as actor include *The Spanish Jade* (1915), in the role of Don Bartolomé; *Ramona* (1916), in the role of Lieutenant Francis Ortegna; *Germatic Love* (1916, Vogue Films, Inc., dir. Rube Miller, also starring Madge Kirby and Henry Kernan [film held by LC]); *The Eyes of the World* (1917), as the convict; *Mothers of Men* (1917), as Giuseppe; *The Savage* (1917), as Joe Bedotte; *Hungry Eyes* (1918), as Scotty; and *Fortune's Mask* (1922), as Vicenti. His credits as film editor, both in Hollywood English-language and Spanish-language films, include *Lilies of the Field, The Perfect Flapper, Single Wives,* and *So Big* (1924); *Chickie, The Knockout, The Making of O'Malley, The Necessary Evil, Scarlet Saint,* and *The Unguarded Hour* (1925); *Men of Steel, Puppets, The Savage,* and *Too Much Money* (1926); *Sombras de gloria* (1929); *Oriente y occidente* (starring Lupe Vélez) and *Así es la vida* (1930); and *Don Juan diplomático, Drácula* (starring Carlos Villarías and Lupita Tovar), *East of Borneo, The Homicide Squad,* and *Strictly Dishonorable* (1931).

Virgilio Teixera

Spanish actor. He appeared in a number of films in the 1960s, primarily shot in Spain, including *The Boy Who Stole a Million* (1960), *The Happy Thieves* (1961), *Face of Terror* and *The Fall of the Roman Empire* (both 1964), *Doctor Zhivago* and *The Redeemer* (1965), *A Man Could Get Killed* and *Return of the Seven* (1966), and *Saul and David* (1968).

Rick Tejada Flores

Director, born in Bolivia. He is noted for his documentaries including *Sí se puede* (1973), which records César Chávez's twenty-four-day fast in Arizona to protest antistrike legislation; *Low 'N Slow: The Art of Lowriding* (screened at the 1984 San Antonio film festival); *Rivera in America* (1988), on Diego Rivera's murals painted in the United States during the 1930s; and *Spreading Beauty Wherever I Go* (1995). He worked on the feature film, *Screamers* (1996).

Carlos Thompson

(Juan Carlos Mundin Schafter) Actor, born in Argentina, June 7, 1923 [PHH has 1913], died November 10, 1990 (suicide), married to actress Lilli Palmer. After having succeeded in several Argentine films, he appeared in *Fort Algiers* (1953, costarring opposite Yvonne De Carlo), *Flame and the Flesh* (1954), *Valley of the Kings* (1954), as Franz Liszt, *Raw Wind in Eden* (1958), and *The Last Rebel* and *The Spessart Inn* (both 1961).

Rachel Ticotin

Actress, born in the Bronx, New York, November 1, 1958, to Dominican parents. She attended the High School of Music and Art and began to work in film as a production assistant on *The Wanderers* (1979), *Dressed to Kill* (1980), and *Raging Bull* (1980). She debuted as an actress in a small role in *King of the Gypsies* (1978) and appeared in *Fort Apache, The Bronx* (1981) as a heroin-addicted nurse with whom Paul Newman falls in love. She has appeared in *When the Bough Breaks* (TV film) and *Critical Condition* (both 1986); *Spies Lies and Naked Thighs* (1988); *Total Recall* (1990); *One Good Cop, Prison Stories: Women on the Inside* (TV film, also with Talisa Soto), and *F/X 2: The Deadly Art of Illusion* (1991); *Keep the Change* and *Where the Day Takes You* (1992); *Falling Down* (1993, starring Michael Douglas), as a policewoman; and *Don Juan de Marco* (1995). On television she regularly appeared in the series *For Love and Honor, Ohara,* and *Crime and Punishment.*

Amílcar Tirado

Puerto Rican filmmaker. He directed *El puente* (1954), about a community that solves the overflowing of a river by building a bridge, and *El santero* (1956, written by Ricardo Alegría), about a devoted *santero* who struggles to compete with mass-produced commercial plaster images.

Romualdo Tirado

Spanish actor and writer, born September 3, 1880, died October 17, 1963. He appeared mostly in major or supporting parts, but occasionally in a starring role, in at least 32 Hollywood Spanish-language films, including *Charros, gauchos y manolas* (1930, Hollywood Spanish Pictures Co.); *Un fotógrafo distraído* (1930, Hollywood Spanish Pictures Co., dir. Xavier Cugat, in a starring role, with Carmen Guerrero and Don Alvarado costarring), a Spanish-language original short (2 reels); *La jaula de los leones* (1930, Producciones Ci-Ti-Go, presented by J. H. Hoffberg Co., Inc., costarring Matilde Liñán), a Spanish-language original based on a screenplay by Romualdo Tirado; *¡De frente, marchen!* (1930, MGM), as Pepe Alegría; *El caballero de la noche* (1932, Fox), as Barón Fenwick; *El rey de los gitanos* (1933, Fox), as Remetz; *Dos noches* (1933, Fanchon Royer Pictures, Inc., presented by J. H. Hoffberg Co., Inc.), as Paul Denisy; *La melodía prohibida* (1933, Fox), as Al Martin; *Angelina o el honor de un brigadier* (1935, Fox), as Dr. D. Elías; *Alas sobre el Chaco* (1935, Universal), as "Cracker"; *De la sartén al fuego* (1935, 20th Century-Fox), as Alfred Gibbons; *Tengo fe en ti* (1940, RKO-Radio Pictures), as León León; *La vida bohemia* (1937, Columbia), as Colline, el filósofo; and *El milagro de la Calle Mayor* (1939, 20th Century-Fox), as Pepito. He also appeared in *A Message to Garcia* (1936).

Lia Torá

Actress, born in Rio de Janeiro. She starred in a few Hollywood Spanish-language films including *A media noche* (1930, Fox, costarring Juan Torena), a Spanish-language original based on "Evidence Only" by Ethel Clifton; *Don Juan diplomático* (1931, Universal, costarring opposite Miguel Faust Rocha), a Spanish-language version of *The Boudoir Diplomat* (1930, starring Betty Compson and Mary Duncan); *Soñadores de la gloria* (1931, United Artists, dir. Miguel Contreras Torres, costarring opposite Miguel Contreras Torres), a Spanish-language original based on a screenplay by Miguel Contreras Torres; *Eran trece* (1931, Fox), as Sybil Conway; and *Hollywood, ciudad de ensueño* (1931, Universal, costarring opposite José Bohr), a Spanish-language original based on a screenplay by José Bohr. She was also in the English-language films *Making the Grade* and *The Veiled Woman* (both 1929).

Juan Torena

Actor. He appeared in starring or major roles in at least 23 Hollywood Spanish-language films, including the first and second such films produced: *Sombras habaneras* (1929,

Above: Romualdo Tirado, Enrique de Rosas, Rina de Liguoro, Ligia de Golconda, and Andrés de Segurola in *Angelina o el honor de un brigadier* (1935, Fox)

Hispania Talking Film Corp., presented by All-Star Exchange), as Pedro, and *Sombras de gloria* (1929, Sono-Art Productions, Ltd.), as Jack. Additional film credits include *El hombre malo* (1930, First National Pictures), as Alberto; *Del mismo barro* (1930, Fox, costarring opposite Mona Maris), a Spanish-language version of *Common Clay* (1930, starring Constance Bennett and Lew Ayres); *El valiente* (1930, Fox, costarring Angelita Benítez), a Spanish-language version of *The Valiant* (1929, starring Paul Muni and Marguerite Churchill); *A media noche* (1930, Fox, costarring opposite Lia Torá), a Spanish-language original based on Ethel Clifton's work, "Evidence Only"; *Del infierno al cielo* (1931, Fox, dir. Richard Harlan, costarring María Alba), a Spanish-language version of *The Man Who Came Back* (1931, dir. Raoul Walsh, starring Janet Gaynor and Charles Farrell); *El impostor* (1931, Fox, costarring Blanca de Castejón), a Spanish-language version of *Scotland Yard* (1930, starring Edmund Lowe and Joan Bennett); *Eran trece* (1931, Fox, costarring opposite Manuel Arbó), a Spanish-language version of *Charlie Chan Carries On* (1931, starring Walter Oland and John Garrick); *La cruz y la espada* (1933, Fox), as José Antonio Romero; *Nada más que una mujer* (1934, Fox, costarring opposite Berta Singerman), a Spanish-language version of *Pursued* (1934, starring Rosemary Ames and Victor Jory); *El crimen de media noche* (1935, Reliable Pictures), as Alberto Burke; *De la sartén al fuego* (1935, 20th Century-Fox, costarring opposite Rosita Moreno), a Spanish-language version of *We're in the Legion Now* (1935, also released as *The Rest Cure,* starring Reginald Denny and Esther Ralston); *Verbena trágica* (1938, Columbia), as Claudio; and *Mis dos amores* (1938, Paramount), as *fiscal* José Miranda. He also appeared in a number of Hollywood English-language films including *The Gay Caballero* (1932); *Pleasure Cruise*

(1933); *The Eagle's Brood* and *Storm Over the Andes* (both 1935); *The Devil on Horseback, Meet Nero Wolfe,* and *A Message to Garcia* (1936); *Espionage, Love Under Fire,* and *Wallaby Jim of the Islands* (1937); and *Flight to Nowhere* (1938).

Antonio Torres

Puerto Rican actor. He appeared in *Thunder Island* (1963, also with Miriam Colón) and *Harbor Lights* (1964, also with José de San Antonio), both filmed in Puerto Rico.

Edwin Torres

Writer and judge, born in 1930 in New York. He attended City College of New York and Brooklyn Law School and became a justice of the New York State Supreme Court in 1979. As a novelist he wrote *Carlito's Way* and its sequel *After Hours,* both of which were the basis for the film *Carlito's Way* (1993, starring Al Pacino). Another novel was adapted for the feature film *Q & A* (1990, dir. Sidney Lumet).

Liz Torres

Comic actress, born in the Bronx, New York, September 27, 1947, to a Puerto Rican father and a Venezuelan mother. She has appeared in a number of films, including *You've Got to Walk It Like You Talk It or You'll Lose That Beat* (1971, filmed 1968), *America* (1986), *Thieves of Fortune* (1989), *Lena's Holiday* (1991), *Bloodfist IV: Die Trying* (1992), and the notable thriller *Just Cause* (1995, starring Sean Connery). On television she was featured on *All in the Family* and costarred on *Phyllis,* in addition to guest-starring on numerous other series. She was nominated for an Emmy award as Best Supporting Actress, Comedy Series, for her role in *The John Larroquette Show* (NBC). She also received Emmy nominations for the TV films *Kate's Secret* and *Poker Alice* (1987, starring Elizabeth Taylor), and she was in the TV film *More Wild Wild West* (1980).

Luis Torres

Producer. He has often worked in collaboration with Jesús Salvador Treviño. His credits include the documentary *Birthwrite* (1989, dir. Jesús Salvador Treviño).

Nancy Torres

Actress and singer, born in Guadalajara, Mexico, in 1910. She appeared in a few Hollywood Spanish-language films in supporting roles or as a singer, including *El rey del jazz*

(1930, Universal, a musical review in which she appeared as the soloist for the number "Sucedió en Monterrey"); *¡Hola Rusia!* (1930, Universal, starring Slim Summerville), as *la chica; Carne de cabaret* (1931, Columbia), as Eunice; and *Mi último amor* (1931, Fox), as Lupe.

Raquel Torres

(Marie Paula Osterman) Actress, born in Hermosillo, Sonora, Mexico, November 11, 1908, raised in Los Angeles, died in Malibu, California, August 10, 1987. At age 19, she was chosen to costar in *White Shadows in the South Seas* (1928), MGM's first feature that fully synchronized dialog, music, and effects. She was in *The Bridge of San Luis Rey* (1929) in the role of Pepita; *The Desert Rider* (1929, MGM, dir. Nick Grinde, also starring Tim McCoy and Bert Roach [film held at EH]); *The Sea Bat* and *Under a Texas Moon* (both 1930); *Aloha* (1931); and *Duck Soup, So This Is Africa,* and *The Woman I Stole* (1933). After appearing in the British feature *The Red Wagon* (1934), she retired from the screen except for an occasional appearance, as in *Tampico* (1944). She also costarred opposite Buster Keaton in the Hollywood Spanish-language film *Estrellados* (1930, MGM), a version of *Free and Easy* (1930, starring Buster Keaton and Anita Page). Her second husband was actor Jon Hall (whom she married in 1959).

Renée Torres

Actress. She starred or had major roles in several Hollywood Spanish-language films including *La rosa de fuego* (1930, Tom White Productions, costarring opposite Don Alvarado), a Spanish-language original based on a screenplay by Eustace Hale Ball; *La gran jornada* (1931, Fox); *Amor que vuelve* (1934, Latin American Pictures, Inc.,

Above: Renée Torres with Don Alvarado (left) in *Amor que vuelve* (1934)

presented by Kinematrade, Inc., costarring opposite Don Alvarado), a Spanish-language original based on a screenplay by Eustace Hale Ball; and *El otro soy yo* (1939, Paramount), as María Ramírez. She was also in the following Hollywood English-language films: *Under the Pampas Moon* (1935), *The Devil on Horseback* (1936), and *God's Country and the Woman* and *Submarine D-1* (both 1937).

José Luis Tortosa

Actor. He had several supporting roles in Hollywood Spanish-language films including *El día que me quieras* (1935, Paramount); *Tango Bar* (1935, Paramount), as *el capitán*; *No matarás* (1935, Hispano International Film Corporation); *El crimen de media noche* (1935, Reliable Pictures), as James A. Sullivan; *De la sartén al fuego* (1935, 20th Century-Fox), as Henri Rilet; *El capitán tormenta* (1936, MGM), as Dr. Kelly; *El otro soy yo* (1939, Paramount); and *Cuando canta la ley* (1939, Paramount), as Señor Vázquez. He was also in the following Hollywood English-language films: *A Message to Garcia* (1936), *Love under Fire* (1937), *Law of the Texan* (1938), and *Code of the Secret Service* (1939).

José Torvay

Character actor, born in Durango, Mexico, in 1910, died in 1973. He worked both in Mexican films and Hollywood productions shot in Mexico including *The Fugitive* (1947); *Border Incident* (1949); *Borderline* (1950); *My Outlaw Brother* (1951); *The Brave Bulls* (also 1951, starring Mel Ferrer, Anthony Quinn, and Miroslava), in the role of a small time *impresario*; *My Man and I* (1952, starring Ricardo Montalbán); *The Littlest Outlaw,* in the role of the comic *bandido,* Buitre, and *The Hitch-Hiker* (both 1953); *Strange Lady in Town,* as the humble father whose son is cured by the character played by Greer Garson, and *Untamed* (1955); *Bandido* (1956, starring Robert Mitchum and Gilbert Roland, also with Rodolfo Acosta); *Serenade* (1956, starring Mario Lanza and Sarita Montiel, also with Martín Garralaga); *Woman's Devotion* (1957, filmed on location in Acapulco, also with Rosenda Monteros and

Carlos Riquelme); *Last Sunset* (1961, starring Kirk Douglas and Rock Hudson); and *Two Mules for Sister Sara* (1970).

Lupita Tovar

Actress, born in Tehuantepec, Mexico, July 27, 1910 [R has 1915]. She starred in the first Mexican sound film, *Santa* (1932). She came to Hollywood in 1930 and starred in many of the Hollywood Spanish-language productions including *Drácula* and *El rey del jazz* (1930). She also appeared in sexy or exotic stereotypical roles in numerous English-language films throughout the 1930s and 1940s. Her Hollywood Spanish-language film credits include *El rey del jazz* (1930, Universal), a musical review in which she shared honors as master/mistress of ceremonies with Martín Garralaga; *La voluntad del muerto* (1930, Universal, dir. George Melford, costarring Antonio Moreno), a Spanish-language version of *The Cat Creeps* (1930, dir. Rupert Julian, starring Helen Twelvetrees and Raymond Hackett); *Drácula* (1931, Universal, dir. George Melford, costarring opposite Carlos Villarías), a Spanish-language version of *Dracula* (1931, dir. Tod Browning, starring Bela Lugosi, David Manners, and Helen Chandler); *El tenorio del harem* (1931, Universal, costarring opposite Slim Summerville), a Spanish-language version of *Arabian Knights* (1931, starring

Above: Lupita Tovar and Barry Norton in *Drácula* (1931, Universal)

Slim Summerville, Tom Kennedy, and Sally Blane); *Carne de cabaret* (1931, Columbia, dir. Christy Cabanne, costarring Ramón Pereda), a Spanish-language version of *Ten Cents a Dance* (1931, dir. Lionel Barrymore, starring Barbara Stanwyck and Ricardo Cortez); *Estamos en París* (1931, Universal, costarring opposite Slim Summerville and Eddie Gribbon), a Spanish-language version of *Parisian Gaieties* (1931, starring Slim Summerville, Eddie Gribbon, and Sally Blane); *Alas sobre el Chaco* (1935, Universal, dir. Christy Cabanne, costarring opposite José Crespo), a Spanish-language version of *Storm Over the Andes* (1935, dir. Christy Cabanne, starring Jack Holt, Antonio Moreno, and Mona Barrie); and *El capitán tormenta* (1936, MGM, costarring Fortunio Bonanova), a Spanish-language version of *Captain Calamity* (1936, also released as *Captain Hurricane,* starring George Houston and Marion Nixon). Her English-language roles include *Border Law,* as a cantina girl, *East of Borneo,* and *Yankee Don* (all 1931); *Mr. Robinson Crusoe* (1932); *Old Spanish Custom* (1936, British production, also released as *The Invader,* costarring opposite Buster Keaton); *Blockade* (1938); *The Fighting Gringo, Tropic Fury,* and *South of the Border* (1939); *Green Hell* and *The Westerner* (1940); *Two Gun Sheriff* (1941); and *Gun to Gun* (1944).

Bill Travilla

Costume designer, born in 1923 in Avalon, Santa Catalina, died November 21, 1990. He worked first for Warner Brothers and subsequently for 20th Century-Fox. During his career he did the costume design for most of Marilyn Monroe's films and for *The Adventures of Don Juan* (1949, for which he won an Academy Award for Best Costume Design), *Viva Zapata!* (1952), *How to Marry a Millionaire* (1953, nominated for an Oscar for Best Costume Design), *There's No Business Like Show Business* (1954, nominated for an Oscar for Best Costume Design), and *The Stripper* (1963, nominated for an Oscar for Best Costume Design). On television he did *The Loretta Young Show, Dallas* (for which he won an Emmy Award for Costume Design in 1985), and the miniseries *Evita Perón* and *Jacqueline Bouvier Kennedy* (both 1981), *The Thorn Birds* (1983), and *My Wicked, Wicked Ways* (1985). He is recognized for having designed the white chiffon dress worn by Marilyn Monroe in *The Seven Year Itch* (1955).

Jesús Salvador Treviño

Director, producer, and writer, one of the best-known Chicano filmmakers, born March 26, 1946, in El Paso, Texas. His films include *Raíces de sangre* (1977, starring Richard Yñíguez, funded by the Mexican government), which evokes border life and the *maquiladoras* (twin plants); *Seguín* (1982, starring Henry Darrow and Edward James Olmos), a PBS presentation of a Hispanic perspective on the Alamo; and documentaries and docudramas including *Salazar Inquest* and *Chicano Moratorium* (both 1970); *America Tropical* (1971); *Carnalitos* (Bobby Páramo, coproducer), *La Raza Unida,* and *Yo Soy Chicano* (all 1972); *Somos Uno* (1973); *Have Another Drink, Ese* (1977); *One Out of Ten* (1979); *Yo Soy/I Am* (1985, with José Luis Ruiz); and *Gangs* (winner of the Director's Guild of America award in the dramatic daytime television show category), *Date Rape,* and *Birthwrite* (all 1989). His most recent credits include directing episodes of the television series *Gabriel's Fire, Lifestories, Mathnet, Sweet Justice, Babylon 5* (UPN), *New York Undercover* (Fox), *Space: Above and Beyond* (Fox), *Seaquest DSV,* and *N.Y.P.D. Blue.* He was coexecutive producer of *Chicano! History of the Mexican American Civil Rights Movement* (1996, documentary TV series). Beginning in the late 1960s and early 1970s in his role as producer and host of two of the earliest Chicano public affairs television series, *Ahora!* and *Acción Chicano,* and continuing through the present within the Director's Guild of America, Treviño has been an important spokesman for and booster of Latino talent in the film industry.

Jorge Treviño

(Also George) Actor, born in Monterrey, Mexico. He appeared in *The Beast of Hollow Mountain* (1956), *The Bottom of the Bottle* (1956, starring Van Johnson), *Ghost Diver* (1957, about searching for underwater South American treasure, also with Rodolfo Hoyos, Jr.), *Last of the Fast Guns* (1958, starring Gilbert Roland and Linda Cristal), and *The Third Voice* (1960).

Fernando Trueba

Spanish director. His *Belle Époque* (1992, starring Fernando Fernán Gómez and Jorge Sanz), about an army deserter in the pre-Franco, Republican Spain of 1931, won the Oscar for Best Foreign Film. Subsequently he directed his first American feature, *Two Much* (1995, starring Antonio Banderas, Melanie Griffith, and Daryl Hannah).

Felipe Turich

(Felipe Turriche) Character actor, born December 5, 1898, died March 9, 1992. He appeared in *We Were Strangers*

Above: Jesús Salvador Treviño (left), director

(1949), *Crisis* and *The Lawless* (both 1950), *My Favorite Spy* (1951), *Giant* (1956), *One-Eyed Jacks* (1961), *Jesse James Meets Frankenstein's Daughter* (1966), *Hook, Line and Sinker* (1969), and *Walk Proud* (1979). He also appeared in supporting roles in two Hollywood Spanish-language films: *Un hombre peligroso* (1935, Criterion Films) and *La Inmaculada* (1939, United Artists), as Nacho.

Rosa Turich

Character actress, married to Felipe Turich. She usually played Mexican mothers or *doñas*. Her film credits include *Clipped Wings, Rose of the Rio Grande,* and *Starlight Over Texas* (all 1938); *Drifting Westward* (1939); *Rangers of Fortune* (1940); *Bowery Buckaroos* (1947); *The Loves of Carmen* (1948); *The Lawless, The Kid from Texas, On the Isle of Samoa,* and *Tripoli* (all 1950); *Havana Rose* (1951, starring Estelita Rodríguez); *Rancho Notorious* (1952, starring Marlene Dietrich); *The Hitch-Hiker* (1953); *Passion* (1954, starring Cornel Wilde); *Move Over Darling* (1963); and *Jesse James Meets Frankenstein's Daughter* (1966). She had a supporting role in the Hollywood Spanish-language film *Papá soltero* (1939, Paramount), as Romualda.

RECOVERING RAQUEL TORRES

Educated in a Los Angeles convent, Mexican-born Raquel Torres had major roles in the early sound period before she retired from the screen.

Top left: Raquel Torres and Emily Fitzroy (right) in *The Bridge of San Luis Rey* (1929)

Bottom left: Raquel Torres

Below right: Raquel Torres in *White Shadows in the South Seas* (1928, MGM)

Above: Raquel Torres

Enrique Uhthoff

Writer. He translated into Spanish or wrote original screenplays for a few Hollywood Spanish-language films including *El milagro de la Calle Mayor, El otro soy yo,* and *Papá soltero* (all 1939) and *Cuando canta la ley* (1940).

Natividad Vacío

Actor, born in El Paso, Texas. Working first as a teacher and musician, he made his film debut in *The Loves of Carmen* (1948, starring Rita Hayworth) and has appeared in numerous films including *Branded* (1951), *Escape from Red Rock* (1957), *The Magnificent Seven* (1960), *The Gun Hawk* (1963), *Castle of Evil* (1966), *The Pink Jungle* (1968), and *The Milagro Beanfield War* (1988).

David Valdés

Producer. He rose through the ranks especially through his collaborations with Francis Ford Coppola and Clint Eastwood. He was assistant director on *The Outsiders* and *Rumble Fish* (both 1983) and first assistant director on *Any Which Way You Can* (1980), *Firefox* (1982), *Sudden Impact* (1983), *City Heat* (1984), and *Tightrope* (also 1984). He served as associate producer of *Pale Rider* (1985) and *Ratboy* (1986) and producer of *Pink Cadillac* and *The Dead Pool* (both 1988). He was executive producer of *Bird* (1988), *Black Heart* (1990), *Unforgiven* (1992), and *A Perfect World* (1993); coproducer of *Like Father, Like Son* (1987); and coexecutive producer of *Gardens of Stone* (1987). In 1996 he was a producer for Rysher Entertainment.

Daniel Valdez

Songwriter, singer, and actor, born in 1949, the brother of Luis Valdez. He starred as Henry Reyna in the film *Zoot Suit* (1981) and appeared in *Which Way Is Up* (1971), *The China Syndrome* (1979), and *La Bamba* and *Born in East L.A.* (both 1987). He was also associate producer on *La Bamba*. He was in *Corridos* (1987, TV film, dir. Luis Valdez) as the Lavaplatos and the PBS feature production *. . . and the earth did not swallow him* (1995, Severo Pérez, director-writer).

Luis Valdez

Director, playwright, and screenwriter, born June 26, 1940. Valdez spent his childhood as a migrant farm worker, and after graduating from San Jose State College he spent a year with the San Francisco Mime Troupe. Subsequently he joined the United Farm Workers under César Chávez, formed El Teatro Campesino, which was the theatrical arm of the union, and in 1966 was the principal author of the influential "Plan of Delano." He was the major force in the conception of the many *actos* and *mitos* that were produced by El Teatro Campesino, which currently has its own theater in San Juan Bautista, California. He also produced one of the earliest Chicano films, *I Am Joaquín* (1969), based on Rodolfo "Corky" Gonzales's notable poem, followed by *Los Vendidos/The Sellouts* (1972), a filming of the Teatro Campesino *acto*. In 1978, Valdez expanded into more conventional theater; he wrote and directed the musical drama *Zoot Suit* about *pachucos* and the Sleepy Lagoon Riots during World War II, which was a hit in Los Angeles and the first play by a Chicano writer to appear on Broadway. In 1981, he wrote and directed the film version, which was nominated for a Golden Globe for best musical picture. Valdez's second feature, *La Bamba* (1987, starring Lou Diamond Phillips, Esai Morales, Rosana De Soto, and Elizabeth Peña), about the life and career of Ritchie Valens, was highly successful in both mainstream and Hispanic markets. It was the first major film that was simultaneously produced and distributed in both English and Spanish. For television he wrote and directed the Christmas fantasy *La Pastorela: A Shepherd's Play,* a PBS production (1991, starring Linda Ronstadt, Cheech Marín, Paul Rodríguez, Robert Beltrán, Freddy Fender, and Flaco Jiménez), and *The Cisco Kid* (1994, starring Jimmy Smits and Cheech Marín, also with Pedro Armendáriz, Jr.). Recently he has written two plays: *I Don't Have to Show You No Stinking Badges,* which had a successful run in Los Angeles, and *Bandido,* a musical melodrama that premiered at the Mark Taper Forum in Los

Above: Luis Valdez, director

Angeles in 1994. Additional film credits include *Which Way Is Up* (1977, bit part) and, as a director, *Corridos! Tales of Passion and Revolution* (1987, starring Linda Ronstadt).

Miguelito Valdez

Afro-Cuban singer, died November 9, 1978, in Bogotá, Columbia, during a performance. He is best known for introducing the "Babalu" song later made famous by fellow Cuban Desi Arnaz. He appeared in *Suspense* (1946, Monogram, one of this humble studio's most expensive productions), a vehicle to showcase the ice-skating star Miss Belita. He also appeared in the musical short *Miguelito*

Valdez (1950, Columbia, which introduced Valdez, the De Castro sisters, and other Latin entertainers).

Ritchie Valens

(Richard Valenzuela) Pop star, born in Pacoima, California, May 13, 1941, died in Mason City, Iowa, February 3, 1959, in the airplane crash that killed Buddy Holly and others. He was the subject of the notable bio pic *La Bamba* (1987, dir. Luis Valdez). His only film appearance was in *Go, Johnny Go!* (1959), in which rock promoter Alan Freed molds a young orphan into rock sensation "Johnny Melody." He played himself in the film's musical performances as did Eddie Cochran, Jackie Wilson, Chuck Berry, The Cadillacs, and others.

Harry Vallejo

(Also E. J. Vallejo; Enrico; Enrique; Enrique Juan; born Enrique Juan Vallejo) Cameraman, born in 1883 and raised in Mexico City, retired in 1935, died May 10, 1950. He came to the United States at age 19, where he worked as a cameraman for D. W. Griffith, Charlie Chaplin, Mack Sennet, Douglas Fairbanks, Sr., and Mary Pickford. In 1927 he returned to Mexico and made a series of promotional films for the Mexican oil industry. Film credits include *The Spanish Jade* (1915); *Ramona* (1916); *The Eyes of the World* (1917); *The Romance of Tarzan* and *Tarzan of the Apes* (1918); *The Shepherd of the Hills* (1919); *The Dwelling Place of Light, The Money-Changers, Riders of the Dawn,* and *The U.P. Trail* (1920); *The Millionaire, The Spenders, The Killer, The Lure of Egypt,* and *The Rage of Paris* (1921); *The Three Must-Get-Theres* (1922); *Don Q, Son of Zorro* (1925); and *Her Sacrifice* (1926).

Víctor Vallejo

Son of Harry Vallejo, born in 1907. He began as a costumer at Warner Brothers from 1937 to 1957 and became, progressively, second assistant director, first assistant director, and unit manager at Warner Brothers. He was responsible

207

for such TV series as *Cheyenne, Maverick, Hawaiian Eye,* and *77 Sunset Strip.* He had a bit part as a child in *Ramona* (1916), in which his father served as cameraman.

Rafael Valverde

Actor. He had a few supporting roles in Hollywood Spanish-language films including *La fuerza del querer* (1930, Paramount); *Del mismo barro* (1930, Fox); *Cuando el amor ríe* (1930, Fox), as Alonso; and *Soñadores de la gloria* (1931, United Artists).

César Vanoni

Actor. He had roles in several Hollywood Spanish-language films including *Sombras de gloria* (1929, Sono-Art Productions, Ltd.), as *el fiscal del distrito*; *Así es la vida* (1930, Sono-Art Productions, Ltd.); *¡Huye, faldas!* (1930, MGM); *El presidio* (1930, MGM), as El Lobo; and *Hollywood, ciudad de ensueño* (1931, Universal). He also appeared in the English-language films *All Men Are Enemies* (1934) and *The Buccaneer* (1938).

Amanda Varela

Actress. She costarred in two Hollywood Spanish-language films: *Papá soltero* (1939, Paramount, opposite Tito Guízar), a Spanish-language original based on a screenplay by Dana Wilma, and *El otro soy yo* (1939, Paramount, opposite Tito Guízar), a Spanish-language original based on a screenplay by Mortimer Braus and Dana Wilma.

Nina Varela

Character actress, born in Mexico in 1908 [PHH has 1899], died February 13, 1982. Initially trained in Europe as an opera singer, she appeared in numerous films as a Mexican mother or *doña.* Her film credits include *Viva Zapata!* (1952); *The President's Lady, The Woman They Almost Lynched* (dir. Allan Dwan), and *Niagara* (1953); *Jubilee Trail* (1954); *Love with the Proper Stranger* (1963); and *Madigan* (1968).

Jacob Vargas

Actor, born August 18, 1970. His film credits include *Ernest Goes to Camp* and *The Principal* (both 1987), *American Me* and *Gas, Food, Lodging* (1992), and *Mi Vida Loca* (1994).

John Vargas

Actor, born in the Bronx, New York, April 24, 1944, of Puerto Rican heritage. He has appeared in *Only When I*

Laugh (1981), *Star Trek II: The Wrath of Khan* (1982), *Mass Appeal* (1984), *Hanoi Hilton* (1987), and *Seduced by Evil* (1994, TV film, starring Suzanne Somers, also with Julie Carmen). He appeared regularly on the TV series *At Ease* and guest-starred in various television episodes and in the made-for-television film *The Jesse Owens Story* (1984).

Joseph B. Vásquez

Writer and director, born in 1963 in the South Bronx, New York, of Puerto Rican heritage, died in San Diego, December 16, 1995, of AIDS-related causes. He attended the Picker Film Institute at the City College of New York and entered the industry as an assistant film editor. With $30,000 of his own money, Vásquez made his first feature, *Street Story* (1986, subsequently released as *Street Hitz,* 1991, starring Angelo López and Lydia Ramírez), followed by *Bronx War* (1989, starring Fabio Urena and Charmain Cruz), in which he also appeared, and the well-received *Hangin' With the Homeboys* (1991, starring John Leguizamo), which was produced by New Line and shared the screenwriting award at the 1991 Sundance Film Festival. Vásquez's last film, *Manhattan Merengue,* debuted at the 1995 Cannes Film Festival.

Roberta Vásquez

Actress. She first received attention as a *Playboy* magazine centerfold and then appeared in several sexploitation and action vehicles made by Malibu Bay films, often with south-of-the-border drug-dealer plots: *Picasso Trigger* (1988), *Guns* (also with Erik Estrada as an international arms dealer) and *Do or Die* (both 1991), *Hard Hunted* (1992), and *Fit to Kill* (1993). She also was in a motorcycle gang film, *Easy Wheels* (1989), *The Rookie* (1990, starring Clint Eastwood, Charlie Sheen, Raúl Juliá, Pepe Serna, and Marco Rodríguez), and *Street Asylum* (1990, starring G. Gordon Liddy in a pathetic performance as an evil genius).

Isela Vega

Actress, born in Sonora, Mexico, in 1940. She became well-known in Mexican film in the 1960s as a sex symbol. In the United States she has had roles in *Rage* (1966); *The Deadly Trackers* (1973); *Bring Me the Head of Alfredo García* (1974), costarring in the role of Elita; *Joshua,* a Western revenge drama, and *Drum* (both 1976); *The Streets of L.A.* (1979, TV film), as a suffering Mexican mother; *Bordello* (1979, TV film, starring Chuck Connors), a spoof about cowboys and shady ladies; and *Barbarosa* (1982), as an aristocratic Mexican wife.

Sylvia Vega Vásquez

Costume designer. She has worked on *La Bamba* (1987) and *American Me* (1992).

Jerry Velasco

Actor, born in Mexico, January 31, 1953. He has appeared in *The Jerk* (1979), *Boulevard Nights* (1979), and *Heart-breaker* (1983).

Eddie Vélez

(Edwin Vélez) Actor, born in New York City, June 4, 1958; he attended the High School of Art and Design and served in the U.S. Air Force. His film credits include *Repo Man* (1984); *Doin' Time* (1985); *The Women's Club* (1987); *Split Decisions* (1988), as a boxer; *Rooftops* (dir. Robert Wise, with a Hispanic girl and white youth plot, but a long way from the director's earlier *West Side Story*) and *Romero* (both 1989); and *Bitter Vengeance* (1994, TV film). On television he appeared in the series pilot film *For Love and Honor* (1983) and was a regular on various series including *Bay City Blues, Berenger's, Charlie & Co.,* and the final season of *The A-Team,* as Frankie Santana. He starred as a young lawyer in the series *Trial and Error.*

Lupe Vélez

(María Guadalupe Vélez de Villalobos) Actress, born July 18, 1908, in San Luis Potosí, Mexico, died in Beverly Hills, California, December 14, 1944. Originally a dancer, she debuted in film in 1926 under Hal Roach's direction and became a star as the leading lady in *The Gaucho* (1928), opposite Douglas Fairbanks. She played a girl of dubious morals in *Lady of the Pavements* (1929, dir. D. W. Griffith). Known as a fiery leading lady both in silent and sound film, she made positive use of her Spanish-accented English during the sound period to reposition herself as a comedienne in the "Mexican Spitfire" series. She also did several important Hollywood Spanish-language films. Her volatile personal life, including a romance with Gary Cooper and marriage to Johnny Weismuller, ended in suicide. Additional English-language film credits include *Sailors, Beware* (1927); *Stand and Deliver* (1928); *Tiger Rose, Where East Is East,* as the half-caste daughter of Lon Chaney, and *Wolf Song* (all 1929); *East Is West, Hell Harbor* (dir. Henry King, costarring Gibson Gowland and Jean Hersholt), *Mad About Money,* and *The Storm* (1930); *Resurrection, The Squaw Man,* as an Indian maiden, and *The Cuban Love Song* (1931); *The Broken Wing, The Half Naked Truth,* and *Kongo* (1932); *Mr. Broadway* and *Hot Pepper* (1933); *Hollywood*

Party (dir. Allan Dwan, starring Jimmy Durante, Stan Laurel, and Oliver Hardy), *Laughing Boy, Hell's Harbor* (costarring Jean Hersholt, possibly related to her 1930 *Hell Harbor*), *Palooka,* and *Strictly Dynamite* (1934); *Gypsy Melody* (1936, British production); *High Flyers* (1937); *The Girl from Mexico* (1939); *Mexican Spitfire, Mexican Spitfire/Smartest Girl in Town* (double feature; in the first, a man impersonates an English lord in order to save a contract for the spitfire's husband, while in the second, a photographer's model mistakes a millionaire for a fellow model), and *Mexican Spitfire Out West* (1940); *Six Lessons from Madame La Zonga, Playmates,* and *Mexican Spitfire's Baby* (1941); *Honolulu Lu* (with Leo Carrillo; in the film she does some notable, allegedly "malicious," impersonations in her broken English of Katharine Hepburn and Marlene Dietrich), *Mexican Spitfire at Sea, Mexican Spitfire Sees a Ghost,* and *Mexican Spitfire's Elephant* (1942); *Mexican Spitfire's Blessed Event, Ladies Day* (a baseball film starring Eddie Albert), in the role of Pepita Zorita, "a bundle of Mexican dynamite," and *Redhead from Manhattan* (1943); and *Nana* (1944, Mexican production).

Her Hollywood Spanish-language films include *Oriente y occidente* (1930, Universal, dir. George Melford, costarring Barry Norton), a Spanish-language version of *East Is West* (1930, dir. Monta Bell, starring Lupe Vélez, Lew Ayres, and Edward G. Robinson); *Resurrección* (1931, Universal, dir. Edwin Carewe, costarring Gilbert Roland), a Spanish-language version of *Resurrection* (1931, dir. Edwin Carewe, starring Lupe Vélez and John Boles); and *Hombres en mi vida* (1932, Columbia, costarring Gilbert Roland), a Spanish-language version of *Men in Her Life* (1931, starring Lois Moran and Charles Bickford).

Eduardo Venturini

(Also Edward, E. D.) Director. He directed both English-language (silent and sound period) films and a few Hollywood Spanish-language films. His English-language credits as director include *God's Country and the Law* (1921), *The Headless Horseman* (1922, starring Will Rogers), *The Old Fool* (1923), *In Old Mexico* (1938), and *The Llano Kid* (1939). He was associate director on *The False Madonna* (1931) and *The Love Captive* (1934), and he did preproduction research on *Madame Butterfly* (1932). His Spanish-language credits as director include *El dios del mar* (1930, Paramount, starring Ramón Pereda and Rosita Moreno), a Spanish-language version of *The Sea God* (1930, dir. George Abbott, starring Richard Arlen and Fay Wray); *Gente alegre* (1931, Paramount, starring Roberto Rey and Rosita Moreno), a Spanish-language original based on a screenplay by Henry Myers; and *El príncipe gondolero*

(1931, Paramount, starring Roberto Rey and Rosita Moreno), a Spanish-language version of *Honeymoon Hate* (1927, dir. Luther Reed, starring Florence Vidor and Tullio Carminati).

Elena Verdugo

Actress, born April 20, 1927, in Paso Robles, California [PHH has born in 1925 in Beaumont, Texas]. Allegedly a descendent of one of the old *Californio* families, her first appearance as an entertainer was as a child dancer. At age 17 she recorded the song "Tico Tico" with Xavier Cugat's orchestra, and she debuted on film at age 13 in *Down Argentine Way* (1940, starring Don Ameche and Betty Grable). Her first major role was as a Tahitian beauty in *The Moon and Sixpence* (1942). She also appeared in *Belle Starr* (1941); *Rainbow Island* and *House of Frankenstein* (1944); *Strange Voyage* (starring Eddie Albert, also with Martín Garralaga) and *The Frozen Ghost* (both 1945); *Little Giant* (1946, starring Abbott and Costello); *Song of Scheherazade* (1947); *The Big Sombrero* (starring Gene Autry, also with Martín Garralaga), *Tuna Clipper, The Lost Volcano,* and *El Dorado Pass* (all 1949); *Cyrano de Bergerac* (1950, starring José Ferrer); *The Thief of Damascus* and *The Pathfinder* (1952); *Knights of the Round Table* (1954); *Panama Sal* (1957); *Day of the Nightmare* (1965); *How Sweet It Is!* (1968); and *Angel in My Pocket* (1969). On television she starred in a very popular series, *Meet Millie,* in the early 1950s, and later she received two Emmy nominations as Best Supporting Actress while costarring for seven years on *Marcus Welby, M.D.,* as the nurse, Consuelo López. She was a guest star on numerous shows including *The Red Skelton Show* and *The Bob Cummings Show,* and she costarred on *The Phil Silvers Show.*

Noah Verduzco

Child actor. Following appearances in various commercials, he has had roles in *Radio Flyer* and *Kickboxer 3: The Art of War* (both 1992) and *Bound by Honor* (1993).

John Verros

Actor. He appeared in *Pocket Money* (1972, starring Paul Newman and Lee Marvin, also with Héctor Elizondo) and *The Outlaw Josey Wales* (1976), in the role of Chato.

Manuel Vico

Spanish actor. He had a few supporting roles in Hollywood Spanish-language films: *La fiesta del diablo* (1930, Para-mount), as Ezra Stone; *La pura verdad* (1931, Paramount), in the role of Apolodoro; and *¿Cuándo te suicidas?* (1931, Paramount), as Grillard.

James Victor

Actor, born July 27, 1939, in the Dominican Republic. He immigrated to New York at age four. His film credits include *Rolling Thunder* (1977), as López, a barroom brawler; *Boulevard Nights* (1979), as an auto shop owner; *Defiance* (1980), as a Puerto Rican priest; *Borderline* (1980, starring Charles Bronson), in which he costarred as Mirández, the truck driver; and *Losin' It* (1983), in the role of a shady lawyer opposite Shelley Long. On television he starred in *Viva Valdez* (1976), the first prime-time network series to feature a Hispanic family. In 1982 he had the role of a grandfather in the series *Condo.* He spent four seasons in Spain in the role of the bumbling Sergeant García in New World Television's *Zorro* series starring Duncan Regehr.

Antonio Vidal

(Antonio A. Vidal) Spanish actor. He had supporting roles in at least 18 Hollywood Spanish-language films including *El presidio* (1930, MGM); *La llama sagrada* (1931, Warner), as Dr. Hart; *El comediante* (1931, Paramount), as Dixon; *Eran trece* (1931, Fox), as Paul Nielson; *El rey de los gitanos* (1933, Fox), as *el primer ministro*; *La buenaventura* (1934, First National Pictures), as Conde de Molnar; *El cantante de Nápoles* (1934, Warner), as Profesor Rubini; and *Rosa de Francia* (1935, Fox), as Duque de Pópoli. He also appeared in a few English-language films including *Men in Her Life* (1931), *A Wicked Woman* (1934), and *When You're in Love* (1937).

Christina Vidal

Puerto Rican child actress. She starred in *Life with Mikey* (1993) opposite Michael J. Fox.

Juan Emilio Viguié Cajas

First-known Puerto Rican filmmaker. In 1912 he took the earliest shots of Puerto Rico in Ponce. His filmmaking career was primarily involved in doing newsreels for continental U.S. enterprises such as Pathé, Fox Movietone, and MGM. Among his works were films on Charles A. Lindbergh's trip to Puerto Rico in 1927 and the San Ciriaco hurricane of 1928. He did many documentaries for the government, the first of which was *La colectiva* (1920), about the tobacco industry. His *Romance tropical* (1934) was the first Puerto Rican feature of the sound period, about a lovesick young musician who attempts to seek his fortune at sea.

Juan Emilio Viguié, hijo

Son of Juan Emilio Viguié Cajas, the first-known Puerto Rican filmmaker. In 1951, he founded, together with Manuel R. Navas, Viguié Film Productions, the first large Puerto Rican film production company.

Roberto Vila

Argentine film star. He was brought to the United States during World War II in an attempt to make films that would "further the cause of hemispheric solidarity." Initially expected to star, after the screen test he was relegated to second banana (actually second gaucho) status in *They Met in Argentina* (1941, starring Maureen O'Hara as a Latina). He returned to Argentina, where prospects were better.

Ernesto Vilches

Actor, born in Tarragona, Spain, February 6, 1879, died in Barcelona, December 7, 1954. He starred in all but one of his several Hollywood Spanish-language films including *Galas de la Paramount* (1930, Paramount, a musical review); *Cascarrabias* (1930, Paramount, costarring Carmen Guerrero and Barry Norton), a Spanish-language version of *Grumpy* (1930, starring Cyril Maude and Phillips Holmes); *Wu Li Chang* (1930, MGM, costarring Angelita Benítez), a Spanish-language version of *Mr. Wu* (1927, starring Lon Chaney and Louise Dresser); *Su última noche* (1931, MGM, costarring Conchita Montenegro), a Spanish-language version of *The Gay Deceiver* (1926, starring Lew Cody and Marceline Day); *Cheri-Bibi* (1931, MGM, dir. Carlos F. Borcosque, costarring María Ladrón de Guevara), a Spanish-language version of *The Phantom of Paris* (1931, starring John Gilbert and Leila Hyams); and *El comediante* (1931, Paramount, costarring Angelita Benítez), a Spanish-language original based on the work "Sullivan" by E. V. Domínguez, with screenplay by Ernesto Vilches.

Reynaldo Villalobos

Cinematographer, born in Los Angeles. His father was a painter on movie sets. He began as a photographer and entered the studios as a laborer and painter, then became assistant cameraman for *The Young Lawyers* (1969), and was quickly promoted to first assistant cameraman. He began as

Above: José Crespo, Conchita Montenegro, Edgar Neville, and Ernesto Vilches, under contract to MGM in the early 1930s

a cinematographer on *Urban Cowboy* (1980) and has done important work including the cinematography for *9 to 5* (1980), *The Ballad of Gregorio Cortez* and *Risky Business* (both 1983), *Punchline* (1988), *Major League* (1989), *Coupe de Ville* (1990), *American Me* (1992), and *A Bronx Tale* (1993). On television he has directed episodes of *Tour of Duty* and *Midnight Caller*. He directed the made-for-television film *Conagher* (1991, starring Sam Elliott and Katharine Ross, also with Daniel Quinn).

Carlos Villar

(Carlos Villarías) Actor, born in Córdoba, Spain, July 7, 1892. He is best known for his starring role in Universal's Spanish-language version of *Drácula* (1931). He had occasional parts in English-language films throughout the 1930s and 1940s and had the role of the headwaiter in *Bordertown* (1935). Additional English-language credits include *The*

California Trail (1933); *Goin' to Town* (1935); *California Frontier, Flirting with Fate, Rose of the Rio Grande, Starlight Over Texas,* and *Tropic Holiday* (1938); *Frontiers of '49, Paris Honeymoon,* and *Tropic Fury* (1939); and *Meet the Wildcat* (1940). His Hollywood Spanish-language film credits are numerous. While he only starred in *Drácula,* he had major or supporting roles in at least 34 other Hollywood Spanish-language films including *El cuerpo del delito* (1930, Paramount), as John F. X. Markham, *el fiscal del distrito; El hombre malo* (1930, First National Pictures), as Dobbs; *El valiente* (1930, Fox), as *el director de la cárcel; Cuando el amor ríe* (1930, Fox), as Don José Alvarado; *Drácula* (1931, Universal, dir. George Melford, costarring Lupita Tovar and Barry Norton), a Spanish-language version of *Dracula* (1931, dir. Tod Browning, starring Bela Lugosi, David Manners, and Helen Chandler); *El código penal* (1931, Columbia), as Mart Brady; *El impostor* (1931, Fox), as Arnold Bronson; *El pasado acusa* (1931, Columbia), as Carlos Morán; *Tres amores* (1934, Universal), as *el abogado* Nelson; *El diablo del mar* (1935, Theater Classic Pictures), as *el capitán; Mis dos amores* (1938, Paramount), as Don Antonio Santiago; *El milagro de la Calle Mayor* (1939, 20th Century-Fox), as *el médico;* and *La Inmaculada* (1939, United Artists), as Dr. Torres.

Daniel Villarreal

Actor, born November 19, 1960. He played a gang member in *Stand and Deliver* (1988) and in *American Me* (1992).

Julio Villarreal

Actor, born in Madrid in 1885, died in Mexico City, August 4, 1958. He appeared in over 200 films in Mexico. He had numerous supporting roles in Hollywood Spanish-language films including *Del mismo barro* (1930, Fox); *El dios del mar* (1930, Paramount), as Korff; *La gran jornada* (1931, Fox), as Carson; *El código penal* (1931, Columbia), as Dr. Rinewulf; *El impostor* (1931, Fox), as Jerry Palmer; *La ley del harem* (1931, Fox), as Hassan; *Eran trece* (1931, Fox), as Dr. Lofton; and *El rey de los gitanos* (1933, Fox), as Gran Duque Alejandro. He was active in the Mexican film industry, costarring in a Buñuel film released in the United States with the title *A Woman Without Love* (1951), and he appeared in a Hollywood film shot in Mexico, *Honeymoon* (1947).

Lucio Villegas

Actor, born in Lota, Chile, February 25, 1883, died July 20, 1968. He had at least 17 supporting roles in Hollywood Spanish-language films including *La voluntad del muerto*

Above: Blanca de Castejón, Carlos Villar, and Tito Guízar in *Mis dos amores* 1938, Paramount)

(1930, Universal); *Oriente y occidente* (1930, Universal); *A media noche* (1930, Fox), as Alberto Martin; *Del infierno al cielo* (1931, Fox), as Carlos Reisling; *La cruz y la espada* (1933, Fox), as *el padre superior; Nada más que una mujer* (1934, Fox), as Dr. Steiner; *Te quiero con locura* (1935, Fox), as Tío Daniel; *El crimen de media noche* (1935, Reliable Pictures), as Dr. Kelly; *El trovador de la radio* (1938, Paramount), as *el cirujano jefe;* and *Papá soltero* (1939, Paramount), as Don Pedro. He also appeared in a number of English-language films including *The Notorious Sophie Lang* (1934); *Bride of Frankenstein, Goin' to Town, Storm Over the Andes,* and *Under the Pampas Moon* (1935); *Fatal Lady, The Invisible Ray, A Message to Garcia,* and *Robin Hood of El Dorado* (1936); *I'll Take Romance* (1937); *The Renegade Ranger* and *Yellow Jack* (1938); *The Fighting Gringo, Only Angels Have Wings,* and *The Real Glory* (1939); and *Down Argentine Way, The Light of Western Stars, The Mark of Zorro,* and *Three Men from Texas* (1940).

Jorge Villoldo

Actor, active in the Argentine film industry. He appeared in *The Avengers* (1950, with Mona Maris and Fernando Lamas) and *Way of the Gaucho* (1952, starring Rory Calhoun and Gene Tierney), both filmed in Argentina.

Blanca Vischer

Actress. She had several supporting roles in Hollywood Spanish-language films including *El caballero de la noche* (1932, Fox); *El tango en Broadway* (1934, Paramount), as Laurita; and *El carnaval del diablo* (1936, MGM). She also appeared in several English-language films including *Caravan, Now I'll Tell, 365 Nights in Hollywood,* and *Wild*

Gold (1934); George White's 1935 Scandals and Under the Pampas Moon (1935); The Bohemian Girl, The Devil on Horseback, Follow the Fleet, A Message to Garcia, Strike Me Pink, and Swing Time (1936); Dangerous to Know, Daughter of Shanghai, Sing You Sinners, Thrill of a Lifetime, Tropic Holiday, and You and Me (1938); Another Thin Man (1939); and Billy the Kid's Gun Justice and The Ghost Breakers (1940).

Mike Vitar

Actor, born in 1979. He had the role of Benny Rodríguez in The Sandlot (1993). He also appeared in television on CBS's Brooklyn Bridge series.

Sam Vlahos

Actor, born in San Diego, California, August 10, 1935, to a Greek father and Mexican mother. He appeared in Summer and Smoke (1961), The Milagro Beanfield War (1988), Powwow Highway (1989), Kiss Me a Killer (1991), and . . . and the earth did not swallow him (1995). On television he has appeared in numerous series as a guest star including Hawaiian Eye, Hill Street Blues, and Key West.

LUPE VÉLEZ, BEFORE AND DURING HER "MEXICAN SPITFIRE" SERIES

After beginning her film career as a fiery Latina dancer, in 1938, playing upon her frequent appearances in the scandal press, she was able to achieve a second cycle of success as a malaprop-spouting, extremely stereotypical "Mexican Spitfire."

Above right: Cover of sheet music, "Yo Te Amo Means I Love You," song sung by Lupe Vélez in Wolf Song (1929, Paramount)

Right: Lupe Vélez (opposite Douglas Fairbanks, Sr.) in The Black Pirate (1926)

Left: Leon Errol and Lupe Vélez, in the role of "The Mexican Spitfire," in the first film of the series, *The Girl from Mexico* (1938)

Below: Film poster, *Mexican Spitfire* (1939)

Raoul Walsh

(Albert Edward Walsh) Director and actor, partly Hispanic on his mother's side, born in New York City, March 11, 1887, died in Simi Valley, California, December 31, 1980. He was given his first directorial assignment by D. W. Griffith: *The Life of General Villa* (1914, Biograph, in collaboration with Christy Cabanne), a seven-reel mixture of staged scenes and authentic footage of Pancho Villa's military

Above: Raoul Walsh in the role of Villa in *The Life of General Villa* (1914)

campaign, starring the Mexican bandit himself. Walsh's most notable appearance as an actor was in the role of John Wilkes Booth in Griffith's *The Birth of a Nation* (1915). He subsequently appeared occasionally in films but largely devoted himself to a career as a director. He directed, sometimes acted in, wrote the story, or earned other credits in the following: *The Mystery of the Hindu Image, The Double Knot, The Greaser, A Bad Man and Others,* and *Carmen* (1914); *Pillars of Society* and *The Serpent* (1916); *The Conqueror, Betrayed, The Silent Lie,* and *The Innocent Sinner* (1917); *The Woman and the Law* (1918); *Evangeline* (1919); *The Deep Purple* (1920); *Serenade* (1921); *The Thief of Bagdad* (1924); *The Spaniard* (1925); *What Price Glory* (1926, starring Dolores del Río); *The Loves of Carmen* (1927, starring Dolores del Río); *Sadie Thompson* and *Me Gangster* (1928); *In Old Arizona* (1929, codirected, inasmuch as he lost an eye in an accident while shooting this film, starring Warner Baxter as the Cisco Kid); *The Big Trail* (1930); *Women of All Nations* (1931); *For Me and My Gal/Pier 13* (1932); *The Bowery* and *Going Hollywood* (1933); *Under Pressure* (1935); *Klondike Annie* (1936); *Artists and Models* and *Hitting a New High* (1937); *St. Louis Blues* and *The Roaring Twenties* (1939); *Dark Command* and *They Drive by Night* (1940);

Above: Raoul Walsh playing the Cisco Kid in *In Old Arizona* (1929), before his accident and replacement in the role by Warner Baxter

They Died With Their Boots On, High Sierra, and *Strawberry Blonde* (1941); *Desperate Journey* and *Gentleman Jim* (1942); *Background to Danger* and *Northern Pursuit* (1943); *Uncertain Glory* (1944); *Objective Burma!* and *The Horn Blows at Midnight* (1945); *The Man I Love* and *Pursued* (1947); *Silver River* and *Fighter Squadron* (1948); *Colorado Territory* (starring Virginia Mayo as a "half-breed" Mexican woman) and *White Heat* (1949); *Along the Great Divide, Captain Horatio Hornblower,* and *Distant Drums* (1951); *Glory Alley, The World in His Arms,* and *Blackbeard the Pirate* (1952); *The Lawless Breed, Sea Devils,* and *A Lion Is in the Streets* (1953); *Saskatchewan* (1954); *Battle Cry* and *The Tall Men* (1955); *The Revolt of Mamie Stover* and *The King and Four Queens* (1956); *Band of Angels* (1957); *The Naked and the Dead* (1958); *A Private's Affair* (1959), *Marines Let's Go!* (1961); and *A Distant Trumpet* (1964).

Aissa Wayne

(Aissa María Morrison) Actress, Hispanic on her mother's side, born in Los Angeles, March 31, 1956, daughter of John Wayne. She appeared in *The Comancheros* (1961) and *McClintock!* (1963).

Ethan Wayne

(Also John Ethan; John Ethan Morrison) Actor, born in Newport Beach, California, February 22, 1962, the youngest son of John Wayne and his Peruvian-born wife, Pilar Pallett, brother of actors Aissa, Antonia, Michael, and Patrick Wayne. As a young boy he appeared in *Big Jake* (1971), as a kidnapping victim. He was also in *Scream* and *Escape from El Diablo* (both 1983), *Operation Nam* (1985), and *The Manhunt* (1986). On television he starred in *Adam 12* and has guest-starred in several TV series episodes.

Michael Wayne

(Michael Morrison) Producer, Hispanic on his mother's side, born in Los Angeles, California, November 23, 1934. He produced many of his father's later films made by the family's Batjac production company.

Patrick Wayne

(Patrick Morrison) Actor, Hispanic on his mother's side, born in Los Angeles, California, July 15, 1937, son of John Wayne and brother of Aissa, Antonia, Ethan, and Michael Wayne. He has appeared in numerous films including *The Long Gray Line* and *Mister Roberts* (1955); *The Searchers* (1956); *The Alamo* (1960); *The Comancheros* (1961); *Donovan's Reef* and *McClintock* (1963); *Cheyenne Autumn* (1964); *Shenandoah* (1965); *An Eye for an Eye* and *Talion* (1966); *The Green Berets* (1968); *The Deserter, Ride to Glory,* and *Big Jake* (1971); *The Gatling Gun* (1972); *Beyond Atlantis* (1973); *The Bears & I* (1974); *Mustang Country* (1976); *Sinbad and the Eye of the Tiger, Texas Detour,* and *The People That Time Forgot* (1977); *Rustler's Rhapsody* (1985); *Revenge* (1986); *Young Guns* (1988); *Her Alibi* (1989); and *Blind Vengeance* and *Chill Factor* (1990).

Raquel Welch

(Raquel Tejada) Actress, born September 5, 1940, in Chicago to a Bolivian-born engineer father and mother of

Above: Raquel Welch in *One Million Years B.C.* (1966)

Above: Raquel Welch in *100 Rifles* (1969)

Shelly Winters). She gained attention as a sexy prehistoric woman in *One Million Years B.C.* (1967). Other films include *A Swingin' Summer* (1965); *Fantastic Voyage, The Lovely Ladies,* and *Shoot Loud, Louder . . . I Don't Understand!* (all 1966); *Bedazzled* (British production) and *Fathom* (1967); *The Biggest Bundle of Them All, Bandolero!,* as María, a Mexican woman, *Lady in Cement, The Oldest Profession,* and *The Queens* (1968); *100 Rifles,* notable for its interracial sex, as Sarita, a Mexican Yaqui woman, and *Flareup* (1969); *Myra Breckinridge* and *The Magic Christian* (1970); *Kansas City Bomber, Hannie Caulder, Restless, Fuzz,* and *Bluebeard* (1972); *The Last of Shiela* (1973); *The Three Musketeers* (1974); *The Four Musketeers* and *The Wild Party* (1975); *Mother, Jugs, and Speed* (1976); *The Prince and the Pauper* (1978); *Stunt-woman* (1981); and *The Naked Gun 33 1/3: The Final Insult* (1994). On television she has appeared in important productions that often better highlight her acting abilities, including *The Legend of Walks Far Woman* (1982); *Right to Die* (1987), as a victim of Lou Gehrig's disease; *Trouble in Paradise* and *Scandal in a Small Town* (1988); and *Tainted Blood* (1993).

English background. Despite a very difficult and inauspicious beginning, a phenomenally successful 1963 publicity tour in Europe that she devised with her second husband, former child actor Patrick Curtis, made her a major international personality within two years without having appeared in a single important film. In 1965 *Time* magazine called her "The Nation's Number One Sex Symbol." She was known first as a voluptuous sex goddess, subsequently also as a comedienne. Welch debuted in a small role as a college student in *Roustabout* (1964, starring Elvis Presley) and played a bordello girl in *A House Is Not a Home* (1964, starring

Tahnee Welch

Actress, born in 1962, daughter of Raquel Welch. She has appeared in *Cocoon* (1985), *Lethal Obsession* (1987), *Cocoon: The Return* (1988), *Cannon Movie Tales: Sleeping Beauty* (1989), and *Night Train to Venice* (1993, starring Hugh Grant).

David Yáñez

Actor. Beginning as a child he appeared in numerous TV episodes and films of the late 1970s and 1980s, usually as a Native American or Hispanic youth. His credits include the television miniseries *Centennial* (1978) and the film *Born in East L.A.* (1987).

Alfred Ybarra

Art director, born in 1907 in Los Angeles. He worked on numerous films including *The Fugitive* (1947), *The Bullfighter and the Lady* (1951), *Track of the Cat* and *The High and the Mighty* (both 1954), *Blood Alley* (1955), *The Alamo* (1960), *Marines, Let's Go!* and *The Comancheros* (1961), *Five Weeks in a Balloon* (1962), *Kings of the Sun* (1963), *Major Dundee* (1965), *Duel at Diablo* and *The Rare Breed* (1966), *Hour of the Gun* and *The Young Warriors* (1967), and *The Pink Jungle* (1968). He also worked on numerous Mexican films in the mid-1940s. He retired in 1968.

Rocky Ybarra

Cowboy actor and stuntman, born September 30, 1900, died in Hollywood, December 12, 1965. He worked in numerous films including *Viva Zapata* (1952).

Richard Yñíguez

Actor, born December 8, 1946, in Firebaugh, California. He began in television, where he appeared in 1968 in the daytime show *Canción de la Raza* (PBS), the first Chicano-written and -produced series on television. He appeared in TV films including *Tribes* (1970); *Sniper,* as a police officer, and *The Deadly Tower* (both 1975); *Shark Kill* (1976); *River of Promises* (1977); *The Dirty Dozen: The Fatal Mission* (1988, starring Telly Savalas); and *Jake Spanner Private Eye* (1989). He played the lead in Jesús Salvador Treviño's *Raíces de Sangre* (Mexico, 1977) and starred in *Boulevard Nights* (1979). He directed and starred in *La negrita* (1985), an artistic and financial failure about the miracle of Our Lady

of Los Ángeles in Costa Rica. He has had many guest-starring appearances on television including *The Lucy Show, Marcus Welby, M.D., Bonanza, Hawaii Five-O, The Streets of San Francisco,* and *Simon and Simon.*

Joe Yrigoyen

Basque stuntman. He worked at Republic Pictures from 1935 to 1958 and doubled for Roy Rogers in many Westerns. Credits include *Square Shooter* (1935); *Winds of the Wasteland* (1936); *The Old Wyoming Trail, Outlaws of the Prairie,* and *Two Fisted Sheriff* (1937); *The Man from Music Mountain* (1938); *Melody Ranch* (1940); *The Sons of Katie Elder* (1965); and *Alvarez Kelly* (1966).

Del Zamora

Actor, born in Roswell, New Mexico. He was one of the Castillo brothers in *Repo Man* (1984) and has appeared in *Private School* (1983), *Sid and Nancy* and *Heat Street* (both 1986), and *Born in East L.A., RoboCop,* and *Walker* (all 1987).

Carmen Zapata

Mexican American actress, born in New York City, July 15, 1927, cofounder of the Bilingual Foundation of the Arts, a resident theater company in Los Angeles. Zapata has had a successful career as both a film and stage actress and as a producer. She began in 1946 on the Broadway stage in the musical *Oklahoma!,* followed by other musicals including *Bells Are Ringing* (1956) and *Guys and Dolls* (1957). She appeared in many film roles including *Sol Madrid* (1968), *Hail, Hero!* (1969), *Pete and Tillie* (1972), *The Last Porno Flick* (1974), *Boulevard Nights* (1979), *Vultures* (1983), and *Sister Act* (1992). On television she had the role of Carmen Castillo on the soap opera *Santa Barbara* and appeared in recurring roles in *Flamingo Road* and *The Dick Van Dyke Show.* She starred in the series *Viva Valdez* and also starred for nine seasons in the PBS bilingual children's series *Villa Alegre*. She was in *Daniel and the Towers* (year unconfirmed but 1990s, part of the Wonderworks series).

Daphne Zúñiga

Actress, born in San Francisco, November 28, 1962, after her father, Joaquín Alberto Zúñiga, a left-wing Guatemalan philosophy professor, migrated to Berkeley and participated in the 1960s Free Speech Movement. She appeared in *The Dorm That Dripped Blood* (1981); *The Initiation* (1983); *The Sure Thing*, as a college student, and *Vision Quest* (1985); *Modern Girls* (1986); *Spaceballs* (1987), as a space princess; *Last Rites* (1988), as a Mexican temptress; *The Fly II,* in a leading role, *Staying Together,* and *Gross Anatomy* (1989); *Eyes of the Panther* (1990); *800 Leagues Down the Amazon* (1993, dir. Luis Llosa); and *Charlie's Ghost* (1994, also with Cheech Marín in the role of the ghost). On television she has appeared in the TV films *Quarterback Princess* (1983), *Stone Pillow* (1985, opposite Lucille Ball), and *Prey of the Chameleon* (1992), and she starred as Jo Reynolds in the series *Melrose Place*.

Frank Zúñiga

Director, born March 20, 1936, in New Mexico. He began his career at Walt Disney as a cameraman and later a director on a number of wildlife films, turning more recently to Latino-focused plots. His credits include *Further Adventures of the Wilderness Family, Part 2* (1977); *Heartbreaker* (starring Fernando Allende, also with Miguel Ferrer, Pepe Serna, Rafael Campos, and Apollonia), about gang turf wars in East Los Angeles, and *The Golden Seal* (both 1983); and *Fist Fighter* (1988, starring George Rivero).

Above: Daphne Zúñiga

Marcos Zurinaga

Puerto Rican director. His credits include the notable *La gran fiesta* (1987), about Puerto Rico in 1942, and *Tango Bar* (1988, Argentine-Puerto Rican coproduction, starring Raúl Juliá).

THE LATIN LOVER

The Latin Lover was a standard character in the late sound period, and some of these roles were actually played by Latins!

Left: Romaine Fielding with Mary Ryan in *Rattlesnake* (1913)

Below left: Rudolph Valentino in *Blood and Sand* (1922)

Below center: Antonio Moreno in *The Border Legion* (1924, Paramount)

Below right: John Barrymore in *Don Juan* (1926, Warner Brothers)

Opposite page, top left: Douglas Fairbanks, Sr., and Katherine MacDonald in *Headin' South* (1918)

Top right: Douglas Fairbanks, Sr., in *The Gaucho* (1922)

Bottom left: Rudolph Valentino in the famous tango scene with Beatrice Domínguez in *The Four Horsemen of the Apocalypse* (1921)

Bottom right: Gilbert Roland with Mary Astor in *Rose of the Golden West* (1927, First National)

221

BIBLIOGRAPHY

This general bibliography includes all of the titles that appear in the companion volume, *Hispanics and United States Film: An Overview and Handbook.*

PERIODICALS, TRADE JOURNALS, AND NEWSPAPERS

This research has made use of numerous trade journals, newspapers, and other periodicals including the titles that follow. If not otherwise noted, the serials were (or are) published in the United States. For clarity, the U.S. city of publication is occasionally given as well.

ABC (Madrid), *Academy of Motion Picture Arts and Sciences Bulletin* (and *Supplements*), *Agenda, American Cinematographer, American Projectionist, Arte y Cinematografía* (Barcelona), *Aztlán, Baltimore Sun, Billboard, The Bioscope, Boston Gazette, Boston Herald, Brooklyn Eagle, Cámara* (Madrid), *Cámara* (Mexico City), *Caminos, El Carbayón* (Oviedo, Spain), *Cartel* (Mexico City), *Celuloide* (Mexico City), *Chicago Inter-Ocean, Chicago Tribune, Cine* (Mexico City), *El Cine* (Barcelona), *Cine Acción News, Cine al Día* (Caracas), *Cine Cubano* (Havana), *Cinegramas* (Madrid), *Ciné Journal, Cine Mexicano* (Mexico City), *Cinelandia* (Los Angeles), *Cinema* (Madrid), *Cinema: The Magazine of the Photoplay, Cinema Arts, Cinema News, Cinema Progress: The Film and Life, La Cinématographie* (Paris), *Cinematography, Cinemonde, Cine Mundial* (New York), *Cineteca Nacional* (Mexico City), *Cleveland Plain Dealer, El Correo Español—El Pueblo Vasco* (Bilbao, Spain), *Detroit Free Press, The Eclair Bulletin, Edison Kinetogram, Educational Film Magazine, Essanay News, Excelsior* (Maracaibo, Venezuela), *Excelsior* (Mexico City), *The Exhibitor, Exhibitor's Trade Review Film Index* (early issues, *Views and Film Index), Film Daily, Film Daily Production Guide, Film Daily Year Book, Film Music Notes, Filmográfico* (Mexico City), *Filmópolis* (Cuba), *Films* (Cuba), *Films de Amor* (Barcelona), *Film History, Film Literature Index, The Film Renter and Moving Picture News, Films Selectos* (Barcelona), *The Film Spectator, Los Grandes Films Mudos y Sonoros* (Barcelona), *Harrison's Reports, Hartford Courant, Heraldo de Aragón* (Zaragoza, Spain), *Hispanic,*

Hispanic Business, Hispano América (San Francisco), *Hollywood Filmograph, Hollywood Reporter, Hollywood Spectator, Hoy* (Havana), *El Imparcial* (San Juan, Puerto Rico), *Imparcial Films* (Argentina), *International Index to Film Periodicals, International Projectionist, International Sound Technician, Kalem Kalendar, Kinematograph Weekly, Latin Heat, Los Angeles Evening Express, Los Angeles Evening Herald, Los Angeles Examiner, Los Angeles Times, Lubin Bulletin, Madrid Cinematográfico, La Mañana* (Montevideo, Uruguay), *Los Mejores Films* (Barcelona), *Mensajero Paramount* (New York), *El Mercurio* (Santiago, Chile), *México* (Chicago*), México Cinema* (Mexico City), *Monthly Film Bulletin* (London), *Motion Picture Age, Motion Picture Almanac, Motion Picture Classic, Motion Picture Daily, The Motion Picture Director, Motion Picture Magazine, Motion Picture News Booking Guide, Motion Picture Herald, Motion Picture Projectionist, Motion Picture Story Magazine, Motion Picture Studio Insider, Motography, The Moving Picture Weekly, The Moving Picture World, El Mundo* (San Juan, Puerto Rico), *La Nación* (Buenos Aires), *El Nacional* (Chicago), *New Orleans Picayune, The New York Clipper, New York Daily Tribune, The New York Dramatic Mirror, New York Evening Post, New York Herald, New York Journal and Advertiser, New York Mail and Express, New York Sun, New York Times, New York World, The Nickelodeon* (became *Motography* in 1911), *Nuestro, Ondas Sonoras* (Los Angeles), *La Opinión* (Los Angeles), *Pathe Messenger, La Película* (Argentina), *Philadelphia Record, Photoplay, Picture Play Magazine, Photoplay Journal, Photo-Play World, Pittsburgh Dispatch, Pittsburgh Post, La Prensa* (Buenos Aires), *La Prensa* (New York), *La Prensa* (San Antonio, Texas), *Primer Plano* (Madrid), *Las Provincias* (Valencia, Spain), *Reel and Slide, Reel Life, Reseña* (Madrid), *San Francisco Chronicle, San Francisco Examiner, Saint Louis Republic, Screen Achievements Bulletin, The Screen Writer, The Script, Show World, Siempre* (Mexico City), *The Silent Picture, Silver Screen, Sound Waves, Teatros y Cines* (Madrid), *Tras la pantalla* (Madrid), *The Triangle, La Unión* (Seville), *El Universal* (Mexico City), *Universal Weekly* (also called *Moving Picture Weekly), Variety, Variety Bulletin, Vitagraph Life Portrayals, La Voz de Galicia* (La Coruña, Spain), *Wid's Film Daily, Wid's Yearbook, Views and Film Index, Washington Evening Star, Washington Post,* and *Writer's Monthly.*

EXHIBITION PROGRAMS, CD-ROMS, VIDEOTAPES, AND SOFTWARE PROGRAMS

The programs and accompanying materials of Le Giornate del Cinema Muto and of the San Antonio Cine Festival (often published in *Tonantzín,* the newsletter of The Guadalupe Cultural Arts Center in San Antonio, Texas) have been of critical importance to this research. Also highly valuable have been the CD-ROM *International Film Archive,* produced by FIAF, the *VideoHound Multimedia* companion to *VideoHound's Golden Movie Retriever,* and the diskette version of *Leonard Maltin's 1966 Movie & Video Guide.* The following films on videotape have been of use:

The Library of Congress Video Collection. 6 vols. Vol. 1, *The African American Cinema I.* Vol. 2, *Origins of the Gangster Film.* Vol. 3, *Origins of American Animation.* Vol. 4, *Origins of the Fantasy Feature.* Vol. 5, *The African American Cinema II.* Vol. 6, *America's First Women Filmmakers.*

Musser, Charles. *Before the Nickelodeon,* 1982. Distributed by First-Run Features.

ARCHIVAL MATERIALS AT THE LIBRARY OF CONGRESS AND ELSEWHERE

The materials (usually one-page synopses) deposited during the silent period with the Library of Congress for copyright purposes have proved very valuable to this research. Unfortunately, these materials are not complete. Originally, films were submitted for copyrighting by means of the deposit of synopses and perhaps supporting materials, but not the deposit of actual films. The condition of many of the synopses is poor because they were deposited with unstable photographic stills that, as they deteriorated, sometimes burned through the paper materials.

Also, mention should be made of the files of loose materials such as clippings and programs in the possession of the Library of Congress, which have been of considerable help.

Additionally, this research has benefited from the materials contained in or otherwise obtained from the following archives:

American Film Institute Library, Los Angeles
Archives of the Archdiocese of Los Angeles, San Fernando, California
Bureau of Motion Pictures (domestic and overseas branches), Office of War Information, Record Group 208, Washington National Records Center, Suitland, Maryland
Cineteca Nacional, Mexico City, Mexico
George Eastman House, Rochester, New York

Franklin Institute of Arts and Sciences, Philadelphia
Margaret Herrick Library of the Academy of Motion Picture Arts and Sciences, Beverly Hills, California
Will Hays Papers (microfilm), University Publications of America
Library of Congress Manuscript Division
Daniel H. Lord Papers, Jesuit Missouri Province Archives, Missouri Province of the Society of Jesus, St. Louis
Louis B. Mayer Library of the American Film Institute, Los Angeles
Motion Picture Division of New York State Archives, Albany, New York
Museum of Modern Art, New York City
National Archives, Washington, DC (particularly Office of Censorship, Record Group 216 and Public Relations Branch of the U.S. Army, Record Group 44)
National Board of Review of Motion Picture Collection, New York Public Library
Martin J. Quigley Papers, Special Collections Division, Georgetown University Library
Franklin D. Roosevelt Library, Hyde Park, New York
Billy Rose Theatre Collection, New York Public Library at Lincoln Center
Special Collections, Doheny Library, University of Southern California, Los Angeles
Special Collections and the Theater Arts Library, University Research Library, University of California at Los Angeles
Walter Wanger Papers, Special Collections, University of Wisconsin, Madison, Wisconsin
The Wisconsin Center for Film and Theater Research at the Wisconsin State Historical Society, Madison, Wisconsin.

GENERAL BIBLIOGRAPHY

Abaeove, Henry, et al., eds. *The Lesbian and Gay Studies Reader.* New York: Routledge, 1993.

Abella, Alex. "The New Rhythm of Florida." *Los Angeles Times Magazine,* 23 May 1993, 38.

Abrash, Barbara, and Catherine Egan. *Mediating History.* New York: New York University Press, 1992.

Ackerman, Carl W. *George Eastman.* Boston: Houghton Mifflin Co., 1930.

Ackerman, Forrest J. *Lon of a 1000 Faces.* Beverly Hills, CA: Morrison, Raven-Hill Col., 1983.

Adams, Les, and Buck Rainey. *Shoot-Em-Ups, The Complete Reference Guide to Westerns of the Sound Era.* New Rochelle, NY: Arlington House, 1978.

Adelman, Alan, ed. *A Guide to Cuban Cinema.* Latin American Monograph and Document Series 4. Pittsburgh: Center for Latin American Studies, University of Pittsburgh, 1981.

Admari, Ralph. "The House that Beadle Built, 1859-1869." *American Book Collector* 4 (November 1933): 223-25.

Agan, Patrick. *The Decline and Fall of the Love Goddesses.* Century City, CA: Pinnacle Books, 1979.

Agee, James. *Agee on Film.* 2 vols. New York: McDowell, Obelensky Co., 1958.

Agel, Henri. *Le Western.* Paris: Lettres Modernes, 1969.

Agramonte, Arturo. *Cronología del cine cubano.* Havana: ICAIC, 1966.

Aitken, Roy E., and Al P. Nelson. *The Birth of a Nation Story.* Middleburg, VA: Denlinger, 1965.

Alcalá, Manuel. *Buñuel (Cine e ideología).* Madrid: Editorial Cuadernos para el Diálogo, 1973.

Alexander, Francis W. "Stereotyping as a Method of Exploitation in Film." *Black Scholar,* May 1976.

Alexander, William. "Class, Film Language, and Popular Cinema." *Jump Cut* 30 (March 1985).

Allen, Richard. "Hollywood Corner." *Framework* 26-27 (1985): 86-89.

Allen, Robert C. "Motion Picture Exhibition in Manhattan, 1906-1912: Beyond the Nickelodeon." *Cinema Journal* 18 (spring 1979): 2-15.

_____. *Speaking of Soap Operas.* Chapel Hill: University of North Carolina Press, 1985.

_____. *Vaudeville and Film, 1895-1915: A Study in Media Interaction.* New York: Arno Press, 1980.

Allen, Robert C., and Douglas Gomery. *Film History: Theory and Practice.* New York: Alfred A. Knopf, 1985.

Allen, William D. "Spanish-Language Films in the U.S." *Films in Review* 1 (July-August 1950): 42-45.

Allgood, Jill. *Bebe and Ben.* London: Robert Hale and Co., 1975.

Allsup, Carl. "Who Done It? The Theft of Mexican-American History." *Journal of Popular Culture* 17, no. 3 (winter 1983): 150-55.

Allvine, Glendon. *The Greatest Fox of Them All.* New York: Lyle Stuart, 1969.

Almendros, Néstor. "A los dictadores les gusta el cine." *Noticias de Arte* [New York] (September 1987): 10-12.

_____. "The Cinema in Cuba." *Film Culture* 3 (1956): 21.

_____. *Cinemanía.* Barcelona: Seix Barral, 1992.

_____. *Conducta impropia.* Madrid: Editorial Playor, 1984.

_____. *A Man with a Camera.* Trans. from the Spanish by Rachel Phillips Belash. New York: Farrar, Straus, Giroux, 1984.

_____. "P.M." *Bohemia* 53, no. 21 (21 May 1961).

Almoina, Helena. *Bibliografía del cine mexicano, 1960-1985.* Mexico City: Filmoteca de la UNAM, 1985.

_____. *Notas para la historia del cine en México.* 2 vols. Mexico City: Filmoteca de la UNAM, 1980.

Altman, Diana. *Hollywood East: Louis B. Mayer and the Origins of the Studio System.* New York: Carol Publishing Group, 1992.

Altman, Rick. *The American Film Musical.* Bloomington: Indiana University Press, 1989.

Altomara, Rita Ecke. *Hollywood on the Palisades: A Filmography of Silent Features Made in Fort Lee, New Jersey, 1903-1927.* New York: Garland Publishing, 1983.

Alvarado, Jennie. "Knowing What You Want Is the First Step." *Caminos* 5, no. 7 (July-August 1984): 42-44.

Amador, María Luisa, and Jorge Ayala Blanco. *Cartelera cinematográfica, 1930-1939.* Mexico City: Filmoteca de la UNAM, 1982.

_____. *Cartelera cinematográfica, 1960-1969.* Mexico City: Textos de Humanidades, 1986.

Amador, Omar G. "Latin Lovers, Lolita, and *La Bamba.*" *Americas* (July-August 1988): 2-9.

Amar Rodríguez, Víctor Manuel. *Héctor Babenco: una propuesta de lectura cinematográfica.* Madrid: Dyckinson, 1994.

Amenegual, Barthélmy. *Que Viva Eisenstein!* Lausanne: Éditions l'Âge d'Homme, 1980.

The American Film Institute Catalog of Feature Films, 1921-1930. Ed. Kenneth Munden. New York: R. R. Bowker Co., 1971.

The American Film Institute Catalog of Feature Films, 1961-1970. Executive ed. R. P. Krafsur. New York: R. R. Bowker Co., 1976.

The American Film Institute Catalog of Motion Pictures Produced in the United States. Feature Films, 1911-1920. Executive ed. Patricia King Hanson. Berkeley: University of California Press, 1988.

The American Film Institute Catalog of Motion Pictures Produced in the United States. Feature Films, 1931-1940. Executive ed. Patricia King Hanson. Berkeley: University of California Press, 1993.

The American Film Institute Catalog of Motion Pictures Produced in the United States. Film Beginnings, 1893-1910. Comp. Elias Savada. Metuchen, NJ: Scarecrow Press, 1995.

"American Me." *Variety,* 10 March 1992, 2, 29.

Andersen, Christopher. *Citizen Jane: The Turbulent Life of Jane Fonda.* New York: Henry Holt and Co., 1990.

Anderson, Benedict. *Imagined Communities.* Rev. ed. London: Verso, 1991.

Anderson, Gillian. *Music for Silent Films: 1894-1929.* Washington, DC: Library of Congress, 1988.

Anderson, Robert. "The Role of the Western Film Genre in Industry Competition, 1907-1911." *Journal of the University Film Association,* spring 1979, 19-26.

Anderson, Robert G. *Faces, Forms, Films: The Artistry of Lon Chaney.* South Brunswick, NJ, and New York: A. S. Barnes, 1971.

Andrade-Watkins, Claire, and Mbye B. Cham, issue editors. "Critical Perspectives on Black Independent Cinema." *Blackframes,* special issue. Cambridge: MIT Press, 1988.

Anger, Kenneth. *Hollywood Babylon.* New York: Bell, 1975.

Aranda, Francisco. *Luis Buñuel: A Critical Biography.* Trans. and ed. David Robinson. New York: Da Capo, 1976.

Arce, Hector. *Groucho.* New York: G. P. Putnam's Sons, 1979.

Argüelles, Lourdes, and Ruby Rich. "Homosexuality, Homophobia, and Revolution: Notes toward an Understanding of the Cuban Lesbian and Gay Experience." Parts 1 and 2. *Signs: Journal of Women in Culture and Society* 9, no. 4 (1984): 683-99; 11, no. 1 (1985): 120-36.

Armes, Roy. *French Cinema.* New York: Oxford University Press, 1985.

_____. *Third World Filmmaking and the West.* Berkeley: University of California Press, 1987.

Arnaz, Desi. *A Book.* New York: William Morrow and Co., 1976.

Aros, Andrew A. *An Actor Guide to the Talkies, 1965 through 1974.* Metuchen, NJ: Scarecrow Press, 1977.

_____. *A Title Guide to the Talkies, 1965 through 1974.* Metuchen, NJ: Scarecrow Press, 1977.

_____. *A Title Guide to the Talkies, 1975 through 1984.* Metuchen, NJ: Scarecrow Press, 1986.

Arreaza-Camero, Emperatriz. "Movimientos, comunicación y resistencia popular: cine chicano." *Comunicación: Estudios venezolanos de comunicación* 73 (first trimester 1991): 70-86.

Arvey, Verna. "Present Day Musical Films and How They Are Made Possible." *Etude* 49 (January 1931): 16-17, 61, 72.

Askenazy, Natalia. "Movieland Stretches Southward: A Newsletter from Mexico City." *Films in Review* 1 (May-June 1950).

———. "The Two Kinds of Mexican Movies." *Films in Review* 2 (May 1951).

Aspland, Uno. *Chaplin's Films.* Trans. from the Swedish by Paul Britton Austen. South Brunswick, NJ, and New York: A. S. Barnes, 1976.

Astor, Mary. *A Life on Film.* New York: Delacorte Press, 1967.

Astre, Georges-Albert, and Albert-Patrick Hoarau. *Univers de Western.* Paris: Éditions Seghers, 1973.

Aufderheide, Pat. "Awake Argentina." *Film Comment,* April 1986, 51-55.

Aumont, Jean-Pierre. *Sun and Shadow.* New York: W. W. Norton, 1972.

Austin, Bruce A. *The Film Audience: An International Bibliography of Research.* Metuchen, NJ: Scarecrow Press, 1983.

"Authentic Pachuco." *Time,* 10 July 1944, 72.

Ayala Blanco, Jorge. "Artenstein y el mito del cine chicano." *El Financiero,* 10 September 1990, 71.

———. *La aventura del cine mexicano.* Mexico City: Ediciones Era, 1968. Reprint, Mexico City: Editorial Posada, 1985.

———. *La búsqueda del cine mexicano (1968-1972).* 2 vols. Cuadernos de Cine 22. Mexico City: UNAM, Dirección General de Difusión Cultural, 1974.

———. *La condición del cine mexicano (1973-1985).* Mexico City: Editorial Posada, 1986.

———. *La disolvencia del cine mexicano: entre lo popular y lo exquisito.* Mexico City: Editorial Grijalbo, 1991.

———. *Falaces fenómenos fílmicos: algunos discursos cinematográficos a fines de los 70.* 2nd ed. Mexico City: Editorial Posada, 1988.

———. "Pancho Villa en el jardín de los senderos que trifurcan." *Siempre,* 15 September 1982.

Aylesworth, Thomas G. *Broadway to Hollywood.* New York: Bison Books, 1985.

Bainbridge, John. *Garbo.* Garden City, NY: Doubleday, 1955.

Baker, Fred, and Ross Firestone. *Movie People.* New York: Lancer Books, 1973.

Baker, Houston A. "Spike Lee and the Commerce of Culture." *Black American Literature Forum* 25, no. 2 (summer 1991): 237-52.

Balázs, Béla. *Theory of the Film.* Trans. Edith Bone. New York: Dover, 1970.

Balio, Tino, ed. *The American Film Industry.* Madison: University of Wisconsin Press, 1976. Rev. ed., 1985.

———. *United Artists: The Company Built by the Stars.* Madison: University of Wisconsin Press, 1976.

Ball, Eustace Hall. *Photoplay Scenarios: How to Write and Sell Them.* New York: Hearst's International Library Co., 1917.

Balshofer, Fred J., and Arthur C. Miller. *One Reel a Week.* Berkeley: University of California Press, 1967.

Barbour, Alan G. *Cliffhanger: A Pictorial History of the Motion Picture Serial.* Secaucus, NJ: Citadel Press, 1977.

———. *Days of Thrills and Adventure.* New York: Macmillan, 1970.

———. *Saturday Afternoon at the Movies.* New York: Bonanza Books, 1986.

———. *The Thrill of it All.* New York: Collier, 1971.

Bardèche, Maurice, and Robert Brasillach. *Histoire du Cinéma.* Vol. 2, *Le Cinéma parlant.* Paris: André Martel, 1954, 430-36.

———. *History of the Film.* Trans. and ed. Iris Barry. New York: W. W. Norton/Museum of Modern Art, 1938.

Barnard, Tim. *Argentine Cinema.* Toronto: Nightwood, 1986.

Barnett, Louis K. *The Ignoble Savage: American Literary Racism, 1790-1890.* Westport, CT: Greenwood Press, 1975.

Barr, Charles. *Laurel and Hardy.* Berkeley: University of California Press, 1968.

Barrios, Gregg. "Boulevard Knights in Hollywood Satin." *Caracol* 5, nos. 11-12 (July-August 1979): 8-10, 22.

———. "Efraín Gutiérrez y el nuevo cine chicano." *La Opinión* (Los Angeles), 18 August 1985, "La Comunidad" section, 3.

———. "El Indio's Golden Era of Movies." *Los Angeles Times,* 28 August 1983.

———. "Latinos en Hollywood: Ahora y antes." *Más* 1, no. 1 (1989): 54-59.

———. " 'Old Gringo': Romance, Revolution, Sex, Passion." *Los Angeles Times,* 24 April 1988.

———. "Very Old Gringo." *Variety,* 27 August 1989.

Barry, Iris. *D. W. Griffith: American Film Master.* New York: Museum of Modern Art, 1940.

———. *Let's Go to the Movies.* New York: Payson and Clarke, 1926.

Barrymore, John. *Confessions of an Actor.* Indianapolis: Bobbs-Merrill Co., 1926.

Barrymore, Lionel, with Cameron Shipp. *We Barrymores.* New York: Appleton-Century-Crofts, 1951

Barson, Michael. *The Illustrated Who's Who of Hollywood Directors.* Vol. 1, *The Sound Era.* New York: Farrar, Straus & Giroux, 1995.

Bas de Tamayo, Xenia. "Las grandes estrellas hispanas en el cine de Hollywood." *Réplica* 21, no. 882, (June 1990): 6-11.

Basten, Fred E. *Glorious Technicolor: The Movies' Magic Rainbow.* New York: Barnes, 1980.

Bataille, Gretchen, and Bob Hicks. "American Indians in Popular Films." In *Beyond the Stars: Characters in American Popular Film,* ed. Paul Loukides and Linda K. Fuller. Bowling Green, OH: Bowling Green State University Popular Press, 1990.

Bataille, Gretchen M., and Charles L. P. Silet. *Images of American Indians on Films: An Annotated Bibliography.* New York: Garland Publishing, 1985.

———. *The Pretend Indians: Images of Native Americans in the Movies.* Ames: Iowa State University Press, 1980.

Batman, Richard Dale. "The Founding of the Hollywood Motion Picture Industry." *Journal of the West* 10 (October 1971): 609-23.

Batty, Linda, ed. *Retrospective Index to Film Periodicals, 1930-1971.* New York: R. R. Bowker Co., 1971.

Baudrillard, Jean. *Seduction.* New York: St. Martin's Press, 1979.

Baudry, Jean-Louis. "Ideological Effects of the Basic Cinematographic Apparatus." Trans. Alan Williams. In *Narrative, Apparatus, Ideology: A Film Theory Reader,* ed. Phil Rosen, 286-98. New York: Columbia University Press, 1986.

Baudry, Pierre. "Les Aventures de l'idée (sur 'Intolérance')." Parts 1 and 2. *Cahiers du cinéma* 240 (July-August 1972): 51-58; 241 (September-October 1972): 31-45.

Baudy, Mary L., ed. *The Dawn of Sound.* New York: Museum of Modern Art, 1989.

Bawden, Liz-Anne, ed. *The Oxford Companion to Film*. New York and London: Oxford University Press, 1976.

Baxter, John. *The Cinema of John Ford*. New York: A. S. Barnes, 1971.

_____. *The Hollywood Exiles*. New York: Taplinger, 1976.

_____. *Hollywood in the Thirties*. New York: A. S. Barnes and Co., 1968.

_____. *King Vidor*. New York: Monarch Press, 1976.

Baym, Nina. *Woman's Fiction: A Guide to Novels By and About Women in America, 1820-1870*. Ithaca, NY: Cornell University Press, 1978.

Bazin, André. *Orson Welles: A Critical View*. New York: Harper and Row, 1978.

_____. *What Is Cinema?* Trans. Hugh Gray. 2 vols. Berkeley: University of California Press, 1971.

Beaton, Welford. *Know Your Movies: The Theory and Practice of Motion Picture Production*. Hollywood: Howard Hill, 1932.

Beaupree, Lee. "One-Third Film Public: Negro: Columbia and UA Pitch for Biz." *Variety*, 29 November 1967.

Behlmer, Rudy, ed. *MEMO from David O. Selznick*. New York: Viking Press, 1972.

Belafonte, Dennis, and Alvin H. Marrill. *The Films of Tyrone Power*. New York: Citadel Press, 1979.

Bell, Geoffrey. *The Golden Gate and the Silver Screen: San Francisco in the History of the Cinema*. Cranbury, NJ: Fairleigh Dickinson University Press (Associated University Presses), 1984.

Bellour, Raymond, ed. *Le Western*. Paris: Union Général d'Éditions, 1966.

Belton, John. *Cinema Stylists*. Metuchen, NJ: Scarecrow Press, 1983.

Benayoun, Robert. *John Huston*. Col. Cinéma d'aujourd'hui. Paris: Éditions Seghers, 1966.

Benítez-Rojo, Antonio. *The Repeating Island: The Caribbean and the Postmodern Perspective*. Durham, NC: Duke University Press, 1992.

Bennett, D. M. *Anthony Comstock: His Career of Cruelty and Crime*. 1878. Reprint, New York: Da Capo Press, 1971.

Bennett, Lerone, Jr. "The Emancipation Orgasm: Sweetback in Wonderland." *Ebony* 26 (September 1971): 106-16.

Beranger, Clara F. "The Photoplay—A New Kind of Drama." *Harper's Weekly* 56, no. 2907 (7 September 1912): 13.

Berelson, Bernard R. *Content Analysis in Communication Research*. Glencoe, IL: Free Press, 1952.

Berg, Charles M. *An Investigation of the Motives for and Realization of Music to Accompany the American Silent Film, 1897-1927*. New York: Arno Press, 1976.

Bergan, Ronald. *The United Artists Story: The Complete History of the Studio and Its 1581 Films*. London: Octopus Books, 1986.

Bergman, Andrew. *We're in the Money: Depression America and Its Films*. New York: New York University Press, 1971.

Bergman, David, ed. *Camp Grounds: Style and Homosexuality*. Amherst: University of Massachusetts Press, 1993.

Berkhofer, Robert, Jr. *The White Man's Indian*. New York: Vintage Books, 1979.

Berry, Chris, ed. *Perspectives on Chinese Cinema*. London: British Film Institute, 1991.

Berry, Gordon L., and Claudia Mitchell-Kernan. *Television and the Socialization of the Minority Child*. New York: Academic Press, 1982.

Bertsch, Marguerite. *How to Write for Moving Pictures: A Manual of Instruction and Information*. New York: George H. Doran Co., 1917.

Besas, Peter. *Behind the Spanish Lens: Spanish Cinema under Fascism and Democracy*. Denver: Arden Press, 1985.

_____. "Crossovers Vie for Megabuck Tortilla: Latinos and Anglos Seek to Break Ethnic Barriers." *Variety*, 23 March 1988, 43+.

Best-Mangard, Adolfo. "Mexico into Cinema." *Theatre Arts Monthly*, November 1932, 926.

Beynon, George. *Musical Presentation of Motion Pictures*. New York: Schirmer, 1921.

Biberman, Herbert. *Salt of the Earth: The Story of a Film*. Boston: Beacon Press, 1965.

Bielby, William, and Denise Bielby. *The 1987 Hollywood Writers' Report: A Survey of Ethnic, Gender, and Age Employment Practices*. Los Angeles: Writers Guild of America West, 1987.

_____. *The 1989 Hollywood Writers' Report: Unequal Access, Unequal Pay*. Los Angeles: Writers Guild of America West, 1989.

Bilbao, Elena, and María Antonieta Gallart. *Los chicanos*. Mexico City: Editorial Nueva Imagen, 1981.

Billops, Camille, Ada Griffin, and Valerie Smith, eds. "Special Issue on Black Film." *Black American Literature Forum* 25, no. 2 (summer 1991).

Birchard, Robert S. *King Cowboy: Tom Mix and the Movies*. Burbank, CA: Riverwood Press, 1993.

Birri, Fernando. "For a Nationalist, Realist, Critical, and Popular Cinema." *Screen* 26, nos. 3-4 (May-August 1985): 89-91.

Bishop, W. H. "Story-Paper Literature." *Atlantic* 44 (September 1879): 387.

Bitzer, Billy. *His Story: The Autobiography of D. W. Griffith's Master Cameraman*. New York: Farrar, Straus and Giroux, 1973.

Black, Gregory D., and Clayton R. Koppes. "OWI Goes to the Movies: The Bureau of Intelligence's Criticism of Hollywood, 1942-1943." *Prologue* 6 (1974): 42-57.

Blades, Rubén. "The Politics Behind the Latino's Legacy." *New York Times*, 19 April 1992, H31.

Blanco, Carlos. *Don Quijote cabalga de nuevo*. Madrid: Editorial Fragua, 1973.

Blesh, Rudy. *Keaton*. New York: Macmillan, 1966.

Bloem, Walter S. *The Soul of the Moving Picture*. New York: E. P. Dutton, 1924.

Bluestone, George. "The Changing Cowboy: From Dime Novel to Dollar Film." *Western Humanities Review* 14 (summer 1960): 331-37.

_____. *Novels into Film: The Metamorphosis of Fiction into Cinema*. Berkeley: The University of California Press, 1957.

Blum, Daniel. *A New Pictorial History of the Talkies*. New York: G. P. Putnam's Sons, 1968.

_____. *A Pictorial History of the Silent Screen*. New York: Grosset and Dunlap Publishers, 1953.

Bobo, Jacqueline. "The Subject is Money: Reconsidering the Black Film Audience as a Theoretical Paradigm." *Black American Literature Forum* 25 (summer 1991): 421-32.

Bodeen, De Witt. "Dolores del Río." *Films in Review* 18 (May 1967): 266-83.

_____. *From Hollywood*. Cranbury, NJ: A. S. Barnes & Co., 1976.

_____. *More From Hollywood*. South Brunswick, NJ, and New York: A. S. Barnes & Co., 1977.

_____. "Ramón Novarro." *Films in Review* 18 (November 1967): 528-47.

Boetticher, Budd. *When in Disgrace.* Santa Barbara, CA: Neville Publishing, 1989.

Bogdanovich, Peter. *Allan Dwan: The Last Pioneer.* New York: Praeger, 1971.

_____. *John Ford.* Berkeley: University of California Press, 1968. 2nd ed., 1978.

Bogle, Donald. *Toms, Coons, Mulattoes, Mammies, and Bucks: An Interpretative History of Blacks in American Film, 1900-1941.* New York: Viking Press, 1973.

_____. "Uptown Saturday Night: A Look at Its Place in Black Film History." *Freedomways* 14 (1974): 320-30.

Bohr, José. *Desde el balcón de mi vida.* 2nd ed. Buenos Aires: Editorial Sudamericana/Planeta, 1987.

_____. *¡Luz! ¡Cámara! ¡Acción! (Retrospectiva de una vida).* Santiago de Chile: Editorial del Pacífico, 1976.

Bojarski, Richard, and Kenneth Beale. *The Films of Boris Karloff.* Secaucus, NJ: Citadel Press, 1974.

Bold, Christine. *Selling the Wild West: Popular Western Fiction, 1860-1960.* Bloomington: Indiana University Press, 1987.

_____. "The Voice of the Fiction Factory in Dime and Pulp Westerns." *Journal of American Studies* 17, no. 1 (1984): 29-46.

Bollman, Gladys, and Henry Bollman. *Motion Pictures for Community Needs.* New York: Henry Holt, 1922.

Borde, Raymond, ed. *Le Cinéma français muet dans le monde.* Perpignan, France: Cinémathèque de Toulouse and Institut Jean Vigo, 1989.

Bordwell, David. "Eisenstein's Epistemological Shift." *Screen* 15, no. 4 (winter 1974-75): 29-46.

_____. "The Idea of Montage in Soviet Art and Film." *Cinema Journal* 11, no. 2 (spring 1972): 9-17.

_____. "Narration and Scenography in the Later Eisenstein." *Millennium Film Journal* 13 (fall-winter 1983-84): 62-80.

_____. *Narration in the Fiction Film.* Madison: University of Wisconsin Press, 1985.

Bordwell, David, Janet Staiger, and Kristin Thompson. *The Classical Hollywood Cinema: Film Style and Mode of Production to 1960.* New York: Columbia University Press, 1985.

Boskin, Joseph. *Sambo: The Rise and Demise of an American Jester.* New York: Oxford University Press, 1986.

Bosworth, Patricia. *Montgomery Clift.* New York: Bantam Books, 1978.

Bourdieu, Pierre. *Distinction.* Cambridge, MA: Harvard University Press, 1984.

Bowers, Q. David. *Nickelodeon Theatres and Their Music.* Vestal, NY: Vestal Press, 1986.

Bowser, Eileen. "Racial/Racist Jokes in American Silent Slapstick Comedy." *Griffithiana* 18, no. 53 (1995): 35-44.

_____. *The Transformation of Cinema, 1907-1915.* Vol. 2 of *History of the American Cinema,* Charles Harpole, gen. ed. New York: Charles Scribner's Sons, 1990.

_____, ed. *Biograph Bulletins 1908-1912.* New York: Farrar, Straus and Giroux, 1973.

_____, ed. *Film Notes.* New York: Museum of Modern Art, 1969.

Branch, E. Douglas. *The Cowboy and His Interpreters.* New York: D. Appleton and Co., 1926.

Branigan, Edward R. *Point of View in the Cinema: A Theory of Narration and Subjectivity in Classical Film.* Amsterdam: Mouton Publishers, 1984.

Brauer, Ralph, with Donna Brauer. *The Horse, the Gun, and the Piece of Property: Changing Images of the TV Western.* Bowling Green, OH: Bowling Green State University Popular Press, 1975.

Bronner, Edwin J. *The Encyclopedia of the American Theater, 1900-1975.* San Diego and New York: A. S. Barnes and Co., 1980.

Brooks, Louise. *Lulu in Hollywood.* New York: Alfred A. Knopf, 1982.

Brooks, Tim, and Earle Marsh. *The Complete Directory to Prime Time Network and Cable TV Shows, 1946-Present.* 6th ed. New York: Ballantine Books, 1995.

Brown, Gene. *Movie Time: A Chronology of Hollywood and the Movie Industry from Its Beginnings to the Present.* New York: Macmillan, 1995.

_____, ed. *New York Times Encyclopedia of Film, 1896-1928.* New York: New York Times Books, 1984.

Brown, Karl. *Adventures with D. W. Griffith.* Edited by Kevin Brownlow. New York: Farrar, Straus and Giroux, 1973.

Brown, Peter Harry. *Kim Novak: The Reluctant Goddess.* New York: St. Martin's Press, 1986.

Brown, Peter H., and Jim Pinkston. *Oscar Dearest: Six Decades of Scandal, Politics and Greed Behind Hollywood's Academy Awards, 1927-1986.* New York: Harper and Row, 1987.

Brownlow, Kevin. *Hollywood: The Pioneers.* New York: Alfred A. Knopf, 1979.

_____. *The Parade's Gone By. . . .* New York: Alfred A. Knopf, 1968.

_____. *The War, the West, and the Wilderness.* New York: Alfred A. Knopf, 1978.

Brownlow, Kevin, and John Kobal. *Hollywood: The Pioneers.* New York: Alfred A. Knopf, 1979.

Broyles-González, Yolanda. "What Price 'Mainstream'? Luis Valdez's *Corridos* on Stage and Film." *Cultural Studies* 4, no. 3 (October 1990): 281-93.

Bruce-Novoa, Juan. "The Hollywood Americano in Mexico." In *Mexico and the United States: Intercultural Relations in the Humanities,* ed. Juanita Luna Lawhen et al., 19-34. San Antonio, TX: San Antonio College, 1984.

Buache, Freddy. *The Cinema of Luis Buñuel.* Trans. Peter Graham. New York: A. S. Barnes, 1973.

Buñuel, Luis. *Mi último suspiro (memorias).* Mexico City: Plaza y Janés, 1982.

_____. *My Last Sigh.* New York: Alfred A. Knopf, 1983.

Burch, Noël. *Theory of Film Practice.* Trans. Helen R. Lane. New York: Praeger, 1973.

Burgin, Victor, James Donald, and Cora Kaplan. *Formations of Fantasy.* New York: Routledge, 1989.

Burns, Archibaldo. "Dolores del Río: de sus cenizas, la leyenda." *Proceso* 337 (18 April 1983).

Burns, E. Bradford. *Latin American Cinema: Film and History.* Los Angeles: Latin American Center, 1975.

Burton, Jack. *The Blue Book of Hollywood Musicals.* New York: Century House, 1953.

Burton, Julianne. "Marginal Cinemas and Mainstream Critical Theory." *Screen* 26, no. 3 (1985): 2-21.

_____. "Transitional States: Creative Complicities with the Real in *Man Marked to Die: Twenty Years Later* and *Patriamada.*" *Studies in Latin American Popular Culture* 7 (1988): 139-55.

_____, ed. *Cinema and Social Change in Latin America: Conversations with Filmmakers*. Austin: University of Texas Press, 1986.

_____, comp. *The New Latin American Cinema: An Annotated Bibliography of Sources in English, Spanish, and Portuguese (1960-1980)*. New York: Smyrna Press, 1983.

_____, ed. *The Social Documentary in Latin America*. Pittsburgh: University of Pittsburgh Press, 1990.

Buscombe, Edward, ed. *The BFI Companion to the Western*. New York: Atheneum, 1988.

Bustillo Oro, Juan. *Vida cinematográfica*. Mexico City: Cineteca Nacional, 1984.

Bustos, Víctor. "Entrevista con María Novaro." *Dicine* 40 (July 1991).

Butler, Ivan. *Silent Magic: Rediscovering the Silent Film Era*. London: Columbus Books, 1987.

Butler, Judith. *Gender Trouble*. New York: Routledge, 1990.

Butler, Ron. "Cantinflas: Príncipe mexicano de la comedia." *Américas,* April 1981.

Butsch, Richard, ed. *For Fun and Profit: The Transformation of Leisure into Consumption*. Philadelphia: Temple University Press, 1990.

Cabrera Infante, Guillermo. "Cuba's Shadow." *Film Comment* 21 (1985): 43-45.

Cagin, Seth, and Philip Dray. *Sex, Drugs, Violence: Hollywood Films of the Seventies*. New York: Harper & Row, 1984.

"Caja de sorpresas." *Tiempo,* 30 March 1945, 39.

Calder-Marshall, Arthur. *The Innocent Eye*. New York: Harcourt, Brace, & Co., 1966.

Calderón, Héctor, and José David Saldívar. *Criticism in the Borderlands*. Durham, NC: Duke University Press, 1991.

Campbell, Craig W. *Reel America and World War I: A Comprehensive Filmography and History of Motion Pictures in the United States, 1914-1920*. Jefferson, NC: McFarland & Co., 1985.

Candelaria, Cordelia. "Film Portrayals of La Mujer Hispana." *Agenda* 11, no. 3 (June 1981): 32-36.

Canham, Kingsley. *The Hollywood Professionals*. New York: A. S. Barnes, 1973.

Cantor, Eddie, as told to David Freedman. *My Life Is in Your Hands*. New York: Harper and Brothers, 1928.

Cantor, Eddie, with Jane Kesner Ardmore. *Take My Life*. New York: Doubleday, 1957.

Caparrós Lera, José María, and Rafael de España. *The Spanish Cinema: An Historical Approach*. Trans. Carl J. Mora. Barcelona: Centre for Cinematic Research "Film-Historia," 1987.

Capra, Frank. *The Name above the Title*. New York: Macmillan, 1971.

Carbo, Rosie. "Amor in the Afternoon." *Hispanic,* September 1994, 46-50.

Cárdenas, Don, and Suzanne Schneider, eds. *Chicano Images in Film*. Denver, CO: Denver International Film Festival, 1981.

Cardoso, Abel, Jr. *Carmen Miranda*. São Paulo: Símbolo S.A. Indústrias Gráficas, 1978.

Careaga, Gabriel. *Erotismo, violencia y política en el cine*. Mexico City: Joaquín Mortiz, 1981.

Carey, Gary. *Brando*. New York: Pocket Books, 1973.

_____. *Doug & Mary: A Biography of Douglas Fairbanks & Mary Pickford*. New York: E. P. Dutton, 1977.

Carlson, Jerry W., guest ed. "Contemporary Latin American Film," special issue. *Review: Latin American Literature and Arts* 46 (fall 1992).

Carmen, Ira H. *Movies, Censorship, and the Law*. Ann Arbor: University of Michigan Press, 1966.

Carpozi, George, Jr. *The John Wayne Story*. New Rochelle, NY: Arlington House, 1972.

Carr, C. *On Edge: Performance at the End of the Twentieth Century*. Hanover, NH: Wesleyan University Press, 1993.

Carr, Catherine, ed. *The Art of Photoplay Writing*. New York: Hannis Jordan Co., 1914.

Carr, Larry. *More Fabulous Faces: The Evolution and Metamorphosis of Dolores del Río, Myrna Loy, Carole Lombard, Bette Davis, and Katherine Hepburn*. Garden City, NY: Doubleday, 1979.

Carr, Nick. *The Western Pulp Hero*. San Bernardino, CA: Borgo Press, 1990.

Carrier, Esther Jane. *Fiction in Public Libraries 1876-1900*. New York: Scarecrow Press, 1965.

Carrillo, Leo. *The California I Love*. Englewood Cliffs, NJ: Prentice-Hall, 1951.

Carro, Nelson. *El cine de luchadores*. Mexico City: Filmoteca de la UNAM, 1984.

Cassady, Ralph. "Monopoly in Motion Picture Production and Distribution, 1908-1915." *Southern California Law Review,* no. 32 (summer 1959): 325-45.

Castro, Antonio. *El cine español en el banquillo*. Valencia, Spain: Fernando Torres Editor, 1974.

Casty, Alan. *The Films of Robert Rossen*. New York: Museum of Modern Art, 1969.

Catalog of Copyright Entries, Cumulative Series: Motion Pictures, 1912-1939. Washington, DC: Library of Congress, Copyright Office, 1951.

Cawelti, John. *Adventure, Mystery, and Romance*. Chicago: University of Chicago Press, 1976.

_____. *The Six-Gun Mystique*. Bowling Green, OH: Bowling Green State University Popular Press, 1971.

Cawley, John, and Jim Korkis. *The Encyclopedia of Cartoon Superstars*. Las Vegas: Pioneer Books, 1990.

Ceplair, Larry, and Steven Englund. *The Inquisition in Hollywood: Politics in the Film Community, 1930-1960*. Berkeley: University of California Press, 1983.

Césarman, Fernando. *El ojo de Buñuel: Psicoanálisis desde una butaca*. Barcelona: Anagrama, 1976.

Cham, Mbye B. *Critical Perspectives on Black Independent Cinema*. Cambridge, MA: MIT Press, 1988.

_____, ed. *Ex-Isles: Essays on Caribbean Cinema*. Trenton, NJ: Africa World Press, 1992.

Chanan, Michael. *Chilean Cinema*. London: British Film Institute, 1976.

_____. *The Cuban Image: Cinema and Cultural Politics in Cuba*. London: British Film Institute, 1985.

_____. *The Dream That Kicks*. London: Routledge and Kegan Paul, 1981.

_____. *Twenty-Five Years of the New Latin American Cinema*. London: British Film Institute, 1983.

_____, ed. *Memories of Underdevelopment: Tomás Gutiérrez Alea, Director*. New Brunswick, NJ: Rutgers University Press, 1990.

Chaplin, Charles. *My Autobiography.* New York: Simon and Schuster, 1964.

Chatman, Seymour. *Story and Discourse: Narrative Structure in Fiction and Film.* Ithaca, NY: Cornell University Press, 1978.

Chavarría, Elvira. *Chicano Film Guide.* 2nd ed. Austin: University of Texas at Austin, Mexican American Library Program, Benson Latin American Collection, 1983.

Chávez, Carlos. "Films by American Governments: Mexico." *Films* 3 (summer 1940).

Chávez, John R. *The Lost Land: The Chicano Image of the Southwest.* Albuquerque: University of New Mexico Press, 1984.

Chávez, Stephanie, and Greg Braxton. "Anti-Gang Crusader Slain in Driveway." *The Sacramento Bee,* 15 May 1992, B8.

Cherchi-Usai, Paolo, ed. *Vitagraph Company of America: Il cinema prima di Hollywood.* Pordenone, Italy: Edizioni Studio Text, 1987.

Chinea-Varela, Migdia. "In Hollywood, Diversity Programs Create the Illusion of Fairness." *Hispanic Business,* July 1995, 8.

Chinoy, Helen Kritch, and Toby Cole. *Directors and Directing: A Source Book of the Modern Theater.* Indianapolis: Bobbs-Merrill, 1976.

Chirat, Raymond. *Catalogue des films français de long métrage: Films de fiction 1940-1950.* Luxembourg: Imprimerie Saint-Paul, 1981.

———. *Catalogue des films français de long métrage: Films sonores de fiction 1929-1939.* 2nd ed. Brussels: Cinémathèque Royale de Belgique, 1981.

Chirat, Raymond, and Roger Icart. *Catalogue des films français de long métrage: Films de fiction 1919-1929.* Toulouse, France: Cinémathèque Royale de Belgique, 1981.

Christensen, Terry. *Reel Politics.* New York: Basil Blackwell, 1987.

Christie, Ian, and David Elliott, eds. *Eisenstein at 90.* Oxford: Museum of Modern Art, 1988.

Ciment, Michel. *Kazan por Kazan.* Madrid: Editorial Fundamentos, 1974.

Cine-Aztlán. *La Raza Film Bibliography.* Santa Barbara, CA: Cine-Aztlán, 1974.

Cini, Zelda, and Bob Crane. *Hollywood: Land and Legend.* Westport, CT: Arlington House, 1980.

Clair, René. *Reflections on the Cinema.* London: William Kimber, 1953.

Clapham, Walter C. *Western Movies.* London: Octopus Books, 1974.

Clarens, Carlos. *Crime Movies: From Griffith to the Godfather and Beyond.* New York: W. W. Norton and Co., 1980.

Clark, Cedric C. "Television and Social Controls: Some Observations on the Portrayals of Ethnic Minorities." *Television Quarterly* 8 (spring 1969): 18-22.

Coatsworth, John H., and Carlos Rico, eds. *Images of Mexico in the United States.* La Jolla, CA: University of California, San Diego, Center for U.S.-Mexican Studies, 1989.

Coe, Brian. *The History of Movie Photography.* Westfield, NJ: Eastview Editions, 1981.

Cohen, Keith. *Film and Fiction: The Dynamics of Exchange.* New Haven, CT: Yale University Press, 1979.

Cohen, Sandy. "Racial and Ethnic Humor in the United States." *Amerika Studien/American Studies* 30 (1985): 204.

Cohen, Sarah Blacher. *From Hester Street to Hollywood: The Jewish American Stage and Screen.* Bloomington: Indiana University Press, 1986.

Colectivo Alejandro Galindo. "El cine mexicano y su crisis." Parts 1-3. *Dicine* 19 (May-June 1987); 20 (July-August 1987); 21 (September-October 1987).

Coleman, Todd. "Ethnicity on the American Screen: Where Are the Latinos?" *Cine Acción News* 13, no. 1 (February 1996): 1+.

———. "Latinos Are the Most Stereotyped Ethnic Group on TV." *Cine Acción News* 13, no. 2 (March 1996): 1+.

Colina, Enrique, and Daniel Díaz Torres. "Ideología del melodrama en el viejo cine latinoamericano." *Cine Cubano* 73-75 (1971): 14-26.

Collins, Francis A. *The Camera Man.* New York: Century, 1919.

Coma, Javier. *Diccionario del cine de aventuras.* Barcelona: Plaza y Janés, 1994.

Combs, James. *American Political Movies.* New York: Garland Publishing Co., 1990.

"The Coming of Age of Hispanic Broadcasting: Special Report." *Broadcasting,* 3 April 1989.

Comisión Nacional de Cinematografía. *El libro de oro del cine mexicano, 1949.* Mexico City: Comisión Nacional de Cinematografía, 1949.

Comito, Terry, ed. *Touch of Evil: Orson Welles, Director.* New Brunswick, NJ: Rutgers University Press, 1985.

Comstock, Anthony. "Vampire Literature." *North American Review* 153 (August 1891): 164.

Comstock, George. *The Impact of Television on American Institutions and the American Public.* Honolulu: East-West Communications Institute, East-West Center, 1977.

Conant, Michael. *Antitrust in the Motion Picture Industry: Economic and Legal Analysis.* Berkeley: University of California Press, 1960.

Conn, Peter. *The Divided Mind: Ideology and Imagination in America, 1898-1917.* Cambridge: Cambridge University Press, 1983.

"Connecting with the American Experience: An Interview with Luis Valdez." *Hispanic Business,* July 1987, 10-13.

Connor, Edward. "The Genealogy of Zorro." *Films in Review,* Aug.-Sept. 1957, 330-33, 343.

Conot, Robert. *A Streak of Luck: The Life and Legend of Thomas Alva Edison.* New York: Seaview Books, 1979.

Contreras Torres, Miguel. *El libro negro del cine mexicano.* Mexico City: Editora Hispano-Continental Films, 1960.

Cook, David A. *A History of Narrative Film.* New York: W. W. Norton & Co., 1981.

Cooke, Alistair. *Douglas Fairbanks: The Making of a Screen Character.* New York: Museum of Modern Art, 1940.

Cooper, Miriam, with Bonnie Herndon. *Dark Lady of the Silents: My Life in Early Hollywood.* Indianapolis: Bobbs-Merrill, 1973.

Coppedge, Walter. *Henry King's America.* Metuchen, NJ: Scarecrow Press, 1986.

Corey, Melinda, and George Ochoa, comps. *A Cast of Thousands: A Compendium of Who Played What in Film.* 3 vols. New York: Facts on File, 1992.

Coria, José Felipe. "Un cine popular mexicano. El progreso de un libertino." *Intolerancia* 7 (November-December 1990).

Corliss, Richard. "Born in East L.A.: Hollywood Can Be a Tough Town for Non-Anglos." *Time,* 11 July 1988, 66-67.

———. *The Hollywood Screenwriters.* New York: Discuss Books, 1972.

———. *Talking Pictures.* Woodstock, NY: Overlook Press, 1974.

Corman, Roger, with Jim Jerome. *How I Made a Hundred Movies in Hollywood and Never Lost a Dime.* New York: Random House, 1990.

Corneau, Ernest N. *The Hall of Fame of Western Stars.* North Quincy, MA: Christopher Publishing House, 1969.

Corrigan, Timothy. *A Cinema Without Walls: Movies and Culture After Vietnam.* New Brunswick, NJ: Rutgers University Press, 1991.

Cortés, Carlos E., "Chicanas in Film: History of an Image." In *Chicano Cinema: Research, Review, and Resources,* ed. Gary D. Keller, 94-108. Binghamton, NY: Bilingual Review/ Press, 1985.

_____. "Chicanos y medios masivos de comunicación." *Plural,* January 1993, 50-59.

_____. "Empowerment through Media Literacy: A Multicultural Approach." In *Empowerment Through Multicultural Education,* ed. Christine E. Sleeter. Albany: State University of New York Press, 1991.

_____. "*The Greaser's Revenge* to *Boulevard Nights:* The Mass Media Curriculum on Chicanos." In *History, Culture, and Society: Chicano Studies in the 1980s,* ed. National Association for Chicano Studies. Ypsilanti, MI: Bilingual Press, 1983.

_____. "The History of Ethnic Images in Film: The Search for a Methodology." In *Ethnic Images in Popular Genres and Media,* special issue of *MELUS: The Journal of the Society for the Study of the Multi-Ethnic Literature of the United States* 11, no. 3 (fall 1984): 63-77.

_____. "The Immigrant in Film: Evolution of an Illuminating Icon." In *Stock Characters in American Popular Film,* vol. 1 of *Beyond the Stars,* ed. Paul Loukides and Linda K. Fuller, 23-34. Bowling Green, OH: Bowling Green State University Popular Press, 1990.

_____. "Italian-Americans in Film: From Immigrants to Icons." In *Italian-American Literature,* special issue of *MELUS: The Journal of the Society for the Study of the Multi-Ethnic Literature of the United States* 14, nos. 3-4 (fall-winter 1987): 107-26.

_____. "The Role of Media in Multicultural Education." *Viewpoints in Teaching and Learning* 56, no. 1 (winter 1980): 38-49.

_____. "The Societal Curriculum: Implications for Multiethnic Education." In *Education in the 80s: Multiethnic Education,* ed. James A. Banks, 24-32. Washington, DC: National Education Association, 1981.

_____. "To View a Neighbor: The Hollywood Textbook on Mexico." In *Images of Mexico in the United States,* ed. John H. Coatsworth and Carlos Rico, 91-118. San Diego: Center for U.S.-Mexican Studies, University of California, San Diego, 1989.

_____. "Who Is María? What Is Juan? Dilemmas of Analyzing the Chicano Image in U.S. Feature Films." In *Chicanos and Film: Essays on Chicano Representation and Resistance,* ed. Chon A. Noriega, 83-104. New York: Garland Publishing Co., 1992.

Cotten, Joseph. *La vanidad te llevará a alguna parte.* Barcelona: Parsifal Ediciones, 1992.

Coulson, Thomas. "Philadelphia and the Development of the Motion Picture." *Journal of the Franklin Institute* 262 (July 1956): 1-16.

Cowan, Lester, ed. *Recording Sound for Motion Pictures.* New York: McGraw-Hill, 1931.

Cowie, Peter, ed. *International Film Guide.* London: Tantivy Press, 1968–.

_____, ed. *World Filmography.* South Brunswick, NJ, and New York: A. S. Barnes and Co., 1977.

Cox, Alex, Richard Peña, and Michael Tolkin. "Mexican Cinema." *Film Comment* 31, no. 6 (Nov./Dec. 1995): 26-35.

Crafton, Donald. *Before Mickey: The Animated Film (1898-1928).* Cambridge: MIT Press, 1982.

Crawford, Christina. *Mommie Dearest.* New York: William Morrow and Co., 1979.

Crawford, Paul J. "Movie Habits and Attitudes of the Under-Privileged Boys of the All Nations Area in Los Angeles." Master's thesis, University of Southern California, 1934.

Cripps, Thomas. *Black Film as Genre.* New York: Oxford University Press, 1977.

_____. "Black Films and Film Makers: Movies in the Ghetto, B.P. (Before Poitier)." *Negro Digest,* February 1969, 25.

_____. "The Myth of the Southern Box Office: A Factor in Racial Stereotyping in American Movies, 1920-1940." In *The Black Experience in America: Selected Essays,* ed. James C. Curtis and Louis L. Gould. Austin: University of Texas Press, 1970.

_____. *Slow Fade to Black: The Negro in American Film, 1900-1942.* New York: Oxford University Press, 1977.

Crosby, Ted. *Story of Bing Crosby.* Cleveland: World Publishing Co., 1946.

Crowther, Bosley. *Hollywood Rajah: The Life and Times of Louis B. Mayer.* New York: Holt, Rinehart and Winston, 1960.

_____. *The Lion's Share: The Story of an Entertainment Empire.* New York: E. P. Dutton, 1957.

Crowther, Bruce. *Charlton Heston: The Epic Presence.* London: Columbus Books, 1986.

Croy, Homer. *How Motion Pictures Are Made.* New York: Harper, 1918.

_____. *Star Maker: The Story of D. W. Griffith.* Introd. Mary Pickford. New York: Duell, Sloan and Pearce, 1959.

Crusz, Robert. "Black Cinemas, Film Theory, and Dependent Knowledge." *Screen* 26 (May-August 1985): 152-56.

40 aniversario del cine sonoro mexicano. Mexico City: Comisión Organizadora de los Actos Conmemoratorios del 40 Aniversario del Cine Sonoro Mexicano, 1971.

"La cuestión cinematográfica." *La Crónica,* 2 November 1911, 1.

Cumbow, Robert C. *Once Upon A Time: The Films of Sergio Leone.* Metuchen, NJ: Scarecrow Press, 1987.

Currie, Barton W. "Nickel Madness." *Harper's Weekly,* 24 August 1907, 1246-47.

Czitrom, Daniel J. *Media and the American Mind: From Morse to McLuhan.* Chapel Hill: University of North Carolina Press, 1982.

_____. "The Redemption of Leisure: The National Board of Censorship and the Rise of Motion Pictures in New York City, 1900-1920." *Studies in Visual Communication* 10 (fall 1984): 2-5.

Da, Lottie, and Jan Alexander. *Bad Girls of the Silver Screen.* New York: Carroll & Graf Publishers, 1989.

Dandridge, Dorothy, and Earl Conrad. *Everything and Nothing: The Dorothy Dandridge Tragedy.* New York: Abelard-Schylman, 1970.

Daniels, Bebe, and Ben Lyons. *Life with the Lyons.* London: Odhams, 1953.

Dardis, Tom. *Harold Lloyd: The Man on the Clock.* New York: Viking Press, 1983.

_____. *Keaton: The Man Who Wouldn't Lie Down.* New York: Charles Scribner's Sons, 1979.

_____. *Some Time in the Sun: The Hollywood Years of Fitzgerald, Faulkner, Nathanael West, Aldous Huxley, and James Agee.* New York: Charles Scribner's Sons, 1976.

Dávalos Orozco, Federico, and Esperanza Vazques Bernal. *Filmografía general del cine mexicano.* Puebla, Mexico: Universidad de Puebla, 1985.

Daves, Philip, and Brian Neve, eds. *Cinema, Politics, and Society in America.* New York: St. Martin's Press, 1981.

Davis, Bette. *The Lonely Life.* New York: Lancer Books, 1962.

Davis, Michael. *The Exploitation of Pleasure: A Study of Commercial Recreations in New York City.* New York: Russell Sage Foundation, 1911.

Dawes, Amy. "Hispanic Mart Promises Big B.O. But Studio Pursestrings Tight." *Variety,* 23 March 1986, 86.

Dearborn, Mary V. *Pocahontas's Daughters: Gender and Ethnicity in American Culture.* New York: Oxford University Press, 1986.

deCordova, Richard. "The Emergence of the Star System in America." *Wide Angle* 6, no. 4 (1985): 4-13.

_____. *Picture Personalities: The Emergence of the Star System in America.* Urbana: University of Illinois Press, 1991.

de Hughes, Phillipe, and Dominique Muller, eds. *Gaumont: 90 ans de cinéma.* Paris: Ramsaye, 1986.

de la Colina, José. *Miradas al cine.* Mexico City: Sep/Setentas, 1972.

de la Colina, José, and Tomás Pérez-Turrent. *Luis Buñuel: Prohibido asomarse al interior.* Mexico City: Joaquín Mortiz/Planeta, 1986.

del Amop, Álvaro. *Comedia cinematográfica española.* Madrid: Editorial Cuadernos para el Diálogo, 1975.

De la Teja Ángeles, Ileana. "Hemerografía chicana sobre medios de comunicación masiva." *Revista mexicana de ciencia política* ca 5, no. 1 (January 1984): 6-7.

de Lauretis, Teresa. *Alice Doesn't: Feminism, Semiotics, Cinema.* Bloomington: Indiana University Press, 1984.

_____. "Guerrilla in the Midst: Women's Cinema in the 80s." *Screen* 31, no. 1 (spring 1990): 6-25.

_____. *Technologies of Gender.* Bloomington: Indiana University Press, 1987.

de Lauretis, Teresa, and Stephen Heath, eds. *The Cinematic Apparatus.* New York: St. Martin's Press, 1980.

De la Vega Alfaro, Eduardo. *José Bohr: pioneros del cine sonoro 3.* Cineastas de México, no. 8. Guadalajara, México: Universidad de Guadalajara-CIEC, 1993.

De León, Arnoldo. *They Called Them Greasers: Anglo Attitudes towards Mexicans in Texas, 1821-1900.* Austin: University of Texas Press, 1983.

De León, Darcy. "Rising to the Top [Elizabeth Peña]." *Hispanic,* November 1994, 16-17.

DelGaudio, Sybil. "The Mammy in Hollywood Film, I'd Walk a Million Miles for One of Her Smiles." *Jump Cut* 28 (April 1983): 23.

del Moral González, Fernando. *El rescate de un camarógrafo: las imágenes perdidas de Eustasio Montoya.* Mexico City: Arqueología Cinematográfica, Archivo General de la Nación, 1994.

De los Reyes, Aurelio. *Cine y sociedad en México, 1896-1930.* Mexico City: UNAM, Instituto de Investigaciones Estéticas, 1981.

_____. *Con Villa en México.* Mexico City: UNAM, Instituto de Investigaciones Estéticas, Colección especial, 1984.

_____. "Con Villa en México." *Encuadre: Revista de cine y fotografía* (Caracas) no. 43 (1994). Offprint, 44 pp.

_____. *Filmografía del cine mudo mexicano, 1896-1931.* 3 vols. Mexico City: Filmoteca de la UNAM, 1986.

_____. *Medio siglo de cine mexicano (1896-1947).* Mexico City: Editorial Trillas, 1986.

_____. *Los orígenes del cine en México.* Mexico City: Colección SEP 80, 1983.

_____. "Las películas estadounidenses denigrantes y el gobierno mexicano." *Intermedios* (Mexico, Dirección General de Radio, Televisión y Cinematografía) 5 (1993): 58-68.

_____. "With Villa in Mexico: On Location." *Performing Arts Annual* (Washington, DC: Library of Congress) no. 1 (1986): 98-132.

_____. "With Villa North of the Border. On Location." *Performing Arts Annual* (Washington, DC: Library of Congress) no. 2 (1987): 124-52.

Delpar, Helen. "Goodbye to the 'Greaser': Mexico, the MPPDA, and Derogatory Films, 1922-1926." *Journal of Popular Film and Television* 12 (1984): 34-41.

DeMille, Cecil B. *The Autobiography of Cecil B. DeMille.* Ed. Donald Hayne. Englewood Cliffs, NJ: Prentice-Hall, 1959.

deMille, William. *Hollywood Saga.* New York: E. P. Dutton, 1939.

Dempsey, Michael, and Udayan Gupta. "Hollywood's Color Problem." *American Film* 7 (April 1982).

Dench, Ernest A. *Advertising by Motion Pictures.* Cincinnati: Standard Publishing Co., 1916.

_____. *Making the Movies.* New York: Macmillan, 1915.

Denning, Michael. *Mechanic Accents: Dime Novels and Working-Class Culture in America.* London: Verso, 1987.

Depue, Oscar A. "My First 50 Years in Motion Pictures." *American Cinematographer,* April 1948, 124-27.

Deslandes, Jacques. *Le Boulevard du cinéma.* Paris: Éditions du Cerf, 1963.

_____. *Histoire comparée du cinéma.* Vol. 1, *De la cinématique au cinématographe, 1826-1896.* Tournai, Belgium: Casterman, 1966.

Deslandes, Jacques, and Jacques Richard. *Histoire comparée du cinéma.* Vol. 2, *Du cinématographe au cinéma, 1896-1906.* Tournai, Belgium: Casterman, 1968.

de Usabel, Gaizka S. *The High Noon of American Films in Latin America.* Ann Arbor, MI: UMI Research Press, 1982.

Dever, Susan. "Re-Birth of a Nation: On Mexican Movies, Museums, and María Félix." *Spectator* 13, no. 1 (fall 1992).

Dey, Tom. "Gabriel Figueroa: Mexico's Master Cinematographer." *American Cinematographer* (March 1992): 34-40.

Diakite, Madubuko. *Film, Culture, and the Black Filmmaker: A Study of Functional Relationships and Parallel Developments.* New York: Arno Press, 1980.

Diawara, Manthia. *African Cinema: Politics and Culture.* Bloomington: Indiana University Press, 1992.

_____. "Black Spectatorship: Problems of Identification and Resistance." *Screen* 29 (fall 1988): 66-72.

_____. "Noir by Noirs: Towards a New Realism in Black Cinema." *African American Review* 27, no. 4 (winter 1993): 525+.

_____, ed. *Black American Cinema.* New York: Routledge, 1993.

_____, ed. "Special Issue on Black Cinema." *Wide Angle* 13, nos. 3-4 (July-October 1991).

Diawara, Manthia, and Phyllis Klotman. "*Ganja and Hess:* Vampires, Sex, and Addictions." *Jump Cut* (April 1990): 35.

Díaz, Eduardo. "Latino Cinema in the U.S." In *Latin American Visions: Catalogue,* ed. Pat Aufderheide, 46-47. Philadelphia: The Neighborhood Film/Video Project of International House of Philadelphia, 1989.

Díaz, Katharine A. "Outrageous!" *Caminos* 6, no. 3 (April 1985): 10-12.

_____. "A Sense of Decorum: José Ferrer." *Caminos* 6, no. 2 (March 1985): 24-26, 28.

Dibbell, Julian. "Notes on Carmen." *Village Voice,* 29 October 1991, 43-45.

Dick, Bernard. *The Star-Spangled Screen: The American World War II Film.* Lexington: University Press of Kentucky, 1985.

Dickens, Homer, ed. *The Films of Gary Cooper.* New York: Citadel Press, 1970.

Dickson, William Kennedy Laurie. *The Biograph in Battle.* London: T. Fisher Unwin, 1901.

_____. *History of the Kinetograph and Kinetophonograph.* 1895. Reprint, New York: Arno Press, 1970.

Dickson, William Kennedy Laurie, and Antonio Dickson. *The Life and Inventions of Thomas Alva Edison.* New York: Thomas Y. Crowell, 1894.

di Claudio, Cianni. *Il cinema Western.* Rome: Libreria Universitaria Editrice, 1986.

Di Lauro, Al, and Gerald Rabkin. *Dirty Movies: An Illustrated History of the Stag Film, 1915-1970.* New York: Chelsea House, 1976.

Dimick, Howard T. *Modern Photoplay Writing: Its Craftsmanship.* Franklin, OH: James Knapp Reeve, 1922.

di Nubila, Domingo. *Historia del cine argentino.* Vol. 1. Buenos Aires: Edición Cruz de Malta, 1959.

Dixon, Wheeler W. *The "B" Directors: A Biographical Directory.* Metuchen, NJ: Scarecrow Press, 1985.

Doane, Mary Anne. "Film and the Masquerade: Theorizing the Female Spectator." *Screen* 23, nos. 3-4 (September-October 1982): 74-87.

_____. "Masquerade Reconsidered: Further Thoughts on the Female Spectator." *Discourse* 11, no. 1 (1988-89): 42-54.

Doane, Mary Anne, Patricia Mellencamp, and Linda Williams, eds. *Revision: Essays in Feminist Criticism.* Los Angeles: American Film Institute, 1984.

Dobkins, J. B. "Treatment of Blacks in Dime Novels." *Dime Novel Round-Up* 580 (August 1986): 50-56.

Dockser, Amy, Edward James Olmos, and Tom Bower. "Making Sure There Are Alternatives: The Ballad of Edward James Olmos, Tom Bower, and Gregorio Cortez." *Imagine* 1, no. 1 (summer 1984): 1-9.

Dodds, John W. *The Several Lives of Paul Fejos.* New York: Wenner-Gren Foundation, 1973.

Domínguez, Erika. "Disección del cine mexicano." *Plural* 139 (April 1983).

_____. "Emilio García Riera: Un sexenio de cine mexicano." *Plural* 135 (December 1982).

Domínguez, Sebastián. "*El Super,* Cuban Cinema in Exile Maturing: An Interview with León Ichaso and Orlando Jiménez-Leal." *Film Library Quarterly* 12, no. 4 (1979): 16-21.

Donahue, Suzanne Mary. *American Film Distribution: The Changing Marketplace.* Ann Arbor, MI: UMI Research Press, 1987.

Donohue, John J. *Warrior Dreams: The Martial Arts and the American Imagination.* Westport, CT: Bergin and Garvey, 1994.

Doring, Richard, and Charles Rich. "María Montez." *Films in Review,* March 1963.

Dorr, Rheta Childe. *What Eight Million Women Want.* Boston: Small, Maynard, 1910.

Douglas, Ann. *The Feminization of American Culture.* New York: Avon Books, 1978.

Douglas, Helen W. "The Conflict of Cultures in First Generation Mexicans in Santa Ana, California." Master's thesis, University of Southern California, 1928.

Douglas, María Eulalia. *Diccionario de cineastas cubanos, 1959-1987.* Havana/Mérida: Cinemateca de Cuba/Universidad de los Andes, 1989.

Dowdy, Andrew. *The Films of the Fifties: The American State of Mind.* New York: William Morrow and Co., 1973.

"Down Argentine Way." *Variety,* 9 October 1940.

Downing, John H. "Ethnic Minority Radio in the United States." *The Howard Journal of Communications* 2 (spring 1990): 135-48.

_____. *Film and Politics in the Third World.* New York: Praeger, 1987.

Doyle, Billy H. *The Ultimate Directory of Silent Screen Performers: A Necrology of Births and Deaths and Essays on 50 Lost Players.* Metuchen, NJ: Scarecrow Press, 1995.

Dreifus, Claudia. "Carlos Fuentes: When Eternity Moves." *Film Comment,* June 1986.

Drew, Bernard, with Martin H. Greenberg and Charles G. Waugh. *Western Series and Sequels: A Reference Guide.* New York: Garland Publishing Co., 1986.

Drew, William M. *D. W. Griffith's Intolerance: Its Genesis and Its Vision.* Jefferson, NC: McFarland & Co., 1986.

Drinkwater, John. *The Life and Adventures of Carl Laemmle.* London: Heinemann, 1931.

Du Bois, W. E. B. *The Souls of Black Folk.* 1903. Reprint, New York: Penguin, 1990.

Dunne, John Gregory. *The Studio.* New York: Bantam Books, 1969.

Durgnat, Raymond, and Scott Simmon. *King Vidor, American.* Berkeley: University of California Press, 1988.

Durham, Philip, ed. *Dime Novels.* New York: Odyssey Press, 1966.

Durham, Philip, and Everett L. Jones. *The Negro Cowboys.* New York: Dodd, Mead and Co., 1965.

Durxman, Michael B. *Make It Again, Sam: A Survey of Movie Remakes.* South Brunswick, NJ: A. S. Barnes, 1975.

Dvon, Louis. "Douglas Fairbanks." *Films in Review,* May 1976, 267-83.

Dworkin, Susan. *Double De Palma: A Film Study with Brian De Palma.* New York: Newmarket Press, 1984.

Dyer, Frank, Thomas Martin, and William Meadowcraft. *Edison: His Life and Inventions*. New York: Harper and Brothers, 1929.

Dyer, Richard. *Heavenly Bodies: Film Stars and Society*. New York: St. Martin's Press, 1986.

———. *Now You See It: Studies on Lesbian and Gay Film*. New York: Routledge, 1990.

———. *Stars*. London: British Film Institute, 1979.

———. "White." *Screen* 29 (fall 1988): 44-64.

———, ed. *Gays and Film*. New York: Zoetrope, 1984.

Eames, John Douglas. *The MGM Story: The Complete History of Fifty-Seven Roaring Years*. 2nd rev. ed. New York: Crown Publishers, 1985.

———. *The Paramount Story*. New York: Crown Publishers, 1985.

Easton, Carol. *The Search for Sam Goldwyn: A Biography*. New York: William Morrow and Co., 1976.

Ebert, Roger. Film review of *El Norte*. *Migration Today* 12, no. 2 (1984): 35.

———. "Redford's New Movie Sports 'A Lot of Levels.'" *Mesa (AZ) Tribune*, 27 March 1988.

Eberwein, Robert T. *Film and the Dream Screen: A Sleep and a Forgetting*. Princeton, NJ: Princeton University Press, 1984.

Eby, Lois. *Shirley Temple*. Derby, CT: Monarch Books, 1962.

Eckert, Charles W. "The Anatomy of a Proletarian Film: Warner's *Marked Woman*." *Film Quarterly* 27 (winter 1973-74): 10-24.

Eckhardt, Joseph P., and Linda Kowall, guest cocurators. *Peddler of Dreams: Siegmund Lubin and the Creation of the Motion Picture Industry, 1896-1916*. Program of an exhibition of the National Museum of American Jewish History in cooperation with the Free Library of Philadelphia, 1984.

Edmunds, I. G. *Big U: Universal in the Silent Days*. New York: A. S. Barnes and Co., 1977.

Edwards, Gregory J. *The International Film Poster: The Role of the Poster in Cinema Art, Advertising, and History*. Salem, NH: Salem House, 1985.

Eels, George. *Hedda and Louella*. New York: Warner Books, 1973.

Eisenstein, Sarah. *Give Us Bread But Give Us Roses: Working Women's Consciousness in the United States, 1890 to the First World War*. London: Routledge & Kegan Paul, 1983.

Eisenstein, Sergei. *Eisenstein on Disney*. Ed. Jay Leyda. Trans. Alan Upchurch. New York: Methuen, 1988.

———. *Eisenstein 2*. Ed. Jay Leyda. Trans. Alan Upchurch et al. New York: Methuen, 1988.

———. *Film Essays and a Lecture*. Ed. Jay Leyda. Princeton, NJ: Princeton University Press, 1982.

———. *Film Form: Essays in Film Theory*. Trans. and ed. Jay Leyda. New York: Harcourt, Brace and World, 1949.

———. *The Film Sense*. Ed. and trans. Jay Leyda. New York: Harcourt, Brace and World, 1947.

———. *Immoral Memories: An Autobiography*. Trans. Herbert Marshall. Boston: Houghton Mifflin Co., 1983.

———. "Letters from Mexico." Trans. Tanaqauil Taubes. *October* 14 (fall 1980): 55-64.

———. *¡Que viva México!* Mexico City: Ediciones Era, 1971.

———. *Que Viva Mexico!* London: Vision Press, 1951. Reprint, New York: Arno Press, 1972.

———. *Three Films*. Ed. Jay Leyda. Trans. Diana Matias. New York: Harper, 1974.

"Eisenstein Says 'Adios.'" *Los Angeles Times*, 7 December 1930.

Elizondo, Salvador. "El nuevo cine mexicano y la crisis." In *Hojas de cine: Testimonios y documentos del nuevo cine latino americano*. Vol. 2. Mexico City: Fundación Mexicana de Cineastas, 1988.

Ellis, Don Carlos, and Laura Thornborough. *Motion Pictures in Education: A Practical Handbook for Users of Visual Aids*. New York: Crowell, 1923.

Ellis, Jack C., Charles Derry, and Sharon Kern. *The Film Book Bibliography 1940-1975*. Metuchen, NJ: Scarecrow Press, 1979.

Ellis, Kirk. "Stranger than Fiction: Emilio Fernández's Mexico." *Journal of Popular Film and Video* 10, no. 1 (spring 1982): 27-36.

Ellison, Mary. "Blacks in American Film." In *Cinema, Politics and Society in America*, ed. Philip Davies and Briane Neve. Manchester: Manchester University Press, 1981.

Elsaesser, Thomas, with Adam Barker. *Early Cinema*. London: British Film Institute, 1990.

Emerson, John, and Anita Loos. *How to Write Photoplays*. New York: James A. McCann Co., 1920.

Enciclopedia del cine mexicano. Mexico City: Publicaciones Cinematográficas, 1955.

Enciclopedia ilustrada del cine. Barcelona: Editorial Labor, 1969.

Engelhardt, Tom. "Ambush at Kamikaze Pass." *Bulletin of Concerned Asian Scholars* 3, no. 1 (winter-spring 1971).

Enloe, Cynthia. *Bananas, Beaches, and Bases: Making Feminist Sense of International Politics*. Berkeley: University of California Press, 1990.

Epstein, Julia, and Kristina Straub, eds. *Body Guards*. New York: Routledge, 1991.

Epstein, Lawrence J. *Samuel Goldwyn*. Boston: Twayne Publishers, 1981.

Erens, Patricia. *Issues in Feminist Film Criticism*. Bloomington: Indiana University Press, 1990.

———. *The Jew in American Cinema*. Bloomington: Indiana University Press, 1984.

———, ed. *Sexual Stratagems: The World of Women in Film*. New York: Horizon Press, 1979.

Ernst, Morris L., and Pare Lorentz. *Censored: The Private Life of the Movies*. New York: Cape and Smith, 1930.

Esenwein, J. Berg, and Arthur Leeds. *Writing the Photoplay*. Springfield, MA: Home Correspondence School, 1913.

"Esparza/Katz Skeds Seven Pix in 16 Months with $68 Mil Slate." *Variety* 228, no. 55 (21 August 1990).

"The Essanay Company Out West." *Moving Picture World* 5 (4 December 1909): 800-802.

Essoe, Gabe. *Tarzan of the Movies: A Pictorial History of More Than Fifty Years of Edgar Rice Burroughs' Legendary Hero*. New York: Citadel Press, 1968.

Evans, Mark. *Soundtrack: The Music of the Movies*. New York: Hopkinson & Blake, 1975.

Everson, William K. *American Silent Film*. New York: Oxford University Press, 1978.

———. *The Bad Guys: A Pictorial History of the Movie Villain*. New York: Citadel Press, 1964.

———. *The Films of Hal Roach*. New York: Museum of Modern Art, 1971.

_____. *The Films of Laurel and Hardy.* New York: Citadel Press, 1967.

_____. *A Pictorial History of the Western Film.* New York: Citadel Press, 1969.

Ewen, Elizabeth. "City Lights: Immigrant Women and the Rise of the Movies." *Signs* 5, no. 3, supplement (1980): S45-65.

Ewen, Stuart. *Captains of Consciousness: Advertising and the Social Roots of the Consumer Culture.* New York: McGraw-Hill, 1976.

Ewen, Stuart, and Elizabeth Ewen. *Channels of Desire: Mass Images and the Shaping of American Consciousness.* Minneapolis: University of Minnesota Press, 1982.

Eyles, Allen. *The Western.* Rev. ed. London: Tantivy Press, 1975.

Eyman, Scott. "Lubitsch, Pickford, and the *Rosita* War." *Griffithiana* 15, nos. 44-45 (May-September 1992): 176-89.

_____. *Mary Pickford: America's Sweetheart.* New York: Donald I. Fine, 1990.

La fábrica de sueños: Estudios Churubusco 1945-1985. Mexico City: Instituto Mexicano de Cinematografía, 1985.

"El fabuloso 'Tin-Tan.'" *Mañana* 29 (May 1976): 56.

Fadiman, William. "Cowboys and Indies." *Films and Filming* 10, no. 6 (March 1964): 51-52.

Fadiman, William J. "Books into Movies." *Publishers' Weekly* 126, no. 10 (8 September 1934): 753-55.

Fairbanks, Douglas. *Laugh and Live.* New York: Britton, 1917.

Fairbanks, Douglas, Jr., and Richard Schickel. *The Fairbanks Album.* Boston: Little, Brown, 1975.

"Famous Authors with Universal." *The Moving Picture World,* 5 September 1914, 1356.

Famous Players-Lasky Corporation. *The Story of the Famous Players-Lasky Corporation.* New York: Famous Players-Lasky Corporation, 1919.

Farber, Stephen. "Peckinpah's Return." *Film Quarterly* 23 (fall 1969): 2-11.

Faulkner, Robert R. *Hollywood Studio Musicians: Their Work and Careers in the Recording Industry.* Chicago: Aldine, Atherton, 1971.

Faulkner, William. *Faulkner's MGM Screenplays.* Ed. Bruce F. Kawin. Knoxville: University of Tennessee Press, 1982.

Featherstone, Mike, ed. *Global Culture: Nationalism, Globalization and Modernity.* London: Sage, 1990.

Fein, Seth. "Hollywood, U.S.-Mexican Relations, and the Devolution of the Golden Age of Mexican Cinema." *Film-Historia* 3 (1994): 103-35.

Feldman, Charles Mathew. *The National Board of Censorship (Review) of Motion Pictures, 1909-1922.* New York: Arno Press, 1977.

Feldman, Simón. *El director de cine: mitos y sometimientos.* Buenos Aires: Granica Editor, 1974.

Fell, John L. *Film and the Narrative Tradition.* Norman: University of Oklahoma Press, 1974.

_____. *A History of Films.* New York: Holt, Rinehart and Winston, 1979.

_____. "Motive, Mischief and Melodrama: The State of Film Narrative in 1907." *Film Quarterly* 23 (spring 1983): 30-37.

_____. ed. *Film before Griffith.* Berkeley: University of California Press, 1983.

Fenin, George N., and William K. Everson. *The Western.* New York: Orion Press, 1962.

_____. *The Western from Silents to Cinerama.* New York: Bonanza Books, 1972.

_____. *The Western from Silents to the Seventies.* New York: Penguin, 1973.

Fernández, Adela. *El Indio Fernández: vida y mito.* 3rd ed. Mexico City: Panorama Editorial, 1986.

Fernández, Carlos. "Nuevamente sobre el cine mexicano." *Cine Cubano* 17 (January 1964).

_____. "Unas palabras sobre el cine mexicano." *Cine Cubano* 7 (1961).

Fernández, Dominique. *Eisenstein.* Paris: Grasset, 1975.

Fernández, Enrique. "Miami's Autores." *Film Comment* 21, no. 3 (May-June 1985): 46-48.

_____. "Parting Ways. A Cuban-American View." *Cineaste* 23 (1986): 39.

_____. "Spitfires, Latin Lovers, Mambo Kings." *New York Times,* 19 April 1992, H1, H30.

Fernández, Sandra, and Dory Lightfoot. "Entrevista with Filmmaker Lourdes Portillo." *Alambraso: Chicano Studies Program Newsletter* (University of Wisconsin-Madison) 9, no. 1 (fall 1994): 4+.

Ferrera-Balanquet, Raúl. "Sites of Struggle: Exile and Migration in the Cuban-Exile Audiovisual Discourse." *FELIX: A Journal of Media Arts and Communication* 2, no. 1 (1995): 46-55.

_____. "The Videotapes of the Latino Midwest Video Collective: A Manifesto." *Cinematograph* 4 (1991): 149-52.

Feuer, Jane. *The Hollywood Musical.* Bloomington: Indiana University Press, 1982.

_____. "Hollywood Musicals: Mass Art as Folk Art." *Jump Cut* 23 (October 1980): 23-25.

Field, Martin. "Type-Casting Screen-Writers." *Penguin Film Review* 6 (April 1948): 29-32.

Fielding, Raymond. *The American Newsreel, 1911-1967.* Norman: University of Oklahoma Press, 1972.

_____, ed. *A Technological History of Motion Pictures and Television.* Berkeley: University of California Press, 1967.

Films with a Purpose: A Puerto Rican Experiment in Social Film, April 23-May 3, 1987. Museum of Modern Art, Collective for Living Cinema, New York University, El Museo del Barrio, Bronx Museum of Art, El Instituto de Cultura Puertorriqueña. New York: Exit Art, 1987.

Finch, Christopher. *The Art of Walt Disney: From Mickey Mouse to the Magic Kingdom.* New York: Harry N. Abrams, 1973.

Finch, Christopher, and Linda Rosenkrantz. *Gone Hollywood: The Movie Colony in the Golden Age.* New York: Doubleday, 1979.

Fine, Richard. *West of Eden: Writers in Hollywood, 1928-1940.* Washington, DC: Smithsonian Institution Press, 1993.

Finler, Joel W. *Stroheim.* Berkeley: University of California Press, 1967.

Fishbein, Leslie. "Harlot or Heroine? Changing Views of Prostitution, 1870-1920." *Historian* 43, no. 1 (November 1980): 23-35.

Fisher, Kim N., ed. *On the Screen: A Film, Television, and Video Research Guide.* Littleton, CO: Libraries Unlimited, 1986.

Fisher, Robert J. "Film Censorship and Progressive Reform: The National Board of Censorship of Motion Pictures, 1909-1922." *Journal of Popular Film* 4 (1975): 143-56.

Fiske, John. *Television Culture.* London: Methuen, 1987.

Flamini, Roland. *Ava: A Biography.* New York: Coward, McCann & Geoghegan, 1983.

Flexner, Eleanor. *Century of Struggle: The Woman's Rights Movements in the United States.* Cambridge, MA: Harvard University Press, 1959.

Flori, Monica. "A Selected and Annotated Filmography on Latin American Women." *Third Woman* 2, no. 2 (1984): 117-21.

Florey, Robert. *Hollywood d'hier et d'aujourd'hui.* Paris: Éditions Prisma, 1948.

Folsom, James K. *The American Western Novel.* New Haven, CT: College and University Press, 1966.

Font, Domènec. *Del azul al verde: El cine español durante el franquismo.* Barcelona: Editorial Avance, 1976.

Ford, Charles. *Histoire du Western.* Paris: Albin Michel, 1976.

_____. *Historia popular del cine.* Trans. from the French by Leoncio Sureda Goyto. Barcelona: Editorial AHR, 1956.

_____. "Paramount at Joinville." *Films in Review,* November 1961, 541-50.

Ford, Dan. *Pappy: The Life of John Ford.* Englewood Cliffs, NJ: Prentice-Hall, 1979.

Fordin, Hugh. *The Movies' Greatest Musicals: Produced in Hollywood USA by the Freed Unit.* New York: Frederick Ungar, 1984.

_____. *The World of Entertainment! Hollywood's Greatest Musicals.* Garden City, NY: Doubleday, 1975.

Forman, Henry James. *Our Movie Made Children.* New York: Macmillan, 1933.

Fosdick, Raymond B. *A Report on the Condition of Motion Picture Shows in New York.* New York: City of New York, Office of the Commissioner of Accounts, 1911.

Fountain, Leatrice Gilbert. *Dark Star: The Untold Story of the Meteoric Rise and Fall of the Legendary John Gilbert.* New York: St. Martin's Press, 1985.

Fowler, Gene. *Father Goose: The Story of Mack Sennett.* New York: Covici-Friede, 1934.

_____. *Good Night, Sweet Prince.* New York: Ballantine Books, 1950.

Fox, Claire. "Hollywood's Backlot: Carlos Fuentes, *The Old Gringo,* and National Cinema." *Iris* 13 (summer 1991): 63-86.

Fox, Stuart, comp. *Jewish Films in the United States: A Comprehensive Survey and Descriptive Filmography.* Boston: G. K. Hall & Co., 1976.

Franco, Jean. "The Incorporation of Women: A Comparison of North American and Mexican Popular Narrative." In *Studies in Entertainment: Critical Approaches to Mass Culture,* ed. Tania Modleski. Bloomington: Indiana University Press, 1986.

_____. *Plotting Women: Gender and Representation in Mexico.* New York: Columbia University Press, 1989.

Franklin, Harold B. *Motion Picture Theater Management.* New York: Doran, 1927.

_____. *Sound Motion Pictures from the Laboratory to their Presentation.* Garden City, NY: Doubleday, Doran & Co., 1930.

Franklin, Joe. *Classics of the Silent Screen.* New York: Citadel Press, 1959.

Frantz, Joe B., and Julian Ernest Choate, Jr. *The American Cowboy: The Myth and the Reality.* Norman: University of Oklahoma Press, 1955.

Frase-Blunt, Martha. "Everything's Rosie." *Hispanic,* April 1993, 14-16.

Frayling, Christopher. *Spaghetti Westerns: Cowboys and Europeans from Karl May to Sergio Leone.* London: Routledge and Kegan Paul, 1981.

Frazer, John. *Artificially Arranged Scenes: The Films of Georges Méliès.* Boston: G. K. Hall, 1979.

Frederickson, George M. *The Black Image in the White Mind.* New York: Harper & Row, 1972.

Freeburg, Victor Oscar. *The Art of Photoplay Making.* New York: Macmillan, 1918.

_____. *Pictorial Beauty on the Screen.* New York: Macmillan, 1923.

Fregoso, Rosa Linda. "*Born in East L.A.* and the Politics of Representation." *Cultural Studies* 4, no. 3 (October 1990): 264-80.

_____. *The Bronze Screen: Chicana and Chicano Film Culture.* Minneapolis: University of Minnesota Press, 1993.

_____. "Chicana Film Practices: Confronting the Many-Headed Demon of Oppression." In *Chicanos and Film: Essays on Chicano Representation and Resistance,* ed. Chon A. Noriega, 189-204. New York: Garland Publishing Co., 1992.

_____. "The Mother-Motif in *La Bamba* and *Boulevard Nights.*" In *Building with Our Hands: New Directions in Chicana Scholarship,* ed. Beatriz M. Pesquera and Adela de la Torre. Los Angeles: University of California Press, 1993.

_____. "La quinceañera of Chicana Counter Aesthetics." *Centro: Boletín del Centro de Estudios Puertorriqueños* 3, no. 1 (winter 1990-91): 87-91.

_____. "The Representation of Cultural Identity in *Zoot Suit.*" *Theory and Society* 22, no. 5 (October 1993): 659-74.

_____. "*Zoot Suit* and *The Ballad of Gregorio Cortez.*" *Crítica* 1, no. 2 (spring 1985): 126-31.

Fregoso, Rosa Linda, and Angie C. Chabram. "Introduction: Chicana/o Cultural Representations: Reframing Alternative Critical Discourse." *Cultural Studies* 4, no. 3 (October 1990): 203-12.

French, Philip. *The Movie Moguls.* London: Weidenfield and Nicholson, 1969.

_____. *Westerns.* Rev. ed. London: Secker and Warbur, 1977.

"French-Spanish Versions for 20 Paris Pictures." *Film Daily,* 5 September 1930.

French, Warren. "The Cowboy in the Dime Novel." *Texas Studies in English* 30 (1951): 219-34.

Freund, Elizabeth. *The Return of the Reader: Reader-Response Criticism.* London: Methuen, 1987.

Frewin, Leslie. *Dietrich: The Story of a Star.* New York: Stein and Day, 1967.

Friar, Ralph E., and N. A. Friar. *The Only Good Indian.* New York: Drama Book Specialists, 1972.

Friedman, Lester D. *Hollywood's Image of the Jew.* New York: Frederick Ungar Publishing, 1982.

_____, ed. *Unspeakable Images: Ethnicity and the American Cinema.* Urbana: University of Illinois Press, 1991.

Friedrich, Otto. *City of Nets: A Portrait of Hollywood in the 1940's.* New York: Harper & Row, 1986.

Fuentes, Carlos. "El rostro de la escondida." In *Dolores del Río,* ed. Luis Gasca. San Sebastián, Spain: 24th Festival Internacional del Cine, 1976.

_____. "Velázquez, Plato's Cave, and Bette Davis." *New York Times,* 15 March 1987.

Fuentes, Carlos, and C. Dreifus. "When Eternity Moves." *Film Comment* 22, no. 3 (1986): 48-52.

Fuentes, Víctor. "Luis Valdez: De Delano a Hollywood." *Xalmán* 2 (1979): 7-8

_____. "Luis Valdez, Hollywood y Tezcatlipoca." *Chiricú* 5, no. 2 (1988): 35-39.

Furhammer, Leif, and Folke Isaksson. *Politics and Film.* Trans. Kersti French. New York: Praeger, 1971.

Fusco, Coco. "Ethnicity, Politics and Poetics: Latinos and Media Art." In *Illuminating Video: An Essential Guide to Video Art,* ed. Doug Hall and Sally Jo Fifer, 304-16. New York: Aperture/BAVC, 1990.

_____. "The Latino 'Boom' in Hollywood." *Centro de Estudios Puertorriqueños Bulletin* 2, no. 8 (1990): 48-56.

_____, ed. *Reviewing Histories: Selections from the New Latin American Cinema.* Buffalo, NY: Hallwalls Contemporary Arts Center, 1987.

Gabbard, Krin, and Glen O. Gabbard. *Psychiatry and the Cinema.* Chicago: University of Chicago Press, 1987.

Gaberscek, Carlo. *Il West di John Ford.* Feletto Umberto, Italy: Arti Grafiche Friulane, 1994.

Gabler, Neal. *An Empire of Their Own: How the Jews Invented Hollywood.* New York: Crown Publishers, 1988.

_____. "The Jewish Problem." *American Film* 13, no. 9 (July-August 1988): 37-44.

Gabriel, Teshome. "Colonialism and 'Law and Order' Criticism." *Screen* 24 (March-April 1983): 60-64.

_____. *Third Cinema in the Third World: The Aesthetics of Liberation.* Ann Arbor, MI: UMI Research Press, 1982.

Gagne, Paul R. *The Zombies That Ate Pittsburgh: The Films of George A. Romero.* New York: Dodd, Mead, and Co., 1987.

Gaines, Jane. "*The Scar of Shame:* Skin Color and Caste in Black Silent Melodrama." *Cinema Journal* 26 (summer 1987): 3-21.

_____. "White Privilege and Looking Relations: Race and Gender in Feminist Film Theory." *Cultural Critique* 4 (1986): 59-81.

_____. "Women and Representation." *Jump Cut* 29 (February 1984): 25-27.

Gaines, Jane, ed. *Classical Hollywood Narrative: The Paradigm Wars.* Durham, NC: Duke University Press, 1992.

Galbraith, Jane. "Book, Film Tie-in Whetting Appetites for 'Chocolate.'" *Los Angeles Times,* 29 May 1993, F2.

Galindo, Alejandro. *El cine, genocidio espiritual: De 1900 al "crash" de 29.* Mexico City: Editorial Nuestro Tiempo, 1971.

_____. *El cine mexicano.* Mexico City: Edamex, 1985.

_____. *¿Qué es el cine?* Mexico City: Editorial Nuestro Tiempo, 1975.

_____. *Una radiografía histórica del cine mexicano.* Mexico City: Fondo de Cultura Popular, 1968.

_____. *Verdad y mentira del cine mexicano.* Mexico City: Aconagua Ediciones y Publicaciones, 1981.

Gallagher, Tag. *John Ford: The Man and His Films.* Berkeley: University of California Press, 1986.

Gamboa, Harry, Jr. "El barrio en la pantalla." *La Opinión* (Los Angeles), 16 November 1980, 6-7.

_____. "Past Imperfecto." *Jump Cut* 39 (June 1994): 93-95.

_____. "Silver Screening the Barrio." *Forum* 6, no. 1 (November 1978): 6-7.

Gang Exploitation Film Committee. *A Reader and Information Packet on the "Gang Exploitation Films."* Monterey Park, CA: East Los Angeles College M.E.Ch.A. (Movimiento Estudiantil Chicano de Aztlán), 1979.

Gansberg, Alan L. "The Dealmakers: Methods, Money, Movies!" *Hispanic Business,* July 1991, 32-37.

_____. "Raúl Juliá: One of the Busiest Actors in America." *Hispanic Business,* July 1992, 48-52.

Garbicz, Adam, and Jacek Klinowski. *Cinema, the Magic Vehicle: A Guide to Its Achievement. Journey One: The Cinema Through 1949.* New York: Schocken Books, 1983.

García, Guy. "Frente a frente con Edward James Olmos." *Más,* March-April 1991, 59-64.

_____. "A Tale of Two Movies." *Premiere,* April 1992, 38-42.

García, Juan R. "Hollywood and the West: Mexican Images in American Films, 1894-1983." In *Old Southwest, New Southwest,* ed. Judy Nolte Lensink. Tucson, AZ: Tucson Public Library, 1988.

García, Kino. "Puerto Rico: Hacia un cine nacional." *Centro de Estudios Puertorriqueños Bulletin* 2, no. 8 (1990): 80-90.

García, Rocío. "Andy García debuta como director." *Aquí New Orleans,* January 1994, 16.

García Berúmen, Frank Javier. *The Chicano/Hispanic Image in American Film.* New York: Vantage Press, 1995.

García Riera, Emilio. *Arturo Ripstein habla de su cine.* Guadalajara, Mexico: Universidad de Guadalajara, Centro de Investigación y Enseñanza Cinematográficas, 1988.

_____. *El cine mexicano.* Mexico City: Ediciones Era, 1963.

_____. *El cine y su público.* Mexico City: Fondo de Cultura Económica, 1974.

_____. "Cuando el cine mexicano se hizo industria." In *Hojas de cine: Testimonios y documentos del nuevo cine latino americano.* Vol. 2, *México,* 11-20. Mexico City: Secretaría de Educación Pública, 1986.

_____. *Emilio Fernández, 1904-1986.* Guadalajara, Mexico: Universidad de Guadalajara, 1987.

_____. "En la frontera mexicana fue. . . ." *Dicine* 1, no. 4 (January 1984): 6-9.

_____. *Historia del cine mexicano.* Mexico City: SEP/Foro 2000, 1986.

_____. *Historia documental del cine mexicano 1926/1966.* 10 vols. Mexico City: Ediciones Era, 1969-78.

_____. *Howard Hawks.* Guadalajara, Mexico: Universidad de Guadalajara, 1988.

_____. "Medio siglo de cine mexicano." *Cine Cubano,* nos. 31-33 (1966).

_____. *México visto por el cine extranjero.* Vol. 1, *1894-1940;* vol. 2, *1906-1940, Filmografía;* vol. 3, *1941-1969;* vol. 4, *1941-1969, Filmografía;* vol. 5, *1970-1988;* vol. 6, *1970-1988, Filmografía.* Mexico City: Ediciones Era, 1987-90.

_____, coordinator. *Filmografía mexicana de medio y largo metrajes: 1906-1940.* Mexico City: Cineteca Nacional, 1985.

García Riera, Emilio, and Fernando Macotela. *La guía del cine mexicano: De la pantalla grande a la televisión, 1919-1984.* Mexico City: Editorial Patria, 1984.

Gardner, Gerald. *The Censorship Papers: Movie Censorship Letters from the Hays Office, 1934 to 1968.* New York: Dodd, Mead & Co., 1987.

Garfield, Brian. *Western Films.* New York: Rawson Associates, 1982.

Garrison, Lee C., Jr. *The Composition, Attendance Behavior and Needs of Motion Picture Audiences: A Review of the Literature.* UCLA Management in the Arts Program, no. 12. Los Angeles: University of California, 1971.

Gartenberg, Jon. "The Brighton Project: The Archives and Research." *Iris* 2 (spring 1984): 5-16.

————. "Camera Movement in Edison and Biograph Films, 1900-1906." *Cinema Journal* 19 (spring 1980): 1-16.

————. "Vitagraph before Griffith: Forging Ahead in the Nickelodeon Era." *Studies in Visual Communication* 10 (fall 1984): 7-23.

Gasca, Luis. *Las estrellas: Historia del cine en sus mitos.* Barcelona: Ediciones Urbión, 1981.

Gaudreault, André. "The Infringement of Copyright Laws and Its Effects, 1900-1906." *Framework* 29 (1985): 2-14.

————, ed. *Ce que je vois de mon ciné: La représentation du régard dans le cinéma des premiers temps.* Saint-Étienne, France: Impression Dumas, 1988.

Gayle, Addison, Jr., ed. *The Black Aesthetic.* Garden City, NY: Doubleday, 1972.

Geduld, Harry M. *The Birth of the Talkies: From Edison to Jolson.* Bloomington: Indiana University Press, 1975.

————. *Focus on D. W. Griffith.* Englewood Cliffs, NJ: Prentice-Hall, 1971.

————, ed. *Authors on Film.* Bloomington: Indiana University Press, 1972.

Geduld, Harry M., and Ronald Gottesman, eds. *Sergei Eisenstein and Upton Sinclair: The Making and Unmaking of Que Viva Mexico!* Bloomington: Indiana University Press, 1970.

Gehring, Wes D. *The Marx Brothers: A Bio-Bibliography.* New York: Greenwood Press, 1987.

Gelman, Barbara, ed. *Photoplay Treasury.* New York: Crown Publishers, 1972.

Georgakas, Dan. "*Improper Conduct.*" *Cineaste* 14, no. 1, (1985): 45-48.

————. Review of *El Super. Cineaste* 9, no. 4 (1979): 49-51.

Georgakas, Dan, and Lenny Rubinstein. *Art, Politics, Cinema: The* Cineaste *Interviews.* London: Pluto Press, 1995.

George Kleine Collection of Early Motion Pictures in the Library of Congress. Prepared by Rita Horwitz and Harriet Harrison, with the assistance of Wendy White. Washington, DC: Library of Congress, 1980.

Gerald, Yvonne. "The Comedy of Cantinflas." *Films in Review* 9 (January 1958).

Gerlach, John, and Lana Gerlach, eds. *The Critical Index.* New York: Teachers College Press, 1974.

Gever, Martha, John Greyson, and Pratibha Parmar, eds. *Queer Looks.* New York: Routledge, 1993.

Gibson, Gloria. "The Cultural Significance of Music to Black Independent Filmmakers." Ph.D. diss., Indiana University, 1986.

Gibson-Hudson, Gloria J. "African American Literary Criticism as a Model for the Analysis of Films by African American Women." *Wide Angle* 13, nos. 3-4 (July-October 1991): 44-55.

Giebler, A. H. "News of Los Angeles and Vicinity." *The Moving Picture World,* December 1917, 727.

Gifford, Denis. *The British Film Catalogue, 1895-1970.* Newton Abbot, England: David and Charles, 1973.

Gil-Montero, Martha. *Brazilian Bombshell: The Biography of Carmen Miranda.* New York: Donald I. Fine, 1989.

Gilbert, James. *A Cycle of Outrage: America's Reaction to the Juvenile Delinquent in the 1950's.* New York: Oxford University Press, 1986.

Gilman, Sander L. *Jewish Self-Hatred: Anti-Semitism and the Hidden Language of the Jews.* Baltimore: Johns Hopkins University Press, 1986.

Giroux, Henry. *Border Crossings.* New York: Routledge, 1989.

Gish, Lillian. *Dorothy and Lillian Gish.* Ed. James E. Frasher. New York: Macmillan, 1973.

Gish, Lillian, with Ann Pinchot. *Lillian Gish: The Movies, Mr. Griffith and Me.* Englewood Cliffs, NJ: Prentice-Hall, 1969.

Gladston, Jim. "*La Bamba:* Valdez, Valens and the American Dream." *Calendar Magazine,* August 1987.

Gleason, Philip. "Confusion Compounded: The Melting Pot in the 1960 and 1970s." *Ethnicity* 6 (March 1979): 10-20.

Gledhill, Christine, ed. *Home Is Where the Heart Is: Melodrama and the Woman's Film.* London: British Film Institute, 1987.

Goldman, Emma. *The Traffic in Women and Other Essays in Feminism.* New York: Times Change Press, 1970.

Goldwyn, Sam. *Behind the Screen.* New York: George H. Doran, 1939.

Gomery, Douglas. *The Hollywood Studio System.* New York: St. Martin's Press, 1986.

————. "Movie Audiences, Urban Geography, and the History of the American Film." *Velvet Light Trap,* no. 19 (1982): 23-29.

————. *Shared Pleasures: A History of Movie Presentation in the United States.* Madison: University of Wisconsin Press, 1992.

Gomezjara, Francisco Javier, and Delia Selene de Dios. *Sociología del cine.* Colección SEP-Setentas Diana, no. 110. Mexico City: Editorial Diana, 1981.

Gómez Mesa, Luis. *La literatura española en el cine nacional.* Madrid: Filmoteca Nacional de España, 1978.

Gómez-Peña, Guillermo. "A Binational Performance Pilgrimage." *The Drama Review* 35, no. 3 (fall 1991): 39-40.

————. "Death on the Border: A Eulogy to Border Art." *High Performance* 14, no. 1 (spring 1991): 8-9.

————. "Documented/Undocumented." In *The Graywolf Annual Five: Multi-Cultural Literacy,* ed. Rick Simonson and Scott Walker, 130. Saint Paul, MN: Graywolf Press, 1988.

————. "The Free Art Agreement/*El tratado de libre cultura.*" *High Performance* 16, no. 3 (fall 1993): 58-63.

————. "From Art-mageddon to Gringostroika." *High Performance* 14, no. 3 (fall 1991): 21.

————. "The Multicultural Paradigm: An Open Letter to the National Arts Community." *High Performance* 12, no. 3 (fall 1989): 21.

————. "The New World (B)order." *High Performance* 15, nos. 2-3 (summer-fall 1992): 60.

————. "The New World Border: Prophecies for the End of the Century." *The Drama Review: The Journal of Performance Studies* 38, no. 1 (spring 1994): 119-42.

Gómez-Peña, Guillermo, and Jeff Kelley, eds. *The Border Arts Workshop: Documentation of Five Years of Interdisciplinary Art Projects Dealing with U.S.-Mexico Border Issues, 1984-1989.* New York: Artists Space; La Jolla, CA: Museum of Contemporary Art, 1989.

Gonzales, Rodolfo "Corky." *I Am Joaquín/Yo soy Joaquín.* New York: Bantam Books, 1972.

González, Satir. "The Golden Eagle Awards: A Continuing Tradition." *Caminos* 5, no. 8 (September 1984): 9-10.

Goodwin, James. "Eisenstein: Ideology and Intellectual Cinema." *Quarterly Review of Film Studies* 3, no. 2 (spring 1978): 169-92.

_____. *Eisenstein, Cinema, and History.* Urbana: University of Illinois Press, 1993.

_____. "The Object(ive)s of Cinema: Vertov (Factography) and Eisenstein (Ideography)." *Praxis* 4 (1978): 223-30.

_____. "Plusieurs Eisensteins: Recent Criticism." *Quarterly Review of Film Studies* 6, no. 4 (fall 1981): 391-412.

Goulart, Ron. *Cheap Thrills.* New Rochelle, NY: Arlington House, 1972.

Graham, Cooper C., Steven Higgins, Elaine Mancini, and João Luiz Vieira. *D. W. Griffith and the Biograph Company.* Metuchen, NJ: Scarecrow Press, 1985.

Graham, Sheila. *Confessions of a Hollywood Columnist.* New York: Bantam Books, 1968.

Grant, Barry Keith, ed. *Film Genre Reader.* Austin: University of Texas Press, 1986.

_____. *The Business Man in the Amusement World.* New York: Broadway, 1910.

Grau, Robert. *The Theatre of Silence: A Volume of Progress and Achievement in the Motion Picture Industry.* New York: Benjamin Blom, 1914.

Gray, Chris Hables, Heidi J. Figueroa-Sarriera, and Steven Mentor, eds. *The Cyborg Handbook.* New York: Routledge, 1995.

Gray, Herman. "Recodings: Possibilities and Limitations in Commercial Television Representations of African American Culture." *Quarterly Review of Film and Video* 13, nos. 1-3 (1991): 117-30.

Green, Abel, and Joe Laurie, Jr. *Show Biz: From Vaude to Video.* New York: Henry Holt, 1951.

Green, Fitzhugh. *The Film Finds Its Tongue.* New York: Putnam's, 1929.

Green, Stanley. *Encyclopedia of the Musical Film.* London and New York: Oxford University Press, 1981.

Greenberg, Bradley S., and Pilar Baptista-Fernández. "Hispanic Americans: The New Minority on Television." In *Life on Television: Content Analysis of U.S. TV Drama,* ed. Bradley S. Greenberg, 3-12. Norwood, NJ: Ablex Publishing Corp., 1980.

Greenberg, Bradley S., Michael Burgoon, Judee K. Burgoon, and Felipe Korzenny. *Mexican Americans and the Mass Media.* Norwood, NJ: Ablex Publishing Corp., 1983.

Greenfield, Gerald Michael, and Carlos E. Cortés. "Harmony and Conflict of Intercultural Images: The Treatment of Mexico in U.S. Feature Films and K-12 Textbooks." *Estudios Mexicanos* 7, no. 2 (1991): 45-56.

Greenfield, Jeff. *Television, the First Fifty Years.* New York: Crescent Books, 1981.

Gregory, Carl Louis. *Condensed Course in Motion Picture Photography.* New York: New York Institute of Photography, 1920.

_____. *Motion Picture Photography.* Ed. Herbert C. McKay. 2nd ed. New York: Falk, 1927.

Griffith, Albert J. "The Scion, the Señorita, and the Texas Ranch Epic: Hispanic Images in Film." *Bilingual Review/Revista Bilingüe* 16, no. 1 (Jan.-April 1991): 15-22.

Griffith, D. W. *The Man Who Invented Hollywood: The Autobiography of D. W. Griffith.* Ed. and annotated by James Hart. Louisville, KY: Touchstone Publishing, 1972.

_____. *The Rise and Fall of Free Speech in America.* 1916. Reprint, Los Angeles: Larry Edmunds, 1967.

Griffith, Linda Arvidson. *When the Movies Were Young.* 1925. Reprint, New York: Dover Publications, 1969.

Griffith, Richard. *Samuel Goldwyn: The Producer and His Films.* New York: Museum of Modern Art Library, 1956.

Griffith, Richard, and Arthur Mayer. *The Movies.* New York: Simon and Schuster, 1957.

Grimstead, David. *Melodrama Unveiled: American Theater and Culture, 1800-1850.* Chicago: University of Chicago Press, 1968.

Grindon, Leger. *Shadows on the Past.* Philadelphia: Temple University Press, 1994.

Grobel, Lawrence. *The Hustons.* New York: Charles Scribner's Sons, 1989.

Grover, Ron. *The Disney Touch: How a Daring Management Team Revived an Entertainment Empire.* Homewood, IL: Richard D. Irwin, 1991.

Gruber, Frank. "The Basic Western Novel Plots." *Writer's Year Book,* 1955, 49-53.

_____. *The Pulp Jungle.* Los Angeles: Sherbourne Press, 1967.

_____. "The 7 Ways to Plot a Western." *TV Guide* 6 (30 August 1958): 5-7.

Gruening, Ernest. *Mexico and Its Heritage.* New York: Appleton-Century, 1928.

Grupenhoff, Richard. *The Black Valentino: The Stage and Screen Career of Lorenzo Tucker.* Metuchen, NJ: Scarecrow Press, 1988.

Gubern, Román. *Benito Perojo, pionerismo supervivencia.* Madrid: Filmoteca Española, 1994.

_____. *Cine español en el exilio, 1936-1939.* Barcelona: Editorial Lumen, 1976.

_____. *El cine sonoro en la República, 1929-1936. Historia del cine español II.* Barcelona: Editorial Lumen, 1977.

_____. "La guerra hispano-yanqui y los orígenes del cine político." *Historia y vida* 25 (April 1970): 36-38.

Guernica, Antonio José. "Chicano Production Companies: Projecting Reality, Opening the Doors." *Agenda: A Journal of Hispanic Issues* 8, no. 1 (January-February 1978): 12-15.

Guerrero, Ed. "AIDS as Monster in Science Fiction and Horror Cinema." *Journal of Popular Film & Television* 18, no. 3 (fall 1990): 86-93.

_____. *Framing Blackness: The African American Image in Film.* Philadelphia: Temple University Press, 1993.

_____. "Spike Lee and the Fever in the Racial Jungle." In *Film Theory Goes to the Movies: Cultural Analyses of Contemporary Film,* ed. Ava Collins, Jim Collins, and Hilary Radner. London: Routledge, 1992.

Guerrero Suárez, Jorge. *El cine sonoro mexicano: sus inicios, 1930-1937.* Cuadernos de la Cineteca Nacional. Mexico City: Cineteca Nacional, 1987.

Guibbert, Pierre, ed. *Les Premiers Ans du cinéma français.* Perpignan, France: Institut Jean Vigo, 1985.

Guiles, Fred Lawrence. *Marion Davies: A Biography.* New York: McGraw-Hill, 1972.

Guillermoprieto, Alma. *Samba.* New York: Random House, 1990.

Gunning, Tom. "The Cinema of Attraction: Early Film, Its Spectator, and the Avant-Garde." *Wide Angle* 8, nos. 3-4 (1986): 63-70.

——. *D. W. Griffith and the Origins of American Narrative Film*. Urbana: University of Illinois Press, 1991.

——. "The Narrator's Incision: The Legacy of Griffith's Biograph Films." Paper presented at the colloquium on D. W. Griffith at the Université de Paris, n.d. Archives of the Museum of Modern Art, New York.

——. "Non-Continuity, Continuity, Discontinuity: A Theory of Genres in Early Films." *Iris* 2 (spring 1984): 101-12.

——. "'Primitive' Cinema: A Frame-up? or the Trick's on Us." *Cinema Journal* 28, no. 2 (winter 1989): 3-12.

——. "Weaving a Narrative: Style and Economic Background in Griffith's Biograph Films." *Quarterly Review of Film Studies* (winter 1981): 11-21.

Gutiérrez, Félix, and Clint C. Wilson II. "The Demographic Dilemma." *Columbia Journalism Review* (Jan.-Feb. 1979): 53.

Gutiérrez, Félix F. "Spanish-Language Media in America: Background, Resources, History." *Journalism History* 4 (February 1977): 34-41.

Gutiérrez, Félix F., and Jorge R. Schement. *Spanish-Language Radio in the Southwestern United States*. Monograph No. 5. Austin: University of Texas, Center for Mexican American Studies, 1979.

Gutiérrez Alea, Tomás. *Dialéctica del espectador*. Mexico City: Federación Editorial Mexicana, 1983.

Gutiérrez-Jones, Carl. "Legislating Languages: *The Ballad of Gregorio Cortez* and the English Language Amendment." In *Chicanos and Film: Essays on Chicano Representation and Resistance,* ed. Chon A. Noriega, 219-32. New York: Garland Publishing Co., 1992.

Gutman, Herbert G. *Work, Culture and Society in Industrializing America: Essays in American Working Class and Social History.* New York: Vintage Books, 1966.

Habegger, Alfred. *Gender, Fantasy, and Realism in American Literature*. New York: Columbia University Press, 1982.

Hacker, Leonard. *Cinematic Design*. Boston: Photographic Publishing Co., 1931.

Haddad García, George [George Hadley-García]. "Dolores de mi corazón." *Nuestro,* April 1979, 31-33.

Hadley-Freydberg, Elizabeth. "Prostitutes, Concubines, Whores and Bitches: Black and Hispanic Women in Contemporary American Film." In *Women of Color: Perspectives on Feminism and Identity,* ed. Audrey T. McCluskey, 46-65. Bloomington: Indiana University, Women's Studies Program, 1985.

Hadley-García, George. *Hispanic Hollywood: The Latins in Motion Pictures.* (Simultaneous Spanish-language version: *Hollywood Hispano.*) New York: Citadel Press, 1990.

Hall, Benjamin. *The Golden Age of the Movie Palace: The Best Remaining Seats.* New York: Clarkson N. Potter, 1961.

Hall, Hal, ed. *Cinematographic Annual.* 2 vols. Hollywood: American Society of Cinematographers, 1930-31.

Hall, Stuart. "Cultural Identity and Cinematic Representation." *Framework* 36 (1980): 68-81.

——. "New Ethnicities." *ICA Documents* 7 (1988): 27-31.

Halliwell, Leslie. *Halliwell's Film Guide.* Rev. and ed. by John Walker. New York: HarperCollins, 1991.

Ham, Debra Newman. *The African-American Mosaic: A Library of Congress Resource Guide for the Study of Black History and Culture.* Washington, DC: Library of Congress, 1993.

Hammond, Paul. *Marvelous Méliès.* New York: St. Martin's Press, 1975.

——, ed. *The Shadow and Its Shadow: Surrealist Writing on Cinema.* London: British Film Institute, 1978.

Hampton, Benjamin. *History of the American Film Industry from Its Beginnings to 1931.* Reprint of his 1931 *A History of the Movies.* New York: Dover Publications, 1970.

Hancock, Ralph, and Letitia Fairbanks. *Douglas Fairbanks: The Fourth Musketeer.* New York: Holt, Rinehart, 1953.

Handel, Leo. *Hollywood Looks at Its Audience.* Urbana: University of Illinois Press, 1950.

Hanisch, Michael. *Western: Die Entwicklung eines Filmgenres.* Leipzig, Germany: Henschelverlag, 1984.

Hansen, Miriam. *Babel and Babylon: Spectatorship in American Silent Film.* Cambridge: Harvard University Press, 1991.

——. "Early Silent Cinema: Whose Public Sphere?" *New German Critique* 29 (winter 1983): 147-184.

——. "Pleasure, Ambivalence, Identification: Valentino and Female Spectatorship." *Cinema Journal* 25 (summer 1986): 6-32.

Hanson, Patricia King, and Stephen L. Hanson, eds. *The Film Review Index.* Vol. 1, *1882-1949.* Phoenix, AZ: Oryx Press, 1986.

Haraway, Donna. *Simians, Cyborgs and Women: The Reinvention of Nature.* New York: Routledge, 1991.

Harbison, W. A. *George C. Scott.* New York: Pinnacle Books, 1977.

Harcourt, Peter. "Luis Buñuel: Spaniard and Surrealist." *Film Quarterly* 20 (spring 1967): 2-19.

Hardy, Phil. *The Encyclopedia of Science Fiction Movies.* Minneapolis, MN: Woodbury Press, 1984.

——. *The Western.* New York: William Morrow and Co., 1983.

Harley, John Eugene. *World-Wide Influences of the Cinema: A Study of Official Censorship and the International Cultural Aspects of Motion Pictures.* Berkeley: University of California Press, 1940.

Harmetz, Aljean. "Hollywood Gamble en Español." *New York Times,* 18 July 1987, I9.

——. "Math Stars in a Movie." *Los Angeles Times,* 20 March 1988, sec. 2, 1.

Harrington, John. *Film and/as Literature.* Englewood Cliffs, NJ: Prentice-Hall, 1977.

Harris, Charles W., and Buck Rainey. *The Cowboy: Six-Shooters, Songs and Sex.* Norman: University of Oklahoma Press, 1976.

Hart, James, ed. *The Man Who Invented Hollywood: The Autobiography of D. W. Griffith.* Foreword by Frank Capra. Louisville, KY: Touchstone Publishing Co., 1972.

Hart, John Mason. *Revolutionary Mexico: The Coming and Process of the Mexican Revolution.* Berkeley: University of California Press, 1987.

Hart, William S. *My Life East & West.* New York: Benjamin Blom, 1929.

Hart, William S., and Mary Hart. *Pinto Ben and Other Stories.* New York: Britton, 1919.

Harvey, Charles M. "The Dime Novel in American Life." *Atlantic Monthly* 100 (July 1907): 44.

Haskell, Molly. *From Reverence to Rape: The Treatment of Women in the Movies.* New York: Holt, Rinehart and Winston, 1974.

Hausheer, Cecilia, and Christoph Settele, eds. *Found Footage Film.* Lucerne, Switzerland: Viper/Zyklop Verlag, 1992.

Haver, Ronald. *David O. Selznick's Hollywood.* New York: Alfred A. Knopf, 1980.

Havránek, Bohuslav. "The Functional Differentiation of the Standard Language." In *A Prague School Reader on Esthetics, Literary Structure and Style,* ed. Paul L. Garvin. Washington, DC: Georgetown University Press, 1964.

Hawaii Film Board. *Celebration of the 80th Anniversary of the First Film Showing in Hawaii.* Honolulu: Hawaii Film Board, 1977.

Hay, Peter. *MGM: When the Lion Roars.* Atlanta: Turner Publishing, 1991.

Hayakawa, Sessue. *Zen Showed Me the Way.* Indianapolis: Bobbs-Merrill, 1961.

Hayden, Sterling. *Wanderer.* New York: Alfred A. Knopf, 1963.

Hays, Will H. *The Memoirs of Will H. Hays.* Garden City, NY: Doubleday, 1955.

_____. *See and Hear.* New York: Motion Picture Producers and Distributors of America, 1929.

Heath, Stephen. *Questions of Cinema.* Bloomington: Indiana University Press, 1981.

Heider, Karl G. *Ethnographic Film.* Austin: University of Texas Press, 1976.

Heinink, Juan B., and Robert G. Dickson. *Cita en Hollywood.* Bilbao, Spain: Ediciones Mensajero, 1990.

Heller, Michele A. "Off the Air: Why Aren't Hispanics on the Networks?" *Hispanic,* August 1994, 30-34.

Hembus, Joe. *Western Geschichte, 1540-1894.* Munich: Wilhelm Heyne Verlag, 1979.

_____. *Western-Lexikon.* Munich: Hanser Verlag, 1976.

Hemming, Roy. *The Melody Lingers On: The Great Songwriters and Their Movie Musicals.* New York: Newmarket Press, 1986.

Henderson, Brian. "A Musical Comedy of Empire." *Film Quarterly* 35 (winter 1981-82): 2-16.

Henderson, Robert M. *D. W. Griffith: His Life and Work.* New York: Oxford University Press, 1972.

_____. *D. W. Griffith: The Years at Biograph.* New York: Farrar, Straus and Giroux, 1970.

Hendricks, Gordon. *Beginnings of the Biograph.* New York: Beginnings of the American Film, 1964. Reprint, New York: Arno Press, 1972.

_____. *Eadweard Muybridtge: The Father of the Motion Picture.* New York: Grossman, 1975.

_____. *The Edison Motion Picture Myth.* Berkeley: University of California Press, 1961. Reprint, New York: Arno Press, 1972.

_____. *The Kinetoscope: America's First Commercially Successful Motion Picture Exhibitor.* 1966. Reprint, New York: Arno Press, 1972.

Hennebelle, Guy, and Alfonso Gumucio-Dragón, eds. *Les Cinémas de L'Amérique Latine.* Paris: Nouvelles Éditions Pierre Lherminier, 1981.

Hernández, Beatriz Johnston. "Ramón Menéndez: A Filmmaker Possessed." *Vista,* 18 February 1989, 6-12.

Hernández, Guillermo. Film review of *The Ballad of Gregorio Cortez. Crítica* 1, no. 2 (spring 1985): 122-26.

Hernández, Luis Alberto. "The Origins of the Consumer Culture in Puerto Rico: The Pre-Television Years (1898-1954)." *Centro de Estudios Puertorriqueños Bulletin* 3, no. 1 (winter 1990-91): 38-54.

Hernández, Ricardo, and Edith Sánchez, eds. *Cross-Border Links.* Albuquerque, NM: Inter-Hemispheric Education Resource Center, 1992.

Herndon, Booton. *Mary Pickford and Douglas Fairbanks: The Most Popular Couple the World Has Ever Known.* New York: W. W. Norton and Co., 1977.

Herrera, Juan Felipe, and Bobby Páramo. "*Cerco Blanco, The Balloon Man* and *Fighting City Hall*: On Being a Chicano Filmmaker." *Metamorfosis,* 3, no. 2 (1980-81): 77-82.

Herzog, Charlotte. "The Archeology of Cinema Architecture: The Origins of the Movie Theatre." *Quarterly Review of Film Studies* 9 (winter 1984): 11-32.

Hicks, Emily D. *Border Writing.* Minneapolis: University of Minnesota Press, 1991.

Higashi, Sumiko. *Cecil B. DeMille: A Guide to References and Resources.* Boston: G. K. Hall & Co., 1985.

_____. *Cecil B. DeMille and American Culture: The Silent Era.* Berkeley: University of California Press, 1994.

_____. *Virgins, Vamps, and Flappers: The American Silent Movie Heroine.* Montreal: Eden Press, 1979.

Higginbotham, Virginia. *Spanish Film under Franco.* Austin: University of Texas Press, 1988.

Higham, Charles. *Cecil B. DeMille.* New York: Charles Scribner's Sons, 1973.

_____. *Celebrity Circus.* New York: Dell Books, 1980.

_____. *The Celluloid Muse.* New York: Signet Books, 1969.

_____. *The Films of Orson Welles.* Berkeley: University of California Press, 1970.

_____. *Hollywood Cameramen.* Bloomington: Indiana University Press, 1970.

_____. *Marlene: The Life of Marlene Dietrich.* New York: W. W. Norton & Co., 1977.

_____. *Merchant of Dreams: Louis B. Mayer and the Secret Hollywood.* New York: Donald I. Fine, 1993.

_____. *Orson Welles: The Rise and Fall of an American Genius.* New York: St. Martin's Press, 1985.

_____. *Warner Brothers.* New York: Charles Scribner's Sons, 1975.

Higham, Charles, and Joel Greenberg. *Hollywood in the Forties.* New York: A. S. Barnes, 1968.

Higham, John. *Send These to Me: Immigrants in Urban America.* 2nd ed. Baltimore: Johns Hopkins University Press, 1984.

_____. *Strangers in the Land: Patterns of American Nativism, 1860-1925.* New Brunswick, NJ: Rutgers University Press, 1955.

Hilger, Michael. *The American Indian in Film.* Metuchen, NJ: Scarecrow Press, 1986.

Hill, Laurance L., and Silas E. Snyder. *Can Anything Good Come out of Hollywood?* Los Angeles: Times-Mirror Press, 1923.

Hinxman, Margaret, and Susan d'Arcy. *The Cinema of Dirk Bogarde.* South Brunswick, NJ: A. S. Barnes and Co., 1974.

Hirschorn, Clive. *The Columbia Story: The Complete History of the Studio and All Its Films.* New York: Crown Publishers, 1990.

_____. *The Warner Brothers Story.* New York: Crown Publishers, 1979.

"Hispanic Owners Band Together." *Broadcasting,* 20 May 1991.

Hoagland, Herbert Case. *How to Write a Photoplay.* New York: Magazine Maker Publishing Co., 1912.

Hoberman, J., and Jonathon Rosenbaum. *Midnight Movies.* New York: Harper and Row, 1983.

Hobsbawm, Eric. *Bandits*. Rev. ed. New York: Pantheon Books, 1981.

Hochman, Stanley, ed. *From Quasimodo to Scarlett O'Hara: A National Board of Review Anthology, 1920-1940*. New York: Frederick Ungar Publishing, 1982.

Holden, Stephen. "A Visionary Cuba: When Believers Still Believed." Review of *I Am Cuba. New York Times,* 8 March 1995.

Holm, Bill, and George Irving Quimby. *Edward S. Curtis in the Land of the War Canoes: A Pioneer Cinematographer in the Pacific Northwest*. Seattle: University of Washington Press, 1980.

Holman, Roger, comp. *Cinema 1900-1906: An Analytical Study by the National Film Archive (London) and the International Federation of Film Archives*. Vol. 1, *Brighton Symposium, 1978*. Vol. 2, *Analytical Filmography (Fiction Films), 1900-1906*. Brussels: Fédération internationale des archives du film, 1982.

Homenaje a los iniciadores del cine en México 1896-1938. Cuadernos de la Cineteca Nacional, no. 9. Mexico City: Cineteca Nacional, 1979.

Honig, Piet Hein, and Hanns-Georg Rodek. *100001. Die Showbusiness-Enzyklopädie des 20. Jahrhunderts*. Fielderstadt, Germany: Showbizdata Deutschland, 1992.

Hopewell, John. *Out of the Past: Spanish Cinema after Franco*. London: BFI Books, 1986.

Hopwood, Henry V. *Living Pictures*. 1899. Reprint, New York: Arno Press, 1970.

Horsman, Reginald. *Race and Manifest Destiny: The Origins of American Racial Anglo-Saxonism*. Cambridge: Harvard University Press, 1981.

Horwitz, James. *They Went Thataway—Old-Time Hollywood Cowboys*. New York: E. P. Dutton, 1976.

Horwitz, Rita. *An Index to Volume 1 of "The Moving Picture World and View Photographer."* Introduction by Lawrence Karr. Los Angeles, CA: American Film Institute, 1974.

Houseman, Victoria. *Made in Heaven: The Marriages and Children of Hollywood Stars*. Chicago: Bonus Books, 1991.

Huaco, George A. *The Sociology of Film Art*. New York: Basic Books, 1965.

Huaco-Nuzum, Carmen. "Matilde Landeta: An Introduction to the Work of a Pioneer Mexican Filmmaker." *Screen* 28, no. 4 (fall 1987): 96-105.

Hubbard, Kim. "Beating Long Odds, Jaime Escalante Stands and Delivers, Helping to Save a Faltering High School." *People Weekly,* 11 April 1988, 57-58.

Hudson, Richard M., and Raymond Lee. *Gloria Swanson*. South Brunswick, NJ, and New York: A. S. Barnes and Co., 1970.

Huerta, Jorge. *Chicano Theater: Themes and Forms*. Ypsilanti, MI: Bilingual Press, 1982.

Huettig, Mae D. *Economic Control of the Motion Picture Industry*. Philadelphia: University of Pennsylvania Press, 1944.

Huff, Theodore. *Charlie Chaplin*. New York: Schuman, 1951.

Hughes, Lawrence A., ed. *The Truth about the Movies by the Stars*. Hollywood: Hollywood Publishers, 1924.

Hulfish, David Sherrill. *Cyclopedia of Motion-Picture Work*. 1915. Reprint, New York: Arno Press, 1970.

———. *The Motion Picture: Its Making and Its Theater*. Chicago: Electricity Magazine Corporation, 1909.

———. *Motion Picture Work*. Chicago: American School of Correspondence, 1913.

Hurst, Richard Maurice. *Republic Studios: Between Poverty Row and the Majors*. Metuchen, NJ: Scarecrow Press, 1979.

Huston, John. *An Open Book*. New York: Alfred A. Knopf, 1980.

Hyams, Jay. *The Life and Times of the Western Movie*. New York: Gallery Books, 1983.

Hyatt, Marshall, comp. *The Afro-American Cinematic Experience: An Annotated Bibliography and Filmography*. Wilmington, DE: Scholarly Resources, 1983.

Idar, Nicasio. "El cinematógrafo." *La Crónica,* 19 October 1911, 3.

Iglesias, Norma. *Entre yerba, polvo y plomo: lo fronterizo visto por el cine mexicano*. Tijuana, Mexico: El Colegio de la Frontera Norte, 1991.

———. *La visión de la frontera a través del cine mexicano*. Tijuana, Mexico: Centro de Estudios Fronterizos del Norte de México, 1985.

———. "La visión de la frontera a través del cine mexicano." In *Times of Challenge: Chicanos and Chicanas in American Society,* ed. National Association for Chicano Studies, 125-33. Houston, TX: University of Houston, Mexican American Studies Program, 1988.

Iglesias Prieto, Norma V. "El desarrollo del cine fronterizo: análisis de los últimos tres sexenios." In *Frontera norte: chicanos, pachucos y cholos,* ed. Luis Hernández Palacios and Juan Manuel Sandoval, 501-24. Mexico City: Ancien Régime, 1989.

"Los indios norteamericanos protestan malos efectos del cinematógrafo." *La Crónica,* 2 March 1911, 5.

International Directory of Film and Television Documentation Centers. Chicago: St. James Press, 1988.

International Motion Picture Almanac, 1928-1945. New York: Quigley Publishing Co., 1928-45.

Iris 13 (summer 1991). Issue dedicated to Latin American cinema.

Irwin, Will. *The House That Shadows Built*. Garden City, NY: Doubleday, Doran and Co., 1928.

Jacobs, Lea. *The Wages of Sin: Censorship and the Fallen Woman Film, 1928-1942*. Madison: University of Wisconsin Press, 1991.

Jacobs, Lewis. *The Emergence of Film Art*. New York: Hopkinson and Blake, 1974.

———. *Introduction to the Art of the Movies*. New York: Noonday Press, 1960.

———. *The Rise of the American Film: A Critical History*. New York: Harcourt Brace and Co., 1939.

———. *The Rise of the American Film: A Critical History, with an Essay, Experimental Cinema in America 1921-1947*. Studies in Culture and Communication. New York: Teachers College Press, 1968.

James, David. *Allegories of Cinema: American Film in the Sixties*. Princeton, NJ: Princeton University Press, 1989.

Jameson, Fredric. *The Geopolitical Aesthetic: Cinema and Space in the World System*. Bloomington: Indiana University Press, 1992.

Janney, O. Edward. *The White Slave Traffic in America*. New York: National Vigilance Committee, 1911.

Jarvie, I. C. *Movies and Society*. New York: Basic Books, 1970.

Jeanne, René, and Charles Ford. *Historia ilustrada del cine*. 3 vols. Madrid: Alianza Editorial, 1974.

Jeffords, Susan. *Hard Bodies: Hollywood Masculinity in the Reagan Era*. New Brunswick, NJ: Rutgers University Press, 1994.

_____. *The Remasculinization of America: Gender and the Vietnam War.* Bloomington: Indiana University Press, 1989.

Jenks, George C. "Dime Novel Makers." *Bookman* 22 (October 1904): 112.

Jerome, V. J. *The Negro in Hollywood Films.* New York: Masses and Mainstream, 1950.

Jesionowski, Joyce E. *Thinking in Pictures: Dramatic Structure in D. W. Griffith's Biograph Films.* Berkeley: University of California Press, 1987.

Jewell, Richard B., and Vernon Harbin. *The RKO Story.* London: Arlington House, 1982.

Jiménez, Lillian. "First Steps to Latino Alternatives." *The Independent* 6 (July-August 1983): 19.

_____. "From the Margin to the Center: Puerto Rican Cinema in the United States." *Centro de Estudios Puertorriqueños Bulletin* 2, no. 8 (1990): 28-43.

_____. "Moving from the Margin to the Center: Puerto Rican Cinema in New York." *Jump Cut* 38 (June 1993): 60-66.

_____. "Puerto Rican Video Artist: Interview with Edin Vélez." *Jump Cut* 39 (June 1994): 99-104, 106.

Jiménez, Luis. "Cambia la imagen del latino en Hollywood." *La Opinión* (Los Angeles), 9 June 1985, "La Comunidad" section, 14-15.

Jiménez-Rueda, Julio. "El cine sonoro: Otra opinión sobre la cuestión del lenguaje español y las películas habladas—el problema fundamental." *La Opinión* (Los Angeles), 14 January 1930, 14.

Jobes, Gertrude. *The Motion Picture Empire.* Hamden, CT: Archon Books, 1966.

Johansen, Jason C. "El cine chicano, redefiniendo su crecimiento." *La Opinión* (Los Angeles), Suplemento Cultural, 16 November 1980.

_____. "El cine chicano: Una breve reseña." In *Hojas de cine: Testimonios y documentos del nuevo cine latino americano,* vol. 1. Mexico City: Universidad Autónoma Metropolitana, Fundación Mexicana de Cineastas, 1988.

_____. "Notes on Chicano Cinema." *Jump Cut* 23 (October 1980): 9-10.

Johanssen, Albert. *The House of Beadle and Adams and Its Dime and Nickel Novels: The Story of a Vanished Literature.* 2 vols. Norman: University of Oklahoma Press, 1950.

Johnson, Martin. *Camera Trails in Hollywood.* New York: Century, 1924.

Johnson, Randal, and Robert Stam, eds. *Brazilian Cinema.* Austin: University of Texas Press, 1988.

Johnston, Claire. "Femininity and the Masquerade: Anne of the Indies." In *Psychoanalysis and Cinema,* ed. E. Ann Kaplan, 64-72. New York: Routledge, 1990.

"Joinville Makes 110 in 12 Languages." *Film Daily,* 26 August 1930.

Jones, Charles Reed, ed. *Breaking into the Movies.* New York: Unicorn Press, 1927.

Jones, Daryl. *The Dime Novel Western.* Bowling Green, OH: Popular Press, 1978.

Jones, Dorothy B. "The Hollywood War Film: 1942-1944." *Hollywood Quarterly* 1 (1945): 1-19.

Jones, G. William. *Black Cinema Treasures: Lost and Found.* Denton: University of North Texas Press, 1991.

Jorgens, Jack. *Shakespeare on Film.* Bloomington: Indiana University Press, 1977.

Josephson, Matthew. *Edison.* New York: McGraw-Hill, 1959.

Joskowitz, Alejandro. "¿Sabe usted quién es el culpable de la situación en que se encuentra el cine mexicano hoy?" *Pantalla* 10 (winter 1988).

Jowett, Garth S. *Film: The Democratic Art.* American Film Institute Series. Boston: Little, Brown, 1976.

_____. "The First Motion Picture Audiences." *Journal of Popular Film* (winter 1974): 39-54.

Jowett, Garth, and James Linton. *Movies as Mass Communication.* Beverly Hills, CA: Sage Publications, 1980.

Julien, Isaac, and Kobena Mercer, eds. "The Last 'Special' Issue on Race?" *Screen* 29, no. 4 (1988).

Kaminsky, Stuart. *American Film Genres.* New York: Pflaum, 1974.

Kanellos, Nicolás. "Brief History of Hispanic Theater in the United States." In *Handbook of Hispanic Cultures in the United States: Literature and Art,* ed. Francisco Lomelí. Houston, Texas: Arte Público Press and Instituto de Cooperación Iberoamericana, 1993.

_____. *A History of Hispanic Theater in the United States: Origins to 1940.* Austin: University of Texas Press, 1990.

_____. "Theater." In *The Hispanic-American Almanac,* ed. Nicolás Kanellos, 505-41. Detroit: Gale Research, 1993.

Kaplan, E. Ann. *Motherhood and Representation: The Mother in Popular Culture and Melodrama.* London: Routledge, 1992.

_____, ed. *Women in Film Noir.* London: British Film Institute, 1978.

Karetnikova, Inga, in collaboration with Leon Steinmetz. *Mexico according to Eisenstein.* Albuquerque: University of New Mexico Press, 1991.

Karney, Robyn, ed. *Who's Who in Hollywood.* London: Bloomsbury Publishing Group, 1993.

Karney, Robyn, et al. *Chronicle of the Cinema.* London: Dorling Kindersley, 1995.

Karr, Kathleen. "The Long Square-up: Exploitation Trends in the Silent Films." *Journal of Popular Film* (spring 1974): 107-28.

Kasson, John F. *Amusing the Millions: Coney Island at the Turn of the Century.* New York: Hill and Wang, 1978.

Katz, Ephraim. *The Film Encyclopedia.* New York: Thomas Y. Crowell, 1979. Rev. ed., New York: HarperCollins, 1994.

Kaufmann, Stanley, ed., with Bruce Henstall. *American Film Criticism from the Beginnings to Citizen Kane. Reviews of Significant Films at the Time They First Appeared.* New York: Liveright, 1972.

Kay, Karyn, and Gerald Peary. *Women and the Cinema.* New York: E. P. Dutton, 1977.

Kazan, Elia. "Letters to the Editor." *The Saturday Review* 35 (5 April 1952): 22.

Kearney, Jill. "The Old Gringo." *American Film* 13, no. 5 (March 1988): 26-31, 67.

Keen, Sam. *Faces of the Enemy: Reflections of the Hostile Imagination.* New York: Harper & Row, 1986.

Keil, Charles. "Transition through Tension: Stylistic Diversity in the Late Griffith Biographs." *Cinema Journal* 28 (spring 1989): 22-40.

Keller, Gary D. "The Boom in Ethnic Cinema and the Breakthrough in Its Analysis." *Bilingual Review/Revista Bilingüe* 20, no. 1 (Jan.-April 1995): 77-89.

_____. "Film." In *The Hispanic-American Almanac,* ed. Nicolás Kanellos, 543-94. Detroit: Gale Research, 1993.

_____. *Hispanics and United States Film: An Overview and Handbook.* Tempe, AZ: Bilingual Review/Press, 1994.

_____. "La representación de los chicanos en la filmografía de los Estados Unidos y el surgimiento de la filmografía chicana." In *Culturas hispanas en los Estados Unidos de América,* ed. María Jesús Buxó Rey and Tomás Calvo Buezas, 695-705. Madrid: Ediciones de Cultura Hispánica, 1990.

_____, ed. *Chicano Cinema: Research, Reviews, and Resources.* Binghamton, NY: Bilingual Review/Press, 1985.

_____, ed. *Cine chicano.* Mexico City: Cineteca Nacional, 1988.

Kelley, Ken. "Luis Valdez: The Interview." *San Francisco Focus,* September 1987, 104-5.

Kelley, Kitty. *Elizabeth Taylor: The Last Star.* New York: Simon and Schuster, 1981.

Kellner, Douglas, and Michael Ryan, eds. *Camera Politica: The Politics and Ideology of Contemporary Hollywood Film.* Bloomington: Indiana University Press, 1988.

Kellner, Elena. "Everything's Coming Up Rosie." *Hispanic Business,* July 1994, 28-30.

Kelman, Steven G. "Cine San Antonio." *Texas Observer,* 26 January 1990, 20-21.

Kennedy, Joseph P., ed. *The Story of Films.* Chicago: A. W. Shaw, 1927.

Kernan, Lisa. "Keep Marching, Sisters: The Second Generation Looks at *Salt of the Earth.*" *Nuestro* 9, no. 4 (May 1985): 23-25.

Kerr, Paul, ed. *The Hollywood Film Industry.* London: Routledge and Kegan Paul, 1986.

Kerr, Walter. *The Silent Clowns.* New York: Alfred A. Knopf, 1979.

Ketchum, Richard M. *Will Rogers: His Life and Times.* New York: American Heritage Publishing Co., 1973.

Keyser, Les. *Hollywood in the Seventies.* La Jolla, CA: A. S. Barnes, 1981.

Keyser, Les, and Barbara Keyser. *Hollywood and the Catholic Church: The Image of Roman Catholicism in American Movies.* Chicago: Loyola University Press, 1984.

Kindem, Gorham, ed. *The American Movie Industry: The Business of Motion Pictures.* Carbondale: Southern Illinois University Press, 1982.

King, John. *Magical Reels: A History of Cinema in Latin America.* London: Verso, 1990.

King, John, Ana M. López, and Manuel Alvarado, eds. *Mediating Two Worlds: Cinematic Encounters in the Americas.* London: British Film Institute, 1993.

King, John, and Nissa Torrents, eds. *The Garden of Forking Paths: Argentine Cinema.* London: British Film Institute, 1987.

Kirkley, Donald H. *A Descriptive Study of Network Television Westerns during the Seasons 1955-6–1962-3.* New York: Arno Press, 1979.

Kirkpatrick, Sidney. *A Cast of Killers.* New York: E. P. Dutton, 1986.

Kitses, Jim. *Horizons West: Anthony Mann, Budd Boetticher, Sam Peckinpah: Studies in Authorship within the Western.* Bloomington: Indiana University Press, 1969.

Kleine, George. *Catalogue of Educational Motion Picture Films.* Chicago: Kleine Optical Co., 1910.

Klotman, Phyllis Rauch. *Frame by Frame: A Black Filmography.* Bloomington: Indiana University Press, 1979.

Klumph, Inez, and Helen Klumph. *Screen Acting: Its Requirements and Rewards.* New York: Falk, 1922.

Knight, Alan. *The Mexican Revolution.* 2 vols. Cambridge: Cambridge University Press, 1986.

Kobal, John. *The Art of the Great Hollywood Portrait Photographers, 1925-40.* New York: Harrison House, 1980.

_____. *A History of Movie Musicals.* London: Octopus Publishing Group, 1988.

_____. *Rita Hayworth: The Time, the Place and the Woman.* New York: W. W. Norton and Co., 1977.

_____. *Romance in the Cinema.* London: Studio Vista, 1973.

Kobal, John, and V. A. Wilson. *Foyer Pleasure: The Golden Age of Cinema Lobby Cards.* London: Aurum Press, 1982.

Kobler, John. *Damned in Paradise: The Life of John Barrymore.* New York: Atheneum, 1977.

Koestenbau, Wayne. *The Queen's Throat: Opera, Homosexuality, and the Mystery of Desire.* New York: Poseidon Press, 1993.

Kolkler, Robert. *The Altering Eye: Contemporary International Cinema.* New York: Oxford University Press, 1983.

Konder, Rodolfo. "The Carmen Miranda Museum: The Brazilian Bombshell Is Still Box Office in Rio." *Americas* 34, no. 5 (1982): 17-21.

Koppes, Clayton R., and Gregory D. Black. *Hollywood Goes to War.* Berkeley: University of California Press, 1987.

_____. "What to Show the World: The Office of War Information and Hollywood, 1942-1945." *Journal of American History* 64 (1977): 87-105.

Koszarski, Diane. *There's a New Star in Heaven . . . Valentino.* Berlin: Verlag Volker Spiess, 1979.

Koszarski, Diane Kaiser. *The Complete Films of William S. Hart: A Pictorial Record.* New York: Dover Publications, 1980.

Koszarski, Richard. *The Astoria Studio and Its Fabulous Films.* New York: Dover Publications, 1980.

_____. *An Evening's Entertainment: The Age of the Silent Feature Picture, 1915-1928.* Vol. 3 of *History of the American Cinema,* Charles Harpole, gen. ed. New York: Charles Scribner's Sons, 1990.

_____. *The Man You Loved to Hate: Erich von Stroheim and Hollywood.* Oxford: Oxford University Press, 1983.

_____. "60 Filmographies: The Men with the Movie Cameras." *Film Comment* 8, no. 2 (summer 1972): 27-57.

_____. *Universal Pictures: 65 Years.* New York: Museum of Modern Art, 1977.

_____, ed. *Hollywood Directors: 1914-1940.* New York: Oxford University Press, 1976.

_____, ed. *Hollywood Directors: 1941-1976.* New York: Oxford University Press, 1977.

_____, ed. *The Rivals of D. W. Griffith.* Minneapolis: Walker Art Center, 1976.

Kotsilibas-Davis, James. *The Barrymores: The Royal Family in Hollywood.* New York: Crown Publishers, 1981.

Kotz, Liz. "Unofficial Stories: Documentaries by Latinas and Latin American Women." *Centro de Estudios Puertorriqueños Bulletin* 2, no. 8 (1990): 58-69.

Krauze, Enrique. "The Guerrilla Dandy." *The New Republic* 198, no. 26 (27 June 1988): 28-38.

Krippendorff, Klaus. *Content Analysis: An Introduction to Its Methodology.* Beverly Hills, CA: Sage Publications, 1980.

Kronke, David. "A Brush with Success—This Funny Business Has Paid Off for Animator Phil Roman." *Hispanic Business,* February 1993, 22-24.

Kyrou, Ado. *Luis Buñuel.* Paris: Éditions Seghers, 1970.

La Fuente, María Isabel. *Índice bibliográfico del cine mexicano (1930-1965).* Vol. 1. Mexico City: Editorial América, 1967.
_____. *Índice bibliográfico del cine mexicano (1966-1967).* Vol. 2. Mexico City: Editorial América, 1968.
Lahue, Kalton C. *Bound and Gagged: The Story of Silent Serials.* Cranbury, NJ: Barnes, 1968.
_____. *Continued Next Week: A History of the Moving Picture Serial.* Norman: University of Oklahoma Press, 1964.
_____. *Dreams for Sale: The Rise and Fall of the Triangle Film Corporation.* South Brunswick, NJ, and New York: A. S. Barnes and Co., 1971.
_____. *Mack Sennett's Keystone: The Man, the Myth and the Comedies.* South Brunswick, NJ, and New York: A. S. Barnes and Co., 1971.
_____. *Motion Picture Pioneer: The Selig Polyscope Company.* South Brunswick, NJ: A. S. Barnes, 1973.
_____. *Riders of the Range.* New York: Castle Books, 1973.
_____. *Winners of the West.* New York: A. S. Barnes, 1970.
_____. *World of Laughter.* Norman: University of Oklahoma Press, 1966.
Lahue, Kalton C., and Terry Brewer. *Kops and Custards: The Legend of Keystone Films.* Norman: University of Oklahoma Press, 1964.
Lahue, Kalton C., and Sam Gill. *Clown Princes and Court Jesters.* Cranbury, NJ: Barnes, 1970.
Lamarque, Libertad. *Libertad Lamarque, autobiografía.* Buenos Aires: Javier Vergara Editor, 1986.
Lamb, Blaine P. "The Convenient Villain: The Early Cinema Views the Mexican American." *Journal of the West* 14 (October 1975): 75-81.
Lamster, Frederick. *Souls Made Great through Love and Adversity: The Film Work of Borzage.* Metuchen, NJ: Scarecrow Press, 1981.
Landy, Marcia, ed. *Imitations of Life: A Reader on Film and Television Melodrama.* Detroit: Wayne State University Press, 1991.
Lane, Tamar. *What's Wrong with the Movies?* Los Angeles: Waverly, 1923.
Lang, Robert. *American Film Melodrama: Griffith, Vidor, Minelli.* Princeton, NJ: Princeton University Press, 1989.
_____, ed. *The Birth of a Nation. D. W. Griffith, Director.* New Brunswick, NJ: Rutgers University Press, 1993.
Langman, Larry. *A Guide to Silent Westerns.* New York: Greenwood Press, 1992.
Laprevotte, Gilles, ed. *Les Indiens et le cinéma: Des Indiens d'Hollywood au cinéma des Indiens.* Amiens, France: Trois Cailloux, Maison de la culture d'Amiens (Festival international du film d'Amiens), 1989.
Lardner, James. *Fast Forward: Hollywood, the Japanese, and the Onslaught of the VCR.* New York: W. W. Norton & Co., 1987.
Larkin, Rochelle. *Hail, Columbias!* New Rochelle: Arlington House, 1975.
Larson, Randall D. *Films into Books: An Analytical Bibliography of Film Novelizations, Movie and TV Tie-Ins.* Metuchen, NJ: Scarecrow Press, 1995.
Lash, Vivian. "Experimenting with Freedom in Mexico." *Film Quarterly* 19 (summer 1966).

_____. " Las películas mexicanas en los EEUU." *Tiempo,* 27 April 1945.
Lasky, Betty. *RKO: The Biggest Little Major of Them All.* 2nd ed. Santa Monica, CA: Roundtable Publishing, 1989.
Lasky, Jesse L., with Don Weldon. *I Blow My Own Horn.* Garden City, NY: Doubleday & Co., 1957.
Latham, Aaron. *Crazy Sundays: F. Scott Fitzgerald in Hollywood.* New York: Viking Press, 1970.
"Latin Americans Urge Film Care." *Variety* 6, November 1940, 1, 22.
"Latina-Run Firm Wins Film Award." *Nuestro* 8, no. 6 (August 1984): 13.
"Latin Ladies—Hollywood Is Invaded by Talent South of the Rio Grande." *Life,* 3 February 1941.
Latino Film and Video Images. Special issue. *Centro* 2, no. 8 (spring 1990). (Centro de Estudios Puertorriqueños, Hunter College/CUNY.)
Latinos and the Media. Special issue. *Centro* 3, no. 1 (winter 1990-91). (Centro de Estudios Puertorriqueños, Hunter College/CUNY.)
Lauritzen, Einar, and Gunnar Lundquist. *American Film Index, 1908-1915.* Stockholm: Film-Index (University of Stockholm), 1976.
_____. *American Film Index, 1916-1920.* Stockholm: Film-Index (University of Stockholm), 1984.
Lawston, Richard. *A World of Movies: 70 Years of Film History.* New York: Bonanza Books, 1974.
Lax, Eric. *Woody Allen: A Biography.* New York: Alfred A. Knopf, 1991.
Lazo, Rod. "*Latino:* Haskell Wexler's Controversial New Movie Released." *Caminos* 6, no. 9 (November 1985): 10-11.
Leab, Daniel J. *From Sambo to Superspade: The Black Experience in Motion Pictures.* Boston: Houghton Mifflin Co., 1975.
Leahy, James. *The Cinema of Joseph Losey.* New York: A. S. Barnes & Co., 1967.
Leaming, Barbara. *If This Was Happiness: A Biography of Rita Hayworth.* London: Sphere Books, 1990.
_____. *Orson Welles: A Biography.* New York: Penguin, 1985.
Leblanc, Edward. "American Dime Novel Reprints in Europe." *Dime Novel Round-Up,* no. 612 (December 1991): 111-13.
Lee, Spike. *Inside Guerrilla Filmmaking. She's Gotta Have It.* New York: Fireside, 1987.
Lee, Spike, with Lisa Jones. *Uplift the Race: The Construction of School Daze.* New York: Simon and Schuster, 1988.
Lees, David, and Stan Berkowitz. *The Movie Business.* New York: Vintage Books, 1981.
Lehman, Peter. "Stenches, Flies, Drunks, and Impostors: The Eclair Company in Tucson." *Griffithiana* 16, no. 47 (1993): 181-88. [One of several articles on an issue dedicated to the Eclair Company.]
Leiner, Marvin. *Sexual Politics in Cuba: Machismo, Homosexuality and AIDS.* Boulder, CO: Westview Press, 1993.
Lenihan, John H. *Showdown: Confronting Modern America in the Western Film.* Urbana: University of Illinois Press, 1980.
Lenning, Arthur, ed. *The Sound Film: An Introduction.* Troy, NY: Walter Snyder, 1969.
Lent, John. *The Asian Film Industry.* Austin: University of Texas Press, 1990.
Leonard, William Torbet. *Masquerade in Black: Blackface Biographies.* Metuchen, NJ: Scarecrow Press, 1986.

Lerner, Jesse, and Clark Arnwine. "The Pre-Cortesian Codices as 'Mexican' Film Language in *Retorno a Aztlán.*" *Spectator* 13, no. 1 (fall 1992): 86-91.

Lescale, Aurora. "México indígena." *Cine Cubano* 103 (1984).

Lescarboura, Austin. *Behind the Motion Picture Screen.* New York: Munn, 1919.

Leutrat, Jean-Louis. *L'Alliance brisée.* Lyon, France: Presses Universitaires de Lyon, 1985.

_____. *Le Western.* Paris: Armand Colin, 1973.

Levine, Felicia, and Andrew Paxman. "Telemundo's New Destiny." *Variety,* 27 March-2 April 1995.

Levine, Paul G. "Remember the Alamo? John Wayne Told One Story. PBS's *Seguín* Tells Another." *American Film,* Jan.-Feb. 1982, 47-48.

Levy, David. "Edwin S. Porter and the Origins of the American Narrative Film, 1894-1907." Ph.D. diss., McGill University, 1983.

Levy, Mark, ed. *The VCR Age: Home Video and Mass Communication.* Newbury Park, CA: Sage Publications, 1989.

Lewels, Francisco J. "Racism in the Media—Perpetuating the Stereotype." *Agenda: A Journal of Hispanic Issues,* 1978, 4-6.

Lewis, Howard T. *Cases on the Motion Picture Industry.* New York: McGraw-Hill, 1930.

_____. *The Motion Picture Industry.* New York: Van Nostrand, 1933.

Leyda, Jay. "Eisenstein's Notes for the Epilogue of *Que Viva Mexico!*" *Sight & Sound* 6 (1958): 306.

_____. *Kino: A History of the Russian and Soviet Film.* London: Allen and Unwin, 1960; New York: Collier, 1973.

_____, ed. *Eisenstein 2: A Premature Celebration of Eisenstein's Centenary.* Calcutta: Seagull Books, 1985.

Leyda, Jay, and Charles Musser, eds. *Before Hollywood: Turn-of-the-Century Film from American Archives.* Catalog for the touring film exhibition. New York: American Federation of the Arts, 1986.

Leyda, Jay, and Zina Voynow. *Eisenstein at Work.* New York: Pantheon Books/Museum of Modern Art, 1982.

Library of Congress. *Wonderful Inventions: Motion Pictures, Broadcasting, and Recorded Sound at the Library of Congress.* Washington, DC: Library of Congress, 1985.

Lichter, S. Robert, and Daniel R. Amundson. *Distorted Reality: Hispanic Characters in TV Entertainment.* Washington, DC: Center for Media and Public Affairs, 1994.

Lightfoot, Dory. "Entrevista with Filmmaker Juan Frausto." *Alambraso: Chicano Studies Program Newsletter* (University of Wisconsin-Madison) 10, no. 1 (spring 1995): 4+.

Limbacher, James L. *Haven't I Seen You Somewhere Before? Remakes, Sequels and Series in Motion Pictures and Television, 1896-1978.* Ann Arbor, MI: Pierian Press, 1979.

Limerick, Patricia Nelson. *The Legacy of Conquest: The Unbroken Past of the American West.* New York: W. W. Norton and Co., 1987.

Limerick, Patricia Nelson, Clyde A. Milner II, and Charles E. Rankin, eds. *Trails: Toward a New Western History.* Lawrence: University Press of Kansas, 1991.

Limón, José. "Stereotyping and Chicano Resistance: An Historical Dimension." *Aztlán: International Journal of Chicano Studies Research* 4, no. 2 (fall 1973): 257-70.

Lindsay, Shelley Stamp. "Wages and Sin: *Traffic in Souls* and the White Slavery Scare." *Persistence of Vision* 9 (1991): 90-102.

Lindsay, Vachel. *The Art of the Motion Picture.* 1915. Reprint, New York: Liveright, 1970.

Linet, Beverly. *Alan Ladd: A Hollywood Tragedy.* New York: Berkley Books, 1979.

Lipsitz, George. *Time Passages.* Minneapolis: University of Minnesota Press, 1990.

List, Christine. "Chicano Images: Strategies for Ethnic Self-Representation in Mainstream Cinema." Ph.D. diss., Northwestern University, 1992.

_____. "*El Norte:* Ideology and Immigration." *Jump Cut* 34 (March 1989): 27-31.

_____. "Self-Directed Stereotyping in the Films of Cheech Marín." In *Chicanos and Film: Essays on Chicano Representation and Resistance,* ed. Chon A. Noriega, 205-18. New York: Garland Publishing Co., 1992.

Livingston, Don. *Film and the Director.* New York: Macmillan, 1953.

Lizalde, Eduardo. *Luis Buñuel.* Mexico City: UNAM, Dirección General de Difusión Cultural, 1962.

Llano, Tod. "Movie Maze: How Hispanic Films Make It to the Big Screen." *Hispanic,* July 1995, 22-26.

Lloyd, Ann, ed. *Movies of the Silent Years.* London: Orbis, 1984.

Lloyd, Harold. *An American Comedy.* New York: Longman, Green, 1928. Reprint, with an introduction by Richard Griffith, New York: Dover Publications, 1971.

Lomas, H. M. *Picture Play Photography.* London: Ganes, 1914.

Long, Robert. *David Wark Griffith: A Brief Sketch of His Career.* New York: D. W. Griffith Services, 1920.

Loos, Anita. *Cast of Thousands.* New York: Grosset & Dunlap, 1927.

_____. *A Girl Like I.* New York: Viking Press, 1966.

_____. *Kiss Hollywood Goodbye.* New York: Viking Press, 1974.

_____, *The Talmadge Girls: A Memoir.* New York: Viking Press, 1978.

López, Ana M. "Are All Latins from Manhattan? Hollywood, Ethnography, and Cultural Colonialism." In *Unspeakable Images: Ethnicity and the American Cinema,* ed. Lester D. Friedman, 404-24. Urbana: University of Illinois Press, 1991.

_____. "Celluloid Tears: Melodrama in the 'Old' Mexican Cinema." *Iris* 13 (summer 1991): 29-52.

_____. "The Melodrama in Latin America: Films, Telenovelas and the Currency of a Popular Form." *Wide Angle* 7, no. 3 (1985): 8.

_____. "The 'Other' Island: Cuban Cinema in Exile." *Jump Cut* 38 (June 1993): 51-59.

_____. "Setting the Stage: A Decade of Latin American Film Scholarship." *Quarterly Review of Film and Video* 13, nos. 1-3 (1991).

López, Oliva M. "Proyección chicana en *Raíces de Sangre.*" *Cine Cubano* 100 (1981): 75-80.

Lott, Tommy L. "A No-Theory Theory of Contemporary Black Cinema." *Black American Literature Forum* 25 (summer 1991): 221-36.

Lottman, Herbert R. *The Left Bank: Writers, Artists, and Politics from the Popular Front to the Cold War.* Boston: Houghton Mifflin Co., 1982.

Loughney, Patrick G. "A Descriptive Analysis of the Library of Congress Paper Print Collection and Related Copyright Records." Ph.D. diss., George Washington University, 1988.

_____. "In the Beginning Was the Word: Six Pre-Griffith Motion Picture Scenarios." *Iris* 2 (spring 1984): 17-32.

_____. "Still Images in Motion: The Influence of Photography on Motion Pictures in the Early Silent Period." In *The Art of Moving Shadows,* ed. Annette Michelson et al., 31-47. Washington, DC: National Gallery of Art, 1989.

Lounsbury, Myron. *The Origins of American Film Criticism, 1909-1939.* New York: Arno Press, 1973.

Lovelace, Linda, with Mike McGrady. *Out of Bondage.* Secaucus, NJ: Lyle Stuart, 1986.

Lovell, Glenn. "Hispanic Film's Brutality Stirs Praise, Outrage." *San Jose Mercury News,* 29 February, 1992, 1+.

_____. "Stand Out and Deliver: Edward James Olmos Commits Himself to a Tough Look at Life's Imprisonment." *San Jose Mercury News,* Eye Weekly Entertainment Guide, 13 March 1992, 12.

Low, Rachel. *The History of the British Film, 1906-1914.* London: Allen & Unwin, 1948.

_____, *The History of the British Film, 1914-1918.* London: Allen & Unwin, 1950.

_____. *The History of the British Film, 1918-1929.* London: Allen & Unwin, 1971.

Low, Rachel, and Roger Manvell. *The History of the British Film, 1896-1906.* London: Allen & Unwin, 1948.

Lowrey, Carolyn. *The First One Hundred Noted Men and Women of the Screen.* New York: Moffat, Yard, 1920.

Lozoya, Jorge Alberto, ed. *Cine mexicano.* Barcelona: Lunwerg Editores and Instituto Mexicano de Cinematografía, 1992.

Luhr, William. *Raymond Chandler and Film.* New York: Frederick Ungar Publishing, 1982.

_____. "The Scarred Woman behind the Gun: Gender, Race, and History in Recent Westerns." *Bilingual Review/ Revista Bilingüe* 20, no. 1 (Jan.-April 1995): 37-44.

Lund, Karen C., comp. *American Indians in Silent Film: Motion Pictures in the Library of Congress.* Mimeographed manuscript. Library of Congress, August 1992 (updated April 1995).

Lutz, E. G. *Animated Cartoons.* New York: Scribner's, 1920.

_____. *The Motion-Picture Cameraman.* New York: Scribner's, 1927. Reprint, New York: Arno Press, 1972.

Lynn, Kenneth J. "The Torment of D. W. Griffith." *American Scholar,* spring 1990, 255-64.

Lyon, Christopher, ed. *The International Dictionary of Films and Filmmakers.* Chicago: St. James Press, 1984.

Lyons, Timothy. *Charles Chaplin: A Guide to References and Resources.* Boston: G. K. Hall & Co., 1979.

_____. *The Silent Partner: The History of the American Film Manufacturing Company, 1910-1921.* New York: Arno Press, 1974.

Lytton, Grace. *Scenario Writing Today.* Boston: Houghton Mifflin Co., 1921.

MacBean, James Roy. *Film and Revolution.* Bloomington: Indiana University Press, 1975.

McBride, Joseph. *Frank Capra: The Catastrophe of Success.* New York: Simon & Schuster, 1992.

_____. *Orson Welles.* New York: Viking Press, 1972.

McBride, Joseph, and Michael Wilmington. *John Ford.* New York: DaCapo Press, 1975.

McCaffrey, Donald W. *Focus on Chaplin.* Englewood Cliffs, NJ: Prentice-Hall, 1971.

MacCann, Richard Dyer. *The First Film Makers.* Metuchen, NJ: Scarecrow Press, 1989.

_____. *Hollywood in Transition.* Boston: Houghton Mifflin Co., 1962.

_____. "The Independent Producer: Independence with a Vengeance." *Film Quarterly* 15 (summer 1962): 14-21.

_____. *The People's Films: A Political History of U.S. Government Motion Pictures.* New York: Hastings House, 1973.

MacCann, Richard Dyer, and Ted Perry, eds. *The New Film Index.* New York: E. P. Dutton, 1975.

McCarthy, Todd, and Charles Flynn. *Kings of the Bs: Working within the Hollywood System.* New York: E. P. Dutton, 1975.

McCarty, Clifford. "Filmusic for Silents." *Films in Review* 8, no. 3 (March 1957): 117-18, 123.

_____. "Filmusic Librarian." *Films in Review* 3, no. 5 (June-July 1957): 292-93.

McCarty, John. *The Complete Films of John Huston.* New York: Citadel Press, 1990.

McClelland, Doug. *The Golden Age of the B Movies.* New York: Bonanza Books, 1981.

_____. *Hollywood on Hollywood.* Boston: Faber and Faber, 1985.

McClure, Arthur F., and Ken D. Jones. *Heroes, Heavies and Sagebrush.* New York: A. S. Barnes, 1972.

McCormick, Ruth. "*Salt of the Earth* Revisited." *Cineaste* 5 (fall 1972): 53-55.

McDonald, Archie P., ed. *Shooting Stars.* Bloomington: Indiana University Press, 1987.

MacDonald, J. Fred. *Who Shot the Sheriff? The Rise and Fall of the Television Western.* New York: Praeger, 1987.

McDonald, Gerald D., Michael Conway, and Mark Ricci. *The Films of Charlie Chaplin.* New York: Bonanza Books, 1977.

McGee, Mark Thomas. *Fast and Furious: The Story of American International Pictures.* Jefferson, NC: McFarland & Co., 1984.

McGee, Mark Thomas, and R. J. Robertson. *The J.D. Films.* Jefferson, NC: McFarland & Co., 1982.

McGilligan, Pat. *Backstory: Interviews with Screenwriters of Hollywood's Golden Age.* Berkeley: University of California Press, 1986.

Macgowan, Kenneth. *Behind the Screen.* New York: Delacorte Press, 1965.

Macgowan, Kenneth, and William Melnitz. *The Living Stage: A History of the World Theater.* Englewood Cliffs, NJ: Prentice-Hall, 1955.

Maciel, David R. *El bandolero, el pocho, y la raza: Imágenes cinematográficas del chicano.* Mexico City: Cuadernos Americanos/UNAM, 1994.

_____. "Braceros, Mojados, and Alambristas: Mexican Immigration to the United States in Contemporary Cinema." *Hispanic Journal of Behavioral Sciences* 8 (1986): 369-85.

_____. *The Celluloid Frontier: The U.S.-Mexico Border in Contemporary Cinema, 1970-1988.* Renato Rosaldo Lecture Series Monograph, no. 5, 1987-88. Tucson: University of Arizona, Center for Mexican American Studies, 1989, 1-34.

_____. "The Cinematic Renaissance of Contemporary Mexico, 1985-1992." *Spectator* 13, no. 1 (fall 1992).

_____. "Latino Cinema." In *Handbook of Hispanic Cultures in the United States: Literature and Art,* ed. Francisco Lomelí,

312-32. Houston: Arte Público Press and Instituto de Cooperación Iberoamericana, 1993.

————. *El Norte: The U.S.-Mexican Border in Contemporary Cinema.* San Diego, CA: San Diego State University, Institute for Regional Studies of the Californias, 1990.

————. *La otra cara de México: el pueblo chicano.* Mexico City: Ediciones "El Caballito," 1977.

McMillan, Terry, and others. *The Films of Spike Lee: Five for Five.* New York: Stewart, Tabori & Chang, 1991.

McVay, Douglas. *The Musical Film.* New York: A. S. Barnes, 1967.

McWilliams, Carey. *Southern California: An Island on the Land.* 1946. Reprint, Santa Barbara, CA: Peregrine Smith, 1973.

Madrid, Francisco. *Cincuenta años de cine: Crónica del séptimo arte.* Buenos Aires: Ediciones del Tridente, 1964.

Madsen, Axel. *William Wyler.* New York: Crowell, 1973.

Maffer, Sergio. "México en tres niveles." *Cine Cubano,* nos. 63-65 (1970).

Magaña Esquivel, Antonio. *'El Cine', México, cincuenta años de revolución.* Mexico City: Fondo de Cultura Económica, 1962.

Magill, Frank N., ed. *Magill's Survey of Cinema. Silent Films.* Englewood Cliffs, NJ: Salem Press, 1982.

Magliozzi, Ron, ed. *Treasures from the Film Archives: A Catalog of Short Silent Fiction Film Held by FIAF Archives.* Metuchen, NJ: Scarecrow Press, 1988. [A publication of the Fédération Internationale des Archives du Film.]

Mahieu, Agustín. *Breve historia del cine nacional, 1896-1974.* Buenos Aires: Alzamor Editores, 1976.

Mair, George. *Inside HBO.* New York: Dodd, Mead and Co., 1988.

Malthête, Jacques, ed. *Le Voyage autour du monde de la G. Méliès Manufacturing Company.* Paris: Association "Les Amis de Georges Méliès," 1988.

Malthête-Méliès, Madeleine, ed. *Méliès et la naissance au spectacle cinématographique.* Paris: Meridiens Klincksieck, 1984.

Maltin, Leonard. *The Art of the Cinematographer: A Survey and Interviews with Five Masters.* Rev. ed., New York: Dover Publications, 1978.

————. *The Disney Films.* New York: Crown Publishers, 1973.

————. *Leonard Maltin's Movie Encyclopedia.* New York: Penguin, 1994.

————. *Leonard Maltin's Movie and Video Guide.* 1996 edition. New York: Penguin, 1995.

————, ed. *Hollywood: The Movie Factory.* New York: Popular Library, 1976.

Manchel, Frank. *Film Study: A Resource Guide.* Rutherford, NJ: Fairleigh Dickinson University Press, 1973.

Manchell, Fred. *Cameras West.* Englewood Cliffs, NJ: Prentice-Hall, 1971.

Manvell, Roger. *The Film and the Public.* Baltimore: Penguin Books, 1955.

————. *Shakespeare and the Film.* South Brunswick, NJ: A. S. Barnes and Co., 1979.

————. *Theater and Film.* Rutherford, NJ: Fairleigh Dickinson University Press, 1979.

Manvell, Roger, and John Huntley. *The Technique of Film Music.* London: Focal Press, 1957.

Mapp, Edward. *Blacks in American Films: Today and Yesterday.* Metuchen, NJ: Scarecrow Press, 1972.

Marchetti, Gina. *Romance and the "Yellow Peril": Race, Sex, and Discursive Strategies in Hollywood Fiction.* Berkeley: University of California Press, 1994.

Marcossan, Isaac F., and Daniel Frohman. *Charles Frohman: Manager and Man.* New York: Harper and Brothers, 1916.

Marcuse, Herbert. *The Aesthetic Dimension: Toward a Critique of Marxist Aesthetics.* Boston: Beacon, 1978.

"María Montez in *Arabian Nights.* She Does the Dance of the Single Veil." *Life,* 28 December 1942.

Marion, Frances. *How to Write and Sell Film Stories.* New York: Covici-Friede, 1937.

————. *Off with Their Heads: A Serio-Comic Tale of Hollywood.* New York: Macmillan, 1972.

Marrill, Alvin H. *The Films of Anthony Quinn.* Secaucus, NJ: Citadel Press, 1975.

————. *Samuel Goldwyn Presents.* South Brunswick, NJ, and New York: A. S. Barnes and Co., 1976.

Marsh, Mae. *Screen Acting.* Los Angeles: Photo-Star Publishing Co., 1921.

Martin, Laura. "Language Form and Language Function in *Zoot Suit* and *The Border:* A Contribution to the Analysis of the Role of Foreign Language in Film." *Studies in Latin American Popular Culture* 3 (1984): 57-69.

Martin, Mick, and Marsha Porter. *Video Movie Guide 1996.* New York: Ballantine Books, 1995.

Martin, Olga J. *Hollywood's Movie Commandments: A Handbook for Motion Picture Writers and Reviewers.* New York: Wilson, 1937.

Martínez, Eliud. "*I Am Joaquín* as Poem and Film: Two Modes of Chicano Expression." *Journal of Popular Culture* 13 (spring 1980): 505-15.

Martínez, Josefina. *Los primeros veinticinco años de cine en Madrid, 1896-1920.* Madrid: Filmoteca Española, 1992.

Martínez, Max. "Who Is That Sweetback and Why Is He Carrying That Terrible Thing?" *Magazin* 1, no. 3 (December 1971): 61-62, 72.

Martínez, Thomas M. "Advertising and Racism: The Case of the Mexican American." *El Grito: A Journal of Contemporary Mexican-American Thought* 2, no. 4 (summer 1969): 3-13.

Martínez, Walter. "Our Man in Hollywood—Cheech Marín." *Latin Style,* August 1994, 31-34.

Martínez Carril, Manuel. "*Raíces de sangre,* Jesús Treviño." In *Antología del cine latinoamericano,* 160-65. Valladolid, Spain: Semana Internacional de Cine de Valladolid, 1991.

Martínez de Flask Vélez, Patricia. *Directores de cine. Proyección de un mundo oscuro.* Mexico City: Instituto Mexicano de Cinematografía y CONEICC, 1991.

Martínez Pardo, Hernando. *Historia del cine colombiano.* Bogotá, Columbia: Editorial América Latina, 1978.

Martínez Torres, Augusto, and Manuel Pérez Estremera. *Nuevo cine latinoamericano.* Barcelona: Editorial Anagrama, 1973.

Marx, Arthur. *Goldwyn: A Biography of the Man behind the Myth.* New York: W. W. Norton & Co., 1976.

Marx, Groucho. *Groucho and Me.* New York: Random House, 1959.

Marx, Harpo, with Roland Barber. *Harpo Speaks.* New York: Bernard Geis, 1961.

Marx, Samuel. *A Gaudy Spree: Literary Hollywood When the West Was Fun.* New York: Franklin Watts, 1987.

_____. "The Last Writes of the 'Eminent Authors.'" *Los Angeles Times,* 12 March 1977, 3.

_____. *Mayer and Thalberg: The Make-Believe Saints.* New York: Random House, 1975.

Maslin, Janet. "Charting Generations of East L.A.'s Gangs." Review of *American Me. New York Times,* 13 March 1992.

Massoud, Paula J. "Mapping the Hood: The Genealogy of City Space in *Boyz N the Hood* and *Menace II Society." Cinema Journal* 35, no. 2 (winter 1996): 85-97.

Mast, Gerald. *'Can't Help Singin': The American Musical on Stage and Screen.* Woodstock, NY: Overlook Press, 1987.

_____. *The Comic Mind: Comedy and the Movies.* 2nd ed. Chicago: University of Chicago Press, 1979.

_____. "Film History and Film Histories." *Quarterly Review of Film Studies* 1 (Aug. 1976): 297-314.

_____. *Howard Hawks, Storyteller.* New York: Oxford University Press, 1982.

_____. *A Short History of the Movies.* 4th ed. New York: Macmillan, 1986.

_____, ed. *The Movies in Our Midst: Documents in the Cultural History of Film in America.* Chicago: University of Chicago Press, 1982.

Mast, Gerald, and Marshall Cohn, eds. *Film Theory and Criticism.* 3rd ed. New York: Oxford University Press, 1985.

Matthews, Leonard. *History of Western Movies.* New York: Crescent Books, 1984.

May, Lary Linden. *Screening Out the Past: The Birth of Mass Culture and the Motion Picture Industry.* New York: Oxford University Press, 1974.

Mayer, Michael F. *Foreign Films on American Screens.* New York: Arco, 1964.

Maynard, Richard A., ed. *The American West on Film: Myth and Reality.* Rochelle Park, NJ: Hayden Book Co., 1974.

_____, ed. *The Black Man on Film: Racial Stereotyping.* Rochelle Park, NJ: Hayden Book Co., 1974.

Mayne, Judith. "Immigrants and Spectators." *Wide Angle* 5, no. 3 (1982): 32-40.

Mehr, Linda, ed. *Motion Pictures, Television, and Radio: A Union Catalogue of Manuscript and Special Collections in the Western United States.* Boston: G. K. Hall & Co., 1977.

Mejías-Rentas, Antonio. "Latinos Prominent in New Movie Releases." *Nuestro* 9, no. 1 (Jan.-Feb. 1985): 43-44.

Mejías-Rentas, Antonio, and Armando Nevárez. "Life after *La Bamba:* When Will Hollywood Give Stories and Actors a Chance to Shine?" *Hispanic Business,* July 1993, 18-24.

Mekas, Adolfas. "A Letter from Mexico." *Film Culture* 20 (1959).

Mellen, Joan, ed. *The World of Luis Buñuel.* New York: Oxford University Press, 1978.

Menard, Valerie. "An American Tale" [on *Mi Familia*]. *Hispanic,* May 1995, 28-30.

_____. "Color in Latin" [on John Leguizamo]. *Hispanic,* May 1995, 16-18.

Méndez, José Carlos. "Cine mexicano: Utopía y realidad." *Plural* 127 (April 1982).

_____. "Mexican Cinema: A Panoramic View." *Film Quarterly* 18 (summer 1965).

Méndez Leite, Fernando. *Historia del cine español.* Madrid: Ediciones Rialp, 1965.

Mendoza, Rick. "Is Hollywood Finally Coming Around?" *Hispanic Business,* July 1994, 16-20.

Mercer, Jane. *Great Lovers of the Movies.* London: Hamlyn Publishing Group, 1975.

Merman, Ethel, as told to Pete Martin. *Who Can Ask for Anything More.* New York: Doubleday, 1955.

Merritt, Russell. "Dixon, Griffith, and the Southern Legend." *Cinema Journal* 12 (fall 1972): 26-45.

_____. "The Impact of D. W. Griffith's Motion Pictures from 1908 to 1915 on Contemporary American Culture." Ph.D. diss., Harvard University, 1970.

_____. "Nickelodeon Theaters, 1905-1914: Building an Audience for the Movies." In *The American Film Industry,* ed. Tino Balio. Madison: University of Wisconsin Press, 1985.

Merritt, Russell, and J. B. Kaufman. *Walt in Wonderland: The Silent Films of Walt Disney.* Gemona, Italy: Le Giornate del Cinema Muto/La Cineteca del Friuli, 1993; distributed by Johns Hopkins Press.

Metz, Christian. *Film Language: A Semiotics of the Cinema.* Trans. Michael Taylor. New York: Oxford University Press, 1974.

_____. *The Imaginary Signifier: Psychoanalysis and the Cinema.* Trans. Celia Britton et al. Bloomington: Indiana University Press, 1982.

"Mexico Bars Any Film of Charlie's [Chaplin] or Doug's [Fairbanks], Punishing for Kidding Country in Past Pictures." *Motion Picture World,* 27 January 1923.

Meyer, Doris L. "Early Mexican American Responses to Negative Stereotyping." *New Mexico Historical Review* 53, no. 1 (1978).

Meyer, Eugenia, coord. *Testimonios para la historia del cine mexicano.* 8 vols. Mexico City: Dirección de Cinematografía de la Secretaría de Gobernación, 1976.

Meyer, William R. *The Making of the Great Westerns.* New Rochelle, NY: Arlington House, 1979.

Michel, Manuel. *Al pie de la imagen: Críticas y ensayos.* Mexico City: UNAM, Dirección General de Difusión Cultural, 1968.

_____. *El cine y el hombre contemporáneo.* Xalapa, Mexico: Universidad Veracruzana, 1962.

_____. "Mexican Cinema: A Panoramic View." *Film Quarterly* 18, no. 4, (1965): 46-65.

Michener, Charles. "Black Movies." *Newsweek* 80 (23 October 1972): 74.

Millard, André. *Edison and the Business of Innovation.* Baltimore: Johns Hopkins University Press, 1990.

Miller, Clyde. "Filmmakers in Churubusco." *Américas,* April 1974, 15-20.

Miller, Don. *"B" Movies.* New York: Curtis Books, 1973.

_____. *Hollywood Corral.* New York: Popular Library, 1976.

_____. *Hollywood Corral.* Revised and updated by Packy Smith and Ed Hulse. Burbank, CA: Riverwood Press, 1993.

Miller, Jim. "Chicano Cinema: An Interview with Jesús Treviño." *Cineaste* 8, no. 3 (1978).

Miller, Lee O. *The Great Cowboy Stars of Movies and Television.* New Rochelle, NY: Arlington House, 1979.

Miller, Mark Crispin. *Boxed In: The Culture of Television.* Evanston, IL: Northwestern University Press, 1988.

_____. "In Defense of Sam Peckinpah." *Film Quarterly* 28 (spring 1975): 2-17.

Miller, Randall M., ed. *Ethnic Images in American Film and Television.* Philadelphia: Balch Institute, 1978.

———, ed. *The Kaleidoscopic Lens: How Hollywood Views Ethnic Groups.* Englewood, NJ: Jerome S. Ozer, 1980.

Miller, Tom. "Salt of the Earth Revisited." *Cineaste* 13, no. 3 (1984): 31-36.

Milne, Peter. *Motion Picture Directing: The Facts and Theories of the Newest Art.* New York: Falk, 1922.

Milne, Tom. *Losey on Losey.* Garden City, NY: Doubleday & Co., 1968.

Mindiola, Tatcho, Jr. "*El corrido de Gregorio Cortez*: The Challenge of Conveying Chicano Culture through the Cinematic Treatment of a Folk Hero." *Tonantzín* 4, no. 1 (November 1986): 14-15.

———. "Film Critique: *The Ballad of Gregorio Cortez.*" *La Red/The Net,* no. 80 (May 1984): 11-17. Rpt. in *Southwest Media Review* 3 (1985): 52-56, and *Tonantzín* 4, no. 1 (November 1986): 14-15.

Mintz, Marilyn D. *The Martial Arts Films.* Rutland, VT: Charles E. Tuttle and Co., 1983.

Mistron, Deborah E. "A Hybrid Subgenre: The Revolutionary Melodrama in the Mexican Cinema." *Studies in Latin American Popular Culture* 3 (1984): 47-56.

———. "Re-evaluating the Revolution: Mexican Cinema of the Echeverría Administration (1970-1976)." *Studies in Latin American Popular Culture* 4 (1985): 218-27.

———. "The Role of Pancho Villa in the Mexican and the American Cinema." *Studies in Latin American Popular Culture* 2 (1983): 1-13.

Mitchell, Alice M. *Children and Movies.* Chicago, IL: University of Chicago Press, 1929.

Mitchell, C. H., ed. *Assistant Director's Compendium.* Hollywood: Jesse L. Lasky Feature Play Co., April 1916.

Mitchell, George. "Sidney Olcott." *Films in Review* 5 (1954): 175-81.

Mitchell, Lofton. *Black Drama: The Story of the American Negro in Theatre.* New York: Hawthorn Books, 1967.

Mitry, Jean. *Bibliographie internationale du cinéma et de la télevision.* Vol. 7, *Espagne et pays de langue espagnole et portugaise.* Paris: Institut des Hautes Études Cinématographiques, 1968.

———. *Esthétique et psychologie du cinéma.* 2 vols. Paris: Éditions Universitaires, 1966.

———. *Histoire de cinéma: Art et industrie.* Vol. 1, 1895-1914. Paris: Éditions Universitaires, 1967.

Mix, Paul E. *The Life and Legend of Tom Mix.* South Brunswick, NJ: A. S. Barnes and Co., 1972.

Moews, Daniel. *Keaton: The Silent Features Close Up.* Berkeley: University of California Press, 1976.

Moley, Raymond. *The Hays Office.* Indianapolis: Bobbs-Merrill, 1945.

Monaco, James, et al. *The Encyclopedia of Film.* New York: Perigee Books, 1991.

Monaco, Paul. *Ribbons in Time: Movies and Society Since 1945.* Bloomington: Indiana University Press, 1987.

Monaghan, Jay. *The Great Rascal: The Life and Adventures of Ned Buntline.* Boston: Little, Brown, 1952.

Monroy, Douglas. " 'Our Children Get So Different Here': Film, Fashion, Popular Culture and the Process of Cultural Syncretization in Mexican Los Angeles, 1900-1935." *Aztlán, A Journal of Chicano Studies* 19, no. 1 (spring 1988-90): 79-108.

Monsiváis, Carlos. *Amor perdido.* Mexico City: Ediciones Era, 1977.

———. "Cantinflas: de la esencia popular al moralismo pedagógico." *Prensa Hispana,* 17 June 1993, 2, 6, 8-9. First published in *Proceso,* no. 860 (26 April 1993).

———. "El cine nacional." In *Historia general de México.* Vol. 4. Mexico City: El Colegio de México, 1976.

———. "The Culture of the Frontier: The Mexican Side." In *Views Across the Border: The United States and Mexico,* ed. Stanley R. Ross. Albuquerque: University of New Mexico Press, 1978.

———. "De México y los chicanos, de México y su cultura fronteriza." In *La otra cara de México: el pueblo chicano,* ed. David R. Maciel, 1-19. Mexico City: Ediciones "El Caballito," 1977.

———. "Discovering Images: Establishing Point of View." Trans. Roberto Tejada. *Artes de Méjico* 2 (winter 1988).

———. *Escenas de pudor y liviandad.* Mexico City: Editorial Grijalbo, 1988.

———. "El fin de la diosa arrodillada." *Nexos,* February 1992.

———. " 'Landscape, I've Got the Drop on You!': On the Fiftieth Anniversary of Sound Film in Mexico." Trans. Julianne Burton and Manuel Rivas. *Studies in Latin American Popular Culture* 4 (1985).

———. "¡Órale, arriba! de Speedy González a don Juan." *La cultura en México,* supplement of *Siempre,* 7 Feb. 1979.

———. "Ya veo salir a Speedy González: México, ¿nación de chicanos?" *El Financiero,* 22 June 1990, 74.

Montagu, Ivor. *Con Eisenstein en Hollywood.* Mexico City: Ediciones Era, 1976.

———. *With Eisenstein in Hollywood.* New York: International Publishers, 1976.

Montoya, José. "Thoughts on la cultura: The Media, Con Safos and Survival." *Caracol* 5, no. 9 (May 1979): 6-8, 19.

Moore, Colleen. *Silent Star.* New York: Doubleday, 1968.

Moore, Daniel S. " '95 Watershed for Latinos in Hollywood." *Variety,* 27 March-2 April 1995, 43+.

Mora, Carl J. "Alejandro Galindo: Pioneer Mexican Filmmaker." *Journal of Popular Culture* 18, no. 1 (summer 1984): 101-12.

———. "Feminine Images in Mexican Cinema: The Family Melodrama; Sara García 'The Mother of Mexico'; and the Prostitute." *Studies in Latin American Popular Culture* 4 (1985): 228-35.

———. "Mexican Cinema in the 1970s." In *Mexican Art of the 1970s.* Ed. Leonard Folgarait. Nashville, TN: Vanderbilt University, Center for Latin American and Iberian Studies, 1984.

———. *Mexican Cinema: Reflections of a Society, 1896-1980.* Rev. ed. Berkeley: University of California Press, 1989.

———. "Mexico's Commercial Films: Sources for the Study of Social History." *PCCLAS Proceedings* 6 (1977-79).

———. "Spain's Cinema of the 'Autonomies.'" *New Orleans Review* 13, no. 2 (summer 1986): 32-42.

———. "The Odyssey of Spanish Cinema." *New Orleans Review* 14, no. 1 (spring 1987): 7-20.

Morales, Miguel Ángel. *Cómicos de México.* Mexico City: Panorama Editorial, 1987.

Morales, Sylvia. "Filming a Chicana Documentary." *Somos* 2, no. 3 (June 1979): 42-45.

Morán, Julio. "Films: Chicanos in a New Era." *Somos* 2, no. 3 (March 1979): 12-15.

Mordden, Ethan. *The Hollywood Studios: House Style in the Golden Age of the Movies.* New York: Alfred A. Knopf, 1988.

_____. *Movie Star: A Look at the Women Who Made Hollywood.* New York: St. Martin's Press, 1983.

Morella, Joe, and Edward Z. Epstein. *The "It" Girl.* New York: Delacorte Press, 1976.

Morin, Georges-Henri. *Le circle brisé: L'Image de l'Indien dans le Western.* Paris: Payot, 1977.

Morsberger, Robert E., ed. *Viva Zapata! (The Original Screenplay by John Steinbeck).* New York: Viking Press, 1975.

Morton, Carlos. "Motion Picture: *El Norte,* a Classic American Epic." *National Hispanic Journal* 3, no. 2 (spring-summer 1984): 23.

Mosley, Leonard. *Zanuck: The Rise and Fall of Hollywood's Last Tycoon.* Boston: Little, Brown, 1984.

Motion Pictures 1912-1939. Washington, DC: Library of Congress, Copyright Office, 1951.

Mott, Frank Luther. *Golden Multitudes: The Story of Best Sellers in the United States.* New York: Macmillan, 1947.

_____. *A History of American Magazines, 1885-1905.* Vols. 4-5. Cambridge, MA: Harvard University Press, 1957-68.

Mottet, Jean. *D. W. Griffith: Colloque international sous la direction de Jean Mottet.* Publications de la Sorbonne. Paris: Éditions L'Harmattan, 1984.

_____. *D. W. Griffith: Études sous la direction de Jean Mottet.* Publications de la Sorbonne. Paris: Éditions L'Harmattan, 1984.

Mould, David H. *American Newsfilm 1914-1919: The Underground War.* New York: Garland Publishing Co., 1983.

Moussinac, Leon. *Sergei Eisenstein.* New York: Crown Publishers, 1970.

Mull, Martin, and Allen Rucker. *The History of White People in America.* New York: G. P. Putnam's Sons, 1985.

Muñoz, Sergio, ed. "Cine chicano: primer acercamiento." *La Opinión* (Los Angeles), Suplemento Cultural no. 20, 16 November 1980, 1-15.

Munsterberg, Hugo. *The Photoplay: A Psychological Study.* New York: D. Appleton and Co., 1916.

Munsterberg, Margaret. *Hugo Munsterberg: His Life and Work.* New York: D. Appleton and Co., 1922.

Murillo, Fidel. "Dolores del Río se ha negado a filmar una cinta denigrante." *La Opinión* (Los Angeles), 24 May 1931.

Murray, James P. *To Find an Image: Black Films from Uncle Tom to Super Fly.* Indianapolis: Bobbs-Merrill Co., 1973.

Musser, Charles. "American Vitagraph, 1897-1901." *Cinema Journal* 22 (spring 1983): 4-46.

_____. *Before the Nickelodeon.* Berkeley: University of California Press, 1991.

_____. "The Early Cinema of Edwin S. Porter." *Cinema Journal* 19 (fall 1979): 1-38.

_____. *The Emergence of Cinema: The American Screen to 1907.* Vol. 1 of *History of the American Cinema,* Charles Harpole, gen. ed. New York: Charles Scribner's Sons, 1990.

_____. "Ethnicity, Role-playing, and American Film Comedy: From *Chinese Laundry Scene* to *Whoopee* (1894-1930)." In *Unspeakable Images: Ethnicity and the American Cinema,* ed. Lester D. Friedman, 39-81. Urbana: University of Illinois Press, 1991.

_____. *A Guide to "Motion Picture Catalogs by American Producers and Distributors, 1894-1908: A Microfilm Edition."* Frederick, MD: University Publications of America, 1985.

_____. "The Nickelodeon Era Begins: Establishing the Framework for Hollywood's Mode of Representation." In *Early Cinema: Space/Frame/Narrative,* ed. Thomas Elsaesser. London: British Film Institute, 1990.

_____. *Thomas A. Edison and His Kinetographic Motion Pictures.* New Brunswick, NJ: Rutgers University Press, 1995.

_____. "The Travel Genre in 1903-4: Moving Toward Fictional Narrative." *Iris* 2 (spring 1984): 47-60.

_____, ed. *Motion Picture Catalogs by American Producers and Distributors 1894-1908: A Microfilm Edition.* Frederick, MD: Thomas A. Edison Papers, 1985.

Musser, Charles, with Carol Nelson. *High Class Motion Pictures: Lyman H. Howe and the Traveling Exhibitor.* Princeton, NJ: Princeton University Press, 1989.

"Must Talkies Stay at Home?" *Literary Digest,* 29 December 1930.

Muwakkil, Salim. "Spike Lee and the Image Police." *Cineaste* 17, no. 4 (1988), 48.

Myerson, Michael, ed. *Memories of Underdevelopment: The Revolutionary Films of Cuba.* New York: Grossman Publishers, 1973.

"Myrtle González Dead." *Los Angeles Times,* 23 October 1918, sec. 2, 1.

Nachbar, Jack. *Western Films: An Annotated Critical Bibliography.* New York: Garland Publishing Co., 1975.

_____, ed. *Focus on the Western.* Englewood Cliffs, NJ: Prentice-Hall, 1974.

Naficy, Hamid. "Exile Discourse and Televisual Fetishization." *Quarterly Review of Film and Video* 13, nos. 1-3 (1991): 85-116.

Naremore, James. *The Magic World of Orson Welles.* New York: Oxford University Press, 1978.

Nash, Jay Robert, and Stanley Ralph Ross. *The Motion Picture Guide.* Vols. 1-12. New York: R. R. Bowker Co., 1987. Succeeding guides published annually.

National Film Archive Catalogue: Silent Fiction Films, 1895-1930. London: British Film Institute, 1966.

Naumberg, Nancy, ed. *We Make the Movies.* New York: W. W. Norton and Co., 1937.

Navarro, Ray, and Catherine Saalfield. "Not Just Black and White." *The Independent,* July 1989, 18-23.

Naylor, David. *American Picture Palaces.* New York: Van Nostrand Reinhold, 1981.

_____. *Great American Movie Theaters.* Washington, DC: Preservation Press, 1987.

Neale, Steve. *Genre.* London: British Film Institute, 1980.

_____. "Questions of Genre." *Screen* 31, no. 1 (spring 1990): 46.

Negri, Pola. *Memories of a Star.* New York: Doubleday, 1970.

Negrón-Muntaner, Frances. "Making Films in the Puerto Rican Community." *Centro de Estudios Puertorriqueños Bulletin* 3, no. 1 (winter 1990-91): 81-85.

Nelson, John. *The Photo-Play.* Los Angeles: Photoplay Publishing Co., 1913.

Nelson, Richard Alan. *Florida and the American Motion Picture Industry 1898-1980.* New York: Garland Publishing Co., 1983.

Nericcio, William Anthony. "Autobiographies at la Frontera: The Quest for Mexican-American Narrative." *The Americas Review* 16, nos. 3-4 (1988): 165-87.

_____. "Of Mestizos and Half-Breeds: Orson Welles's *Touch of Evil*." In *Chicanos and Film: Essays on Chicano Representation and Resistance,* ed. Chon A. Noriega, 189-204. New York: Garland Publishing Co., 1992.

Nesteby, James R. *Black Images in American Films, 1896-1954.* Washington, DC: University Press of America, 1982.

Newman, Kathleen. " 'Based on a True Story': Reaffirming Chicano History." *Tonantzín* 7, no. 1 (Jan.-Feb. 1990): 16, 19.

_____. "Latin American Cinema in North American Film Scholarship." *Iris* 13 (summer 1991): 1-4.

_____. "Steadfast Love and Subversive Acts: The Politics of *La ofrenda: The Days of the Dead*." *Spectator* 13, no. 1 (fall 1992).

Newman, Kim. *Wild West Movies.* London: Bloomsbury Publishing, 1990.

Newton, Esther. *Mother Camp: Female Impersonators in America.* Chicago: University of Chicago Press, 1972.

Newton, Huey P. "He Won't Bleed Me: A Revolutionary Analysis of 'Sweet Sweetback's Baadasssss Song.' " *Black Panther* 6 (19 June 1971): A-L.

The New York Times Directory of the Film. Introd. Arthur Knight. New York: Arno Press/Random House, 1971.

The New York Times Encyclopedia of Film. Ed. Gene Brown. New York: Times Books, 1984.

The New York Times Film Reviews, 1913-1994. 19 vols. New York: The New York Times, 1971–. [Available through Garland Publishing Co., New York.]

The New York Times Theater Reviews, 1870-1994. 28 vols. New York: The New York Times, 1974–. [Available through Garland Publishing Co., New York.]

Nichols, Bill. *Ideology and the Image: Social Representation in the Cinema and Other Media.* Bloomington: Indiana University Press, 1981.

_____. *Representing Reality.* Bloomington: Indiana University Press, 1991.

_____, ed. *Movies and Methods.* Berkeley: University of California Press, 1976.

_____, ed. *Movies and Methods II.* Berkeley: University of California Press, 1985.

Nichols, Roger L. "The Indian in the Dime Novel." *Journal of American Culture* 5 (1982): 49-55.

Nicholson, Irene. "Mexican Films: Their Past and Future." *Quarterly of Film, Radio and Television* 10 (1955-56).

Nicoll, Allardyce. *Film and Theater.* New York: Crowell, 1936.

Nisbett, Alex. *The Technique of the Sound Studio.* New York: Hastings House, 1962.

Niver, Kemp R. *D. W. Griffith: His Biograph Films in Perspective.* Los Angeles: John D. Roche, 1974.

_____. *Early Motion Pictures: The Paper Print Collection in the Library of Congress.* Washington, DC: Library of Congress, 1985.

_____. *The First Twenty Years: A Segment of Film History.* Los Angeles: Artisan Press, 1968.

_____. *Klaw and Erlanger Present Famous Plays in Pictures.* Ed. Bebe Bergsten. Los Angeles: Locare Research Group, 1976.

_____. *Motion Pictures from the Library of Congress Paper Print Collection, 1894-1912.* Berkeley: University of California Press, 1967.

_____, ed. *Biograph Bulletins, 1896-1908.* Los Angeles: Locare Research Group, 1971.

Noble, Gil. *Black Is the Color of My TV Tube.* Secaucus, NJ: Lyle Stuart, 1981.

Noble, Peter. *Hollywood Scapegoat: The Biography of Erich von Stroheim.* London: Fortune Press, 1950.

_____. *The Negro in Film.* London: Skelton Robinson, 1948. Reprint, New York: Arno Press, 1970.

Noriega, Chon. " 'Above All Raza Must Speak': Chicano Cinema, 1969-1981." In *National Latino Film and Video Festival Catalogue.* New York: Museo del Barrio, 1991.

_____. "The Aesthetic Discourse: Reading Chicano Cinema Since *La Bamba*." *Centro de Estudios Puertorriqueños Bulletin* 3, no. 1 (winter 1990-91): 55-71.

_____. "Café Órale: Narrative Structure in *Born in East L.A.*" *Tonantzín* 8, no. 1 (February 1991): 17-18.

_____. "Chicano Cinema and the Horizon of Expectations: A Discursive Analysis of Film Reviews in the Mainstream, Alternative and Hispanic Press, 1987-1988." *Aztlán, A Journal of Chicano Studies* 19, no. 2 (fall 1988-90): 1-32.

_____. "Citizen Chicano: The Trials and Titillations of Ethnicity in the American Cinema, 1935-1962." *Social Research* 58, no. 2 (summer 1991): 413-38.

_____. "Essay." In "*Cine de Mestizaje*: The National Latino Film and Video Festival, 1991." Pamphlet, unpaginated. New York: El Museo del Barrio, 1991.

_____. "Godzilla and the Japanese Nightmare: When *Them!* Is U.S." *Cinema Journal* 27, no. 1 (fall 1987): 63-77.

_____. "El hilo latino: Representation, Identity, and National Culture." *Jump Cut* 38 (June 1993): 45-50.

_____. "In Aztlán: The Films of the Chicano Movement, 1969-79." *New American Film and Video Series* 56. Pamphlet no. 56, 9-27 January 1991. New York: Whitney Museum of American Art.

_____. "The Numbers Game." *Jump Cut* 39 (June 1994): 107-11.

_____. "Road to Aztlán: Chicanos and Narrative Cinema." Ph.D. diss., Stanford University, 1991.

_____. "Talking Heads, Body Politic: The Plural Self of Chicano Video." In *Resolutions: Contemporary Video Practices,* ed. Michael Renov and Erika Suderburg, 207-28. Minneapolis: University of Minnesota Press, 1996.

_____. "This Is Not a Border." *Spectator* 13, no. 1 (fall 1992): 6.

_____. " 'Waas Sappening?': Narrative Structure and Iconography in *Born in East L.A.*" *Studies in Latin American Popular Culture* 14 (1995): 107-28.

_____. "What Is Hispanic Cinema?" *Tonantzín* 7, no. 1 (January-February 1990): 18.

_____. *Working Bibliography of Critical Writings on Chicanos and Film.* Working Bibliography Series, no. 6. Stanford, CA: Stanford University Libraries, Mexican-American Collections, 1990.

_____, ed. "Border Crossings, Mexican and Chicano Cinema." Special edition. *Spectator* 13, no. 1 (fall 1992).

_____, ed. *Chicanos and Film: Essays on Chicano Representation and Resistance.* New York: Garland Publishing Co., 1992. Reprint, Minneapolis: University of Minnesota Press, 1992.

_____, ed. "U.S. Latinos and Media." Special edition. *Jump Cut,* no. 38 (June 1993).

Noriega, Chon, and Lillian Jiménez. "La indirecta directa: Two Decades of Chicano and Puerto Rican Film and Video." *New American Film and Video Series,* no. 61. New York: Whitney Museum of American Art, 1992.

Noriega, Chon, and Ana M. López, eds. *The Ethnic Eye: Latino Media Arts.* Minneapolis: University of Minnesota Press, 1996.

Noriega, Chon, and Steven Ricci, eds. *The Mexican Cinema Project.* Los Angeles: UCLA Film and Television Archive, 1994.

North, Joseph H. *The Early Development of the Motion Picture: 1887-1909.* New York: Arno Press, 1973.

Nuiry, Octavio Emilio. "The Hollywood-Washington Connection." *Hispanic,* October 1993, 15-22.

Null, Gary. *Black Hollywood: The Black Performer in Motion Pictures.* New York: Citadel Press, 1975.

Nunn, Curtis. *Marguerite Clark: America's Darling of Broadway and the Silent Screen.* Fort Worth: Texas Christian University Press, 1981.

Nye, Russel B. *The Unembarrassed Muse: The Popular Arts in America.* New York: Dial Press, 1970.

Oberfirst, Robert. *Valentino, the Man behind the Myth.* New York: Citadel Press, 1962.

Oberholtzer, Ellis Paxon. *The Morals of the Movie.* Philadelphia: Penn Publishing Co., 1922.

Ochling, Richard A. "Hollywood and the Image of the Oriental." *Film and Film History* 7 (May 1978).

O'Connor, John E. *The Hollywood Indian: Stereotypes of Native Americans in Film.* Trenton: New Jersey State Museum, 1980.

_____. "TV: *Seguín*: True Tale of the Texas Revolution." *New York Times,* 26 January 1982, Arts/Entertainment section.

O'Dell, Paul. *Griffith and the Rise of Hollywood.* New York: International Film Guide Series, 1970.

O'Dell, Scott. *Representative Photoplays Analyzed.* Hollywood: Palmer Institute of Authorship, 1924.

O'Hara, Kenneth. "The Life of Thomas H. Ince." *Photoplay,* June 1917, 34-47.

Okuda, Ted. *The Monogram Checklist: The Films of Monogram Pictures Corporation, 1931-1958.* Jefferson, NC: McFarland & Co., 1987.

O'Leary, Liam. *Rex Ingram: Master of the Silent Cinema.* Dublin: Academy Press, 1980. Reprint copublished by Le Giornate del Cinema Muto (Gemona, Italy) and British Film Institute, 1993.

_____. *The Silent Cinema.* New York: E. P. Dutton, 1965.

Olivares, Juan. Film review of *The Ballad of Gregorio Cortez. Metamorfosis* 4 (1982-83): 68-69.

Olivas, Michael A. "Of *Mestizaje,* Bricolage, and Tergiversators." *Bilingual Review/Revista Bilingüe* 20, no. 3 (Jan.-April 1995): 72-76.

_____. "Of Pachucos, Yeguas, Greasers, and Coffee and Eggs: Chicanos and Film Criticism." *Bilingual Review/Revista Bilingüe* 19, no. 1 (Jan.-April 1994): 75-77.

Oliver, María Rosa [Marie Rose]. "Cantinflas." *Hollywood Quarterly* 2 (1946-47).

_____. "The Native Films of Mexico." In *The Penguin Film Review.* London and New York: Penguin Books, 1948.

Olson, Stuart. *The Ethnic Dimension in American History.* New York: St. Martin's Press, 1979.

Onoski, Tim. "Monogram: Its Rise and Fall in the Forties." *Velvet Light Trap* 5 (summer 1972): 5-9.

Ordóñez, Elizabeth J. "La imagen de la mujer en el nuevo cine chicano." *Caracol* 5, no. 2 (October 1978): 12-13.

Orona-Córdova, Roberta. "*Zoot Suit* and the Pachuco Phenomenon: An Interview with Luis Valdez." *Revista Chicano-Riqueña* 11 (1983): 98-108.

Ortman, Marguerite G. *Fiction and the Screen.* Boston: Marshall Jones Co., 1935.

Osborne, Robert. *Fifty Golden Years of Oscar: The Official History of the Academy of Motion Picture Arts and Sciences.* La Habra, CA: ESE California Books, 1979.

Oseas Pérez, Joel. "*El Norte:* imágenes peyorativas de México y los chicanos." *Chiricú* 5, no. 1 (1987): 13-21.

Oshana, Maryann. *Women of Color: A Filmography of Minority and Third World Women.* New York: Garland Publishing Co., 1985.

Paine, Albert Bigelow. *Life and Lilian Gish.* New York: Macmillan, 1932.

Palmer, Frederick. *Photoplay Plot Encyclopedia: An Analysis of the Use in Photoplays of the Thirty-Six Dramatic Situations and Their Subdivisions.* 2nd ed., rev. Los Angeles: Palmer Photoplay, 1922.

_____. *Photoplay Writing Simplified and Explained.* Los Angeles: Palmer Photoplay Corporation, 1918.

Páramo, Bobby. "Silver Screening the Barrio." *Forum* 6, no. 1 (November 1978): 6-7.

Paredes, Américo. *"With His Pistol in His Hand": A Border Ballad and Its Hero.* Austin: University of Texas Press, 1958.

Paris, Barry. *Louise Brooks.* New York: Alfred A. Knopf, 1989.

Parish, James Robert. *Actors' Television Credits, 1950-1972.* Metuchen, NJ: Scarecrow Press, 1973.

_____. *The George Raft File.* New York: Drake Publishers, 1973.

_____. *Great Western Stars.* New York: Ace Books, 1976.

_____. *The MGM Stock Company.* New York: Bonanza Books, 1977.

_____. *The Paramount Pretties.* Secaucus, NJ: Castle Books, 1972.

_____. *The RKO Girls.* New Rochelle, NY: Arlington House, 1974.

_____, ed. *The Great Movie Series.* Cranbury, NJ: A. S. Barnes and Co., 1971.

Parish, James Robert, and George H. Hill. *Black Action Films.* London: McFarland & Co., 1989.

Parish, James Robert, and Michael R. Pitts. *The Great Western Pictures.* Metuchen, NJ: Scarecrow Press, 1976.

_____. *The Great Western Pictures II.* Metuchen, NJ: Scarecrow Press, 1988.

Parish, James Robert, and Gregory W. Mank. *The Hollywood Reliables.* Westport, CT: Arlington House Publishers, 1980.

Parish, James Robert, and Don E. Stanke. *Hollywood Baby Boomer.* New York: Garland Publishing Co., 1992.

Parkinson, Michael, and Clyde Jeavons. *A Pictorial History of Westerns.* London: Hamlyn, 1972.

Parks, Riat. *The Western Hero in Film and Television.* Ann Arbor, MI: UMI Research Press, 1982.

Parsons, Louella. *How to Write for the "Movies."* Chicago, IL: A. C. McClurg and Co., 1915.

Pastor Legnani, Margarita, and Rosario Vico de Peña. *Filmografía uruguaya.* Montevideo, Uruguay: Cinemateca Uruguaya, 1973.

Pathé, Charles. *De Pathé Frères à Pathé Cinéma.* Nice, France, 1940. Reprint, Paris: Premier Plan, 1970.

Patterson, Francis Taylor. *Cinema Craftsmanship.* New York: Harcourt, Brace, and Howe, 1920.

———. *Scenario and Screen.* New York: Harcourt, Brace & Co., 1928.

Patterson, Lindsay, ed. *Black Films and Film-makers: A Comprehensive Anthology from Stereotype to Superhero.* New York: Dodd, Mead and Co., 1975.

Paul, Jeff. Film review of *The Ballad of Gregorio Cortez. Lector* 2, no. 2 (Sept.-Oct. 1983): 23.

Peacocke, Captain Leslie T. *Hints on Photoplay Writing.* Chicago: Photoplay Publishing Co., 1916.

Pearson, Edmund. *Dime Novels: Or Following an Old Train in Popular Literature.* Boston: Little, Brown, 1929.

Pearson, Roberta. "Cultivated Folks and the Better Classes: Class Conflict and Representation in Early American Film." *Journal of Popular Film and Television* 15 (fall 1987): 120-28.

———. "The Modesty of Nature: Performance in Griffith's Biographs." Ph.D. diss., New York University, 1986.

Peden, Charles. *Newsreel Man.* New York: Doubleday, Doran, 1932.

Peiss, Kathy. *Cheap Amusements: Working Women and Leisure in Turn-of-the-Century New York.* Philadelphia: Temple University Press, 1986.

"Las películas mexicanas en los EE.UU." *Tiempo* 27 (April 1945): 36-37.

Pérez, Ismael Diego. *"Cantinflas," genio del humor y del absurdo.* Mexico City: Editorial Indo-Hispana, 1954.

Pérez, Richie. "Committee against *Fort Apache: The Bronx* Mobilizes against Multinational Media." In *Cultures in Contention,* ed. Douglas Kahn and Diane Neumaier. Seattle, WA: Real Comet Press, 1985.

———. "From Assimilation to Annihilation: Puerto Rican Images in U.S. Films." *Centro de Estudios Puertorriqueños Bulletin* 2, no. 8 (1990): 8-27.

Pérez Arnay, Antonio, and Terenci Moix. *María Montez: La reina del tecnicolor.* Canary Islands, Spain: Filmoteca Canaria, 1995.

Pérez Turrent, Tomás. *"La Bamba." El Universal,* 29 December 1987, 1, 4.

Perry, Louis B., and Richard S. Perry. *A History of the Los Angeles Labor Movement.* Berkeley: University of California Press, 1963.

Peterson, Ruth C., and L. L. Thurstone. *Motion Pictures and the Social Attitudes of Children.* New York: Macmillan, 1933.

Petrova, Olga. *Butter with My Bread: The Memoirs of Olga Petrova.* Indianapolis: Bobbs-Merrill Co., 1942.

Pettit, Arthur G. *Images of the Mexican American in Fiction and Film.* College Station: Texas A&M University Press, 1980.

———. "Nightmare and Nostalgia: The Cinema West of Sam Peckinpah." *Western Humanities Review* 29 (spring 1975): 105-22.

Phillips, Gene. *Stanley Kubrick: A Film Odyssey.* New York: Popular Library, 1977.

Phillips, Henry Albert. *The Feature Photoplay.* Springfield, MA: Home Correspondence School, 1921.

———. *The Photodrama.* Larchmont, NY: Stanhope-Dodge Publishing Co., 1914.

Photoplay Arts Portfolio of Eclair Moving Picture Stars with Biographies and Autographs. New York: Photoplay Artists Company, 1914.

Photoplay Arts Portfolio of Kalem Moving Picture Stars with Biographies and Autographs. New York: Photoplay Artists Company, 1914.

Photoplay Arts Portfolio of Thanhouser Moving Picture Stars with Biographies and Autographs. New York: Photoplay Artists Company, 1914.

Photoplay Research Society. *Opportunities in the Motion Picture Industry.* Los Angeles: Photoplay Research Society, 1922.

Pic, Zuzana M. *The New Latin American Cinema: A Continental Project.* Austin: University of Texas Press, 1993.

Pickard, Roy. *The Hollywood Studios.* London: Frederick Muller, 1978.

Pickford, Mary. *Sunshine and Shadow.* London: William Heinemann, 1956.

Pilkington, William T., and Don Graham, eds. *Western Movies.* Albuquerque: University of New Mexico Press, 1979.

Pines, Jim. *Blacks in Film: A Study of Racial Themes and Images in the American Film.* London: Cassell & Collier Macmillan, 1975.

Pines, Jim, and Paul Willemen, eds. *Questions of Third Cinema.* London: British Film Institute, 1989.

Pinsky, Mark I. "Racism, History and Mass Media." *Jump Cut* 28 (April 1983): 67.

Pinto, Alfonso. "Cuando Hollywood habló en español." *Américas,* October 1980, 3-8.

———. "Hollywood's Spanish Language Films." *Films in Review* 24 (October 1973): 474-83, 487.

———. "Lupe Vélez, 1909-1944." *Films in Review* 31, no. 3 (November 1977): 513-24.

———. "Mona Maris." *Films in Review* 31, no. 3 (November 1977): 146-59.

Pitkin, Walter B., and William M. Marston. *The Art of Sound Pictures.* New York: D. Appleton & Co., 1930.

Pitt, Leonard. *The Decline of the Californios.* Berkeley: University of California Press, 1966.

Pitts, Michael R. *Hollywood and American History: A Filmography of over 250 Motion Pictures Depicting U.S. History.* Jefferson, NC: McFarland & Co., 1984.

———. *Western Movies.* Jefferson, NC: McFarland & Co., 1986.

Place, J. A. *The Western Films of John Ford.* Secaucus, NJ: Citadel Press, 1974.

Platt, Agnes. *Practical Hints on Acting for the Cinema.* New York: E. P. Dutton, 1923.

Podeschi, John. "The Writer in Hollywood." Ph.D. diss., University of Illinois at Urbana-Champaign, 1971.

Poitier, Sidney. *This Life.* New York: Alfred A. Knopf, 1980.

Posada, Pablo Humberto. *Apreciación del cine.* Mexico City: Universidad Iberoamericana-Alhambra Mexicana, 1980.

Poussaint, Alvin F. "Cheap Thrills That Degrade Blacks." *Psychology Today* 7 (February 1974).

Powdermaker, Hortense. *Hollywood: The Dream Factory.* Boston: Little, Brown, 1950.

Powell, Ardon Van Buren. *The Photoplay Synopsis.* Springfield, MA: Home Correspondence School, 1919.

Pratt, George C. *Spellbound in Darkness: A History of the Silent Film.* Greenwich, CT: New York Graphic Society, 1966.

Prawer, S. S. *Karl Marx and World Literature.* Oxford: Oxford University Press, 1976.

Prendergast, Roy M. *A Neglected Art: A Critical Study of Music in Films.* New York: New York University Press, 1977.

Pribram, Deidre, ed. *Female Spectators: Looking at Film and Television.* New York: Verso, 1988.

Prida, Dolores. *"El Norte*—a Landmark Latino Film." *Nuestro* 8, no. 4 (May 1984): 48-51.

Pristin, Terry. "Olmos Puts a Warning Out to Gang Members." *Los Angeles Times,* 24 February 1992, F1+.

"Profile of Actress Julie Carmen." *Caminos* 6, no. 10 (December 1985): 24.

Pryluck, Calvin. "The Aesthetic Relevance of the Organization of Film Production." *Cinema Journal* 15, no. 2 (spring 1976): 1-6.

———. "The Itinerant Movie Show and the Development of the Film Industry." *Journal of the University Film and Video Association* 36 (fall 1983): 11-22.

Purdy, Jim, and Peter Roffman. *The Hollywood Social Problem Film: Madness, Despair, and Politics from the Depression to the Fifties.* Bloomington: Indiana University Press, 1981.

Pye, Michael, and Lynda Myles. *The Movie Brats: How the Film Generation Took Over Hollywood.* New York: Holt, Rinehart & Winston, 1979.

Quart, Leonard, and Albert Auster. *American Film and Society Since 1945.* New York: Praeger, 1984.

Quigley, Martin. *Decency in Motion Pictures.* New York: Macmillan, 1937.

Quinlan, Sterling. *Inside ABC: American Broadcasting Company's Rise to Power.* New York: Hastings House, 1979.

Quinn, Anthony. *The Original Sin.* Boston: Little, Brown, 1972.

Quintana, Alvina. "Politics, Representation and the Emergence of a Chicana Aesthetic." *Cultural Studies* 4, no. 3 (October 1990): 257-63.

Quirk, Lawrence J. *The Films of Gloria Swanson.* Secaucus, NJ: Citadel Press, 1984.

———. *The Films of Myrna Loy.* Secaucus, NJ: Citadel Press, 1980.

———. *The Films of Paul Newman.* Secaucus, NJ: Citadel Press, 1971.

———. *The Films of Robert Taylor.* Secaucus, NJ: Citadel Press, 1975.

Rabinovitz, Lauren. "Temptations of Pleasure: Nickelodeons, Amusement Parks, and the Sights of Female Sexuality." *Camera Obscura* 23 (May 1990): 71-88.

Radway, Janice A. *Reading the Romance: Women, Patriarchy, and Popular Literature.* Chapel Hill: University of North Carolina Press, 1987.

Rafferty, Terrence. "Panic and Propaganda: 'Outbreak' and 'I Am Cuba.'" *The New Yorker,* 20 March 1995.

Ragan, David. *Who's Who in Hollywood 1900-1976.* New Rochelle, NY: Arlington House Publishers, 1976.

Rahill, Frank. *The World of Melodrama.* University Park: Pennsylvania State University Press, 1967.

Rainey, Buck. *The Fabulous Holts: A Tribute to a Favorite Movie Family.* Nashville, TN: Western Film Collector Press, 1976.

———. *Heroes of the Range: Yesterday's Saturday Matinee Movie Cowboys.* Metuchen, NJ: Scarecrow Press, 1987.

———. *Saddle Aces of the Cinema.* New York: A. S. Barnes, 1980.

———. *The Shoot-Em-Ups Ride Again. A Supplement to Shoot-Em-Ups.* Metuchen, NJ: Scarecrow Press, 1990.

Ramírez, Arthur. "Anglo View of a Mexican-American Tragedy: Rod Serling's *Requiem for a Heavyweight." Journal of Popular Culture* 13, no. 3 (spring 1980): 501-4.

———. Review of *Chicano Cinema,* by Gary D. Keller. *Americas Review* 14, nos. 3-4 (1986): 160-61.

Ramírez, Gabriel. *El cine de Griffith.* Mexico City: Ediciones Era, 1972.

———. *Crónica del cine mudo.* Mexico City: Cineteca Nacional, 1980.

———. *Lupe Vélez: la mexicana que escupía fuego.* Mexico City: Cineteca Nacional, 1986.

Ramírez Berg, Charles. "*Bordertown,* the Assimilation Narrative and the Chicano Social Problem Film." In *Chicanos and Film: Essays on Chicano Representation and Resistance,* ed. Chon A. Noriega, 33-52. New York: Garland Publishing Co., 1992.

———. *Cinema of Solitude: A Critical Study of Mexican Film, 1967-1983.* Austin: University of Texas Press, 1992.

———. "Cracks in the *Macho* Monolith: *Machismo,* Man, and Mexico in Recent Mexican Cinema." *New Orleans Review* 16, no. 1 (spring 1989): 67-74.

———. "Figueroa's Skies and Oblique Perspective: Notes on the Development of the Classical Mexican Style." *Spectator* 13, no. 1 (fall 1992).

———. "The Image of Women in Recent Mexican Cinema." *Journal of Latin American Popular Culture* 8 (1989).

———. "Images and Counterimages of the Hispanic in Hollywood." *Tonantzín* 6, no. 1 (November 1988): 12-13.

———. "Immigrants, Aliens, and Extraterrestrials: Science Fiction's Alien 'Other' as (Among Other Things) New Hispanic Imagery." *CineAction!* 18 (fall 1989): 3-17.

———. "Mexican Cinema: A Study in Creative Tension." *New Orleans Review* 10, no. 2 (summer-fall 1983): 149-52.

———. "Stereotyping in Film in General and of Hispanics in Particular." *Howard Journal of Communications* 2, no. 3 (summer 1990): 286-300.

———. "*Ya basta con* the Hollywood Paradigm!—Strategies for Latino Screenwriters." *Jump Cut* 38 (June 1993): 96-104.

Ramón, David. *Sensualidad. Las películas de Ninón Sevilla.* Mexico City: Universidad Nacional Autónoma de México, 1989.

Ramón, David, María Luisa Amador, and Rodolfo Rivera. *80 años de cine en México.* Mexico City: UNAM, Dirección General de Difusión Cultural, 1977.

Ramsaye, Terry. *A Million and One Nights.* New York: Simon and Schuster, 1926. Reprint, London: Frank Cass, 1964.

Randall, Richard S. *Censorship of the Movies.* Madison: University of Wisconsin Press, 1968.

Rapee, Erno. *Motion Picture Moods for Pianists and Organists.* New York: Schirmer, 1924.

Rasche, William Frank. *The Reading Interests of Young Workers.* Chicago: University of Chicago Libraries, 1937.

Rathbun, John B. *Motion Picture Making and Exhibiting.* Los Angeles: Holmes, 1914.

Raths, Louis E., and Frank N. Trager. "Public Opinion and 'Crossfire.'" *Journal of Educational Sociology* 21, no. 6 (1948): 345-68.

Ravage, John W. *Television: The Director's Viewpoint.* Boulder, CO: Westview Press, 1978.

Reade, Eric. *Australian Silent Films: A Pictorial History, 1896-1929.* Melbourne: Landsowne Press, 1970.

Reader, Keith. *Cultures on Celluloid.* London: Quartet Books, 1981.

Rebello, Stephen, and Richard Allen. *Reel Art: Great Posters from the Golden Age of the Silver Screen.* New York: Abbeville, 1988.

Reed, Joseph W. *Three American Originals: John Ford, William Faulkner, and Charles Ives.* Middletown, CT: Wesleyan University Press, 1984.

Rehrauer, George. *The Macmillan Film Bibliography.* New York: Macmillan, 1982.

Reid, Mark A. *Redefining Black Film.* Berkeley: University of California Press, 1993.

_____. "The U.S. Black Family Film." *Jump Cut* 36 (1991): 81-88.

Reid-Pharr, Robert. "The Spectacle of Blackness." *Radical America* 24, no. 4 (1993): 51-64.

Reilly, Adam. *Harold Lloyd, the King of Daredevil Comedy.* New York: Macmillan, 1977.

Reisz, Karel, and Gavin Millar. *The Technique of Film Editing.* New York: Hastings House, 1968.

Renov, Michael. *Hollywood's Wartime Woman: Representation and Ideology.* Ann Arbor, MI: UMI Press, 1988.

Reyes, Alfonso, Martín Luis Guzmán, and Federico de Onís. *Frente a la pantalla.* Mexico City: UNAM, Dirección General de Difusión Cultural, 1963.

Reyes, Luis. "Hispanic-American Cinema Lights Up the Silver Screen." *Hispanic Times,* Oct.-Nov. 1981, 28-29.

_____. "Hispanics in the Movies." *Hispanic Times,* May-June 1983, 52-53.

_____. "The Magical Way of 'Chico' Day." *DGA* [Director's Guild of America] *Magazine* 20, no. 3 (July-August 1995): 30-31.

_____. "The Mexican's Turn to Remember the Alamo." *Los Angeles Times,* 24 Aug. 1982, 1.

_____. "Year of Hispanics at Universal Studios." *Hispanic Times,* March-April 1982, 36.

Reyes de la Maza, Luis. *El cine sonoro en México.* Mexico City: UNAM, Instituto de Investigaciones Estéticas, 1973.

_____. *Memorias de un pentonto.* Mexico City: Editorial Posada, 1984.

_____. *Salón Rojo.* Mexico City: Ediciones Cuadernos de Cine, UNAM, Dirección General de Difusión Cultural, 1968.

Reyes Nevares, Beatriz. "Cine mexicano: Habla Ricardo Garibay." *Siempre,* 13 December 1972.

_____. "El cine mexicano es hoy de mejor calidad." *Siempre,* 27 December 1972.

_____. "Entre cretinos y voraces naufraga el cine mexicano." *Siempre,* 3 January 1973.

_____. *The Mexican Cinema: Interviews with Thirteen Directors.* Trans. Carl J. Mora and Elizabeth Gard. Albuquerque: University of New Mexico Press, 1976.

_____. "Salomón Liter: Profeta de un nuevo cine." *Siempre,* 24 January 1973.

_____. *Trece directores del cine mexicano.* Mexico City: Sep/Setentas, 1973.

Reynolds, Quentin. *The Fiction Factory: Or, From Pulp Row to Quality Street.* New York: Random House, 1955.

Rheuban, Joyce. *Harry Langdon: The Comedian as Metteur-en-scène.* Rutherford, NJ: Fairleigh Dickinson University Press, 1983.

Rich, Ruby. "Bay of Pix." *American Film* 7, no. 9 (July-August 1984): 57-59.

Richard, Alfred Charles, Jr. *Censorship and Hollywood's Hispanic Image: An Interpretive Filmography, 1936-1955.* Westport, CT: Greenwood Press, 1993.

_____. *Contemporary Hollywood's Negative Hispanic Image: An Interpretive Filmography, 1956-1993.* Westport, CT: Greenwood Press, 1994.

_____. *The Hispanic Image on the Silver Screen: An Interpretive Filmography from Silents into Sound, 1898-1935.* New York: Greenwood Press, 1992.

Richardson, Frank Herbert. *Handbook of Projection.* 5th ed. 2 vols. New York: Chalmers, 1927.

_____. *Motion Picture Handbook: A Guide for Managers and Operators of Motion Picture Theatres.* New York: Moving Picture World, 1910.

Richardson, Robert. *Literature and Film.* Bloomington: Indiana University Press, 1969.

Rico, María Elena. "Anatomía de un éxito loco: *Allá en el rancho grande.*" *Contenido,* June 1976.

Riess, Steven. "A Fighting Chance: The Jewish-American Boxing Experience, 1890-1940." *American Jewish History* 74 (March 1985): 2-11.

Rieupeyrout, Jean-Louis. *La Grande Aventure du Western.* Paris: Éditions du Cerf, 1964.

Rigdon, Walter. *The Biographical Encyclopedia & Who's Who of the American Theater.* New York: James H. Heineman, 1965.

Riggens, Stephen Harold, ed. *Ethnic Minority Media: An International Perspective.* Newbury Park, CA: Sage Publications, 1992.

Ringgold, Gene. *The Films of Rita Hayworth.* Secaucus, NJ: Citadel Press, 1974.

Ringgold, Gene, and DeWitt Bodeen. *The Films of Cecil B. DeMille.* Secaucus, NJ: Citadel Press, 1974.

Ríos, Alejandro. "Otro cine cubano de hoy." *Cine Cubano* 133 (November-December 1991): 53-57.

Ríos-Bustamante, Antonio. "An Idea Whose Time Has Come." *Caminos* 5, no. 7 (July-Aug. 1984): 39-41.

_____. "Latino Participation in the Hollywood Film Industry, 1911-1945." In *Chicanos and Film: Essays on Chicano Representation and Resistance,* ed. Chon Noriega, 21-32. New York: Garland Publishing Co., 1992.

_____. "Latinos and the Hollywood Film Industry, 1920s to 1950s." *Americas 2001* 1, no. 4 (January 1988): 18-21.

Rivera, Héctor. "*El Indio,* tan intenso en la furia como en la ternura." *Proceso* 11 (August 1986).

Rivera, Lucas. "Mambo King of Comedy." *Hispanic,* March 1992, 11-15.

Rivera, Tomás. "*The Ballad of Gregorio Cortez.*" *Hispanic Times,* Oct.-Nov. 1983, 22.

_____. Film review of *The Ballad of Gregorio Cortez. Migration Today* 12, no. 1 (1984): 22.

Riviere, Joan. "Womanliness as Masquerade." In *Formations of Fantasy,* ed. Victor Burgin, James Donald, and Cora Kaplan, 35-44. New York: Routledge, 1989.

Rivkin, Allen, and Laura Kerr. *Hello, Hollywood!* Garden City, NY: Doubleday, 1962.

Roberts, John Storm. *The Latin Tinge: The Impact of Latin American Music on the United States.* New York: Oxford University Press, 1979.

Roberts, Shari. " 'The Lady in the Tutti-Frutti Hat': Carmen Miranda, a Spectacle of Ethnicity." *Cinema Journal* 32, no. 3 (spring 1993): 3-23.

Robertson, Patrick. *The Guinness Book of Movie Facts and Feats.* New York: Abbeville Press, 1991.

_____. *Movie Clips.* 2nd ed. London: Guinness Books, 1989.

Robinson, Cecil. *Mexico and the Hispanic Southwest in American Literature.* Tucson: University of Arizona Press, 1977.

_____. *With the Ears of Strangers: The Mexican in American Literature.* Tucson: University of Arizona Press, 1969.

Robinson, David. *Buster Keaton.* Bloomington: Indiana University Press, 1969.

_____. *Chaplin: His Life and Art.* New York: McGraw-Hill, 1985.

_____. *Chaplin: The Mirror of Opinion.* Bloomington: Indiana University Press, 1984.

_____. *The History of World Cinema.* New York: Stein and Day, 1973.

_____. *Hollywood in the Twenties.* New York: Barnes, 1968.

Robinson, Henry Norton. "Mr. Beadle's Books." *Bookman* 60 (March 1929): 22.

Robinson, Leroy. "Media Invisibles." *Crisis* 92, no. 6 (June-July 1985): 36-39.

Robinson, W. R., ed. *Man and the Movies.* Baton Rouge: Louisiana State University Press, 1967.

Rockefeller, Nelson. "Fruits of the Good Neighbor Policy." *New York Times Magazine,* 14 May 1944, 15.

Rodríguez, Elena. *Dennis Hopper: A Madness to His Method.* New York: St. Martin's Press, 1988.

Rodríguez, Jorge Luis. "Los santos en el celuloide americano." *La Opinión* (Los Angeles)*,* 26 March 1988, 1-2.

Rodríguez, Roberto. "Interview with Stars of Controversial *Latino.*" *Caminos* 6, no. 19 (December 1985): 26-27, 30.

_____. *Rebel without a Crew, or, How a 24-Year-Old Filmmaker with $7,000 Became a Hollywood Player.* New York: E. P. Dutton, 1995.

Rodríguez Flores, Juan. Review of *Stand and Deliver. La Opinión* (Los Angeles), 2 March 1988, sec 2, 1+.

Rodríguez y Galván, Rolando. *Cantinflas, torero.* Mexico City: Editorial Clío, 1995.

Roeder, George H., Jr. "Mexicans in the Movies: The Image of Mexicans in American Films, 1894-1947." University of Wisconsin, 1971. Unpublished manuscript; highly faded copy in possession of Gary D. Keller.

Roffman, Peter, and Jim Purdy. *The Hollywood Social Problem Film.* Bloomington: Indiana University Press, 1981.

Roffman, Peter, and Bev Simpson. "Black Images on White Screens." *Cineaste* 13 (June 1984): 14-21.

Rogin, Michael. "Blankface, White Noise: The Jewish Jazz Singer Finds His Voice." *Critical Inquiry* 18 (spring 1992): 417-53.

_____. "The Great Mother Domesticated: Sexual Difference and Sexual Indifference in D.W. Griffith's *Intolerance.*" *Critical Inquiry* 15 (spring 1989).

_____. *Ronald Reagan, the Movie and Other Episodes in Political Demonology.* Berkeley: University of California Press, 1987.

Rollins, Peter C. *Will Rogers: A Bio-Bibliography.* Westport, CT: Greenwood Press, 1984.

_____, ed. *Hollywood as Historian, American Film in a Cultural Context.* Lexington: University of Kentucky Press, 1983.

_____, guest editor. Special issue: *The Hollywood Indian. Film and History* 23, nos. 1-4 (1993).

Romaguera i Ramio, Joaquim. *Diccionario filmográfico de directores de España, Portugal y Latinoamérica.* Barcelona: Laertes, 1994.

Román, Ernesto, and MariCarmen Figueroa Pérez. *Premios y distinciones otorgados al cine mexicano en festivales internacionales, 1938-1984.* Mexico City: Cineteca Nacional, 1986.

Rosales, Arturo. *Chicano! History of the Mexican American Civil Rights Movement.* Published in conjunction with the documentary *Chicano!* Houston: Arte Público Press, 1996.

Rose, Brian G. *TV Genres.* Westport, CT: Greenwood Press, 1985.

Rosen, David. *Off-Hollywood: The Making and Marketing of Independent Films.* New York: Grove Weidenfeld, 1990.

Rosen, David, and Nancy Sher. "Independent Features: Supporting and Promoting Narrative Films." *Benton Foundation Bulletin* 4 (1990): 2.

Rosen, Irwin C. "The Effect of the Motion Picture 'Gentlemen's Agreement' on Attitudes Toward Jews." *Journal of Psychology* 26 (1948): 525-36.

Rosen, Marjorie. *Popcorn Venus: Women, Movies and the American Dream.* New York: Coward, McCann and Georghegan, 1973.

Rosenbloom, Nancy J. "Between Reform and Regulation: The Struggle over Film Censorship in Progressive America, 1908-1922." *Film History* 1, no. 4 (1987): 307-25.

_____. "In Defense of Moving Pictures: The People's Institute, the National Board of Censorship, and the Problems of Leisure in Urban America." *American Studies* 33, no. 2 (fall 1992): 41-61.

_____. "Progressive Reform, Censorship, and the Motion Picture Industry, 1909-1917." In *Popular Culture and Political Change in Modern America,* ed. Ronald Edsforth and Larry Bennett, 41-59. Albany, NY: SUNY Press, 1991.

Rosenfelt, Deborah. "Ideology and Structure in *Salt of the Earth.*" *Jump Cut* 12-13 (1976): 19-22.

Rosenstone, Robert A., ed. *Revisioning History: Film and the Construction of a New Past.* Princeton, NJ: Princeton University Press, 1995.

Rosenzweig, Roy. *Eight Hours for What We Will: Workers and Leisure in an Industrial City, 1870-1920.* Cambridge: Cambridge University Press, 1983.

Ross, Lillian. *Picture.* New York: Rinehart & Co., 1952.

Ross, Murray. *Stars and Strikes: The Unionization of Hollywood.* New York: Columbia University Press, 1941.

Rossi, Eduardo A. "Veinte años del cine argentino." *Otrocine* 3 (July-September 1975): 44-52.

Rosten, Leo. *Hollywood, the Movie Makers, the Movie Colony.* New York: Harcourt, Brace, 1941.

Rotha, Paul. *The Film till Now: A Survey of the Cinema.* New York: Jonathon Cape and Harrison Smith, 1930.

Rothel, David. *The Singing Cowboys.* New York: A. S. Barnes, 1978.

_____. *Those Great Cowboy Sidekicks.* Metuchen, NJ: Scarecrow Press, 1984.

Rouse, Roger. "Mexican Migration in the Social Space of Postmodernism." *Diaspora* 1, no. 1 (spring 1991): 8-23.

Rowland, Donald W., ed. *History of the Office of the Coordinator of Inter-American Affairs.* Washington, DC: Government Printing Office, 1947.

Rubia Barcia, J. "Luis Buñuel's *Los olvidados.*" *Quarterly of Film, Radio & Television* 7 (1952-53): 392-401.

Russell, Rosalind. *Life is a Banquet.* New York: Grossett and Dunlap, 1977.

Russo, Vito. *The Celluloid Closet: Homosexuality in the Movies.* New York: Harper & Row, 1981.

Rutland, J. R. *State Censorship of Motion Pictures.* New York: Wilson Co., 1923.

Ruy Sánchez, Alberto. "Cine mexicano: producción social de una estética." *Historia y Sociedad* 18 (summer 1978): 71-83.

_____. *Mitología de un cine en crisis.* Mexico City: Premia Editora, 1981.

Ryan, Michael, and Doug Kellner. *Camera Politica.* Bloomington: Indiana University Press, 1988.

Ryan, Roderick T. *A History of Motion Picture Color Technology.* New York: Focal Press, 1977.

Saalfield, Catherine, and Ray Navarro. "Not Just Black and White: AIDS, Media and People of Color." *Centro de Estudios Puertorriqueños Bulletin* 2 (spring 1990): 70-78.

Sadoul, Georges. *British Creators of Film Technique.* London: British Film Institute, 1948.

_____. *Dictionary of Films.* Translated, edited, and updated by Peter Morris. Berkeley: University of California Press, 1972.

_____. *Georges Méliès: Présentation et bio-filmographie: choix de textes et propos de Méliès.* Col. Cinéma d'aujourd'hui. Paris: Éditions Seghers, 1961.

_____. *Histoire général du cinéma.* 2 vols. Vol. 1, *L'Invention du cinéma, 1832-1897.* Vol. 2, *Les Pionniers du cinéma: De Méliès à Pathé, 1897-1909.* Paris: Denoël, 1947-48.

_____. *Louis Lumière.* Coll. Cinéma d'aujourd'hui. Paris: Éditions Seghers, 1964.

_____. *Lumière et Méliès.* Revised and augmented by Bernard Eisenhitz. Paris: L'Herminier, 1985.

Sadownick, Doug. "Two Different Worlds: Luis Alfaro Bridges the Gap between Gay Fantasies and Latino Reality." *L.A. Weekly* 11, no. 29 (1989): 62-63.

St. Charnez, Casey. *The Films of Steve McQueen.* Secaucus, NJ: Citadel Press, 1984.

Salcedo Silva, Hernando. *Crónicas del cine colombiano 1897-1950.* Bogotá, Colombia: Carlos Valencia Editores, 1981.

Salt, Barry. "Film Form, 1900-1906." *Sight and Sound* 47 (summer 1978): 148-53.

_____. *Film Style and Technology: History and Analysis.* London: Starwood, 1983.

_____. "What Can We Learn from the First Twenty Years of Cinema?" *Iris* 2 (spring 1984): 83-90.

Sammons, Jeffrey T. *Beyond the Ring: The Role of Boxing in American Society.* Urbana: University of Illinois Press, 1988.

Sampson, Henry T. *Blacks in Black and White.* Metuchen, NJ: Scarecrow Press, 1977.

Sánchez-Jankowski, Martín. *Islands in the Street.* Berkeley: University of California Press, 1991.

Sánchez Vidal, Agustín. *Luis Buñuel.* Madrid: Cátedra, 1991.

Sandburg, Carl. *Carl Sandburg at the Movies.* Ed. Dale Fetherling and Doug Fetherling. Metuchen, NJ: Scarecrow Press, 1985.

Sands, Pierre Norman. *A Historical Study of the Academy of Motion Picture Arts and Sciences (1927-1947).* New York: Arno Press, 1973.

Sanerson, Richard Arlo. "A Historical Study of the Development of American Motion Picture Content and Techniques Prior to 1904." Ph.D. diss., University of Southern California, 1961.

Sands, Pierre Norman. *A Historical Study of the Academy.* New York: Arno Press, 1966.

Sanjek, Russell. *American Popular Music and Its Business: The First Four Hundred Years.* Vol. 3, *From 1900 to 1984.* New York: Oxford University Press, 1988.

Santiago, Chiori. Film review of *Frida: Naturaleza Viva. High Performance* 9, no. 3 (1986): 101.

Saragoza, Alex M. "The Border in American and Mexican Cinema." *Cultural Atlas of Mexico-United States Border Studies.* Ed. Raymond Paredes. Los Angeles: UCLA Latin American Center Publications, 1990.

_____. "Mexican Cinema in the United States, 1940-1952." In *History, Culture and Society: Chicano Studies in the 1980s,* ed. National Association for Chicano Studies, 107-24. Ypsilanti, MI: Bilingual Press, 1983.

Sargent, Epes Winthrop. *Picture Theatre Advertising.* New York: Moving Picture World, Chalmers Publishing Co., 1915.

_____. *The Technique of the Photoplay.* 2nd ed. New York: Moving Picture World, 1913.

Sarris, Andrew. *Interviews with Film Directors.* New York: Avon Books, 1967.

_____. *The John Ford Movie Mystery.* Bloomington: Indiana University Press, 1976.

Savage, William W. *The Cowboy Hero: His Image in American History and Culture.* Norman: University of Oklahoma Press, 1979.

Schaefer, Claudia. *Textured Lives: Women, Art, and Representation in Modern Mexico.* Tucson: University of Arizona Press, 1992.

Schatz, Thomas. *The Genius of the System: Hollywood Filmmaking in the Studio Era.* New York: Pantheon Books, 1988.

_____. *Hollywood Genres: Formulas, Filmmaking, and the Studio System.* New York: Random House, 1981; Philadelphia: Temple University Press, 1981.

_____. *Old Hollywood/New Hollywood: Ritual, Art, and Industry.* Ann Arbor, MI: UMI Research Press, 1983.

Schechter, Harold, and David Everitt. *Film Tricks: Special Effects in the Movies.* New York: Harlin Quist, 1980.

Schement, Jorge R., and Ricardo Flores. "The Origins of Spanish-Language Radio: The Case of San Antonio, Texas." *Journalism History* 4 (February 1977): 56-58.

Schick, Frank L. *The Paperbound Book in America.* New York: R. R. Bowker Co., 1958.

Schickel, Richard. *D. W. Griffith: An American Life.* New York: Simon and Schuster, 1984.

_____. *Harold Lloyd: The Shape of Laughter.* Boston, MA: New York Graphic Society, 1974.

_____. *His Picture in the Papers: A Speculation on Celebrity Based on the Life of Douglas Fairbanks, Sr.* New York: Charterhouse, 1973.

_____. *Intimate Strangers: The Culture of Celebrity.* New York: Fromm, 1986.

Schmitt, Robert C. "Movies in Hawaii, 1897-1932." *Hawaiian Journal of History* 1 (1967).

Schnitman, Jorge A. *Film Industries in Latin America: Dependency and Development.* Norwood, NJ: Ablex Publishing Co., 1984.

Schulberg, Budd. *Moving Pictures: Memories of a Hollywood Pioneer.* New York: Stein and Day, 1981.

Schulman, Irving. *Valentino.* New York: Trident Press, 1967.

Schumach, Murray. *The Face on the Cutting Room Floor: The Story of Movie and Television Censorship.* New York: William Morrow & Co., 1964.

Schurman, Lydia. "Anthony Comstock's Lifelong Crusade against 'Vampire Literature.'" *Dime Novel Round-Up,* no. 600 (December 1989): 81-88.

1Bibliography1

2Schuster, Mel, ed. *Motion Picture Directors: A Bibliography of Magazine and Periodical Articles, 1900-1972.* Metuchen, NJ: Scarecrow Press, 1973.

Schwartz, Nancy Lyon, completed by Sheila Schwartz. *The Hollywood Writers' Wars.* New York: Alfred A. Knopf, 1982.

Scott, Evelyn F. *Hollywood: When Silents Were Golden.* New York: McGraw-Hill, 1972.

"Screen Credit for Dubbed Voices by UA." *Variety,* 27 November 1929.

Seabury, William M. *Motion Picture Problems: The Cinema and the League of Nations.* New York: Avondale Press, 1929.

_____. *The Public and the Motion Picture Industry.* New York: Macmillan, 1926.

Seawell, Molly Elliot. *The Ladies' Battle.* New York: Macmillan, 1911.

Sedgewick, Eve Kosofsky. *The Epistemology of the Closet.* Berkeley: University of California Press, 1990.

_____. *Tendencies.* Durham, NC: Duke University Press, 1993.

See, Carolyn. "The Hollywood Novel: An Historical and Critical Study." Ph.D. diss., University of California, Los Angeles, 1963.

Seelye, John. "The American Tramp: A Version of the Picaresque." *American Quarterly* 15 (1963): 535-53.

Seiter, Ellen. "The Promise of Melodrama: Recent Women's Films and Soap Opera." Ph.D. diss., Northwestern University, 1981.

_____. "Stereotypes and the Media: A Re-evaluation." *Journal of Communication* 36, no. 2 (spring 1986): 14-26.

Seiter, Ellen, et al., eds. *Remote Control: Television, Audiences and Cultural Power.* New York: Routledge, 1989.

Seldes, Gilbert. *The Seven Lively Arts.* New York: Harper, 1924.

Selznick, Irene Mayer. *A Private View.* New York: Alfred A. Knopf, 1983.

Sennett, Mack, with Cameron Shipp. *King of Comedy.* Garden City, NY: Doubleday, 1954.

Sennett, Ted. *Warner Bros. Presents.* New Rochelle, NY: Arlington House, 1971.

Shale, Richard. *Academy Awards: An Ungar Reference Index.* New York: Frederick Ungar, 1978.

Shaler, Tom, et al. *The American Film Heritage: Impressions from the American Film Institute Archives.* Washington, DC: Acropolis Books, 1972.

Shankman, Arnold. "Black Pride and Protest: The Amos 'N' Andy Crusade." *Journal of Popular Culture* 12 (fall 1979): 236-52.

Sharaff, Irene. *Broadway and Hollywood.* New York: Van Nostrand Reinhold, 1976.

Sharp, Dennis. *The Picture Palace and Other Buildings for the Movies.* New York: Praeger, 1969.

Sheeha, Peter Poore. *Hollywood as a World Center.* Hollywood: Hollywood Citizen Press, 1923.

Shepherd, Donald, and Robert Slatzer, with Dave Grayson. *Duke: The Life and Times of John Wayne.* Garden City, NY: Doubleday, 1985.

Sheppard, Dick. *Elizabeth.* New York: Warner Books, 1974.

Sherman, Eric. *Directing the Film: Film Directors on Their Art.* Boston: Little, Brown, 1976.

Shohat, Ella. "Gender and Culture of Empire: Toward a Feminist Ethnography of the Cinema." *Quarterly Review of Film and Video* 13, nos. 1-3 (1991): 45-84.

Shove, Raymond. *Cheap Book Production in the United States, 1870 to 1891.* Urbana: University of Illinois Library, 1937.

Shull, Michael S., and David E. Wilt. *Doing Their Bit: Wartime Animated Short Films, 1939-1945.* Jefferson, NC: McFarland & Co., 1987.

Sidney, George. "Faulkner in Hollywood: His Career as a Scenarist." Ph.D. diss., University of New Mexico, 1959.

Sieben, Pearl. *The Immortal Jolson.* New York: Frederick Fell, 1962.

Silva, Fred, ed. *Focus on The Birth of a Nation.* Englewood Cliffs, NJ: Prentice-Hall, 1971.

Silver, Alain, and Elizabeth Ward. *Film Noir: An Encyclopedia Reference to the American Style.* Woodstock, NY: Overlook Press, 1979.

Simcovitch, Maxim. "The Impact of Griffith's *The Birth of a Nation* on the Modern Ku Klux Klan." *Journal of Popular Film* 1 (winter 1972): 45-54.

Simmon, Scott. *The Films of D. W. Griffith.* Cambridge: Cambridge University Press, 1993.

Simmons, Garner. *Peckinpah: A Portrait in Montage.* Austin: University of Texas Press, 1976.

Simmons, Michael K. "Nationalism and the Dime Novel." *Studies in the Humanities* 9, no. 1 (1981): 39-44.

Simonds, Cylena. "Public Audit: An Interview with Elizabeth Sisco, Louis Hock, and David Avalos." *Afterimage* 22, no. 1 (summer 1994): 8-11.

Sinclair, Andrew. *John Ford: A Biography.* New York: Dial, 1979.

Sinclair, John. "Dependent Development and Broadcasting: 'The Mexican Formula.'" *Media, Culture and Society* 8 (1986): 81-101.

Sinyard, Neil. *Silent Movies.* New York: W. H. Smith Publishers, 1990.

Sitney, P. Adams. *Visionary Film: The American Avant-Garde.* New York: Oxford University Press, 1974.

_____, ed. *The Essential Cinema: Essays on Film in the Collection of Anthology Film Archives.* New York: New York University Press, 1975.

Skal, David J. *Hollywood Gothic: The Tangled Web of* Dracula *from Novel to Stage to Screen.* New York: W. W. Norton & Co., 1991.

Sklar, Robert. *Movie-Made America: A Cultural History of American Movies.* New York: Random House, 1975.

_____. "Oh! Althusser!: Historiography and the Rise of Cinema Studies." *Radical History Review* 41 (1988): 11-35.

Sklar, Robert, and Charles Musser. *Resisting Images: Essays on Cinema and History.* Philadelphia: Temple University Press, 1990.

Slatta, Richard. *Bandidos: The Varieties of Latin American Banditry.* Westport, CT: Greenwood Press, 1987.

Slevin, James. *On Picture-Play Writing: A Hand-book of Workmanship.* Cedar Grove, NJ: Farmer Smith, 1912.

Slide, Anthony. *Aspects of American Film History Prior to 1920.* Metuchen, NJ: Scarecrow Press, 1978.

_____. *Early American Cinema.* New York: A. S. Barnes, 1970.

_____. *Early American Women Film Directors.* New York: A. S. Barnes and Co., 1984.

_____. "The Evolution of the Film Star." *Films in Review* 25 (December 1974): 591-94.

_____. *The Griffith Actresses.* South Brunswick, NJ, and New York: A. S. Barnes and Co., 1975.2

259

_____. *The Idols of Silence.* New York: A. S. Barnes, 1976.

_____. *The Kindergarten of the Movies: A History of the Fine Arts Company.* Metuchen, NJ: Scarecrow Press, 1980.

_____. "The Thanhouser Company." *Films in Review* 26 (November 1975): 441-45.

_____, ed. *The American Film Industry.* Westport, CT: Greenwood Press, 1986.

_____, ed. *Selected Film Criticism, 1912-1920.* Metuchen, NJ: Scarecrow Press, 1982.

Slide, Anthony, with Alan Gevinson. *The Big V: A History of the Vitagraph Company.* Rev. ed. Metuchen, NJ: Scarecrow Press, 1987.

Slide, Anthony, and Edward Wagenknecht. *Fifty Great American Silent Films, 1912-1920: A Pictorial Survey.* New York: Dover Publications, 1980.

Sloan, Kay. *The Loud Silents: Origins of the Social Problem Film.* Urbana: University of Illinois Press, 1988.

Slotkin, Richard. *Gunfighter Nation: The Myth of the Frontier in Twentieth-Century America.* New York: Atheneum, 1992.

Smith, Albert E., in collaboration with Phil A. Koury. *Two Reels and a Crank.* Garden City, NY: Doubleday, 1952.

Smith, H. Allen. *The Life and Legend of Gene Fowler.* New York: William Morrow, 1979.

Smith, Henry Nash. "The Dime Novel Heroine." *Southwest Review* 34 (spring 1949): 182-88.

_____. *Virgin Land.* Cambridge, MA: Harvard University Press, 1950.

_____. "The Western Hero in the Dime Novel." *Southwest Review* 33 (summer 1948): 276-84.

Smith, James L. *Melodrama.* London: Methuen, 1973.

Smith, Norman D. "Mexican Stereotypes on Fictional Battlefields: or Dime Novel Romances of the Mexican War." *Journal of Popular Culture* 13, No. 3 (1980): 526-40.

Smith, Paul, ed. *The Historian and Film.* New York: Cambridge University Press, 1976.

Smith, Ralph. "Barred by the Post Office." *Dime Novel Round-Up,* no. 145 (October 1944): 1-3.

Smith, Ronald Lande. *Cosby.* New York: St. Martin's Press, 1986.

_____. *The Stars of Stand-up Comedy.* New York: Garland Publishing Co., 1986.

Snydert, Robert. *The Voice of the City: Vaudeville and Popular Culture in New York.* New York: Oxford University Press, 1990.

Sobchack, Vivian. *Screening Space: The American Science Fiction Film.* 2nd ed. New York: Frederick Ungar, 1987.

Solanas, Fernando E., and Octavio Getino. *Cine, cultura y descolonización.* Buenos Aires: Siglo XXI, 1973.

Sonnichsen, C. L. *From Hopalong to Hud.* College Station: Texas A&M University Press, 1978.

Sopocy, Martin. "A Narrated Cinema: The Pioneer Story Films of James A. Williamson." *Cinema Journal* 18 (fall 1978): 1-28.

Souto, H. Mario Raimondo. *The Technique of the Motion Picture Camera.* 3rd rev. and enlarged ed. New York: Hastings House, 1977.

Span, Paula. "Emilio Estévez, Seriously." *Nuestro* 9, no. 8 (October 1985): 12-16.

Spatz, Jonas. *Hollywood in Fiction.* The Hague: Mouton Press, 1969.

Spears, Jack. "Edwin S. Porter." *Films in Review* 31 (June-July 1970): 327-54.

"Special Issue on Black Cinema." *The Black Scholar* 21, no. 2 (March-May 1990).

Spehr, Paul C. "Filmmaking at the American Mutoscope and Biograph Company, 1900-1906." *Quarterly Journal of the Library of Congress* 37 (summer-fall 1980): 413-21.

_____. *The Movies Begin: Making Movies in New Jersey, 1887-1920.* Newark, NJ: Newark Museum in cooperation with Morgan and Morgan, 1977.

Spelling, Ian. "Voyage to a New Frontier." *Hispanic,* April 1995, 14-16.

Springer, Claudia. "Black Women Filmmakers." *Jump Cut* 29 (February 1984).

Springer, John. *All Talking! All Singing! All Dancing!* New York: Citadel Press, 1966.

Springhall, John. "The Dime Novel as Scapegoat for Juvenile Crime: Anthony Comstock's Campaign to Suppress the 'Half-Dime' Western of the 1880s." *Dime Novel Round-Up,* no. 613 (February 1992): 7-16.

Staiger, Janet. *Bad Women: Regulating Sexuality in Early American Cinema.* Minneapolis: University of Minnesota Press, 1995.

_____. "Combination and Litigation: Structures of U.S. Film Distribution, 1896-1917." *Cinema Journal* 23 (winter 1983): 41-71.

_____. "Dividing Labor for Production Control: Thomas Ince and the Rise of the Studio System." *Cinema Journal* 18, no. 2 (spring 1979): 16-25.

_____. *Interpreting Films: Studies in the Historical Reception of American Cinema.* Princeton, NJ: Princeton University Press, 1992.

_____. "The Politics of Film Canons." *Cinema Journal* 24 (spring 1985): 4-23.

Stam, Robert. *Reflexivity in Film and Literature: From Don Quixote to Jean-Luc Godard.* Ann Arbor, MI: UMI Research Press, 1983.

_____. *Subversive Pleasures: Bakhtin Cultural Criticism and Film.* Baltimore: Johns Hopkins University Press, 1989.

Stam, Robert, and Louise Spence. "Colonialism, Racism, and Representation: An Introduction." *Screen* 24, no. 2 (1983): 2-20.

Stanfield, Peter. "The Western, 1909-14: A Cast of Villains." *Film History* 1 (1987): 97-112.

Stanley, Robert H. *The Celluloid Empire: A History of the American Movie Industry.* New York: Communication Arts Books, 1978.

Stanley, Robert H., and Charles S. Steinberg. *The Media Environment: Mass Communications in American Society.* New York: Hastings House, 1976.

Staples, Robert, and Terry Jones. "Culture, Ideology, and Black Television Images." *Black Scholar* 16, no. 3 (May-June 1985).

Steckmesser, Kent Ladd. *The Western Hero in History and Legend.* Norman: University of Oklahoma Press, 1965.

Stedman, Raymond William. *Shadows of the Indian: Stereotypes in American Culture.* Norman: University of Oklahoma Press, 1982.

Steele, Joseph Henry. *Ingrid Bergman.* New York: Popular Library, 1959.

Steele, Richard. *Propaganda in an Open Society: The Roosevelt Administration and the Media, 1933-1941.* Westport, CT: Greenwood, 1985.

Stein, Arlene, ed. *Sisters, Sexperts, Queers: Beyond the Lesbian Nation.* New York: Penguin Books, 1993.

Steinberg, Corbett. *Reel Facts: The Movie Book of Records.* New York: Vintage Books, 1982.

Steinberg, Stephen. *The Ethnic Myth: Race, Ethnicity, and Class in America.* Boston: Beacon Press, 1989.

Stenn, David. *Clara Bow: Running Wild.* Garden City, NY: Doubleday, 1988.

Sterling, Bryan B., and Frances N. Sterling. *Will Rogers in Hollywood.* New York: Crown Publishers, 1984.

Stern, Gary M. "The Reel World: Hispanic Directors Struggle in Hollywood." *Hispanic,* January-February 1992, 11-14.

Stern, Seymour. "The Birth of a Nation." *Film Culture* 36 (spring-summer 1965).

Sternberg, Meir. *Expositional Modes and Temporal Ordering in Fiction.* Baltimore: Johns Hopkins University Press, 1978.

Sterrit, David. "Puerto Rico: New Presence in Film." *The Christian Science Monitor,* 21 August 1987, 19-20.

Steven, Peter, ed. *Jump Cut: Hollywood Politics and Counter Cinema.* Toronto: Between the Lines, 1985.

Stewart, John, ed. *Filmarama I: The Formidable Years, 1893-1919.* Metuchen, NJ: Scarecrow Press, 1975.

Strait, Raymond. *The Tragic Secret Life of Jayne Mansfield.* Chicago: Henry Regnery Co., 1974.

Strasser, Susan. *Satisfaction Guaranteed: The Making of the American Mass Market.* New York: Pantheon Books, 1989.

Strebel, Elizabeth Grottle. *French Social Cinema of the Nineteen Thirties: A Cinematographic Expression of Popular Front Consciousness.* New York: Arno Press, 1980.

Streetback, Nancy. *The Films of Burt Reynolds.* Secaucus, NJ: Citadel Press, 1982.

Subervi, Federico. *"Media."* In *The Hispanic-American Almanac,* ed. Nicolás Kanellos, 621-74. Detroit: Gale Research, 1993,

Swanberg, W. A. *Citizen Hearst.* New York: Bantam Books, 1961.

Swanson, Gloria. *Swanson on Swanson.* New York: Random House, 1980.

"Sylvia Morales: Faith Even to the Fire." *Booklist,* 15 December 1992.

Tafolla, Carmen. *To Split a Human: Mitos, Machos y la Mujer Chicana.* San Antonio, TX: Mexican American Cultural Center, 1985.

Tafoya, Eddie. *"Born in East L.A.:* Cheech as the Chicano Moses." *Journal of Popular Culture* 26, no. 4 (spring 1993): 123-29.

Taibo I., Paco Ignacio. *"Indio" Fernández: el cine por mis pistolas.* Mexico City: Joaquín Mortiz/Planeta, 1986.

———. *María Félix: 47 pasos por el cine.* Mexico City: Joaquín Mortiz/Planeta, 1985.

Takaki, Ronald T. *Iron Cages: Race and Culture in 19th-Century America.* Seattle: University of Washington Press, 1979.

Talbot, Daniel, ed. *Film: An Anthology.* New York: Simon and Schuster, 1959.

Talbot, Frederick A. *Moving Pictures: How They Are Made and Worked.* Philadelphia: Lippincott, 1914. Reprint, New York: Arno Press, 1970.

———. *Practical Cinematography and Its Applications.* London: Heinemann, 1913.

Talmadge, Margaret L. *The Talmadge Sisters: Norma, Constance, Natalie.* Philadelphia: J. B. Lippincott Co., 1924.

Talmey, Allene. *Doug and Mary and Others.* New York: Macy-Masius, 1927.

Tate, Alfred O. *Edison's Open Door.* New York: E. P. Dutton, 1938.

Tatum, Stephen. *Inventing Billy the Kid: Visions of the Outlaw in America, 1881-1981.* Albuquerque: University of New Mexico Press, 1982.

Taubin, Amy. "Girl N the Hood." *Sight and Sound* 3, no. 8 (August 1993): 17.

Taves, Brian. *The Romance of Adventure: The Genre of Historical Adventure.* Jackson: University Press of Mississippi, 1993.

Taylor, Clyde. "The LA Rebellion: New Spirit in American Film." *Black Film Review* 2 (1986): 2.

———. "New U.S. Black Cinema." *Jump Cut* 28 (1983).

———. "The Paradox of Black Independent Cinema." *Black Film Review* 4, no. 4 (fall 1988).

Taylor, Deems. *A Pictorial History of the Movies.* New York: Citadel Press, 1966.

Taylor, Frank J. "Leo the Caballero." *Saturday Evening Post,* 6 July 1946, 26.

Taylor, John Russell, and Arthur Jackson. *The Hollywood Musical.* New York: McGraw-Hill, 1971.

Tello, Jaime. "Notas sobre la política del 'viejo' cine mexicano." In *Hojas de cine: Testimonios y documentos del nuevo cine latino americano.* Vol. 2. Mexico City: Fundación Mexicana de Cineastas, 1988.

Terriss, Tom. *Writing the Sound and Dialogue Photoplay.* Hollywood: Palmer Institute of Authorship, 1930.

Theis, David. "Hollywood on the Río Grande." *Texas Monthly,* August 1987, 118-20.

Thomas, Bob. "Chico Day." *Action,* January-February 1971, 19-21.

———. *Joan Crawford.* New York: Bantam Books, 1978.

———. *King Cohn: The Life and Times of Harry Cohn.* New York: G. P. Putnam's Sons, 1967.

———. *The One and Only Bing.* New York: Grosset and Dunlap, 1977.

———. *Selznick.* New York: Doubleday, 1969.

———. *Thalberg, Life and Legend.* New York: Doubleday, 1976.

———. *Walt Disney: An American Original.* New York: Pocket Books, 1976.

Thomas, Kevin. " 'The earth' Revolves around a Moving Spiritual Odyssey." *Los Angeles Times,* 5 May 1995.

Thomas, Sari, ed. *Culture and Communication: Methodology, Behavior, Artifacts and Institutions.* Norwood, NJ: Ablex Publishing Co, 1987.

Thomas, Tony. *Ustinov in Focus.* New York: A. S. Barnes & Co., 1971.

Thomas, Tony, and Jim Terry. *The Busby Berkeley Book.* New York: New York Graphic Society, 1973.

Thompson, Frank. *Alamo Movies.* East Berlin, PA: Old Mill Books, 1991.

Thompson, Kristin. *Exporting Entertainment: America in the World Film Market, 1907-1934.* London: British Film Institute, 1985.

Tibbetts, John, and James M. Welsh. *His Majesty the American: The Cinema of Douglas Fairbanks, Sr.* New York: Barnes, 1977.

Tibbetts, John C., ed. *Introduction to the Photoplay.* Shawnee Mission, KS: National Film Society, 1977.

Tickner, Lisa. *The Spectacle of Women: Imagery of the Suffrage Campaign, 1907-14.* Chicago: University of Chicago Press, 1988.

Tinting and Toning of Eastman Positive Motion Picture Film. Rochester, NY: Eastman Kodak, 1927.

Toll, Robert. *Blackening Up: The Minstrel Show in 19th-Century America.* New York: Oxford University Press, 1974.

Tompkins, Jane P. *Sensational Designs: The Cultural Work of American Fiction, 1790-1860.* New York: Oxford University Press, 1985.

———. "Sentimental Power: *Uncle Tom's Cabin* and the Politics of Literary History." *Glyph,* no. 5 (1979): 79-102.

Torres, José Artemio. "Cine." In *Puerto Rico A-Zeta,* ed. Lucas Morán Arce. Barcelona: Ediciones Nauta, 1987.

Torres, Luis R. "The Chicano Image in Film." *Caminos* 3 (November 1982): 8-11+.

———. "Distortions in Celluloid: Hispanics and Film." *Agenda: A Journal of Hispanic Issues* 11 (May-June 1981): 37-40.

———. "Getting a Word in Edgewise." *Hispanic Business* 7, no. 5 (May 1985): 22-23.

———. "Hollywood and the Homeboys: The Studios Discover Barrio Gangs." *Nuestro* 3 (April 1979): 27-30.

———. "*Raíces de Sangre:* First Feature Film Directed by a Chicano." *Somos,* 1978, 16-19.

Toulet, Émmanuelle. *Domitor Bibliographie internationale du cinéma des premiers temps: Travaux des members.* Quebec: Domitor, 1987.

Tovares, Joseph. "Mojado Like Me." *Hispanic,* May 1995, 20-24.

Trelles Plazaola, Luis. *El cine visto en Puerto Rico (1962-1973).* Colección Uprex. Río Piedras: Universidad de Puerto Rico, Editorial Universitaria, 1975.

———. *South American Cinema: Dictionary of Filmmakers.* Trans. Yudit de Ferdinandy. Río Piedras: Editorial de la Universidad de Puerto Rico, 1989.

Treviño, Jesús Salvador. "Chicano Cinema." *New Scholar* 8 (1982): 167-80.

———. "Chicano Cinema Overview." *Areíto* 10, no. 37 (1984): 40-43.

———. "Cinéma Chicano aux États-Unis." In *Les Cinémas de l'Amérique Latine,* ed. Guy Hennebelle and Alfonso Gumucio-Dragón, 493-99. Paris: Nouvelles Éditions Pierre Lherminier, 1981.

———. "El desarrollo del cine chicano." In *Hojas de cine: Testimonios y documentos del nuevo cine latino americano.* Vol. 1, *Centro y Sudamérica,* 277-84. Mexico City: Fundación Mexicana de Cineastas/Universidad Autónoma Metropolitana, 1988.

———. "Jesús Salvador Treviño habla para *Cine Cubano*: Entrevista." *Cine Cubano* 83 (1977-78): 11-16.

———. "Latino Portrayals in Film and Television." *Jump Cut* 30 (March 1985): 14-16.

———. "Latinos and Public Broadcasting: The 2% Factor." *Jump Cut* 28 (1983): 65.

———. "Lights, Camera, Action." *Hispanic* 5 (August 1992): 76.

———. "Mirando hacia América Latina: Entrevista." *Cine Cubano* 94 (1979): 26-37.

———. "The New Mexican Cinema." *Film Quarterly* 32, no. 3 (1979).

———. "Presencia del cine chicano." In *A través de la frontera,* ed. Ida Rodríguez Prampolini, 194-201. Mexico City: UNAM,

Centro de Estudios Económicos y Sociales del Tercer Mundo and Instituto de Investigaciones Estéticas, 1983.

———, ed. "Feature Section on Chicano Films." *Caminos* 3, no. 10 (November 1983): 6-20.

Trimble, Marian Blackton. *J. Stuart Blackton: A Personal Biography by His Daughter.* Metuchen, NJ: Scarecrow Press, 1985.

Trudgill, Eric. *Madonnas and Magdalens: The Origins and Development of Victorian Sexual Attitudes.* New York: Holmes and Meier, 1976.

Truitt, Evelyn Mack. *Who Was Who on Screen.* 3rd ed. New York: R. R. Bowker Co., 1983.

Tuñón, Julia. *En su propio espejo.* Mexico City: Metropolitan University Press, 1988.

Turan, Kenneth. "*American Me* Delivers." *Los Angeles Times,* 13 March 1992, F1, F10, F12.

Turner, Frederick Jackson. *The Frontier in American History.* New York: Holt, Rinehart and Winston, 1962.

———. "The Significance of the Frontier in American History." In *Annual Report, American Historical Association, 1893.* Washington, DC: Government Printing Office, 1894.

Tuska, Jon. *The American West in Film.* Westport, CT: Greenwood Press, 1985.

———. *The Filming of the West.* Garden City, NY: Doubleday, 1976.

Tuska, Jon, and Vicki Piekarski, eds. *Encyclopedia of Frontier and Western Fiction.* New York: McGraw-Hill, 1983.

Tyler, Parker. *The Hollywood Hallucination.* New York: Simon & Schuster, 1970.

———. *Magic and Myth of the Movies.* New York: Simon & Schuster, 1970.

Tynyanov, Yur. "Plot and Story-line in the Cinema." *Russian Poetics in Translation* 5 (1978): 20-21.

Ulla, Jorge, Lawrence Ott, and Miñuca Villaverde. *Dos filmes del Mariel: El éxodo cubano de 1980.* Madrid: Editorial Playor, 1986.

The United States Government v The Motion Picture Patents Company. Equity no. 889, District Court, Eastern District of Pennsylvania. 6 vols., 1913-14 (Library of the Museum of Modern Art, New York).

Uricchio, William, and Roberta E. Pearson. *Reframing Culture: The Case of the Vitagraph Quality Film.* Princeton, NJ: Princeton University Press, 1993.

Valdez, Armando, ed. *Telecommunications and Latinos: An Assessment of Issues and Opportunities.* Stanford, CA: Stanford Center for Chicano Research, 1985.

Valdez, Luis. "Hollywood y Tezcatlipoca." *Chiricú* 5, no. 2 (1988): 35-39.

Valenti, Peter. *Errol Flynn: A Bio-Bibliography.* Westport, CT: Greenwood Press, 1984.

Valle, Víctor. "*La Bamba* May Change Film Marketing." *Los Angeles Times,* 20 July 1987, sec. 6, 5.

———. "Latino: Hollywood Opens Door As 'La Bamba' Leads Way." *Mesa Tribune* (Arizona), 6 April 1988, D2. (Article picked up from *Los Angeles Times.*)

———. "The Latino Wave: More Show Biz Doors Are Opening Since *La Bamba.*" *Los Angeles Times,* 2 April 1988, sec. 6, 1.

———. "Real-Life Flashback to 'Stand, Deliver.'" *Los Angeles Times,* 17 March 1988, sec. 6, 1.

———. "Ritchie Valens Film Boosts Prospects of Dubbing, Subtitles." *Los Angeles Times,* 24 July 1987, sec. 6, 1+.

Valverde, Umberto. *Reportaje crítico al cine colombiano.* Bogotá, Colombia: Editorial Toronuevo, 1978.

Vanden Heuvel, Hon, and Everette E. Dennis. *Changing Patterns: Latin America's Vital Media.* New York: Columbia University, Freedom Forum Media Studies Center, 1995.

Vanderwood, Paul J. "An American Cold Warrior: *Viva Zapata!*" In *American History/American Film: Interpreting the Hollywood Image,* ed. John E. O'Connor and Martin A. Jackson, 183-201. New York: Frederick Ungar, 1979.

———, ed. *Juárez* [film script]. Madison: University of Wisconsin Press, 1983.

Van Peebles, Melvin. *The Making of Sweet Sweetback's Baadasssss Song.* New York: Lancer Books, 1972.

Van Zile, Edward. *That Marvel—The Movie.* New York: Putnam Sons, 1923.

Vardac, A. Nicholas. *From Stage to Screen: Theatrical Method from Garrick to Griffith.* Cambridge, MA: Harvard University Press, 1949. Reprint, New York: Benjamin Blom, 1968.

Varela, Jesse "Chuy." "Luis Valdez—The Frida Fracaso." (Interview.) *Cine Acción News* 9, no. 3 (September 1992): 8.

Varela, Willie. "Chicano Personal Cinema." *Jump Cut* 39 (June 1994): 96-99.

Vargas, Lucila. Film review of *El Norte. The Americas Review* 14, no. 1 (1986): 89-91.

Variety Film Reviews (1907-86). New York: Garland Publishing Co., 1983–.

Variety Movie Guide. One vol. *Variety* staff writers, with consulting ed. Derek Elley. New York: Prentice Hall, 1992.

Variety Obituaries (1905-1990). New York: Garland Publishing Co., 1988–.

Variety Television Reviews (1923-1994). Ed. Howard H. Prouty. New York: Garland Publishing Co., 1989–.

Vaughn, Robert. *Only Victims: A Study of Show Business Blacklisting.* New York: G. P. Putnam's Sons, 1972.

Veciana-Suárez, Ana. *Hispanic Media: Impact and Influence.* Washington, DC: Media Institute, 1990.

———. *Hispanic Media, USA.* Washington, DC: Media Institute, 1987.

Veloso, Caetano. "Caricature and Conqueror, Pride and Shame." *New York Times,* 20 October 1991, sec. H34.

Vermilye, Jerry. *Burt Lancaster: A Pictorial Treasury.* New York: Fallon Enterprises, 1971.

Victor, James. "My Cousin the Actor." *Caminos* 6, no. 8 (Sept.-Oct. 1985): 22-23.

Vidal, Gore. "Who Makes the Movies?" *New York Review of Books,* 25 November 1976, 35-39.

Vidor, King. *A Tree Is a Tree.* New York: Harcourt, Brace and World, 1954.

Viera, Mark A. *Hollywood Portraits: Classic Scene Stills 1929-41.* Greenwich, CT: Bison Books, 1988.

Viñas, Moisés. *Historia del cine mexicano.* Mexico City: Universidad Nacional Autónoma de México and UNESCO, 1987.

———. *Índice cronológico del cine mexicano, 1896-1992.* Mexico City: UNAM, Dirección General de Actividades Cinematográficas, 1992.

Vinson, James, ed. *Twentieth-Century Western Writers.* London: Macmillan, 1982.

"Las vistas cinematográficas y los mexicanos." *La Crónica,* 12 October 1911, 1.

Vogel, Amos. *Film as a Subversive Art.* New York: Random House, 1974.

Vogel, Harold L. *Entertainment Industry Economics: A Guide for Financial Analysis.* 2nd ed. New York: Cambridge University Press, 1990.

Volman, Dennis. " 'We Are Losing Our Identity': An Interview with Mexican Director Marcela Fernández Violante." *Film Literature Quarterly* 15, no. 1 (1987).

von Sternberg, Josef. *Fun in a Chinese Laundry.* New York: Macmillan, 1965.

Wagenknecht, Edward. *The Movies in the Age of Innocence.* New York: Ballantine Books, 1971.

———. *The Stars of the Silents.* Metuchen, NJ: Scarecrow Press, 1987.

Wagenknecht, Edward, and Anthony Slide. *The Films of D. W. Griffith.* Foreword by Lillian Gish. New York: Crown Publishers, 1975.

Wagner, Rob. *Film Folk.* New York: Century, 1918.

Walker, Alexander. *Rudolph Valentino.* New York: Stein and Day, 1976.

———. *The Shattered Silents: How the Talkies Came to Stay.* New York: William Morrow & Co., 1979.

———. *Stardom: The Hollywood Phenomenon.* London: Michael Joseph, 1970.

Wall, Howard Lamarr. *Motion Pictures, 1894-1912 (Identified from the Records of the United States Copyright Office).* Washington, DC: Library of Congress, 1953.

Waller, Gregory A. "Another Audience: Black Moviegoing, 1907-16." *Cinema Journal* 31, no. 2 (1992): 3-25.

Walley, Wayne. "*La Bamba* Wakes Up Hollywood: Hispanic Market Potential Pondered." *Advertising Age,* 10 August 1987, 41.

Walsh, Raoul. *Each Man in His Time: The Life Story of a Director.* New York: Farrar, Straus and Giroux, 1974.

Wanamaker, Mark. "Historic Hollywood Movie Studios." Part 1 of a series of articles. *American Cinematographer,* May 1976, 280-83, 286-88, 297.

Wanger, Walter. "Hollywood and the Intellectual." *Saturday Review,* 5 December 1942, 6, 40.

Ward, Larry Wayne. *The Motion Picture Goes to War: The U.S. Government Film Effort during World War I.* Ann Arbor, MI: UMI Research Press, 1985.

Warner, Jack L., with Dean Jennings. *My First Hundred Years in Hollywood.* New York: Random House, 1964.

Warshaw, Robert. *The Immediate Experience.* Garden City, NY: Anchor Books, 1964.

Wasko, Janet. *Movies and Money.* Norwood, NJ: Ablex Publishing Co., 1982.

Watts, Stephen, ed. *Behind the Screen: How Films Are Made.* New York: Dodge Publishing Co., 1938.

Wayn, Jane Ellen. *Stanwyck.* New York: Arbor House, 1985.

Weales, Gerald. *Canned Goods as Caviar: American Film Comedies of the 1930s.* Chicago: University of Chicago Press, 1985.

Weaver, John T., comp. *Twenty Years of Silents, 1908-1928.* Metuchen, NJ: Scarecrow Press, 1971.

Wees, William C. *Recycled Images.* New York: Anthology Film Archives, 1993.

Weigman, Robyn. "Feminism, the Boyz, and Other Matters Regarding the Male." In *Screening the Male: Exploring Masculinities in Hollywood Cinema,* ed. Steven Cohan and Ina Rae Hark. New York: Routledge, 1993.

Weiss, Jason. "An Interview with Guillermo Gómez Peña." *Review: Latin American Literature and Arts* 45 (July-December 1991): 8-13.

Weiss, Ken, and Ed Goodgold. *To Be Continued . . .* New York: Crown Publishers, 1972.

Weiss, Rachel, and Alan West. *Being América: Essays on Art, Literature, and Identity from Latin America.* Fredonia, NY: White Pine, 1991.

Weitzel, Edward. *Intimate Talks with Movie Stars.* New York: Dale Publishing Co., 1921.

Welbon, Yvonne. "Calling the Shots: Black Women Directors Take the Helm." *The Independent* 15, no. 2 (March 1992): 18-22.

Welch, Jeffry Egan. *Literature and Film: An Annotated Bibliography, 1909-1977.* New York: Garland Publishing Co., 1981.

Welker, Robert H. "New Image of American Black." *Variety,* 1 Feb. 1961, 7, 19.

Wellek, René, and Austin Warren. *Theory of Literature.* 3rd ed. New York: Harcourt, Brace and World, 1956.

Welsh, Robert Emmett. *A.B.C. of Motion Pictures.* New York: Harper and Bros., c. 1916.

Weltman, Manuel, and Raymond Lee. *Pearl White, the Peerless Fearless Girl.* Cranbury, NJ: Barnes, 1969.

Wenden, D. J. *The Birth of the Movies.* New York: E. P. Dutton, 1974.

West, Dennis. "Mexican Cinema in 1977: A Commentary on the Mexican Film Festival Presently Touring the U.S." *The American Hispanist* 2 (May 1977).

West, Dennis, and Gary Crowdus. "Cheech Cleans Up His Act." *Cineaste* 16, no. 3 (July 1988): 37.

West, Mae. *Goodness Had Nothing to Do with It.* Englewood Cliffs, NJ: Prentice-Hall, 1959.

Westmore, Frank, and Muriel Davidson. *The Westmores of Hollywood.* Philadelphia: Lippincott, 1976.

Wexman, Virginia Wright. "Suffering and Suffrage: Birth, the Female Body, and Women's Choices in D. W. Griffith's *Way Down East.*" *The Velvet Light Trap,* no. 29 (spring 1992): 53-65.

Wheaton, Christopher. "A History of the Screen Writers Guild (1920-1942)." Ph.D. diss., University of Southern California, 1974.

White, Armond. "Figueroa in a Landscape." *Film Comment* (January-February 1992): 60-63.

_____. "The New Players: Hollywood's Black Filmmakers Observe the Rules of the Game." *Emerge,* August 1992, 42.

White, Arnold. "Films in Focus: Néstor Almendros." *Films in Review* 35 (December 1984): 607-9.

White-Hensen, Wendy, comp. *Archival Moving Image Materials: A Cataloging Manual.* Washington, DC: Library of Congress, Motion Picture, Broadcasting, and Recorded Sound Div., 1984.

Whitney, John. "Image Making in the Land of Fantasy." *Agenda, A Journal of Hispanic Issues* 8, no. 1 (Jan.-Feb. 1978): 7-11.

Who Was Who in the Theatre: 1912-1976. Detroit: Gale Research Co., 1978.

Wiley, Mason, and Damien Bona. *Inside Oscar: The Unofficial History of the Academy Awards.* New York: Ballantine Books, 1986.

Wilkerson, Tichi, and Marica Borie. *The Hollywood Reporter: The Golden Years.* New York: Coward-McCann, 1984.

Williams, Alan. *Republic of Images: A History of French Filmmaking.* Cambridge: Harvard University Press, 1992.

Williams, Linda. "Type and Stereotype: Chicano Images in Film." In *Chicano Cinema: Research, Reviews, and Resources,* ed. Gary D. Keller, 59-63. Binghamton, NY: Bilingual Press, 1985.

_____. "Type and Stereotype: Chicano Images in Film." *Frontiers: A Journal of Women's Studies* 5, no. 2 (summer 1980): 14-17.

Williams, Martin. *Griffith: First Artist of the Movies.* New York: Oxford University Press, 1980.

Williams, Raymond. *Marxism and Literature.* Oxford: Oxford University Press, 1977.

Williamson, Judith. *Consuming Passions: The Dynamics of Popular Culture.* London: Marion Boyars, 1987.

Wilson, Clint C., II, and Félix Gutiérrez. *Minorities and Media: Diversity and the End of Mass Communication.* Beverly Hills, CA: Sage Publications, 1985.

Wilson, George M. *Narration in Light: Studies in Cinematic Point of View.* Baltimore: Johns Hopkins University Press, 1986.

Wilson, Michael, and Deborah Rosenfelt Silverton. *Salt of the Earth.* Old Westbury, NY: Feminist Press, 1978.

Windeler, Robert. *Sweetheart: The Story of Mary Pickford.* New York: Praeger, 1974.

Winkler, Allan. *The Politics of Propaganda: The Office of War Information, 1942-1945.* New Haven, CT: Yale University Press, 1978.

Winkopp, C. G. *How to Write a Photoplay.* New York: C. G. Winkopp, 1915.

Winokur, Mark. "Improbable Ethnic Hero: William Powell and the Transformation of Ethnic Hollywood." *Cinema Journal* 27 (fall 1987): 5-22.

_____. " 'Smile Stranger': Aspects of Immigrant Humor in the Marx Brothers' Humor." *Literature/Film Quarterly* 13, no. 3 (1985): 161-71.

Winston, Michael R. "Racial Consciousness and the Evolution of Mass Communications in the United States." *Daedalus: Journal of the Academy of Arts and Sciences* 3, no. 4 (fall 1982): 171-82.

Woll, Allen L. "Bandits and Lovers: Hispanic Images in American Film." In *The Kaleidoscopic Lens: How Hollywood Views Ethnic Groups,* ed. Randall M. Miller, 54-72. Englewood, NJ: Jerome S. Ozer, 1980.

_____. *The Hollywood Musical Goes to War.* Chicago: Nelson-Hall, 1983.

_____. "Hollywood's Good Neighbor Policy: The Latin American Image in American Film, 1939-1946." *Journal of Popular Film* 3 (fall 1974): 283-85.

_____. *The Latin Image in American Film.* Los Angeles: University of California, Latin American Center, 1977.

_____. "Latin Images in American Films." *Journal of Mexican History* 4 (1974): 28-40.

_____. Review of *Chicano Cinema,* by Gary D. Keller. *Journal of American Ethnic History* 6, no. 1 (fall 1986): 111-12.

_____. *Songs from Hollywood Musical Comedies, 1927 to the Present: A Dictionary.* New York: Garland Publishing Co., 1976.

Woll, Allen L., and Randall M. Miller, eds. *Ethnic and Racial Images in American Film and Television: Historical Essays and Bibliography.* New York: Garland Publishing Co., 1987.

Wong, Eugene Franklin. "On Visual Media Racism: Asians in the American Motion Pictures." Ph.D. diss., University of Denver, Graduate School of International Studies, 1977. Reprint, New York: Arno Press, 1978.

Wood, Joe. *Malcolm X, in Our Own Image.* New York: St. Martin's Press, 1992.

Wood, Leslie. *The Romance of the Movies.* London: William Heinemann, 1937.

Wood, Michael. *America in the Movies.* New York: Basic Books, 1975.

Wood, Robin. "The American Nightmare: Horror in the 70s" and "Normality and Monsters: The Films of Larry Cohen and George Romero." Chaps. 5 and 6 in *Hollywood from Vietnam to Reagan.* New York: Columbia University Press, 1986.

_____. *Hitchcock's Films Revisited.* New York: Columbia University Press, 1989.

_____. "*Rancho Notorious:* A *Noir* Western in Colour." *Cine-Action!,* summer 1988, 84.

Woodbridge, Elizabeth. *The Drama: Its Laws and Its Techniques.* Boston: Allyn & Bacon, 1898.

Wright, Lyle. *American Fiction, 1774-1850: A Contribution toward a Bibliography.* San Marino, CA: Huntington Library, 1969.

_____. *American Fiction, 1851-1875: A Contribution toward a Bibliography.* San Marino, CA: Huntington Library, 1978.

_____. *American Fiction, 1876-1900: A Contribution toward a Bibliography.* San Marino, CA: The Huntington Library, 1978.

Wright, Will. *Sixguns and Society: A Structural Study of the Western.* Berkeley: University of California Press, 1975.

Wright, William Lord. *The Motion Picture Story: A Textbook of Photoplay Writing.* Chicago: Cloud Publishing Co., 1914.

_____. *Photoplay Writing.* New York: Falk Publishing Co., 1922.

Writers' Program of the Work Projects Administration, City of New York, comp. *The Film Index: A Bibliography.* 3 vols. New York: Museum of Modern Art, 1966-85. Reprint, White Plains, NY: Kraus International Publications, 1985-88.

"Xavier Cugat, la música de unos años." *El Europeo,* no. 3 (July-August, 1988): 91-107.

Yacowar, Maurice. "Aspects of the Familiar: A Defense of Minority Group Stereotyping in Popular Film." *Film Literature Quarterly* 2, no. 2 (spring 1974): 129-39.

Yallop, David A. *The Day the Laughter Stopped: The True Story of Fatty Arbuckle.* New York: St. Martin's Press, 1976.

Ybarra Frausto, Tomás. "The Chicano Alternative Film Movement." *Centro de Estudios Puertorriqueños Bulletin* 2, no. 8 (1990): 44-47.

Yearwood, Gladstone L. "The Hero in Black Film." *Wide Angle* 5, no. 2 (1983).

_____, ed. *Black Cinema Aesthetics: Issues in Independent Black Filmmaking.* Athens: Ohio University, Center for Afro-American Studies, 1982.

Young, Freddie, and Paul Petzold. *The Work of the Motion Picture Cameraman.* New York: Hastings House, 1972.

Zambrano, A. L. *Dickens and Film.* New York: Gordon Press, 1977.

Zavarzadeh, Mas'ud. *Seeing Films Politically.* New York: SUNY Press, 1991.

Zeitlin, Ida. "Sous American Sizzler." *Motion Picture,* September 1941.

Zheutlin, Barbara, and David Talbot. "The Whole World Is Watching: Jesús Salvador Treviño." In *Creative Differences: Profiles of Hollywood Dissidents,* 345-52. Boston: South End Press, 1978.

Zierold, Norman. *Garbo.* New York: Stein and Day, 1969.

_____. *The Moguls.* New York: Coward-McCann, 1969.

_____. *Sex Goddesses of the Silent Screen.* Chicago: Henry Regnery, 1973.

Ziff, Larzer. *Literary Democracy: The Declaration of Cultural Independence in America.* New York: Viking Press, 1981.

Zinman, David. *Saturday Night at the Bijou.* New Rochelle, NY: Arlington House, 1973.

Zito, Stephen. "The Black Film Experience." In *American Film Heritage: Impressions from the American Film Institute Archives,* ed. Tom Shales and Kevin Brownlow. Washington, DC: Acropolis Books, 1972.

Zmijewsky, Boris, and Lee Pfeiffer. *The Films of Clint Eastwood.* New York: Citadel Press, 1982.

Zoglin, Richard. "Awaiting a Gringo Crumb." *Time,* 11 July 1986, 76.

Zolotow, Maurice. *Billy Wilder in Hollywood.* New York: G. P. Putnam's Sons, 1977.

_____. *Shooting Star: A Biography of John Wayne.* New York: Simon and Schuster, 1975.

Zubiri, Nancy. "Pionero de Hollywood. (Jesús Salvador Treviño)." *Los Angeles Times,* 14 June 1995, Section, 8-9.

Zukor, Adolph, with Dale Kramer. *The Public Is Never Wrong: The Autobiography of Adolph Zukor.* New York: G. P. Putnam's Sons, 1953.

INDEX OF INDIVIDUAL AND GROUP NAMES

This index has been alphabetized using the letter-by-letter system. Roman numeral I refers to *Hispanics and United States Film: An Overview and Handbook;* II refers to the present volume. The variations on an individual's name that appear in the two volumes are incorporated within the same index entry (e.g., Acosta, Rodolfo "Rudy" [Rudolph]). In cases where an individual uses a stage name different from the birth name, the latter is found in the text entry; this index includes only stage names. This index corrects the occasional mistakes in the spelling of names that appeared in volume I.

INDEX OF FILM AND TV SHOW TITLES

This index is alphabetized using the word-by-word system. Roman numeral I refers to *Hispanics and United States Film: An Overview and Handbook;* II refers to the present volume. Definite and indefinite articles in Spanish, French, etc. (*el, la, los, las, un, una, le, l'*) appear at the end of the title, like their English counterparts (*the* and *a/an*), except in the case of titles commonly considered as a unit: *La Traviata, El Dorado, El Greco.* This index corrects the occasional mistakes in titles that appeared in the text of volume I.